SOVEREIGNTY DISRUPTED

Cultural Memory | *in the Present*

Hent de Vries, Editor

SOVEREIGNTY DISRUPTED

Spinoza and the Disparity of Reality

Gilah Kletenik

STANFORD UNIVERSITY PRESS
Stanford, California

Stanford University Press
Stanford, California

© 2025 by Gilah Kletenik. All rights reserved.

No part of this book may be reproduced or transmitted in any form or by any means, electronic or mechanical, including photocopying and recording, or in any information storage or retrieval system, without the prior written permission of Stanford University Press.

Library of Congress Cataloging-in-Publication Data
Names: Kletenik, Gilah, author.
Title: Sovereignty disrupted : Spinoza and the disparity of reality / Gilah Kletenik.
Other titles: Cultural memory in the present.
Description: Stanford, California : Stanford University Press, 2025. | Series: Cultural memory in the present | Includes bibliographical references and index.
Identifiers: LCCN 2025018706 (print) | LCCN 2025018707 (ebook) | ISBN 9781503644151 (cloth) | ISBN 9781503644465 (paperback) | ISBN 9781503644472 (ebook)
Subjects: LCSH: Spinoza, Benedictus de, 1632-1677. Ethica. | Sovereignty—Philosophy. | Immanence (Philosophy) | Political science—Philosophy.
Classification: LCC B3974 .K53 2025 (print) | LCC B3974 (ebook)
LC record available at https://lccn.loc.gov/2025018706
LC ebook record available at https://lccn.loc.gov/2025018707

Cover design: Bob Aufuldish, Aufuldish & Warinner
Cover art: Oleksander Roitburd, *Spinoza in Tuscany*, 2016; oil on linen, private collection. Reproduced by permission of Betsheva Roitburd.

The authorized representative in the EU for product safety and compliance is: Mare Nostrum Group B.V. | Mauritskade 21D | 1091 GC Amsterdam | The Netherlands | Email address: gpsr@mare-nostrum.co.uk | KVK chamber of commerce number: 96249943

In gratitude to MaBa

Contents

Acknowledgments		xi
Preface		xv
	Introduction	1
1	Substance Is Insubstantial	40
2	Nature Is Not All	76
3	Not for Nothing	124
4	Serves No Purpose	167
5	Splitting the Difference	219
6	Off Subject	263
7	Human Interest	310
	Abbreviations and Citational Practices	363
	Notes	365
	Bibliography	415
	Index	431

Acknowledgments

It is gratifying to have reached this juncture. Yet surfacing at this moment—amidst devastating wars; the ravages of neoliberalism; surging racism, xenophobia, and transphobia; accelerating ecological destruction; and the consolidation of authoritarianism and fascism—elicits in me a sense of disparity. This project emerges from the privileges conferred upon me. While these are largely structural, here I pause to recognize specific institutions and individuals who have supported this book and me.

I am grateful to the Skirball Department of Hebrew and Judaic Studies at New York University. David Engel was instructive and supportive throughout my graduate studies and magnanimously served as an additional member of my committee. Warren Montag was also an additional member who has since been giving with constructive feedback and encouragement. As a member of the committee, Hent de Vries offered valuable perspective. Judith Butler tendered incisive feedback as a member of the committee and has subsequently been most generous with their wisdom, guidance, and support. Elliot R. Wolfson—my advisor and chair of the committee—supported the project from its nascence. Over these years he has been responsive and reinforcing. I thank him for paving a path of thinking that is unsparing in rigor, uncompromising in integrity, and unapologetic in complexity.

I began writing this book as an Alan M. Stroock Fellow at the Center for Jewish Studies at Harvard University. My thanks to David Stern, Jay Harris, and the Starr Fellow cohort. My tenure as postdoctoral associate at the Elie Wiesel Center for Jewish Studies at Boston University allowed me to write in earnest. I am grateful to Deanna Klapper and Kecia Ali for their clarity and care.

The Stroum Center for Jewish Studies at the University of Washington is an accommodating intellectual home. The Center has supported this book, subsidizing a stay at the Whiteley Center for writing, defraying the costs of indexing, and offering a subvention grant. I am grateful to the staff, my students, and colleagues in both Jewish Studies and Philosophy, especially Mika Ahuvia, Noam Pianko, Devin Naar, Noga Rotem, Nick Baar, Liora Halperin, Sasha Senderovich, and Sara Goering.

Ideas in this book have been presented at Manchester Metropolitan University, Harvard University, Boston University, the University of Michigan, the University of Washington, and the North American Spinoza Society. I appreciate these audiences and conversations. Points in the book's second chapter were published in "To Infinity, Not Beyond: Spinoza's Ontology of the Not One," in *New Paths: Essays in Honor of Professor Elliot Wolfson*, edited by Glenn Dynner, Susannah Heschel, and Shaul Magid (Purdue University Press, 2024). My thanks for permission to reprint these.

Exchanges with fellow Spinozists have been generative. I look forward to debating infinity, ad infinitum, with Luce deLire. Willi Goetschel has been discerning and most encouraging, while Idit Dobbs-Weinstein's work has been a salve.

I thank Betsheva Rojtburd for permission to feature her father's—Oleksandr Rojtburd's—painting *Spinoza's Journey to Tuscany* (2016) on the cover of this book. The oil on linen painting is currently in a private collection.

My thanks to Stanford University Press. I am immensely grateful to the two very generous readers who offered kind feedback on the manuscript. It has been a delight to work with the series editor Hent de Vries and publisher Erica Wetter. I appreciate Catherine Mallon's able copyediting and the efforts of the rest of the team at Stanford. Sarahh Scher's capable indexing is also much appreciated.

Our communities in Seattle remain enriching. I am grateful to so many for their warmth, the opportunities to study, and to wine and dine together. Many friendships have sustained me, I particularly thank: Zalman Rothschild for the camaraderie; Dani Passow for the provocations; Deborah and David Leschinsky for their kindness; Jason Stanley for the sarcasm; and Abby Brockman for the laughs.

My gratitude to Daphna Stroumsa. To Elul and Tuvi, too. Rafi Neis remains a most rewarding interlocutor, unruly collaborator, and reliable confidante.

Thank you, Tali, Noch, Marley, Zoharah, and Liav for your energy and interest. And Savti, for your affection. My thanks to Peshy, Chesky, Avidan, Rachel, and Ilan for your vibrancy and good humor; Shya for becoming the physician of the family so I could be its metaphysician; and Eli, Devorah, Chayah, Boruch, Sarah, Leib, and Rochel for your perceptiveness and wit. MaBa thank you for being my first, foremost, and forever teachers. You have trained me to read texts with precision and conviction, curiosity and possibility, while modeling a life of generous teaching and ethical responsibility. Elisha, Saadiah, and Shai Shai, you keep us on our toes while never failing to remind me that there is much fun to be had outside the study. My profoundest gratitude to Samuel for being at my side over these years. Life with you is ablaze. Thank you for always imagining otherwise.

Preface

This book critiques sovereignty. It uncovers how "Western"[1] philosophy is anchored in the logics of sovereignty, tracing the ways in which its hierarchical rationales subsidize forms of human exceptionalism, cishetsexism, and colonialism. Such purports suffuse liberalism and neoliberalism and pervade contemporary theory. Spinoza's disruption of sovereignty commences with his repudiation of a Sovereign god, which dismantles the imbricated hierarchies of Mind over body, Human over nature, Self over other. This draws from the naturalism *or* materialism of medieval Islamic and Jewish philosophy, which was repressed by "Western," Christian philosophy. Like his sources, Spinoza's work has also been suppressed. It has been denounced as Jewish and "Oriental," and discredited for disabling "the agency of Christianity"[2] and "the Western principle of individuality."[3]

The cover art of *Sovereignty Disrupted* engages these concerns. *Spinoza's Journey to Tuscany* (2016), by the late Jewish-Ukrainian artist Oleksandr Rojtburd, depicts Spinoza in royal attire with scepter in hand. Yet unlike in, say, Diego Velázquez's *Equestrian Portrait of Philip IV* (1635–1636), Spinoza is not bestride a horse but a zebra, who is not curvetting, ready to charge, but remains in a "natural" pose. Instead of a sovereign triumphing over animal or land, perched atop a cliff, eyes fixed ahead, Spinoza faces the viewer, gaze askance, as he casually gestures in the opposite direction. The hues are vibrant and he appears *of* his surrounds, not apart from them, let alone dominant over them. By contrast, Kehinde Wiley's *Equestrian Portrait of Philip IV* (2017) replaces the king with a young Black man, retaining the pose of dominance.

Spinoza's biography is anything but glamorous: his mother died when he was six, his older brother when he was seventeen, and his father when he was twenty-two. This burdened him with immense debt from which he was ultimately relieved, but the process likely contributed to his excommunication from the Amsterdam Jewish community. Spinoza's lifestyle was humble. He seems never to have ventured beyond the borders of the Dutch Republic. There is scant indication that he enjoyed a buzzing social or intimate life. By his death at forty-four, Spinoza was marginalized and his theories deemed scandalous, including his critique of absolutist power and endorsement of democracy. The latter distinguished him from "Western" philosophers stretching back to Plato, including Machiavelli of Tuscany. Thus, depicting Spinoza in a royal pose is decidedly ironic. Rojtburd plays with the tropes of monarchical portraits, depriving Spinoza of certain accoutrements of power and the posture of conquest. This reimagining complements Rojtburd's absurdist portraits of René Descartes steering an automobile (*Rene Descartes and a Moving Matter*, 2017), Adam Smith lounging by a swimming pool (*Siesta Adam Smith*, 2017), and Arthur Schopenhauer beside brachiosauruses (*Schopenhauer's Misanthropy as Will and Presentation*, 2017).

Notwithstanding Rojtburd's subversion of the genre, the depiction of a European atop a zebra cannot be disaggregated from the brutal history of European colonialism in Africa. Whether or not the artist was conscious of this is partly beside the point, but it speaks to the project this book undertakes: to expose the "Western" philosophical adoration of sovereignty and demonstrate how it has sponsored arrogations of power, licensing dominations such as European supremacy, colonialism, and racism. Throughout, it also discerns these rationales in the scholarship on Spinoza, which is littered with Christian supremacy, Eurocentrism, and anti-Judaism.

Spinoza reconfigures the concepts he inherits from medieval Jewish philosophy. Accordingly, in reading Spinoza through fresh lenses, this book engages the scholarship but is not constrained by it. It seeks both to understand Spinoza's philosophy and to think *with* him. Much as Rojtburd's portrait leans on the works that came before it, recasting their motifs, allowing us to perceive them and Spinoza differently, this book revisits Spinoza with hopes that doing so might allow us to see his philosophy and our worlds differently.

Introduction

> All that philosophy can do is destroy idols. And that means not creating a new one—say in the "absence of an idol."
>
> —LUDWIG WITTGENSTEIN[1]

Is it possible to dispense with sovereignty? *Sovereignty Disrupted* is stimulated by this question, which it refracts through the lenses of Spinoza's philosophy. By introducing an ontology dispossessed of sovereign pretenses, Spinoza, I demonstrate, effectively denaturalizes sovereignty. This move conditions his epistemology and his ethics, which are similarly divested of the logics and features of sovereignty. Reading Spinoza's philosophy as disrupting sovereignty proffers a fresh interpretation of his thought, while positioning it as indispensable to abiding questions about the nature of reality, the status of reason, and the condition of being human. Although I make the case for a particular exposition of Spinoza's philosophy, I am simultaneously intent on thinking *with* Spinoza, exploring the possibilities that his capacious project opens, adapting his ideas, pressing them in ways that he may not have anticipated. Such a move, I trust, renders his philosophy all the more compelling and vital, as pertinent and controversial as ever. This book is both interpretive and theoretical. It tenders a careful but novel reading of Spinoza's philosophy that is steeped in the voluminous and diverse scholarship on it. It also delivers a constructive analysis of the concept of sovereignty and a speculative critique of its logics.

Sovereignty has conventionally been quarantined within the confines of legal and political theory. Though understandable, this classification is misleading because the rationale and force of sovereignty are manifest across the domains of so-called "Western" philosophy, anchoring its approaches to reality, reason, and humans. The hierarchy that underpins sovereignty and the superiority it secures configure familiar "Western" dominations, such as cishet male supremacy, white supremacy, and human supremacy. These supremacies are promoted by additional doctrines enrooted in sovereignty, to wit, that nature is hierarchically arranged and that reason is supreme. Considering as much, rather than attending to the conspicuously political aspects of sovereignty, this book concentrates on its understudied sway over matters ontological, epistemological, and ethical. Although Spinoza's explicitly political writings—the *Theological-Political Treatise* and *Political Treatise*—consider and critique political sovereignty, the focus here centers on how Spinoza's philosophy as laid out in his *Ethics* dismantles the logics and mechanisms of sovereignty. Tracking Spinoza's subversion of sovereignty equips this book to expose the hegemony that sovereignty maintains across "Western" philosophy and interrogate the alternative that he inculcates.

The determination to study the concept of sovereignty in this manner is, minimally, a methodological and scholarly decision reflective of my contention that sovereignty and its features consolidate predominant "Western" approaches to the nature of reality, the scope of reason, and the condition of being human. Consequently, to properly apprehend certain predominant "Western" ontologies, epistemologies, and ethical theories, much less to critique them, entails confronting the concept of sovereignty and dissecting its preeminence. This book is trussed by this postulate. Such a program enhances not merely our grasp of the ontological, epistemological, and ethical, but it also has ramifications for the political, social, and juridical study of sovereignty. Most obviously, this is because contextualizing sovereignty as this book does, uncovering its pervasiveness, and implicitly advocating for a more expansive treatment of it also contributes to the multidisciplinary discourse on sovereignty. Admittedly, the resolve to treat sovereignty outside the fixed contours of the political—which to some might seem idiosyncratic—is a political decision. Doing so concurrently uncloaks the politics subsidizing the division of "Western" philosophy into distinct branches, including ontology, philosophy of knowledge or epistemology, philosophy of religion or theology, ethics and moral philosophy, anthropology or social philosophy, and political philosophy. The erection of these sovereign boundaries, even if driven by organizational concerns, is hardly neutral. These divisions configure auxiliary hierarchies by privileging certain questions. So it is that First Philosophy—metaphysics or theology or ontology—has historically taken precedence, while since René Descartes, and certainly Immanuel Kant, concerns regarding the conditions of knowledge and the human capacity to know have positioned epistemology as foremost. Such divisionary perimeters cordon off the political and the social from what and how reality is and what and how humans know. Currently, the field of philosophy—like the humanities more broadly—appears to be facing certain pressures to address matters of justice by (finally) taking concerns like sexism and racism seriously. Yet the routine eviction of such content to secluded domains counterproductively reinforces the mistaken notion that issues of mind and metaphysics transcend these seemingly more concrete interests. Moreover, relegating these matters to subfields like ethics conveniently insulates other areas of study from confronting them. Against this custom and informed by Spinoza's anti-dualism, which conceives the mind as the idea of body—human thought as inseparable from its material conditions—this book considers thinking and being as imbricated. Likewise, by examining how the logics of sovereignty configure "Western" ontology and epistemology, it also exposes the conceits of such neat divisions and the hierarchical rationales that underwrite them.

Spinoza's thought partially emerges from a medieval Jewish and Islamic philosophical tradition uncommitted to certain precepts of "Western," that is, Christian philosophy. Amongst these is the exclusion of the political from the philosophical. Or when not technically barred, political matters are simply included by means of subordination to what have been deemed loftier, more fundamental concerns of being or knowing. By contrast, Spinoza names his magnum opus the *Ethics*, even as he seems to grant pride of place to ontological and epistemological concerns, only later turning to address the affects, being human, and how best to live. Too many commentators over the centuries, sedimented within the "Western," Latin, Christian philosophical tradition, have mostly ignored the ethical aspects of this book called the *Ethics* or simply puzzled over its moniker, unable to understand why a work initially concerned with what seem like "philosophical," that is, ontological or epistemological questions is, at its core, ethical. Further bafflement stems from the fact that Spinoza actively critiques and largely dispenses with the features most constitutive of modern "Western" ethics: personal choice, individual autonomy, natural law, and normative standards. Nevertheless, certain readers across the centuries, often those situated on the margins of "Western" philosophy, have glimpsed his attempts. To wit, Moses

Hess intuits that Spinoza's "magnum opus was no mere metaphysics but an ethics."[2]

In the rivulets of medieval Jewish and Islamic philosophy to which Spinoza is heir, the philosophical *is* political and the political *is* philosophical. This orientation tracks back to their ancient Greek sources. Plato's *Republic* and *Laws* were preserved in Arabic—after being translated in the ninth century—while remaining lost to the Latin "West" only to be "discovered" in the fifteenth century. Accordingly, while the Christian "West" censored the more naturalist or materialist elements in Aristotle, medieval Islamic philosophy, across its elaborate commentaries, often accentuated these elements. The multiple Arabic translations of Aristotle's *Metaphysics* and the positioning of it at the center of the Islamic philosophical curriculum, especially as promoted by al-Farabi and later Ibn Sina (Latinized as "Avicenna"), cemented the mark of Aristotelian science and rationalism on this heritage. These factors contributed to distinct interpretative priorities: "In the circles of the mediaeval Judeo-Islamic commentators, the reception of Aristotle . . . has taken a direction significantly divergent from the Western privileging of *episteme* as the primary, purest philosophical mode."[3] This emphasis, coupled with historical contingencies, is reflective of and contributed to what in strands of medieval Jewish and Islamic philosophy is the inseparability of philosophy from politics. In these traditions, speculative concerns, which in "Western" philosophy are commonly referred to as "scholastic" matters, are inherently social and political, "practical" and ethical. So it is, for example, that the *Guide of the Perplexed*—penned in Judeo-Arabic in 1190 by Moshe ben Maimon or Mūsā bin Maimūn (Latinized as "Maimonides")—allocates dozens of chapters to philological, epistemological, theological, and ontological matters, all of which, it becomes apparent, serve to steer readers towards living rightly. As its denouement renders visible, acting justly and kindly is a natural consequence of philosophical thinking. The ideas we cogitate and the convictions we cherish occasion concrete repercussions. For Maimonides, like al-Farabi, following Plato but also Aristotle, philosophy is not separable from individual and communal life; it is indispensable to societal functioning. The upshot is that a book like this one, which explores the concept of sovereignty without explicitly centering political, legal, statist matters is at home in these *other* traditions. Arguably, it is only from a certain "Western," Christian philosophical standpoint that such a methodological course might even appear curious, let alone in need of defense.

Denaturalizing Sovereignty

A core thesis of this book is that how we perceive reality has consequences for how we perceive much else, if not all else. And further, how we perceive reality is shaped by a constellation of perceptions that we have and commitments that we hold. This is why, I contend, sovereignty is also, if not especially, even principally, an ontological concern. The historic and ongoing segregation of social and political philosophy from ontology in predominant clusters of "Western" thought conceals this critical linkage. Spinoza's *Ethics*, both in content and form, endorses a different approach. It opens with what is categorized as ontology, segues to what is classified as epistemology, then turns to what is considered the anthropological or social. Yet for Spinoza, all of these coalesce. So it is that part I, "Of God," which concerns the nature of reality, bears an appendix that essentially translates its main points into an alternate language. It addresses the "prejudices" that inhibit a reader from grasping the preceding eight definitions, seven axioms, and thirty-six propositions and their attendant demonstrations, corollaries, and scholia. In this appendix, rather than the explicitly "ontological" talk of substance, attributes, and modes, we hear of human freedom, good and evil, religious and political authority, imagination and reason, selfishness and narcissism. To certain readers this transition may strike them as incongruent, which no doubt accounts for its deemphasis in sectors of the scholarship. But this appendix merely restates what has already been articulated throughout part I, albeit in a different idiom. For Spinoza, adequate perception of the nature of reality has immediate "practical" implications for how to live. In turn, how we actually live impacts these perceptions because the actual, concrete, material circumstances of being human condition our thinking.

Although various prejudices inhibit our perceptions of reality, there is a specific miscalculation that Spinoza identifies and correcting for it, this book demonstrates, stands at the center of his project. "For no one will be able to perceive rightly the things I maintain unless they[4] take great care not to confuse God's power with the human power or right of kings."[5] The problem is that "ordinary people" mistakenly conceive "God as a human, or as like a human," empowered with "free will" and a "right over all things which are."[6] But God, which for Spinoza is substance *or* nature—meaning, reality—is not sovereign. These misbeliefs surfaced, as the appendix tells it, because humans looked at nature and concluded "that there was a ruler, or a number of rulers of nature, endowed with human freedom."[7] Humans manufactured God in their own image by coronating God as sovereign and investing God with absolute freedom. This anthropomorphic move—which derives from the conceits of anthropocentrism—is not the only error here. There is a more rudimentary misstep, arising from a misperception that humans maintain of themselves: "that they act from a free decision of the mind."[8] This "prejudice," Spinoza writes, is so prevalent and entrenched that we "are not easily freed of it."[9] Since humans believe themselves free, they anthropomorphically refract their presumed freedom onto reality by supposing that a Free being, a Sovereign, presides over it. Thereby, humans project both their senses of themselves and their structures of governance onto reality. This effectively *naturalizes* sovereignty: making it seem *as if* there is a sovereign in nature. It also naturalizes the fiction of freedom: making it seem *as if* freedom as such exists. Furthermore, this naturalization of sovereignty and its prized trait of freedom circularly reinforces the human constructs that initially produced them. A purportedly Sovereign god, reigning over reality, operatively validates human institutions that exercise sovereignty, making it seem as if sovereignty is natural, rather than being the anthropic invention that it is. Similarly, the attribution of free will to God suggests that freedom is natural, when it too is a human construct. Refuting these assertions that sovereignty and freedom exist in reality—naturally, ontologically—is the initial stride toward what I maintain is Spinoza's denaturalization of sovereignty.

Sovereignties promote further sovereignties. To Spinoza, the investiture of human monarchs leads to the reflection of this institution onto nature—the installation of God as Supreme—while the claim to human free will conditions its replication through the attachment of it to God. But this is only the beginning. This book registers the ways in which purports to sovereignty and the arrogation of its traits promote ever more sovereignties. Consequently, disrupting sovereignty entails identifying, analyzing, and critiquing it in the multiplicity of its diverse manifestations. A crucial thrust of the appendix is that doctrines as well as ideas are never disinterested or neutral. Our knowledge of ourselves, other singular things, and reality more generally is mediated through the bodied minds or minded bodies that we are. This renunciation of dualism means that no idea or theory can be disaggregated from its contexts. Claims that sovereignty is natural—that it exists in reality independent of the human contrivance of it—not only license its exercise but serve the interests of those who already hold sovereignty. In the most obvious sense, it benefits actual seats of authority that exercise sovereignty: the state, the law, the ruler, or in a democracy, the people. But this is also the case in all sorts of other more and less subtle realms in which sovereignty is presumed to exist.

By now, it is fair to ask, what is meant by *sovereignty*? In this book, it broadly stands for the condition of being a controlling influence and independent force—often so a priori and innately—that maintains supremacy in rank, domination, or authority. Throughout, distinct features of sovereignty are detected and scrutinized. These include oneness, unity, indivisibility, autonomy, precedence, exceptionalism, self-sameness, free will, preeminence, alterity, and independence. These are all, to varying degrees, acknowledged traits of the most classic "Western" exemplars of sovereignty: God and monarch. What I show is that Spinoza does not merely dispossess substance—God, nature, reality—of these sovereignties but refrains from refurbishing them by refusing to furnish alternate beings with these attributes. Not only is substance not endowed with sovereignty, but neither, as we have seen, are humans. These are the most readily discernible purports to sovereignty that Spinoza repudiates. I demonstrate how these disavowals participate in a much wider and more comprehensive disruption of sovereignty that has remained unacknowledged. In some ways, this is shown through analysis that descries several further manners in which Spinoza disbands the sovereignty of God *or* substance *or* nature. For example, I evince how reality is divested of the trait of oneness and nature deprived of regulatory laws. These instances typify a fundamental stimulus of Spinoza's philosophy: his renouncement of transcendence and teleology. I enrich the understanding of these acclaimed critiques by revealing how both transcendence and teleology rest on the logics of sovereignty. Transcendence depends on exceptionalism, the supposition that someone—typically, God or human—is exempted from causal determinism. So it is that God is said to perform miracles by overturning nature or humans are perceived as having minds that override their bodies. These avowals of transcendence rely on hierarchy and superiority: that God or humans are above causal necessity and either wholly or partly above corporeal nature. Concomitantly, these purports underwrite supremacy: the notion that God is supreme over reality or that a part of humans—mind or will—is supreme over the rest of themselves and other beings. Teleology accordingly relies on the rationales of sovereignty by presupposing that a force—traditionally, God—maintains dominion over reality, captaining it towards purposive ends, in a process that often presumes God has the freedom to choose and the autonomy to deliver on its desires. Similarly, the very notion of a telos subordinates the existence or functioning of a given thing to its supposed Purpose. The end is taken as sovereign, and all else becomes subservient to it. When humans nominate certain features that they happen to possess, like the capacity to reason or the ability to reproduce, they crown these as their purpose for being, which hierarchically subsumes all other aspects of who they are to these capabilities.

By resisting transcendence and teleology, Spinoza positions the dislocation of various purports to sovereignty, while disclosing the mutually reinforcing logics that anchor them. This primes us to unfurl the fantasies of domination that saturate our conceptions of reality and our perceptions of ourselves. There is, Spinoza insists—contra not only Cartesianism but an entire current of "Western" philosophy that it seizes and concretizes—"no dominion within a dominion."[10] Here, Spinoza is specifically repelling dualisms that see the mind as exempted from causal determinism, humans as exceptional, exclusively invested with a free will that allows them to dominate their minds and control their bodies. This is correspondingly seen as a mark of human essentialized difference—like God, who is superlatively Different—a sign of human superiority over other beings and thus a sanction to supremacy. Spinoza's rejection of this doctrine is emblematic of a commitment that I espy as pulsating through his entire philosophy: a resistance to the logics and logistics of sovereignty. Particularly, the claim to an essential distinction from some other being and correlatively, the authority to exercise supremacy over this other. By denaturalizing hierarchy and unmasking the interested desires that underpin them, Spinoza delivers an ontology that is radically non-sovereign, while tendering resources for us to continue his critique.

This book probes the manners in which Spinoza pointedly deposes the sovereign God and the sovereign Human, alongside the less obvious ways in which he divests reality and reason of sovereignty. Crucially, this book consolidates and extends Spinoza's critique by applying it to different seats of sovereignty, to other entities routinely arrogated sovereignty, including the cishet male human, the able-bodied human, the white human, and the "Western" human. While Spinoza does not directly address the sovereignties assumed by several of these particular identities, his philosophy, as I detail, submits integral resources for discrediting these entitlements to sovereignty and the supremacies they instantiate. I register how the rationales of sovereignty and the exercise of it direct streams of "Western" philosophy, evincing how sovereignty is not restricted to the realms of the political or theological as is conventionally assumed. This exemplifies my theory that sovereignties amass in coalitions, that the bestowal of sovereignty or its features onto an entity, tends to effectuate further purports to sovereignty. To depict as much, consider the aforementioned example: avowals that God is sovereign emerge from and further spawn professions that humans—uniquely forged in God's image—are sovereign, which then yield additional purports to sovereignty, including the sovereignty of human modes over other modes, the sovereignty of certain humans over other humans, and the sovereignty of parts of humans (minds) over other parts (bodies). Stated differently, admitting hierarchy into reality naturalizes it, promoting its reproduction. By contrast, Spinoza's ontology, which dispels and denaturalizes hierarchies, reprobates the "Western" philosophical fidelity, even fetishization of autonomy, domination, and supremacy.

The Supremacy of Spirit

The religious and theological underpinnings of "Western" modernity, science, and politics have been uncovered,[11] including the purported "secularization" of political sovereignty.[12] I expand on these observations in two manners. The first—as the foregoing expounds—is by augmenting our grasp of sovereignty to encompass not only the strictly political but, perforce, the ontological, epistemological, and ethical, all of which, Spinoza teaches, are intertwined. This approach helps uncover how the rationales and instruments of sovereignty—which are seen as imported from religious quarters, especially medieval Christian domains[13]—suffuse "Western" philosophy.

The second way in which this book supplements theories of "secularization" is by elucidating how the theological character of "Western" philosophy and modernity is distinctly Christian. Although this might seem obvious, it bears stressing because the Christological nature of Descartes's, Kant's, and G. W. F. Hegel's projects is obscured precisely because of their place in *modern* philosophy. By ventilating the logics of sovereignty that condition much of "Western" thought, this book uncovers the Christian origins of entitlements to supremacy. And here I refer not specifically to Christian supremacy in the "religious" sense as instantiated by doctrines of supersession and historically enforced through coerced conversions, inquisitions, and massacres. Nor do I refer to the supremacist imperialism of colonizing missions, which violently impelled Christianity onto indigenous peoples across the globe, slaughtering multitudes, while pilfering their lands, resources, and ideas. But rather I refer to certain supremacist logics, engrained in Christian theology—although not exclusive to it—that continue to inform predominant "Western" approaches to matters ontological and epistemological. For example, as this book unpacks, the rationales of Christian dualism that crown Spirit or Reason as supreme have facilitated the naturalization of sexgendered and racialized differences. If it is by now recognized that "Western" philosophy speaks predominantly from the particularity of the cishet white Christian man of European association who presumptuously takes himself to represent Universality, I signal that such a purport to superiority is uncoincidental, insomuch as the logics of sovereignty, which manifest in the mechanisms of hierarchy, domination, and supremacy, permeate "Western" philosophy. This is an animating theory of the book. Significantly, I make the case that an alternative to this regime is potentiated by Spinoza's denaturalization of sovereignty and destabilization of its sponsoring logics. This book leans on his insights to think reality otherwise, to think reason otherwise, to think being human, otherwise.

The alternative that Spinoza cultivates is deeply indebted to his medieval Jewish and Islamic forebears. Latin, Christian, "Western" philosophy has systematically marginalized these traditions, especially the more naturalist or materialist approaches they endorse. These repressed sources and their flashes of immanence enable the resistance to sovereignty that I spot and magnify in Spinoza's philosophy. Relatedly, the aforementioned medieval Jewish and Islamic rebuff to the quarantining of politics from philosophy fuels his project, facilitating its ethical pith. These legacies ignite Spinoza's refusal to partition minds from bodies and ideas from material conditions, which incubates his trenchant critique of the logics of sovereignty. Concomitantly, probing this non-Christian, non-"Western" tradition accentuates the pervasive theoretical hold that sovereignty maintains over "Western" philosophy. If Augustine had not denigrated the earthly City, segregating it from the superior City of God, if Descartes had not subordinated the body to the hegemony of the transcendent *cogito*, if Hegel had not sublated difference in the teleological advance of Spirit, perhaps the ubiquity of sovereignty in "Western" thought might not have persisted unnoticed. Yet the fact that matters are not otherwise is the point and the problem.

The "Western" positioning of politics as *other* to philosophy, I venture, camouflages the dominance that "political" concerns maintain across its domains. This "Western" stance is cinched by its beloved fictions of neutrality, disinterestedness, and objectivity. Such conceits, Spinoza allows us to see, are secured by the sovereign trait of transcendence. Disavowing transcendence catalyzes his unrelenting critique of Cartesian dualism, which positions mind as sovereign over body, ideas as unconditioned, and free will as emancipated from and so dominant over materiality. With this move, Descartes ratifies centuries of Christian dualism that construe Spirit as regnant and matter as damned, earthly concerns as subordinate to the supersensible. By contrast, in upholding the dependence of the human mind on its body, Spinoza confirms human thinking as embedded in time and space. This renders it natural rather than supernatural, material rather than immaterial, historical rather than ahistorical. Our ideas do not exist in a transcendent realm insulated from embodied circumstances. On the contrary, since there is no escape from the "infinite connection of causes,"[14] from reality, what we think and how we think are impacted by our conditions and continuously impact those conditions. This not only means that our thoughts can never be "neutral" or entirely "objective"—segmented from matter—but also that our ideas *matter*. How we perceive reality has ramifications for how we perceive everything else, and in turn how we perceive everything else shapes how we perceive reality. This is why I maintain that Spinoza's most innovative and generative move is his denaturalization of sovereignty. By dethroning the Sovereign god, Spinoza exposes the anthropocentric conceits that condition this fiction, forestalling the reproduction of further purports to sovereignty. It is because thinking is *of* nature, immanent rather than transcendent, that the conceptualization of sovereignty cannot be sequestered from its material enactment, let alone from the material conditions that foment it. This intuition prompts my interconnected theories that sovereignty governs "Western" philosophy and that its rationales sponsor predominant approaches to reality, reason, and humans, which in turn underwrite certain hierarchies and dominations that remain with us.

Subversive Sources

As this book critiques sovereignty, its methodology or approach, not coincidentally, also agitates against it. Spinoza's philosophy, I contend, has been victim to the liberties of "Western" Christian supremacy. This is discernible in three interconnected facets of its reception, which are delineated here and in the ensuing three sections. The first is the continued occlusion of the medieval Jewish and Islamic philosophical heritages to which Spinoza is heir. Specifically, the more naturalist or materialist interpretation of Aristotle explicated by Ibn Rushd (Latinized as "Averroes") and Ibn Sina (Latinized as "Avicenna"), extrapolated by Maimonides and his close reader, the fourteenth-century Provençal philosopher Levi ben Gershom (Latinized as "Gersonides") through which Spinoza accessed it. While Louis Althusser is right to position Spinoza as a participant in a "repressed"[15] materialist tradition that includes, amongst others, Lucretius, Niccolò Machiavelli, Thomas Hobbes, and Karl Marx, he is mistaken to omit such key figures as Ibn Rushd and Gersonides. This is not a mere oversight. It reflects the willful ignorance that sustains "Western" philosophy, which is supported by its repression of entire libraries of thought. The Condemnation of 1277, issued by the bishop of Tempier, rendered "radical Aristotelianism"—the naturalist interpretation of Aristotle promulgated by Ibn Rushd and other non-"Western," non-Christian thinkers—heretical. Hundreds of years earlier, Justinian's edict in 529 shuttered the Neoplatonic Academy of Athens over suspicions that it was cultivating theories heretical to Christianity. By contrast, not only did the school in Alexandria persist longer, but its emphasis on the more naturalist elements in Aristotle facilitated the naturalist orientations of certain Islamic philosophers centuries later, including Ibn Sina and Ibn Rushd. These traditions, which inform Spinoza's celebrated naturalism or materialism were actively censored by the Latin, Christian, West. This book contributes to the recuperation of these persecuted voices, specifically as refracted through the medieval Jewish philosophers centered in its interpretation of Spinoza.

Even as Christian Europe strained to suppress the naturalism or materialism of medieval Islamic and Jewish Aristotelianism, its subversive forces proved irrepressible. This tradition was pivotal to the development of modern "Western" materialism. Overturning dominant reception histories, Ernst Bloch tracked as much by identifying an influential materialist current stretching from Aristotle to Marx, which he dubbed the "Aristotelian Left."[16] The inaugural philosophers in this lineage, according to Bloch, are Ibn Sina, Ibn Rushd, and Solomon Ibn Gabirol (Latinized as "Avicebron"). Their combined insights reconfigured the soul by denying bodily resurrection; universalized reason by rendering all humans as participants in the active intellect, while refusing to place religion *above* reason; and conceived matter as active, rather than passive. To Bloch, these elements, especially the latter, pack emancipatory potential by imbuing matter with dynamic vitality, positioning material conditions as open to transformation. By contrast, the "Right" Aristotelianism of Christian Scholastics was committed to resurrection, the Church monopoly on reason, and the idealist denigration of matter. Bloch tags Giordano Bruno (influenced by Ibn Sina and Ibn Gabirol) and Spinoza (influenced by Maimonides, including his uptake of Ibn Sina and Ibn Rushd) as decisive figures in this alternative leftist movement, to which Marx and modern "Western" materialism are indebted. This book amplifies Spinoza's distinct contributions to this heritage.

Resisting Binaries

A century ago, Harry Austryn Wolfson pronounced: "We cannot get the full meaning of what Benedictus says unless we know what has passed through the mind of Baruch."[17] While this statement is true insofar as it recognizes the formative influence that Jewish thought had on Spinoza's philosophy, it mistakenly erects a binary between these identities, implying a teleological progression from Baruch to Benedictus. This is accentuated by Wolfson's classification of the former as "the last of the medievals" and the latter as "the first of the moderns."[18] Although his work instructively plumbs Jewish sources to contextualize Spinoza's ideas—supplying an unparalleled resource to students of Spinoza—his method is compromised by its dichotomy between the medieval and modern. This leads to an excavation of the Jewish, Christian, and Islamic backgrounds to Spinoza that glosses over distinctions between these heritages and the disparate thinkers comprising them. Its most lamentable casualty is the stifling of precisely those cadences of Jewish immanence that so aroused Spinoza. Not dissimilarly, Leo Strauss, whose own project is trained on the related and no less regrettable binary of philosophy and religion, reduces Spinoza's philosophy to this confrontation, while minimizing its continuity with medieval Jewish philosophy.[19] By contrast, I follow the lead of Leon Roth, who in 1924 adumbrated the distinctly Maimonidean nature of Spinozism, deciphering that it forms "the grounds of its opposition to and rejection of Cartesianism."[20] More recently, Warren Zev Harvey,[21] Idit Dobbs-Weinstein,[22] and Heidi Ravven[23] have illuminated the indispensable role that Maimonides occupies in the development of Spinoza's philosophy.[24] Harvey and Dobbs-Weinstein, alongside Julie R. Klein, have also instructively turned attention to Gersonides,[25] whose philosophy, penned in Hebrew, also inspired Spinoza. These scholars have constructively shown not only the significance of the Jewish and Islamic naturalism[26] that informs Spinozism, but specifically how it stands in opposition to and tenders a critique of the Platonic, Christian, Latin tenets of "Western" thought.

At issue here is not merely a matter of Spinoza's intellectual setting, of getting the details of his influences straight, which is surely important to any scholarly encounter with his work. Rather, this is also a matter of politics and ethics, not simply because for Spinoza matters intellectual can never be fully disconnected from such concerns, but more pointedly because the dismissal of Spinoza's Jewish and Islamic forebears is a form of Christian, "Western" supremacy. This is so in cases of omission due to simple ignorance on the part of the commentator because such obliviousness is enabled by a system constructed upon the devaluing of traditions deemed other to it. Similarly, when informed commentators—whether personally Jewish or not—downplay Spinoza's Jewish sources or reduce them merely to broader trends in "Western" philosophy, their maneuvers cannot be divorced from this wider Christian supremacist context.

By crediting Jewish thinkers as primary contributors to the development of Spinoza's philosophy, I refer specifically to the signal theory for which he is known: immanence, which prompts his naturalism or materialism. These commitments are exactly what has rendered his thought both controversial in "Western" thought and galvanic. The strands of Jewish immanence that Spinoza inherits primarily from Maimonides and Gersonides, alongside varieties of rationalism imbibed from Abraham ibn Ezra and Hasdai Crescas, position his most pivotal ideas. Often, Spinoza seizes the glints of resistance to transcendence and teleology that percolate in their philosophies and escorts them to more extreme conclusions. Stated plainly, the signature aspects of Spinoza's thought are grounded in the immanence of his Jewish and Islamic predecessors. By recuperating these sources, which have been historically censored and continually sidelined by Christian, "Western" philosophy, this book may be seen as participating in a certain practice of decolonizing.[27] Or minimally, it de-Christianizes and de-"Westernizes"—if these can be meaningfully disaggregated from coloniality—Spinoza's philosophy. Beyond amplifying his non-Christian and non-"Western" influences, this book rebuts still common interpretations of Spinoza derived from the muscled imposition of Christian or "Western" ideas onto his thought. It also rebuts critiques of Spinozism founded on Christian precepts foreign to it. Yet I hazard that this book aligns with certain decolonial aims on a more conceptual register, too. The formative principles that Spinoza inherits from his medieval Jewish predecessors, namely, their revision of the Aristotelian naturalism of Islamic commentators, especially its protests against teleology and transcendence, position Spinoza's confutation of the human exceptionalism, hierarchical dualism, and individualistic freedom that remain sinews of "Western" philosophy. These commitments and the liberties they license have been deemed by decolonial and antiracist philosophy as complicit in colonialism and racism.[28] Crucially, Spinoza's rejection of these postulates of Christian, Cartesian, "Western" philosophy condition what I theorize to be his renouncement of sovereignty and critique of its rationales.

The aspects of Spinoza's immanence that disavow Cartesian dualism and liberal individualism have been lauded by Gilles Deleuze, Louis Althusser, Pierre Macherey, Étienne Balibar, and Antonio Negri. Their work is elucidative and spoors of this book are oriented by their collective, varying insights. However, their readings overlook the Jewishness of Spinoza's philosophy. Barring customary remarks about his Jewish background, routinely accompanied by titillating references to his excommunication, meager attention is granted to the intellectual significance of this heritage.[29] I register instances wherein their disregard and ignorance of Jewish ideas leads to misreadings and the concomitant disfiguring of his philosophy by assimilating it to Christian predicates. This expunging of Spinoza's Jewish sources is all the more glaring considering that earlier thinkers who were similarly aroused by the precise aspects of Spinozism that animate these scholars were at least attuned to its hints of Jewishness. To wit, German-Jewish intellectuals of the nineteenth century, including Heinrich Heine, Berthold Auerbach, Moses Hess, Karl Marx, and Jakob Stern turned to Spinoza, descrying in his philosophy critical resources for thinking differently about identity, autonomy, and being human. These and other modern socialist thinker-activists,[30] Tracie Matysik shows,[31] leaned on Spinoza's materialism to critique bourgeois individualism, the exploitations of capitalism, and the oppressions of liberalism.[32] Crucially, the complexities of their Jewishness, especially the lack of civil rights it conferred upon them—acutely so for Heine, Hess, and Marx as Rhenish Jews whose generation underwent de-emancipation[33]— informed their radical politics and Spinoza's attractiveness to them. Withal, it arguably becomes increasingly difficult to dissociate Spinoza's Jewishness and the Jewishness of his ideas from their appeal to these Jewish thinkers and, in turn, the Jewishness of their contributions to critiques of liberalism, Christian metaphysics, capitalism, and individualism.

The Spinoza-Marx nexus, often refracted through his twentieth-century French partisans like Deleuze and Althusser, continues to motivate divergent reorientations in thinking, including current feminisms, antihumanisms, and New Materialisms. Yet the medieval Islamic and Jewish roots of the immanence or naturalism or materialism that such theorists hail remain indefensibly absent in their engagements. Recently, a couple of scholars, resisting hegemonies of reception histories and the history of philosophy more broadly, have excavated the Jewish background to Spinoza's ideas, while expounding the expansive pertinence of his Jewish philosophical reception to "Western" thought. Spinoza's philosophy sparked a current of German-Jewish thought—starting with Moses Mendelssohn—which has been indispensable to formulating the questions and concepts that have spurred conduits of modern philosophy and its twentieth-century offshoot, Critical Theory.[34] In this vein, Willi Goetschel confirms a lineage that links Spinoza, Hess, Marx, and Theodor Adorno.[35] Likewise, Dobbs-Weinstein positions Marx, Adorno, and Walter Benjamin as heirs to Spinoza's "Jewish form of concrete, material, historical freedom,"[36] which she grounds in medieval Islamic and Jewish Aristotelianism. Spinoza's materialist disruption of the sovereign human ego and the transparent, rational self have also been affined with Freud's materialism.[37] The common indifference to the intellectual significance of Spinoza's Jewishness, incognizance of its Jewish reception, and in turn, insouciance concerning its major impacts on the course of modern "Western" philosophy exemplify the ways in which supremacist postures are reinforcing and perennially reproducing.

By highlighting Spinoza's Jewish sources, I do not mean to reduce him to them. Certain scholarship that is rightly cognizant of his debt to Jewish philosophers, regrettably, at times reads too much of them into his thought. This is patent in readings that uncritically affix Maimonides's ideas onto Spinoza, obfuscating the ways in which he mostly *reconceives* rather than merely receives the thoughts of his predecessors. Spinoza's studious disposal of early drafts of the *Ethics* as well as his notes exhibits the lengths he undertook to cover his tracks. Even a cursory encounter with his writings betrays the degree to which he resigns from citing other philosophers. Those rare occasions when Spinoza does name other thinkers, more often than not, occur in the context of critique. Jewish thinkers are no exception here. However, and Spinoza would be the first to insist on this point, ideas—like everything—do not sprout forth ex nihilo. What we think is profoundly shaped by our pasts, especially our early exposures, encounters, and educations. Spinoza's formal schooling, from early childhood until the age of fourteen or fifteen, occurred in Amsterdam at the Portuguese Jewish community's Talmud Torah. The study of Hebrew Scripture and its medieval commentaries were staples of the curriculum. In the classroom and beyond—in study groups, sermons, and conversations—the young Spinoza would have also studied rabbinic literature, *halakhah*, as well as Jewish medieval philosophers, including Maimonides and Gersonides.[38] Spinoza would have also been introduced, albeit less programmatically, to other sources in the eclectic, burgeoning archive of Jewish thought, including Kabbalah. Not only did Spinoza and his brothers receive what at the time constituted a solid Jewish education, he seemed inclined towards it: "All the earliest sources for Spinoza's life, including comments of his own, agree that his chosen initial sphere of study over many years was the Hebrew language, Bible, and rabbinic law."[39] After leaving the community—at the age of twenty-three—we know that these ideas stayed with Spinoza, literally, as testified by his library, which included, amongst other Jewish tomes: a 1551 printing of Maimonides's *Guide of the Perplexed* in Hebrew translation; a volume of Nissim of Gerona's Talmudic commentary and halakhic glosses; *Halikhot Olam*, a guide to the Talmud; and two tracts of Joseph Solomon Delmedigo, *Sefer Elim* and *Ta'alumot Hokhmah*, a collection of Kabbalistic texts.[40]

It is not clear to what degree Spinoza would have seen himself as a "Jewish philosopher," robustly construed, or to what extent this even matters. Such a label, like all tags, is the type of contrived "mode of thinking" against which he continuously remonstrates. Moreover, Spinoza upholds the particularity of thought: ideas are particularized in being thought by a particular individual whose thinking is primed by the various particularities of that specific person, their conditions, and intra-connections. And further, for Spinoza, adequate thinking is of the particular rather than the general, since abstractions and universals are of the imagination, not reason. As this book trumpets the Jewish aspects of Spinoza's philosophy, it does so while insisting on the particularity of his thinking, underscoring the ways in which he transforms received concepts, intensifying their immanence through reconceptualizations that redound in singularity. Pertinently, my qualifications about classifying Spinoza's project and hesitations to stick a binary label onto his philosophy have nothing to do with the perceived heresies of his theories. Indeed, it is difficult to identify an original thinker in the history of Jewish ideas whose texts were not condemned for supposed heterodoxy. Here I do not refer to the vigorous history of Christian persecutions, censorships, and burnings of Jews and their books. This goes without saying. Rather, I am referencing the reception of Jewish thinkers and texts within certain Jewish circles, including figures like Maimonides and Gersonides, not to mention Kabbalah. By thinking subversively and radically, Spinoza is decidedly in good company with his primary Jewish influences and with the subsequent modern Jewish revolutionary thinkers he inspired. Whatever Spinoza may have thought about the Jewishness of his own thinking, we can be sure that he would hasten to remind us that such designations say more about the one rendering them than the one about whom they are rendered.

The Scandal of Jewishness

The second interrelated concern with regard to the reception of Spinoza's philosophy is the scandal of his Jewishness, by which is meant the ways in which the perceived Jewishness of his ideas has been weaponized in order to discredit his philosophy, specifically by condemning it as pantheist or atheist, a claim historically supported by linking it to Kabbalah. This connection was solidified by the 1699 publication of Johann Georg Wachter's polemical tract *Der Spinozismus im Judenthumb*, which alleged that Spinoza was a closeted Kabbalist, that Judaism is reducible to Kabbalah, that Kabbalah is atheistic, and so Judaism is nothing but atheism. This facilitated Gottfried Wilhelm Leibniz's association of Spinoza with Kabbalah, though he avouched that Spinoza corrupted its teachings, much as he perverted Cartesianism to develop his "monstrous" doctrine.[41] In this, Leibniz and many others were encouraged by Pierre Bayle's influential dictionary entry on Spinoza, which opens with this neat, teleological account: "Juif de naissance, et puis déserteur du judaïsme, et enfin athée" (a Jew by birth, and then a deserter from Judaism, and finally an atheist).[42] The validity of claims to Spinoza's atheism notwithstanding, this label cannot be detached from the doctrinal Christian incrimination of Jews for rejecting Jesus. Hence, "Spinoza's detractors could draw on fifteen hundred years of research attributing Jewish origins to skepticism, materialism, and atheism. These genealogies could be telegraphed in brief allusions."[43] Accordingly, the scandals that encased Spinoza's philosophy from the outset, the fearmongering about its dangers, unrivaled efforts to censor and suppress it, likewise instantiate centuries of Christian suspicions that Jews will seduce them astray. In this entry and throughout the dictionary, Bayle classifies Spinozism as "Oriental" and Eleatic. This allying of Spinoza's philosophy with these "Eastern" philosophies, much like associations of it with Kabbalah, is fostered by and in turn promotes centuries of Christian anti-Judaism and "Western," Christian supremacy.

Portraying Spinoza's philosophy as inherently Jewish became a trope in the eighteenth century. It was popularized by Friedrich Heinrich Jacobi's assault on Enlightenment reason, which he conflated with Spinozism and "Jewish reason." These—the Enlightenment, Spinozism, and Jewish reason—Jacobi claimed, posed a satanic threat to Christian faith and "Western" philosophy. To counter these diabolical forces, Jacobi undertook an inquisition by accusing the deceased Gotthold Ephraim Lessing of having been a Spinozist, with the intention of discrediting the brand of Enlightenment of which he had been a proponent. Jacobi launched these attacks in a series of antisemitic-laden missives to Moses Mendelssohn. With the legacy of Mendelssohn's dear friend Lessing maligned, their Enlightenment project assailed, and Mendelssohn's advocacy for Jewish emancipation imperiled, he had no choice but to respond to Jacobi's attacks. Instead of disavowing Jacobi's charges about the Jewishness of Spinozism, Mendelssohn hailed them, arguing that a "refined" version of Spinoza's philosophy is compatible with Judaism and so also with Mendelssohn's universally accessible religion of reason. This public controversy sank Mendelssohn's reputation, the strains of which precipitated his untimely death in 1786. Yet rather than relegating Spinoza's philosophy to the sidelines, this catapulted it onto center stage of the German intellectual scene. Such prominence exposed the still young but soon to be pivotal German Romantics such as Johann Wolfgang von Goethe, Johann Gottfried Herder, Friedrich Wilhelm Joseph Schelling, Friedrich Hölderin, and Novalis to Spinozism. Crucially, what appealed to these thinkers was less Spinoza's actual philosophy than their systematic baptism of it. Indeed, "it was by virtue of this Christianization that Spinoza suddenly became fashionable and was subsequently embraced."[44] Whereas Leibniz and Jacobi underscored the Jewishness of Spinoza's philosophy in order to attack it as a foreign other contaminating Christian, "Western" philosophy—while simultaneously expropriating it—this generation of thinkers simply purged Spinozism of its Jewishness, forcibly converting its concepts into comportment with Christian doctrines. This was hardly a new technique, yet its most relevant precedent was the Christianization of Kabbalah, inaugurated by *Kabbala Denudata*, a seventeenth-century compendium of Kabbalistic texts in Latin translation. This compilation became an easily adaptable weapon for Christian scholars to deploy in discrediting Spinoza's philosophy. Wachter cited from it to burnish his claims that Spinozism was Kabbalistic and so atheistic, while Anne Conway relied on the work to construct her philosophy by Christianizing Kabbalistic ideas, positioning her own system as "diametrically opposed" to what she regarded as the heretical pantheism of Spinozism.[45]

The tendentious Christian reception of Spinoza—especially Jacobi's polemics in the *Spinozastreit*—braced Hegel to mount his misreading, which categorizes Spinoza's philosophy as "Oriental" and condemns it as compromised by the purported oneness, identity, and rigidity of substance. This is expected, Hegel tells us, because Spinoza is a "Jew," so his philosophy is perforce an "echo from Eastern lands."[46] Consequently, it disables the dynamicity of the Trinity and "the Western principle of individuality."[47] This is not merely an overdetermined, anti-Jewish, Christian appraisal. Rather, such marginalization strategically positions Hegel to appropriate the signal concepts of Spinoza's philosophy, namely the self-causation, infinity, and immanence of substance, which he deftly exploits to correct for what he concocts to be its deficits. Its allegedly paralyzing negativity—"Oriental" immobility—is dialectically transmuted by means of Hegel's deployment of Spinoza's immanence and self-causation into the self-mediating, teleologically advancing, Absolute. Christian Hegelianism sublates Jewish Spinozism, positioning universal Christian Spirit to supersede the particularity of Jewish staidness. Thusly, substance *becomes* Subject.

While Hegel has a penchant for interested readings that promote his own theses, his denunciation and concomitant embezzlement of Spinoza's philosophy is unmatched in his oeuvre. The Jewishness of Spinoza and the perceived Jewishness of his ideas subsidize this maltreatment. Recall that Hegel's complementary projects on the philosophy of history and history of philosophy are structured on the hierarchical European contrivance of an "East" and "West," "Orient," and "Occident." This fabricated binary, which serves to position European, Christian, white society as fundamentally different from and therefore superior to other cultures, was commonplace in German letters at the time and was exploited by Goethe, Herder, and Schlegel, amongst others. Yet this European supremacist, Christian supremacist, white supremacist device occupies an unparalleled place in Hegel's system. This sovereign binary and the sovereignties that it spawns were staples of European Christian imperialism and colonialism, licensing its assault on people and the ransacking of their cultures and resources the world over. Withal, this hegemonic posture is transposed with particularity in Hegel's system, wherein the *history* of philosophy *is* philosophy: ideas manifest and reason *becomes* historically, progressively, and teleologically. The history of philosophy is the becoming of Spirit, which forms a single totality. In Hegel's telling, "Western" philosophy originates in "Eastern" lands, advancing from the "Oriental," to the Greek, and eventually to German philosophy, the culmination of which is Hegel's own project. As with traditional Christian supersessionism, whereby the Jewish is absorbed and overcome by the Christian, Hegel expands this calculus to encompass "Oriental" cultures and concepts, the best of which are supplanted through sublation in the teleological, free triumph of "Western" Spirit. "Western" philosophy—like history—develops by dialectically confiscating and converting "Eastern" concepts, none of which is more decisive for Hegel's own project than those of Spinoza. So it is that Spinoza, Hegel says, is the "testing-point in modern philosophy"[48] and "to be a follower of Spinoza is the essential commencement of all Philosophy."[49] This Jewish beginning of modern philosophy stations Hegel's adept despoiling and supersession of Spinozism, as Spirit consummates *as* Hegelianism.

More startling than Hegel's "Western" and Christian supremacist maltreatment of Spinoza is both the silence about this in the literature—save the valuable interventions of a few Jewish scholars[50]—and its uninterrogated reproduction within the wider scholarship. In the most compelling and sustained rebuttal to Hegel, Macherey's *Hegel or Spinoza*, there is nary a mention of the Christian, "Western" supremacy underpinning Hegel's critique. This is so, even as Macherey cites the most impeachable of Hegel's passages regarding the "Oriental" nature of Spinozism: Spinoza's Jewishness and his disavowal of individual Christian consciousness and disallowance of the Trinity.[51] Similarly, while Althusser pinpoints the concept of Spinoza's that Hegel most fails to appreciate—anti-teleology—Althusser duplicates its sovereign logics by speaking of "Spinoza's anticipation of Hegel."[52] In this formulation, Spinoza's philosophy functions as but the means to the ends of Hegelianism. Jewish Spinoza is the vehicle through which Christian Hegel ascends to prominence.

The impact of the German Idealist misreadings of Spinoza, especially Hegel's, pervade the scholarship, extending far beyond the aforementioned works that directly contend with them. Countless interpretations of Spinoza uncritically perpetuate their suppositions. Whether done wittingly or unwittingly, such readings cannot be disaggregated from the anti-Jewish and Christian supremacist contexts that initially sponsored their promotion. For example, Deleuze's portrayal of substance as a univocity, his attribution of idealism to Spinoza, and his hierarchical construal of substance-attributes-modes reprise the staples of Hegel's Christian supremacist rendition, which was informed by Christian denunciations linking Spinozism to Kabbalah and atheism. Similar presuppositions remain staples of the more "analytic" literature on Spinoza, including assertions of its monism, idealism, and parallelism. While this book rebuts such readings and the sovereign logics that underwrite them on exegetical grounds, what bears emphasis here is not so much the intellectual merits or demerits of such accounts. But the indifference or ignorance on the part of scholars concerning the origins of such interpretations and the ideologies that supported them.

The problem here is not merely current work that reprises prejudiced readings flagrantly rooted in Christian, "Western" supremacy. It is that alternative paths of interpretation that make a strong case against, say, monism, idealism, and parallelism are oriented by Spinoza's Jewish predecessors. This is also the case for alternatives to what have been dubbed "Platonizing interpretations"[53] as well as the misattribution of teleology and normativity to Spinoza. Had "Western" philosophy historically, and still now, not sidelined Jewish philosophy, if it actually *studied* Jewish thinkers such as Maimonides and Gersonides, then some of these errors might have been avoided. The unquestioned imposition of "Western" categories and constructs *onto* his philosophy, not to mention a rubric that evaluates it based on Christological tenets, whether explicitly so, or as is often the case, merely implicitly, is responsible for these misinterpretations. This demands a reckoning and concerted rectification. Critical examinations throughout this book are modest contributions towards this desideratum.

Conflict of Interest

The third intertwined concern of reception is how the scholarship on Spinoza remains bedeviled by what has been termed a "conflict of interpretations,"[54] a circumstance wherein the same texts and ideas are construed antipodally. While incompatible readings of any body of philosophical work can emerge, and such turns often bespeak the capaciousness, nuance, and energy of a given thinker, the case of Spinoza's reception exceeds this expected, even exciting prospect. Not only do conflicting takes stretch back to the earliest readings, but their durability, scope, and reputability are singular. To name but the most acknowledged of such contradictions: to some, Spinoza is an idealist while to others a materialist, his philosophy is seen by some as "God intoxicated" and by others as atheistic, his theories are perceived by some as promoting liberalism and by others as endorsing socialism. Indeed, Spinoza remains "a fundamental reference for so many completely opposed philosophical trends."[55] This reality of conflicting readings has been explained as reflective of the ways in which Spinoza's philosophy defies pat classifications and disrupts neat binaries.[56] It has also been attributed to the diverse range of philosophical traditions from which he draws.[57] These are contributing factors, to be sure, as is Warren Montag's insight that Spinoza's philosophy "never definitively closes upon itself" but remains open to "unforeseeable theoretical elements that arrive from beyond its boundaries."[58]

While these explanations are fair, they are not the full story. The "conflict of interpretations" also reflects the interests of Spinoza's readers. By this I mean not merely the aforementioned early Christian reception typified by Leibniz, Bayle, and Conway nor the German Romantic baptizing and German Idealist critiques, but twentieth-century and contemporary scholarship wherein Spinoza's philosophy "is often appropriated piecemeal and second-hand in order to serve as justification for the motives of authors who, precisely, eschew any close reading of Spinoza's text."[59] This is a symptom of certain presentations, across the gamut of the literature, several of which are exposed and rebutted in this book. Such interpretive violence cannot be dissociated from its long history, exemplified by its pivotal offenders—Jacobi and Hegel—and the Christian supremacy that sponsored their denunciations and expropriations. Yet Spinoza's Jewishness is not merely a factor that contributes to the wanton pillaging of his philosophy. Rather, I maintain that his Jewishness, which has been central to the reception of his philosophy ab initio, remains an unrecognized facet undergirding the predicament of divergent interpretations. Historically and still today, it seems that Spinoza's Jewishness licenses scholars to remake him in whatever image suits their ends. Here I do not refer merely to ungenerous or appropriative readings but also to earnest work that liberally sees in Spinoza commitments that simply are not really there. Much of this is subsidized by past and present Christianizing and "Westernizing" readings, which sovereignly impose their presuppositions onto it. Beyond this, however, I suspect that precisely Spinoza's Jewishness feeds the font of conflicting readings. In the eyes of his interpreters, Spinoza is the Jew, the other who is without true substance. As Derrida, glossing Paul Celan, has it: "The Jew is the other who has no essence . . . whose own essence is not to have one."[60] Like Hegel's indictment of modes as "nothing in and for themselves,"[61] Spinoza's ideas, from the vantage of his Christian readership, are without essential features or basic commitments. Jewish Spinoza, much as Hegel alleges of substance, is divested of "individuality, personality, the moment of self-consciousness."[62] Spinoza, as Jew, is not yet Subject.

Lest it seem that I am here only to pillory Christian supremacist philosophers for manipulating and mutilating Spinoza's ideas, it is pertinent to punctuate that Jewish philosophy has not been especially impartial or hospitable to Spinoza. At least since Jacobi's crusade against Mendelssohn against Spinozism against Kabbalah against Jewishness, Jewish interpretations of Spinoza's philosophy have been overdetermined, either in affirming Spinoza's Jewishness and the Jewishness of his thought as Mendelssohn[63] and Salomon Maimon do,[64] or in disaffirming its Jewishness and rebuffing its theories. Hermann Cohen's polemical reading of the *Theological-Political Treatise* (hereafter referred to as *TTP*) is emblematic of this approach,[65] as is Emmanuel Levinas's appropriation of Hegel's critiques of Spinoza.[66] Their misapprehensions of Spinoza's thought cannot be disjoined from the broader "Western," Christian supremacist treatment of Spinoza nor from the commitments of their own projects and their respective stakes in specific varieties of Jewishness. Several prominent modern Jewish philosophers mostly ignore Spinoza, including Franz Rosenzweig and Hannah Arendt, while Martin Buber offers minimal engagement.[67] A similar avoidance exists in the work of Rosa Luxemburg and Adorno, which, considering their Marxist commitments, is especially palpable and a missed opportunity. Spinoza's reception across the wider spectrum of Jewish thought is complex, encompassing critique, appropriation, and inspiration.[68] Much of it focuses more on Spinoza's work in the *TTP*, especially his interpretation of Hebrew Scripture and his remarks on religion, than on his philosophy as explicated in the *Ethics*. The experiences of his own life, chiefly the writ of *ḥerem* issued him by the leaders of his synagogue also figure prominently in the centuries of Jewish reception of his texts and legacy. To certain readers this was rousing, while to others, scandalizing.

The fact that Spinoza's Jewishness has been weaponized to demonize his philosophy as atheistic does not detract from the fact that it does, indeed, discrown the Sovereign god. Claims to its atheism, therefore, are not unjustified. What is important to stress, however, is how such charges have historically been imbricated with Spinoza's Jewishness and linkages of it to the presumed atheism of Kabbalah. Moreover, although Spinoza's views have been deemed as undercutting conventional Jewish theology, within the context of specific streams of Jewish thought, they are not quite as radical as they may seem. Certain texts in Kabbalah do undermine the divine sovereignties of transcendence and unity assumed by some as theologically fundamental.[69] Yet even more direct influences on Spinoza's project have equally been deemed heretical, including the work of Ibn Ezra, Maimonides, and Gersonides. Often, Spinoza escorts their ideas to more radical conclusions, some of which they likely could neither have anticipated nor accepted. Nevertheless, the historicism, rationalism, and immanence that he inherits and intensifies from these Jewish philosophers valuably contextualizes more popular depictions that punctuate the supposedly unprecedented heterodoxy of his ideas.

Without entangling ourselves in the complexities of Spinoza's excommunication and the amalgam of social, political, economic, legal, and theological factors that precipitated it, the invocation of this episode from Spinoza's life by commentators, like accusations of his atheism, especially by Christian readers, is seldom neutral. At times, such treatment assumes the kind of taut, teleological take as seen above in Bayle's telling or in Henry More's: "Spinoza, a Jew first, after a Cartesian, and now an atheist."[70] Not only do such simplistic formulae rely on centuries of Christian damnations of Jews for rejecting Christ. Here, rather than a Jew overcoming their corporeality by moving towards Jesus, as Christianity doctrinally ordains and has violently enforced—as with Spinoza's converso ancestors—we have a Jew so obstinate that he reverts to atheism. Such a telling not only weaponizes Spinoza's Jewishness to denounce his ideas but presumes that Spinoza could not have been a Jew when he developed his philosophy. This is precisely the point when over a hundred and seventy years later, Bruno Bauer, in his screed against Jewish emancipation declaims: "Spinoza was no longer a Jew when he created his system."[71] For Bauer—influenced by Hegel—Jews are not only outside of history but due to their particularity, actively forestall its progress and so, he contends, are unworthy of civil rights. Denying Spinoza's Jewishness allows Bauer to claim "not one Jewish name" has contributed to cultural, political, or societal progress.[72] By contrast, in contemporary work, mentions of Spinoza's Jewishness and the *ḥerem* tend towards the admiring, if at times idolizing. Girding for his own Christian/Hegelian denunciation of Spinozism, Slavoj Žižek snarkily indexes this habit: "Who can be against a lone Jew who, on top of it, was excommunicated by the 'official' Jewish community itself?"[73]

Pockets of Resistance

Stating that Spinoza critiques sovereignty is an uncontroversial assertion. Even as scholars disagree about the degree to which his political theory undercuts sovereignty, there is no denying that in his life and in his philosophy, Spinoza was outspoken about the ways in which power is exploitive, tyranny oppressive, and subjugation unethical. Accordingly, he displayed scant regard for the weight of authority and resisted popular superstitions, prejudices, and myths. By corroborating that Spinoza's *Ethics* stages a thoroughgoing disruption of sovereignty, this book at once contextualizes these acknowledged strands in Spinoza's theories and expands the scope and significance of this resistance. This is achieved on two complementary planes. The first is by identifying the conjunctive ways in which Spinoza's philosophy exposes as false a variety of purported sovereigns and the traits of sovereignty they assume—most obviously, the sovereign God. While this is unmistakable, I enrich the understanding of this by demonstrating its breadth, evincing how Spinoza divests God, that is reality, of not merely transcendence and supremacy but a variety of coadunated sovereign features, including Alterity, Preeminence, and Oneness. Such analysis turns attention to the more subtle ways in which the mechanisms of sovereignty pervade not simply the scholarship on Spinoza but "Western" philosophy more broadly. Accordingly, I uncover how by stripping God of sovereignty, Spinoza effectively disburdens nature or reality of sovereign pretense, which means that there are no Laws of Nature or Natural Laws, no normativity or norms in reality. This facilitates a consideration of the ways in which such notions continue to sponsor certain sexist, racist, and ableist ideologies that serve to secure the domination of certain people over others. Similarly, I enrich the understanding of Spinoza's celebrated rejection of free will and sovereign individualism by considering its pertinence for redressing contemporary neoliberal policies and ethea.

The second is by demonstrating how as Spinoza dispenses with established sovereigns—God, Human, Reason—he also resigns from recycling their sovereignties. For example, he dispossesses God of will, transcendence, and freedom without rehabilitating these features by attaching them to other entities such as reality itself or humans or certain features possessed by humans, such as reason. This is especially significant because much of the analysis throughout this book interrogates the ways in which readers of Spinoza attach commitments to him that reproduce the sovereignties he disavows. These include assertions of Spinoza's normativism, parallelism, and idealism, which, I show, rely on the very logics of sovereignty that he vitiates. Similarly, while Spinoza's ontology resists sovereign oneness and identity, I evidence how this does not devolve into the erasure of difference wherein individual particularity is dissolved in totality. This would amount to nothing more than an inversion that renders the universal, rather than the particular, supreme.

Considerable attention is also tendered to competing philosophical stances through investigations that expose the logics and logistics of sovereignty that subtend them. This is done by contending with positions that Spinoza himself critiques, most prominently Cartesianism, as well as the approaches of his critics, including Hegel's teleological dialecticism. But more revealingly, by analyzing contemporary ontologies, including Object-Oriented Ontology and New Materialism, decoding how, rather than abjuring ontotheological sovereignties, often these approaches merely refurbish them. Furthermore, exposing and exploring Spinoza's assault on the logics of sovereignty position me to extrapolate his critique by discerning and critiquing the sovereign rationales that underpin current enterprises, including feminisms of sexual difference, evolutionary biology, and deep ecology.

Following Maimonides, Spinoza regards language as a repository of prejudices.[74] But since there are no effective means of dispensing with language or seamlessly wresting readers of their sedimented, often unconscious, prejudices, Spinoza turns to a strategy of subversive redefinition, which seizes certain familiar theological and philosophical terms and reframes them. This technique, while rhetorically savvy, has also freighted his thought in confusion, facilitating misconstructions, many of which are entrenched in hegemonic Christian, "Western" suppositions. Consider his most famous deployments: "God *or* substance"[75] and "God *or* nature."[76] God *or* substance *or* nature. This formulation captures, on the one hand, Spinoza's widely recognized—and criticized—unthroning of a sovereign God from its transcendent pedestal. Yet, on the other hand, it also signifies a further, if more subtle disruption, for it is not merely God that is redefined but also substance and nature and not simply because such an equation by default tenders a redefinition of all its terms. Rather, his use of the metaphysical term *substance*, I evidence, defies its common usage as does the valence carried by *nature*. This means that substance is not substantial in the classic sense nor is there nature as such. Other common terms that Spinoza uses, but redefines in ways that dilute their sovereign pretenses, include *essence, attribute, power, affect, desire,* and *conatus*.

A further consequential way in which Spinoza fractures conventional habits of thought is his overturning of binaries, the most famous of which is his uncompromising rejection of Christian, Augustinian, Cartesian dualism, which places mind over body, spirit over matter, thinking over being. Yet alongside this, Spinoza also dismantles the binaries of subject and object, self and other, mind and body. While these have been noted in the literature, other less known binaries that Spinoza razes include culture and nature, natural and unnatural, ends and means, past and present. This book also revises certain suppositions in the scholarship by advocating for the dissolution of ostensible binaries particular to the commitments of his program, such as that between substance and modes, cause and effect, potential and actual, essence and existence, passivity and activity, feeling and thinking. Furthermore, I corroborate that Spinoza's abolition of binaries is expressive of, and critical to, his overall assault on sovereignty, not only because the unhinging of these obdurate binaries undoes the supremacies routinely afforded one over the other, say, the sovereignty of the mind over the body, but insomuch as it calibrates our theorizing of binary logics. Throughout this book, I excavate the sovereign logics that underpin binary rubrics and the exercises in supremacy they serve to ratify. Binaries presume an a priori, immutable, essentialized difference, which promotes and often naturalizes hierarchy. These ranks are then enforced through the maintenance of boundaries, which are in turn perceived as sovereign, that is, given, unchanging, and commanding. This functionally validates forms of domination and subordination. Scrutinizing the sovereign rationale that shores binaries allows us to interrogate not merely notorious "Western" binaries like that between "man" and "woman" but also how even thinkers militating against the oppressiveness of this precise binary at times reinscribe its logics. This is most egregiously the case with feminisms of sexual difference and TERFism (trans-exclusionary radical feminism), but also in certain liberatory stances. To wit, the just work to destigmatize transness is popularly accompanied by the installation of a further binary: that between transness and cisness. While this serves to promote trans visibility, it risks reifying cisness as the natural, normative default and transness as non-normative, unnatural, and exceptional. This also presumptuously forces all those who are not or not yet trans into the straitjacket of cisness. The uptake of these reflections on binary rationales is that sovereign distinctions of this kind, even well-intentioned ones, hazard counterproductively perpetuating the supremacies endemic to binaries. By contrast, Spinoza's resistance to binaries, classifications, and the contingency of all "modes of thinking" solicits us to think outside of binary logic.

Breaking with Convention

This book is not the first to assert that certain presumptions associated with sovereignty orient core "Western" tenets, the most commonly acknowledged of these being doctrines of individualism and voluntarism. Scholars have instructively outlined the significance of Spinoza's critique of these principles, specifically in his rebuttals to Cartesianism. Extending this work, I demonstrate how this impulse pervades Spinoza's entire project, well beyond these recognized nodes. Accordingly, I corroborate how purports to sovereignty orient the predominant strains of "Western" philosophy that he critiques. This casting of "Western" thought is revelatory and foments a refreshed theoretical confrontation with it. At the same time, by probing the logics of sovereignty and unraveling how it structures particular streams of "Western" philosophy, this book gestures towards the ramifications of this state of affairs. It does so most patently by interrogating certain sites in which the logics of sovereignty remain operative, including through ableist, sexist, transphobic, and racist practices. In so doing, this book implicitly questions the fitness of a system—"Western," Christian thought—contrived on the rationales of supremacy and hierarchy to overcome, let alone to actively correct for, such injustices. Although countless factors contribute to the tragic reality that equality, not to mention the conditions promoting the flourishing of historically and still oppressed individuals and groups of individuals, remains elusive, this book intimates that an element in this calculus is the fact that certain prized "Western," Christian, liberal ideas are founded on the logics of sovereignty. Until there is a genuine confrontation with how these principles continue to underwrite a certain "Western" ethos, the dismantlement of supremacies and the forms of sexgendered, racial, ethnic, social, religious, and economic domination they license may remain beyond our reach. Such a predicament is poignantly captured by Audre Lorde's verdict: "The master's tools will never dismantle the master's house."[77] Crucially, this book unclasps the prospect of an otherwise by uncovering and expanding upon Spinoza's philosophy, which divests reality, reason, and humans of pretensions to sovereignty. Not coincidentally, the hints of immanence promoted by his Jewish forebears, which were actively censored by "Western," Christian thought, position Spinoza's vitiation of sovereignty. It likewise seems uncoincidental that several aspects of Spinoza's philosophy, which I evince as indispensable to his philosophy *or* to his insurrection against sovereignty, have been occluded by scholarly interpretations rooted in the logics of hierarchy.

Spinoza repudiates a dominant conceit of "Western" philosophy: that philosophy is sovereign, which is to say that it thinks—like the Cartesian *cogito*—autonomously, universally, objectively. This amounts to the claim that thought is unconditioned by its circumstances, unconstrained by its particularity, and unhindered by its standpoint. The naturalist or materialist strand in Jewish philosophy to which Spinoza is heir furnishes him with the frame through which to resist the hegemony of this "Western" stance and the privileges that it has come to validate. This book is therefore committed to the Spinozist principle which takes our perceptions of reality seriously precisely because they are *not neutral* and because they have lived repercussions. Accordingly, Spinoza's nondualism resists the "Western" sequestering of epistemology from ethics, thinking from being. Knowledge begins with the body—the imagination—which means that it is entrenched in place and time. Thinking is affective or emotional, which is also why reason is social and public and so necessarily a matter of ethics and politics. Spinoza devotes considerable attention to understanding affects and desires because thinking is embodied and *of* its conditions. While this stance inspires this book's critique of "Western" philosophy and its pervasive reliance on the logics and mechanisms of sovereignty, Spinoza's own miscues are not exempted from critique. Spinoza is unsparing in his criticism of the superstitions and prejudices that propel many philosophical, religious, cultural, historical, and moral beliefs. When confronted by the signs of his own prejudices, this book follows his guidance to recognize them, contextualize them, and critique them.

In their correspondence, Hugo Boxel vainly attempted to persuade Spinoza to accede to the existence of ghosts. To bolster his case, Boxel asserted, "all the Philosophers, both ancient and those of our time" believed in their veridicality.[78] Spinoza not only discredited Boxel's conviction, with no small amount of sarcasm, but declared: "To me the authority of Plato, Aristotle, and Socrates is not worth much."[79] I, too, do not seek the authority of Spinoza to confirm, for example, my anti-cishetsexism and my antiracism. Moreover, I remain suspicious of efforts to plumb the so-called canon merely to excavate materials that might confirm or burnish the truths that many are only now coming to fully appreciate. But I am keen to think *with* Spinoza, which encompasses critiquing his trafficking in sexist and racist stereotypes and registering his family's colonial enterprises. Doing so unapologetically does not negate the force of his thinking to help us deconstruct the very sovereignties that he at times perpetuates. While Spinoza evidently did not see as much, his critique of teleology, transcendence, binary logic, and "modes of thinking"—his denaturalization of sovereignty—furnishes us with valuable conceptual resources for deconstructing the power and traction of these oppressions, the violence they license, and the possibilities available for dismantling them.

The aspersions that Spinoza casts upon the need to rely on the authority of other philosophers to certify his views encapsulates his disregard for inherited customs of thought and the injurious submission to convention. Throughout his writings, he seldom refers to other philosophers, and when he does, he is mostly critical. Yet even as Spinoza's influences remain unmentioned, their presence is palpable as he studiously renovates and remodels their ideas, often extending them to conclusions they likely did not expect nor would condone. Since all thinking is situated and conditioned, Spinoza recognized the ways in which the weight of prejudices informed and distorted the conceptions of his predecessors. There is then both a certain irony and vindication to the fact that the interpretation of Spinoza's philosophy continues to be subject to the imposition of various prejudices and received verdicts. Such awareness, coupled with keen attunement to his Jewish sources, allows this book to read Spinoza in ways that may seem unfamiliar to those firmly situated in the mainstream scholarship, whether ensconced in so-called analytic or continental quarters. Despite their differences and even with admirable recent strides to elevate traditions on their margins, both philosophical domains remain predominantly attached to Latin, Christian, "Western" modalities of thinking. This manifests in the attribution to Spinoza of doctrines such as idealism, monism, and parallelism. It accordingly surfaces in scholarship that renders Spinoza's reality as a totality; construes substance, attributes, and modes hierarchically; sustains a strict dualism between substance and modes; and undercuts modal existence. These interpretations are steeped in centuries of criticism of Spinoza that were motivated by anti-Judaism and Christian supremacy. By punctuating this history, this book attempts a redress. At issue here is not only the matter of disreputable origins but also interpretative validity. Several of these readings and many further connected renderings impose specific Christian, "Western" presuppositions and constructs onto Spinoza's philosophy. Tending to Spinoza's Jewish sources proffers salient background, which elicits alternative readings. Doing so also exposes the sovereign logics that underwrite several predominant approaches, especially of the dualist, idealist, parallelist variety. Thinking beyond these and other "Western" philosophical models unveils a *different* Spinozist ontology and epistemology and so also ethics.

Through its theorizing with Spinoza, this book steers his ideas into untrammeled territory, incubating analyses, inducing conclusions, and inciting questions that may strike readers as unexpected, even unwarranted. Here, too, I follow Spinoza's lead, who pushed his inherited sources to facilitate inferences that they surely would have deemed excessive, and brought their ideas to bear on the concerns of his moment and into conversation with his contemporaries. In this spirit, for example, I use Spinoza's critique of teleology to debunk the "Western" axiom of gender as the *truth* of the self, to discredit the liberal dogmas of progress, and to dissect the discourse surrounding the emergence of COVID. If such interventions appear idiosyncratic when conjoined with this book's close textual exegesis, immersion in the vast scholarship on Spinoza, and steadied analysis of his ideas, all I can say is that here too, Spinoza is to blame. His entire project, aligned with the example set by Maimonides, realizes the inseparability of ideas from material states, thinking from being, philosophy from politics. Of course, this also means that my readings are no less conditioned and my concerns no less particularized and my priorities no less impacted. There is merit to Althusser's (defensive) remark that "to be a heretical Spinozist is almost orthodox Spinozism."[80] The fact that Spinoza's philosophy continues to accommodate uncanny readings and discordant uptakes bespeaks its openness, its promise, its disparity. Even after centuries of exploitive and overdetermined readings, nuanced and informed readings, dull and uninteresting readings, revelatory and insightful readings—and sometimes all of these in the very same reading!—there is still much to say about Spinoza *or* with Spinoza.

On Disparity

In thinking disparity as signaled by the subtitle of this book, what is meant is a sense of difference and incongruity, which is distinct from the logics of the binary, wherein two things are taken as opposed, contrasting, divided, which induces hierarchy, domination, and supremacy. It alludes to how this book limns the ways in which Spinoza dispenses with binary thinking, while hinting at its theorizing of difference outside of binary logics. Such disparity also speaks to how Spinoza's philosophy resists the supremacist logics of final ends, which manifest in liberalisms of inevitable progress and celebrations of the triumph of reason, either individually or societally. There is no transition from unreason to reason, irrationality to rationality. Reality is uncontained and uncontrolled and inconsistent. Reality is disparate. We are subject to forces within us and outside of us that far exceed our comprehension, let alone our control. We too, are disparate. Spinoza's lifework strives to cultivate the conditions for humans to flourish, "not so they may be slaves, but that they may do freely the things that are best."⁸¹ Yet this campaign for emancipation from supremacist domination and oppressive hierarchies, be they political, religious, or social, is tempered by his recognition of its obstacles, especially the prejudices and superstitions, histories and habits, selfishness and greed that hinder equality, the common good, and living well. Ethics depends upon our capacities to enact more "agreements" rather than "disagreements" with others, particularly those with whom we most share a nature, other humans. Spinoza reminds us that there is no resort from our predicaments and particularities, which means that disagreements, differences, and disparities are inevitable.

A further impediment to individual thriving, which for Spinoza is necessarily collective, is the fiction of our freedom. While he resisted the sovereign exercises by authorities to circumscribe freedoms, Spinoza equally theorized the ways in which humans, like all modes, are not really free. With this, he assails the freedom adulated by Augustine and Descartes, Christian theology and "Western" philosophy, liberalism and, now, neoliberalism. Such freedom, he stresses, relies on and verifies the delusive sovereignty of human exceptionalism, the conceit of transcendence from corporeality, and the fiction of escape from causal determinism, all of which promote fantasies of autonomous, atomistic individualism. The freedom *from* constraint licenses the freedom *to* dominate. Yet in vitiating this variety of Christian, Cartesian, "Western" freedom, Spinoza is also deflating its seemingly less sovereign but no less damaging instantiations. Free will, as Augustine and Descartes argue, renders humans individually culpable for their deeds and so punishable by a Sovereign god. The remnants of this theology are palpable today in liberal mythologies of "rugged individualism," in a neoliberalism that blames individuals for their sorry circumstances in place of implicating structures, and in pop psychologies that pronounce: "You can be whatever you want to be." Against this abiding delusion, Spinoza delivers the sobering truth: we are not free. While appealing, conceits of freedom are fundamentally disempowering. We humans are not sovereign over ourselves, our circumstances, our feelings, our thoughts, our memories, our desires, and our actions. Recognizing as much—dispensing with this delusion—is a prerequisite to realizing Spinoza's non-transcendent, non-sovereign, non-teleological ethics. Such immanent ethics accepts thinking as affective, living as collective, and doing good as not merely possible, but necessary.

Cutting a Path

Chapter 1, "Substance Is Insubstantial," is oriented by Spinoza's admonition: "No one will be able to perceive rightly the things I maintain unless they take great care not to confuse God's power with the power or right of kings."[82] This reflects his refusal of the sovereign traits routinely attached to God, especially Transcendence, Freedom, Will, and Agency. Through a close reading of part I of the *Ethics*, I document how this program is more expansive. Spinoza divests God *or* nature *or* substance of several further sovereignties by foreclosing its status as First Cause and Origin and stripping it of Primacy, Alterity, and Essence. This denaturalization of sovereignty rebuts the dominant thrust of "Western" philosophy, which arrays reality on mechanisms of preeminence, hierarchy, and exceptionalism as typified by the Christian dualism consolidated by Cartesian metaphysics. Against this, Spinoza introduces an ontology that is without priority, rank, or essentialized difference. To launch this revolution, he leans on medieval Jewish and Islamic Aristotelianism, especially as refracted by Maimonides. I demonstrate how Spinoza extracts the naturalist currents of this tradition—its notion of God as the necessary existent, its conception of God as unlimited, its construal of God as coincident with God's actions—and extends them further. These induce his interlaced claims that substance is self-caused, infinite, and immanent, which I delineate as more innovative and egalitarian than has been acknowledged. To depict as much, I introduce an interpretation of substance—all that is—as infinite, indeterminate power that exists only *as* its finite, determinate acts, which *are* its modes. Reality is an infinite matrix of intra-active causation. This levels the hierarchical binaries of cause and effect, freedom and necessity, form and matter, activity and passivity, doing and being. Thereby, Spinoza releases substance from the metaphysical supremacies routinely attached to it, rendering it "insubstantial." The chapter ends by theorizing the implications of Spinoza's immanent ontology, which confirms reality as non-hierarchical, non-exceptionalist, and non-sovereign.

Chapter 2, "Nature Is Not All," develops an innovative take on Spinoza's conception of infinity, confirming it as the unrecognized anchor of his philosophy. By construing the infinity of substance as indeterminacy—which I detail as partly indebted to medieval Jewish philosophy—Spinoza liberates infinity from the fetters of sovereign properties. This resists the Christian, "Western" philosophical relegation of infinity to the Transcendent and its routine impoundment within the confines of unity, oneness, and identity.

In upholding immanent reality as infinite, Spinoza refuses such hierarchy and exceptionalism, unleashing an ontology that I delineate as unbounded. Reality is not One, it is not Whole, and it is not a Totality. All that is, is not All. Modes too, are disburdened of sovereign Oneness: no mode constitutes an isolated One, a bounded Unity, or a staid Identity. To advance such an ontology, I confront the centuries of scholarship that have linked Spinoza's substance to "Oriental" oneness and Kabbalah's Ein Sof. While I expose the anti-Judaism and Christian supremacy that subsidize these claims, including their imbrication with the Christianization of Kabbalistic texts, I also confront the complexities of Mendelssohn's and Maimon's construals. This contextualizes what I descry as the Christian, "Western" supremacy that sponsors Hegel's misreading of Spinoza. What I show is that Hegel's Christian/"Western" supremacy positions him to criticize, assimilate, and then overcome Jewish/"Oriental" Spinozism. This supersession is not coincidental but is endemic to his dialectical system, which I evince as founded on and fueled by supremacy: the Absolute is a totality that subsumes the finite as a moment in its infinite, teleological advance to becoming Subject. By contrast, Spinoza refuses to conceive the infinite and finite binarily: infinite power only exists *as* its finite acts. To conclude, the chapter registers how the contemporary literature continues to miss Spinoza's nonbinary take on infinity, which surfaces in hierarchical construals of substance, attributes, and modes; claims that substance is "One"; portrayals of Spinoza's ontology as a "system"; and classifications of it as "monist." Such readings are not only mistaken but cannot be disaggregated from their Christian, "Western" supremacist histories and derive partly from the erasure of Spinoza's medieval Jewish sources, which inform his alternative, nonbinary conception of infinity.

Chapter 3, "Not for Nothing," probes the conceptual implications of Spinoza's nonbinary conception of infinity, which suspends the binaries of Something and Nothing, Positive and Negative, Being and Nonbeing. Against the "Western" philosophical tendency to ground reality in a supreme Presence or its total Absence, Spinoza's novel approach to infinity refuses this choice by declining to invest either with sovereignty. Yet the reception of Spinoza's philosophy remains freighted in fidelity to this false choice. Whereas Hegel critiques Spinozism by aligning it with the presence, identity, and positivity of Eleaticism, recent proponents of Spinoza have responded by spotlighting his supposed alignments with atomism. Both Deleuze and Althusser exploit Lucretius's clinamen to defend Spinozism against these Hegelian charges.

Examining their glosses and their roots in Marx's dissertation positions me to perpend with the void and its associated concepts: identity and difference, unity and multiplicity, stability and generativity. What Deleuze and Althusser discover in Spinoza complements their respective philosophies more than it reflects his own commitments. In fact, Spinoza, I evidence, follows medieval Jewish and Islamic Aristotelianism as well as Cartesianism in voiding the vacuum. However, unlike these traditions, Spinoza's invalidation of the void neither bolsters the singularity of a sovereign God nor promotes the Positive as primary. Moreover, examining Crescas's advocacy of an infinite vacuum exemplifies the ontotheological sovereignties that sponsor its construction. Proponents of nothingness, both past and present, who perceive it as primary, originary, and supremely constitutive of what is, furnish it with the sovereign traits traditionally attached to God. Withal, contemporary scholarship has not tired of the vacuum, the void, the nothing. I discern as much by probing Timothy Morton's Object-Oriented Ontology, unveiling the sovereignties that certify their ontology: transcendence, apophaticism, and nothingness. This audit positions analysis of Hegel's legacy as manifest in the work of Alain Badiou and Žižek, both of whom leverage Lucretius to criticize Spinozism. I register their missteps, while revealing the sovereign, Christian logics that secure their respective programs. Whereas dominant clusters of ancient, medieval, early modern, and contemporary "Western" philosophy rely on the binary of being and nonbeing to make sense of reality, Spinoza's ontology fosters an unrecognized alternative. By discounting the hierarchies, supremacies, and essentialized differences that anchor this contrived binary, it upholds reality as nonbinary.

Chapter 4, "Serves No Purpose," elucidates anew Spinoza's acclaimed critique of teleology, which divests reality of End, Design, and Order, emancipating it from subjugation to a Plan and submission to a Purpose. It dissects the anthropocentrism that undergirds teleology and undresses the sovereign rationales that sponsor it, highlighting Spinoza's debt to and divergence from Maimonides on these questions. For Spinoza, the infinity of reality forecloses its subordination to a transcendent being or blueprint. I evince how this immanence renders nature unregulated, without sovereign Laws and Norms. Nature is divested of normativity: nothing is *meant* to be, so no mode is not as it should be. This reprobates against tendencies in the literature—both analytic and "continental"—that smuggle teleology into Spinoza's philosophy. Thinking with Spinoza—while pressuring certain feminist readings—I consider the implications of this non-teleological ontology for theorizing sexgender. Contra biological essentialism, sovereign binarism, and reductionist normativity, Spinoza, I evince, invites a queering of sexgender. I further register how Spinoza's critique of teleology furnishes resources for countering the teleology that underwrites certain forms of racism and ableism. Whereas the transcendence of Christian/Cartesian/"Western" dualism imagines an escape from corporeal "nature," Spinoza's immanence entangles all modes in the "infinite connection of causes." This derogates the hierarchical binaries of culture and nature, unnatural and natural, present and past, much as it rebuts Christian, "Western," liberal notions of History as sequestered from "nature," contentions that it carries Meaning, and that it Progresses. I deconstruct how these notions rely on mechanisms of sovereignty like rank and instrumentalization that sanction exercises in supremacy. Thinking on this front, the chapter concludes by interrogating the anthropocentrism and teleology that moor evolutionary biology, philosophies of "longtermism," and the management of the COVID pandemic.

Chapter 5, "Splitting the Difference," pivots to epistemology. Whereas much of "Western" philosophy—in the wake Descartes, Kant, and Hegel—invests reason with supremacy, conceiving it as the measure and determinant of all, Spinoza's rejection of transcendence and teleology, I deduce, proscribes as much. The infinity attached to the attributes, it is demonstrated, means that neither extension nor thought is ontologically privileged or preeminent. Contra much of the scholarship, this means that reality cannot be subordinated to Reason. Rather, for Spinoza, thought and extension—mind and body—are different, irreducible aspects of the same. Yet readers of various orientations continue to miss this. To redress this misunderstanding, I examine Deleuze's reading of Spinoza and Deleuze's own philosophy, exposing how they are both marred by the sovereignties of Identity and Idealism. The chapter then presents its conception of Spinoza's non-supremacist approach to reason, which takes mind and body in humans as interdependent and irreducible. Spinoza's contention that all thinking is embodied and particularized, exists in time and space, has roots in Gersonides's naturalism. Sustained disregard for the mark of medieval Jewish and Islamic Aristotelianism on Spinoza's philosophy, I evince, drives the continued scholarly assimilation of it to parallelism, idealism, and the Principle of Sufficient Reason. Against these currents, this chapter reconfirms the immanence of Spinoza's epistemology, upholding it as tendering a significant rejoinder to the dominant "Western" investiture of reason as Sovereign and the supremacies concomitant therewith.

Chapter 6, "Off Subject," further probes Spinoza's epistemology by unpacking his critique of Cartesianism, specifically the claims that humans are essentially thinking beings, uniquely endowed by God with an internal mind that is distinct from its external body, over which it sovereignly rules through the exercise of free will. With this, I show, Descartes ratifies the dualisms promoted by Augustine's Platonic-inflected Christianity, which organizes reality through hierarchical binaries: God and nature, Spirit and matter, Man and woman, Human and animal, Self and other. By contrast, Spinoza's rejection of these dualisms derives from medieval Jewish Aristotelianism. The chapter scrutinizes the complicity of Cartesianism with sexism, racism, and colonialism, as Sylvia Wynter, Enrique Dussel, Emmanuel Chukwudi Eze, and Aimé Césaire aver. Although Descartes upholds the transcendence of reason as securing its Universality, rendering it accessible to all humans, I document how such egalitarianism is undercut by the inherently supremacist rationales of dualism. Hence, the weaponization of Cartesian "objectivity" and "rationalism" by colonial racism and the German Idealist monopolization of reason to exclude its "Oriental" Jewish others. Such compromising logics, I demonstrate, also surface in Conway's vital monism. Its ligature to Christian binaries that privilege Spirit, light, and "maleness" forestall its egalitarian potential. By contrast, Spinoza's immanence reputes the "Western" conceits that Reason can be neutral, absolute, and universal. This not only dislodges the dualist hierarchy of mind and body, but also its allied binaries: subject and object, active and passive, internal and external, self and other, theory and practice. I show how Spinoza delivers an epistemology divested of the "Western" sovereignties of Truth, Method, and the Subject. While Descartes prescribes a formalized Method for capturing Truth, seeking to transform his individual readers into Cartesian Subjects, Spinoza resists such a teleological, individualistic, and supremacist approach to reason. Rather, thinking is an immanent activity that is unguaranteed. It emerges from recognizing our embeddedness in the infinite connection of causes and our interdependence with others. To conclude, the chapter punctuates the emancipatory prospects of Spinoza's anti-dualist epistemology, which Marx and Hess deployed to dislodge certain supremacist dominations of "Western" philosophy.

The book closes with chapter 7, "Human Interest," which explores Spinoza's approach to living well, accentuating its pointed, yet unrecognized departure from "Western" models. I elucidate how Spinoza introduces an ethics divested of transcendent sovereignties like God, the Good, Natural

Law, and Morality. It likewise does not defer teleologically to Duty, Ideal, and Principle. Accordingly, Spinoza's ethics does not submit to sovereign Rationality nor is it moored to conceits of Self-control, Willpower, or Goal-setting. This reprobates the sovereignties that suture the Christian/Cartesian stance, which upholds humans as uniquely rational and invested with free will, as exceptional, superior to nonhuman animals, and so individually culpable for their actions. These logics, I show, remain with us, financing neoliberal values and policies. Similarly, I demonstrate how brands of contemporary New Materialism undertaking to decenter humans reproduce oppressive "Western" sovereignties, most notably, Jane Bennett's program, which I document as undermined by Christian supremacy, anthropomorphism, and the erasure of difference. By contrast, Spinoza's ethics is uncompromised by purports to supremacy. It achieves as much by intensifying the immanence that flickers through Maimonides's and Gersonides's philosophies. Through his practice of redefinition, Spinoza, I detail, reconstrues the meaning of conatus, affect, and desire, stripping them of sovereign pretenses. This dismantles the hierarchical binaries of thinking and feeling, being and doing, essence and existence. For Spinoza, everything we do is causally determined—not sovereignly decided—partly driven by our desires, which I evince as particularized and singular. Reason can influence our actions not by dint of its sovereignty but due to its affectivity: what we think impacts who we are, what we desire, and so *how* we are. This new interpretation positions me to clarify Spinoza's misappraised approach to self-esteem and suicidality, underscoring our lack of sovereignty over our feelings, ideas, and desires. The chapter elucidates how Spinoza's ethics is fastened by his redefinition of *good* as that which makes us *feel* good, which is good for us and so also for those like us, other humans. Such good is realized by enacting "agreements" with other humans. This confirms the particularity of different kinds of modes, accentuating the constraints of connecting meaningfully with nonhuman animals, which pressures New Materialisms that erase such difference. By rereading part V of the *Ethics*, discrediting its absorption to Christian, "Western," liberal frames, I construe Spinoza's redefinition of freedom as the recognition of our fundamental nonfreedom. Accepting our non-sovereignty, our entrenchment in nature, our imbrication with others, our lack of control over ourselves—the insuperable disparity that is us—is what makes ethics not only possible, but immanently necessary.

ONE

Substance Is Insubstantial

> Indeterminacy is an un/doing of identity that
> unsettles the very foundations of non/being.
>
> —KAREN BARAD[1]

Spinoza cautions: "No one will be able to perceive rightly the things I maintain unless they take great care not to confuse God's power with the power or right of kings."[2] This advice reflects at once the unprecedented ways in which his ontology dispels the rationales of sovereignty and, concomitantly, the barriers that might inhibit readers from absorbing these disavowals. Of concern to Spinoza are the prejudices epitomized by doctrines that misconstrue God as invested with free will, omnipotence, and dominion over reality. Yet, these are not the only traits of sovereignty that Spinoza discredits. Through a steady exploration of part I of the *Ethics*, this chapter demonstrates how Spinoza pointedly divests reality of a series of obvolute sovereignties. Substance is denied the status of First Cause and Origin, stripped of Primacy, Alterity, and Agency, while the notions of Essence and Freedom are redefined in ways that gut their sovereign purports. This feat is secured by overturning several of the constelled hierarchical binaries that gird "Western" ontology: cause and effect, form and matter, thought and extension, being and doing, essence and existence, freedom and necessity, activity and passivity.

The ontological revolution that Spinoza foments is epitomized by his formulation: "God *or* substance"[3] or "God *or* nature."[4] This reflects his acclaimed dethronement of God, which disfurnishes it of the sovereign traits of transcendence and exceptionalism, relieving it of such traditional purports as exemption from causal determinism and exclusion from corporeality. The upshot is that God does not possess free will and is not above nature or excluded from its ways. These are the most unmissable strides in Spinoza's campaign against sovereignty. But there is more. Not only does he reframe what is meant by *God*—vitiating the properties conventionally definitive of it—but so too does he revise the valence of *substance*, reversing the primacy and hierarchy classically afforded it. Substance is not a being or thing, form or matter, but rather infinite power that is only actualized, never in reserve. This infinite and so immanent power, I evince, only exists *as* finite modes. With this, Spinoza presents a conception of reality that does not rest on priority, independence, and preeminence but rather predication and imbrication.

How we perceive reality has expansive ramifications. It at once reflects but continuously and circularly reconfirms our conceptions of ourselves and so also, all else. By discarding the sovereignties philosophically, religiously, culturally afforded to God, Spinoza is concomitantly dismantling the conceptual apparatus that supports it and is reciprocally supported by it. This is why his admonition "not to confuse God's power with the power or right of kings" is so important. Indeed, the repudiation of such misperceptions underpins Spinoza's entire program. Construing God as Sovereign and invested with its classic bevy of properties—autonomy, transcendence, free will, exceptionalism, priority—is never just about God. Rather, it underwrites entire worldviews, which Spinoza repeatedly underscores are humanly constructed and irreversibly anthropocentric. To wit, attributing these features to God has entailed the attribution of them to humans, in lesser degrees, yet nevertheless enough to distinguish them from other beings. So, humans are taken as possessive of a mind or free will that transcends nature and is exempt from causal determinism. This positions humans as essentially different from and consequently superior to other beings. It also promotes the installation of further hierarchies, whereby humans are differentiated from each other based on the extent to which they supposedly possess or exercise these sovereignties. Denuding God of sovereignty is the decisive strike in Spinoza's assault on sovereignty, on the entire infrastructure of beliefs that rely on it and upon which it relies.

By rendering God as substance as nature—what he dubs "the infinite connection of causes"—Spinoza effectively deprives reality of the features and properties of sovereignty. This inducts an ontology that is without hierarchy, essentialized difference, and exceptions. There are no confirmed ranks in nature: humans are not inherently superior to nonhumans, and thought is not inherently superior to matter. Accordingly, nothing exists beyond the infinite connection of causes, and the immanence of its causal ways is without exclusion. There is no privilege in nature, nor privileged resort from it. Sovereignty is thereby *denaturalized*. Reality is deprived of all priority and exception. As with God, so with humans. Nothing, it will be demonstrated, exists independently, atomistically, or freely. There are no inherent boundaries and borders demarcating here from there, this from that. You and me, the microbiota in my belly and the microchip in your computer, my dream last night and your assessment of this point are equally *of* the infinite connection of causes and subject to its ways, without exception. This is only a sampling of the implications that redound from Spinoza's unprecedented denaturalization of sovereignty. Identifying, dissecting, and theorizing its expansive repercussions are the mainstays of this book, all of which emerge from the initial arguments of the *Ethics*, which confirm reality as infinite, self-caused, and immanent. Delineating and contextualizing these intertwined points are the enterprise of this chapter.

Common Rules

Spinoza develops his ontology in direct opposition to dominant "Western" approaches. Rather than relying on the properties of sovereignty, especially transcendence, hierarchy, essentialized difference, free will, and priority, he rejects these constructs and turns attention to the anthropic conceits that produce them. While certain aspects of these moves are unmistakable, further elements have evaded comprehensive, not to mention accurate exposition, in the literature. Several intertwined factors have contributed to these lapses. The first oversight concerns misapprehensions of Spinoza's rhetorical methods, specifically his strategy of redefinition, whereby he deploys familiar philosophical or theological terms only to redefine their meaning. Most famously, "God *or* substance" or "God *or* nature." Yet in so doing, as this chapter traces, Spinoza not only redefines God, ridding it of transcendence and essentialized difference, he also modifies the meaning of *substance* in a move that similarly divests it of sovereign pretenses. Accordingly, he dispossesses reality of several other sovereignties by dismantling the staid binaries of cause and effect, activity and passivity, freedom and necessity, doing and being. This inaugurates an ontology that is evicted of purports to sovereignty. The unprecedentedness of this stride is the second element that has contributed to scholarly misrecognitions of it. Precisely because dominant "Western" ontologies are so reliant on hierarchies, precedence, and essentialized differences, scholars tend to miss Spinoza's discreditation of these, while simultaneously coercing them onto his program. This imposition—be it witting or unwitting—bespeaks a certain unfamiliarity and plain discomfort with an ontology that is without priority, a reality divested of sovereignty. This is why, for example, the scholarship has not tired of installing rank into Spinoza's philosophy, construing substance, as over and above, prior to, and distinct from its attributes and modes. This state of affairs is not simply due to the regrettable, though forgivable, phenomenon of flawed readings nor to the constraints that our contexts, exposures, and desires—what Spinoza calls "prejudices"—place on our interpretations. Rather, these miscues coalesce with a third component: the willful ignorance or active disregard for Spinoza's Jewish repertory and the medieval Jewish and Islamic sources that inform him. To redress these compounding facets, this chapter elucidates the critical arguments of part I of the *Ethics*. It demonstrates how Spinoza's ontology dismantles the sovereignties that secure the dominant Christian, Cartesian, "Western" scheme and how, in order to do so, he relies on the sparks of naturalism or immanence that flicker through medieval Jewish Aristotelianism. Furthermore, in mounting its case about Spinoza's denaturalization of sovereignty, this chapter twice defers to passages from Spinoza's unfinished *Hebrew Grammar* that unexpectedly illuminate his ontology. The inattention to this work—which has been excluded from some collections of Spinoza's writings—reflects not only the contemporary "Western" supremacist denigration of and concomitant ignorance of classical languages that are not Greek and Latin, but also the corresponding philosophical devaluation of work that defies the narrow form deemed appropriate for articulating content of theoretical import.

While Spinoza is oriented by medieval Jewish philosophy, most prominently the work of Maimonides, he is not a mere recipient or amplifier of its principles. On the contrary, he reads, reformulates, and vigorously reconceives these sources. Mostly, Spinoza corrals their ideas, descrying their potential, while demonstrating that his predecessors failed to discern the sweeping consequences of their own commitments. More often than not, this is because they retain fidelity to certain traits of sovereignty, including transcendence, hierarchy, and preeminence. Through steadfast critique, Spinoza exposes the inconsistencies and tensions in their ideas, while purposefully ushering them towards less sovereign, more immanent conclusions. Admittedly, Spinoza is not exactly open about his procedures, and none of these influences are explicitly mentioned in the *Ethics*. In fact, barring a single mention of Descartes—by way of critique—no philosopher is. However, there are certain signals of Spinoza's Jewish influences, as when he echoes specific positions, albeit without named attribution, or his reference to "some of the Hebrews"[5] in a most decisive passage. Beyond this, certain ruminations elsewhere in his oeuvre, even in their embryonic form, furnish crucial, clarifying background. In elucidating Spinoza's ontology as laid out in part I of the *Ethics*, this chapter tags such allusions and tracks their connections. Of especial focus is its exploration of and tarrying with the medieval Jewish, especially Maimonidean, sources from which Spinoza draws to develop his ontology. Tending to these texts not only illuminates core aspects of Spinoza's conception of reality, correcting for the continued inattention to these non-"Western," non-Christian influences. It also punctuates the novelty of Spinoza's program by identifying and expositing the ways in which he deliberately renovates what he receives, consolidating the immanence, while repelling the remnants of transcendence shading the reasoning he inherits. This technique proves indispensable to his ontological divesture of sovereignty, which starts with his recasting of causation.

Without Exception

Nowhere is the purported sovereignty of God more apparent than in accounts of how reality has come to be and, correlatively, what it is. Classic "Western" approaches conceive the origin of reality by leaning on such properties of sovereignty as preeminence, hierarchy, exception, free will, and essentialized difference. Hebrew Scripture opens by portraying God as the source of all, whose agency effectuates the universe. Implicitly, this narrative confirms that while God causes, God is not caused. Moreover, reality, in its telling, hinges on hierarchy: God appears to maintain hegemony over its creations and is endowed with a degree of heteronomy in relation to them. Other ancient traditions also rely on causal rank and essentialized difference to account for all that is. Platonic Forms are seen as transcendent to physical reality, perfect, simple, and responsible for the essence of all inferior entities. Similarly, Aristotle's Unmoved Mover is upheld as the eternal, uncaused Cause of everything, which sustains it as Distinct. The One of Plotinus is foremost and singular and unified; it is the cause of all that is but is itself not caused. It is over and above reality. These features of sovereignty coalesce in various traditions including that of Augustine, which positions God as preceding all that is, freely effectuating it out of absolute nothingness, and continuously maintaining "the whole universe which is under the control of his sovereign law."[6] To Augustine, God is the Supreme Ruler who voluntaristically oversees nature, while remaining transcendent to it and thus immutable, immaterial, and invulnerable. This heritage informs Descartes's metaphysics, which conceives God as the independent and incorporeal source of all that exists, who freely and willfully causes all else to be, presiding over it "just as a king lays down laws in his kingdom."[7]

What distinguishes Spinoza from the aforementioned approaches is that although they all maintain that generally, according to the principles of reason, in order for something to be, something must have *caused* it to be, they inscribe an exception to this principle. In fact, their differentiated ontologies are grounded in this exclusion, this sovereign exception, which deems everything as ultimately effectuated by a cause that itself is excluded from having been caused. To them, reality is caused, yet by a being that is uncaused. Spinoza reprobates these logics of exceptionalism and the coalition of sovereignties imbricated therewith: preeminence, hierarchy, and essentialized difference. By refusing these features, he forestalls the installation of further sovereignties by denaturalizing sovereignty. This becomes patent by probing Spinoza's unusual position, his indebtedness to, yet simultaneous departure from, the medieval Aristotelianism of his predecessors as well as Cartesian metaphysics.

To Aristotle, there is an exception to causal norms: "The first mover ... of necessity exists."[8] In prominent streams of medieval Jewish and Islamic philosophy, Aristotle's first mover is upheld as God.[9] By construing God's existence as necessary, these thinkers obviate questions concerning *how* God has come to be. To Ibn Sina, "if what is in itself a necessary existent were to have a cause, it would not be in itself a necessary existent. Thus ... the Necessary Existent has no cause."[10] Maimonides echoes as much: "Everything that is necessarily existent in respect to its own essence has no cause for its existence."[11] Attaching a cause to the existence of God suggests that its existence could have been otherwise. Equally so, a cause implies that God has *come* to be and has not always been. Spinoza reconfigures this calculus. If for Ibn Sina and Maimonides, the necessity of God's existence is taken to foreclose its having been caused, Spinoza emphasizes that the veridicality of its existence commands as much. To exist is to have a cause[12] and to say that God is not caused is to say that God does not exist, since "there must be, for each existing thing, a certain cause on account of which it exists."[13] Therefore, substance is caused. But, on account of its *necessary* existence, this means that it is its own cause. As the inaugural definition of the *Ethics* states: "By *causam sui*—cause of itself—I understand that whose essence involves existence, *or* that whose nature cannot be conceived except as existing."[14] Substance is such a cause. Notice how Spinoza inverts the traditional argument: it is not that the necessary existence of God precludes its having been caused; rather, necessary existence *confirms* that it is caused. This is verified by his axiom: "What cannot be conceived through another, must be conceived through itself."[15] Hence, "By substance I understand what is in itself and conceived through itself."[16] Since another substance cannot exist—because substance is infinite[17]—its cause must be its own self.[18] This self-causation is an efficient causation.[19]

Whereas Spinoza's commitment to the rationalist principles of causation and therefore to the self-causation of substance is uncompromising, Descartes equivocates. Although he maintains that reason commands that everything must have a cause[20] and implies that God is *causa sui*,[21] in his *Replies*, he attenuates this position. Thus, he asserts that concerning God "the immensity of his nature is the cause or reason why he needs no cause in order to exist."[22] Similarly, he qualifies the sense in which he takes God to be *causa sui*, suggesting he means it only by way of analogy or as referring to formal causation, rather than efficient causation.[23] Both sustain God as transcendent to the rationales of causation, an exception to causal logics, an exemption from the dictates of reason. Furthermore, although for Descartes a hierarchy adheres between a cause and effect—the active and the passive—he avouches that his downgraded conception of *causa sui* preserves God's superiority: "We have ascribed to God the dignity inherent in being a cause in such wise that no indignity inherent in being an effect would follow thence in him."[24]

From a conventional theological stance, positing that God is caused—has not always been—undercuts its status as eternal and so its stature as Supreme. This is why medieval Islamic and Jewish philosophers, as we have seen, conceive God as the necessary of existence and the Scholastics testify that God is the cause that is not caused. However, to say that God is caused albeit self-caused—as does Descartes, however tepidly—in a certain sense, actually upholds God's sovereignty by construing it as Singular. *Only* God is self-caused. *Only* God has the power to self-generate. *Only* God has an essence coincident with its existence. The exclusively Self-caused is then *also* the

Cause of all else. Moreover, the Cartesian impulse to render God self-caused derives from a commitment to reason, which either adjusts God to align with and become Sovereign over reason *or* subsumes God under the supremacy of Reason.[25] Either way—and it need not be either/or—a clear sovereign is sustained. This tension was not lost on Martin Heidegger, who characterizes the *causa sui* as "the right name for the God of philosophy."[26] Since conceiving God as self-caused pivots on the difference between "Being as the ground, and beings as what is grounded," it typifies the "onto-theological constitution of metaphysics."[27] Glossing this passage, Derrida remarks that as *causa sui* "God then becomes the highest being, the most elevated, the supreme foundational being... who grounds everything in reason."[28]

While the Cartesian *causa sui* positions God as singular, exclusively self-caused and the cause of all else, which certifies its sovereignty and comports its status with reason, Spinoza's embrace of the concept remains immune from such concerns. Although the *Ethics* begins with a definition of *causa sui*, it is not a First Principle nor even a property of substance.[29] Moreover, by considering Spinoza's *causa sui* together with its constellated postulates—that substance is *causa immanens* and *infinitus*—a starkly contrasting portrayal emerges. Rather than reaffirming the "God of philosophy," Spinoza's program deposes it and deprives reality of its sovereignties.

Inside Job

For Spinoza, substance is the cause of itself and the cause of everything that exists. While this latter point sounds conventional—it seems like the traditional notion that God is the cause of reality—it is not. This is because "God must be called the cause of all things in the same sense in which God[30] is called the cause of itself."[31] The repercussions of this are considerable. Rather than elevating the status of substance—as Singular, First, and Primary—Spinoza levels it. Such causation, it will be shown, resists the rank, hierarchy, and exceptionalism of competing theories. In order to grasp how Spinoza does this, initial attention must be tendered to his theory of causal immanence, the contours of which are sketched roughly here and will be refined as our analysis unfolds.

The immanence that is a signature of Spinoza's philosophy is captured by this formulation: "Whatever is, is in God, and nothing can be or be conceived without God."[32] Everything is *of* substance: "All things, I say, are in God."[33] This is because "particular things are nothing but the affections of

God's attributes, *or* modes by which God's attributes are expressed in a certain and determinate way."[34] Everything that exists is substance "*or* what is the same,"[35] its attributes and affections. Indeed, "there is nothing except substances and their affections."[36] Substance *is* reality and everything that exists is *of* it or more strongly, *is* it. Spinoza means this literally, not formally. It applies to matter as much as thought. Everything that exists—this idea, the ink with which it is written, the eyes that are now reading it—are equally *of* substance, which is their immanent cause. This immanence follows directly from the positions that Spinoza progressively verifies in the preceding propositions. Everything has a cause. However, on account of the infinity of substance[37]—which precludes the existence of other substances[38] and confirms the necessity of its existence[39]—it follows that substance is the cause of itself and the cause of all else.[40] So, "God is the immanent, not the transitive, cause of all things."[41] Gestations of this argument surface in the *Short Treatise on God, Human and Well-Being*, where Spinoza maintains that God "does everything in itself, and not outside itself (because outside it there is nothing),"[42] and clarifies: "an immanent or internal cause (which is all one, according to me)."[43] To say that substance is an immanent cause of all that exists means that all that is inheres in it, is *of* it, not apart from it.

By rendering substance as the immanent cause of all that is, Spinoza rejects models configured on transcendence. Specifically, the kind of essentialized difference and naturalized hierarchy that buttress competing accounts that uphold reality as the product of a Being which stands above it, beyond it, presiding over it. This elevation of God traditionally entails its exclusion from corporeal nature, the claim of incorporeality. God is divested of matter, yet not of reason, thought, or intellect. Such identification of God with reason alone installs thought as not merely superior but Supreme. Spinoza's immanence undoes this dualist hierarchy, which traces back at least to Plato. The refusal to exempt substance from extension accentuates how the induction of a sovereign relies on and promotes further sovereignties. By refusing a Sovereign, as will become apparent, Spinoza simultaneously reprobates a variety of its conjunctive sovereignties.

Through a Cloud

Immanence is an equalizer that reverses the essentialized differences and naturalized ranks concomitant to doctrines of transcendence. Spinoza's causal immanence dislodges a coalition of symbiotic binary hierarchies rooted in the purported superiority of God over nature, thought over extension, and form over matter. These dualisms condition Descartes's Christian metaphysics, which, by elevating Spirit over matter, conceives God as transcendent to nature, entirely free, and sovereign over it. To counter such transcendence and the sovereignties it calcifies, Spinoza confers with medieval Jewish philosophy. By deferring to his Jewish predecessors, he unlocks the rationales of immanence latent in their ontologies.

For Spinoza, causal immanence confirms that infinite substance is uniformly the cause of all things: anything that exists—all modes—are the determinate affections of indeterminate substance. What this means is that both matter and mind or things and thoughts are equally the modifications of substance. This is because extension and thought are attributes of "one and the same substance."[44] They do not comprise different, gradational substances as Cartesianism has it. Consequently, "a mode of extension and the idea of that mode are one and the same thing, but expressed in two different ways."[45] Mind and body are not hierarchically ordered, neither is more real or essentially superior for they are differentiated expressions of the same, immanent reality. In explicating as much, Spinoza allows: "Some of the Hebrews seem to have seen this, as if through a cloud, when they maintained that God, God's intellect, and the things understood by God are one and the same."[46]

The doctrine of "some of the Hebrews" was embraced by Ibn Ezra,[47] Maimonides,[48] and Gersonides.[49] Appreciating what Spinoza is positing, and how adeptly he appropriates this position, requires a brief sashay into Aristotelian metaphysics and its uptake by medieval Jewish philosophy. To Aristotle, "the act of contemplation is what is most pleasant and best."[50] Thinking, specifically active thinking, is foremost. Such thinking occurs when "thought thinks itself . . . so that thought and object of thought are same."[51] While humans experience this[52] "in the case of things that have no matter,"[53] God is in a constant state of such contemplation, which is immaterial and indivisible. This is so because if God's thinking depended on something else—an external object—"it cannot be the best substance" and "the act of thinking cannot be the best of things."[54] Notice how Aristotle's construal endows God with the sovereignties of preeminence and independence, arrogating in the highest degree the sovereignties afforded to thinking: priority, unity, and indivisibility. This privileging of thinking over matter coincides with the hierarchization of activity over potentiality: "Always the active is superior to the passive factor, the originating force to the matter."[55] Aristotle's portrayal of God as constantly thinking itself, coupled with the claim of the identity between thinking and that which is thought, figure prominently in medieval Islamic and Jewish speculations concerning how exactly God is the cause of all that is.

In his *Guide of the Perplexed*,[56] Maimonides[57] theorizes "the dictum of the philosophers" that God "is the intellect as well as the intellectually cognizing subject and the intellectually cognized object."[58] Like Aristotle, he maintains that humans at times experience such thinking as when cognizing "pure" or "abstract" form,[59] whereas God "is always an intellect in actu" such that "He and the thing thought are one thing, which is Himself"[60] or His essence.[61] Since God is always thinking actively, this means that the thinking, the thinking subject, and the thought object form "one single notion in which there is no multiplicity."[62] Though God knows all that is, in its variety and multiplicity, this knowledge is one. It does not change, even as it apprehends things that do change, much as it is not finite, although it knows finite things.[63] Withal, God's knowledge "is not of the same species as ours ... but a totally different thing."[64] To wit, God's knowledge of things does not derive from them, but things "follow upon His knowledge, which preceded and rendered them as they are."[65] Therefore, "through knowing the reality of his own immutable Self, He also knows all that follows from His acts."[66] Everything "is disclosed to His knowledge, which is Himself" or His essence.[67] As the *Mishneh Torah* has it, God knows things "*mahmat atsmo, because of Himself*" *or* on account of His own essence. God knows all in merely knowing God's own self; if matters were otherwise, then God would be deficient rather than perfect, contingent rather than necessary, limited rather than unlimited. By knowing self, God knows all "for the being of everything relies on His existence."[68] Much as God is one, "this whole of being is one individual."[69]

The purport to God's unity is a pillar of Maimonides's thought, hermeneutic support for which he finds in a Scriptural verse,[70] which he thusly glosses: "*God lives [hay]* and not, *by the life of God [hei]*. For His life is not something other than Him" or His essence.[71] God's life *is* God.[72] Indeed, with God, "the notion of knowledge ... is identical with the notion of life."[73] This life that is God is responsible for all life, in being "the ultimate form for all that exists."[74] To Maimonides, following al-Farabi and Ibn Sina, "God has ... with reference to the world, the status of a form."[75] Because God is the form of the world—the Form of forms—God is "*hei ha-olam*" (life of the world).[76] It is specifically as Form that God is considered to be the Cause of everything that exists, its life. How precisely God as Form effectuates everything else is not explicated by Maimonides, although here and in subsequent passages he speaks of *shef'a* (overflow): "The world derives from the overflow of God."[77] Somehow, through God's activity of thinking, everything comes to be.[78] The notion that God's action—thinking—amounts to the world finds expression in a further remark of Maimonides: "ki-she-titbonein be-pe'ulot ha-'elohiyot, rotseh lomar, ha-pe'ulot ha-tivi'ot" (if you contemplate godly actions, which is to say, natural actions).[79]

In a section of *Cogitata Metaphysica* entitled "Of God's Intellect," Spinoza reprises several of these Maimonidean arguments. To affirm the perfection of God's intellection, he stresses: "God has never had a potential intellect."[80] Likewise, God's "ideas are not determined, as ours are, by objects placed outside God."[81] In fact, all things have been "determined by God's intellect."[82] God is "the object of God's knowledge, or rather is God's own knowledge."[83] Like Maimonides, Spinoza maintains: "God's power is not distinguished from God's essence."[84] Accordingly, "they speak best who call God life. Some Theologians think it was for this reason i.e., that God is life, and is not distinguished from life, that the Jews, when they swore, said *ḥai* Yahweh but not *ḥaiyei* Yahweh."[85] God—God's power, God's essence—is also not distinguished from God's intellect.[86] Those who suppose otherwise are befuddled in "absurdity ... confusing the divine intellect with the human intellect and frequently comparing God's power with the power of kings."[87] Furthermore, God's "simplicity" disallows for composition or multiplicity. "*In God there is only one simple idea*," and this is "the idea of God's self," and this is "nothing but God's essence."[88] Even as things are multiple, God's knowledge is not; therefore, "if we attend to the proportion of the whole of nature, we can consider it one being, and consequently there will only be one idea of God, *or* decree concerning *natura naturata*."[89]

These passages showcase the depth of Spinoza's familiarity with the doctrines of "some of the Hebrews" and indicate the significant influence that Maimonides's ideas had on the development of his ontology. From this tradition, Spinoza extrapolates: the identity of God, God's thinking and God's thoughts, and correlatively, the identity of God's power with God's essence with God's intellect. Other Maimonidean elements undergo considerable evolution in Spinoza's hands: Maimonides's claims that God's act of thinking projects all that is into being, remaining simple, undivided, and "one," develops into the more immanent conception of substance advocated in the *Ethics*. Withal, it is unsurprising that Mendelssohn, in his defenses of Spinozism, portrays it in a Maimonidean vein, emphasizing the unity of all in the Divine intellect, promoting an idealism that, he asserts, eludes suspicions of atheism.[90] More recently, commentators have rightly observed how this variety of Maimonidean immanence prompts Spinoza's *causa immanens*.[91] This is verily the case. Yet what proves decisive for Spinoza is the insufficiency of Maimonides's rendition, especially its reliance on the sovereign traits of hierarchy, exception, and difference, which is to say transcendence, specifically transcendence *from* corporeality.

What's the Matter?

The purport to God's incorporeality is a pillar of Maimonides's philosophy. In his estimation, attributing corporeality to God undercuts several interrelated principles that rely on certain Aristotelian suppositions concerning the nature of matter. Matter, according to Aristotle, is divisible. To Maimonides, such divisibility subverts God's unity. Similarly, bodies, he maintains, are finite and so only possess finite power.[92] Whatever has limitation and definition has limited power. Since God's power has no limit, God cannot have a body.[93] Relatedly, to Maimonides, material bodies also entail change, which if attributed to God, would undermine God's immutability. Further, potentiality rather than actuality obtains in matter and, as Aristotle affirms: "Matter does not move itself."[94] These premises lead Maimonides to reason that there must be an immaterial and so not finite power that is actual, rather than merely potential, which moves the sphere eternally. To him, this is God, whose power derives from God alone, for God is the necessary existent, which is necessarily an exclusive status.[95]

While Maimonides has Aristotelian metaphysics on his side, he does not have Hebrew Scripture. This is why much of the *Guide* is trained on reconstruing Scriptural verses that describe God in corporeal terms. According to Maimonides, such portrayals place limitations on God's power because matter is limited and limiting. What stands behind Scripture's misleading depictions, he claims, are the limitations of the multitude, people who cannot but rely on corporeal anthropomorphisms to make sense of God. To address these anthropic constraints, Scripture "ascribed to Him, may He be exalted, everything that in our opinion is a perfection in order to indicate that He is perfect,"[96] without deficiency. For example, since to the multitude, "motion belongs to the perfection of a living being," Scripture ascribes this capacity to God even though God cannot move, as motion requires magnitude, which is divisible, and God is not divisible and so also not material. While by the rubrics of his own theology such depictions limit God, to Maimonides, such verses emphasize the obverse by figuring God's perfection in a manner accessible to all readers.

The measure of Spinoza's disappointment with Maimonides and his allies is apparent from the aforementioned remark about "some of the Hebrews" who "seem to have seen this, as if through a cloud."[97] With this, he flags how they are right to conceive God as the immanent thinking, thinker, and thought-about yet falter by not extending this immanence to materiality. It seems—at least to my sardonic intuitions—that Spinoza's "cloud" is a riff on Maimonides's invocation of clouds in his explications proscribing God's corporeality. Hebrew Scripture describes prophetic encounters wherein God manifests in clouds and darkness. To reconcile such verses with his commitments, Maimonides insists that they are not literal, and they do not mean that God "is a body surrounded by mist or an enveloping cloud or a heavy cloud."[98] This is because "a body cannot be one, but is composed of matter and form; it is also divisible."[99] If God were comprised of matter, this would undermine God's unity and indivisibility.[100] Therefore, the meaning of Scriptural passages that patently suggest otherwise is that "we are separated by a veil from God and that He is hidden from us by a heavy cloud, or by darkness or by a mist or by an enveloping cloud."[101] This is due to "our incapacity to apprehend Him because of matter."[102] Not only do Scriptural allusions to clouds not imply that God manifests corporeally, but according to Maimonides, these actually reinforce God's incorporeality by alluding to "the tenebrous character of our substance," which renders apprehension of the immaterial God "impossible."[103] Spinoza wittily turns Maimonides's imagery back at him. Indeed, people, that is *certain* people, *are* enveloped in a cloud that prevents them from apprehending the true nature of God; these are people like Maimonides, who fail to grasp that God is not only the form but also the matter of all. Extension, as well as thought, and all other attributes in reality, are *of* substance.

Extending Credit

To Spinoza, the ontology of his medieval Jewish predecessors is not only befogged in confusion, it is beclouded in discrepancy. In mounting his case for conceiving extension as an attribute of substance, he seizes their reasoning and exposes how it actually supports his position. Spinoza pinpoints their privileging of intellection and immateriality as undercutting their commitments to the necessity, perfection, and limitlessness of God's existence.

Recall that Maimonides confirms God's transcendence from corporeality in order to substantiate God's perfection as without limitation and potentiality. Spinoza corrals these claims and extends their scope to demonstrate why extension must be of substance as much as thought is. This hinges on the avowal—fundamental to his ontology—that substance is infinite and that such infinity is constitutive: "Every substance is necessarily infinite."[104] Hence, "by God I understand a being absolutely infinite . . . a substance consisting of an infinity of attributes."[105] The reason that substance must be of infinite attributes is because the infinity of substance entails the necessity of its existence and precludes the existence of other substances,[106] which means that everything that exists must follow from the "necessity of its existence."[107] Since thought and extension exist, they must either be "attributes of God" or "affections of God's attributes."[108] Spinoza recapitulates the point: "Except God, no substance can be or be conceived, and hence we have concluded that extended substance is one of God's infinite attributes."[109] This argument seizes the rationales of his forebears that God is the necessary of existence. Yet to Spinoza, their conception of God as only the form, rather than also the matter of all that is, undermines God's necessity. For if extension adheres in reality and extension is not of substance, this would mean that something *else* is responsible for it, indicating that substance is not truly the necessary of existence. Their concern for subverting God's unity, singularity, and preeminence—driven by Aristotelian presumptions regarding the nature of matter—leads "some of the Hebrews" to compromise on the necessity of God's existence.

According to Maimonides, God is without deficiency or limitation; God is perfect. This is why God knows and knows all, because if God did not know all, let alone not know anything at all, this would constitute a defect.[110] Likewise, since God is perfect, all good things must exist in God.[111] Spinoza appropriates these points to prove that "all good things" must include not merely thought but also extension, for "the more reality or being each thing has, the more attributes belong to it."[112] This is because "being able to exist is power."[113] As such, "the more reality belongs to the nature of a thing, the more powers it has . . . to exist,"[114] which is why substance must have an "absolutely infinite power of existing."[115] Correlatively, a lack of power amounts to a deficit in being. If substance did not have infinite attributes, including extension, it would be deficient, limited, and imperfect. With this, Spinoza demonstrates how the Aristotelian and Maimonidean exclusion of extension from God subverts God's perfection and limitlessness.

This reasoning is rehearsed in his correspondence with Johannes Hudde, wherein Spinoza argues that definition and determination are forms of negation, indicating "something is lacking to a thing which pertains to its nature" and so amounts to imperfection.[116] Accordingly, "since the nature of God does not consist in a definite kind of being, but in a Being which is *absolutè indeterminatum*, its nature also requires everything which expresses *being* perfectly, since otherwise its nature would be *determinata*, and deficient."[117] Therefore, if something exists, like extension, it "will pertain to God, or it will be something which expresses God's nature in some way."[118] If there is something that is not of substance—say, extension—this implies that it is *beyond* substance, suggesting that substance is lacking, restricted, circumscribed.

With this reasoning, Spinoza evinces how excluding the attribute of extension from God effectively subverts its necessity, unlimitedness, and perfection. The cloud that obscures "some of the Hebrews" is their misrecognition of this. Moreover, by extending Maimonides's own principles, Spinoza demonstrates how close his Jewish predecessors come to his own conclusion. Yet because of their Aristotelian prejudices concerning not simply matter—its presumed divisibility, passivity, potentiality, and inferiority—but also thought—its supposed preeminence and superiority—rather than enhancing God's power, they vitiate it. By rendering God transcendent to matter, excluding matter from God's attributes, Maimonides as much as Descartes and countless allied theologians derogate God's power. Ordering reality on the sovereignties of hierarchy, priority, and essentialized difference, Spinoza makes patent, is not only misguided but counterproductive to their own aims.

"Some of the Hebrews" falter by taking God as only the Form of all that is, restricting God to thought. Spinoza turns attention to the snag of such arrangements: "If things have nothing in common with one another, one of them cannot be the cause of the other."[119] Substance cannot be the cause of all that is, including extension, if it transcends extension. Negotiating this challenge—how a supposedly incorporeal God causes that which is corporeal—stretches back to Aristotle's *Metaphysics* and loomed prominently in medieval speculations. Hence this gave rise to claims of creation ex nihilo, whereby God is perceived as effectuating the world from absolutely nothing, or emanationist accounts of overflow, whereby materiality is born through a series of intermediaries that ultimately trace back to the Immaterial. Spinoza will have none of this and refuses to countenance any causation absent commonality. With this, he discounts the essentialized difference underpinning such accounts, confirming that substance is not constitutionally other to its effects, for if it were, it could not be their cause.

By rendering extension of substance as much as thought, Spinoza overturns the "Western" philosophical elevation of intellect and its concomitant denigration of matter. To Aristotle: "Life also belongs to God; for the actuality of thought is life, and God is that actuality."[120] The reason that God must have life is because God thinks and thought is life. Spinoza cites and critiques this doctrine. Instead, he defines life as "the *force through which things persevere in their being*."[121] This applies to God as much as it does to amoebas, viruses, and humans. The problem with competing definitions of life is their exclusions, which bestow upon humans and gods exceptional status.

Will Away

In Hebrew Scripture, God is portrayed as speaking the cosmos into being. This depiction has sponsored the doctrine that God exercises free will, which has been promoted by diverse thinkers, including Philo and Crescas, Augustine and Descartes, and al-Kindi and al-Ghazâlî. Spinoza departs from such conceptions by denuding substance of the sovereign traits of Will, Volition, and Agency. On this score too, he is oriented by the Aristotelianism promulgated by Ibn Sina and Maimonides, which as ever, he extrapolates and extends. Spinoza dedicates considerable and repeated attention to dispossessing substance of will. This focus does not derive solely from the celebration of God's will by thinkers both antecedent to and contemporaneous with him. Rather, the stakes of this issue are steep for Spinoza as dispelling the attribution of volition to substance is critical to his denaturalization of sovereignty and denunciation of its qualities, especially transcendence, hierarchy, and exceptionalism.

The reason that people mistakenly attach will and intellect to God, Spinoza argues—appropriating Maimonides—is because "they know nothing they can ascribe to God more perfect than what is the highest perfection in us."[122] Such anthropomorphizing is misguided; rather than bolstering God's power, it attenuates it. This stance is counterproductive because saying that God understands "in the highest degree" implies that God is able to think more than God is able to do: "that God cannot bring about everything to which God's power extends."[123] This limits God's power, purporting that God has potentiality that is not actualized. Spinoza identifies an additional constraint to this doctrine: the ascription of will to God attaches imperfection to God. If God chooses to act, this indicates that the action is contingent; that it could have been otherwise and thus that God is not perfect. Even more troublesome than assigning will to God is the supposition "that God does all things for the sake of the good."[124] To posit as much is "to place something outside God, which does not depend on God, to which God attends, as a model, in what God does, and at which God aims, as at a certain goal."[125] This suggests that there is something transcendent to God to which God yields. Professing that God has a Goal, be it the Good or any other, abrogates infinity. Neither the Good nor God is sovereign.

Though Spinoza mounts his case against the ascription of Will, Agency, and Intellect to God by exposing its logical inconsistencies, he is also intent on disassembling its supports: "By God's power ordinary people understand God's free will and right over all things. . . . they say that God has the power of destroying all things and reducing them to nothing. Further, they very often compare God's power with the power of Kings."[126] The ascription of free will to God is an unambiguous form of anthropomorphism. Humans imagine that they possess will and esteeming this will, they attach it to God in the most eminent degree. The problem is that not only is this false—God does not have will—but in supposing as much, people *think* that they are esteeming God by saluting God's supreme power. But this subverts God's power, rendering God's actions contingent. While this is a reiteration of the points that Spinoza has already explicated, he underscores a deeper root of the problem: people "compare God's power with the power of Kings." On account of this misstep of anthropomorphosis, the most apt manifestation of God's power is perceived to be the attribution of absolute will, the misknowledge that God acts in the manner of a human monarch, the acme of whose power is taken to be their capacity to do as they please, to transcend accepted norms, to rule by fiat. Since humans equip their monarchs with such power, they imagine God as King, as possessive of a transcendent Will, as endowed with absolute Agency. This mistake is so incompatible with Spinoza's philosophy that, as cited above, he admonishes: "No one will be able to perceive rightly the things I maintain unless they take great care not to confuse God's power with the power or right of Kings."[127] It is impossible to correctly apprehend substance so long as one envisions it as a Sovereign invested with the freedom to will and the agency to decide. Spinoza reprises this in the appendix to part I, identifying the source of the interlaced prejudices that he disentangles as the misbelief that "God directs all things to some certain end," which derives from the conviction "that there is a ruler, or a number of rulers of nature, endowed with human freedom."[128] Disproving this anthropocentric conferral of agency, freedom, and volition onto God and invalidating these constructs are fundamental to Spinoza's comprehensive denaturalization of sovereignty.

Bare Necessities

What is the alternative that Spinoza assembles? As he straightforwardly puts it: "God acts from the laws of God's nature, alone, and is compelled by no one."[129] The actions of substance derive from itself. Substance is not compelled to act by something external, since infinity forecloses an outside. Accordingly, its actions are not *caused* by anything, even something internal. Rather, "God alone exists only from the necessity of God's nature ... and acts from the necessity of God's nature."[130] Thus, "God alone is a free cause."[131] What is meant by "free" is that substance acts in the absence of compulsion or submission. It does not mean free to choose, free to decide, free to enact what it desires. On the contrary, for Spinoza, the freedom of substance *is* its necessity, its lack of contingency and choice. Therefore, "will cannot be a free cause, but only a necessary one,"[132] since "in whatever way it is conceived, whether as finite or as infinite, it requires a cause by which it is determined to exist and produce an effect."[133] Here, Spinoza emphasizes that everything has a cause, which is to say that no action is without predication. If substance acts, these actions are necessary, which means they are causally determined rather than contingent. This reduction of substance to necessity opposes conceptions of God and understandings of reality that rely on the rationales of supremacy, most prominently exemplified in the construct of the miracle, the belief that God interrupts the causal ways of nature. Such doctrines of sovereignty rely on the purport that God transcends nature, stands *over* it and is *other* to it. In these approaches, constitutive difference and the rank that it enshrines subsidize the bestowal of absolute power onto the Sovereign, validating domination.

Spinoza's disavowal of God's will and endorsement of causal determinism contributed to accusations of his atheism. Lambertus van Velthuysen leveled such claims in an extended letter to Spinoza, asserting that he "secretly introduces Atheism" as for him "God is subjected to fate; no room is left for any divine governance or providence; the whole distribution of punishments and rewards is destroyed."[134] This accurately identifies an upshot of Spinoza's program: the divestment of God's sovereignty, discreditation of doctrines that God presides over reality like a Ruler, meting out rewards and punishments. In his careful response, Spinoza denies that he "subjects God to fate" and thusly defends himself: "I've maintained that everything follows with inevitable necessity from God's nature in the same way everyone maintains that it follows from God's nature that God understands God's self."[135] Indeed, everyone supposes, "God understands God's self completely freely, even if necessarily."[136] With this, Spinoza adeptly presents his stance as compatible with traditional doctrines, maintaining that the necessity of God's intellect is no different from the necessity of all else attributed to God. He then proceeds to attack van Velthuysen's Cartesianism, identifying the contradiction in supposing that God sovereignly preordains all that is and yet invests humans with free will, a point that Descartes himself concedes exceeds our comprehension.[137]

Spinoza's most proximate target in his attacks on God's volitional sovereignty is Descartes, whose approach to these questions is underpinned by a thread of Christian theology that stretches back centuries, striving to reconcile the sovereignty and freedom of a transcendent God with natural causation and purports to human freedom. These concerns had fresh relevance with the rise of the New Science. Descartes is committed to the kind of unbounded, free will of God advocated by Augustine, for whom God's "will is what imposes necessity on things."[138] God's providence, he maintains, governs everything through a dualistic hierarchy of natural and voluntaristic activity, which is duplicated in humans who are comprised of matter that is subject to natural activity and a soul with free will that transcends nature. Descartes consolidates such free will in both God and human.

To Descartes, everything is by dint of Divine fiat, not by necessity. Against certain Scholastics, he conceives God's will as Sovereign over reason itself, the Designer of and so the Dictator over mathematical and eternal truths, for God "has laid down these laws in nature just as a king lays down laws in his kingdom."[139] So, God "could change them as a king changes his laws."[140] These do not exist "independent of God."[141] If they did, then God would be subordinated to their dominion. Moreover, Descartes explains, the veridicality of these truths depends on God's diktat. Truths only exist and exist as true because "from all eternity he willed and understood them to be, and by that very fact he created them."[142] This is why God is "free to make it not true that all the radii of the circle are equal."[143] In fact, because "the power of God cannot have any limits," even the laws of noncontradiction do not encroach on God's will.[144] Moreover, Descartes figures that "since every basis of truth and goodness depend on his omnipotence, I would not dare to say that God cannot make a mountain without a valley, or bring it about that 1 and 2 are not 3."[145] Everything—reason, truth, logic—result from and so are subordinate to God's absolute freedom. God's sovereignty reigns supreme.

Spinoza's resistance to the willful contingency and unbounded supremacy constitutive of Descartes's God is oriented by strands of reasoning unfurled by Maimonides, whose own negotiation of this complex is conflicted. Certain passages in the *Guide* seem to uphold a robust construal of God's will or at least purposiveness.[146] Yet these cannot be read independent of additional comments that clarify what precisely Maimonides signifies by the will of God: "His will and His volition or His wisdom not being things extraneous to His essence [she-'ein retsono ve-heftso 'o hohkmato devarim yots'eim huts le-'atsmo]. I mean to say that they are not something other than His essence"[147] or Himself. Notice the equivalence signaled by "His volition *or* His wisdom," which reflects how "volition too is consequent upon wisdom; all these being one and the same thing—I mean His essence and His wisdom—for we do not believe in attributes."[148] Or, "the divine will—if you prefer you can also say . . . the divine wisdom."[149] God's will is God's wisdom, which is God's essence.[150] To be sure, for Maimonides, like Ibn Sina, the asset of such identity is that it upholds God's unity. This Maimonidean coincidence of God's will, intellect, and essence, it has been suggested, "effectively strips the concept of God's will of any cognitive meaning."[151]

Spinoza is guided by Maimonides in nullifying God's will. This is unmistakable in *Cogitata Metaphysica*, when Spinoza asserts: "Both the essence and the existence of things have been made from God's intellect *or* will."[152] Not only does the purport of this statement align with Maimonides's thesis, but Spinoza's "intellect *or* will," is uncannily close to Maimonides's "His volition *or* His wisdom." Maimonides is similarly present in this phrasing: "God's intellect, and power and will . . . are not distinguished from one another in any way, except in regard to our thought."[153] Spinoza leans on this point in the *Ethics* to rebut the notion that God could sovereignly decree matters to be otherwise, say, by making it that the three angles of a triangle do not equal two right angles. "God's intellect," he explains, "insofar as it is conceived to constitute God's essence is really the cause both of the essence and the existence of things."[154] Spinoza continues: "This seems also to have been noticed by those who asserted that God's intellect, will and power are one and the same."[155] Those who have noticed as much are "some of the Hebrews" and Spinoza in his earlier writings. Whereas Descartes regards God's free will as sovereign, deciding to render truths necessary, Spinoza references the Maimonidean identity of God's intellect and will as that which make truths and everything necessary, necessarily.

To further appreciate the import of Spinoza's elimination of the will of God within the context of his campaign against sovereignty, it is instructive to consider the justification of it formulated by Abraham Cohen de Herrera in *Gate of Heaven*. Herrera wrote this work in Spanish during his years in Amsterdam, which Aboab de Fonseca—who Spinoza likely knew, possibly even "fairly well"[156]—translated into Hebrew in 1635. Therein, Herrera devotes a section to substantiating that "the infinite First Cause does not act by necessity or in accordance with its nature but rather following the counsel of its understanding and the free choice of its own will and consent."[157] Free will is "most appropriate for the most superior primary maker" who "is absolutely Master of itself and of its effects, which it produces when and how it wishes, being capable of not producing them or of producing others."[158] Mastery over self and over reality encompasses not only the capacity to freely and voluntarily choose without constraint but to dominate reality, to be sovereign over it. This is precisely the reasoning that Spinoza confutes.

By depriving substance of freedom, in reducing its acts to causal necessity, Spinoza strips it of agency and volition. Whereas conventionally, God's omnipotence is epitomized by its capacity to do as it pleases, to choose, to be an Agent, Spinoza inverts this logic, arguing that specifically *this* presumption undercuts God's power by rendering it subject to contingency. Moreover, by reducing the acts of substance or substance itself to causal determination, Spinoza is affirming that substance is nothing but these necessary determinations, these acts. While the ensuing analysis further explores this advance, here it is pertinent to underscore that in so doing, Spinoza is developing a conception of substance as devoid of the forms of independent action and agential behavior routinely associated with subjects, not to mention Subjects, such as Herrera's "Master" and Descartes's "King." This is not merely a rejection of the pervasive anthropomorphizing of God but a more comprehensive assault on the very construct of God. Spinoza refuses to perceive reality as subordinated to any Being or aspect of a Being. Instead of decisions, plans, and miracles, there is the necessity of causal determinism. Inextricable to the conception of sovereignty is the contention that the sovereign has absolute power, and indispensable to such power is the supposition that it is unhindered. The sovereign is free to act as it pleases, and nothing prevents it from so doing. This is why a sovereign is positioned as Supreme. In the case of God this means regnant *over* reality, while with regard to human monarchs this means hegemonic *over* their subjects. Not only does Spinoza repudiate this calculus by dispossessing substance of subjecthood, arguing that it is not a Being that wants and wills and wishes, but he also demonstrates that freedom as such is a conceit. Reality is nothing but itself, there is not desire and *then* action, there is no goal to foreground its doing.

Breaking Rank

In standard—that is linear and sequential—renditions of causation, a cause is deemed wholly responsible for an effect. It preexists its effect, is independent of it, and *other* to it. The action of a cause on its effect is considered unilateral, and its status is upheld as superior. Often, this also entails the supposition that the cause is not impacted by its effectuation of the effect and is accompanied by the classification of the cause as active and the effect as passive. This hierarchical binary of cause and effect relies on and reinforces the further hierarchical binaries of precedent and subsequent, active and passive, all of which derive their status from the imposition of fixed temporal, spatial, or conceptual boundaries. These sovereign features are hallmarks of conventional versions of what it means to think God as Cause.

Conventional "Western" accounts maintain that God is preeminent, existing independently and chronologically prior to that which it subsequently effectuates. This situates God as essentially different from its effects, installing a hierarchy between the Cause and its effects, which fortifies God's stature as Supreme. Certain emanationist renditions temper the transcendence of such accounts yet nevertheless retain elements of transcendence and the intractable rank concomitant to it. To wit, the One for both Plotinus and Proclus is the cause of being that remains beyond Being, begetting it through descending tiers. This hierarchy is preserved in diverse Jewish sources inflected with Neoplatonism, including Samuel ibn Gabirol and Isaac Israeli but also Maimonides's "overflow" as well as the disparate musings of Kabbalah. By contrast, Spinoza's immanence dispenses with the alterity, precedence, and rank underpinning such schemes.

Through his theorization of causal immanence, Spinoza disbands the sovereignties and binaries that suture predominant theories of causation. In place of independence, essentialized difference, and priority, he regards causation through notions of imbrication, interconnection, and intra-action.[159] This reverses the sovereignties commonly attendant to accounts of how reality has come to be and continues to be. This further decimates the supremacies signified by the appellation "God." Concomitantly, Spinoza denaturalizes these sovereignties by presenting an ontology divested of such purports. This delivers a reality—an "infinite connection of causes"—wherein causation is anchored in mutuality, agency is synergistic, and borders are provisional and so mutable.

The *Ethics* opens with several axioms focused on causation. After confirming that effects follow from their determinate causes, it affirms: "The knowledge of an effect depends on, and involves, the knowledge of its cause."[160] The succeeding axiom elaborates: "Things that have nothing in common with one another also cannot be understood through one another, *or* the concept of the one does not involve the concept of the other."[161] This idea explains, as noted above, why substance must be of infinite attributes and not of thought alone. What is pertinent to emphasize here is the invocation of involvement, which links causation to notions of concertedness, entanglement, and intra-connection. This clarifies how infinite substance causes finite modes: "Each idea of each body, or of each singular thing which actually exists, necessarily *involvit* an eternal and infinite essence of God."[162] Therefore, singular things have substance as a cause "insofar as . . . their ideas must involve the concept of their attribute," meaning they "must *involvere* an eternal and infinite essence of God."[163] At issue here is an element of dependence,[164] but involvement connotes a deeper and less hierarchical linkage.

Substance cannot be considered a "remote cause" of its effects, that is, "not conjoined in any way with its effect."[165] Rather, "all things that are, are in God."[166] This is the upshot of causal immanence: everything that is inheres in substance, which means that substance is conjoined with its modes, its effects. Such conjoining undercuts the binary adhering between cause and effect: if the effects of substance are conjoined with it, involve it, inhere within it, they are not other to it. Claims to alterity are obviated. This accordingly pressures further binaries correlated with cause and effect, namely, those of activity and passivity, subject and object. If the effects of substance do not exist separately from it, distinctions between an Active cause and a passive effect, a Subject and the object upon which it acts, dissolve. When substance effectuates modes, this action is therefore of, to, or upon itself. This is exactly the point that Spinoza makes, en passant, in an understudied passage in *Hebrew Grammar*.

Introducing his discussion of the seven different noun—actually verb—constructions in the Hebrew language,[167] Spinoza explains how each of these "express an action in either an active or passive relationship."[168] To wit, "to visit [*visitare*] someone" is active, whereas "to be visited [*visitari*] by someone is passive."[169] In Latin—and English—the difference in nominative and accusative states is signaled by modifying word order and pronouns. In Hebrew such active/passive and subject/object distinctions are expressed by conjugating the root word—*to visit*—in different grammatical structures. The seventh structure—התפעל—Spinoza explains, captures how "it frequently happens that one and the same person is both the actor and the person acted upon,"[170] as when someone visits themself.[171] To represent this active reflexive state "it was necessary to devise another form of infinitive which would express an action related to the active mood *sive causam immanentem*" (or immanent cause), which is signaled by the prefix unit הִתְ. Notice how Spinoza describes reflexive activity as "immanent cause." Reflexive action unsettles the hierarchical binaries and fixed boundaries adhering between causes and effects, subjects and objects, acting and being acted upon. This is what it means to be an immanent cause.

When Spinoza describes substance as the immanent cause of modes, it seems fair to infer that he means this reflexively, akin to actions conjugated in התפעל. In these instances, cause and effect, subject and object, are one and the same. When substance effectuates modes, it is not effectuating things other to it, outside of it, or even subordinate to it. Rather, substance is acting reflexively, for "all things are in God."[172] This is relayed in the *Short Treatise* amidst Spinoza's multipronged defense of attributing extension to substance. Retorting the Aristotelian, Maimonidean, and Cartesian suppositions that matter is passive, rather than active and therefore unsuitable of God, Spinoza explains: "One can never say of an agent, which acts in itself, that they have the imperfection of being acted on, because they are not acted on by another."[173] Reflexive action—immanent action—undoes the binaries of object and subject, passive and active. Indeed, as substance "is an immanent cause, who would dare say that it is imperfect when it is acted on by itself?"[174]

Staying Power

Considering what has been established concerning substance as reflexively causing modes, which inhere in it, which *are* it, it is fair to ask: What exactly is God *or* substance *or* nature? And, correlatively, what are modes? I propose that Spinoza presents an even more innovative conception than has been recognized, and that in so doing, he divests substance of Substantiality, wresting it of additional sovereignties. To accomplish this, here too, he exploits the ideas of "some of the Hebrews." Yet in Spinoza's hands, and within the framework of his ontology, this leads to a radical conclusion: substance is nothing *but* its modes. Infinite, indeterminate substance only exists *as* its finite, determinate modes.

The *Ethics*, as noted above, defines substance as "a being absolutely infinite." Such infinity is constitutive: "Every substance is necessarily infinite."[175] If substance were not infinite, its necessary existence would be undermined, "it would be limited by something else."[176] This cannot be, for limitation is antithetical to infinitude and definitional to finitude.[177] As Spinoza elaborates in a letter: "Something whose definition affirms existence, cannot be conceived as *determinatum*."[178] Determination is a limitation. Therefore, substance is not "a definite kind of being."[179] Infinity forecloses definition, determination, and delimitation.[180] Spinoza is not asserting that substance is a Being with unlimited power in the conventional sense as epitomized by claims of God's omnipotence. Rather, he is advancing the logic of this doctrine by maintaining that *any* form of being, *any* determination, *any* definiteness undercuts the infinity of that which is absolutely infinite. Substance is that which is not determinate, defined, or delimited. It is indeterminate. The ramification of this, I submit, is that it forecloses substance from being a thing or Being, a Container of things or font that energizes things, as these entail the definiteness and delimitation ingenerate to determination. This bears stressing because certain readers, across the centuries, have construed Spinoza's substance in precisely such a manner.

Correlative to Spinoza's insistence that substance is indeterminate and indefinite stands the affirmation that it "expresses *being* perfectly."[181] This is the purport of his remark that "God's *Infinity*, in spite of what the term suggests, is something most positive."[182] Hence, the infinity of substance means that it is "of an infinity of attributes, of which each one expresses an eternal and infinite essence,"[183] because "the more reality belongs to the nature of a thing, the more powers it has, of itself, to exist."[184] Consequently, substance "has an absolutely infinite power of existing."[185] This infinity of attributes not only mandates that substance is of extension as well as thought—as examined above—it requires that substance be of infinite other attributes too, of unlimited, indeterminate power. Anything less, say, only thought or just thought and extension, would amount to a constraint, a limit on its "power of existing." Power is constitutive of substance, hence this equivalence: "God's absolute nature, *or* infinite power."[186] Substance *is* infinite power. Power is not a feature or quality that substance possesses but *is* it. Following Maimonides, for Spinoza, "God's power is God's essence itself."[187] Its "existence and essence are one and the same" such that "its existence is nothing but its essence."[188] This existence or essence *is* power. Significantly, this power is affined with Maimonides's Aristotelian construal of God's mind as constantly *in actu*: "God's power is nothing except God's active essence."[189] Substance is the actualization of infinite power, which is only realized, never in reserve. Hence, "it is as impossible for us to conceive that God does not act as it is to conceive that God does not exist."[190] Infinite substance is the expression, performance, enactment of infinite power, which is only actualized.[191] Substance is action, act, activity, *in actu*.

How does such action happen or more aptly, how *is* such action? "God's power, by which God and all things are and act, is God's essence itself."[192] The power that is substance is that power by which all things exist and act. In positing as much, however, Spinoza is not parroting traditional claims that everything that exists is so by dint of God's power. Rather, on account of his immanence, the assertion is sharper, not merely that God's power is actualized in "all things," but *as* all things: "Whatever exists expresses the nature, *or* essence of God in a certain and determinate way . . . whatever exists expresses in a certain and determinate way the power of God."[193] As such, "particular things are nothing but affections of God's attributes, *or* modes by which God's attributes are expressed in a certain and determinate way."[194] Finite, determinate modes are the particularized expressions of infinite, indeterminate power. The infinite, indeterminate power that is substance exists *as* its finite, determinate modes. What this means, I venture, is that modes are the actions of substance, its acts. More specifically, infinite, indeterminate power only exists *as* its finite, determinate modes, which are *how* its power actualizes. This does not mean that by acting, substance effectuates a mode but rather that its very actions *are* modes—modes *are* the acts of substance.

In discussing Hebrew nouns, Spinoza writes:

By a noun I understand a word by which we signify or indicate something that is understood. However, among things that are understood there can be either things and attributes of things, modes and relationships, or actions, and modes and relationships of actions. Hence, we sum up easily the various kinds of nouns. For example, the noun איש *man*; חכם *learned*, גדול *big*, etc., are attributes of a man; הולך *walking*, יודע *knowing*, are modes; בין *between*, תחת *under*, על *above*, etc., are nouns which show the relationship a man has to other things.[195]

Notice the description of "walking" and "knowing" as "modes and relationships, or actions." Modes *or* actions: modes *are* actions. The noun *man* has the attribute of being *learned* and is doing the action of *knowing*, which is a mode. Knowing, like all actions, is a mode. Applied to substance, this would mean that it does the action of knowing and that this action is a mode. Its knowing is modal. As explained in the *Ethics*: "When we say that the human mind perceives this or that, we are saying nothing but that God, not insofar as God is infinite but insofar as God is explained through the nature of the human mind, *or* insofar as God constitutes the essence of the human mind, has this or that idea."[196] When modes think, these are God thinking, that is, substance as modified, as determined, as finite. But I suggest that Spinoza is saying even more, or at least that if we follow the implications of his arguments, what emerges is that substance *only* thinks modally, *only* does anything modally, *only* exists modally, for modes *are* its actions. Substance is only ever modified because modes are the enactment of its power, which *is* it.[197]

A further reason I am suggesting that infinite, indeterminate substance *only* exists as its finite, determinate modes is because otherwise, how else are we to understand Spinoza's insistence that substance is infinite—without definition, delimitation, and determination—yet also only exists as actualized power? How might indeterminate power be actual without being defined, delimited, or determined? What is an act, if not a form of determination, if not determinate? Moreover, substance cannot preexist its actions—its modes—as this would undermine its existence, which is its essence, which is its power, rendering it not actualized. This is an upshot of Spinoza's remark that "it is as impossible for us to conceive that God does not act as it is to conceive that God does not exist."[198] Or, "since, in eternity, there is neither *when*, nor *before*, nor *after*, it follows ... that God was not before God's decrees, and cannot be without them."[199] If modes are the actions—"decrees"—of substance, this means that substance never was nor can ever be without its modes.[200] Substance is not akin to a battery of power that exists independent of and precedes the things that it powers. Rather, substance *is* the very enactment of the power that is it, which only is modal. The actions of substance *are* it; not only do they inhere in it, as *causa immanens* necessities but substance cannot be more than them, for then it would have to preexist them or have power that is in reserve and not yet realized.

Although Spinoza refers to substance and modes as if they are distinct, "except for substance and modes there is nothing"[201] or "in nature there is nothing except substances and their affections."[202] These are not separate entities, by which is meant, not the irrefutable point that all modes inhere in substance, but that substance and modes coincide. "By mode," Spinoza clarifies, "I understand the affections of substance."[203] And the affections of substance are the same with it: "substances *or* what is the same ... their attributes and affections."[204] These are the same only "distinguished by reason."[205] When Spinoza refers to infinite substance and finite modes distinctly, he is doing so in order to convey specific points about the nature of reality and being human. Really, though, these are the same, distinguished *only* by reason, not actually. As examined above, "some of the Hebrews," in order to uphold or at least not undercut God's unity, argue that differences in God's attributes are only notional. Spinoza echoes as much in discussing the attributes, especially in his earlier works. I suggest that he extends this by supposing that substance is not really distinguished from modes because these modes are its power, enacted. Indeed, this is the only way in which its power—which *is* it—is actualized, for any other option would subvert its infinity, its indeterminacy, since infinite, indeterminate power only *is*, *as* its finite, determinate acts.

Rightly perceived,[206] substance is "what is in itself and is conceived through itself, i.e. that whose concept does not require the concept of another thing."[207] Hence, *natura naturans* is "what is in itself and is conceived through itself, *or*... God insofar as God is considered a free cause."[208] "Free" means unlimited, unconstrained, "determined to act by itself alone."[209] These actions, as we have seen, are modes. For the "absolutely infinite" power that is substance cannot be without being actualized; its power is only *in actu*. Logically, substance cannot be without its modes, without its acts, which *are* it—hence, Spinoza's "insofar as." We can speak of substance *as if* it is separated from, independent of, prior to its modes, but this is only a way of speaking, a "being of reason."[210] Modes are "what is in another, those things whose concept is formed from the concept of the thing in which they are."[211] Accordingly, *natura naturata* refers to "whatever follows from the necessity of God's nature, *or* . . . all the modes of God's attributes insofar as they are considered as things which are in God, and can neither be nor be conceived without God."[212] Modes are whatever follow from the necessity of substance, its power, which *is* its essence. These can be considered "as things which are in God," taken "insofar as" they are *in* substance and only conceivable through it. Yet really, modes are more than this, they *are* substance, the determinate ways in which its indeterminate essence, which *is* it, is. Substance as *natura naturans* is substance as *natura naturata*; *natura naturata* is substance as *natura naturans*. These terms reflect different ways of perceiving, describing, construing the same thing, the same reality, whatever is. But these are not ontologically distinct, they do not reflect a hierarchical arrangement or tiered reality. On the contrary, taking substance as nothing *but* its actions, which are its modes, tenders a reality that is without priority, essentialized difference, and rank. This is why "God must be the cause of all things in the same sense in which God is called the cause of itself,"[213] not because substance is a sovereign power responsible for all subsidiary things but since it only *is* these other things. Thus, "from the necessity alone of God's essence it follows that God is the cause of itself and of all things."[214] The necessary existence of substance, which is its essence, which is its infinite power, only exists as active, as modes. This is why all things follow from the same necessity as its very existence, as "all things" are how it *is*.

Reality is nothing more than its singular things, its modes. These finite modes exist as the actualization of a power that is infinite, yet a power that is proscribed from being prior to, independent of, and more than its finite actions. Crucially, due to the infinity that is substance, this means there can be no a priori curbs or conditions on how these modes are, on how reality is. The response to the question of how have things come to be, from this Spinozist perspective, is that reality is nothing but infinite power actualized finitely. What has been—colliding waves of energy so many eons ago, a warm pool of festering microbes billions of years ago, a split from chimpanzee-bonobos millions of years ago—are the countless singular, finite modal acts of infinite power, which is only realized finitely. What exists, therefore, is what it is and is so due only to itself, the infinite connection of causes, countless intra-acting modes.

In on the Act

Let us take stock of what this all means. Substance is nothing *but* its modes. Not only is all that it does reflexive, such that the binaries of cause and effect, subject and object, active and passive are dislodged. Such immanence further means that substance does not exist prior to, otherwise than, independent of its modes, which are its actions, how the infinite, indeterminate power that is substance actualizes.

This rendition is distinguished from readings that recognize how Spinoza disrupts hierarchical and unilateral approaches to causation yet retains a certain priority or alterity. For example, Friedrich Engels writes, "Spinoza: substance is *causa sui* strikingly expresses the reciprocal action."[215] More recently, Klein has described Spinoza's "nonhierarchical immanence" as pivoting on the "reciprocal implication" of cause and effect.[216] Such mutuality is also reflected in Negri's depiction: "God is the world that constitutes itself ... The mode is both the world and God."[217] Similarly, to Macherey, "if no determinations at all were given in God, it is the existence of things and his own specific existence that would be called into question."[218] These renditions echo a subtle purport of Scripture: at the beginning, God creates, not because there can be no creation without God, but since there can be no God without creation. Yet Spinoza is not merely saying that substance needs modes in order to be substance, that being a Cause requires an effect, nor the further point that substance exists only by dint of its modes, that "it is nothing other than the act of expressing itself immediately in all its modes."[219] Rather, I posit that Spinoza dismantles the hierarchy further by leveling the binary of substance and modes such that substance is the very action that *is* modes and not that modes are the instruments through which it acts or that its acts simply inhere in it. This is because substance is power *in actu*.

Construing substance as infinite power that only exists as finite modes, which are its acts, levels essentialized difference and rank. There is no Cause that precedes its effects, existing independently of them. This has been missed by generations of readers. To wit, Hegel, criticizing Spinoza, portrays the liaison of substance, attributes, and modes as emanationist, "*one after the other.*"[220] Deleuze, similarly maintains that "Spinoza's substance appears independent of the modes, while the modes are dependent on substance."[221] If substance cannot exist without its actions because it is its active essence, this means that substance is not independent of modes. It only exists *as* them. There is no succession or supremacy, hegemony or primacy.

Readers who continue to puzzle over how the infinite "transitions" into or begets the finite miss this innovation. There is no transition because indeterminate power only exists determinately. Moreover, power is not a thing or capacity that is possessed but only exists as its actualization. This means that power does not precede action but is its very performance. Likewise, agency is not a capacity that preexists its exercise but *is* its actualization. Reality, nature, all that exists, is not a what—a thing—so much as it is a how. Construing substance as infinite, indeterminate power enacted finitely and determinately also sidesteps questions of identity and suspicions of self-sameness be it of substance with itself or modes. Since it is not a being or thing or power but only action *in actu*—doing—concerns of containment, presence, and coincidence, as the following chapter more closely unpacks, are obviated.

Substance is not really Substantial. It is not an *ousia* in the classic sense, as it is not matter and form, nor matter or form, as these rely on definiteness and determination. Besides, such categories amount to constraints, delimitations that vitiate infinity. Substance, as Spinoza repeatedly emphasizes, is without a telos, and so it definitely cannot be a substance in the Aristotelian sense. Substance is also not substantial in the colloquial sense, as it cannot be solely a *material* thing, as matter is necessarily determined, defined, and delimited. But more remarkably, as we follow Spinoza's arguments, it becomes apparent that his own definition of substance is more nuanced than initially appears. For substance as "what is conceived through itself" can only be as the modes that are it. The infinite power that is substance can only exist as enacted, as its acts, which are its modes. Substance, therefore, is not an underlying substance, a ground, a being that underpins what is. *What* it is, is what *is*. Through his utilization of the term *substance*, Spinoza modifies its meaning, denuding it of metaphysical pretenses, divesting it of the sovereignties of preeminence, priority, and predominance.

Common Cause

By extrapolating from the rationales of his predecessors, Spinoza tenders a radically non-sovereign conception of reality, the valence of which is strategically cloaked in the familiar vocabularies of traditional metaphysics. Yet each term or concept—God, nature, substance, attribute, mode, cause, effect, power, freedom, necessity—is revised such that reality amounts to infinite power that only exists as its finite enactments. The ramifications of this innovation are expansive, and the pages that follow register, complexify, and refine this picture. However, at this juncture, several of these are lightly sketched here to offer a sense of Spinoza's ontology.

Reality is doing. Rather than grounding all that exists in an independent, preeminent, Origin, Cause, or Being, Spinoza reframes it. There is no infinite Beyond being but only infinite being, which is nothing but finite activity. This strips reality of the essentialized difference, hierarchy, supremacy, independence, preeminence, and binarity associated with conventional approaches to causality and competing ontologies. Whereas Descartes considers reality the passive effects of a sovereign God who stands above it and imbues it with vitality, Spinoza reverses this equation by taking substance as existing only as the actions that are finite modes. To exist is to be active, to be is to do. This is accentuated by the coincidence of being and doing, of essence and existence, which not only applies to substance but also to modes, whose essence is also their power, which is their *conative* persistence in being, nothing but their actual doing.[222] Moreover, since infinite, indeterminate substance only exists as its finite, determinate modes, this means that all that exists, whatever is, reality itself, is nothing but singular things. A singular thing is "an affection, *or* mode, which expresses God's nature in a certain and determinate way."[223] That is, the "certain and determinate"[224] actualizations of indeterminate, infinite power.

While part I commences by confirming substance as the immanent cause of all else, it concludes by dispersing such causality to all modes: "Nothing exists from whose nature some effect does not follow."[225] Everything that exists is the determinate effect of countless different causes and itself also the determinate cause of countless different effects "and so on, to infinity."[226] This is what it means to consider substance as the cause of what is: it is cause *as* the doing that is determinate, singular things. All things are "determined by *infinito causarum nexu*—an infinite connection of causes—to exist and produce effects."[227] Reality, for Spinoza, is an infinite connection of causes, an immanent matrix of causes and effects, effects and causes, which Balibar notes, "cannot be represented by an addition of independent linear series, or genealogies of causes and effects ... only by an infinite network of singular modulations."[228] This captures the nonhierarchical character of intra-action, which applies to all that exists. Everything is imbricated, implicated, and involved, entangled in the infinite connection of causes, which as infinite must be without beginning or end, purpose or plan. There is no above or below, interior or exterior, center or margins.

The infinite connection of intra-action that is reality is without privilege or exception. There is no transcendence from it and no escape from causal interconnections. All that is, is *of* it. This means that nothing is exempt from the necessity of causal determinism or immanence. Thought is causally determined as much as extension is. Much as God is divested of sovereign freedom, so too are modes. Everything is caused to be and caused to be *as* it is, rather than sovereignly chosen, elected, or decided to be so. Nothing we do, or think, or feel is Free, unconditioned, or decontextualized. There is no escape from imbrication, no transcendence from the infinite connection of causes.

Accordingly, humans are *of* the infinite connection of causes. Their imaginations and ideations are of it, not apart from it. Indeed, the ways in which reality acts, "according to which all things happen ... are always and everywhere the same."[229] This refusal of exceptionalism, a priori difference, and fixed boundaries are crucial to Spinoza's campaign against sovereignty. Everything is equally of nature, which is reality. Substance *or* nature. Substance is neither other to nor excepted from nature. As Spinoza reflects: "I do not separate God from nature as everyone known to me has done."[230] As with substance, so too with modes; nothing is an exception to nature and its causal ways. Moreover, there is no hierarchy or separation between what is colloquially termed "nature" and that which is deemed other to it: a kangaroo is of nature, much as a phantasm of a kangaroo is of nature, as is a plastic figurine of a kangaroo, a cantata about a kangaroo. These are all equally *of* nature. Everything is *of* nature, *of* substance, *of* reality and subject to its immanent, intra-active ways, without exception.

Substance *as* its modes means that all that exists are modes and modes are singular things. Everything, every force, every entity, every being is a mode. There are modes of extension: this keyboard. There are modes of thought: this idea. There are modes that are a coming together of both thought and extension: me, and you, and your nibling. There surely might be modes that are not of extension or thought because reality is of infinite attributes. Since everything that is, is a mode, this also means that modes are not just objects like this book. They can be structures like capitalism and ideologies like trans misogyny. Or the feeling of nausea I had yesterday. Your recollection of experiencing ecstasy, your sensation of it, your fantasy of it, and your desire to experience it once more. These are all modes.

Although everything is a mode and modes are singular things, the identities of singular things fluctuate since modes are interconnected, not isolated.

What is considered an "individual" mode varies based on perspective: you are a mode but you are "highly composite" as you are "composed of a great many individuals,"[231] including cells and memories, muscles and synapses, musings and sensations. Modes are determined in "infinite ways" and "compelled to undergo infinitely many variations."[232] Much like all the nerves in your nervous system are themselves configured of countless modes that combine to comprise your nervous system, so too, many different individuals—say, you, your dentist, and their nemesis—can collaborate together, such that you can be perceived as comprising "one body *or* individual."[233] Your mutual intra-activity dissolves the provisionary boundaries taken as dividing you from them, them from each other. Much as we can refer to your nervous system *and* to you—as separate—so too, all of reality can be conceived more particularly or more generally, as everything is a singularized actualization of infinite power. Such permeability can be quite fraught, unintended, and injurious, as when a bee stings you, a whiff of rosewater prompts recall of a traumatic experience, or a bot in your social feed thrusts fascistic content upon you. All of us, all that exists, is impacted "by external bodies in very many ways."[234] Such intra-actions effectuate all sorts of things, sometimes salubrious and sometimes insalubrious. Spinoza describes these intra-actions in terms of "coherence," "agreement," and "adaptation."[235] This recognition engenders considerable epistemological and ethical implications, positioning him to theorize living well as maintaining "agreements" rather than "disagreements" with other modes, stressing how doing so is necessarily *of* our natures, immanent to us.

By construing God *as* substance *as* nature, Spinoza dethrones God from its traditional perch of privilege. This is but the initial movement in his comprehensive denaturalization of sovereignty. For not only is God divested of sovereignty and its traits, so too, is reality. What exists is so without an Origin or First Cause, is deprived of Freedom and Agency, Alterity and Primacy. These do not adhere ontologically. There is no given Privilege nor a priori Hierarchy, much as reality is without fixed boundaries and essentialized differences. Everything is entangled in the infinite connection of causes, equally conditioned and confined by it. Although everything is *of* the infinite connection of causes and imbricated with others, this infinite connection of causes does not exist independently, prior to, or beyond the finite modes or singular things that *are* it. All that exists are singular things, particularized actualizations of the power that is reality, the finite determinations of infinite, indeterminate substance. To deliver this non-sovereign reality, Spinoza unhinges the binaries securing conventional "Western" alternatives, including cause and effect, form and matter, thought and extension, being and doing, essence and existence, freedom and necessity, activity and passivity.

Disrupting sovereignty entails not simply overthrowing Sovereigns but dismantling the infrastructure and instruments that support them, much as it entails overturning the logics that underwrite the concept of sovereignty. This is why denaturalizing sovereignty is so vital; it exposes sovereignty as constructed, anthropically contrived, conditioned by human desires. Doing so not only discredits the conceit of sovereignty. It forestalls its reproduction because the naturalization of sovereignty validates sovereignty, conceptually and practically, fomenting its proliferation. Delegitimizing the circular authorization derived from the pervasive, delusive naturalization of sovereignty and its traits means that reality can no longer be leaned upon to license hierarchy, domination, and supremacy. This matters because such naturalization continues to sponsor—if often unknowingly—its theoretical and tangible promotion. Liberating reality from all purports to and properties of sovereignty, as this book ventilates, not only allows us to see reality otherwise but to descry what is possible once we detach from our prejudices to predominance.

TWO

Nature Is Not All

> The oneness of being, therefore, embraces the truth that being is not one.
> —ELLIOT R. WOLFSON[1]

The radicality of Spinoza's ontology derives from the contention that substance is infinite. Rather than anchor reality in a being that is One and Beyond, he reasons that infinity forecloses all limitations, which means that it cannot be contained to certain boundaries or constrained to specific confines. Infinity commands immanence by rendering all that exists *of* the infinite connection of causes and, correlatively, by sustaining this immanent reality as limitless. With this, Spinoza liberates infinity from impoundment in the ontotheological, stripping it of sovereignties. Not only is infinity not tethered to a transcendent One that is *other*, but infinite reality is disburdened of sovereign Oneness and its constellated features. What this means is that substance is not One, it is not Whole, and it is not a Totality. Reality is boundless and open. It is not All. Significantly, modes are also divested of sovereign Oneness. No mode is an isolated One, a uniform Identity, or an enclosed Unity. By sustaining reality as infinite and by releasing infinity from the fetters of sovereignty, Spinoza confers the resources for a thorough recalibration of reality. Such an ontology solicits us to consider what it means to approach reality without resort to sovereignty and to contemplate the subversive consequences of such a move.

By resolving that substance is not One and deriving that it is dispossessed of such associated traits as Unity, Allness, and Identity, this chapter resists truisms about Spinozism that have circulated for centuries. Since its earliest reception and still today, with select exceptions, Spinoza has been interpreted as delivering an ontology of oneness. I contest this by tracking his conception of infinity, revealing how the indeterminacy and limitlessness constitutive of it proscribe as much. But this is only part of the present enterprise because to debunk the pervasive misportrayal of Spinoza's ontology demands reckoning not merely with the content of these misconstructions but also their context.

The most influential misreading of Spinoza is that of Hegel, who posits that substance is One, constitutes an identity, is deprived of movement, precludes individual actuality, and has an infinity that is complete. He links this to "Oriental" thought, contraposing it to "Western" Christian individuality. Spinoza, "the Jew," disallows for the dynamicity of Christian Trinitarianism. Thus, Spinoza's philosophy is to be sublated and superseded. Hegel is neither the first to deliver this verdict nor to connect it to Spinoza's Jewishness. The conjecture that substance is One and the coupling of this to "Oriental" and Jewish ideas has proliferated since the publication of Spinoza's *Ethics*. During the late seventeenth century, throughout the eighteenth century, and thereafter, this assertion was corroborated by aligning substance with Kabbalah's Ein Sof. Our exploration exposes the conditioned nature of this posited connection. Nowhere were these imbricated concerns more consequential than in the tragic *Spinozastreit* of the 1780s. Briefly surveying this controversy uncovers the ways in which Spinoza's Jewishness and that of his thought were weaponized to discredit his philosophy by portraying it as atheistic. In Jacobi's crusading missives to Mendelssohn—which influenced Hegel—Spinozism featured as the menace that Christian, "Western" culture must confront and through which it is defined.

Scrutinizing the anti-Judaism that has sponsored the reception of Spinoza's philosophy is necessary for several interconnected reasons. The first is the simple imperative to set the record straight by uncloaking the Christology and anti-Judaism that underwrites "Western" philosophy and proves indispensable to its treatment of Spinoza. This is historically the case and its legacy persists, which is the second reason that attention to this complex is crucial. The scholarship on Spinoza has mostly failed to register the anti-Judaism subtending the interpretation of his philosophy. Not only have the anti-Judaism, Christology, and colonialism of Hegel's misappraisal of Spinoza been largely ignored, but contemporary scholars perpetuating Hegel's interpretations effectively reproduce the violence of his maltreatment. If these scholars are doing this wittingly, their culpability demands to be prosecuted. If they are doing so unwittingly, the privilege of their ignorance must be cited, and the systemic Christian supremacy by which "Western" philosophy is sustained, and upon which the modern discipline of philosophy is founded, warrants indictment. It is hard to overstate the scope of this phenomenon as many of the German Idealist construals, especially as pronounced by Hegel, remain commonplace in the literature. I not only disprove these but unmask their prejudicial underpinnings. When scholars read Spinoza as an idealist; reduce his philosophy to monism; render his reality a totality; construe substance, attributes, and modes hierarchically; sustain a strict dualism between substance and modes; and undercut modal existence, they are sustaining centuries of criticism of Spinoza that was motivated by anti-Judaism and Christian supremacy. Scholars must reckon with their complicity in this legacy, irrespective of their supposed "intellectual" merits or the personal commitments of particular scholars.

Tarrying with Hegel serves a further purpose in this chapter: it furnishes a salient depiction of the mechanics and logics of sovereignty. This is readily discernible when Hegel, following Jacobi, positions Spinozism as *other* to "Western" philosophy, as hostile to the Christology structuring it. In so doing, he leans on sovereign constructs such as the essentialization of difference, the contrivance of hierarchy, and the imposition of binary distinction to certify the preeminence of that which he deems "Western," Christian, European. Moreover, it is the marginalization of Spinoza that licenses the assimilation and subsequent overcoming of his ideas by Hegelianism. These tactics of sovereignty are not unique to Hegel, although they assume unprecedented centrality within the context of his project in two salient manners. The first concerns his history of philosophy and philosophy of history, which are contrived upon the manufactured difference and implicit hierarchy between that which is seen as "Western" and that which is deemed "Oriental." For Hegel, the "West" absorbs the signal concepts and contributions of the "Orient," which facilitates its ascent, securing its supremacy. This relates to the second critical aspect of Hegel's exercises in sovereignty. As will become clear, the Hegelian dialectical system is founded upon and fueled by the logics of supremacy. Lingering with Hegel in this chapter supplies an instructive depiction of the logics and logistics of sovereignty, which accentuates, by contrast, what I determine to be the assets of Spinoza's alternative. This is evident not merely in the supremacies that sponsor Hegelianism but in its negotiations of the traits of sovereignty at the center of this chapter, specifically Oneness, Allness, and Sameness and their conjunction with infinity.

Contending with Hegel and his partisans enables us to rebut their misconceptions, to recuperate aspects of Spinoza's ontology that have been repressed, and to contemplate the expansive theoretical consequences thereby unlocked. Against the consensus supposing that substance is One, I demonstrate that it is neither quantitatively nor qualitatively One. The former follows directly from Spinoza's remarks on the matter and from his reservations concerning the inadequacies of signification. The latter emerges from an elaboration of the infinity attached to substance outlined in the previous chapter, which construes infinity as indeterminacy, infinite substance only *as* its finite modes. This understanding is consolidated by tending to the limitlessness implied by the infinity of substance, which I reason, precludes suspicions of identity, allness, and closure. These cannot obtain when substance is infinite act. This is the meaning, I demonstrate, of Spinoza's endorsement of an actual infinite: infinity is actual as *act*. Anticipating potential rebuttals, I decipher that the supposed indivisibility of substance amounts to its dynamicity rather than the immutability of an identity and correlatively deduce that substance is not a circumscribed Individual nor a totalized Whole. Like substance, modes too, are not numerically One nor are they endowed with the qualities of Oneness. Particular modes are not isolated, their confines are not stable, and they do not comprise a unity.

To Spinoza, nothing is already One or Whole or Same. This is because these are anthropic constructs that fail to adequately signify reality. Further, these are comparative terminologies that presuppose the existence of that which is other to them: the One is precipitated by the many, the Whole presumes an outside, the Same depends upon what is different. The One is only One over and against the Many, the Whole is only Whole relative to what it excludes, the Same is only Same over and against that which is Different. These rely on the sovereign presuppositions of an originary state and a transcendent, essentialized distinction, which presume and perpetuate hierarchy. This reasoning underpins what I discern as a primary theoretical asset of Spinoza's conception of infinity: it empowers us to approach infinity without resort to sovereign binarization. Binary rationale subverts infinity by rendering it contingent upon the finite; it constrains infinity, undercutting its limitlessness. But there is more here. Thinking with Spinoza positions us to expose the supremacies that sponsor binary reasoning, including the privilege, preeminence, and predominance that it inscribes. By contrast, I advocate for conceiving infinity nonbinarily, for upholding reality as nonbinary. Taking substance as infinite power enacted finitely, rather than its prominent alternatives—an infinite Origin that *begets* the finite; an infinite Ground that *contains* the finite; an infinite Being *opposed to* the finite—accommodates this scheme. It enables us to accept infinity as actual and reality itself as infinite, without circumscribing infinity or subordinating the finite to it.

For Spinoza's critics, substance is One, All, and Same. Spinozist infinity is deficient. This conception of reality originates, they allege, in "Oriental" and Jewish thought. Not only is this assessment prejudiced and erroneous, I evince that it is precisely Spinoza's *Jewish* sources that inform his refusal to attach sovereign Oneness to substance. These accordingly condition his account of infinity as eluding all forms of limitation, which emancipates substance from confining boundaries and constraining enclosure. Unmooring Spinoza's infinity from its Christian supremacist reception discloses reality as non-same, non-contained, and non-total, confirming it as not All.

All for One

What is? To broach this question, "Western" thought has tended to lean on the notion of Oneness and its constellated traits: unity, identity, and indivisibility. Eleatic philosophy is credited with initiating this trend. Xenophanes insists that the One is god. To Parmenides, being is one and so indivisible and same. Democritus multiplies the ones: being is reducible to countless ones—atoms moving about the void—that are indivisible and internally same. This tide persists with Plato's Demiurge and notion of the Good, which differentially arrogate such affined features of oneness as unity, identity, and indivisibility. Aristotle's Unmoved Mover is foremost and exclusively one, responsible for the unity of all, and possessive of an Intellect that maintains identity and indivisibility. Plotinus and then Proclus compound this current by proclaiming the One as the origin of itself and all else. Hebrew Scripture credits reality to a God deemed singular and so exclusively worthy of worship. Since at least Philo, it has been axiomatic in Jewish thought that God is One, which has amounted to the insistence that God is a unity, indivisible, and immutable, though the contours of said oneness are contested. This fierce trust in—if not fetishization of—the One as the ground and reason for reality becomes entangled with infinity such that

Oneness and infinity are intertwined in the One god that is Infinite or the Infinite god that is One. This is epitomized by the Kabbalistic appellation Ein Sof, which was initially an adverbal abbreviation for "until infinity" or "up to no end" and later became a proper noun.

The enticements of Oneness are perceptible. In order to organize a reality that is multiple, disparate, and chaotic, it seems reassuring to attribute it to an originary unit or unifying ground. Conceivably, it is comforting to construe reality as contained and constrained. Despite these assets, the trouble with Oneness is that it is not a neutral construct. It is freighted with baggage. Most obvious are those traits that the ancients readily associated with it: identity, immutability, and indivisibility. Positioning all that exists as One appears to imprison and immobilize reality, subordinating it to the supremacy of the Same. If all that exists is One, what of difference and development? And if reality is considered the product of an *other*, a Being that is One—rather than itself One—this instantiates transcendence, installing hierarchy, rank, and distinction. These suspicions likewise recur when the oneness of God or Being is transferred to *specific* beings as when humans are conceived as atomistic ones: independent, isolated by impermeable boundaries, invested with an indivisible, stable identity.

Considering as much, it is unsurprising that the concept of sovereignty is often associated with oneness, with the attestation that the Sovereign—god, monarch, state, or self—is endowed with oneness, unity, and identity. This pretense tames the disparities of reality by crediting them to a shared origin or by uniting them under common rule. Most conventionally this is the contention that what is either originates in or is overseen by a Being or Principle that precedes all else and is supreme over it. This status tends to be secured by underscoring the uniqueness, the originality, and the singularity or difference of this very being. Such distinction tends to be tethered to claims not only of the precedence of this being or principle but also of the immutability of its boundaries or its being. Thereby, the variety of reality is coalesced and its variability cohered through submission to the supremacy of this origin or unifying force. Consider, for example, the familiar case with states: the heterogeneity of the collective is typically integrated through a hegemonic identity that dissolves or at least marginalizes difference. Likewise, the particularities endemic to the collective are assimilated and united in and through allegiance to a single authority. The corresponding legitimacy of both the collective and its sovereign are consolidated through the demarcation of territorial and identitarian boundaries united by containing an "inside" constructed upon the exclusion of that which lies "outside." These mechanisms are similarly operative in the hierarchical and nontransferable stature of the sovereign.

This pervasive adulation for the One as a founding or unifying principle of reality has not escaped contestation. In his critique of classic metaphysics, Heidegger pinpoints the decisive sway of oneness: "The essential constitution of metaphysics is based on the unity of beings as such in the universal and that which is highest."[2] More recently, Badiou has constructed an ontology resisting oneness, endeavoring to wrest infinity from theological monopolization by the One. To do so, he capitalizes on "the secularization of infinity"[3] purportedly enacted by mathematics. In declaring "the One is not,"[4] Badiou asserts that oneness is never given but only ever an effect. Spinoza's conception of infinity, I demonstrate, inaugurates this line of critique and delivers an ontology unencumbered by the constraints of oneness and its cognate sovereignties.

Hegel's Negativity

It is hard to overstate the influence of Hegel's misreading of Spinoza. The accusations that he presses, while not original, are substantially responsible for continued dismissals of Spinoza's theories. Hegel's construal of Spinoza's philosophy rests on the assertion that it reprises "the oriental theory of absolute identity."[5] This is expected, Hegel implies at the start of his treatment of Spinoza in his *Lectures on the History of Philosophy*, because he is a "a Jew," so his philosophy is perforce "an echo from Eastern lands."[6] Thus, in Spinoza's thought—which itself comprises a "profound unity"—Spirit manifests "as the identity of the finite and the infinite in God, instead of God's appearing related to these as a Third."[7] Spinoza's Jewish heritage sponsors his purported theoretical commitment to oneness and identity, while his biography reputedly also reflects this allegiance. As Hegel crudely sees it, Spinoza's lens-grinding vocation "was no arbitrary choice . . . it represents in the material sphere the absolute identity which forms the Oriental view of things."[8] In a correspondingly ludicrous Hegelian concretization of Spirit, Hegel proclaims that Spinoza's cause of death—consumption (*Schwindsucht*)—"was in harmony with his system of philosophy, according to which all particularity and individuality pass away [*verschwindet*] in the one substance."[9]

Only after marginalizing Spinoza as a Jew, reducing his thought to his Jewishness—the "Oriental"—and construing his life and death through this reified conceptual prism, does Hegel turn in his *Lectures* to Spinoza's actual ideas. What he contends is that for Spinoza, substance is "one absolute Being."[10] Reality is an "absolute unity,"[11] constituted by attributes that form a "totality," are "identical and infinite," and comprise "true completion."[12] This proves damning: "The world has no true reality" for it is "cast into the abyss of the one identity."[13] All that exists is "the positive, the affirmative, and consequently the one substance,"[14] marred by a "rigid motionlessness" that disallows for "the moment of negativity."[15] Substance has a "single form of activity": the divestment of all "determination and particularity."[16] Thus "all differences and determinations of things and of consciousness simply go back into the One substance... cast down into this abyss of annihilation."[17] Modes, therefore are "nothing in and for themselves,"[18] while substance itself lacks "the principle of spiritual freedom" and remains "only the Idea taken altogether abstractly, not in its vitality."[19]

Allegedly, Spinoza admits only the One, which he deprives of the capacity to become, while denying all else of individuality. The interests driving this condemnatory reading and its stakes are rendered patent as Hegel elaborates: "God is conceived only as Substance, and not as Spirit... The independence of the human soul is therein also denied, while in the Christian religion every individual appears as determined to salvation. Here... the individual spirit is only a mode, an accident, but not anything substantial."[20] Spinozism, like Eleaticism, lacks "the agency of Christianity," which allows for "concrete individuality."[21] It abjures "the Western principle of individuality,"[22] "the principle of spiritual freedom,"[23] and "the independence of the human consciousness."[24] Accordingly, like modes, substance is without "liberty"[25] and "comes to no vitality, spirituality or activity."[26] As "not yet spirit," substance is "rigid and unyielding."[27] Indeed, "the reason that God is not spirit is that He is not the Three in One."[28] Hegel reprises these points, maintaining that Spinozism is marred by its disregard for "Christian consciousness,"[29] which is appropriate, as "Spinoza was a Jew by descent"; consequently, "what finds expression... in his philosophy is in general the oriental intuition according to which everything finite appears merely as something transient, as something vanishing."[30] Jewish Spinoza—in person and thought—is immured by Oneness, by the staidness of a Unity that is immobile, contradistinctive to the dynamic unity of the Christian Trinity and the vitality of Spirit. The "Oriental" Jew deprives humans of "Western," Christian individuality.

This reproach of Spinozism is furthered in *The Science of Logic*, which contends: "For Spinoza substance and its absolute unity has the form of an unmoved unity, that is, a unity which is not self-mediated, a rigidity in which there is no place yet for the concept of the negative unity of the self, of subjectivity."[31] Due to the absence of generative negativity, substance is unable to *become*, to produce modal actuality, genuine subjectivity. Spinozism is here linked to "the *oriental* representation of *emanation*," wherein generation is really degradation, "a progressive loss" since "the negative ... does not revert back to the original light."[32] This correlates with the supposed deficiency of Spinoza's infinity, amounting to "the positive which has complete and present in itself an absolute multiplicity which has no Beyond."[33] The Presence and Completion of substance disallows for the negativity integral to development. Spinoza's infinity is impeded by its Oneness and the posited Infinite disables the production of the finite.

This construal of the Jewish Spinoza and the deficits of his philosophy correlate with Hegel's indictments of Judaism: "The Jews possess that which makes them what they are, through the *One:* consequently the subject has no freedom for himself."[34] Indeed, "The subject does not exist in and for itself"[35] and "never comes to the consciousness of his independence."[36] Accordingly, in Judaism, Hegel alleges, God's wisdom remains "abstract," rather than "truly concrete spirit." As such, "what is posited or determined by God subsists at once in the form of an unmediated other" and "is not yet posited as internal to itself."[37] In Judaism, "God is explicitly the One, the one power as inwardly determined"[38] and not yet "self-developing within itself."[39] Accordingly, "The world is grasped ... as a manifestation that is not affirmative,"[40] while "the particular" is characterized by "externality and dependence."[41] The problem with Spinoza is that he is just *too* Jewish. And to Hegel at least, this is why Spinozism is not atheism but acosmism, much as classic Jewish, Islamic, and related conceptions of God "as unknowable, supreme, and otherworldly"[42] are not strictly atheistic so much as insufficient, incomplete in not confirming God as Spirit concretely, that is, Christologically.

There are several factors that condition Hegel's deprecations of Spinoza's philosophy, including anti-Judaism and the demands of his own history of philosophy, which combine to position his artful supersession of Spinoza.[43] Through this maneuver, it will be shown, Hegel is able to simultaneously denounce Spinoza's "Oriental" thought, while appropriating its most generative concepts in order to advance his "Western" project. The next few sections contextualize Hegel's reading, and the analysis towards the end of the chapter more pointedly grapples with his operation and its place within his overall project. Before doing so, it is imperative to unpack the Christian, "Western" standpoint that Hegel occupies and champions.

The binary of the "Orient" and the "Occident" was common in German scholarship of the time: Herder, Schlegel, and Goethe employ it. The construct functions to situate "Western," European, Christian society as distinct from what is deemed as other: China, Persia, and India; paganism and Hinduism; Judaism and Islam; indigenous peoples and cultures of Africa and the Americas. Essentially, all that is not adjudged to be Christian, "Western," European, and white. But rather than a wholesale denunciation of the Orient, especially in Hegel, the Orient is perceived as the origin of the West; its ideas are absorbed and possessed. This is the purport of Hegel's declaration: "World history travels from East to West, for Europe is quite the end of history, Asia the beginning."[44] In his account, "the Jewish" occupies a pivotal role, commanding "the break between East and West," whereby "spirit descends into the depths of its own being and recognizes the abstract fundamental principle as the spiritual,"[45] even as its spirituality remains unrealized, lacking the subjectivity and freedom that only emerges with Christianity. Across his oeuvre, Hegel leans on Christology, specifically its doctrines of supersessionism to theorize politics, religion, art, history, and philosophy. The role that Spinoza occupies in his philosophy is a particular instance of this "universal" Hegelian thematic. In so doing, Hegel instantiates the ways in which German Orientalism more broadly functionally refurbished the Christian supersessionism of Judaism, updating it to map onto the Eurocentric supersession of the "East." Within such Orientalism: "The Jew is not only always one particular type of Oriental, but the prefiguration, as it were, of a position of the Oriental in general as a prefiguration of the West."[46]

Spinoza is acutely destabilizing to such Christian, "Western" orientations because he is at once a Jew, but also a Jew seen as spurned by his Jewish community and thus not fully Jewish. Moreover, his philosophy is interpreted as pantheist or atheist, which is perceived as a return to paganism. This unsettles the neat teleological progression from paganism to Jewish monotheism and then to Christian Trinitarianism. It is also what positions Hegel to see Spinoza as the turning point that must be overcome in the contrived teleological advance of modern philosophy in and as Spirit. The imprecision of these categorizations and constructions, rather than undercutting the prejudicial disparagements of Spinozism, seem to reinforce them through rhetorically strategic obfuscation and confusion.

One and All

While Hegel is vociferous in his denunciations of Spinozism as a purported theory of Oneness and strident in linking it to Spinoza's Jewishness, these are not innovative criticisms. Spinoza's Jewish identity, the Jewishness of his philosophy, and their imbrication with its presumed oneness and by extension its purported atheism, have been central to the reception of his thought. Precisely the Jewish roots of Spinoza and that of his project are what clinched its supposed atheism and warranted its censorship. Without reckoning with this history, it is impossible to adequately study his philosophy because these conclusions and dismissals have commanded its interpretation for centuries and continue to impact the scholarship, a reality that is seldom acknowledged, let alone engaged. The scholarly inattention to this fact is itself a form of anti-Jewishness, whether committed intentionally or not. Precisely the normalization of anti-Judaism or its erasure facilitates such disregard. Consequently, before foraying into Spinoza's ontology to evince that substance is neither One nor possessive of the qualities associated with oneness, we must first peruse the pervasive claims to the contrary and index the manners in which his Jewishness has been marshaled to certify as much.

Pierre Bayle's influential dictionary entry on Spinoza opens by succinctly delivering the decisive connection: "a Jew by birth, and then a deserter from Judaism, and finally an atheist." It explains that Spinoza was a "systematic atheist" and that his thinking draws from "ancient and modern philosophers, European and Oriental."[47] Considerable space is devoted to debunking Spinozism and discounting its "impiety." Elsewhere in the dictionary, Bayle classifies the Eleatic belief in the unity and immutability of all as "une spéce de Spinozisme."[48]

These precise themes and posture feature in the comments of Gottfried Wilhelm Leibniz. Leibniz had written to Spinoza and seems to have lobbied Spinoza's friends—Schuller and Tschirnhaus—to see drafts of the *Ethics*.[49] Spinoza declined: "I judge it ill-advised to entrust my writings to him so quickly."[50] These instincts proved sound, for although Leibniz manufactured a meeting with Spinoza at The Hague in 1676, as Leibniz's assessments of Spinozism attest, he was not commendatory of it. Leibniz writes that "Spinoza undertook to demonstrate that there is only one substance in the world."[51] In another correspondence he refers to this belief as "a doctrine of most evil repute, which a writer who was subtle indeed but irreligious, in recent years imposed upon the world, or at least revived."[52] Spinoza, Leibniz maintains, tried "to make out of God the nature of the world itself, by causing created things to disappear into mere modifications of the one divine substance."[53] Such beliefs are "fraught with dangerous consequences" and result in "monstrosities," which detract from the "glory" of God.[54] Much of this is echoed in his *Theodicy*,[55] which assails Spinozism for its "blind and geometrical necessity, with complete absence of capacity for free choice, for goodness and for understanding."[56] Such "necessity blind and absolute," like that of Epicurus, "would subvert piety and morality."[57] Leibniz also cites the claim, which had been gaining traction, that "Spinoza revived the ancient Cabalah of the Hebrews."[58] For "Spinoza recognizes only substance in the world, whereof individual souls are but transient modifications."[59]

The presentations of Spinozism—as atheistic and aligned with "Oriental" or Kabbalistic ideas—are interlaced. Despite the potential merits of a connection between Spinoza and Kabbalah, such pronouncements are not neutral and, as will be further demonstrated, have been weaponized to discredit Spinozism. Indeed, the reception of Kabbalah in the Christian "West" has been imbricated with suspicions of atheism, which itself is inseparable from historic anti-Judaism. Kabbalah was first introduced to a Latin readership with *Kabbala Denudata*, a compendium of translated texts, including passages from the Zohar and Lurianic teachings, initiated by Christian Knorr von Rosenroth. It was published in 1677, the same year in which Spinoza's *Opera* was released. Which means that the circulation of Spinoza's philosophy coincided with the first availability of Kabbalah to non-Hebrew and non-Aramaic readers. The initial Christian interest in Kabbalah—as epitomized by the commentary and translations in *Kabbala Denudata*—was bent on converting Jews to Christianity and consistently read Christ *into* Kabbalistic texts. A certain erasure of the influence of Rabbinic literature on Kabbalah and its continuities with Rabbinic Judaism is also discernible in the Christian reception. Moreover, the classification of Kabbalah as ancient, when these texts were actually medieval—despite the claims of Kabbalistic texts to the contrary—reinforced Christian notions that Judaism remained static. All of this is to underline that Christian engagement with and curiosities in Kabbalah were partial and calculated.[60]

The Latin exposure to Kabbalah facilitated the most influential denunciation of Spinozism as Kabbalistic: Johann Georg Wachter's *Der Spinozismus im Judenthumb*, which was published in 1699 and cites passages from *Kabbala Denudata*. This polemical tract was borne from Wachter's disputations with Johann Peter Spaeth, who had collaborated with Rosenroth on the project and later converted to Judaism. Therein, Wachter reduces Judaism to Kabbalah, alleges that Spinoza was a closeted Kabbalist, and maintains that Judaism is atheistic. It is hard to overstate the influence of this work: Leibniz and later Jacobi explicitly cite it in their criticisms of Spinozism. Subsequently, Wachter published, *Elucidarius Cabalisticus*, which contended that both Spinozism and Kabbalah align with Christianity. Another work that solidified the connection of Spinoza with Kabbalah was Jacques Basnage's *Histoire de Juifs* (*History of the Jews*), which places the origin of Spinoza's "One" substance in Kabbalah, asserting that Spinoza is the "Disciple" of Kabbalists, who "having the Art and Dexterity to veil themselves under Mystical Language . . . produce . . . Spiritual Conjectures rather than decisions of faith."[61] Here, the antique opposition between Christian faith and Jewish letter surfaces.

Jews of Speculative Reason

Nowhere is the connection between Spinozism, Jewishness, and atheism more pronounced than in the *Spinozastreit*, the Spinoza controversies instigated by Jacobi who charged, in vociferous exchanges with Mendelssohn that his close friend Lessing had confided in Jacobi before his death in 1781 that he was a Spinozist. To be a Spinozist meant to be an atheist, a fatalist. These posthumous allegations imperiled the legitimacy of Lessing's joint project with Mendelssohn to advance religious tolerance and threatened Mendelssohn's advocacy for Jewish emancipation. The stresses of this controversy precipitated Mendelssohn's tragic death. It is important to reprise a few components of these exchanges, as Jacobi's claims about Spinozism conditioned Hegel's reading of Spinoza, much as they did an entire generation's interpretation of Spinoza and, in varying degrees, embrace of Spinoza, including such thinkers as Goethe, Schelling, Herder, Novalis, Schleiermacher, Hölderlin, and Schlegel. The scandal that Jacobi incited shaped German Idealism and German Romanticism. Crucially, the Spinoza celebrated by these figures was *baptized*, a Christianized version that promoted the personal experience with a pantheistic God, a Spinozism that has been dubbed "Lutheranism without a Bible."[62]

By portraying Lessing, a prominent champion of the German Enlightenment, as a Spinozist, Jacobi intended to discredit Enlightenment reason. In Jacobi's calculus, that which is Jewish is synonymous with reason, over and against Christian faith. Avouching as much in exchanges with Mendelssohn, a preeminent German philosopher, the foremost *Jewish* philosopher at the time, the only such Jewish philosopher "recognized" by the Christian, European, "West" and a proponent of the Enlightenment and religious toleration, encapsulates the stakes of Jacobi's crusade and its anti-Judaism.

Recounting his conversations with Lessing about Spinozism, Jacobi reports having portrayed it as a revival of "the ancient *a nihilo nihil fit* . . . but with more abstract concepts than the philosophers of the cabbala."[63] Indeed, "in place of an emanating *En-Soph* he only posited an *immanent* one, an indwelling cause of the universe eternally unalterable *within itself*, One and the same with all its consequences."[64] More pointedly, "Spinozism is atheism. The *philosophy* of the cabbala . . . is, *as philosophy*, nothing but undeveloped or newly confused Spinozism."[65] In Jacobi's hands, the connection between Spinoza and Kabbalah becomes a weapon for assaulting Enlightenment reason. By connecting Spinoza's philosophy to Kabbalah, Jacobi is arguing that it is genuinely Jewish; the God of Spinozism is Jewish, which means, by extension, that the God of the Enlightenment is Jewish. This is incriminating. If the full valence of these pronouncements is only here implicit, the tenor of Jacobi's subsequent preface to the publication of these letters renders them explicit. There, he links "the Jewish philosophy of emanation" directly to pagan beliefs.[66] Jacobi also connects Islam to paganism.[67] Whatever is not Christian is vilified as pagan and immoral.

Rather than perceiving reality as causally determined, humans as embedded in nature, and God and humans as bereft of free will, Jacobi upheld humans, like God, as free, "supernatural," and unimpeded by causal determinism. This, he claimed, was the true Christian *Glaube*, which Enlightenment reason, "Jewish" reason, undercuts. Instead of fatalism, he proposed faith; instead of determinism, freedom; instead of reason, revelation. Christianity "not only commands, but also impels, each and every man *to believe*, and to accept eternal truths through faith."[68] Especially vexing to Jacobi is Spinoza's denegation of free will. For Jacobi, "to request a demonstration of man's faculty to will is to request a demonstration of his existence."[69] Someone who "does not have an awareness of his faculty to will whenever he acts or desires, is something other than a *Mensch*."[70]

In a jarring passage, Jacobi writes of Spinozism: "A spectre of this system has been making the rounds in Germany. . . . Perhaps we shall live to see a battle over the corpse of Spinoza, just like the one between the Archangel and Satan over the corpse of Moses."[71] The party of the archangel, Jacobi writes to Mendelssohn, will find light in Wachter's *Elucidarius Cabalisti-*

cus.[72] Jeffery Librett explicates this imagery: "Jacobi conflates the corpus of Spinoza, the bad Jew whose thought epitomizes Enlightenment, with the corpse of Moses, the law as rotting carcass, and he does this while addressing himself in polemic to Moses himself—Moses Mendelssohn. He thereby says to Mendelssohn: reason is the letter, the Jew is the dead body of language. You, reason, are the Jew as death itself."[73]

For Jacobi, the dead Jewish letter resurfaces as Enlightenment reason. And Lessing is but the beginning of his inquisition against it. Countless philosophers are suspected of being Spinozists, counted amongst "the Jews of speculative reason."[74] But it is not merely Jews and "Jews of speculative reason" that undermine Jacobi's Christianity; Jesuits and Catholics are threats, as they represent the recrudescence of the Jewish letter, the body, and its rationalism. Attempting to depict the insidiousness of "Hyper-krypto-Jesuitismus" and "philosophischen Papismus," Jacobi turns to scientific racism. He invokes the German scientist Samuel Thomas von Sömmering who is notorious for racist fabrications alleging an association between cranial measurements and intelligence and who declared that Africans, despite being "Menschen," are inferior to Europeans.[75] Jacobi writes that if someone contested as much by proving that Black people are not only not inferior but superior and even if a divine reason confirmed as much, "would we not all laugh and be angry?"[76] Yet, says Jacobi, no one is amused or angered by those who do so in other realms of knowledge. In Jacobi's perverse calculus, Jewish reason and its Catholic and Jesuit reproduction subvert his brand of Protestantism. These are as destabilizing to his worldview as the fact that Black people are no different from Europeans. Jews and their secret disciples—Enlighteners, Spinozists, "Jews of speculative reason," crypto-Jesuits, and Catholics—like Black people, are inferior and irreformable.

Evidently, Jacobi's offensive against the Enlightenment was constructed upon the conflation of Enlightenment reason with Judaism and by extension atheism and nihilism. The controversy that he sparked not only encaged Spinoza's legacy in scandal but it cinched Jacobi's career, introducing him to the public. While Jewish Spinoza, the Jewish origins of his thought, its Jewish rationalism, its purported adherents, especially Jews, and those who befriend them provided Jacobi with an other through which to construct his counter-Enlightenment project.

The Scandal of Jewish Difference

None of this was lost on Mendelssohn. The historical record, theological context, and contemporary stakes of Jacobi's ambuscade were unmistakable. Whereas Jacobi impugns the Enlightenment as "Jewish" and therefore irredeemable, in *To the Friends of Lessing*—his rejoinder to Jacobi—rather than disavowing this, Mendelssohn affirms it, a stratagem that did not aid his cause in the estimation of his contemporaries.[77] Mendelssohn does this by reprising his religion of reason and affirming the Jewishness of Spinozism alongside his own Jewishness. Recall that Mendelssohn's support of Jewish emancipation rests on his claim that Judaism is not a "religion"; that it professes truths attainable through natural reason; that it primarily legislates behavior—"living script"—rather than doctrinal belief and creed. "Now, it seems to me that the certainty of natural religion is just as brilliantly resplendent, just as incontestably sure, to the unspoiled and undeluded common sense of all humans, as any proposition of geometry."[78] With this, Mendelssohn reasserts the universal accessibility of the truths of natural religion promoted by Judaism. To depict this point, he describes an early morning conversation between an indigenous person—who Mendelssohn labels as "Eskimo"—on Kalaallit Nunaat—what he calls "Greenland"—and a colonizing missionary. The indigenous person, upon seeing "the dawn blaze forth between the frozen peaks," declaims: "Look brother, at the young day! How beautiful must he be who has made this!"[79] To Mendelssohn, "this reasoning, which was so convincing for the Greenlander before the pious preacher has led his understanding astray, is also convincing for me."[80] Despite the implicit exoticization of the indigenous person and Mendelssohn's Eurocentric gaze, he likens himself to the indigenous person. Both Mendelssohn and the indigenous person uphold natural truths that are threatened by Christian supremacists: Jacobi is here the colonizing missionary, endeavoring to lead Mendelssohn "astray."[81] Appended to this tale is a citation from Psalms, portraying God as accessible to humans. The message is clear: Judaism allows for a personal and natural connection with God; Christianity corrupts this with its doctrines and intermediaries. The problem is Christian supremacy, not Enlightenment reason, which is open to all.

Rather than disavowing the Jewishness of Spinoza's philosophy, Mendelssohn embraces it, allowing that a "purified" version is compatible with Judaism: "I knew that this purified Spinozism was able to be brought into harmony especially with Judaism, and that Spinoza... would have been able to remain an orthodox Jew if he had not in some of his other writings called into question the authentic core of Judaism."[82] If Lessing was a follower of Spinozism, it would have been this "purified" version:

> The doctrine of Spinoza is obviously much closer to Judaism than it is to the orthodox teaching of Christians ... why then should I not love him all the more when he came closer to Judaism and I recognized him to be a follower of the Jew *Baruch Spinoza?* The appellation "Jew and Spinozist" could never be so startling to me, nor so irksome, as it perchance may be to Mr. Jacobi.[83]

Mendelssohn responds to the anti-Judaism propelling Jacobi's prosecution of Spinozism and besmirching of Lessing's reputation by transforming what was intended as defamatory into that which is salutary.

Mendelssohn's steadfast commitment to his Jewishness and his espousal of Judaism's compatibility with reason epitomized the promises of this strand of German Enlightenment. To its opponents, like Jacobi, this represented its perils. The fact that Mendelssohn never denounced his Judaism but instead promoted its truths, using them to advocate for equal rights, encapsulates precisely what Jacobi found so threatening. Jacobi opposed Jewish emancipation, and the controversy he incited "almost instantaneously destroyed the great reputation of Mendelssohn."[84] Rather than stigmatizing Spinozism, the controversy popularized it: "Overnight, Spinoza's reputation changed from a devil to a saint."[85] These effects are connected: the more Spinoza was baptized by Christian thinkers like Goethe, Herder, and Novalis, "the more Mendelssohn became, for the Christian audience, again simply the *Jewish* and despised philosopher."[86]

The Spinoza controversy evidences the crucial role of Spinoza's Jewishness—and Mendelssohn's—in the interpretation and instrumentalization of Spinozism by "Western" Christian thinkers. Goetschel identifies what subtended the dispute: "the scandal of Jewish difference."[87] Such Jewish difference not only fueled this controversy but shaped at least the next century of German philosophy: "Spinoza's Jewish identity ... figures as the central but suppressed motive in the emergence of German idealism."[88] This is not merely since the question of Jewishness and also the Jewish question were central to these controversies, which configured German Idealism and its critiques, rejoinders, and appropriations of Spinozism, but because German Idealism is anchored in the concepts and supremacies of its Christian, "Western" foundation. Thus, "anti-Judaism remains latent within Kantianism and German Idealism."[89] Or, German Idealism has an "inner" antisemitism.[90]

It is not merely Hegel who needs his Jewish other. As the *Spinozastreit* underscores, German Idealism, indeed "Western" philosophy, needs its "Oriental," Jewish other against and through which to define itself. As with Hegel, the Jewish surfaces alongside a variety of religious, ethnic, geographic, and racial others. Christian, "Western," European, white philosophy and culture is nothing without that which it demarcates as other and determines either to exclude or to plunder and subordinate.

False Identity

Before proceeding, a comment on Kabbalah is merited. Although the hinging of Kabbalah to Spinozism, as evidenced by the foregoing, was propagated by Christian polemicists and thinkers as a means of discrediting it, the weaponization of this potential connection does not in and of itself strip it of all merit. De-Christianizing the study of Spinoza entails disentangling precisely such prejudicial scholarship from what might be legitimate surmises. This is not the place to engage particular affinities between Spinoza's philosophy and Kabbalah, but it is pertinent to mention that Maimon—like Mendelssohn[91]—connected Spinozism to Kabbalah. Not only was Maimon Jewish, but he was a Talmud scholar and student of Kabbalah who even penned a short Kabbalistic treatise. Unlike the aforementioned Christian thinkers, Maimon possessed the requisite knowledge to assess the connections between Kabbalah and Spinozism. Nevertheless, like anyone broaching the fraught reception of Spinozism, especially at that time, his postulates are not impartial.

To Maimon, "the Kabbalah is, in fact, nothing other than an extension of Spinozism."[92] Reflecting upon his initial exposure to Spinoza's philosophy, Maimon writes: "I had, through my reading of Kabbalistic writings, chanced upon the same ideas that underlie his system."[93] Abjuring the classification of Spinozism as atheism, Maimon asserts: "The two systems are diametrically opposed. The atheistic system denies the existence of *God*; Spinoza's denies the existence of the *world*. Thus it should really be acosmic."[94] Atheism "entirely dispenses with a primary cause,"[95] while "Spinoza's system, by contrast, proceeds from the idea that one and the same substance is the immediate cause of all effects."[96] This aligns with Maimon's remark in his Kabbalistic compilation *Livnat ha-Sappir*, wherein he explains, extrapolating from Maimonides, that God's unity means that God alone exists. Maimon then references the Kabbalistic construal of Ein Sof's relation to the world as that of a soul to its body.[97] Such a portrayal of Spinozism as an idealism—wherein only God exists, yet effectuates all else in thinking—is also speculated upon by Mendelssohn in defense of Spinozism against Jacobi's charges of atheism.[98]

Kabbalah is multivocal in contemplating the nature of Ein Sof and its relation to the finite. Despite the assertions cited above, in several divergent Kabbalistic articulations, Ein Sof is not upheld as the One of Identity. Rather, as Elliot R. Wolfson has demonstrated, for certain Kabbalists, Ein Sof is not "the being that is beyond being...it is rather the being that cannot be reduced to or identified with any being.... the one constellated not by the one of singular identity but by the illimitable multiples of the one that is never one."[99] Or as he summarizes: "Through the course of many centuries, kabbalists have contemplated the infinitivity of the One that is not one, the one, that is, within which the henadological manifold is enfolded as the fractional generic of the fragmented whole, what Badiou would call the *multiple of multiples*."[100] The posited alliance between Spinoza and Kabbalah does not result, per se, in the claim that for Spinoza reality is One, Indivisible, and Same. On the contrary, if Spinoza is informed—either directly or indirectly, consciously or not—by Kabbalistic speculations of Ein Sof, there is precedent in this tradition for disrupting the ontotheologies attached to Oneness. If one accepts such contact or correlation, it seems that Spinoza captures these impulses and extends them by positioning substance as insubstantial, the indeterminate infinite as its finite determinations.

To de-Christianize or decolonize the study of Spinoza entails deconstructing the explicit anti-Judaism that sponsored early and still enduring interpretations of his philosophy. It also demands a reckoning with, for example, the colonialist logic, racist asides, and unrestrained Christian supremacy that surfaced in the Spinoza controversy and later in the German Idealist criticism and expropriation of Spinoza. Such an undertaking also encompasses the more delicate labor of trying to dissever the prejudicial espousal of certain scholarly conclusions from what might be their legitimate intellectual grounds. The question of Kabbalah's impact on Spinoza is such an instance. Both Mendelssohn, who was familiar with Wachter's work and Maimon, who was at least aware of Jacobi's controversial statements and references to Wachter, either concede or, in Maimon's case, advocate for this linkage. While their arguments cannot be dissociated from what was by then nearly a century of conditioned interpretations that weaponized Spinoza's Jewishness by coupling his thought to Kabbalah in order to discredit it, this history in and of itself is not enough to discount their assertions.

There is a case to be made for Spinoza's familiarity with certain Kabbalistic concepts. Aside from the presence of a few treatises in his library containing Kabbalistic teachings, he doubtless would have been exposed to Kabbalistic ideas through his schooling and participation within the Amsterdam Jewish community. Certain Kabbalistic texts circulated in the community and were promoted by its leaders. Besides, Spinoza attests to personally knowing certain Kabbalists.[101] Spinoza would unquestionably have encountered Neoplatonic ideas, which inform not only Kabbalah but medieval Jewish philosophy. It is highly probable that Spinoza knew certain speculations about Ein Sof, most likely through Herrera's work, although the extent to which he actively studied Kabbalistic texts, let alone the degree to which these consciously—or not consciously—shaped his ontology, is unclear.

The diverse landscape of Jewish thought is suffused with naturalist, emanationist, and pantheistic tendencies. These verily informed Spinoza, especially in their medieval Jewish philosophical iteration and possibly also in their Kabbalistic expressions. That such ideas were perceived as threatening or undermining of Christian doctrine, not merely in their blatant abjuring of the Trinity but in advancing more naturalist conceptions of reality, especially through such notions as necessary causation and causal determinism, is undeniable. Spinoza was a student of Jewish thought; his philosophy is informed and influenced by it. From this perspective, there is something unmistakably "Jewish" about it. Despite the polemical context and political stakes of Mendelssohn's remarks, his avowal of Spinoza's Jewishness and the Jewishness of his thought is justified. Often, as traced throughout this book, Spinoza extends certain orientations in Jewish thought, leading them to more extreme conclusions. The consequences of this are certainly in tension with a variety of orthodox Christian doctrines, and the resistance by Christian thinkers to these ideas, including Jacobi, is understandable. But evaluating ideas by how they do or do not conform to Christianity is, of course, an exercise in Christian hegemony, which is contextually, if not also inherently, anti-Jewish. These disagreements cannot be disaggregated from a history of Christian persecution, the Christian supremacy that conditions them, and in the instance of the Spinoza controversy, the critical stakes of obtaining civil rights for Jews through emancipation.

One Is Not

Having examined the dominant interpretation of Spinoza's substance as One and reckoned with its anti-Jewish underpinnings and weaponization, we are primed to interrogate its "intellectual" merits. The assertion that Spinoza's substance is One, carries two valences. It suggests that substance is one in the numerical sense or, additionally or alternatively, that substance exhibits qualities of oneness, such as identity, indivisibility, and immutability. Spinoza's conception of infinity actually disallows for both options: substance is neither one in the quantitative sense nor does it possess qualities of oneness.

It is quite curious that the scholarship on Spinoza has mostly failed to register his repudiation of numerical oneness, considering how transparently and repeatedly he asserts it.[102] The overall disregard for his insistences to the contrary suits tendentious interpretive enterprises. Spinoza expostulates against "the terms called transcendental," which are "taken by nearly all Metaphysicians to be the most general Affections of Being."[103] The first of such expressions he addresses is "One": "They say that this term signifies something real outside the intellect," but it is only "a mode of thinking."[104] Spinoza is disinclined to delve any further: "I do not see what more remains to be said about a thing so clear."[105] This is understandable; Descartes, too, maintains that numbers and universals are "simply modes of thinking."[106] But Spinoza continues, explaining that because numbers and terms like "unity" are relative modes of thinking, "God can be called one insofar as we separate God from other beings. But insofar as we conceive that there cannot be more than one of the same nature, God is called unique."[107] Before concluding, he bares: "If we wished to examine the matter more accurately, we could perhaps show that God is only very improperly called one and unique."[108]

While Spinoza evidently considered the inaccuracy of attributing oneness to God to be transparent, this proved less than obvious to Jarig Jelles, who wrote to Spinoza, pressing him to clarify what he meant by this. Spinoza responded, "a thing is said to be one or unique only in relation to its existence, but not to its essence."[109] This is because "we don't conceive things under numbers unless they have first been brought under a common genus."[110] He further expounded:

For example, someone who holds a penny and a dollar in their hand will not think of the number two unless they can call the penny and the dollar by one and the same name, either "coin" or "piece of money." For then they can say that they have two coins or two pieces of money, since they call not only the penny, but also the dollar, by the name "coin" or "piece of money."[111]

Numbers are comparative, presupposing commonality. To speak of "two" pennies or "two" dollars is possible only if the items are conceived as sufficiently alike to comprise a unit: two coins or two pieces of money. But if both cannot be reified into the same category, then there cannot be two and consequently there cannot be one. The same logic applies to the inaccuracy of calling God "one."[112] Spinoza underscores that substance is not a count-for-one: "From this it's evident that nothing is called one or unique unless another thing has been conceived which (as they say) agrees with it."[113] There cannot be *more* than substance or *another* substance because substance is not part of a genus; its absolute infinity forbids the existence of anything beyond it, rendering it singular.[114] But there is a further, perhaps intuitive point that Spinoza is emphasizing: oneness is nothing without that which *exceeds* it. To count as "one," is to presume that there are, minimally, two, if not three, and so on. One never comes first; one is only ever second. If reality is construed as "one" this implies not merely that there are others *like* it but also that said others *precede* it. The claim here is not simply the uncontroversial point that oneness and uniqueness are relative terms. But rather that the very notions of oneness and uniqueness rely upon that which is *more*, the multiple.[115] The many is always originary: the multitude precedes the One, indeed, the One is borne from the multiple. Spinoza closes his treatment of the matter by reprising a related point: since "the existence of God is God's essence," it is not possible to form a "universal idea" of it.[116] Therefore, "someone who calls God one or unique does not have a true idea of God."[117] Universals, like numbers, presuppose commonalities based on agreements between distinct beings but because substance is singular, it escapes such classification.

Spinoza is not the only thinker to adduce that "oneness" is only imprecisely attached to God. Maimonides argues that oneness is predicable of God solely analogously because it is a nonessential and extrinsic designation.[118] Furthermore,[119] "Oneness is not identical with the thing that becomes one, just as number is not identical with the things that are numbered."[120] When adumbrating the essential attributes of God, Maimonides underscores: "These notions are not ascribed to Him and to us in the same sense."[121] This is because "the comparative is used only with regard to things in reference to which the notion in question is used univocally. And if this is so, there is necessarily a likeness between the things in question."[122] Notably, Crescas disputes this[123] and contends that "God is one" and "compared to anything else, more truly and more preeminently called one."[124]

Clearly, Spinoza draws on Maimonides's reasoning in his argument that numbers are comparative and extrinsic denominations. Although he sharpens the point: for there to be one there at least must already be two. One for Spinoza always comes second. Moreover, whereas Maimonides refuses God's oneness in order to uphold God's distinction, for Spinoza, substance is not a God that is *other* but rather the *causa immanens* in which everything inheres. Additionally, it is not merely substance that is not One but as will become apparent, nothing is originally or essentially One. Thusly, Spinoza universalizes the status that Maimonides relegates to God alone, a critical move in what amounts to a substantive assault on the sovereignties of oneness. Significantly, while Hegel—like many others—reduces Spinoza's philosophy to Jewish or "Oriental" oneness and construes this as derivative of his Jewishness, it is precisely Spinoza's Jewish sources that position him to disrupt the ontotheologies of oneness.

Counting Out

Spinoza's resistance to attributing numerical oneness to substance results from his understanding of the specific form of infinity attached to it and from his reservations about the nature of mathematical signification. These aspects surface in Letter 12, Spinoza's "Letter on the Infinite."[125] Our focus concerns two interconnected assertions. The first is that "neither Number, nor Measure, nor Time (since they are aids of the imagination) can be infinite."[126] And the second is the endorsement of "an actual Infinite."[127] With this, Spinoza breaks with theorists who suppose that infinity is quantifiable and splits with Aristotle and Descartes who deny an actual infinite.

Repudiating the quantification of infinity aligns with Spinoza's aforementioned resistance to the imprecision and relativity of numeric and linguistic signification. Thus, "Measure, Time, and Number are nothing but Modes of thinking, or rather, of imagining."[128] Metaphysicians who deny an actual infinite have "confused these three with the things themselves."[129] This results from an elementary misstep: mistaking numbers for *actual* things rather than appreciating that they are *representations* of things. "But let the Mathematicians judge how wretchedly these people have reasoned,"[130] Spinoza exclaims. "For not only have they discovered many things which cannot be explained by any Number—which makes quite plain the inability of numbers to determine all things—they also know many things which cannot be equated with any number."[131] The problem here lies with numbers, not with infinity; the signifier rather than the signified.

Spinoza's reservations about numerical and linguistic signification align with his critique of anthropocentrism. Reality acts due to causal necessity, indifferent to human interests and epistemic incapacities: "Things are not more or less perfect because they please or offend humans' senses, or because they are of use to, or incompatible with, human nature."[132] Just because numbers—human constructs—cannot determine actual infinity, this does not mean that it does not exist.

There is a further aspect to Spinoza's qualms about numbers and their incapacity to adequate infinity that deserves attention. While traditionally, infinity was vouchsafed to the transcendent One certain modern theorists and mathematicians have strained to release infinity from these precincts by promoting mathematical infinity. Georg Cantor undertakes as much in his set theory, which upholds infinity as actual and quantifiable, infinitely countable and comparable through infinite sets.[133] More recently, Badiou has leaned on set theory in his attempts to secularize infinity and reduce ontology to mathematics. Spinoza cannot accept these advances not only because he repudiates quantitative infinity but also since his ontology forecloses as much. Reality is not reducible to mathematics, to numbers, which are modes of thinking, human constructs that inadequately signify reality. Moreover, no discourse or discipline has a monopoly over reality or a privileged rank within it. Fundamental to Spinoza's ontology is the contention that infinite substance is of infinite attributes, each of which is "infinite in its own kind."[134] What this means is that neither thought, nor extension—nor any other attribute—is comprehensively expressive of being. No attribute is favored, superior, or dominant.

Rather than reduce infinite reality to One domain, be it the One God or the One discourse, Spinozist infinity and the immanence that it commands submit a striking alternative by claiming that there is an actual infinite and that it is not quantifiable. This infinity evades quantification not merely because numbers and measures only inadequately approximate it but insomuch as substance by its very nature defies reification. Substance is "the infinite enjoyment of existing *or* (in bad Latin) of being."[135] This aligns with the arguments of the previous chapter, which construe substance as insubstantial, maintaining that it is not a being or thing but rather actualized power *as* its finite modes. Substance is not One because it is only power in *actum*. Beings, objects, and things are measurable and quantifiable but such representations cannot adequately capture enacted power. Substance defies numerical representation "because the nature of the thing cannot admit number without a manifest contradiction."[136]

There Is No One

Not only is substance imprecisely represented by numbers, but "many things" defy numeration for numbers are unable "to determine all things."[137] In fact, nothing is adequately encapsulated by number: "The true definition of each thing neither involves nor expresses anything except the nature of the thing defined."[138] Therefore, "no definition involves or expresses any certain number of individuals."[139] Equally imprecise are "terms called *Transcendental*" such as "Being, Thing" and "notions they call *Universal*, like Human, Horse, Dog, etc."[140] Why is this the case and why does this matter?

Numbers as well as transcendental and universal terms are epistemological devices that we use to order reality. They are helpful but also confusing in that none can adequately express the essence of a singular thing insomuch as they rely on contingencies and comparisons, which erase particularities. Such terms "signify ideas that are confused in the highest degree."[141] These emerge as we are "capable of forming distinctly only a certain number of images at the same time."[142] Consequently, in encountering many different things, the mind imagines them "confusedly, without distinction."[143] It does not appreciate "slight differences" and instead focuses on "what they all agree in."[144] Although it is convenient, even imperative at times to conceive modes "in relation to a certain time and place"[145] and "as greater or less, and divide it into parts" and "reduce them to classes,"[146] doing so is misleading. It confuses modes with "Beings of reason *or* aids of the imagination" by which they "can never be rightly understood."[147] This is because such devices separate the "Affections of Substance from Substance itself,"[148] abstracting modes from the infinite connection of causes. Nothing that exists is aptly signified by numbers, terms, and classes not merely because they are relative and imprecise but insomuch as these abstractions misrepresent how a mode is, erasing differences and dissevering them from the infinite connections of causes in which they are enmeshed.

The upshot of this is that nothing is comprehensively reifiable or reducible to representational signifiers. For Spinoza, One is never already. Neither substance nor modes are constitutionally or inherently One. Reality is not the product of a One. Reality does not comprise a One. Reality is not constituted by Ones. Thusly, Spinoza universalizes the status of not-oneness traditionally vouchsafed to a transcendent God by claiming that one is only ever a provisional effect, it is never given. There is no Originary count-for-one, nothing is already a count-for-one. Accordingly, the multiple *precedes* the One (of course, for Spinoza, even "multiplicity" is contingent and inadequate) for infinite substance only exists as its finite acts.

Off Limits

Now that Spinoza's denial of attaching quantitative oneness to substance has been rendered patent, it is time to probe his repudiation of attributing the qualities of oneness to it. Despite the seeming consensus to the contrary, it will become clear that substance—on account of being absolutely infinite—does not comprise a totality nor does its presumed indivisibility constitute an identity. Substantiating as much is not straightforward. Readers across the centuries who have adduced that substance exhibits certain features of oneness, although tendentious in their interpretations and hasty in their conclusions, were not proposing entirely baseless claims. Spinoza does, for example, state that substance is indivisible. The mistake committed by exegetes, besides certain barefaced prejudices, is in the determination of what exactly is meant by such remarks and, further, how these align with Spinoza's contention that substance is absolutely infinite.

Recall that substance is not substantial, by which I mean that it is not a being or thing, nor matter or form. Rather, as has been adduced, the infinity of substance amounts to its indeterminacy. This is because determination is a feature of limitation,[149] a form of negation,[150] applicable only to finite beings. The infinity of substance amounts to the limitlessness of its power; substance is unhindered and unconstrained. This means not merely that there is no *other* to curtail substance but amounts to infinite power, entirely without constraints. This is why substance is not a *definite* thing, be it an object or Being. It is also the reason that substance is not a Totality or a Whole, which presuppose encompassment and enclosure. To be unlimited is to be without any form of delimitation or determination. Furthermore, the indeterminate, infinite power that is substance only exists as its determinate, finite actions, its modes. Substance is actualized power. This clarifies why infinity renders substance immeasurable: not because it exceeds all measure but since action is not the kind of entity suitably captured by number; it is unquantifiable.

Moreover, insomuch as substance exists as the enacted power—which is only ever realized and never in reserve—that are its modes, this corroborates that substance is not a Plenitude that preexists its particularities nor a Presence that is already.

Coadunated with the proscription on limitation is Spinoza's contention that the infinity of substance is positive, without privation: "Since the nature of God does not consist in a definite kind of being, but in a Being which is absolutely indeterminate, God's nature also requires everything which expresses *being* perfectly."[151] Whereas imperfection "signifies that something is lacking to a thing which pertains to its nature," perfection amounts to the absence of such limitation, which is why substance is an "absolutely indeterminate being."[152] This linkage between indetermination, limitation, and perfection appears to have escaped Hegel and licensed his criticism of Spinoza's infinity, which he construes as positive, complete. The actual meaning of infinity for Spinoza implies the inverse. The infinity of substance amounts to its indeterminacy, which means not only that it cannot be contained but that infinite power exists only as actualized—in action—never in the ready or already. Its perfection is not a Perfection. On the contrary, to say that it is perfect is merely to note that it is without limitations precisely because it is indeterminate. Pertinently, the determination to which Spinoza refers is not the determination that Hegel discerns and seizes upon in his misinterpretation of Spinoza's remark, "determination is negation."[153] Determination, for Spinoza, is a feature of finiteness, whereas indeterminacy is constitutive of an absolute infinite. Crucially, because infinite substance is nothing but its finite acts, it is not a being that exists and subsequently, through negation, begets the finite. It is infinite power actualized *as* its finite modes. There is no state of being that preexists modal existence.

By conceiving the infinity of substance as connoting its limitlessness, Spinoza aligns with a medieval Jewish philosophical sensibility that sustains God as without limitation. This is indispensable to the theology of Maimonides and manifests in the Kabbalistic appellation "Ein Sof." However, Spinoza diverges critically from Maimonides and the most common Kabbalistic construal in claiming that infinity is not bound to the Transcendent One but constitutes its immanence, unboundedness, openness. Rather than constrain infinity to the One, Spinoza positions it as constitutionally not One, actualized only as its finite modes.

Take Apart

Spinoza portrays substance as indivisible. As the *Ethics* has it: "A substance which is absolutely infinite is indivisible."[154] The reason that Spinoza insists on this, however, is complex. Substance is absolutely infinite and this reflects its singularity: that there is no other substance and therefore that there is nothing that is not of it. Hence, there is a substance that is singular—"one"—and it is of infinite, "multiple" attributes. These attributes are the essences of substance and they are inseparable from it: "No attributes of a substance can be truly conceived from which it follows that the substance can be divided."[155] If the attributes were separable from substance, its infinity would be undermined.[156] Either the attributes would retain the nature of the infinity of substance or not. If the former, this would mean that there are multiple substances that are absolutely infinite and infinite by their own cause, which is impossible. And if the latter, wherein the parts have nothing in common with their whole, then there could be neither whole nor parts, because there is no commonality, which is a prerequisite for causal relation. Spinoza further argues that substance is indivisible because "the nature of substance cannot be conceived unless as infinite, and that by a part of substance nothing can be understood except a finite substance, which ... implies a plain contradiction."[157] This is why Spinoza underscores that although substance is of infinite attributes, these attributes are inseparable from it. Indeed, they *are* it.

There is a further complication against which Spinoza must defend his conception of substance. This concerns his commitment to the immanence and infinity of reality: that there is nothing outside or above, beneath or beyond it. Nothing is *other* to it. If anything was external to it, this would undermine its infinity. This is why Spinoza asserts that infinite substance is of infinite attributes. Which means that all the attributes of reality are *of* substance, including that of extension. This innovation counters both the medieval Jewish philosophical tradition that predominantly denies that corporeality is attributable to God and also contests the Cartesian approach. For Descartes, extension comprises its own substance. Spinoza cannot accept this reliance on transcendence and subversion of the infinity of substance. Instead, he maintains that substance is singular: that there is "one" substance, of infinite attributes. The first reason that many thinkers deny that corporeality pertains to God is because "they think that corporeal substance, insofar as it is substance, consists of parts. And therefore they deny that it can be infinite, and consequently, that it can pertain to God."[158] The second argument—Descartes's—is that "God, they say, since he is a supremely perfect being, cannot be acted on. But corporeal substance, since it is divisible, can be acted on. It follows, therefore, that it does not pertain to God's essence."[159] How does Spinoza rebut these claims? And, relatedly, how is he able to uphold the absolute infinity of substance and simultaneously render it *of* infinite attributes, including that of extension?

Spinoza addresses these concerns in a lengthy scholium, the tone of which is strident and polemical. Tactically, he primarily focuses on arguing that despite the general assumption that extension entails divisibility into separable parts, which abrogates infinity, this is not actually the case. Either because extension is not *really* divisible or if it is that such indivisibility is not "unworthy of the divine nature."[160] As he debunks the competing approach and defends his own position, Spinoza divulges aspects of his conception of the infinity of substance that prove indispensable to his ontology. Whereas his opponents contend that corporeal substance is comprised of parts, Spinoza asserts that substance is necessarily "infinite, unique, and indivisible," which implies that "corporeal substance insofar as it is a substance, cannot be divided."[161] The mistake of his disputants is "that they suppose an infinite quantity to be measurable and composed of finite parts."[162] This is simply not the case. The reason that people suppose as much is because "we conceive quantity in two ways: abstractly *or* superficially."[163] "So if we attend to quantity as it is in the imagination, which we do often and more easily, it will be found to be finite, divisible, and composed of parts."[164] However, "if we attend to it as it is in the intellect, and conceive it insofar as it is a substance, which happens with great difficulty... it will be found to be infinite, unique, and indivisible."[165] He clarifies: "Matter is everywhere the same, and that parts are distinguished in it only insofar as we conceive matter to be affected in different ways, so that its parts are distinguished only modally, but not really."[166] The intellect appreciates that substance *itself* is not divisible into separable parts, although modes are certainly divisible and separable. To illustrate as much, he turns to water, explaining, "we conceive that water is divided and its parts separated from one another—insofar as it is water, but not insofar as it is corporeal substance."[167] Accordingly, "water insofar as it is water, is generated and corrupted, but insofar as it is substance, it is neither generated nor corrupted."[168] Separation and division, generation and corruption are features of the finite and do not pertain to substance when conceived independent of its modes. As it happens, Spinoza admits that even if corporeal substance was divisible, as his opponents claim, in and of itself, this is not a reason to argue that extension is not an attribute of substance. After all, it does not disaffirm that "apart from God there can be no substance by which [the divine nature] would be acted on."[169] Divisibility is fine "so long as it is granted to be eternal and infinite."[170]

Spinoza considers this same issue in his *Short Treatise*, clarifying how it is that extension—which is putatively divisible and finite—is nevertheless an attribute of infinite substance. The presumed divisibility of extension does not undermine the perfection of God because "part and whole are not true or actual beings, but only beings of reason; consequently in Nature there are neither whole nor parts."[171] Spinoza continues, noting, "it is impossible that parts could be conceived in an infinite Nature, for all parts are, by their nature, finite."[172] To be *part* of something is, necessarily, to be finite, which is why "division never occurs in the substance, but always and only in the modes of the substance."[173] Finite beings exist and undergo change: they are born and they die, they grow and decay, they expand and contract. These variations in being are real and they are constitutive of finite existence. However, it is inapt to consider such changes as occurring in substance itself because the absolutely infinite *as* infinite is indeterminate.

This establishes that Spinoza does indeed describe substance as indivisible. It is his commitment to the infinity of substance that subsidizes this indivisibility, and significantly, this indivisibility does not amount to the indivisibility associated with totality and identity. On the contrary, it is substance *as* substance that is indivisible as the alternative would undercut its infinity. However, substance is not indivisible *as* its finite modes. Admittedly, as the previous chapter validates, substance does not exist independent of its acts. It is nothing *but* its finite modes. Construing substance as infinite activity, rather than as a Being or Thing also clarifies why it is that substance is indivisible: divisibility is not a feature that can meaningfully pertain to activity. Neither is indivisibility. Both are traits that apply to beings and things rather than to indeterminate power that only exists as its enacted finite acts, which of course are, themselves, divisible and determinate.

A Whole Lot More

For Spinoza, infinite substance is not reifiable as Whole. The temptation to reduce all that exists to a bounded Unity or compassed One functions to ossify and organize reality, to constrain it by construing it in a manner compatible with the human predilection for containment, or at least our desire for the security its conception seems to furnish. By renouncing these intransigent anthropocentricities and their conspiring pretense to transcendence, Spinoza's ontology solicits a sobering alternative. When Henry Oldenburg writes Spinoza asking him to clarify "how each part of Nature agrees with its whole and coheres with the others," Spinoza responds by explaining how reality does not comport with the categories that humans contrive to make sense of it. Our vantage points, he proceeds to expound, are circumscribed, akin to that of a "little worm living in the blood," whose perception is severely truncated. Unaware of what lies beyond its sights, it mistakes the many parts of the body or the body itself for an isolated whole. So too, Spinoza writes, the common interpretation of nature segregates parts, conceiving them as wholes and accordingly miscalculates the nature of their interactive place within the infinite connection of causes. Moreover, this causal matrix that is substance is not reducible to a Whole, "since the nature of the universe is not limited... but is absolutely infinite."[174] To be a Whole is to be contained and constrained and necessarily not really infinite.

While it is clear that substance cannot actually be whole, let alone a Whole, Spinoza nevertheless leans on this language in his attempt to describe the infinite variability of infinite substance: "And if we proceed in this way to infinity, we shall easily conceive that the whole of nature is one individual, whose parts, i.e. all bodies, vary in infinite ways, without any change to the whole individual."[175] This analogy to an "individual" is not Spinoza's own. Furthermore, within the context of his ontology, its meaning is distinct and limited. This is the case not only because of his repeated provisos about the inadequacy of constructs such as "parts" and "whole" to adequate reality but also in virtue of his conception of infinity as defiant of all limitation. It is intriguing, however, to consider the contrasting function that this analogy serves in the thought of his predecessors. Describing reality as akin to an individual being is a fathomable, if problematic, anthropic operation. While this analogy is traceable to Plato and Aristotle, for Spinoza, its place in medieval Jewish philosophy and, I argue, the divergent valence that it carries within the context of his thought, is decisive.

Consider Maimonides's deployment of this homology: "Know that this whole of being is one individual and nothing else."[176] This analogy is hardly neutral. In Maimonides's hands it functionally invests reality with transcendent order, hierarchy, and oversight. Thus, "just as in the body of human there are ruling parts and ruled parts... so are there in the world as a whole ruling parts... and ruled parts require a governor."[177] With such governance comes the presumption of purposiveness in nature, which secures the "orderly arrangement" of certain species and certifies the Distinction of humans over all other animals, being uniquely endowed with a controlling "rational faculty," for only human existence relies on "reflection, perspicacity, and governance of conduct."[178] This representation of being as "one living individual in motion and possessing a soul" serves to prove for Maimonides "that the deity is one" for "the One has created one being."[179] The analogization of reality to one human individual at once procures human exceptionalism and simultaneously crowns the One God as ruler over this One reality.

For Spinoza, infinity and the immanence that it commands combine to configure a reality that remains irreducible to whatever descriptors we apply to it, including its reification into a totality. Not only are the "parts" of reality "compelled to undergo infinitely many variations"[180] since "all bodies, vary in infinite ways."[181] But "the whole individual"[182]—substance—remains uncontainable, constitutionally incapable of being a closed Whole or Individual. Spinoza's employment of this inherited analogy is therefore not to be taken literally both insomuch as he repeatedly tells us that such modes of thinking cannot adequate reality and because his conception of substance as absolutely infinite is irreconcilable with the conventional notion of an Individual, which connotes limits, encompassments, and constraints.

Tangled Up

For Spinoza, nothing already comprises a unity, is invested with a fixed identity, or constitutes a totality. Modes are not atomistic Ones nor are they endowed with static boundaries. By construing reality as the "infinite connection of causes," Spinoza confirms the interconnectedness of all modes, human and nonhuman. What this means is that modal existence is not isolated and that the boundaries demarcating a given mode are porous, unstable, and indeterminate.

In his aforementioned response to Oldenburg, Spinoza unpacks his understanding of how different modes—"parts"—of nature agree with its "whole." After prefacing his remarks by emphasizing the imprecision of these terms, Spinoza presents a picture of reality suffused with instability. "I consider things as parts of some whole to the extent that the nature of the one adapts itself to that of the other so that they agree with one another as far as possible."[183] But when "they disagree with one another, to that extent each forms in our Mind an idea distinct from the others, and therefore it is considered as a whole and not as a part."[184] Modes are interconnected. They act through adaptations that determine fluctuating levels of agreement and disagreement. Reality is open and variable. Similarly, he explains that when bodies, through intra-action, come to constrain each other or collaborate with each other "in a certain and fixed manner," then "we shall say those bodies are united with one another and that they all together compose one body *or* individual."[185]

The boundaries demarcating finite modes are not fixed but in flux. The perimeters marking particular modes—"parts"—are porous and provisional. Modes are not isolatable but already interconnected. Much as reality is not One, it is likewise irreducible to countless ones: "for all bodies are surrounded by others, and are determined by one another to existing and producing an effect."[186] Insomuch as the confines of individual modes are neither predetermined nor prefixed, this implies both that identity is not *given* and that action is already collective rather than independent. Individual modes are in perpetual contact with other modes, "part of the whole universe," intra-acting with other bodies, striving to "agree" and "cohere" with them.[187] It is not merely that individual human modes are neither alienated nor isolated. But a particular human is comprised of countless interacting modes. The human body is "highly composite," comprised of "a great many individuals of different natures," which interact with each other as well as with "external bodies in very many ways."[188] The human mode—as is the case with all modes—is not strictly atomistic nor, considering its divergent parts, is it an autonomous totality. For Spinoza, as Klein explains, "an individual is best described as a concurrence or intersection of individuals."[189]

The "whole" that we comprise is not a Whole, insomuch as its borders are permeable and impermanent. Spinoza understands the labels "parts" and "whole"—of an individual mode in relation to the rest of nature or an individual mode in relation to the modes that form it—as variable and perspectival. The porosities of a mode together with its innumerable interactions, interdependencies, and interlacements position it as a multiplicity. The body, for Spinoza, as Roth described it nearly a hundred years ago, is "an assemblage."[190] This term suggests a temporary coming together of heterogeneous parts through coordinated arrangements, rather than the stability and enclosure of a bounded whole or unity. Furthermore, conceiving a human mode as interconnected with other modes and other life-forms strips it of transcendent boundaries, the prospect of absolute control over itself, and the conceit of a consistent, stable identity. With this, Spinoza tenders a valuable alternative to certain "Western" sovereignties and invites us to consider what follows from the refusal to conceive modes as a Whole, One, or Unity.

For Christ's Sake

To appreciate the assets of Spinoza's conception of infinity and the ramifications of his ontology, it is instructive to return to the errancies of the German Idealists, especially Hegel. As Macherey contends, "it is Spinoza who constitutes the true alternative to Hegelian philosophy."[191] This alternative, as I see it, is that of thinking reality without resort to the logics of supremacy. Hegel proffers the ideal foil to Spinoza's disruption of sovereignty insomuch as Hegel's project is suffused with the rationales and instruments of sovereignty. Hegelianism is paradigmatic of the specific Christian, "Western" philosophical attachment to sovereignty theorized throughout this book, and Hegel's manipulation of Spinoza constitutes a particular instantiation of a more Universal spirit.

Hegel's approach to a number of his predecessors read as selective and reductive. This is expected not solely because partiality is a liability of all interpretative exercises but especially so with Hegel, whose exegeses of philosophers serve his grandiose History, which culminates in its telos, his Philosophy. Yet Hegel's treatment of Spinoza is singular; he recognized his indispensability: "Spinoza is made a testing-point in modern philosophy, so that it may really be said: You are either a Spinozist or not a philosopher at all."[192] He proclaimed—à la Jacobi's attribution to Lessing[193]—"to be a follower of Spinoza is the essential commencement of all Philosophy."[194] To Hegel, this status demands a specific approach: "The only possible refutation of Spinozism can only consist, therefore, in first acknowledging its standpoint as essential and necessary and then raising it to a higher standpoint *on the strength of its own resources.*"[195] Therefore, "effective refutation must infiltrate the opponent's stronghold and meet him on his own ground; there is no point in attacking him outside his own territory and claiming jurisdiction where he is not."[196] This is Hegel's strategy with Spinoza, whose philosophy is to be invaded and occupied and its resources extracted in order to fabricate a "higher system" which "must contain it within as its subordinate."[197] Christian, "Western" Hegel is to conquer, expropriate, and then dominate Jewish, "Oriental" Spinoza. With this, Hegel deftly harnesses that established scheme known as supersession, whereby Christianity negates Judaism, appropriates what it renders worthy, and through such absorption secures its supremacy, all the while defining itself against the perversions of Judaism that it discards. Christian Hegel negates Jewish Spinoza through an expropriation and integration of his most potent ideas, facilitating the advance of Hegelianism, which is constituted through its domination of Spinozism.

How does Hegel do this? He criticizes Spinoza's conception of infinity and then appropriates its most generative aspects, particularly its imbricated notions of *causa sui* and *causa immanens*. He also miscasts and then collars Spinoza's passing comment—*omnis determinatio est negatio*—concerning determination and negation. These concepts, in Hegel's hands, become the tools through which he develops the self-mediation and generative negativity that configure his dialectic. Thereby, Hegel poaches Spinoza's ideas and dispatches them to mend what he perceives to be the immobility of substance and lack of modal reality. Spinoza's *causa sui*, in Hegelianism, becomes the means through which the absolute self-determines as self-negation, immanently and reciprocally, generating difference *as* self-differentiation, movement by means of self-transformation. Thusly, substance *becomes* Subject.

This is not a simple case of taking a previous thinker and refuting or developing their concepts further. Rather, this technique and the status that Hegel confers upon Spinoza's "Oriental" and Jewish philosophy not only license his negations of it but certify his adept Christian, colonial expropriation and overcoming of it. Hegel broadcasts as much through his repeated mentions of Spinoza's Jewishness and the "Oriental" nature of his theories. Moreover, as the foregoing documents, what he finds deficient in Spinozism is precisely what he deems insufficient in Judaism, whose God—like substance—is One, remains abstract rather than concrete, and lacks internal development. Consequently, nature is merely posited and so limited, submitted to a God that remains beyond. This externality in turn deprives humans—like Spinoza's modes—of "freedom," "agency," "Christian consciousness," and "individuality," rendering them not yet subjects. Not only do Hegel's critiques of Spinozism correlate with his assessments of Judaism, but Spinoza is a turning point in philosophy, much as to Hegel, Judaism functions as the necessary step towards true religion, Christianity, which corrects for the one-sidedness, abstraction, and externality of the Jewish God by rendering it as an internally, concretely self-determining Trinity.

Invariably, as is so often the case in situations of exploitation, it has fallen to a few Jewish scholars and scholars of Jewish studies to register the Christian supremacy of Hegel's maltreatment of Spinoza. Yovel allows that "familiar anti-Jewish tones may echo in Hegel's comments on Spinoza."[198] He then observes: "Hegel remains fundamentally faithful to a Christian, even Lutheran outlook," such that he

> puts forth a dialectical form of trinity as the highest philosophical logic . . . stresses the need for God, or spirit, to become "incarnated" in the lives and passions of humanity . . . insists, more generally—and speaking explicitly against the "Jew" Spinoza—on the need for a mediator between God and man, the infinite and the finite, not simply in the form of a church as Christ's mystical body but in the actual life experiences of humanity.[199]

Jewish Spinoza is a particular victim of the universal Christian supremacy that defines Hegel's philosophy, whose "dialectic does to Judaism what the medieval church . . . has done to the synagogue."[200] As Erik-Sven Rose observes: "Hegel's critique of Spinoza condenses his narrative of philosophical supersessionism and posits an implicit analogy between his relationship to the Jewish philosopher from Amsterdam and Christianity's relationship to Judaism."[201]

Similarly, Dobbs-Weinstein tags Hegel's "decisive misreading and misrepresentation"[202] of Spinoza, linking it to Hegel's misconstrual of Maimonides's thought. These showcase how "Hegel's reading of the history of philosophy is thoroughly shaped by his understanding of world history and the place of the Orient within it."[203] Thus, Hegel's approach to both Spinoza and Maimonides parries with his "expulsion of the Jews from world history"[204] and reinscribes it. Consider this rendition of Hegel's, which is emblematic of the Christology underwriting his project, his conception of Judaism, and crucially, presents as a blueprint of precisely his treatment of Spinozism:

> Christianity proceeded from Judaism, from self-conscious abjectness and depression. This feeling of nothingness has from the beginning characterized the Jews; a sense of desolation, an abjectness where no reason was, has possession of their life and consciousness. This single point has later on, and in its proper time, become a matter of universal history, and into this element of the nullity of actuality the whole world has raised itself, passing out of this principle indeed, but also into the kingdom of Thought, because that nothingness has transformed itself into what is positively reconciled.[205]

Spinoza, in Hegel's scheme, is the paradigmatic *other*: marginalized but exploitable, condemnable yet extremely valuable and thus worthy of plunder *or* marginalized in order to warrant exploitation, condemned precisely so as to ordain plunder. Spinoza is the Jew that Hegel's "Western" program needs in order to define itself, absorb, and then overcome. The Hegelian plunder of Spinozism is an extreme and pivotal example of the Spirit that underwrites his entire history of philosophy, which amounts to the imperious Christian, "Western" sublation and subordination of that which it deems as insufficiently or not yet "Western" and Christian. So it is that "philosophy proper commences in the West" where "freedom of self-consciousness first comes forth."[206] Philosophy has its "sphere within the Christian world; for Arabians and Jews have only to be noticed in an external and historic way."[207] To Hegel, "throughout all time there has only been one Philosophy,"[208] which amounts to the "development, the revelation of God, as He knows Himself to be."[209] All difference and particularity are erased in the One. For Hegel, all philosophy has developed through a "necessary succession of stages," arriving at the telos of the present, "the highest stage reached."[210] After "the Oriental whirl of subjectivity, which attains to no intelligibility and therefore to no subsistence," philosophy advances, eventually reaching its "goal" in the present, wherein "spirit accordingly is realized as spirit."[211] Universal spirit is incarnated in the particular Germanic brand of "Western" Christianity that Hegel celebrates such that only his philosophy manifests true Spirit.

What is even more jarring than Hegel's "Western" and Christian supremacist treatment of Spinoza is both the relative silence about this in the scholarship and its uninterrogated reproduction. Nowhere is this indifference more conspicuous than in Macherey's *Hegel or Spinoza*. This otherwise compelling work opens by asserting that Hegel proffers a "formidable misreading" of Spinoza, discerning that it constitutes "a sort of obstinate defense, set against a reasoning that destabilized Hegelian philosophy itself."[212] More still, he grasps the momentousness of this Hegelian maneuver, committing his exploration to uncovering and contesting it. Macherey appreciates how according to Hegel's "evolutionary conception of the history of philosophy," he "proposed himself as the only possible alternative to Spinozism, the forerunner that ceded its place to that which came afterwards, in this movement of ascension that comes ever closer to the spirit itself."[213] Yet for Macherey to crystallize the stakes of Hegel's disparaging and supplanting of Spinoza and their role in consolidating Hegel's self-investiture as Supreme in the history of Philosophy—his "ascension" that approaches "spirit itself"—and to still remain either incognizant of or indifferent to the Christian and "Western" supremacy that sponsor the entire operation is a stunning feat. Indeed, he even cites, in full, some of the most impeachable passages in Hegel's *Lectures*, which reference Spinoza's Jewishness, the "Oriental" nature of his thought, its disallowance of Christian consciousness, and disavowal of the Trinity.[214] This tendency is also discernible in Althusser's reflections, which despite accurately grasping the asset of Spinoza's rejection of teleology, nevertheless reproduces its logics by announcing "Spinoza's anticipation of Hegel,"[215] as if the measure of Spinoza's philosophy lies in its purported teleological preemption of Hegel and its function is but a means to the end of Hegelianism.

This is not the place to unpack Hegel's anti-Judaism nor to probe the ways in which his stance on Jews and Judaism fluctuates across his corpus. Rather, the point is to underscore the role that Hegel's Christological approach to religion, philosophy, history, and the history of philosophy occupy in his interpretation and appropriation of Spinozism. It is important to set the record straight not only for interlaced ethical and epistemic imperatives, but also insomuch as the spirit of Hegel's supersessionism persists in the scholarship. While Macherey and Althusser who are sympathetic to Spinoza—and in the case of the former, actively dispute Hegel's misreading of him—overlook the Christian and "Western" supremacy that underwrite Hegel's abuses, others replicate his maneuver. For example, Žižek[216] extends Hegel's relegation of Spinoza to the "Oriental" and reenacts his supersessionism: "In the history of modern thought the triad of paganism-Judaism-Christianity repeats itself twice, first as Spinoza-Kant-Hegel, then as Deleuze-Derrida-Lacan."[217] Not only is Žižek eager to remind us of Spinoza's Jewishness, but attuned to Hegel, he asserts—in total ignorance of the diversity and complexity of Jewish philosophy—that Spinoza's thinking is "foreign to the Jewish universe."[218] This fallacious proclamation is symptomatic of the forced conversion or baptism of Spinozism undertaken by German Idealism. It also incarnates the enduring arrogance and unearned authority exercised by "Western" thinkers in their appraisals of that which they demarcate as *other*. These currents persist in Žižek's more recent ventures, wherein he proclaims: "Spinoza spoke from the interstices of the social space(s), neither a Jew nor a Christian" and proceeds to assert that "we should act like Saint Paul" by recognizing the constraints of particularity.[219] Here not only is Spinoza's Jewishness indispensable to grasping his thought, but it also warrants Žižek—following Hegel—to parrot that classic Christian critique of Judaism, its particularism. Spinozism thus is to be overcome: "The passage from the Spinozan One *qua* the neutral medium/container of its modes and the One's inherent gap is the very passage from

Substance to Subject."[220] Indeed, philosophy "seems to repeat itself again and again: Oriental spirituality, Parmenides, Spinoza—all stand for the inaugural gesture of philosophy which has to be left behind if we are to progress on the long road from Substance to Subject."[221] Jewish Spinoza and his "Oriental" thinking are to be sublated and superseded as "Western" philosophy marches onwards. Even as "Western" philosophy supposedly advances, its anti-Judaism remains consistent across the centuries.

In an ostensibly more nuanced sortie into this morass, Gregor Moder concedes that Hegel's readings are often tendentious and decontextualized in ways that support his "own philosophical theses."[222] Yet "it would be much too naïve—if not completely wrong—to say that he picked out some Spinozist concepts and productively implemented them."[223] To suppose as much is to miss "Hegelian reading," which takes a text as "a necessary expression of the spirit and that it is therefore in itself already in truth."[224] It "does not measure its text to an external guideline, but insists on an immanent explanation."[225] Thus, in reading, Hegel "seeks to *repeat* the text in its truth; and by repeating its truth it reveals its potentiality, its dynamism."[226] This is a cute defense of a stratagem of tactical occupation, extraction, and usurpation. Such glamorized theorizing about immanent reading—invoking the very immanence that Hegel wrests from Spinoza!—not only condones Hegel's Christian, "Western" supersessionism but celebrates it. Throughout his book, Moder offers considered engagement with Hegel's project and his relation to Spinoza. This includes attention to Hegel's critique of "Oriental" theories of being and his Christian alternative, and his invocation of Spinoza's Jewishness and the "Oriental" character of his ideas. Yet throughout his analyses, there is nary a mention of Eurocentrism, Christian, "Western" supremacy, or anti-Judaism. This disregard undermines the merits of Moder's undertaking—to read Spinoza and Hegel together rather than in opposition—while tendering a particularized instantiation of the sovereignties that continue to suture "Western" philosophy.

Mistaken Identity

The logics and mechanisms of sovereignty configure the Christian, European, "Western" colonialism and supremacy constitutive of Hegel's philosophy of history and history of philosophy. These also manifest acutely in his maltreatment of Spinoza. Yet the Hegelian reliance on sovereignty is more expansive still. I contend that Hegel's alternative to Spinoza—his dialectical system—is constructed on sovereignty, specifically its traits of wholeness, identity, totality, universality, and hierarchy. While Hegel wrongly lambasts Spinozism for possessing several of these features, these not only do not inhere in Spinoza's ontology but form the foundational infrastructure of Hegelianism. Perhaps it was more expedient for Hegel to externalize these anxieties onto his "Oriental," Jewish other instead of confronting their presence in his own program. Yet this is not the place for psychoanalytic speculation, but rather theoretical examination and even a cursory survey of Hegel's claims about Spinozism and his correctives to it exhibit as much.

Hegel alleges that for Spinoza there is first an infinite substance that is positive and only subsequently, finite modes, which are negatively absorbed into an infinite, posited plenitude. This disallows for particularity, dissolving all finite existence in the wholeness, positivity, and identity of infinite substance. It likewise disables all generativity, producing a reality of being rather than becoming. To redress what Hegel mistakenly construes as the degradational and oppositional relation between the infinite and finite, he introduces a dialectical alternative. Through negation of the negative, development is secured by means of the immanent return to self, which effectuates finite determination. Whereas Hegel situates the liaison of the infinite and finite as contrary but ultimately self-relational, deploys the negative as subordinate to the positive—which it positions as supreme—and conceives of being in terms of wholeness, Spinozism, I maintain, overturns these sovereignties. This is because for Spinoza, as we have evidenced, the infinity of substance amounts to its unlimitedness and indeterminacy. Substance is never given nor contained, which is why it simply is not a totalized Whole. Since it does not preexist its finite modes but exists only *as* its finite determinations, this means that substance is not an Identity. It is neither a being nor thing but only actualized power. Although Hegel accuses Spinoza of introducing a reality that is Whole and All, marked by identity, it is actually Hegel's own alternative that is prone to precisely these pressures. In his system, substance *encompasses* subject, as a moment of itself, subsuming it in the beingness of its Wholeness and the Whole of being. Whether being is taken as already whole or only becomes whole dialectically, the Absolute *is* whole. Infinity is bounded to and limited by sovereign Wholeness. For Spinoza, unlike Hegel, unity and identity are not resolved immanently in the infinite Whole that differentiates from the finite within and simultaneously has identity with the totality that is itself, the Absolute. Rather, substance *is* the infinite power that is actualized *as* its finite modes.

"The True is the whole," Hegel contends, by which he means "the whole is nothing other than the essence consummating itself through its development. Of the Absolute it must be said that it is essentially a *result*, that only in the *end* it is what it truly is."[227] This claim to wholeness rests on the rationales of supremacy. Teleology instrumentalizes things as but means to its transcendent end, which is positioned as distinct and superior. This is the case even when the end is not already *given*, if it is not a cause but only an effect, if it is so only retrospectively, for nevertheless what was is measured by or valued only because of what has become. Thereby, it is relegated to a subordinate position over and against the hegemony of its telos, which remains of and yet other to it. Hierarchy is endemic to the Hegelian Whole and the teleology and transcendence that subsidize it. By contrast, as Althusser recognizes, "Spinoza helped us see that the concepts Subject/Goal constitute the 'mystifying side' of the Hegelian dialectic."[228]

Beyond the aforementioned criticisms that Hegel mounts against Spinozism, he also denounces the geometrical method, alleging, "the deficiency that has been recognized here with regard to the *content* proves to be a deficiency at the same time with regard to the *form* as well."[229] Hegel's reproach can aptly be turned back onto his own system: the problem with the content of his thought is mirrored by its form. Both are propelled by supremacist logics. The entire Hegelian system is constructed upon the teleological sublation of that which precedes it, a maneuver of subordination and instrumentalization, predicated upon the purport that "throughout all time there has been only one Philosophy" whereby "in the very process of coming to the knowledge itself it is transformed into the moments of the one Spirit, or the one self-present Spirit."[230] The "various philosophies" are "of necessity one Philosophy in its development, the revelation of God, as He knows Himself to be."[231] This sovereign oneness and the erasure of difference that it entails is amplified in the particular case of Spinoza: Hegel renders Spinoza *other*, defining his own "Western" project over and against the Jewish or "Oriental," which it sovereignly excludes, while simultaneously usurping its signature ideas, transforming them to subsidize the triumphal, teleological ascent of Christian Spirit. Moreover, this exclusion is predicated upon the reduction of Spinoza to his Jewish identity and his philosophy to the "Oriental," which strips him and his ideas of particularity. It concurrently fails to take *seriously* his Jewishness or the Jewishness of his thought, which matters only insomuch as it serves the exigencies of Hegel's "Western" program and the Christological hegemony that it sanctions and sustains.

Reality Is Nonbinary

Subtending Hegel's castigations of Spinozism is the charge that its conception of infinity is deficient. This chapter has already disproved this spurious accusation and disclosed its Christological underpinnings. Substance is not a positive, complete, foundational being that is *given* and then begets finite reality, sequentially and also externally. Rather, substance amounts to infinite power that exists only as its actualized finite modes. This construal of substance disrupts the binary logic to which the Hegelian dialectic is tethered. To think beyond sovereignty is to refuse its array of logics, including, I argue, that of the binary. In Hegel's dialectic, "the negative appears as an intermediary: its immediate appearance is returned, subordinated to the interests of the positive, whose arrival it anticipates."[232] To install a binary is already to fortify a hierarchy: the finite is a mere instrument—moment—of the infinite as it advances towards its teleological resolution, returning to Self. By positioning the infinite and the finite as distinct albeit interdependent elements, Hegel cannot escape the constraints of binary logic. The infinite positive remains supreme, exploiting the finite negative as a means to its own end. Spinoza refuses the sovereign pretenses of this bivalent calculus. This is alluded to when he allows that "there is no proportion between the finite and the infinite."[233] There is no measure between them, not merely because infinite substance defies all measure, but insomuch as indeterminate substance *is* its determinate acts; the infinite exists only *as* its finite actions.

By conceiving infinite, indeterminate substance as nothing but its finite, determinate acts, Spinoza razes the infinite-finite binary. To grasp the assets of his nonbinary construal and its theoretical advantages, it is instructive to survey dominant alternatives and catalog the supremacist logics that sponsor them. Classic approaches—like those mentioned at the start of this chapter—that ground reality in a Being that is One presume its preeminence and priority. All other existences are subordinate to and reliant upon this sovereign Origin and Source. This is accordingly the case with traditional renderings of an infinite God as independent of and transcendent to the finite creatures that it effectuates. In certain early Kabbalistic arrangements, this Infinite God *becomes* finite through gradational emanation, while in the Lurianic rendition, the Infinite contracts through *tsimtsum*, generating space for the finite. Although both of these accounts disrupt transcendence, they uphold its related sovereignties by conceiving the Infinite as preexisting the finite and confirming its originality, supremacy, and alterity. These sovereignties are operative in the scientific and mechanistic programs that gained ascendence in Spinoza's time. The picture of reality as inert and finite, infused with life by a Transcendent being—akin to a clock activated by an external force—relies upon the binary distinction between the infinite and the finite, the origin and that which it begets, the source and its descendants. Hierarchy, essentialized difference, and teleology are intrinsic to such constructions. These sovereignties are likewise indispensable to the Hegelian arrangement wherein the infinite totality—the Absolute—includes, encompasses, and subsumes the finite as moments in its process of becoming Self. Although Hegel contends that his dialectic sidesteps the impasses of the One and the Many, his system is driven by the supremacy of the totality and subordination to its telos. The Infinite is *constituted* by the Finite; the One is *comprised* of the Many; the Finite is *sublated;* and the Many dominated as Spirit *becomes* as concrete unity advancing to its telos. The Infinite and the Finite are constituted binarily, if dialectically tied.

Binary logic is inherently hegemonic. This is showcased in conceptions of reality wherein countless multiplicities are taken as coalescing in the All, gathering together or at least uniting all that is finite. Deleuze's notion of univocity epitomizes as much. It retains the infinite-finite binary and the privilege and supremacy endemic to it. Similarly, although Badiou's ontology endeavors to reverse the classic priority of the One *over* the Many, Unity *over* Multiplicity, he positions the multiple as supreme and originary. What exists for Badiou are multiples, but what presents are ones; one is only ever an effect. The problem with this calculus is that it retains the conventional hierarchy and its binary structure, which it simply inverts. To dispense with the fixtures of sovereignty entails not merely usurping the sovereign—here, multiplicity supplanting oneness—but contesting the rationale of supremacy and priority that underwrite it.

Contradistinctive to these competing approaches, I advocate for overturning the binary logic that still commands the liaison of the infinite and the finite and identify in Spinoza's philosophy the initial resources for doing so. The problem with binaries is that they are intrinsically supremacist; they rely on the logics of sovereignty. A binary instantiates a Distinction that entails the purport to a boundary, which is perceived as already established, as essential, and even transcendent. To be clear, the problem is not difference itself but rather the claim of a Transcendent demarcation of such difference and, further, the hierarchy generally attendant therewith: the presumption of privilege whereby one of the two is taken as primary, preeminent, and predominant. Or, one or both are defined by what is other, either the other of the pair or the other that is the binary itself. Tracking Spinoza's reasoning about the indeterminacy of infinite substance and the determinacy of its finite modes, which are its acts, positions us to think about reality nonbinarily.

Decolonizing Infinity

The actuality that nature is not all reflects its infinity, which releases it from the fetters of transcendent and teleological constraints, confirming it as unenclosed, uncontrolled, and uninhibited. Unfortunately, this aspect of Spinozist infinity and its ramifications for his ontology have escaped recognition by even his more astute readers. For example, Deleuze falters by conceiving substance as a "univocity" and upholding its "ontological unity,"[234] which undercuts its infinity. This facilitates his configuration of substance-attributes-modes into a hierarchy and coincides with the idealism that he lards into Spinozism. Not surprisingly, readers oriented by Deleuze recapitulate this mistake as when Rosi Braidotti ascribes to Spinoza the position that "matter is one, driven by the desire for self-expression."[235] Althusser commits a similar misstep in his early association of Spinozism with structuralism. This formulation and his initial attempts to think the immanent cause as present in its effects retain a sense of totality, while trafficking in the confining binaries of whole/parts or structure/elements. Ultimately, in his later reflections, he presents a more apt conception, speaking of "an unbounded Whole, which is only the active relation between its parts."[236] A cognate lapse surfaces in analytically oriented scholarship that reduces Spinoza's philosophy to a monism and centers its supposed oneness. For example, Michael Della Rocca asserts that for Spinoza "one thing exists."[237] While Jonathan Bennett construes Spinoza's infinity as synonymous with "all," meaning a "totality, the whole, nothing omitted."[238] A further and related slap to the infinity of substance manifests in representations of it as a "system," which connotes both enclosure and stability.

Whether these interpreters realize it or not, their portrayals of the central aspects of Spinoza's ontology reproduce the German Idealist construals and criticisms, which are imbricated with Christian supremacy and a "Western" tradition that shapes itself over and against who and what it excludes. Such interpretations cannot be disaggregated from the role that Spinoza's Jewishness occupied in the approach to his work ab initio as exemplified by partial interpretations, strident denunciations, and incendiary controversies. Purports to its "Oriental" character, its association with Kabbalah's Ein Sof, and claims of its atheism, not to mention its disallowance for particularity, freedom, or development, are inseparable from Spinoza's status as "the Jew" who remains other and outside of, or minimally, merely on the margins of, the Christian, "Western" tradition. As the foregoing demonstrates, I reject most of these contentions, at least as inflected by Hegel, not merely because they originate in and manifest Christian supremacy but primarily because they contravene the plain meaning of Spinoza's philosophy. Had "Western" philosophy historically and still now not sidelined "Jewish" philosophy, if it actually *studied* Jewish thinkers such as Maimonides, then some of these mistakes might have been avoided. The repression and exclusion of medieval Jewish and Islamic philosophy, especially the more naturalist Aristotelian tradition, makes it difficult to grasp certain ostensibly idiosyncratic elements in Spinoza's philosophy. The unquestioned imposition of "Western" categories and constructs *onto* his philosophy, not to mention a rubric that appraises it based on Christological tenets, whether explicitly so, or as is more often the case, merely implicitly, is responsible for these misinterpretations and requires a concerted reckoning. Spinozist infinity needs to be de-Christianized and decolonized. This chapter contributes to such an enterprise.

All Out

Since the infinity of substance preserves it as unconstrained and incomplete, I contend that reality for Spinoza is not only not one but is most aptly captured as not All. What this means is that it is constitutionally incapable of being compassed or contained, curbed or curtailed. Accordingly, it does not constitute an identity or totality. Substance is not a Whole or Unity that gathers together its parts or components; it does not preexist its modes. It is indeterminate, infinite power *as* its determinate, finite acts. Substance is nothing but *this* or *that* mode. It is the infinite, unlimited acts that are its modes. It is not All in that it is not a Being or Container or Thing; it is not All in that its power is inexhaustible; it is not All in that it is without circumscriptions. Substance is an actual infinite: uncontainable, uncountable, unconditioned. Its only constraint is that it cannot be constrained. Its only limitation is being unlimited. While substance is all that exists—infinite power *as* its finite modes—what there is, is never all that can or will be; how what is, is never all that can or will be. Reality is incomplete, not because there is power waiting in reserve nor because there is something excluded from it, but since it is never finished, accomplished, consummated. Accordingly, it is not complete in that it is not total or All. It is not All.

In proposing that reality is not All, I do not mean to imply that it is merely the absence, lack, or negation of allness, that it is not-all. Nor do I mean that it is the opposite of that which is all, that it is un-all. Confessedly, I hesitate with the formulation "not all," lest it appear that I am resorting to an Other against which to determine reality, that it is defined merely by what it is not, or, worse, to imply the existence of an excess that lies Beyond, which contravenes the immanence of Spinozist infinity. Nevertheless, the locution seems to appropriately express the limitlessness and the indeterminacy that Spinoza attaches to the infinity of substance. It signifies the unboundedness constitutive of such infinity by denoting its status as radically open. It likewise speaks to the unbridled and uncontrolled status of such infinity, how there can be no a priori mechanisms restraining or regulating it. "Not all" also carries the rhetorical punch of undercutting precisely the claim of Spinoza's critics—and some of his supporters—that substance amounts to a totalizing All.

Staying Power

The tendency to lean upon sovereign traits is scrutable. Notions such as oneness, wholeness, allness, identity, unity, and totality are devices that enable us to make sense of reality. But as Spinoza reminds us, these are modes of the imagination that inadequately represent reality. They might allow us to provisionally organize an ostensibly chaotic reality, but these can never fully capture infinite nature. Similarly, sovereign constructs might furnish us with a sense, however fleeting, of control as with conceits that reality is bounded and contained, that its multiplicities are united in a whole, that it is anchored in a common origin. While these devices might appear neutral and helpful—even comforting—these not only misrepresent reality, they perpetuate and naturalize ethically debilitating ideas. How we perceive reality at once reflects our anthropic inventions and simultaneously reinforces them. To wit, conceiving reality as the product of a Being that is One installs a hierarchy, while construing reality itself as One suggests that it is subordinated to or controlled by a transcendent demarcation. Likewise, purports that reality is a Unity submit its multiplicities to the supremacy of a unifying force, origin, or boundary; heterogeneity is erased in the hegemony of the Same. Taking finite reality as the *product* of the Infinite, traces what exists back to a transcendent Origin, which installs a hierarchy in nature, as does conceiving the finite as *part of* the infinite, subsumed within it. Both of these rest on a binary distinction, which always brings with it superiority and priority. By contrast, Spinoza's construal of reality as an actual infinite, coupled with his innovations in the interpretation of infinity, empower a radical alternative that is unfettered by the rationales and rubrics of sovereignty. Yet the meaning and ramifications of Spinoza's interventions on this register have been ignored and repressed.

The disregard for Spinozist infinity is not the result of mere scholarly occlusion and interpretive oversight. Spinoza's infinity has been systematically misconstrued and programmatically marginalized by "Western" philosophy. While the foregoing unpacks the anti-Judaism and priorities motivating readers across the centuries to misrepresent substance and the infinity attached to it, here it is instructive to emphasize two further elements. The first point is primarily a reprisal of what has already been thoroughly rendered: the historical reception of Spinoza's philosophy is replete with sovereign exclusions, sovereign tactics, and sovereign violence. The German Idealist approach to Spinoza—like its predecessors and successors—is constructed upon Christian supremacy, cultural hegemony, colonial exploitation, prejudicial distinctions, and oppressive instrumentalization. This is entirely at home within the "Western," Christian, European, colonial milieu and persists within a discipline still underlaid by these commitments. This is emblematic of the ways that "Western" philosophy both promotes and practices sovereignty by pervasively espousing sovereign rationales—as this book tracks—which correlates with its perpetual certification of cultural, religious, geographic, ethnic, racial and social prejudices, subjugations, and hierarchies.

The second aspect connected to the scholarly misrecognition and suppression of the meaning and import of Spinozist infinity has been partially addressed through our analysis of how the Hegelian dialectic reflects and realizes the logics and exploits of sovereignty, instantiating and consolidating the "Western" philosophical ratification of sovereignty. But these are symptomatic of a further contributing factor to the eclipse of Spinozist infinity: the staying power of sovereignty, its captivating appeal. By this I do not mean the blatant ways in which those with power—here Christian, European, "Western," white, colonial philosophy—or those seeking power benefit from the promotion and naturalization of sovereign logics, not to mention their actual deployment. Rather, I am referring to the aversion to entertaining the difficult truth that reality is bereft of sovereignty. Spinoza's early critics, notwithstanding their biases and Christian supremacist motives, were not mistaken to condemn his philosophy as atheistic, even nihilistic. Digesting that reality is not underwritten by a Sovereign power or controlled by fixtures of sovereignty is destabilizing. It reminds us that our autonomy is severely truncated and that reality is without guarantees. Surrendering our commitment to sovereignties is hardly a simple task, which is made harder still by the ignorance regarding its command over "Western" philosophy. The ubiquity of sovereignty paradoxically renders its presence and power almost indiscernible while its naturalization and conventionalization make thinking alternatively nearly impossible. Spinoza's philosophy interrupts these currents and habits. By upholding reality as an actual infinite, as infinite and therefore immanent, as infinite and thus not all, by construing infinite substance *as* its finite acts, reality as radically uncontained, Spinoza disrupts these commitments. The rush to read into his philosophy countless sovereignties—Oneness, Identity, Totality, Presence, Wholeness—perhaps reflects not merely bad reading, biased reading, and boring reading but also bespeaks the formidable barriers to thinking otherwise.

THREE

Not for Nothing

> Faith in nothingness would be as insipid as would faith in Being.
> —THEODOR ADORNO[1]

Why is there something rather than nothing? To this abiding question, the response proffered by Spinozism cannot but leave the questioner unsatisfied. After all, as a philosophy that is without a Why, the most it might muster is: substance. Substance is infinite and immanent. It is *necessary*. Ostensibly, this presents as a non-answer. Yet, in its refusal to capitulate to the enticements of transcendence and teleology—its resistance to sovereignties—Spinozism conditions a forceful alternative for negotiating the puzzles captured by this quandary. It provokes us to contest the predicates of the question itself insomuch as Spinoza's philosophy undermines the binary logic of "something" and "nothing" and, correlatively, the concepts for which they stand: the positive and the negative. Since the German Idealist critique, it has become a cliché to identify Spinozism as failing on account of its neglect of the negative. This is a primary thrust of Hegel's criticism, which continues to animate streams of contemporary discourse as exemplified by the trafficking in the now tired opposition: Hegel *or* Spinoza.

While the previous chapter wrestled with Hegel's overall misreading of Spinoza, here, attention is tendered to the significance and legacies of his contention that Spinozism disallows for negativity. This assertion solicits us to investigate the negative and to consider precisely why it is that Spinoza's philosophy seems to preclude it. It will be demonstrated that Spinozism not only does not exclude the negative, but it also does not uphold the positive.

It resists the binary logic that structures this equation. Infinite, indeterminate substance only exists as its finite, determinate modes. As we have seen, however, substance does not preexist its modes nor is it exhausted by them. Substance is the enacted power that are its modes. Nevertheless, on account of its infinity and indeterminacy, as not-all, substance cannot be entirely coincident with its modes. Yet since the power that is substance is only ever actualized and never in potential, this also means that substance cannot be an excess over its modes or a power that is in reserve, ensconced in some beyond. What this leads to is the realization that substance exists only as its modes and yet is not Same with them, not only because substance is not a thing, matter, or object, the kind of being to which Identity can obtain, but also, insomuch as being entirely coincident with its modes would circumscribe its infinity. This status, I suggest, positions substance as at once not Something and certainly also not Nothing. Rather, by construing substance as the infinite action that is actualized only as its finite modes, Spinoza opens a prospect for perceiving reality that skirts the perennial choice between Something and Nothing.

Although this chapter refines our reading of substance and in the process responds to critiques that Spinozism refuses the negative, its primary focus is fixed on the conceptual issues at stake and their historical resonances. Whereas Hegel links Spinoza to Eleatic philosophy, its denegation of negativity and the identity associated therewith, proponents of Spinoza have connected him to a different ancient tradition: the atomism of Lucretius. Deleuze and Althusser both harness Lucretius's clinamen to defend Spinoza against Hegel's condemnations. Exploring this complex allows us not only to assess the legitimacy of this connection, it forces us to perpend the void and the concepts associated with it: identity and difference, unity and multiplicity, stability and generativity. Despite this purported Spinoza-Lucretius kinship, Spinoza is unequivocally opposed to a vacuum or void in reality. This stance is indebted to medieval Jewish Aristotelianism and Cartesian metaphysics. However, in contradistinction to these traditions, Spinoza's disavowal of the atomistic void does not serve to bolster God's singularity nor does it amount to positing the Positive as primary. On the contrary, it is but an uncompromising embrace of the Parmenidean precept that nothing comes from nothing. The significance of this is accentuated by turning to Crescas's noted advocacy of the void and his retorts to Aristotle. By likening the vacuum to God, Crescas, I argue, exemplifies precisely what is most theoretically problematic with the void: it tends to function as God in disguise. Proponents of nothingness who perceive it as primary, originary, and supremely constitutive of what is, effectively furnish it with traits of sovereignty. It is therefore unsurprising, if underappreciated, that the ascendence of atomism and the vacuum in early modern and modern science was an inheritance from Scholastic theological speculations on precisely the concerns with which Crescas was occupied. The void and the Nothing for which it stands are ontotheological sovereignties.

Despite both the historical and conceptual ontotheological baggage of the void and nothingness, contemporary scholarship has not tired of its recuperation. I discern as much by pivoting to Object-Oriented Ontology as formulated by Timothy Morton. Probing their conception of reality uncovers how it is underpinned by sovereignties, especially transcendence, apophaticism, and the excess that marks nothingness, which Morton deems responsible for what is. This audit positions us to return to the legacy of Hegel's Spinoza as it redounds in the work of Badiou and Žižek. For both, Lucretius proves critical to critiquing Spinozism on account of its supposed declination of the void and the clinamen, the nothingness, and the curvature these represent. I register the missteps in their misinterpretations of Spinoza, while unmasking the ontotheology that sponsors their own respective alternatives. This foray proves invaluable as it allows us to recognize and theorize the ways in which ontotheological sovereignties, specifically transcendence and teleology, sustain their projects.

The reliance on the fixtures and logics of sovereignty by theorists past and present to make sense of reality underscores the salience and singularity of Spinoza's ontology. In the final analysis, the perceived deficiency in Spinozism—its denegation of the negative—is symptomatic of its primary triumph: its suspension of the false choice between Nothing and Something, non-Being and Being, Negative and Positive. Spinozism, I maintain, demands as much because of its disruption of sovereignty. Suspending the binary of being and non-being is necessary because the promotion of non-being—no less than being—is ineluctably supremacist. Refusing this choice, by taking neither the side of Parmenides nor of Democritus, Spinozism tenders an ontology that is radically nonbinary.

Nothing to It

The conflict between the Parmenidean tenet *ex nihilo, nihil fit* and Christian notions of creation *ex nihilo* are resolved for Hegel in his conception of *becoming*. Rather than supposing that something comes from absolutely nothing, Hegel suggests that becoming emerges from being and its negation of nothing, whereby "being has passed over into nothing and nothing into being."[2] In this movement, "they are absolutely distinct yet equally unseparated and inseparable . . . *each* immediately *vanishes in its opposite.*"[3] This dynamic unity, Hegel maintains, contrasts with both Eleaticism and Spinozism,[4] which foreclose this kind of nothingness that is not absolutely nothing: "Those who zealously hold firm to the proposition, nothing is just nothing, are unaware that in so doing they are subscribing to the abstract *pantheism* of the Eleatics and essentially also to Spinoza."[5] In these philosophies, Hegel says, "being is only being, nothing only nothing," which is why these are systems of identity. Indeed, "abstract identity is the essence of pantheism."[6] By disclosing the prospect of something coming from nothing, which disallows for becoming, Spinoza's reality is but "an unmoved unity"[7] wherein all particularity is annulled.

Interpreting Spinoza's passing remark—*omnis determinatio est negatio*—as "the absolute principle of Spinozist philosophy," Hegel proceeds to argue that for Spinoza, the infinite is "the *absolute* affirmation of the concrete existence of any one nature," whereas the finite is its mere "*negation.*"[8] By construing infinite substance as perfect, present, and posited while modes as its mere external negation, Hegel is able to liken Spinozism to "the *oriental* representation of *emanation*," which amounts to "progressive loss."[9] "Being thus becomes progressively obscured and the night, the negative, which is the final term in the progression, does not revert back to the original light."[10] Without the inclusion of the negative into the infinite—"the negative unity of the self, of subjectivity"[11]—all determination is but external degradation and there is no space for progressive *becoming*. "Substance, just as it is immediately construed by Spinoza without the prior dialectical mediation, is, as the universal negative power, only this dark, shapeless abyss, as it were, that swallows up into itself every determinate content as vacuous [*nichtig*] from the outset and produces nothing that has a positive standing [*Bestand*] in itself."[12]

There is no reason to relitigate the errors of Hegel's misreading of Spinoza nor the motivations driving them. What is pertinent to underscore is that Spinoza's purported dismissal of negativity is what, to Hegel, dooms his project. The supposed affirmation and perfection of infinite substance eschew all negativity, leaving finite reality external to it, which forecloses the internal dialectical mediation necessary for becoming, thereby dissolving all that is in the void. Needless to say, this is not the actual nature of Spinoza's substance. Rather than a Being that is given, substance is infinite activity that is only actualized as its finite modes. Having rehearsed Hegel's misconstruction of Spinozism and his association of it with Eleaticism, we are ready for the excursion ahead, which considers the legitimacy of these supposed intersections and deliberates on the legacies of Hegel's calculus.

The Authority of Lucretius

Foreclosing nothingness is, as the story has it, an inaugural gesture of philosophy. Parmenides insists that being is and that nothing is not. Correlative to this stands the notion of being as one, continuous, whole, complete, and same. It lacks nothing. In contrast, the atomism of Democritus conceives of infinite atoms that move about the void. There is always motion. Being is therefore not one, but multiple; what is "not" in fact *is*; change is real. Crucially, while atomism ostensibly resists the Eleatic insistence on the indivisibility and oneness of being, it arguably merely displaces these ideas and attaches them to the atom, the new being that is now indivisible and one. Though the atom as a discrete whole moves, its inside stays soundly static.

The philosophy of atomism, however, is not terminated with Leucippus, Democritus, and Epicurus. In the first century, Lucretius's *De Rerum Natura* infused novelty into Epicureanism. Rather than merely reechoing atomistic tenets, Lucretius introduced several innovations. These modifications are not readily discernible, and those that are have often been met with derision and misappraisal. However, at least since Marx penned his dissertation— "Differenz der demokritischen und epikureischen Naturphilosophie"— Lucretius has not been without his defenders.

If German Idealism derisively links Spinoza to Parmenides, Spinozist partisans have advocated an alternative lineage that connects Spinoza to Epicureanism via Lucretius. To wit, Deleuze and Althusser both leaned on Lucretius in an attempt to defend Spinozism against the deficits that Hegel identifies in it. The associations that they develop between Lucretius and Spinoza emerge amidst a broader revival of Lucretius in French theory. Contemporaneously, thinkers as disparate as Badiou[13] and Derrida[14] engage the Epicurean legacy in their respective negotiations of Hegelianism. Marx's youthful celebration of Lucretius figures—sometimes explicitly, sometimes implicitly—in all of their embraces of Epicureanism. Before scrutinizing what Deleuze and Althusser say about the Lucretius-Spinoza connection—as well as how it reflects their particular relationships with Hegelianism and the exigencies of their respective projects—our own trek into this terrain is in order, especially since Deleuze and Althusser are both elliptical and opaque in elucidating the affinities between Lucretius and Spinoza.

At first glance, contriving a connection between Lucretius and Spinoza strikes as unexpected.[15] Spinoza is notoriously sparing in references to his predecessors and Lucretius is no exception. He is mentioned but once, in response to Boxel's claim that "all the Philosophers, both ancient and those of our time"[16] believe in ghosts. Spinoza retorts: "To me the authority of Plato, Aristotle, and Socrates is not worth much. I would have been amazed if you had mentioned Epicurus, Democritus, Lucretius, or any Atomists, or defenders of particles."[17] Although Spinoza's admiration for Epicureanism and atomism is apparent, a passing remark of this kind, especially considering its context, offers little by way of substantive connection.[18] So, wherefrom the ostensive Spinoza-Lucretius alliance?

There are several thematic points of contact between Lucretius's brand of Epicureanism and Spinozism. They both agree, as Lucretius phrases it, that "nothing ever springs miraculously out of nothing."[19] Debunking supernatural forces is central to both of their projects as is spotlighting the epistemic mistakes that induce such views. Both thinkers tend to the complexities of human cognition, particularly sensation and its roles in perception.[20] Affirming the materiality of human existence and confirming its mortality is of mutual import to their respective projects. Lucretius insists on the infinity of the universe[21] and entertains the prospect of infinite worlds,[22] while Spinoza upholds reality as infinite and of infinite attributes. In light of these connections, it is of little surprise that Strauss commences his *Spinoza's Critique of Religion* by tracing Spinoza's antique forebears, specifically Epicurus and Lucretius.[23] Also noteworthy is how both Lucretius and Spinoza exploit received traditions in order to advance their views, rather than merely rejecting them outright. In so doing, they both harness received terms, which they redefine through use.

An Avoidance Strategy

Notwithstanding their shared naturalism, Spinoza and Lucretius diverge on that for which Lucretius is most known: the void and free will. While they agree that nothing comes from nothing, they disagree on how things do come to be. For Spinoza, there is substance, for Lucretius there is both matter *and* void. Significantly though, he never speaks of atoms. Lucretius does not employ the word *atomus*, the Latin equivalent of the Greek *atomos*. Instead, he prefers *rerum* (things) in addition to *corpora* (matter). Lucretius dispenses with the stasis and oneness of the atom, alternatively emphasizing infinite movement, flux, and interaction.[24] It is of little wonder then that Lucretius underwent a vibrant twentieth-century revival.

The clinamen is the most notorious claim of *De Rerum Natura*. To Lucretius, "when bodies are being drawn downward through the void by their own property of weight, at absolutely unpredictable times and places they deflect slightly from their straight course."[25] This deflection—which is not attested to in other renderings of Epicurus—is critical: "If they were not apt to swerve, all would fall downward through the unfathomable void like drops of rains; no collisions between primary elements would occur, and no blows would be effected, with the result that nature would never have created anything."[26] Lucretius elaborates on the essentiality of the clinamen: "If there is no swerve to initiate movement that can annul the decrees of destiny and prevent the existence of an endless chain of causation, what is the source of this free will possessed by living creatures all over the earth?"[27] If not for this slightest of swerves, there would be no collision of matter and thus no world. In effect, the swerve counteracts the brute determinism of Democritus by sanctioning the scantest trace of indeterminacy.

Lucretius's clinamen has been subject to controversy since his own times. The curiosities of its causation, in particular, have been perceived as problematic. Responding to Aristotle's critique of Democritus, Lucretius introduces the clinamen, which permits bodies to collide, in an otherwise entirely consistent and neutral void. In a sense, the clinamen salvages the void. On the one hand, contra the Eleatic One, Epicurean atomism insists on the void; atoms are many ones separated by the void. Yet on the other hand, the clinamen introduces an additional element into the equation, an aspect that at least seems to insist that the negativity of the void is itself insufficient, that something *else* is needed. To appreciate this tension, let us consider the divergent approaches proffered by Hegel and Marx.

Dismissive of atomism, especially Lucretius's clinamen,[28] Hegel nevertheless acknowledges its assets. Atomism is an advance over Parmenidean being and Heraclitan becoming, although it remains disposed to indifference. As Hegel sees it, the relation between the many atoms in the void remains one of externality and, consequently, mere identity.[29] Despite this deficiency, atomism values the negative: "The view that the void constitutes the ground of movement contains the more profound thought that the ground of becoming, of unrest and self-movement, lies in the negative in general."[30] Even if atomism fails in fully realizing the determinateness of the atoms and their relation with themselves, each other, and the void, it still actualizes the potential of the negative. This is its primary achievement. By placing movement within the void, atomism introduces the notion that the negative is productive; that the infinite encompasses the negative within it by means of its negation of negation.

Marx's doctoral thesis focuses on comparing the approaches of Democritus and Epicurus. Unfortunately, it is incomplete, marred by gaps, and not infrequently requires consultation with the notes for basic clarification. Still, it stages its share of insight. In rejecting the conventional portrayal of Epicurus as "a mere plagiarist of Democritus,"[31] Marx identifies his originality and offers a novel interpretation of Lucretius's clinamen. Moreover, contra the criticism inaugurated by Cicero—that the clinamen is "without cause"—Marx reasons that "a physical cause . . . would throw the declination of the atom back into the domain of determinism."[32] Instead he maintains: "*The atom is by no means complete before it has been submitted to the determination of declination.*"[33] And "to inquire after the cause of this determination means therefore to inquire after the cause that makes the atom a principle—a clearly meaningless inquiry to anyone for whom the atom is the cause of everything, hence without cause itself."[34] If critics perceive the declination of the atom as arbitrary—an external contingency—Marx conceives it as ingenerate to it. The clinamen is internal and it is constitutive of the atom. To question its causation is really to question the atom itself, which as the cause of everything, is itself without cause. Not only is this an effective route for responding to critics of Lucretius, but it arguably also endows the atom with an element of Hegelian self-determination.

Returning to Spinoza, there are certainly theoretical conjunctures between Lucretius's conception of matter and Spinoza's substance. The most obvious is an embrace of immanence. Against the transcendence of an Origin and One, they both insist on the infinity of reality, its interconnection and interaction. By dispensing with the discreteness of the atom and instead conceiving matter as moved and moving, *always*, Lucretius is able to realize an ontology of movement, which is somewhat affined with our construal of substance wherein self-causation *is* immanent causation and the binary adhering between cause and effect collapses. There is a certain similitude with Spinoza's *ordo et connexio* and *infinito causarum nexu*. The void, however, is unavoidable. The interpretations of Hegel and Marx underscore its stakes. If Hegel celebrates the negativity of the atomistic void, Marx champions the clinamen as decisive or so at least the literature sees it. That is, Althusser, Deleuze, and Badiou all turn to Lucretius in negotiating the Hegelian dialectic. For Deleuze and Althusser, connecting Spinoza with Lucretius is central to this effort, while for Badiou, it is the contrast between Spinoza and Lucretius that proves critical.

Althusser or *Deleuze*

Epicureanism conceives of the atom dualistically: there is the internal clinamen and the external void. If Marx celebrates the former as sustaining its self-sufficiency, Hegel commends the latter as epitomizing the generativity of the negative. These components inform and configure the divergent connections that Deleuze and Althusser cultivate between Lucretius and Spinoza. Implicitly, at issue for both of their studies is: What space does Spinozist substance sanction for these concepts? Deleuze espoused Spinozism as an antidote to the identity and negativity ingenerate to Hegelianism. Throughout his writings on Spinoza, Deleuze broadcasts its positivity: "Spinoza's philosophy is a philosophy of pure affirmation,"[35] it is "a philosophy of 'life.'"[36] To Deleuze, the *Ethics* rebuts the dialectic of Sameness, while its philosophy of expressionism proposes an alternative logic of affirmation: "The logic of real distinction is a logic of purely affirmative difference and without negation."[37] By contrast, in Althusser's later writings, the notion of the negative or the void is conceived as vital to Spinoza's philosophy. Although there is much to explore in their approaches, our focus is limited to examining how these divergent approaches feature in their remarks on Lucretius and how in so doing both portray Spinoza as his heir. Expectedly, to a certain extent, Deleuze and Althusser each construe Lucretius and forge Spinoza in their own images.

In "Lucretius and the Simulacrum," Deleuze portrays Lucretius's naturalism as "the production of the diverse inside different and non-totalizable compositions and combinations of the elements of Nature."[38] To Deleuze, Lucretius, like Spinoza, thinks difference through causation: "This is why the *clinamen* manifests neither contingency nor indetermination. It manifests something entirely different . . . the irreducible plurality of causes or of causal series and the impossibility of bringing causes together into a whole."[39] Aligned with Marx, Deleuze discounts the contingency routinely taken as constitutive of the clinamen. Accordingly, he deemphasizes the void: "The *clinamen* is the original determination of the direction of the movement of the atom. It is a kind of *conatus*."[40] Here, Deleuze transforms Lucretius's clinamen into Spinoza's conatus such that atoms are not borne from random swerves in the void but rather from their affirmative, *active* powers. This prepares Deleuze to declaim: "Naturalism makes of thought and sensibility an affirmation. It directs its attack against the prestige of the negative; it deprives the negative of all its power; it refuses to the spirit of the negative the right to speak in the name of philosophy."[41] While this is a characteristically Deleuzian conclusion, it is a curious one to ascribe to Lucretius.[42] In Deleuze's hands, Lucretius, as Spinoza, encapsulates the Deleuzian ethos: difference, power, and affirmation.

In Althusser's earlier writings, Spinoza is associated with structuralism, and by his final essays, Spinoza is positioned as pivotal in "aleatory materialism." A tradition that commences with Epicurus's falling atoms and Lucretius's clinamen and comes to encompass such thinkers as Machiavelli, Hobbes, Spinoza, Rousseau, Marx, Heidegger, and Derrida. Uniting these diverse philosophers is "the idea that the origin of every world, and therefore of all reality and all meaning, is due to a swerve, and that Swerve, not Reason or Cause, is the origin of the world."[43] Dispensing with the Given, this lineage instead commences with chance, contingency, and encounter such that swerving is construed as primary.[44] Opening with God, effectively renders substance as nothing: "By starting with this *beyond-which-there-is-nothing*, which, because it thus exists in the absolute, in the absence of all relation, *is itself nothing.*"[45] To begin with God is tantamount, Althusser reasons, to beginning with nothing. "God *is only* nature. This comes down to saying that He is *nothing* else. He is only *nature.*"[46] This effectively reduces the grand questions of philosophy—origins, causation, and knowledge—to nothing. In this way, Spinoza nominates the object of philosophy as the void. Ultimately, his philosophy "*creates the philosophical void* in order to endow itself with existence."[47]

How do Spinoza's actual theories comport with Althusser's interpretation? Not only is his essay fragmentary but Althusser resigns from genuine exposition. Yet extrapolating from his theme, we might apply the status of substance as not Substantial—that it is nothing but its infinite modifications—as akin to a curving. There is no originary curvature because substance does not *precede* its modes, but rather a perpetual curving as substance actualizes as this or that mode. More problematic, however, is the association of Spinoza with the void, the existence of which he denies while also conceiving negation as privative.[48] Deleuze is therefore not mistaken to associate Spinoza with the affirmative and positive. But it is equally simplistic to conclude as both Hegel and Deleuze—indeed, an uncanny coupling—that Spinozism admits *no* negativity.

Devoiding the Void

It is curious that the void, the negative, and nothingness continue to figure prominently in contemporary discourse. After all, modern physics insists that there is never total nothingness: that an absolute vacuum is impossible. A vacuum is not actually empty. It is suffused with electromagnetic waves.[49] Perhaps this non-existence of an absolute vacuum explains precisely why nothingness lingers yet in the literature. To be sure, even if a literal void is implausible this need not attenuate the conceptual fecundity of thinking the lack. This seems to be what is at issue. Moreover, to risk stating the obvious, all of this depends upon what is meant by "the void." Before analyzing the stakes of this investigation and considering its implications, an inventory of Spinoza's remarks on the matter is necessary.

Spinoza denies the prospect of a physical vacuum, following Descartes[50] to maintain that a vacuum "involves a contradiction" since it means there is extension without corporeal substance, "body without body."[51] Moreover, "nothing has no properties"[52] so nothing cannot be. Spinoza reiterates this position in his correspondences with Henry Oldenburg—then Secretary of the Royal Society—concerning the experiments of Robert Boyle. Relevant to us is Spinoza's remark: "I do not know why he calls the impossibility of a vacuum a Hypothesis, since it follows very clearly from the fact that nothing has no properties."[53] Spinoza has occasion to rehearse this point in the *Ethics*, amidst his defense that substance is infinite yet of extension, which he claims does not require that it be divisible into distinct parts: "Since . . . there is no vacuum in nature . . . but all its parts must so concur that there is no vacuum, it follows that they cannot be really distinguished, i.e., that corporeal substance, insofar as it is a substance, cannot be divided."[54] If substance was divisible into parts, this would undermine its contiguity, indicating a vacuum. Likewise, if substance is constituted by distinct parts, this means that its components are isolatable. But since there is no vacuum in nature this is not possible.

Making a Move

While both Descartes and Spinoza disavow the vacuum, the contexts and motivations of their doing so reflect fundamental divergences in their ontologies. To appreciate as much, it is pertinent to examine Descartes's reasons. Empty space or vacuum, according to Descartes, is not actually empty but constituted by extended substance.[55] When people speak of a void, they simply mean that it contains nothing that is readily perceptible to the senses, although it contains extended substance.[56]

Descartes not only denounces the void, he dispenses with its companion, the atom: "It is impossible that there should exist atoms ... pieces of matter that are by their very nature indivisible."[57] The problem with atoms is their pretense to indivisibility. But, if atoms exist, they are extended and all substance is material and, therefore, divisible. Pressing his point further, Descartes reasons: "Even if we imagine that God has chosen to bring it about that some particle of matter is incapable of being divided into smaller particles, it will still not be correct, strictly speaking, to call this particle indivisible."[58] This is because "God certainly could not thereby take away his own power of dividing it, since it is quite impossible for him to diminish his own power.... Hence, strictly speaking, the particle will remain divisible, since it is divisible by its very nature."[59] Descartes reverts to God to decry atomism. Moreover, unlike atoms, which are of extended substance and therefore divisible, God is upheld as incorporeal and so indivisible, "since being divisible is an imperfection, it is certain that God is not a body."[60] Cartesian physics refuses atoms because only God is Incorporeal and so Indivisible.

Extended substance, for Descartes, is "one and the same."[61] Therefore, "all variety in matter, all the diversity of its forms, depends on motion."[62] Crucially, such motion is not innate but rather lavished on matter by the Immovable: "no other than God himself."[63] "In the beginning <in his omnipotence> he created matter, along with its motion and rest; and now, merely by his regular concurrence, he preserves the same amount of motion and rest."[64] Though God endowed corporeality with movement and change, the incorporeal God is unmoved and unchanging: "God's perfection involves not only his being immutable in himself, but also his operating in a manner that is always utterly constant and immutable."[65]

To reprise, there are three Cartesian points relevant to its foreclosure of atomism and the void. First, empty space is substantial. This means that "nothing" is really in fact some-thing. There is no void. Second, not only is there no void, there are no atoms, which are by nature indivisible and only God is indivisible. Further, since God is indivisible, this also means that God is incorporeal. In contrast, substance is both divisible and corporeal. Third, since there are no atoms, this world is actually comprised of a substance, and insomuch as there is no void, this substance is homogeneous. The source of diversity, however, comes from movement, which is instilled into substance by a transcendent God. Although Spinoza, as we have confirmed, concurs with the Cartesian confutation of a vacuum, several tenets of Spinozism require the rejection of these constellated Cartesian conjectures.

Spinoza repudiates the Cartesian insistence on God's incorporeality and its concomitant supposition that corporeality is endowed with movement by a transcendent God. "For this reason," Spinoza writes, "I did not hesitate, previously, to affirm that Descartes' principles of natural things are useless, not to say absurd."[66] While the Cartesian system rests on a series of interlocking sovereignties that Spinoza must refute, the refuge that Descartes takes in God proves advantageous to his conception. Atoms are rejected on account of the Almighty, and substance is vitalized thanks to the Divine. How is Spinoza able to foreclose the void without reverting to Cartesian transcendence? Wherefrom the diversity and movement in nature if not from Above? What of reality if corporeal substance is taken as indivisible?

Dividing Line

Spinoza's ontology is idiosyncratic. It has unmistakably naturalist aspects indebted to the Aristotelianism of Ibn Sina and Ibn Rushd, refracted through Maimonides, Gersonides, and Crescas. These more naturalist or materialist orientations align with commitments associated with Lucretius. At the same time, Spinoza is also a close reader of Descartes and embraces several of his tenets while disavowing others. These diverse resources informing Spinoza position his ontology to evade neat classification. This has at times befuddled his readers and perplexed his interpreters. Arguably such tensions are nowhere more conspicuous than in capturing the liaison between the infinite and the finite. However, these are not oversights. Rather, Spinoza's ontology is sui generis—I posit—because it dispenses with the mechanisms and rationales of sovereignty. Substance is *causa sui*, *causa immanens*, and *infinitus*, which proscribe the sovereignties of transcendence and teleology. However, although self-causation and immanent causation resolve the problems of transcendence, they engender additional conundrums, namely, how to conceive difference and how to see reality as not already posited, given, and accomplished.

Whereas both Maimonides and Descartes deprive God of corporeality, Spinoza considers extension amongst the infinite attributes of substance yet concurrently upholds substance as infinite and indivisible. The trouble with this is that corporeal parts are considered divisible and divisibility compromises infinity. If substance is divisible this means either that there is *more* than one substance, which undercuts its infinity, or that everything is finite, which also obviously undermines infinity.[67] This indivisibility ostensibly substantiates the ongoing critique of Spinozism by seemingly affirming that substance is akin to the Eleatic One, a mere system of identity. Since everything is God, everything is really nothing. As it happens, in the *Ethics*, Spinoza allows that divisibility need not undercut infinity. This is also an issue addressed in the *Short Treatise* wherein he clarifies how it is that extension—which is putatively divisible and finite—is nevertheless an attribute of infinite substance. The presumed divisibility of extension does not undermine the perfection of God because "part and whole are not true or actual beings, but only beings of reason."[68] Although it might seem that extension is comprised of constituent parts, this is not the case. In and of itself, it is indivisible. Spinoza continues, "it is impossible that parts could be conceived in an infinite Nature, for all parts are, by their nature, finite."[69] To be *part* of something is necessarily to be finite, which is why "division never occurs in the substance, but always and only in the modes of the substance."[70] As such, "when we say that a human perishes, or is destroyed, that is only understood of the human insofar as they are a composite being and mode of substance, and not the substance itself on which they depend."[71] Finite beings exist and undergo change: they are born and they die, they grow and decay, they expand and contract. These variations in being are real and they are constitutive of finite existence. However, it is inapt to consider such changes as occurring in substance itself because the absolutely infinite *as* infinite, is indeterminate. Clearly, for Spinoza, modal existence is actual. Whatever the nature of the indivisibility of substance, such indivisibility does not pertain to modes.

Spinoza certainly describes substance as indivisible. It is his commitment to the infinity of substance that subsidizes this indivisibility. Yet significantly, this indivisibility does not amount to the indivisibility routinely associated with totality and identity. On the contrary, it is substance *as* substance that is indivisible as the alternative plainly undercuts infinity.

However, substance is not indivisible *as* its finite modes. Admittedly, as the previous chapters validate, substance is insubstantial which means that it is not independent of its acts. It is nothing *but* its finite modifications, its individual parts. Upholding substance as infinite activity rather than as a Being or Thing correlates with its resistance to divisibility, which cannot meaningfully obtain to activity, to action, to an act. As it happens, neither can indivisibility. These are both traits that pertain to beings and things rather than to indeterminate power that only exists as its enacted finite acts, which of course, are themselves divisible and determinate. Only some-things are divisible. Substance is not some-thing and certainly not Something. Infinite substance itself is not divisible, though substance, *as* its finite modes, is divisible. Therefore, it might be suggested that substance be conceived as the division into and as its modes. Substance is infinite power actualized—divided—as its finite modes. Everything is divisible, save the division itself.

Better Than Nothing

It is true that Spinoza disavows the vacuum and the void in both the literal and theoretical senses. There is no non-being, there is no nothingness. The *Ethics* commences with substance for being, that is becoming, is already. There is no originary Nothing from which all the somethings emerge. Such construals are transcendent and teleological. However, this does not mean that there is *only* or *already* Something.

The infinity of substance, as we have seen, amounts to its indeterminacy, which upholds substance as infinite power rather than as matter, object, form, or thing. This infinite power is only ever realized, never in reserve. This actualization of power *is* the acts that *are* its finite modes. Conceiving substance as the actualization of infinite power establishes not merely as previously evidenced that substance evades the suspicions of identity, immobility, and totality. It also sidesteps the binary logic of something and nothing. This is because indeterminate substance cannot be Something or some Thing. It is infinite power. Yet infinite power is certainly not nothing, either. Furthermore, because substance is infinite, it does not preexist the actualization of the power that it is, it does not *precede* its modes.[72] There can never have been Nothing. Infinite substance exists as its finite modes, which are its acts. Nevertheless, because substance is infinite—indeterminate—power, it is neither exhausted by its finite enactments nor reducible to them. There is a speck of conceptual asymmetry or disparity that pertains between indeterminate power and its determinate actualization.

If Hegel commences *Logic* with "Being, pure being—without any further determination,"[73] Spinoza insists that in fact, there is no such thing. There is never "pure" being. There is substance—infinite division—which is neither quite something because it is not coincident with its modes nor nothing because nothing comes from nothing. In rejecting the notion of a beginning, Spinoza is also further refusing the abiding opposition between being and nothingness. Instead, he posits a "being"—substance—that is "prior"[74] to its modes but is nothing substantial in and of itself. It is not Something. Yet, it is also not "Nothing" for it is its actualized power *as* division into its modes. Thus, substance retains its status as infinite without being a sovereign Nothing or Something. This strange status of substance—that it is neither *more* than nor *same with* its modes—is its principal asset. It repudiates the false choice between Something and Nothing, Positive and Negative, Being and Non-Being. Spinoza's disruption of sovereignties, I contend, requires that he sustain substance in this state of not nothingness and not somethingness.

To refuse both transcendence and teleology is to dispense not only with gods and origins but also with the ancient opposition between being and nothingness. Spinoza traverses beyond the coincidence of opposites and insists on the disequilibrium of non-parity. Admittedly, it does not make sense to construe substance in a manner that is not already its actualization as its modes. However, I am entertaining this in order to underscore that to follow Spinoza's reasoning requires that substance resist complete identification and coincidence with its modes and yet also demands that it not have an identity that is self-sufficient, over-and-above, or even before its modes. This, I suggest is a result of refusing sovereign logic.

The Idealist criticism of Spinoza identifies an absence in his philosophy: its conspicuous lack of nothingness and of generative negativity. As we have demonstrated and as the ensuing further substantiates, this grain persists in recent discourse, scaffolding the theoretical collisions between Spinozists like Deleuze and Lacanian-inspired thinkers including Badiou and Žižek. For all of them, Spinoza permits no space for the negative, for generative negativity. While for Deleuze this is an asset, for Badiou and Žižek, like Hegel, this is its primary deficit. However, I contend that these readings miss the true asset of substance. It is invested with an inherent tension; it is nothing but its actualized power, which manifests as modes, yet remains irreducible to them. This permits the suspension of the binary of being and nothingness.

Out of Place

It is elucidative to consider our construal of substance within a further conceptual orbit: Crescas's refutations of Aristotle's disavowal of an actual infinite and a vacuum. Contra Aristotle, Crescas argues for the existence of an infinite vacuum or void. As with our Cartesian concerns, considering Crescas's void discloses not so much the similarity between his thinking and Spinoza's but underscores their divergences. Specifically, it will be demonstrated that Spinoza's resistance to the trappings of sovereignty demands that he dispense with Crescas's notion of void. The benefit to our investigation is that Crescas's conception of the void epitomizes the ontotheological sovereignties associated with it. Scholars have emphasized the influence of Crescas's void on Spinoza's substance, contending that Spinoza takes Crescas a step farther than his own commitments permit. While this may be the case, I contend that Spinozism has no choice but to resist the heuristic that scaffolds it. Nevertheless, Crescas's embrace of actual infinity and stance that comparisons between the finite and the infinite cannot obtain, do seem to influence Spinoza.

Aristotle flatly rejects defining place as form, matter, or extension between things. Rather, "place is the boundary of the body which contains it."[75] Accordingly, "place is coincident with the thing, for boundaries are coincident with the bounded."[76] Place is here defined by its capacity to receive body. Without body, there is no place. This positions Aristotle to reject the void because void is "thought to be place with nothing in it," which is to say, no body and "where there is no body, there is nothing."[77] However, since place is that which contains body, and void is perceived as a place *without* body, it plainly follows that there can be no void, since there can be no place without body. Moreover, since void occupies place, when a body is placed into the void, it will occupy a place in it that is equal to itself, but this would then mean that two things occupy the exact same dimensional place, which is absurd.[78] By this same reasoning, because place entails the existence of body, it is impossible for there to be an infinite place because this would suppose an infinite body, which is untenable because divisibility into parts is constitutive of body. This is a further reason to disclose an infinite void and, accordingly, the prospect of infinite worlds.[79]

Crescas builds on the reservations concerning Aristotle's stance developed by al-Ghazali, Ibn Rushd, Gersonides, Joseph Albo, and others but goes much farther by proffering a comprehensive refutation. For Crescas, "the true place of a thing is the interval between the limits of that which surrounds it,"[80] which, contra Aristotle, means that place antecedes body. Place exists independently of body and yet is available to accommodate it, becoming its place. This definition positions Crescas to not only affirm the void but to do so by rendering it coincident with place: "ha-maqom ha-'ameti hu' ha-panui" (true place is the void) since "place must be equal to the whole of its occupant as well as to [the sum of] its parts."[81] Place is an immaterial infinite expanse—the void—which contains material body. The universe is a material body that exists in an infinite, immaterial three-dimensional void. With this, Crescas—like the late-antique Philoponus who also refuted Aristotle's foreclosure of the void—is credited with anticipating the seventeenth-century popularization of the cosmological void by such thinkers as Pierre Gassendi and John Locke. The poignancy of this peaks when Crescas invokes and ontologizes the rabbinic dictum of God as *meqomo shel olam* to liken God (literally, place) to the void: "For as the dimensions of the void permeate through those of the body and its fullness, so His glory blessed be He, is present in all the parts of the world and the fullness thereof."[82] This association rests on an identification that "the ancients" made between the place of a thing and its form: "for place like form determines and individuates the things, the whole as well as its parts."[83] Just as a void—here seen as the intervening space between things—exists and permits their form, their individuation; so too, Crescas argues, God, who is everywhere, enables the individuation of all determinate things. By conceiving void as place and place as Place, Crescas likens—*metaphorically*—God to void. The void determines and individuates, much as the Infinite determines and individuates the finite. The metaphoric link between God and void demonstrates why Spinozism insists on a substance that is neither Something nor Nothing. To conceive of the origin of all as emerging from a vacuum is no different—conceptually—from considering Creation as the genesis of all. Both the void and God are invested with transcendence, alterity, and eminence.

Scholars have investigated the influence of Crescas's notion of God as void as Place on Spinoza's substance. The consensus identifies Crescas as an initial step in the corrosion of God's incorporeality, which paves the path for Spinoza to insist on infinite extension—corporeality—as an attribute of substance.[84] While this is not an unreasonable proposition, for our purposes, it is revelatory to note the constraints of Crescas's position and the corrective that Spinoza presents. Even the metaphoric association of God with void falters on Spinozist logic, not merely because it is only metaphoric and not sufficiently literal, nor even since it retains a notion of God's incorporeality. But rather the void is an inapt analogy for substance because it retains sovereignties. In likening God to the void, Crescas is substantiating the argument that we have been advancing. Indeed, with this metaphor, Crescas actually identifies what others fail to discern in their conceptions of the void: that it is just a different name for God.

With this metaphor, Crescas adds his voice to a vibrant medieval debate concerned with the legacies of Aristotelian metaphysics and the problems that it poses for certain theological precepts. Aristotle's disavowal of a void and related claim to the eternity of the world posed a dilemma to theologians: either the world is eternal and therefore could not have been created by God, or God created the world out of a vacuum. Ibn Rushd, for example, follows Aristotle by upholding the eternity of the world and rejecting the void, while arguing that such eternity does not undercut God's status as First Cause. But for those committed to uncompromising approaches to creation ex nihilo, such eternity is not an option. Yet supposing that God created the world out of a void presents its own problems as this suggests that the void either preceded God or is coterminous with God, either of which seem to undermine Divine omnipresence.

Crescas is certainly not the only thinker to associate God with the void. Conceptually, this claim is reminiscent of the subsequent Lurianic construal wherein Ein Sof is seen as immanently generating the nothing in which and from which the world is then effectuated. This is how, for example, Herrera portrays the primordial *tsimtsum* of Ein Sof: "(speaking metaphorically. . . .) it contracted its enormous light, which filled all possible and imaginable places . . . in such a way that it left inside itself something like a space or vacuum ready and disposed to receive and contain its future effects."[85] With this, Herrera joins the vibrant discourse in Kabbalistic texts concerning the effectuation of the world. In his construal, the nothingness from which God is seen as having forged the world—what Genesis dubs *tohu va-vohu*, emptiness and indeterminateness—is incorporated into God. While the diverse texts within the Lurianic tradition proffer differential articulations of this dynamic, what underpins this overall interpretive stance are concerns regarding God's omnipresence and omnipotence. By conceiving Ein Sof as contracting in order to create space for the world, including the effectuation of the nothingness from which all else is contrived, this approach resolves certain perplexities that pertain to creation ex nihilo. Here, God contracts, producing space for the Nothing from which everything is then effectuated.

This implicitly addresses the puzzles of creating all the somethings from Nothing without undermining the status of God as being everywhere or allowing for the existence of something that preexists or is coterminous with God yet is not God. It rejects Aristotle's eternity of the world, without allowing for the creation of something from nothing.

By embracing the void, advocating for actual infinities, and accepting the prospect of multiple worlds, Crescas steadily corrodes medieval Jewish philosophy's attachment to Aristotelian physical and metaphysical tenets. That Crescas does so in the century following the condemnations of 1277, which denounced Aristotelian and Averroian theses as heretical to Christianity and inaugurated the so-called new physics, has not been lost on scholars. While the extent to which Crescas's philosophy is influenced by Scholasticism is debated, it has been noted that his metaphorical likening of the void to God is similar to a theory proffered by Thomas Bradwardine in the first half of the fourteenth century. Keen to advocate for the void, yet hesitant to undercut Divine omnipresence and omnipotence, Bradwardine speculated that God is everywhere, in the world and in the void beyond it. Although there can be a void without a body, he reasoned, there can be no void without God. As such, if there is an infinite void, it is nondimensional and God is in it. Moreover, if no void exists, this also would undercut God's power; it would mean that God could not create a void. Therefore, an infinite void exists, beyond the world, devoid of everything *but* God.

These speculations about God in the fourteenth and fifteenth centuries—precipitated by condemnations of Aristotelian physics and metaphysics—pushed thinkers to both imagine and even uphold the validity of the void. This background, it has been demonstrated, laid the path for the centuries of science that followed: "Scholastic ideas about space and God form an integral part of the history of spatial conceptions between the late sixteenth and eighteenth centuries. . . . Except for extension, the divinization of space in scholastic thought produced virtually all the properties that would be conferred on space during the course of the Scientific Revolution."[86] These very properties, I argue, remain with us. Although modern thought ultimately jettisoned the explicit identification of God with the void, the current discourse on the void and the Nothing remain suffused with ontotheological sovereignties.

Nothing

It is true that to conceptualize nothingness—to embrace the negative—is to think not merely about origins but to contemplate the productive nature of the lack. The dominant criticism of Spinozism is that it disallows for such negativity. However, although Spinoza refuses to conceive of a primordial nothingness—"whatever is, is either in itself or another"[87]—and refutes the existence of absolute nothingness, this is not to foreclose a theoretical role for the negative. Consider Spinoza's trenchant argument for the immanence of substance. The infinity of substance requires that it is immanent—corporeal—for otherwise this would mean that there is something—the attribute of extension—that is outside of, or beyond, it. This is impossible as it contravenes the necessity of its existence. I suggest that we apply this same reasoning to the notion of nothingness. To argue that nothingness is precluded from substance commits the same misstep. Nothing is outside of substance, including nothing and the negative. If the negative and the lack exist, then they must be *of* substance, for "whatever is, is in God."[88] If there is a void, it is not like the void that is external to the indivisible atoms that move about it nor the void that is God and thus Beyond. Rather, akin to the Marxist construal of the clinamen, the negative—if it exists—must inhere immanently in substance.

It is also worth noting that in considering the negative, or anything, naturally we encounter the perplexity of its definition. Any conception of the negative or negativity that we might proffer remains, irrevocably, as of the human perspective. It is prudent to recall Spinoza's polemic against anthropocentric interpretations of reality, which considers all human judgments as insuperably anthropocentric. Thus, even if Spinozism is in a position to admit the negative—the very notion of negativity and certainly its valuation—remains nothing but a human take. Nothingness is anthropic.

On a Hiding to Nothing

A more recent embrace of nothingness has emerged in streams of Object-Oriented Ontology (OOO). To Morton, "modern philosophy has been preoccupied with where to put the nothingness that seems to ooze out everywhere."[89] While they have rightly pinpointed certain ontotheological commitments that sponsor this treatment of nothingness, Morton's own approach problematically reproduces the very ontotheological sovereignties that I have been critiquing. Rather than upholding the Kantian nothing—the gap—between the mind and reality or reducing what is to Hegelian nothingness, Morton embraces the "*meontic* nothing" that pervades everything,[90] by which is meant: "*Nothingness*, rather than absolutely nothing.... Because a thing withdraws, it disturbs us with an excess over what we can know or say about it—this excess is a nothingness, not absolutely nothing, but not something to which one can point."[91] With this, they effectively democratize and universalize nothingness. Morton's ontology commendably discards a "top object"—a God—"that gives meaning and reality to others," and similarly dispels any "bottom object" like a "fundamental particle or ether from which everything else is derived," and likewise dismisses any "middle object," an "ether or medium ... in which objects float."[92] They nevertheless repurpose the sovereign features historically accorded to God, the atom, or the void. Dispersing the nothingness and even allowing that it is not exclusively correlated with the human standpoint does not fully evacuate its ontotheological features. On the contrary, imbuing all things with just a bit of nothingness only reinforces its status as constitutive of reality, as Sovereign. Moreover, by investing every single thing with a smidgen of nothing and rendering this nothingness exclusively irreducible or most real, Morton seems to embrace the kind of transcendence, essentialism, and uniqueness subtending the ontotheology they purportedly undertake to overcome.

Objects, for Morton—following Graham Harman's appropriation of Heidegger[93]—are "withdrawn" by which they mean "beyond any kind of access, any kind of perception or map or plot or test or extrapolation."[94] I agree that objects evade our full grasps of them and likewise that they are not *given* to human perception or accessible to us in their totality. In fact, I maintain that Spinoza's conception of modes and their particularity means that no mode, or in Morton's terminology, object, is entirely reducible or totalizable nor consistent with itself. Yet I hesitate with the terminology and implications of the OOO notion of withdrawal: "An object never exhausts itself in its appearances—this means that there is always something left over, as it were, an excess that might be experienced as a distortion, gap, or void."[95] This happens "because of the Rift; the being of things is hollowed out from within. It is this Rift that fuels their birth,"[96] and "this Rift provides the impetus for movement and continuity."[97] The capitalization here corroborates my suspicions: despite their notable attempts to dispense with the ontotheological rationales that sponsor correlationism, reductionism, and holism, Morton retains their traces. There is an excess that evades us, is *beyond*, and is responsible for what is. Indeed, the Rift between essence and appearance is constitutive; it alone seems most Real. Moreover, its elusiveness is such that "we can't specify 'where' or 'when' the Rift 'is.' The Rift means that we are confronted with an illusion-like reality"[98] such that "aesthetic experience is real and tangible yet unspeakable."[99] Like the traditional conception of God, who is the Origin of all, the Rift is responsible for what is and likewise transcends our attempts to locate it, let alone to speak of it.

The aesthetic, as introduced by Harman, is central to OOO and its conception of causality.[100] "The problem," Morton says, "with many theories of causality is that they edit out a quintessential element of mystery."[101] These "are preoccupied with explaining things away, with demystification."[102] By contrast, OOO argues that "if things are intrinsically withdrawn, irreducible to their perception or relations or uses, they can only affect each other in a strange region out in front of them, a region of traces and footprints: the aesthetic dimension."[103] Because "objects are withdrawn from one another," the way to make sense of causality is by admitting "some vicarious way in which they affect one another."[104] What happens in reality happens because of objects which "are not just themselves—they are uncanny: they are both themselves and not themselves."[105] That is, "*objects themselves just are inconsistent.*"[106] This is due to the Rift because "the existence of an entity is the existence of a Rift within identity."[107] "The Rift is irreducibly part of a thing: a thing is both itself and not-itself."[108] For Morton, this reflects the "fragility" of a thing, "why a thing can exist at all."[109] Consequently, the cessation of this Rift causes an object to cease to be for "to kill or destroy is *to reduce something to consistency.*"[110]

Morton is committed to setting us straight, to unveiling the "magic, illusion, and display"[111] that constantly surround us. Things, they insist, are not as they seem: "Reality is a trickster and objects behave like playful children."[112] It is apposite, if surprising, that to support their supposition that reality is laden with illusion, Morton turns to Maimonides: "Moses Maimonides argues that the literal level is the superficial one. The figurative level is like a golden apple contained in a superfine filigree of silver. From a distance it looks as if we are seeing a silver apple. What we are really seeing is a fine mesh that only appears to be solid. This is the mesh that lies in front of objects."[113] Morton continues: "The interconnectedness of things is a finely woven tissue that floats in front of . . . all entities."[114] Yet "real objects are the strange strangers," they are "irreducibly uncanny."[115] Reality is this way because "when you only have the meshwork, the mask, without the possibility that there's something real underneath it, then you have no play, no pretense, no illusion, no display, no magic. You *know* it's an illusion—so it isn't an illusion."[116] This is the problem, Morton tells us, with performance and conceptual art, "which ignores the Rift between essence and appearance, reducing the ontological to the merely ontic."[117] Consequently, "an overall atmosphere of jaded cynicism hangs over it."[118] Fortunately, reality does not fall prey to this because "objects don't have to deceive other objects totally."[119] This is because there is something withdrawn, something "real," the Rift, which secures the magic in reality. In fact, "the realness of things is in direct proportion to their weird pretense, the way in which things wear perfect replicas of themselves, so that everything is a masquerade, yet absolutely, stunningly real."[120]

As a consequence of this illusionary play, "whenever we look for essence, we won't find it—because it exists."[121] This corroborates that "an object is not an illusion. But it is not a non-illusion."[122] Thus, "an object is utterly real, *essentially* itself, whose very reality is formally ungraspable. No hidden trapdoors, just a mask with some feathers whose mystery is out in front of itself, in your face. A miracle. Realist magic."[123] The mystery, the illusion, the non-cynicism in reality means that objects are not actively hiding the fact that they are ungraspable, but they seem to flaunt it like a mask with feathers. To Morton, this open declaration preserves all of the magic. Furthermore, such "illusion-like play" is due to "the fundamental Rift between withdrawn essence and aesthetic appearance, a 'place' of profound ambiguity in the being of the thing."[124]

Let us return to Morton's citation of Maimonides. Their representation does not exactly correlate with what Maimonides intends with his allegory of the apple. The remark concerning the golden apple filigreed in silver is a reference to a verse in Proverbs,[125] which actually seems to suggest that a word spoken clearly and precisely is as pleasing as the finest metals, perhaps even as exclusive. But Maimonides construes this verse allegorically in order to support an organizing thesis of the *Guide*, that certain verses in Scripture carry both an internal and an external meaning. This is the case with what Maimonides classifies as a parable, which is intentionally constructed such that "when looked at from a distance or with imperfect attention, it is deemed to be an apple of silver; but when a keen-sighted observer looks at it with full attention, its interior becomes clear . . . he knows that it is gold."[126] The silver filigree—the external meaning—"contains wisdom that is useful in many respects, among which is the welfare of human societies. . . . Their internal meaning, on the other hand, contains wisdom that is useful for beliefs concerned with the truth as it is."[127] Crucially, for Maimonides, this truth is not completely inaccessible, but rather only to most readers. But the philosophically inclined, like Maimonides, as much of his *Guide* undertakes to substantiate, do have access to these veiled truths. Arguably, Maimonides himself employs several of these techniques throughout the *Guide*. Truths in texts are not completely elusive; they are not like the essence of Morton's objects that evade us. Moreover, for Maimonides, the external meaning of the text is not a ruse but purposefully serves a pragmatic function. These particulars seem beside the point to Morton. Yet there is something quite apt about their misguided invocation of Maimonides to support their thesis about the illusionary nature of objects. Maimonides interprets this verse from Proverbs in order to substantiate his exegetical project to harmonize Scripture with philosophy, in order to resolve certain religious perplexities and legitimate religion. As it happens, Morton, likely unknowingly, relies on several of the ontotheological sovereignties that structure the Maimonidean project, including the apophatic,[128] for Maimonides in terms of God, whereas for Morton as concerns the essence of objects; the transcendent, for Maimonides, God, for Morton, the essence of objects; and the One responsible for all that is, which for Maimonides is God, but for Morton, the nothingness that is the Rift.

It is hard for me to overcome my Spinozist aversion to anthropocentrism and anthropomorphism. I cannot help but sense that Morton's escapade into the "stunningly real" and the Rift presumes, counterintuitively, that how things are in reality comports with our aesthetic categories and even our, or at least some of our, preferences. This is similarly the case with their reliance on the mysterious and the magical. Why the need to lean on these devices to argue that matters are not always as they seem, that reality is complex, and that not everything is given towards our epistemic grasp? These are basic observations, indispensable to any speculations on the nature of reality. But the withdrawal and the "weirdness"[129] are not mere rhetorical devices nor allegorical tools for OOO; they are constitutive of reality. For OOO what makes reality what it is, what allows objects to be, to change, and to cease being is that which is not: the gap between essence and appearance, the Rift, the nothingness. This sovereignty is why the real is beyond apprehension and access, and also what makes OOO fundamentally an ontology of the apophatic: that which most *is* transcends approach, is present only in its absence. Such emptiness is not merely epistemic but ontological because objects are fundamentally isolated. Despite Morton's objections to the contrary,[130] this seems quite similar to forms of atomism:[131] "If all objects are unique and enclosed from access, they can never truly be said to touch one another!"[132] There is an insurmountable distance between objects, which are enclosed by unsurpassable, sovereign boundaries, which parries with the supposition that "objects are the ontologically primary entities."[133] With the sovereignty of the object comes the sovereignty of its borders, and the sovereignty of its inaccessibility, and ineffable transcendence. Rather than the clinamen being responsible for change in the void, "in an OOO reality, emergence must be a property of objects, not the other way around."[134] All that happens is due to the nothingness of the Rift within an object and the nothingness that is the gap between objects and the nothingness that exceeds our grasps of objects. The varieties of nothingness, absence, and excess that configure reality in OOO are classic theological sovereignties freshly renovated, dispersed, and universalized.

In the Event of... Nothing

The scholarship continues to ventilate Spinoza's disavowal of the void. Probing Badiou's engagement with this complex, his apprehensions about Spinozism, and the role occupied by the void in his own thought proves revelatory.[135] Not only does it exemplify the conceptual assets of the void, it also positions us to unpack its downsides, specifically the logics and mechanisms of sovereignty that undergird it and suture Badiou's overall philosophy.

Badiou commences his treatment of Spinoza in *Being and Event* by pronouncing his philosophy as "the philosophy *par excellence* which *forecloses the void.*"[136] Yet Badiou proceeds to identify a potential locus for the void in Spinozism, which he discerns in the ostensible gap between the infinite and the finite. To Badiou, "if substance is infinite, and modes are finite, the void is ineluctable, like the stigmata of a split in presentation between substantial being-qua-being and its finite immanent production."[137] By taking substance as a priori and modes as a posteriori—in seeing substance as Substantial and Present—Badiou cannot but perceive a lacuna. Unlike Hegel, for whom this damns Spinozism, for Badiou, the excess of the infinite over the finite is a boon, furnishing space for the void. However, after proposing as much, Badiou precipitately repudiates it. To his credit, this is due to a comparatively more accurate grasp of the liaison between substance and modes. Insomuch as substance produces nothing outside of its modes, he concludes, there is no excess or emptiness in which to welcome the void.[138]

This disclosure of the void is resonant with the Hegelian indictment: substance is positive, complete, and whole; it sanctions no space for that which is not *yet*, for that which is *not*. Badiou lauds Spinoza, who "represents the most radical attempt ever in ontology to identify structure and metastructure, to assign the one-effect directly to the state, and to in-distinguish belonging and inclusion."[139] Yet because everything is *of* substance, this means that presentation and representation coincide: "Everything that belongs is included and everything that is included belongs.... everything presented is represented and reciprocally, *because presentation and representation are the same thing*."[140] Such coincidence eradicates the void.[141]

It is instructive to contextualize Badiou's regard for the void—"the proper name of being"[142]—within his overall philosophy. Being, for Badiou, is pure multiplicity, inconsistent and infinite. Contra ontologies of presence, he undertakes to resist totalization by refusing the count-for-one, declaring: "the one *is not*."[143] However, Badiou is disinclined to completely jettison the One. In deference to the Lacanian inference "il y a de l'un"—there is something of the one—he identifies the effects of oneness in the presentation of multiplicities, which manifest in "situations."

For Badiou, situations are of multiplicities. Yet, akin to the sets of set theory, their structure "prescribes, for a presented multiple, the regime of its count-as-one."[144] Effectively, "the situation envelops existence with the one."[145] It takes inconsistency and renders it consistent: "Nothing is presentable in a situation otherwise than under the effect of structure, that is, under the form of the one and its composition in consistent multiplicities."[146] Nothing comes before presentation—before the count—but for something to be presented—to count as one—presupposes that something is not presented, that something is not countable as one. What is included relies on that which is excluded. Moreover, that which is excluded cannot be something because then it is presentable, countable, and included. Consequently, "what is at stake is an unpresentable yet necessary figure which designates the gap between the result-one of presentation and that 'on the basis of which' there is presentation; that is the non-term of any totality."[147] Badiou regards this as the "unpresentable of presentation," which is subtracted from being: "the void." It is "the nothing from which everything proceeds."[148] This is akin to the null-set—$\emptyset$—in set theory, which itself is without elements, though all sets rest upon it. The void is both that which evades presentation and the foundation of all presentation. It is "nothing other than the unpresentable as such."[149] While "every situation implies the nothing of its all ... the nothing is neither a place nor a term of the situation."[150] If any specifics were attached to the void, it would no longer be the unpresentable inconsistent multiple. In fact, precisely because the void is the name for nothing, nothing can actually be attached to it. As such, being qua being—as void—is neither actually one nor multiple: "This way ontology states that presentation is certainly multiple, but that the being of presentation, the that which is presented, being void, is subtracted from the one/multiple dialectic."[151] The void belongs but is not included. This is crucial, Badiou reflects, because "our entire edifice is based on the distinction between belonging and inclusion."[152]

The elusive status of the void is constitutive of Badiou's philosophy and positions his conception of the event, which is precluded from mathematics: "With the event we have the first concept *external* to the field of mathematical ontology."[153] Such ontology excludes the event because every element of a set is also a subset as "belonging implies inclusion."[154] However, the event—historicity—"is founded on singularity, on the 'on-the-edge-of-the-void,' on what belongs without being included."[155] This renders the event extraordinary and *beyond* ontology—foreclosed by the axiom of foundation—as it counts for itself and belongs to its own set. It founds itself. Hence, the event is historical as opposed to natural: "What is natural is stable or normal; what is historical contains some multiples on-the-edge-of-the-void."[156] The void—its edge—stands for the excess of parts over elements and precipitates the event, positioning its novelty, unexpectedness, and singularity.

Badiou revisits his critique of Spinoza in an essay, the title of which—"Spinoza's Closed Ontology"—broadcasts, without subtlety, its program. At the outset, Badiou explains that all philosophies of being commence with claims of "there is." These take one of two forms: the "evental model" and the "axiomatic model." To depict the former, Badiou leans on Lucretius for whom "there is" is expressed through "an unassignable event: the *clinamen*, or swerve, through which the indifferent trajectories of the atoms enter into relations against the backdrop of the void, in such a way as to compose a world."[157]

By contrast, in mathematics, the "there is" is situated in the empty set, the void. And "the only relation is that of belonging," which is guaranteed by the axioms of the theory and "engenders a universe, the cumulative, transfinite hierarchy of sets."[158] Immediately after introducing these contrasting models of being, Badiou hastens to announce: "Spinoza, who excludes every event by precluding excess, chance and the subject, opts unequivocally for the axiomatic model."[159] In Spinoza, the "'there is' is indexed to a single name:

absolutely infinite Substance, or God. The only relation admitted is that of causality."[160] Taking substance as the axiomatic "there is" leads Badiou to conclude: "We are confronted here with a wholly affirmative, immanent and intrinsic proposition about being... it would seem that difference in particular, which is constitutive of the ontology of Lucretius (there is the void *and* atoms), is here absolutely subordinated."[161] Although Badiou goes on to problematize some of these assertions, ultimately identifying a space for difference, inclusion, heterogeneity, and singularity in Spinoza's philosophy, he nevertheless reaffirms "the circular closure of Spinozist ontology."[162]

Echoing the arguments marshaled in *Being and Event*, Badiou revisits the liaison of the infinite and finite but here focuses on Spinoza's infinite intellect, regarding it as "the gathering together, the collection, of finite intellects."[163] The problem is that the finite is *included* in the infinite, the infinite *comprised* of the finite. Therefore, "the infinite intellect can be designated as the *limit point* of the finitudes it totalizes. Conversely, the finite intellect constitutes a point of composition for its infinite sum."[164] Therefore, "causality is merely an apparent order since it is incapable of leading us out of the finite."[165] The infinite is closed and completed, a mere collection of the finite. Like axiomatic mathematics, which admits belonging and not inclusion, Spinozist infinity secures no space for excess. Consequently, Badiou maintains, the only form of intellection that Spinoza allows is that of common notions: "The only points of truth are axiomatic and general"; a subject can only think "the mathematics of being."[166] Thinking is compassed, given, and posited. Badiou connects this with Spinoza's *more geometrico*, maintaining that for Spinoza, "God has to be understood as mathematicity itself. The name of the 'there is' is the matheme."[167] Limited to the mathematical, Spinozism is without "exception to, or supplement for, the 'there is.'"[168] And "it is precisely at this juncture that we need to introduce what, in the wake of others, I have called 'the event.'"[169] Spinoza's philosophy suffers from the closure of its ontology. It vouchsafes no space for the exceptional, for the *exception*.

Spinozism is doomed. Badiou, like Hegel, critiques Spinoza's conception of the infinite and its purported foreclosure of the negative. If for Hegel the infinity of substance undermines the reality of the finite, for Badiou, the inclusion of the finite intellect within the infinite intellect renders thinking compassed. For Hegel and Badiou, the posited nature of substance means that movement is only ever mere return. Like the Hegelian claim that substance amounts to mere identity—being without becoming—Badiou alleges that substance is already given, without a supplement to the "there is." To reprise, once more, as the previous chapters evince, substance is decidedly *not* already given, let alone closed. Indeed, its infinity renders it not All: unregulated, open, and not yet.

Something of the One

This is not the place to conduct a comprehensive appraisal of Badiou's project. Yet an attempt at basic reciprocity is reasonably appropriate: Badiou's ontology will be assessed in light of the concerns most central to Spinoza's, determining how Badiou's philosophy responds to the pressures of Spinozism. This exercise is decidedly partial and abbreviated, as I reckon only with the aspects of Badiou's ontology most germane to the interests of this chapter. The foregoing discloses that the ostensible puzzle in Spinozism—which Badiou, Hegel, and others criticize—is engendered by an anti-sovereign spirit that actually inoculates it from precisely the problems that bedevil the alternatives that they advance. Despite his commitments to the contrary, Badiou reinstalls a series of ontotheological sovereignties that Spinoza dismantles. Exposing as much illuminates the advantages of the Spinozist approach to the something and the nothing.

There are points of contact between Spinoza's ontology and that of Badiou. While Badiou misrecognizes as much, his own philosophy is partially aligned with our reading of Spinoza's repudiation of Oneness. Spinoza, as the previous chapter evinces, dispenses with Oneness and the wholeness, completion, and totalization attendant to it. Oneness is neither the Origin of all nor its telos, not simply because reality is without origin and end but also because there is no One and there are no Ones. However, compared to Badiou, Spinoza more rigorously disallows for oneness. Although Badiou's insistence that "the one is not" structures his project, he affirms that something of the one remains. In fact, I contend that this something of oneness is more than what Badiou has in mind—its mere effects in presentation—and instead reflects the traits of oneness that his ontology reconfirms. At this junction, Badiou's ontology appears to subvert its own stimulus. If the function of his subtraction is to admit novelty without reverting to the totality of univocity—to the ontotheology of Oneness—his attempt to circumvent such metaphysics, while promising, fails when the nature of the void and that which teeters on its edge, the event, are critically anatomized.

The event and the void embody the sovereignties classically associated with God. This is striking insomuch as Badiou's project strives to cope with the death of God and metaphysics in the wake of Nietzsche and Heidegger. The Badiouian enterprise of dispensing with the One and embracing the multiple is a response to this erasure of the One. Badiou reflects on his inspiration: "Lucretius clearly sees that to subtract oneself from the fear of the gods requires that beneath the multiple, there be nothing. And that beyond the multiple, there be only the multiple once again."[170] However, despite his pledge to repudiate ontotheological oneness, Badiou—much like we have seen with OOO—embraces its archetypal accouterments.

Consider the void: it belongs to itself. This nothing—the empty set—though itself comprised of nothing, is that which founds all other sets. Like God, the void is self-founding and also the foundation of all that exists. Further, Badiou slips into apophaticism by asserting that this nothing is without place or descriptors. The event commands silence, proscribing representation: "The *negative* aspect of the definition of evental sites—to not be represented—prohibits us from speaking of a situation 'in-itself.'"[171] Furthermore, the event is constituted by transcendence: "Even though it can always be *localized* within presentation, it is not as such, presented, nor is it presentable. It is—not being—supernumerary."[172] The event is also both ubiquitous yet inaccessible: "neither local nor global, but scattered all over, nowhere and everywhere: it is such that no encounter would authorize it to be held as presentable."[173] This omnipresence confirms its transcendence and supreme oneness: "The event results from an excess-of-one, an ultra one."[174] The definitive feature of the event, its defiance of being-qua-being, the ontological, validates its alterity. Crucially, this also means that the evental "is the abnormal, the instable, the antinatural."[175] It is an exception; it is exceptional. Aptly, Badiou, in discussing Pascal, remarks: "The miracle—like Mallarme's chance—is the emblem of the pure event as a resource of truth."[176] Accordingly, the event itself cannot be "proved" for its existence evades objective substantiation. Its actuality is attested to solely by its adherents, much like belief in God. Like the miracle—the exception—Badiou's event installs a hierarchy between itself and all that is not it, between the finite, which is countable as one, and that which is not. This binary is conspicuously announced by his choice in title: *Being and Event*. There is being *and* that which exceeds it, event. Badiou has taken pains to defend the event against its transparently miraculous,[177] theological features, yet his insistence belies the plainest interpretation of his project.[178]

The foregoing dissection of the vulnerabilities of Badiou's thinking is not an exercise for its own sake. Rather, our interest is to return to Spinozism and study how it sidesteps these ontotheological sovereignties and, crucially, to unpack how it realizes as much by means of the precise dynamic that Badiou and others disparage. The function of the void and its edge—the event—in Badiou's project is to admit novelty in an otherwise deterministic structure. It seeks to overcome Althusser's structural causality by rethinking the notion of the absent cause such that instead of returning to the same, it irrupts into the new. The problem is that the nothingness of the void functions as the foundation of all else. Instead of Something (say, God), Badiou conceives of the Nothing as the First Cause, End, and Purpose. It is thus less than astonishing that the void and the event arrogate so many attributes traditionally granted to God. By embracing the binary reasoning of something and nothing it becomes impossible for Badiou to escape the entrapments of ontotheological reasoning and its sovereignties. Spinoza, by contrast, refuses this binary and the sovereignties associated therewith. Badiou is not the only contemporary thinker who falters on this score. Before arraying our argument about how Spinoza avoids these pitfalls, let us scrutinize Žižek's appraisal of Spinozism by underscoring its similar lapses.[179]

No Less Than Nothing

Considering his primary influences—Hegel and Lacan—Žižek's intoxication with the lack is expected. His celebration of the lack is conspicuous in his polemics against Deleuze's univocity, affirmationism, and Spinozism. Expectedly, Žižek enlists the Hegelian chorus of critics against Spinoza to decry his denegation of the negative. Fundamentally, his evaluation of Spinoza's philosophy echoes Badiou's verdict.

In his earlier *Organs Without Bodies: On Deleuze and Consequences*, Žižek stridently denounces Spinozism, portraying its signal gesture as "the thorough rejection of negativity,"[180] declaring it "a purely positive network of causes and effects in which, by definition, an absence cannot play any positive role."[181] In his more recent *Less Than Nothing: Hegel and the Shadow of Dialectical Materialism*, Žižek tempers his denunciation and flirts with a relatively less damnatory take. Indebted to Althusser, he concedes: "Substance is not simply the generative process which continues without interruption or cut, but . . . on the contrary, the universalization of a cut or fall (*clinamen*)."[182] However, "if all that there is are interruptions or falls, then the key aspect of surprise, of the intrusion of an unexpected contingency, is lost, and we find ourselves in a boring, flat universe whose contingency is totally predictable and necessary."[183] While Žižek's counterintuitive move to render the contingent *necessary* is commendable, the rationale for rejecting this Althusserian clinamen is unconvincing, at least on Spinozist grounds. Is there anything more anthropocentric than expecting reality to bow to the human perspective, let alone its appetite to be tantalized? That such a world would be "boring" seems not merely presumptuous but an unpersuasive reason for refusing it. This allies with Morton's enthusiasm for a reality suffused with mystery and illusion, rather than the supposed staleness of a world in which objects are what they are, without pretense.

In tarrying with Spinoza, Žižek resurrects the Hegel or Spinoza opposition: "Spinoza, for whom there is no Master-Signifier enacting a cut, marking a conclusion, 'dotting the i,' but just a continuous chain of causes, the Hegelian dialectical process involves cuts, sudden interruptions of the continuous flow, reversals which retroactively restructure the entire field."[184] With this, Žižek reprises the perennial misappraisal that because Spinozism only admits the positive, everything is already given and there is no space for rupture.

To Žižek, "it is precisely apropos the topic of the *clinamen* that the gap separating Hegel from Spinoza can be formulated."[185] Accordingly, "Spinozan Substance can be conceived as the productive force which generates the multiplicity of *clinamina*, and which is as such a virtual entity totally immanent to its products, present and actual only in its products."[186] Thereby, "Substance remains One, a Cause immanent to its effects,"[187] whereas for Hegel, "the actually existing plurality of *clinamina* presupposes a more radical '*clinamen*'—reversal or negativity—in the Substance itself (which is why Substance has to be conceived also as subject)."[188] Hegel presents a substance that admits negativity within, prompting Žižek to suggest "there is no Substance, only the Real as the absolute gap, non-identity, and particular phenomena (modes) are Ones, so many attempts to stabilize the gap."[189]

What Žižek claims is absent in Spinozism is actually what has been highlighted as constitutional to it throughout this book. Substance does not remain One but its absolute infinity renders it not One, much as infinity disallows for the completion and closure of substance, mitigating suspicions of identity, rendering it not All. Moreover, while substance is the cause of its effects, as the first chapter unfurls, immanent causation for Spinoza dismantles the hierarchical binary adhering between causes and effects. Insomuch as infinite, indeterminate substance is nothing but its finite, determinate acts, this means that substance does not preexist its acts nor serve as some container for them. It only is power actualized, never in reserve.

This sortie into Žižek terrain solicits an interrogation of the alternative that he advocates and an evaluation of it through Spinozist lenses. If Badiou constructs a philosophy on the void, Žižek goes farther still. For him, Nothing is not enough. Only "less than nothing" will do. In deference to the *den* of Democritus, Žižek—sent this way by Lacan—refuses to see the origin of all either in Something or in Nothing. *More* is needed. The reason for this move is sensible and partly in concert with our construal of the Spinozist impulse. The trouble, though, is that he ultimately loses step with his own logic, resorting to ontotheological sovereignties. In an attempt to circumvent the coincidence of opposites and uphold the Lacanian non-relationship, Žižek advances his alternative, a "minimal repetition," whereby "we pass from something that one can only designate as 'less than nothing' to Nothing."[190] Before there is Nothing and its opposite Something, there is originally less than nothing. The two need their supplemental third. Actualizing the Hegelian inclination, Žižek maintains that "for Something to emerge, the pre-ontological Nothing has to be negated, i.e., it has to be posited as a direct/explicit emptiness, and it is only within this emptiness that Something can emerge, that there can be 'Something instead of Nothing.'"[191] Accordingly, "the first act of creation is thus the emptying of the space, the creation of Nothing."[192] This means that "*den* is the result of a double negation, the negation of 1 which results in zero plus the subtraction from zero which results in *den*."[193] Žižek extends this logic and applies it to the atom, which is to be conceived as "*less* than nothing" because "*something has to be added to the atom not to make it One but to make it Nothing.*"[194]

Žižek is wedded to the opposition of Nothing and Something. The entire picture that he sketches centers on upholding and then renegotiating their antipodal interplay. But since nothing is really nothing, the original nothing is not quite nothing. It is not enough, hence the need for *another* nothing. Rather than transcending the binary logic of Nothing and Something or Something and Nothing, Žižek merely supplements it. Adding a third element that *precedes* the binary bolsters it, in lieu of toppling it. Trinitarian logic—as ever—is not the solution. It amplifies the force of the binary, merely delaying the opposition. Moreover, positing a pre-ontological less than nothing, which is disturbed, thereby begetting nothing and something, is teleological. Beginning at a pre-beginning is no less a Beginning.

Echoing Badiou's conception of the Lacanian Real, Žižek insists on the exclusion of the Real: "The order of Being and the Real are mutually exclusive: the Real is the immanent blockage or impediment of the order of Being, what makes the order of Being inconsistent."[195] Such attachment to transcendence and alterity correlates with this description: "We touch the Real-in-itself in our very failure to touch it, since the Real *is*, at its most radical, the gap, the 'minimal difference,' that separates the One from itself."[196] Žižek's notion of "the Real" seems nothing but a new moniker for God who is radically Other, and we know that God *is* precisely because God is *other*. A similar transposition is discernible when Žižek extrapolates Lacan's notion of the *object a*: "While *den* is 'less than nothing,' the *object a* is 'more than one, but less than two,' as a spectral supplement that haunts the One, preventing its ontological closure."[197] It is not at all clear why Žižek needs "a spectral supplement" in order to prevent "ontological closure." To wit, Spinoza's infinite substance is open—not All—without reverting to a reality haunted by the specters of an Other. Žižek's specters repurpose the alterity, transcendence, and omnipresence of traditional spirits of both demonic and benevolent strains.

Admittedly, Žižek is justified in asserting that "the starting point, is not zero but less than zero, a pure minus without a positive term with regard to which it would function as a lack/excess."[198] It is appropriate to construe an initial point as that which evades the binary of the positive and the negative, an origin bereft of an opposition through which it would be defined and comparatively affirmed or disaffirmed as more or less. However, in Žižek's montage, this opposition is not erased but deferred since the void is diffracted into two different voids: "The vacuum itself is always split between the 'false' and the 'true' vacuum, a split which originally or constitutively disturbs it."[199] Anticipating dismissal of this picture as gratuitously unitary, Žižek insists that "there is no unity preceding the split."[200] It is not that the One precedes the diffraction but that it constitutes it. Similarly, he insists that "the two vacuums are also not symmetrical: we are not dealing with a polarity, but with the displaced One, a One which is, as it were, retarded with regard to itself, always already 'fallen,' its symmetry always already broken."[201] While these moves to undermine Oneness and symmetrical parity are laudable, they do not go far enough to eradicate ontotheological sovereignties. Žižek retains an original point and process of creation, merely camouflaging them with convoluted mechanisms of displacement, disarray, and delay. Moreover, at the core of his theory stands the hierarchical binary of the negative and positive, the "false" and "true" vacuums, the positive-negative and the truly negative-negative.

Žižek would do well to mind his own remark: "For a true dialectician, the ultimate mystery is not 'Why is there something rather than nothing?' but 'Why is there nothing rather than something?': how is it that, the more we analyze reality, the more we find the void?"[202] Žižek not only inverts this classic question but also its answer. In place of the transcendent God of metaphysics, invested with absolute Being—Something rather than nothing—Žižek delivers its inversion: Nothingness. Rather than overcoming the choice between being and nothingness—between the positive and the negative—he reaffirms it, taking the contrarian side of the void. Even if this void is then doubled into a true and false void and even if it is never at peace with itself, it is still a void. In fact, it is even *more* of a void, because it allows for the false void as the starting point and only then generates its true double. Displacing primordial peace with primordial chaos merely instantiates the false choice between something and nothing.

The reliance on the rationales and instruments of sovereignty is hardly accidental. Despite appearances, Žižek remains loyal to a particular tradition of Christian ontotheology. There is no "pre-Fall non-All proto-reality wherein multiple virtualities happily coexist in their superpositions, and this plural paradise is then ruined by the Fall into a single reality."[203] Instead, "the proto-reality is in itself barred, thwarted, so that the Fall has always already taken place."[204] Even if Žižek refuses the concept of an original Fall—positing instead a primordial state of Fallenness—he remains beholden to the hierarchical sovereign logics of positive and negative. Furthermore, in finding his solution in quantum physics and the Higgs field—the notion that "energetically, it costs something to maintain nothing"[205]—merely takes the traditional God and replaces it with the symmetry-breaking of physics. In the beginning there is the "false" vacuum of "pure symmetry," which is then "switched off."[206] An inaugural state of harmony and identity exists, which is then disturbed, creating reality. Conceptually, this is simply the reverse of a God who organizes primordial chaos to create the world.

To Žižek, "the minimal definition of materialism hinges on the admission of a gap between what Schelling called Existence and the Ground of Existence: prior to fully existent reality, there is a chaotic non-All proto-reality, a pre-ontological, virtual fluctuation of a not yet fully constituted real."[207] Materialism entails a distinction between a primordial chaos that is pre-real and its subsequent generation of the actually Real. There is a decisive Beginning—temporally and spatially—which demarcates a Then and a Now, a Here and a There. Such a rendering is secured by the ontotheological sovereignties of transcendence and teleology.

At the core of Žižek's arguments stands his allegiance to antagonism. Tension marks the original vacuum of pre-ontological chaos and the void; it is what diffracts it into two, what pushes it into one, and the incompletion of the One is what begets its supplemental, shadowy, excess. As Žižek sees it, his conception—informed by Hegel and Lacan—is the only true materialist account. The alternative, as Žižek is wont to remind his readers, is Spinoza's take: "While for Spinoza Substance remains a stable and peaceful immanent frame of the incessant movement of its modes . . . for Hegel, the Substance that engenders its modes is in itself antagonistic, 'barred,' marked by an irreducible inner tension—it is this immanent 'contradiction' that pushes the Substance towards the continuous generation of its particular modes."[208] Žižek accuses Spinoza of retaining a substance that is stable, peaceful, and in blissful harmony. As we have confirmed, this is decidedly not the case, as the infinity of substance refuses a priori presence and forecloses completion, upholding reality as not All. The infinite power that is substance only actualizes modally; it does not preexist its acts nor is it reducible to them. Ironically, Žižek—*not* Spinoza—retains a conception of an originary peace, through his insistence on the "false" vacuum in repose, which is disturbed by means of the "true" vacuum. In contrast, Spinoza is able to retain a non-identity without resorting to peaceful beginnings. Its renunciation of origins refuses such transcendence and teleology. Furthermore, insisting on an original "false" vacuum that is at peace with itself actually places Žižek in the uncomfortable position—which he makes no indication of appreciating—of advocating for an original point of identity, which is only subsequently disturbed by the emergence of his "true" vacuum. Spinozism is committed to the non-closure of substance and achieves as much without recourse to transcendent third elements represented by Žižek's embrace of *den* and the *object a*. Likewise, the infinity of substance requires that it is not One, but accomplishes this in the absence of insisting on an inherent and objective antagonism, not to mention a shadowy excess. It seems that Spinoza presents an ontology that realizes Žižek's ends without compromising on transcendence and teleology.

Despite Žižek's deployment of Spinozism as the alternative to his Hegelian-Lacanian materialism,[209] in the final analysis, Spinoza enacts a philosophy that remains committed to these materialist principles while refusing ontological sovereignties. Žižek's rejections of Spinozism—and its proponent, Deleuze—sustain his project by proffering an Other against which it defines itself. This Other, needless to say, has the most utility when it is wantonly misconstrued and oversimplified. These Žižekian maneuvers recall Macherey's reflection on Hegel's reading of Spinoza: "Hegel is never so close to Spinoza as in the moments when he distances himself from him, because this refusal has the value of a symptom and indicates the obstinate presence of a common object, if not a common project."[210] Hegelianism, even today, cannot positively affirm itself without negating Spinozism. What is striking is that Žižek's heterodox interpretation of Hegel, which is divested of a telos, deprived of its pretense of system, stripped of the "Absolute," and relegated to the contingent is far closer to Spinozism than Hegel's own Hegelianism could have ever been.

Disbanding the Binary

"Western" philosophy commences with the banishment of non-being. Parmenides insists that being *is* and non-being is not. Being is one and indivisible. Change is illusory. Democritus revitalizes non-being by introducing the void. Being is not one, it is comprised of many ones—atoms—which themselves are indivisible and internally unchanged, although their ever-changing configurations account for reality. To a certain extent, current discourses on Spinoza center on these two ancient traditions: Eleaticism and atomism. The issue is constructively framed by the question: Is Spinozism on the side of being, oneness, stasis, and identity or that of the void, the split, change, and difference? While this is a simplification, it captures the thrust of the debate. If Hegel reduces Spinozism to an Eleatic system of identity, modern Spinozists such as Deleuze and Althusser celebrate his Epicurean affinities, specifically his alignment with Lucretius. Substance, their readings suggest, is akin to the clinamen. In Deleuzian deflection, the Lucretian clinamen becomes the Spinozan conatus, rendering the void devoid. The swerve, rather, proves decisive. Such continuous declination is the affirmative power of substance as its immanent generation. While Althusser aligns Lucretius's clinamen with Spinoza's substance, instead of renouncing the void, his aleatory materialism incorporates it. There is no origin that is pure (positive) and then corrupted (negated). Substance is nothing but its ongoing swerving.

Despite the merit and conceptual force of these constructions of Spinoza's substance, their eviction and avoidance of the void is strategic, conditioned, and not entirely convincing. Spinoza is unequivocal in dismissing the existence of a literal void or vacuum in reality and, on this score, is diametrically opposed to the atomist tradition. However, as our reading argues, this also need not position Spinozism as a reproduction of Eleatic monism. On the contrary, Spinoza's philosophy falls neatly into neither category. It is not easily assimilated into either the school of being, oneness, and identity or into that of nothingness, diffraction, and difference. This resistance, I propose, renders Spinozism both severely curious and supremely compelling. Turning to Descartes's theory of substance, and considering Spinoza's criticisms of it, discloses certain ontological idiosyncrasies of Spinozism. Although Spinoza accords with the Cartesian denegation of the void, he rejects its metaphysical commitments on account of their concomitant transcendence. This means that even while negating a vacuum in nature, Spinoza is unable to accept substance as only already Something. It is this rejection of both a primordial Something and, accordingly, a primordial Nothing that reflects what I perceive to be the anti-sovereign ontology of Spinoza.

Even though Spinoza maintains that nothing comes from nothing and that there is no nothingness, this is not an embrace of Being. Despite the insistence on the indivisibility of substance—that it is not comprised of parts—its infinity demands that it is nevertheless not Something. This accordingly requires that substance is never already given, posited, whole, complete, or one. Although substance is nothing *but* its modes, its infinity means that it remains irreducible to them. As the foregoing argues, its status is nothing more or nothing less than its infinite actions—its division—*as* its finite modes. Substance may be figured as the division: the only "thing" that itself is indivisible. It is for this reason that the perceived deficiency of Spinozism—its inadequate account of the relation between the infinite and finite—is its triumph. Althusser is justified in emphasizing Spinozism's refusal of all end, origin, and reason. But there is more. Substance is bereft of beginning because it is not All, which also refuses the sovereignties of Something and Nothing. Substance is never "nothing" because it is necessary of existence, infinite power. On account of its infinity, substance remains irreducible to modes, to its infinite somethings, even as it itself is indeterminate, a power that is only actualized and yet only actualized modally. There is, at least conceptually, an asymmetry or a disparity. Substance is also not something insomuch as it is not a thing or matter, object or form. It is infinite and indeterminate power actualized *as* its finite, determinate modes. Substance can never be compassed, consummated, or completed nor can it fully coincide with its modes. In fact, as indeterminate and infinite, it simply cannot be fully identified with, let alone exhausted by, the determinate modes that are its acts.

The infinity of substance commands immanence, which means that nothing is excluded from it. There is nothing transcendent to substance. Therefore, if negativity exists, it must be *of* substance, a determinate mode of it. As such, the negative cannot function as the inverse of the Positive—a God—transcendent to reality, yet still its First Cause. That said, Spinoza's uncompromising campaign against teleology cautions us against falling prey to the distortions of the conditioned human perspective. "Negative" therefore is relative. There is no absolute "positive" or "negative." The contemporary fetishization of the negative would do well to revisit this Spinozist insight. So, to a certain extent, the accusation that Spinoza banishes all negativity is justified. But only if we accept that he equally forecloses the positive. This is certainly the case on the register of origins, which refuses any concept of Beginning, be it the plenitude of the Positive or the nothingness of the Negative. Nevertheless, at least conceptually, there is still more to contend with in considering the space of the negative in Spinozism. At stake—at least partially—is the Hegelian and now Lacanian insistence on the generativity of the negative, on the productive role of the constitutive lack.

In analyzing these concerns, Moder concludes: "Spinoza's concept of being, if we can put it in these terms, certainly doesn't account for a lack or a rupture or a gap in being."[211] However, he tempers this assertion, suggesting that it "can be explained with the idea of the primary *torsion* of being, according to which *to exist* always already means to be contorted, to be in such and such a mode, to be modified."[212] This interpretation—akin to Althusser's clinamen—is not without merit and opens a space for conceiving substance as more than merely already posited and always positive. But it seems to me that in fact there is a place for a lack, rupture, or gap in being according to Spinoza. Or at least there is an element within Spinozism that accomplishes precisely what these notions signify, even if caution is needed in employing these negatively inflected terms. Recall that the singular constraint on substance is its incapacity to fully become. As infinite, it is never completed, whole, or accomplished. It is constitutionally not All. Though it would be transgressive by Spinozist standards to coin this a "lack," functionally, it is not dissimilar. The only imperfection of substance is its incapacity to be perfected, to be completed. Likewise, although the insubstantiality of substance means that it is nothing beyond its modes, its infinity renders it not same with them. As infinite and indeterminate, it is the indivisible division as its finite determinate modes. That which is indeterminate simply cannot be contained or coincident with that which is determinate. Therefore, as the foregoing affirms, there is a disparity of sorts adhering between substance and modes, even if neither is independent of its other and neither precedes its other. This non-coincidence functions in a manner theoretically not dissimilar to a "gap." Crucially, this disparity is not merely originary, it is always already. It is crucial to underscore, once more, that because substance is the infinite—indeterminate power that is actualized as its finite, determinate modes—coincidence simply cannot obtain. There is no comparison, let alone identity between the infinite and the finite because the former is indeterminate, it is not a matter, form, being or thing, whereas modes are only ever determinate as matter, form, being, or things. Yet indeterminate substance, which is action, exists only *as* its finite, determinate modes, which are its acts. But substance is never in potential, it is only ever actualized. However, on account of its absolute infinity, it simply cannot be exhausted by a coincidence with its modes. This would circumscribe it and undercut its infinity.

Not only is Spinoza's substance not the absolutely positive being that it is mistakenly taken to be, but it seems to incorporate the "negative" elements it is perceived as lacking, and does so without resorting to transcendence and teleology, without positing either Something or Nothing as primary. The metaphor that Crescas advances between void and God is instructive because it epitomizes the asset of Spinozism's reservation from taking neither the side of the void nor that of the plenum as originary. Philosophies that perceive the Beginning as in the void are conceptually little different from those that posit being or Being as primordial. Either option remains irrevocably wedded to a constellation of ontotheological sovereignties. The Scholastic theological embrace of the vacuum, most robustly by Bradwardine who renders God as the void, and its legacies in the early modern and modern philosophical sciences are salient cases in point showcasing the ontotheology that sponsors the void. It comes, therefore, as no surprise to witness Hegel and subsequent thinkers who embrace nothingness do so in ways that seem merely to reproduce God and its sovereign traits in and as the Nothing. Morton's construction of the Rift, its transcendence and its apophatic nature, not to mention its status as responsible for the generation and cessation of all that is, exemplifies as much. Their nothingness is merely

God repurposed as the Rift constitutive of all objects. This ontotheology of nothingness is especially pronounced, as we have seen, in the philosophies of Badiou and Žižek, both of whom criticize Spinoza on precisely these grounds of the nothing and the negative. Yet in grasping firmly to the negative, their ontologies cannot but rely on transcendence and teleology. For Badiou, this most prominently takes shape in his allegiance to the exceptional event, whereas with Žižek it is in his conception of a primordial identity, the teleological transition through the voids, the polarity between Something and Nothing, and the transcendence of the *den* or *object a*. Both perilously induct hierarchy, transcendence, and exceptionalism into reality.

A central thesis of this book is that Spinoza's philosophy can be read as positioning a radical critique of sovereignties, sovereign claims, and sovereign features. Concomitant to this proposition is the contention that in so doing Spinoza's philosophy resists several commitments that have escorted and inspired "Western" philosophy from its earliest gestations. The Parmenidean expulsion of non-being and its crowning of Being as all, one, indivisible, and unchanging is a decisive embrace of sovereign fixtures. Reality is a stable totality, an identity system. Contra this Eleatic paradigm, the atomists insist on the divisibility of being and the reality of non-being. Despite their efforts, the atom still arrogates ontotheological traits: the atom is indivisible and its inside is staid. Lucretius essays an alternative. The clinamen claims that curvature is primordial. Being is not initially consummate and only subsequently corrupted by the admittance of the negative. Rather, it is originally swerved; the negative is within, from the beginning. Being and non-being, something and nothing, come together. "Purity" is not primordial. Arguably, however, this either ignores the negativity of the void altogether—per Deleuze—or it renders the swerve meaningless by universalizing it. No matter how we construe the clinamen, the space of the void *and* the atom still upholds the antagonism between nothing and something, that being is born from its confrontation with non-being, or that non-being is in ongoing opposition with being. Spinozism positions a forceful alternative by allowing us to refuse this false choice; substance is neither quite nothing nor quite something, for either option undercuts infinity and restores sovereignty. The only viable alternative is to accept reality as ontologically nonbinary.

Non-being, negativity, and nothingness, as this chapter traces, historically and still today, arrogate the sovereignties that have traditionally been attributed to God. The urge to organize reality by anointing it with an origin, by identifying an exception to its ways, by perceiving an excess responsible for what is, remains with us. However, rather than confronting the perplexities of reality, change, and difference, these devices merely explain them away, reducing them to a force that is transcendent and, correlatively, teleologically guaranteed. Probing the persistent allure of both transcendence and teleology, alongside its perils, is the project of the next chapter.

FOUR

Serves No Purpose

> Law! Order! Order! Law! This is the cry resounding from all sides... the joyous echo from all the bourgeois camps.
>
> —ROSA LUXEMBURG[1]

"Nature does nothing on account of an end."[2] This claim anchors Spinoza's campaign against teleology. Infinite reality, he tells us, is without End, Design, and Order. What exists is so without serving any Purpose. Therefore, all that is, is perfect. This chapter probes the significance and consequences of this critique. It dissects the anthropocentrism, conceits to human exceptionalism, and fantasies of human freedom that undergird teleology, undressing the sovereign rationales underwriting these beliefs. By vitiating all purposiveness and oversight in nature, Spinoza presents a powerful alternative to certain regnant postulates in "Western" philosophy, alongside the logics of sovereignty that underpin them. Upholding reality as infinite, for example, undercuts assertions that nature is regulated or directed. It is without Laws and Norms. Reality is divested of normativity; nothing is *meant* to be, so no mode is not perfect. Notions of perfection and normativity are human constructs. This perspective has implications for theorizing sexgender. Contra biological essentialism, sovereign binarism, and reductionist normativity, I corroborate that such an ontology solicits a queering of sexgender. Relatedly, I register how Spinoza's denaturalization of teleology and normativity, alongside his anatomization of the supremacies that sponsor them, proffers resources for rebutting certain forms of racism and ableism.

By dismantling teleology, Spinoza dethrones humans from their perch of privilege. In contrast to the transcendence of Cartesianism and the Christian dualism it consolidates, Spinoza's immanence emplaces all modes, including humans, within nature. Humans are not exceptional and there is no retreat from the infinite connection of causes. Such immanence not only dismantles the hierarchical dualism of body and mind, it rebuts the correlated hierarchical binarization of nature and culture, natural and unnatural.

In critiquing teleology, Spinoza leans on the sparks of immanence refracted by medieval Jewish philosophy, especially Maimonides. I educe how these insights pressure specific Christian, "Western," liberal dogmas of Progress. Much as it refuses notions of History as sequestered from nature and claims that it carries Meaning. Spinoza's philosophy forecloses the hierarchies, instrumentalizations, and guarantees staking these conventions. Scrutinizing as much uncovers how teleology remains with us, subsidizing evolutionary biology, philosophies of longtermism, the management of global heating and the COVID pandemic. Spinoza's assault on teleology remains as vital today as in his own time.

Denaturalization

The appendix to part I of the *Ethics* is critical to Spinoza's entire philosophy. It centers on repudiating teleology, the belief that reality is purposive, that it fulfills certain ends or satisfies particular functions. In the process of debunking teleology, he uncovers a series of its allied "prejudices," including anthropocentrism, anthropomorphism, and human exceptionalism. These sponsor teleology and are bolstered by it. Importantly, Spinoza not only disproves these doctrines but deconstructs how they come to be. He unmasks the mutually reinforcing misconceptions that stake these prejudices, while probing the desires that propel them. Althusser discerns in this appendix the "matrix of every possible theory of ideology,"[3] ideologies that as I see it, originate in delusive pretenses to sovereignty.

The aim of the appendix is to "expose" remaining prejudices "that could, and can be a great obstacle to people understanding the connection of things in the way I have explained it."[4] Critiquing these prejudices allows Spinoza to restate, with no small amount of polemical flair, the fundaments of his ontology and to sketch their ramifications. The appendix renders visible the meaning and pertinence of the preceding thirty-six propositions, demonstrations, and scholia. At the root of the prejudices the appendix disproves lies a web of purports to sovereignty: the belief that there is a Sovereign overseeing reality, that this Sovereign is free, that this Sovereign is free like humans, and that humans are free. What spurs this calculus are the symbiotic prejudices of teleology, anthropocentrism, and human exceptionalism. These subsidize the claims to sovereignty that Spinoza devotes the most space to dismantling: a sovereign God, sovereign Nature, and a sovereign Human. The infinity of substance and the immanence it conduces disallow for these and related sovereignties.

While this book contends that Spinoza's ontology is divested of sovereignties, it is equally invested in evincing why this is significant. How we perceive reality is not merely not neutral but is borne from and in turn buttresses a coalition of allied commitments to sovereignty. This is why ontology cannot be disaggregated from politics and ethics, why sovereignty is not an exclusively political or juridical concern. On the contrary, the *naturalization* of sovereignty through prejudices about reality at once reflects certain social, political, ethical conditions and in turn reconfirms them. Sovereignties are constructed upon sovereignties and simultaneously produce further sovereignties.

By disassembling the rationales of sovereignty that subsidize anthropocentrism, teleology, and human exceptionalism, Spinoza models for readers how to sustain his critique. This chapter undertakes as much as it turns attention to matters of our moment, discerning the continued purchase of these prejudices. Doing so verifies an undercurrent of this project: that "religious" or "theological" concerns, in this instance, purports to sovereignty and its rationales, persist through modernity, despite the alleged "secularity" of these epochs. Such interrogation is arguably even more urgent today because the theology undergirding teleological thinking is camouflaged by its "secular," "objective," or "scientific" trappings.

To No End

The ensemble of prejudices repudiated in the appendix are hitched by the misbelief "that all natural things act, as humans do, on account of an end" and "that God directs all things to some certain end."[5] Against this, Spinoza confirms that "nature has no end set before it, and all final causes are nothing but human fictions."[6] Considering the arguments of part I, this comes as no surprise. Teleology contravenes the commitments of Spinoza's ontology: the infinity and immanence of substance validate that there is nothing above or below, beyond or outside of it. There is no transcendence, be it in the form of a god or a goal or any other guise. This disallows for the existence of an entity that might transcend reality, securing a purpose or serving a telos. Moreover, the supposition that substance acts towards an end subverts its "infinite power" and "perfection" because "if God acts for the sake of an end, God necessarily wants something which God lacks."[7]

How do people come to believe that reality is teleological? And why is this conviction so prevalent? The trouble starts with the kindred conceits of anthropocentrism and human exceptionalism. Humans "think themselves free" because they "act on account of an end,"[8] so they suppose that nature also does and that it does so to serve humans. This presumption originates in the recognition that there are in fact aspects of nature advantageous to humans: "eyes for seeing, teeth for chewing, plants and animals for food, the sun for light, the sea for supporting fish."[9] Since "they consider all natural things as a means to their own advantage,"[10] humans suppose that these have been made *specifically* for them. This precipitates a further mistake: "After they considered things as means, they could not believe that things had made themselves."[11] So "they had to infer that there was a ruler, or a number of rulers of nature, endowed with human freedom, who has taken care of all things for them, and made all things for their use."[12] Anthropocentrism engenders anthropomorphism: "Since they had never heard about the temperament of these rulers, they had to judge it from their own."[13] The human construction of a sovereign ruler or rulers is transposed onto nature in order to certify that it exists to minister to humans; in turn, these rulers are imagined as sovereign, in the human image.

This muddle fosters the belief "that the Gods direct all things for the use of humans in order to bind humans to them and be held by humans in the highest honor."[14] This leads them to worship God, "so that God might love them above all the rest" and direct nature to benefit them.[15] Once humans profess the existence of a Sovereign who directs reality to serve them, a perplexity arises: Why are there elements and circumstances in nature that seem to hinder rather than promote human flourishing? To reconcile "inconveniences" like "storms, earthquakes, diseases," believers perceive such phenomena as intended by "angry" gods "on account of wrongs done to them by humans, *or* on account of sins committed in their worship."[16] Despite evidence from daily experience that "conveniences and inconveniences happen indiscriminately to the pious and the impious alike, they did not . . . give up their longstanding prejudice."[17] Instead, they concluded that "the judgments of the Gods far surpass humans' grasp."[18] The belief that a transcendent Being exists and that it sovereignly commands reality carries with it the correlative notion that this Sovereign is Other, its ways *exceed* human comprehension. Its Supremacy is secured by regarding other things—here intelligences—as inferior. Notice the allied claims to supremacy: reality is perceived as overseen by a Supreme being directing it in the service of humans who are seen as superior to other beings and thus worthy of having reality yield to them.

Once humans fabricate a God who Rules over reality, they worship it "so that God might love them above all the rest, and direct the whole of nature according to the needs of their blind desire and insatiable greed."[19] Not only does anthropocentrism install a hierarchy that situates humans above nonhumans, it fosters conflict *between* humans. Admitting exceptionalism and supremacy into reality spurs further arrogations of it. Moreover, projecting the human construction of a Ruler onto reality effectively naturalizes it, making sovereignty, hierarchy, and domination seem ontologically real. Such naturalization validates the forms of domination that already exist amongst humans, which is why setting the record straight is so threatening to those holding power. As Spinoza reflects, from no small amount of personal experience: "It happens that one who seeks the true causes of miracles . . . to understand natural things, not to wonder at them, like a fool, is generally considered and denounced as an impious heretic by those whom the people honor as interpreters of nature and the Gods."[20] This is because "they know that if ignorance is taken away, then foolish wonder, the only means they have of arguing and defending their authority is also taken away."[21] The rejection of a sovereign God destabilizes the established theological-political order, which is founded on the fiction that those in power represent God. Their authority is legitimated by the Authority. This dynamic, I maintain, is not restricted to religiopolitical authorities. Rather, all purports to power—to supremacy over other beings, to domination—result from or rely upon the naturalization of sovereignty. Thrusting a Ruler onto reality naturalizes the very institution of Rulership, authorizing it and in turn those who Rule. Furthermore, Spinoza is not only affirming that our ways of perceiving reality are socially conditioned but that precisely the perceptions of reality that gain traction are those which reinforce the existing power structures in society. As Marx later enunciates: "The ideas of the ruling class are in every epoch the ruling ideas."[22]

Spinoza's commentary exposes the reinforcing fictions that configure prevailing conceptions of reality. Anthropocentrism leads humans to regard nature as purposively serving them; this end, it is claimed, must be the result of a being that is Other who is then imagined as existing and behaving like a human Sovereign. In order to curry favor with this Ruler, to further benefit humans, this Ruler is worshipped. When nature appears to act in ways that harm humans, this is interpreted as punishment for misdeeds. Teleology and theology are conjoined. The belief in an End in nature is inseparable from the belief in a Sovereign commanding and controlling it. Once there is an End that transcends reality, it follows that there is a Transcendent being that guarantees it. Most commonly, this is a God who intervenes in nature and is an Exception to its ways. Traditionally, this features in the construct of the miracle, the claim that the Sovereign, through its Decision, interrupts nature to reward or punish humans. Such notions transgress Spinoza's ontological commitments in two significant manners. The first is by curtailing the perfection of substance, for "if God acts for the sake of an end"[23] this implies a lack in God. Although everything that exists is so due to substance, this is "not from the freedom of the will *or* absolute good pleasure, but from God's absolute nature *or* infinite power."[24] And, second, maintaining that there is an End or Purpose that is *other* to substance or transcends it undercuts its infinity. Teleology, like theology, relies on sovereignties and its hierarchies. The supposition of a transcendent aspect to reality, a Goal in nature or an Order to it, endows this feature with sovereignty, akin to that attributed to God. Grounding nature in a telos that stands above it, is other to it, and has command over it renders it Sovereign over all else. Like a Sovereign god it is *beyond* regulation and yet regulates all that is.

There is circularity to the rationales that Spinoza disentangles. The conceit of transcendent human free will leads to the ascription of a transcendent purpose and plan to reality or to a transcendent God that acts with free will to direct reality to suit humans. This belief is furnished by the fiction of human exceptionalism: that humans are distinct from and superior to other beings and that such distinction manifests in their free will. Such a perspective is further substantiated by the reciprocal supposition that reality benefits humans, existing for the purpose of serving them, and that this very purpose is sponsored by a Sovereign god that itself has the free will to command nature for the unique benefit of humans. The fundamental error here is the misunderstanding of human nature as exceptional and humans as endowed with transcendence, which concomitantly leads to the ascription of exceptionalism and transcendence to a God or Goal that directs reality. In order to secure the pretense of human distinction and exceptionalism, humans force their own social construction of a ruler onto nature, imagining this Sovereign as not only Distinct and Exceptional, but paradoxically both Supreme over all else, yet subservient to the telos of human satisfaction.

Without Rhyme or Reason

The prejudice that nature is purposive arises from the constellated prejudices of anthropocentrism and anthropomorphism: because humans often act towards ends, they suppose that reality does too *and* that it serves humans. Spinoza clarifies not only that reality is not anthropocentric—it does not purposively serve humans—but also that it is not anthropomorphic: it does not act towards *any* end. Reality is without Purpose. Neither substance nor modes exist *for a purpose* nor are they products of a Plan. In the absence of a programmatic blueprint, it is also incoherent to impute Meaning onto reality. Appreciating as much requires examining the ontological commitments that moor Spinoza's rejection of teleology and renunciation of the anthropic conceits that cinch it.

To Spinoza, "*good* and *bad*, *merit* and *sin*, *praise* and *blame*, *order* and *confusion*, *beauty* and *ugliness*, and other things of this kind"[25] are human constructs that do not reflect how reality is. In the preface to part IV, he further dissects "perfection and imperfection, good and bad."[26] These, like all values, are "modes of thinking."[27] Perfection, like all judgments of its kind, is linked to purposiveness: if an object satisfies its stated purpose, humans deem it perfect. However, since there is no "objective" standard of how a given thing should be, any such assessment is subjective, particularized to the inclinations and desires conditioned by the experiences and exposures of the person rendering the judgment. So-called universal ideas or models of, for example, "houses, buildings, towers," are anything but "universal."[28] These reflect individual preferences, and each person has their own ideal model against which the object is measured. Teleology emerges when humans apply this procedure to nature: "They are accustomed to form universal ideas of natural things as much as they do artificial ones."[29] They suppose that "nature does nothing except for the sake of some end" and "looks to them, and sets them before itself as models."[30] As such, "when they see something happen in nature which does not agree with the model they have conceived... they believe that nature itself has failed or sinned, and left the things imperfect."[31] But "Nature does nothing on account of an end."[32] In the absence of a Purpose or Plan nothing in nature can be perfect or imperfect, good or bad.

Referencing part I and its appendix, Spinoza reprises why reality is without a telos. It would undermine the infinity of substance: "The reason, therefore, *or* cause, why god *or* nature, acts and the reason why it exists, are one and the same. As it exists for the sake of no end, it also acts for the sake of no end."[33] Since "it has no principle or end of existing, so it also has none of acting."[34] The imputation of ends, goals, and purposes onto reality are "but a human appetite insofar as it is considered as a principle *or* primary cause, of some thing."[35] Those who suppose that substance acts purposively "seem to place something outside God, which does not depend on God, to which God attends, as a model, in what God does, and at which God aims."[36] Ascribing a purpose to nature subordinates it to the supremacy of this purpose, a purpose that transcends it in order to direct it. But infinite substance cannot be subordinate to anything; if it was, it would not be infinite. This is why the acts of substance are not produced by a will, directed towards a goal, or intended towards a function. What exists and how it exists are by necessity. With this explanation, Spinoza exposes the supremacist logics that subsidize doctrines of teleology and more expansively, as the ensuing traces, all value judgments.

Dispensing with teleology not only disallows for a Sovereign who directs reality but also disclaims that what exists, exists for a *reason*. Presuming a Reason or Purpose for what is presupposes hierarchy, subsuming all existences under the aegis of a particular telos, which directs reality, determining all worth. Thereby, the telos becomes Sovereign. To discern a purpose is at once to determine a Being responsible for said purpose, to attribute a Plan to it, and to position reality as submitting to it. Even in the absence of a particular Sovereign overseeing reality, the notion of a telos functions sovereignly: what exists is subordinated to it. Refusing teleology inducts a reality unencumbered by sovereignties, divested of a sovereign God, Ground, Goal, or Good.

Considering how blatant Spinoza is about the menace of teleology, conceiving it as *the* root of all prejudices, it is curious that certain scholars attenuate Spinoza's anti-teleology. Such resistance and the smuggling of teleology into his thought is prevalent in precincts of the "analytic scholarship."[37] Such commentaries reflect not only the "Western" philosophical conditioning and preferences of particular scholars but a certain insecurity with an ontology and so also an ethics that is without guarantees and guardrails.

A Perfect World

By linking judgments of value to purposiveness, Spinoza not only reminds us that our judgments are conditioned by our conscious and unconscious preferences but that to affirm a purpose in nature is *already* to render a judgment. Furthermore, purposes functionally justify and bolster our particularized opinions of what matters and what qualifies as good and bad, perfect and imperfect, beautiful and ugly. Here too, we encounter circular thinking: subjective preferences determine what is valued, and once these preferences are discerned in nature, their presence comes to reinforce the initial preference, validating it. But there is more here. By disavowing the fiction of a purpose or scheme or design in nature, Spinoza is dislodging the intransigent sovereignties of transcendence and rebutting ideologies that perceive meaning in what and how nature is.

Refusing to conceive substance as acting in accord with a purpose or plan, decision or choice, forecloses attaching meaning, ideals, and values *to* nature. What and how any given mode is, is an effect of its imbrication in the infinite connection of causes. It—a microbe, a mushroom, a manatee—was never *intended* to be any way. Its existence neither reflects nor fulfills any ideals or values. Yet people routinely attach meaning and value to the actualities of nature by labeling "natural things perfect or imperfect more from prejudice than from true knowledge."[38] These "modes of thinking" emerge since humans "compare individuals of the same species or genus to one another," deeming "perfect" what is perceived to "have more being, *or* reality, than others," whereas that which is imperfect is perceived as possessing a "lack of power."[39] These assessments derive from how these beings "affect our mind" and do not reflect "something lacking in them which is theirs."[40] This is because "nothing belongs to the nature of anything except what follows from the necessity of the nature of the efficient cause. And whatever follows from the necessity of the nature of the efficient cause happens necessarily."[41] How any mode exists in reality is a consequence of causal intra-actions, rather than how it measures up to or compares with some contrived metric. No gnat is more perfect than its neighbor; no virus more perfect than its predecessor; no kelp more perfect than its kin. This is why, Spinoza contends, "a horse is destroyed as much if it is changed into a human as if it is changed into an insect."[42] There is no preexisting Ideal of how any being is to be. Thus, "if most people were born grown up . . . then everyone would pity the infants, because they could regard infancy itself, not as a natural and necessary thing, but as a vice of nature, *or* a sin."[43] By contrast, Spinoza regards a mode's "power of acting, insofar as it is understood through its nature,"[44] rather than how it measures up to a contrived universal metric.

By unpacking the manners in which our anthropocentric and accordingly extremely individualized standpoints condition our judgments, Spinoza reminds us of the simple truth that what we see often says more about us—what we *want* to see, what comports with our preconceived notions, what reaffirms our beliefs—than it does about the actual nature of the observed thing. Moreover, because what is and how it is was never intended to be, as it was not planned or commanded to be, it makes no sense to discern in the actualities of nature meaning or prescriptiveness. *How* matters are does not reflect how they *ought* to be. It simply is the result of causal determinations. Spinoza declares: "By reality and perfection I understand the same thing."[45] By this he does not mean that how a thing is, is the *best* way in which it might be, but that it is the *only* way in which it might be. Since power is actualized and never in potential, what happens and what is are perfect.

Laying Ghosts to Rest

Boxel, a Dutch legal scholar, wrote Spinoza requesting "to know your opinion about apparitions and specters or ghosts."[46] The "Ancients" as well as "Modern Theologians and Philosophers," he says, all believed in ghosts. Spinoza explains how there is no evidence to substantiate the existence of ghosts, deeming them "nothing more than children's games or the pastimes of fools."[47] Belief in ghosts is prevalent because of "the desire people commonly have to tell things, not as they are, but as they want them to be."[48]

Spinoza's reaction provokes Boxel who replies by defending his belief in ghosts through four arguments: (1) "it makes for the beauty and perfection of the universe that they exist"; (2) "it is probable that the Creator has created them because they are more like him than corporeal creatures are"; (3) since "there is a body without a spirit, there must be a spirit without a body"; and (4) because "the immeasurable space between us and the stars is not empty," it must be filled with "inhabitants" divided between "the highest and uppermost," which are "true spirits," and "the lowest."[49] Notice the ranked distinctions that subtend each of Boxel's explanations: beauty *over* ugliness; non-corporeality *over* corporeality and the proximity in likeness that ghosts have to God over and against that enjoyed by other creatures; spirit *over* body; and the distinction between high and lower spirits. Having arrayed these reasons in support of ghosts, Boxel synopsizes his stance by offering an exclusionary criterion: "I think there are spirits of every kind, except that possibly there are no female spirits."[50]

Expectedly, Spinoza responds by registering the anthropocentric and teleological suppositions undergirding Boxel's arguments. Retorting his first claim that the beauty and perfection of the universe command the existence of ghosts, Spinoza writes: "Beauty, Sir, is not so much a quality of the object one sees as an effect of the object on one who sees it. . . . things considered in themselves, or in relation to God, are neither beautiful nor ugly."[51] Besides, how exactly, asks Spinoza, would "spirits, or all sorts of monsters, like Centaurs, Hydras, Harpies, Satyrs, Griffins, Argusses and more fancies of that kind" enhance the "adornment and perfection of the world?"[52] Turning to repudiate Boxel's second argument—since ghosts are more like God, it is probable that God created them—Spinoza confesses not knowing how ghosts would be more like God than other creatures. Moreover, "the difference between the greatest, most excellent creature and God is the same as between the least creature and God."[53] Even if ghosts existed, they are no more proximate to God than gametes. To Boxel's third argument since "there is a body without a spirit there must also be a spirit without a body," Spinoza retorts: Would it be "that there is a sphere without a circle, because there is a circle without a sphere?" Regarding his fourth reason, Spinoza refers Boxel to his response to the first argument, addressing the follies of anthropocentrism.

Spinoza also tends to Boxel's sexgender caveat—"there are no female spirits"—regarding it "like the imagination of the common people, who suppose that God is male, not female" and quips: "I'm surprised that those who've seen spirits naked have not cast their eyes on their genitalia."[54] This is worthy of attention not merely because it showcases Spinoza's sense of humor but since it gestures towards his understanding of how beliefs are formed. What people reckon about the nature of gods, spirits, and reality in general reflect their predispositions, reproducing their preferences and preconceived notions. It is not just that it is easy, perhaps even delightful, for Spinoza to dismiss ghosts and to deride Boxel's ranking and sexgendering of them. Rather, Boxel's contention that ghosts exist and his seemingly arbitrary claim that they are exclusively male, though familiar, as Spinoza notes, from the common sexgendering of God, is not coincidental. The sexgendering of gods and ghosts epitomizes the basic anthropomorphism at play in human imaginings in general and concerning divine creatures more specifically. Much like the naturalization of a sovereign Ruler validates and vitalizes the human construction of sovereigns, the sexgendering of ghosts operates similarly. It at once reflects sexgendered differences and simultaneously reinforces them, much as it bolsters the hierarchical worldviews that people maintain.

Undismayed, Boxel clarifies: "I think there are no females among them, because I deny that they procreate."[55] Implicit in this defense is the belief that "females"—presumably humans and nonhuman animals—exist in order to reproduce. Since ghosts and spirits do not procreate, there is no reason to admit "females" into their ranks. While Spinoza remains silent on this score, Boxel's logic epitomizes the purposive thinking that he elsewhere, yet also in these very exchanges, disputes. To presume that "females" exist *only* to reproduce presupposes teleology: that what exists, exists for a reason or purpose. Moreover, this suggests that biological variations within or across species are constitutive of beings. (As yet, "female" humans are unable to procreate by themselves, so Boxel's presumption must be due to the asymmetric burden of reproduction shouldered by those with uteri). Identifying a particular feature that a mode possesses and then concluding that this is *why* the mode exists is teleological; it reverses causes and effects, presuming that how something is, is why it is, which purposively assumes that it was guided to be so by a transcendent goal or god. It is also reductive and essentializing: it perceives a biological variation or a capacity that certain humans possess and then *reduces* them to this capacity, rendering it *essential* to their being, which is then circularly upheld as the reason for their existence. Thereby, the biological feature or capability is rendered Sovereign and the existence of that mode becomes subordinate, subservient, secondary to it.

While Spinoza mocks Boxel's anthropomorphic sexgendering of ghosts, he seems untroubled by the sexgendering of humans. Scattered remarks of his attest to an embrace of sexist norms and stereotypes. Yet Spinoza's own sexism does not negate the force of his thinking to help us critique sexism.

In Spinoza's last epistle to Boxel, he responds to Boxel's attribution of human features to God "in an eminent and metaphysical way."[56] Spinoza writes:[57] "I believe that if a triangle could speak, it would say . . . that God is triangular in an eminent way, and that a circle would say that in an eminent way the divine nature is circular."[58] Not only do humans see reality through anthropic lenses but imagining God in their image glorifies themselves. This is more than a mere lack of imagination; the figuring of God in the human image carries serious consequences for humans and nonhumans.

The Good, the Bad, and the Ugly

By repudiating teleology, Spinoza levels a certain traditional conception of God and of humans: God is not a Sovereign directing reality, and reality does not revolve around humans. These fictions are interlaced with anthropomorphism because human conceits about themselves condition their conceits about God and nature. As Spinoza tells it: "After humans persuaded themselves that everything that happens, happens on their account, they had to judge that what is most important in each thing is what is most useful to them, and to rate as most excellent all of those things by which they were most pleased."[59] So "they had to form these notions, by which they explained natural things: good, bad, order, confusion, warm, cold, beauty, ugliness."[60] Furthermore, "all the notions by which ordinary people are accustomed to explain nature are only modes of imagining, and do not indicate the nature of anything."[61] *How* people are impacted by a given thing determines their perceptions of it. For example, "those which move the sense through the nose, they call pleasant-smelling or stinking; through the tongue, sweet or bitter, tasty or tasteless; through touch, hard, or soft, rough or smooth . . . those which move the ears are said to produce noise, sound or harmony."[62] Independent of human experiences and preferences, nothing is inherently good or bad, beautiful or ugly, or anything else. This polemic against teleology and anthropocentrism is aimed not merely at "ordinary people" but at a significant body of philosophy that reaches back to antiquity but was intensified in medieval Christian thought, especially Scholasticism.

Spinoza's critique of anthropocentrism and teleology draws on Maimonides's theories and "mercilessly pushes everything to its supposed conclusion."[63] Maimonides proclaims: "It should not be believed that all the beings exist for the sake of the existence of man. On the contrary, all the other beings too have been intended for their own sakes."[64] As such, "we shall seek . . . no cause or final end whatever."[65] He decries "the ignoramus and those like him among the multitude" who "imagines that all that exists exists with a view to his individual sake . . . as if there were nothing that exists except him."[66]

Emphasizing the anthropic nature of judgments about reality, Maimonides clarifies that Scripture's description of creations in Genesis as "good" is "an expression applied by us to what conforms to our purpose."[67] Scripture, Maimonides repeatedly underscores, deploys human idioms and comports with human convention. Similarly, he differentiates between true and false, good and evil, explaining that, initially, Adam was endowed with an intellect that "distinguishes between truth and falsehood," which "holds good for all intelligible things."[68] However, after disobeying God, he "became absorbed in judging things to be bad or fine."[69] Such judgments are of the imagination rather than intellection. Therefore, "with regard to what is of necessity, there is not *good* and *evil* at all, but only the *false* and the *true*."[70] Values, for both Maimonides and Spinoza, are human constructs.

Order Is Out

Is it any wonder that in confirming God as Creator, Genesis underscores that Creation emerges from chaos and void? To think of a sovereign God as creating is to presume a sovereign Order. The disorder of reality is steadied through intentional execution: there are distinctions and separations by kind; each day is devoted to particular species; creations are endowed with functions. God's sovereignty is certified through organizing, and meaning is secured through ordering. Order inducts reality with hierarchy and infuses it with purpose. Hence, the creation of the universe culminates with the creation of humans, who are distinct from and superior to nonhuman animals and portrayed as the pinnacle of God's creativity, the telos of creation.

The teleological ordering and ranking in Scripture's portrayal of creation has not been lost on exegetes. To Philo, God creates the world using an incorporeal model and this creation is carefully arranged, "for there is no such thing as beauty in disorder."[71] God creates the world from "disorder and confusion" and invests it with "order, quality, animation, resemblance, identity, arrangement, harmony, and everything which belongs to the more excellent idea."[72] Heaven is created first because it is "the best."[73] Order and hierarchy are intertwined: "Order is a due consequence and connection of things precedent and subsequent . . . it is owing to order that they become accurately defined and stationary, free from confusion."[74] This thematic subtends Kabbalistic speculations. Ein Sof creates the world through hierarchical emanations that radiate through the *sefirot*. To Moses de Leon, from the Nothingness in Ein Sof, creations are forged. Whereas for Isaac Luria, through *tsimtsum*, Ein Sof creates the Nothingness from which all else is forged. To both, before creation there is Nothingness, and through creation, distinction and differentiation are borne. Such ordering solidifies the status of Ein Sof, secures reality, and cinches its telos. Spinoza defects from these traditions by dispossessing reality of Order.

Spinoza devotes especial attention in the appendix to disputing the prejudices of "order and confusion." Beliefs in final causes and ends are entangled with or rely upon presuppositions of its order and orderability. Humans like order, desire it, are pleased by it and so attach it to reality: "Since those things we can easily imagine are especially pleasing to us, humans prefer order to confusion, as if order were anything in nature more than a relation to our imagination."[75] What seems ordered to us humans, much like what might seem beautiful to us, are judgments particular to our standpoints that do not reflect how matters really are. This predilection for order precipitates the anthropocentric and anthropomorphic supposition that God, too, likes order and actively orders reality: "Humans have been so mad as to believe that God is pleased by harmony."[76] They "say that God has created all things in order."[77]

The fiction of Order not only presumes transcendent purposiveness, it entails the presumption that this order serves humans: "When they see the structure of the human body, they are struck by foolish wonder, and because they do not know the causes of so great an art, they infer that it is constructed, not by mechanical, but by divine, or supernatural art."[78] The actualities of nature must have been *made* to be in this seemingly ordered way, which requires an Orderer. As Maimonides pronounces, "every physician and philosopher" knows the human body "is brought about of necessity through a purpose of nature."[79] Thus, "Can someone endowed with intelligence conceive that the humors, membranes, and nerves of the eye—which, as is known, are so well arranged and all of which have as their purpose the final end of this act of seeing—have come about fortuitously?"[80] Needless to say, Spinoza, endowed with no small amount of intelligence, does not think that these emerged through chance nor that these are indicative of an Order and so an Orderer. To Maimonides, such organization comes from "craftsmanlike governance."[81] The Order in nature corroborates that it has a Governor. Spinoza reputes this, contending that what exists is so due to immanent causal necessity without transcendent Guides.

In the appendix, Spinoza invokes the Aristotelian case of a person killed by a stone that falls from a roof. Instead of viewing this death as an unfortunate effect of varied, contingent causes—meteorological patterns, architectural realities, personal timing—people "will not stop asking for the causes until you take refuge in the will of God . . . the sanctuary of ignorance."[82] All of this transpired, they suppose, because God *willed* this person to die. Rather than the sorry effect of sundry causes, this death becomes the very cause of the phenomena that effectuated it, the reason for which the wind blew, the sea tossed, the weather changed, and so on. Observing *how* this man died becomes an explanation for *why* he perished: "What is an effect it considers as a cause."[83] Not only does this confuse the effect—the death—with its causes, it renders them subservient to it, supposing that these various things only happened so this person would die. Teleology is fundamentally hierarchical.

While Spinoza decries the "foolish wonder" and "ignorance" of those who attribute what happens in reality to the whims of a transcendent Ruler who Orders it, it is not difficult to appreciate the allure of such beliefs. Consider the case of the person killed by the stone: to make sense of this tragic death, it may be comforting to believe that it was *meant to be*, intended, directed, and executed by a God sovereignly overseeing reality, much as it may be consoling to maintain that the human body was *made* to be as it is, that its functions were planned and purposive, rather than being the effects of countless modal causes, interacting and coalescing without any Design or Director. There is a certain irony here: precisely our lack of transcendence, our inability to command reality, not to mention, far more narrowly, to fully control ourselves, prompts humans to contrive fictions of transcendence. Being radically *of* nature, embedded in the infinite connection of causes, induces people to imagine an Other who is *beyond* causal determinism, *above* nature. To cope with non-transcendence, humans contrive Transcendences: gods, *teloi*, order.

Breaking the Law

Much as Spinoza vitiates the notion of a Sovereign captaining reality, spurning conceptions of an Order and End in nature, his ontology is accordingly divested of the Laws of Nature. This might sound curious, considering that Spinoza refers to "laws of nature." However, what I am suggesting is that considering both his critique of teleology, combined with his conception of the infinity attached to substance, such "laws" cannot be construed as regulatory, predetermined, or fixed. They are not prescriptive but *descriptive*, signifying the ways in which nature acts—how the infinite connection of causes *is*—not how it ought to be. Likewise, such laws cannot denote ordinances by means of which reality is governed. This is the case for three primary reasons. The first is that the infinity of substance proscribes limitations. There can be no "laws" outside (nothing is beyond substance) or inside substance that constrain it. The second is that laws in the prescriptive sense presuppose antecedence. Yet with infinite substance, "there is neither *when*, nor *before*, nor *after*."[84] Substance does not precede its acts; it *is* its acts. Relatedly, the third ground for why these "laws" cannot be Laws is simply because this would presuppose all of the teleological trappings that Spinoza denounces: a plan to which reality bends, an order that it obeys, a model to which it bows.

Before explicating the valence connoted by "laws of nature" in the *Ethics*, a bit of context is due. The "laws of nature" figure prominently in discussions of Divine providence and power: If nature is ordered and bound by certain laws, then where and how does God's omnipotence figure? Such concerns are irrelevant to Spinoza but vexed many a medieval theologian and their early modern heirs. With the advance of the "Scientific Revolution" these questions gained traction: "Throughout the seventeenth century, a new concept of 'laws of nature' gave a new urgency and vigor to the old, almost exhausted, distinction between God's absolute and ordained power."[85] These factors configured Descartes's influential three laws governing the motion and change of bodies: "The rules by which these changes take place I call the 'laws of nature.'"[86] For Descartes, these laws presuppose a Lawgiver; they are ordained and sustained by God's concurrence and immutability;[87] they order nature; they are consistent; and, finally, knowledge of these laws is possible only because God has endowed humans with the capacity to know them.[88] Though Spinoza is able to concede that laws like Descartes's might signify certain features of reality, he cannot accept the sovereignties anchoring this scheme.

Most of Spinoza's references to "the common *leges* of nature" in the *Ethics* surface in his polemic against Cartesian voluntarism, specifically the claim that the mind transcends the body and is sovereign over it. Humans are not exceptions to nature; their feelings, thoughts, and actions are causally determined because "the laws and rules [*leges et regulae*] of nature, according to which all things happen . . . are always and everywhere the same."[89] Therefore, the "way of understanding the nature of anything . . . must also be the same."[90] Spinoza's point is that humans, like everything, are subject to causal determination. This is what he means in saying, "the *leges* [laws] of nature concern the common *ordinem* [order] of nature, of which human is a part."[91] Or that a human "is a part of the whole of nature, whose *legibus* [laws] human nature is compelled to obey."[92] There is no transcendence from our bodies, no retreat from nature. Reason allows us to appreciate that "all things follow from the necessity of the divine nature . . . according to the eternal *leges et regulas* of nature."[93] Repudiating dualist transcendence also stands behind Spinoza's retort to people who cannot believe that buildings and paintings are caused by "the laws [*legibus*] of nature alone."[94]

In his *Theological-Political Treatise*, Spinoza distinguishes between *legis*, which derive from "a necessity of nature or a human decision"[95] and "*lex* which depends on a necessity of nature," meaning it "follows necessarily from the very nature *or* definition of a thing."[96] To depict such laws, Spinoza mentions, "a universal law of all bodies,"[97] which is essentially Descartes's third law of motion. But Spinoza also offers this example: "a law which necessarily follows from human nature that when a human recalls one thing, they immediately recall another like it, or one they had perceived together with the first thing."[98] Both Descartes's third law of motion and Spinoza's theory of memory association are laws that "follow from a necessity of nature."[99] While the latter has not been identified as a Law and codified like Descartes's, both are equally "laws" to Spinoza in that they describe how modes intra-act due to necessary, immanent, causal determinations.

It is instructive to revisit Spinoza's correspondence with Oldenburg, who extends regards from Robert Boyle. This is noteworthy considering Boyle's embrace of teleology, having penned *A Disquisition About the Final Causes of Natural Things*. Writing on their behalf, Oldenburg presses Spinoza to explain how "each part of nature agrees with its whole."[100] In a previous letter, Spinoza had divulged that he does not know how everything coheres in nature and underscored the constraints of his standpoint, how things in reality do not comport with the ordered models of a "philosophical mind." Spinoza further bared that although he once mocked or bemoaned certain human behaviors, now he accepts "each to live according to their own mentality," for humans are *of* nature, not an exception to its ways.[101]

Spinoza prefaces his response to their pressuring with this admonition: "I attribute to nature neither beauty nor ugliness, neither order nor confusion. . . . For only in relation to our imagination can things be called beautiful or ugly, ordered or confused."[102] Turning to directly address Oldenburg's question, he proceeds: "By the coherence of parts, then, I understand nothing but that the *leges sive* [the laws or] the nature of the one part adapts itself to the laws *or* the nature of the other part so that they are opposed to each other as little as possible."[103] Notice the *sive*, which redefines what is meant by "laws" in reference to nature. Laws are nothing but adaptations and coherences because whatever happens in nature happens due to causal intra-actions.

Through enacting agreements, Spinoza elaborates, singular modes and parts of modes cohere provisionally in ways that can be regarded as forming a "whole," whereas through disagreements, they seem to constitute, to our minds, distinct "parts." The point is not only that "wholes" and "parts" are distinctions of reason but that everything that happens is contingent upon necessary causal effects. Instead of conceiving modal intra-actions as ordained by transcendent regulations and teleological norms, infinity commands their immanence: "Laws" are the indeterminate ways that determinate modes *are*.

Spinoza's reduction of the "laws" of nature to how nature acts[104] coincides with his reduction of the power of substance to its necessity: "God acts from the *legibus* of its nature alone, and is compelled by no one."[105] Thus, "from the necessity of the divine nature alone, or (what is the same thing) from the *legibus* of God's nature alone, absolutely infinite things follow."[106] The "laws" are causal necessity. As with substance, so with modes.

There is a further aspect to Spinoza's resistance to the "laws" of nature: his discreditation of generalities and universals. The reification of the "laws" of nature suffers the constraints of "terms called Transcendental" and "notions they call universal."[107] These misrepresent reality, precipitating confusion. By contrast, understanding things distinctly encompasses knowledge of efficient causation and perception of things in their singularity.[108]

Despite Spinoza's explanatory labors, his non-teleological and non-normative conception of reality was unappreciated by his correspondent: "I do not sufficiently follow how we can eliminate the order and symmetry from nature, as you seem to do."[109] Oldenburg accurately grasps that Spinoza's theory dispenses with "order and symmetry" in nature. This is precisely its point. Order is a mode of the imagination, an anthropic artifice that misrepresents reality. Moreover, Oldenburg also misses what Spinoza communicates about the infinite connection of causes: that *how* things are is *what* they are. That "laws" are immanent and descriptive rather than transcendent and prescriptive. The necessity of the infinite connection of causes is not due to any laws or regulations but simply because it is how things *are*. Why a mode is as it is, is so on account of its imbrication in the causal interconnections that are reality, absent decrees or laws or guarantees. Causes and reasons coincide, and efficient causation is the reason that anything is as it is.

Evidently, Spinoza's employment of the "laws of nature" divests it of sovereign baggage: there is no Lawgiver; these "laws" do not preexist their enactment, which means that they are not ordinances but descriptions of how modes causally intra-act; such "laws" are not fixed and so resist systematization. Infinity and immanence generate an ontology deprived of both a Ruler and Rules. While certain scholars continue to ascribe normativity to Spinoza's ontology,[110] even those who appreciate that his "laws" are merely descriptive retain language that reinforces the very normativity he disrupts. For example, Pina Totaro recognizes that for Spinoza "laws do not establish, but they describe"[111] but proceeds to speak of "causal relations that govern,"[112] "the mandatory character of the mechanical laws of nature,"[113] and "codified praxis."[114] Such terminology of governance, mandates, and codification ratifies the very features of normativity that Spinoza vetoes.

Normativity and norms are inherently supremacist. Even without a Sovereign, the institution of Laws functions sovereignly by presupposing that laws are essentially different from all else in nature and therefore dominant. Normative laws of nature are necessarily transcendent to nature and so contravene immanence. Normative laws are regulatory; they limit, constrain, and contain reality, subverting the infinity constitutive of it. Normative laws are teleological; they function as ends awaiting fulfillment and stand above nature, which undercut immanence and infinity. Normative laws are of the limited anthropic perspective, derived from human desires, experience, and particularities rather than how reality actually is. Spinoza's ontology simply cannot admit normative, fixed, regulatory Laws of nature.

Out with the Ordinary

There is a further aspect to Spinoza's discreditation of the normativity attached to the Laws of nature and his disavowal of the teleological fiction that reality is ordered. This concerns what I suggest amounts to a contestation of another form of normativity: claims that anything in nature is "normative" or "normal." Without a Sovereign controlling nature, without sovereign Laws to regulate it, and without a sovereign End and Order to organize it, there is no space for normativity. The modes that exist and how they exist are so beyond the constraints of the supposed "normal" and "abnormal," "ideal" and "nonideal," "regular" and "irregular," "typical" and "atypical." Without teleology and its sovereignties, these notions cannot obtain ontologically. These constructs, just like that of goodness and badness, ugliness and beauty, perfection and imperfection, are human contrivances that derive from subjective values and do not reflect how reality actually is.

Since reality does not submit to any model and the infinite connection of causes acts without prescription, guidance, or rubrics, normative judgments are invalidated. People "are accustomed to form universal ideas of natural things as much as they do artificial ones.... So when they see something happen in nature which does not agree with the model they have conceived ... they believe that nature itself has failed or sinned, and left the thing imperfect."[115] This is what happens when people compare "individuals of the same species or genus to one another" and "find that some have more being, *or* reality, than others" and thus are more perfect.[116] However, "nothing belongs to the nature of anything except what follows from the necessity of the nature of the efficient cause. And whatever follows from the necessity of the nature of the efficient cause happens necessarily."[117] This is why, as cited above, to Spinoza, "reality and perfection" signify "the same thing."[118] How things are is the only way they can be for there is no potential in nature as power is only ever actualized.

There is a further problematic element in rendering teleological, "normative" judgments: these rely on, as the foregoing notes, "terms called transcendental" which "signify ideas that are confused in the highest degree."[119] To Spinoza, "notions they call Universal, like Human, Horse, Dog, etc.,"[120] mislead and misrepresent by making it seem as if these categories adhere ontologically, independent of anthropic systemizing. Nature is of "particular things," rather than categories, genuses, or classes. This is why it is mistaken to think of the "Human," or the "Horse," or the "Dog," let alone to measure singular humans, horses, and dogs by these confused, subjective, anthropic categories.

"Normativity" cannot obtain ontologically, and its contrivance emerges from epistemic missteps. By approaching reality as infinite and so immanent, Spinoza reputes the transcendence and teleology attendant to notions that what exists is the product of an Overseer, Plan, or Model or that it is secured by regulations, governances, and ordinances. In the absence of these sovereignties, it makes no sense to categorize what modes are and how they are in terms not merely of "normativity" but also through related notions of "deviance" and "divergence." Without an Originary state or an Ordained modality of being, neither Designer nor Design, such notions are incoherent. The appendix, as we have seen, incisively dissects the conditions and rationales subsidizing notions of perfection and imperfection, goodness and badness, normal and abnormal. This proffers, I suggest, a generative frame for critiquing specific forms of sexism, racism, and ableism. To be clear, Spinoza does not address these ideologies, and passing remarks in his writings evidence his embrace of certain sexist, racist,[121] and ableist[122] stereotypes. Nevertheless, his analysis of teleology and the transcendences upon which it rests, coupled with his approach to how people come to hold such beliefs and why they retain them, is salient.

Teleology relies on supremacy; it renders what exists subordinate to a specific purpose, end, or function. This is how causes and effects become confused. The purport that the human body is structured, Spinoza explains, presupposes that its constituent parts—its various organs, different tissues, individual cells—are subservient to the functioning of the Whole. The fiction that nature is ordered implicitly subjects what is, to the sovereignty of an Order. What exists is but a means to a particular telos. Hierarchy is endemic to teleology. To uphold a "normal" or "model" or "perfect" way in which a mode is to be subjects its being to that metric. Moreover, in order for there to be an Ideal, there must be a Modeler—providential Overseer—or at least a Model—supreme Plan—that precedes it and towards which it submits. Sexist, racist, and ableist ideologies are teleological in presuming exactly this: that there are more ideal and less ideal humans. But the teleology and sovereignty associated with these ideologies extends further. Identifying a specific biological feature and then essentializing it grants priority to this specific feature, rendering all of the other features of that person or the "whole" of that person secondary to the priority of that feature.

By discrediting teleology, Spinoza confirms, in the first instance, that nature is without Meaning: how it is and what it is are effects of causal intraactions of the infinite connection of causes. Yet humans, because of anthropocentrism, "believe that all things have been made for their sake, and call the nature of a thing good or evil, sound or rotten and corrupt, as they are affected by it."[123] Rather than accepting that nature is purposeless, directionless, and meaningless, people impute value onto its acts, often without realizing that these are contrived. So, "they had to judge that what is most important in each thing is what is most useful to them, and to rate as most excellent those things by which they were most pleased."[124] Instead of accepting that what exists is so without Reason or Purpose, humans prefer to rate modes of nature based on how they serve *their* needs and satisfy *their* predilections. Such interpretations are driven by human desires and experiences, which presume that what is and how it is are *meaningful*. But such meaning, too, is anthropically contrived. To wit, certain people observe biological variations across different humans and teleologically impute meaning *onto* these differences. Thereby, a particular feature is upheld as a microcosm of its whole or as encapsulating some higher meaning, gesturing towards something essential about that being or how that being is to be.

What is observed in nature is not simply conditioned by our contexts but carries meaning *specific* to that context. Phenomena like "storms, earthquakes, diseases"[125] are seen as punishments by God only because the observer is embedded in a context that believes in a Sovereign god. A fish is perceived as existing for human consumption only within a network of established anthropocentric commitments. Spinoza observes: "Nature created individuals, not nations, individuals who are distinguished into nations only by differences of language, laws and accepted customs. Only the latter two factors, laws and customs, can lead a nation to have its specific mentality, its specific character, and its specific prejudices."[126] Ontologically, only singular modes exist for "only the particulars have a cause, not the universals, because they are nothing."[127] The constructs of Nations, Races, and Sexgenders are universals, transcendentals contrived by humans bent on classifying reality.

Observing variations across different humans and attaching meaning to these is only sensible within the context of a system of already established beliefs. Thus, variations in the amount of melanin present in singular human modes only becomes a *meaningful* difference within a social context and the hierarchies structuring it. Racist ideologies have staying power because they serve those who propagate them. As Spinoza details with regard to miracles, those who disprove miracles are "denounced" because the truth undermines the authority of those in power. Moreover, bodily variations are "observed" *because* they benefit those observing them. What humans notice in nature and how they interpret it are derived from whatever they deem "useful."[128] Our interpretations of nature are anything but neutral. They reflect our preferences and desires, which are shaped by what advantages us. If this point seems transparent to our contemporary standpoints, this is a testament to the influence of the critical theorizing that Spinoza practices and has inspired diverse heirs, including Marx, Nietzsche, Freud, Deleuze, Althusser, and Butler. Spinoza's observations solicit not simply a recognition that nature does not deliver, say, abled bodies, "male" bodies, or white bodies but an interrogation of what drives the construction and naturalization of these hierarchical categories. As Frantz Fanon renders with regard to race: "*It is the racist who creates the inferiorized.*"[129] The division of human modes into racial classes secures the supremacy of those sovereignly contriving these differences. Thus, Achille Mbeme observes: "Modern colonization was a direct outcome of doctrines that consisted in sorting humans into groups:

those who counted and who were counted, on the one hand, and, on the other hand, 'the rest,' those who were called 'detritus of men' or 'wastes of men.'"[130]

Spinoza's entire philosophy is rooted in his ontology. After adumbrating it in part I, the appendix shows readers *why* people maintain false beliefs about reality, which prepares them for his subsequent focus on how we think, how we feel, how we act and, in light of this, how best to live. Therefore, recognizing, for example, that race does not adhere ontologically, that it is not a "natural" category, is only the start to addressing how it has become meaningful, how it has come to matter, and how it licenses exploitation. So, while Spinozism certainly accords with Kwame Anthony Appiah's claim that "nobody has a race" because "there are no races"[131]—that is, ontologically—the critical thrust of Spinoza's project invites a posture more aligned with Charles Mills's recognition that while racial categories "correspond to no natural kinds," they "attain a social reality."[132] Appreciating that race is contrived, constructed, and entirely contingent—that it does not adhere ontologically—is only the start to grappling with the meaning that it obtains and the supremacist functions that it serves.

Unsexing

There is no reason to apologize for, explain away, or diminish Spinoza's sexism. It is real. To be clear, I am suspicious of efforts to plumb the so-called canon merely to excavate materials that might confirm the truths that many have only now come to grasp. Much as Spinoza casts aspersions upon the need to rely on the authority of other philosophers to validate his views,[133] I, too, do not seek the authority of Spinoza to confirm my queer conceptions of sexgender. But I am keen to think *with* Spinoza. I regard his critique of teleology and the epistemic missteps that precipitate it as generative for probing sexgender. I am not alone. Feminist philosophers have turned to Spinoza to theorize sexgender.[134] Here, I build on their contributions, while in the following section, I scrutinize the feminisms of sexual difference that several of them advance.

In the absence of a Sovereign god or Sovereign guidelines, what modes exist and how they exist are so without any model or norm. There is no Order to what is. Despite the anthropic impulse to contrive order by dividing modes into distinct classes and species, to Spinoza these are but "modes of the imagination." The categories of sexgender are no exception. Neither "sex" nor "gender" exist in nature. Spinoza's ontology disallows for *ontological* sexgender, much as it does *ontological* race, *ontological* abledness, *ontological* beauty, or *ontological* goodness. None of this is to deny that different human modes have different anatomical, biological, and chromosomal features. The point is that perceiving such differences as foundational, essential, defining, fixed, or determinate is a teleological delusion. Thus, Moira Gatens is right to allow, "it is arguable that the notion of ontological sexual difference belongs to a system of classification (genus, species, kind) that is quite foreign to Spinoza's thought."[135] But the case is stronger: it is not "arguable," it is so.

Categories are teleological. Transcendent universals presuppose teleological purposiveness. As Spinoza explicates, "it cannot rightly be said that there is confusion in nature" because such beliefs are engendered by "the fact that humans have formed universal ideas, with which they think the particulars must agree in order to be perfect."[136] This is typified by Plato's contention that "universal ideas . . . have been created by God,"[137] or by Aristotle who upholds the actuality of transcendent, universal categories, maintaining that God's "providence does not extend to particulars, but only to kinds."[138] By contrast, for Spinoza, God "is a cause of, and provider for, only particular things."[139] This is because "if particular things have to agree with another nature, they will not be able to agree with their own, and consequently will not be able to be what they truly are."[140] Accordingly, "Peter must agree with the idea of Peter . . . and not with the idea of human."[141] To Spinoza, there are only particular, singular beings each of which is causally necessary and so perfect: "All things and actions which are in nature are perfect."[142] This is why the third way of knowing entails perceiving singular modes non-teleologically: as they exist, in and of themselves, independent of categories, criteria, and classes. Hence, "the more we understand singular things, the more we understand God"[143] *or* nature *or* reality.

In assailing transcendentals and universals, Spinoza underscores how they are "confused in the highest degree."[144] The imaginary category of "human" erases "slight differences" between individual humans, privileging "what they all agree in."[145] Classifying modes based on determinate categories necessarily erases particularities in favor of commonalities. Furthermore, the similarities registered—the features that become sovereign—are those that are "most common" and most "affect the body" of the classifier.[146] What the observer discerns is conditioned by what is familiar to them, based on their own experiences even as they "predicate it of infinite many singulars."[147] These constraints of classification are salient to sexgender. The bioscientific categories of "female" and "male" are not simply transcendent contrivances, which by definition cannot reflect matters as they really are, but this binary system is constitutionally incapable of accommodating the "slight differences" of singular humans. Moreover, as Spinoza underscores, such universal "notions are not formed by all in the same way."[148] Concerning the universal category "human," he writes: "Those who have more often regarded human's stature with wonder will understand by the word human an animal of erect stature. But those who have been accustomed to consider something else, will form another common image of a human—e.g., that a human is an animal capable of laughter, or a featherless biped, or a rational animal."[149] There is no consensus on what "human" signifies, much as there is no agreement on the definition of any universal or transcendent notion as "each will form universal images of things according to the disposition of their body."[150] Therefore, "it is not surprising that so many controversies have arisen among the philosophers, who have wished to explain natural things by mere images of things."[151] And so it is with sexgender: there is no consensus about what qualifies as so-called "male" and "female," not to say the least of "woman" and "man."

The binary system of sexgender classification exemplifies the perils that Spinoza delineates as inherent to universal notions. It also typifies the ways in which nature refuses to bend itself to our categories, repeatedly validating that "order in nature" is nothing but "a relation to our imagination."[152] What is "male" and what is "female"? Much as Spinoza demonstrates with the category "human," determining sex depends on whom you ask: Is the difference anatomical? Chromosomal? Hormonal? Something else? There is no agreement on the matter. The fact that tens of millions of people—at least 1.7 percent of humans[153]—do not "satisfy" the "conventional" metrics for assigning "sex" underscores the imprecision, contingency, and failure of this classificatory system. The routinely perceived "ambiguity" displayed by the anatomical "markers" of certain individuals, not to mention the regular "disagreement" between a given person's "sex traits," betrays the fallaciousness of these sovereign constructs. Moreover, the coerced surgical manipulation of anatomical organs or imposed endocrinal interventions on the bodies of those who do not neatly fit into these narrow strictures epitomizes the dangers of teleology: "When they see something happen in nature which does not agree with the model they have conceived of this kind of thing, they believe that nature itself has failed or sinned, and left the thing imperfect."[154]

The medical policing and manipulation of intersex bodies to accord with the contrived, "universal," sovereign model of what a body should be is a case in point.

Interventions to discipline intersex bodies show not merely the speciousness of binary sexgender categories, they demonstrate a further deficiency in teleological reasoning. According to estimates, the number of intersex people in the world is roughly the same as the number of people with red hair. Now, there is no programmatic effort to police the bodies of redheaded individuals to conform with the rest of us blonde-, brown-, and black-haired people. This is because red hair is not "universally" perceived as "deviant" and thus in need of "correction." Such disparity signifies the contingency, subjectivity, and conditioned nature of which "ideals" are esteemed and which are not. This seems quite obvious. But there is more here: the fact that certain bodily features are perceived as in need of "fixing," whereas other differences are seen as insignificant so as to evade "correction," is a consequence of teleological conceits. Teleology privileges the whole *over* the part, functionalizing constitutive parts as serving the sovereign Whole that in this instance is measured against a transcendent Model. Interventions to "correct" "sex" organs rather than red hair exemplify the extent to which humans essentialize "sex" organs, reducing people to *these* features. This convention relies on the teleological reduction of humans to a specific feature or capacity that they seem to exhibit: often, in such cases, the capacity to procreate. This privileging is underwritten by the implicit assumption that these "organs" exist *in order to* enable procreation. But there is no order or end in nature, no Designer or Design. These so-called sex organs exist and they happen to be crucial to reproduction, but they do not exist *for this purpose*. Moreover, while these organs play an unparalleled role in the *process* of reproduction, they are only able to do so *as parts* of a web of interconnected bodily organs and systems, which intra-act through agreements and disagreements, in the absence of Guidance or Goals.

Similar teleological rationales are operative in related attempts to discipline certain humans by forcing them into conformity with specific transcendent ideals and norms. This is especially apparent in violence against trans individuals, legislation against trans youth, and the resistance to adjusting cisnormative society not only to accommodate trans people but to facilitate their flourishing. While the anti-trans movement is diverse, a trademark of its ideology is the reliance on teleological reductionism and biological essentialism. The notion that bodies are "naturally" sexed is a teleological fiction. Transphobic dogma tends to reduce humans to the so-called reproductive organs, presuming that the presence or absence of certain features determines a person's "sex" and thus also who and how they are to be in life. The teleology in this calculus is threefold. First, the identification of a certain biological feature and the claim that this feature is what "sexes" a person instrumentalize a mode of the human body, assuming that it exists *for a reason*, that it is purposive, intended to be so. The second teleological move is the reduction of the entirety of a given human to this aspect of their body, subordinating their entire being to this feature, which is deemed as *essential*. Here an essence is taken as sovereign over existence. The third is the presumption that all of this amounts to a teleological determination of how a given person is to be: prescribing a purpose, end, or function to them. Of course, the very construct of "sex" teleologically presupposes a transcendent Model or Ideal of what and how a "sexed" human is to be. Accordingly teleological is the notion that nature abides by certain norms, that its acts decide and predetermine how a singular mode is intended to be and so how it *ought* to be.

Reality, for Spinoza is nonbinary. The organs and features that manifest in humans, which humans interpret as "sexed," are not "naturally" so. These are effects of the infinite connection of causes, which exists and acts independent of purpose or plan. There is no "sex" as such in nature. Thus, it is not simply that no one is born a "boy" or "girl." Neither are they born "female" or "male." These are transcendent constructs, sovereign models of how humans *should* be that are contrived by certain humans to justify their regimes of control. Spinoza's ontology, on this score, aligns with Butler's observation that "sex" has been "gender all along."[155] Taking Spinoza's critique of teleology seriously demands the denaturalization of "sex." Crucially, this is not to deny the embodied nature of modal existence. Just because nature does not deliver "sexed" bodies, this does not mean that bodies do not become "sexed," inhabit "sex," or live "sex." But here too, a Spinozist take invites nuance. Since mind and body "are one and the same thing," neither exists without its other and neither is precedent over its other. To be human is to be a bodied mind or minded body. There is no Cartesian transcendence of the mind *from* the body, no thinking that is not attached to a body, no human that is not a body. And bodies, as much as minds, are imbricated with other minds and bodies. No mode exists in isolation. To be, for Spinoza, is always to be with other modes, to be entangled in the infinite connection of causes. And so, sexgender is born.

Spinoza anatomizes transcendent universals, undertaking to clarify "which notions are more useful than the others, and which are of hardly any use and then, which are common, which are clear and distinct only to those who have no prejudices, and finally, which are ill-founded."[156] This critique reminds us of the contingency of our classifications, turning attention to how their very construction serves those who contrive them. Spinoza denaturalizes anthropic classifications of nature, spotlighting the ways in which it facilitates domination, elides differences, and punishes "deviance." From a Spinozist perspective, the construct and classification of "sex" are not exceptional. "Sex" is not inherently different from other universals. There is nothing special, fixed, or essential about it. Furthermore, Spinoza's commentary exposes how taxonomies often fail abysmally; actual human modes tend to defy their strict but extremely subjective criteria. As we have seen, the abstract, transcendent category of "sex" is without a coherent or consistent referent. By spotlighting the subjectivity and contingency of categorizations, Spinoza pushes us to probe which classifications become sovereign and why, to consider whose interests these ratify and whose they disregard. The upshot of this analysis is that "sex" does not exist ontologically and that "sex" is not binary. Only "particular things" exist "not the universals, because they are nothing."[157] Insomuch as "sex" does not adhere ontologically, it may be said to follow that really, all of us are genderqueer.

Pertinently, Spinoza's critique solicits pause with regard to the binary categorization of transgender or "cisgender." This classification effectively fixes everyone who is not trans or not *yet* trans into the straitjacket of "cisness," reifying cisness and ontologizing it. Promoting the flourishing of trans people ought to be possible without coercing everyone else into the rigid, fabricated strictures of "cisness." Furthermore, "cisness" often functions as a default norm, positioning transness as exceptional, deviant, and nonnormative. The promotion of sexgender nonbinariness, similarly, misleadingly implies that binary gender inheres in reality and that everyone who is not nonbinary or not yet nonbinary is binary. Nonbinariness binarily positions its others as its fixed opposite. I am not suggesting that everyone who identifies as nonbinary is binarizing sexgender or that everyone who is not nonbinary is effectively binary. My aim is to underscore the imperfections and repercussions of classifications and highlight not merely their instabilities but the sovereignties they install, whether intended or not. Caution is needed in deploying even categories intended to be liberatory. Queering sexgender, from a Spinozist perspective, entails uncovering the contingency of taxonomical classifications like cisness, interrogating their constraints and effects, much as it encompasses denaturalizing the sexgender binary. It accordingly invites us to affirm not only the variability of sexgender between different people but also within an individual, recognizing how contexts, experiences, and desires continuously shape and reshape our ways of being, including our sexgenders.

Gender Trouble

Spinoza's ontology urges the denaturalization of "sex," recognizing the category as an anthropic contrivance that misrepresents reality. Startlingly, however, certain feminist readers of Spinoza, rather than denaturalizing "sex," renaturalize it. Interrogating their commentaries not only allows us to rectify their missteps but punctuates how readily "sex" is naturalized even by those seemingly committed to its deconstruction. This is the case with the interpretations of Genevieve Lloyd and Gatens, which deploy Spinoza's conception of the imagination and the interconnection of modes to critique patriarchal systems. In so doing, they champion a feminism of sexual difference, claiming support for it in Spinoza's resistance to Cartesianism.

To Descartes, the dualism of mind and body upholds minds as transcendent to bodies, which establishes reason as disembodied and undifferentiated. This indicates, Lloyd adduces, that for Descartes, there are sexed bodies but "sexless minds."[158] By contrast, she argues, "Spinoza's view of the mind-body relationship opens up conceptual space for the possibility that minds are sexually differentiated."[159] What does this mean? As Lloyd sees it: "To the extent that the powers and pleasures of human bodies are sexually differentiated, it will then be quite appropriate for a Spinozist to speak of 'male' and 'female' minds."[160] I confess that to this Spinozist—me—such a contention is unconvincing. It is certainly true, as Lloyd argues, that socialization, for Spinoza, impacts minds, making them "different."[161] The problem is that she does not restrict such differences to socialization but avouches that anatomical "sex" differences "undoubtedly" exist and concludes that we are "differently sexed."[162] To Lloyd, "there is more to being a male or female body than anatomy."[163] But what exactly is it to be a "male" or "female" body? And why is this presumed to be a neutral categorization? As she has it, "sex differences" result from "different ways of experiencing the commonalities of human life, and there is of course more involved in this than the physical differences of male and female bodies."[164] She accepts the physical differences of "male" and "female" as ontologically given, while presuming a consensus on what precisely these are. Lloyd claims: "Sex differences for Spinoza apply to minds no less than to bodies. But that need not involve the affirmation of any male or female content, existing independently of operations of power."[165] While I appreciate her non-essentialism regarding the content of what might make a mind "female" or "male," she problematically leaves these constructs uninterrogated. She allows that the *content* of what it means to be "male" or "female" does not *necessarily* exist outside "operations of power," but nevertheless supposes that there is something biologically, anatomically, ontologically "male" or "female," even if its significance might be predominantly social. Lloyd proclaims, "as embodied human beings, we are embodied as different sexes"[166] but concedes that "such affirmations of difference risk 'naturalizing'—and hence rationalizing and perpetuating—some of the content of existing sexual stereotypes."[167] Lloyd is absolutely right that naturalizing "sex" risks naturalizing the sociocultural stereotypes attached to such differences. The way to avoid this is to *not* naturalize "sex" as she does.

Since for Spinoza, "a mode of extension and the idea of that mode are one and the same thing,"[168] all thinking is embodied and situated. Lloyd is entirely justified in presenting Spinoza as an alternative to Cartesian dualism. To Spinoza, mind only knows *as* its body, which means that its ideas, which are it, are conditioned by concrete social, cultural, economic, and political contexts. While Lloyd recognizes as much, she mistakenly regards "sex" as ontological, supposing that it has ramifications for the mind independent of socialization, which, she alleges, delivers specific, definable, non-trivial "powers and pleasures."[169] Moreover, although she insists that "sex" influences the mind, she never tells us what this is nor accounts for why it would impact the mind more than any other biological feature, in and of itself.

There is a similar naturalization of "sex" operative in Gatens's treatment of Spinoza. While she probes the social mechanisms promoting sexism, she nevertheless, both counterintuitively and counterproductively, renaturalizes "sex" and its binarization. Not only do we hear of "both sexes"[170] and "the opposite sex"[171] but also of "relations between the sexes"[172] and "love between the sexes."[173] What these "sexes" are, why there are but two, and how these categories are determined is left unclarified. Trying to retreat from "dualistic understandings of sexual difference (sex/gender)," Gatens asks, "How would a Spinozist theorize the sex/gender distinction?"[174] Her answer: "Sex, in some sense, must be gender, though 'expressed' or made manifest through the attribute of extension rather than thought."[175] Sex and gender are here conceived as different aspects of the same: "Gender is both a power and an affect of a certain modification of the attribute of extension."[176] The asset of this reading, she says, is that "both sex and gender, as parallel descriptions of modified nature, will be definable in relational terms only."[177] She then qualifies: "Given that there is no causal relation between the attributes, the sex of a body does not and cannot cause its gender."[178]

Whereas Gatens ascribes parallelism to Spinoza's attributes, as the following chapter probes, I pressure as much, recognizing that mind and body are irreducible aspects of the same. Although Gatens is right that "sex" does not *cause* "gender," her presumption that "sex" is strictly a mode of extension, whereas "gender" is a mode of thought, is a claim that she leaves unsubstantiated. What makes "sex" exclusively of the body? And how does "sex," a human classification—a "being of reason"[179]—inhere in extension? With this, Gatens, like Lloyd, renaturalizes "sex" and essentializes bodies to their "sexed" differences, even as she resigns from explicating what it is that "sexes" a body. This is a curious position for Gatens to occupy because elsewhere in this collection of essays—originally published at different times—she allows "that the sexed body is not a product of nature but is rather constituted as dichotomously sexed through elaborate and pervasive practices that act on and through the body."[180] Clearly, she recognizes, at least as a cogent argument, that "sex" is not *given*. Further, for Spinoza, Gatens summarizes, "The body does not have a 'truth' or a 'true' nature ... its meaning and capacities will vary according to its context."[181] In the book's preface, she worries "that an insistence on ontological sexual difference leads into the cul de sac of essentialism, where sexual difference is privileged over all other differences."[182] It is true that implicit to essentialism is the privileging of one difference over all others and the concomitant reduction of an individual to that difference. But essentialism is also present simply in the discernment of a difference and the insistence on its inherent significance, even without electing it as Sovereign over all other differences. This is precisely what Gatens seems to be doing: she assumes such a thing as "biological sex" and supposes that it exists causally separate from "gender." Presuming "sexed" difference independent of "modes of thinking" is essentialist.

Despite what seem like her efforts to render "sex" contingent and constructed, Gatens's analyses naturalize and essentialize it. This is apparent in her 1983 essay, "A Critique of the Sex/Gender Distinction."[183] Therein, she advocates for a "feminism based on difference."[184] Since "there is no neutral body, there are at least two kinds of bodies: the male body and the female body."[185] While I appreciate Gatens's allowance that there might be more than two "sexes"—"at least"—on what basis is she concluding that bodies are inherently "sexed"? Not only does she never tell us what determines "sex," but her reasoning presupposes that whatever it is, it is sufficient to unequivocally *determine* someone's "sex." Furthermore, she professes: "Gender is not the issue; sexual difference is."[186] It is not clear how "sex" could be so easily disaggregated from "gender," nor how someone who set out to unsettle the "sex/gender distinction" could be so eager to reinscribe it. But Gatens continues: "The very same behaviours (whether they be masculine or feminine) have quite different personal and social significances when acted out by the male subject on the one hand and the female subject on the other."[187] This is because "attitudes or, if you will, conditioning acquire different significance when applied to male or female subjects."[188] The argument here is quite circular: "sex" needs to be upheld because "sexed" bodies are conditioned to behave certain ways and behaviors carry differentiated "significance" based on the "sex" of the individual performing them. If this "significance" is conditioned, then why must fidelity to it be retained? And further, why is it that those who question the "naturalness," inevitability, and contingency of "sex" are effectively ignoring that it is socially conditioned? Would they not be suggesting precisely the opposite? *Because* it is conditioned, it is therefore available for "reconditioning."

It is instructive to take a closer look at Gatens's resistance to what she calls "the naive simplicity of degendering."[189] The problem is that "there is a contingent, though not arbitrary, relation between the male body and masculinity and the female body and femininity."[190] To assert this, she contends, "is neither biologism nor essentialism" but "to acknowledge the importance of complex and ubiquitous networks of signification to the historically, psychologically and culturally variable ways of being a man or woman."[191] It is certainly true that sexgender is shaped by context. It is equally true that within the "Western" culture from which she speaks, "femininity" and "masculinity" are conventionally attached to so-called male and female bodies. But to suppose that this is "contingent, though not arbitrary" is ludicrous. It redounds in the dangerous claim she then makes that "masculinity and femininity" are not "conditioned forms of behavior."[192] Instead, "'masculinity' and 'femininity' correspond at the level of the imaginary body to 'male' and 'female' at the level of biology."[193] So, the biological *mirrors* the imaginary, with the caveat that all of this is a matter of "historical specificity."[194] (Here we see the beginnings of what Gatens later maps onto Spinoza's attributes: "sex" is of extension, which is expressed parallelly in thought, as "gender"). If it is the case that such constructs are contingent upon context, what is gained by reinforcing such norms? According to Gatens's calculus, "to deny... the specificity of historical forms of femininity and masculinity in favour of a conception of the subject as essentially sex-neutral will lead to the reproduction of present relations between the sexes."[195] To Gatens, seeking to overcome these oppressive binaries—sex and gender, mind and body, femininity and masculinity—amounts to the denial of the historical conditions that create and sustain these very constructs. On the contrary, only by acknowledging as much can there be a possibility of correcting for its injustices. Moreover, she avouches that moves towards "sex-neutral" postures would reproduce "present relations between the sexes," by which I take it she means hierarchical relations. If "sex" becomes "neutral" then how could it reproduce currently "sexed" conditions? Such a claim is only tenable if one maintains that "sex" is "natural," that it is biologically determined, and that it ordains a whole host of attendant behaviors. This is *precisely* what biological essentialism is, what naturalizing "sex" accomplishes.

Decrying feminists who suppose that certain professions are invested with prestige *because* these professions are predominantly occupied by men, proposing that "social value" is primarily determined by *who* does something rather than what it is that is done, Gatens argues: "The problem is not the socialization of women to femininity and men to masculinity but the place of these behaviors in the network of social meaning and the valorizing of one (the male) over the other (the female)."[196] It is indeed the case that "sexual difference" begets the "valorizing" of the "male." But fortifying the "sex" binary as Gatens does will not rectify this hierarchy. Disrupting this supremacy requires denaturalizing and dismantling the "sex" binary.

To Gatens, "theorists of sexual difference do not take as their object of study the physical body, the anatomical body, the neutral, dead body, but the body as lived, the animate body—the *situated* body."[197] Besides the fact that there is no "neutral" body, why is Gatens not concerned about the "lived" and "*situated*" body of those resisting the transphobia, biological essentialism, and naturalization of sexgender promoted by her theorizing? Why are their bodies, desires, and experiences discounted and discredited? Moreover, how could the suggestion that a body that is not "sexed" is "dead" amount to anything but the essentialization of "sex"? Why are whatever hormones, organs, or chromosomes that Gatens classes as determining "sex" that which renders a body alive? She continues: "To speak of 'acquiring' a particular gender is to be mistaken about the significance of gender and its intimate relation to biology-as-lived in a social and historical context."[198] It is not clear what exactly Gatens means by "acquiring" a "gender," but if she supposes that "gender" is embodied in a social and historical context, would not the *obverse* conclusion follow? Only biological essentialism would proscribe as much by maintaining that "gender" is *determined* by "sex" and is therefore fixed. Reflecting on this essay twenty years later, Gatens clarifies: "I thought the replacement of 'sex' with 'gender' was a bad move politically. . . . like so much else in theory, it was leaving the body and corporeality out of the picture."[199] Why must taking the body seriously devolve into biological essentialism? Would not bringing "the body and corporeality" back into the picture entail accommodating the very embodied and corporeal desires of those who do not comport with her essentialist, hierarchical, fixed binary? Surely it ought to encompass the recognition of the multifarious ways in which people *corporeally* inhabit, resist, enact, occupy, and play with precisely such exclusionary, overdetermined, and sovereign conceptions of sexgender as hers.

Contra Gatens, in Spinozistically denaturalizing "sex," I affirm the significance of the body in four important ways. First, since mind and body for Spinoza are "one and the same individual," this means that everything the mind thinks is not merely embodied but situated in time and space, subject to its particularities. Humans are minded bodies or bodied minds; our feelings and desires are of and as the singular minded bodies or bodied minds that we are. This is why bodies matter, why living *as* the body one desires is so important, why "acquiring" a gender as she calls it, is causally necessitated by the feelings and thoughts, sensations and inclinations, desires and experiences of a given minded body or bodied mind. Taking Spinoza's insights seriously not only does *not* support the kind of transphobia that Gatens promotes but prompts the opposite; it validates the actuality, complexity, and particularity of living sexgender as bodied minds or minded bodies and so the imperative to *live* our desires. To be *as* the bodies we are, to *become* as we please, without teleological injunctions to justify doing so or expectations of consistency in so doing.

Second, because there are no given norms in reality, this means that how one is cannot be expected to conform to transcendent, universal, subjective, anthropically contrived categories. Not only does Gatens miss this, but certain allied feminists, not just TERFs, do as well. As Jules Gill-Peterson observes: "Many of the key achievements of liberal feminism, particularly in the West, have relied on minimizing, if not rejecting or trying to transcend femininity" to submit to the misogynistic devaluation of femininity.[200] By contrast, I maintain that taking difference and desire seriously, as Spinoza insists, entails validating "femininity" in all of its variety, including extraness. While Gatens alleges that "sex-neutral" approaches reinforce the devaluation of "femininity," the opposite is the case: detaching sexgender from her biological essentialism actually promotes and diversifies the very "femininity" she is supposedly committed to not denigrating. This unveils how she is not really concerned with the devaluation of femininity but only a very specific kind of it, which necessarily excludes trans femininity.

This brings us to the third point, since "mind and body are one and the same" everything about us exists as situated, entangled in the infinite connection of causes, which constantly shapes, reshapes, and unshapes our desires, which to Spinoza are *who* we are. No desire is more or less "natural" or "unnatural"; these are socially conditioned because we are imbricated with others and cannot sovereignly control how we are intra-actively constituted. This leads to the fourth point, which concerns Spinoza's resistance to the delusive freedom of Cartesian dualism. Against its conceits of free will, interiority, and individualism, Spinoza upholds humans as non-sovereign over themselves and their contexts. This presents a rejoinder to the liberal assumptions that continue to underwrite certain approaches to sexgender identity, specifically those that rely on atomistic Selfhood or personal Truth, construed as existing independent of context, the products of disembodied sovereign decisionism. Precisely such unfreedom explains the inconsistencies, messiness, and instabilities of living sexgender.

Out of Control

Throughout the appendix, Spinoza emphasizes how certain prejudices spur further misperceptions. The conceits of human exceptionalism condition anthropocentrism, inducing misbeliefs that reality yields to an Order or End that serves human interests. Much as there is no Sovereign who creates or controls reality, individual modes are likewise deprived of sovereignty over themselves. Moreover, just as substance is not transcendent to nature—an Exception to its causal ways—modes too, are non-exceptional. There is no escape from the connection of causes, from the immanence of causal intra-action, from imbrications with others. Indeed, humans do not comprise a "dominion within a dominion" but are *of* nature, not apart from it. Spinoza devotes particular attention to renouncing the Christian, Cartesian supposition that "human disturbs, rather than follows, the order of nature, that they have absolute power over their actions, and that they are determined only by themself."[201]

To contest the human exceptionalism, dualism, and free will promoted by Christian, Cartesian, "Western" thought, Spinoza drew from the nonexceptionalist currents in medieval Jewish philosophy influenced by Islamic Aristotelianism. Against human conceits of freedom *from* nature, Maimonides supposes that all acts, whether of humans or animals, voluntary, accidental, or fortuitous are consequences of a concatenation of causes tracing back to God "who arouses a particular volition in the irrational animal and who has necessitated this particular free choice in the rational animal and who has made the natural things pursue their course."[202] Scholars have noted both the patent equivalence established between humans and nonhuman animals here and also the subsumption of "free choice" into the realms of natural causation.[203] Reducing free "choice" to causal necessity has precedent in the conceptions of both al-Farabi and Ibn Sina concerning the will of the intellect, which "chooses" by necessity. A further salient current in Maimonides's thought is his insistence that *through* nature and knowledge of it, humans access God. Not only is there no escape *from* nature but understanding it enables human perfection.[204] Spinoza is also indebted to Gersonides, whose Ibn Rushd–informed Aristotelianism emplaces humans in nature, resisting epistemic transcendence.[205] Also relevant is the attenuation of the sovereignty of Will in the Ibn Sina–inflected determinism of Jewish Spanish philosophy that conditions the particular strain of causal determinism advanced by Crescas.[206]

Whereas the appendix identifies the misbelief of a Sovereign god who transcends nature as deriving from the human conceit of being transcendent from nature and therefore sovereign over body, over self, over nature, Cartesianism is constructed on these very prejudices. The "image of god" that Spinoza exposes as the circular, delusional, anthropomorphic operation that subsidizes teleology, human exceptionalism, and freedom secures Descartes's program. To him, a sovereign God[207] invests humans with a mind that transcends body[208] and a free will that transcends it,[209] which elevates humans as exceptional, *essentially* their minds,[210] sovereignly free over themselves, their thoughts, and their actions and thus superior to all else.[211] These doctrines of mastery over self finance the Cartesian mission to become "the lords and masters of nature."[212] In doing so, Descartes consolidates the dualist voluntarism of Augustine. For Augustine, reality, which is willfully effectuated and superintended by God—who is Spirit—is governed by the hierarchical binary of spirit and matter. God "subjects all things to himself, and then the bodily creation to the spiritual, the non-rational to the rational, the earthly to the heavenly, the feminine to the masculine, the weaker to the stronger, the needier to the better endowed."[213] God's exclusion from matter and sovereignty over reality installs further sovereignties constructed on the denigration of matter and its submission to Spirit: the mind is supreme over the body, rational beings over non-rational beings, and supposedly more rational humans (men) over those deemed less rational (women). To be like God in this Christian tradition is to be exempted from nature, to transcend matter and dominate it and other beings. Sovereignties induct sovereignties, authorizing ever more forms of subjection.

No Escape

Critical to Spinoza's denaturalization of sovereignty is his contention that humans are *of* nature, not transcendent to it. Like all modes, a human "follows and obeys the common order of nature."[214] The incapacity to escape the immanent connection of causes means that our thoughts and affects, actions and desires are causally determined and elude our full autonomy. Much as the mind does not transcend the body, there are also no transcendent boundaries demarcating human modes from other modes.[215] Humans are connected to, reliant upon, and constituted by so much that is not legibly "human." We are comprised of billions of microbiota and trillions of cells and countless fluids that form and fuel us. Furthermore, as Spinoza explains to Oldenburg, adaptations, agreements, and disagreements render the boundaries between self and other porous. Reality does not deliver predetermined, sovereign boundaries. The porosities of the human mode together with its innumerable interactions and interdependencies and interlacements position it as a multiplicity. All of this is so in the absence of teleology; there is no Layout and no Direction, no Law and no Dominion in nature. Accordingly, nature does not endow beings with fixed properties or predetermined capacities, as this is teleological. As Spinoza puts it: "No one has yet determined what the body can do."[216]

Cancel Culture

Much as Spinoza reputes Cartesian dualism of mind and body, he accordingly disrupts the logics that sponsor a sovereign disseveration of nature from culture or culture from nature, or the "natural" from the "unnatural" or the "natural" from the "artificial." Everything that exists is a mode of infinite reality: substance *or* nature. There is no escape or evolution from a proverbial state of nature. For Spinoza, the civil state is continuous with the *status naturalis*. All that exists, is immanent nature, that is, reality. Whatever happens is therefore "natural," causally determined rather than exceptionally or transcendentally or freely rendered. Vaccines are as "natural" as viruses; cyborgs as "natural" as cells; methamphetamines as "natural" as mushrooms. This does not mean that there is no difference between, say, a tree and a table. It means that both are *of* nature. Since there is no retreat from nature, from immanent reality, it is incoherent from a Spinozist perspective to consider "culture" as an overcoming of nature or other to it. "Cultural" artifacts are as much *of* nature as anything else. Hence, Spinoza dismisses those who think that "buildings ... paintings, and other things of this kind," come to be through supernatural means—a transcendent mind or will—rather than natural, immanent causes.

Hierarchies promote ever more hierarchies and presumptions to supremacy. The purported superiority of mind over body sponsors that of culture over nature, human over nonhuman. These subsidize human exceptionalism, licensing the pillage of all that is "natural" in the service of that which is perceived as superior to it. Thus, as Kim Tallbear and Angela Willey observe: "The so-called natural is always paramount in settler ideas of appropriate ways to relate, control, and allocate rights and resources that reproduce structural inequities."[217]

Spinoza's critique of teleology exposes the interested conceits that sponsor judgments of how things are or are not. In the appendix, as we have seen, he uncovers how political and religious leaders naturalize their authority through elaborate networks of prejudices that sustain their power and promote their interests. Appeals to the "nature" of things or the "natural," especially by naturalizing that which is socially contrived, serve to accredit unjustified arrogations of power or perpetuate specific priorities. Such exercises in legitimization come at the cost of delegitimizing someone, something, some desire, some way of life, or some group of people.

To Spinoza, "everyone shares a common nature—we're just deceived by power and refinement."²¹⁸ Unfortunately, his own writings do not always uphold this principle. This is typified by his exclusion of women from democracy. At the close of his *Political Treatise*, Spinoza writes: "Perhaps someone will ask whether women are under the power of their husbands by nature or by custom. If this happened only by custom, then no reason compels us to exclude women from rule."²¹⁹ While Spinoza is to be credited for considering that "custom" is responsible for this unequal state of affairs, he is to be discredited for concluding: "If we consult experience, we'll see that this occurs only because of their weakness."²²⁰ He proceeds: "If women were by nature equal to men, both in strength of character and native intelligence ... surely among so many and such diverse nations we would find some where each sex ruled equally.... But since this has not happened anywhere, we can say without reservation that women do not, by nature, have a right equal to men's but they necessarily submit to men."²²¹ If only Spinoza could have been a better Spinozist! Rather than grasping how the construction of the sexgender binary *produces* the subordination of women and renders paltry instances of their equal rule alongside men, Spinoza confuses his causes and effects. The submission of women to men that he observes is not the effect of their "natural" inferiority. It is not *caused* by nature but engendered by the innovation and naturalization of sexgender. Spinoza's exclusion of women from democracy is an exemplary case of precisely how the naturalization of sovereign, immutable, essentialized differences serves to benefit those who construct and conserve these very differences.

Not So Fit

Teleology underwrites, as we have seen, certain understandings of race, sexgender, and ableness. It also sponsors diverse scientific, historical, and philosophical approaches to reality that retain currency today. To illuminate as much, it is instructive to consider the teleological and anthropocentric presumptions that structure evolutionary biology, modern science, theories of historical progress, and philosophies of so-called longtermism.

At the center of evolutionary selectionism stands a conflation of causes and effects. A trait expressed in a particular species is viewed as having been the very *reason* this trait persists. The same goes for an entire species that has "survived." What might only be an effect—of any number of factors—is taken to be the *cause* of its "survival." While this circularity has been acknowledged, Spinoza positions a critique of the logics sponsoring it: the combination of anthropocentrism and teleology, which "turns nature completely upside down" by mistaking effects for causes.[222] This also speaks to the tautology at the root of selectionism: that the fittest "survivors" are those who have "survived." Thereby, the "survivors" and their descendants—those who develop and propagate this theory—acclaim their own "Survival." I do not mean to discredit evolutionary biology. In fact, the notion of nature adapting and changing is fundamental to Spinoza's ontology. However, because nature is decentered and unregulated, any notion of change must be explained without resort to teleology.

The scientific mission to systematize and categorize nature—to identity a what and how—catalyzes interest in a *why*. With this, questions of agency surface. Jessica Riskin describes the predicament confronted by modern science: "Do the order and action in the natural world originate inside or outside?"[223] Either option is problematic: " 'Inside' violates the ban on ascriptions of agency to natural phenomena such as cells or molecules, and so risks sounding mystical and magical. . . . 'outside' assumes a supernatural source of nature's order, and so violates . . . the principle of naturalism."[224] To avoid overly anthropomorphic verbs like "want," scientists prefer terms such as "regulate" and "control."[225] Yet these still connote "purposeful action."[226] Like the believers Spinoza describes, contemporary biologists observe nature, and attempting to make sense of it, they attach order to it, which then requires an agent—either inside or outside—to whom purposive action is attributed. People remain incapable of *not* transposing anthropic constructs onto nature. Whether Agency is divinized or naturalized, it is nothing but a human contrivance.

Ending History

The appendix demonstrates how teleology is engendered by anthropocentrism and anthropomorphism. Doctrines that perceive reality as purposively catering to humans reflect anthropic desires rather than how things really are. Such notions are founded upon and in turn fortify purports to human exceptionalism. Yet humans, as Spinoza underscores, are without ontological privilege. Moreover, reality is infinite, it serves no Purpose, has no Plan. Whatever exists and whatever transpires are the effects of the infinite, immanent connection of causes. With this, Spinoza dismantles traditional conceptions of a providential Sovereign overseeing reality and vitiates pretenses to human superiority. Both of these, he shows, are furnished by human narcissism: the fabrication of a God in the human image and the subsequent claim that this God is endowed with the free will that humans fictitiously ascribe to themselves. This spawns a further conceit that humans are distinct from other modes, positioned at the top of an ontological hierarchy. Such claims to constitutional Difference consolidate the conception that human affairs exists beyond or above the domains of "nature" and occupy a superior realm of "culture." These factors and further cognate fictions figure in certain philosophies of History and neoliberal doctrines of Progress.

Spinoza's rejection of teleology counters a current of "Western" philosophy traceable at least to Augustine's conceptions of linear time, the progressive advance towards salvation (or damnation), and the hierarchical separation between the city of God and the city of men. The scientific developments of the sixteenth and seventeenth centuries and the so-called Enlightenment, at once vindicated and reinforced Christian, "Western" commitments to progress. These legacies undergird the triumphalism of Kant's "Idea for a Universal History with a Cosmopolitan Purpose." The essay opens by declaiming that if History "examines the free exercise of the human will *on a large scale*, it will be able to discover a regular progression among freely willed actions."[227] Thus, "what strikes us ... as confused and fortuitous may be recognised, in the history of the entire species, as a steadily advancing but slow development of man's original capacities,"[228] for "all the natural capacities of a creature are destined sooner or later to be developed completely and in conformity with their end."[229] Otherwise, "we are faced not with a law-governed nature, but with an aimless, random process."[230] Kant concludes: "If we assume a plan of nature, we have grounds for greater hopes."[231] It "opens up the comforting prospect" of a future wherein "man's destiny can be fulfilled here on earth."[232] Kant contrasts the "history of mankind" with "the non-rational sphere of nature."[233] This analysis displays the teleological thinking that Spinoza denounces. Nature, he clarifies, is bereft of ends and plans, humans are not other to nature, and nature does not serve humans. Reality, accordingly, is without Potential—for power is only actualized—and divested of all *teloi*, including Destiny. Kant's rallying for History instructively encapsulates the appeal of teleology: it supplies humans with a sense of superiority and purpose, secured by the fiction of free will, much as it tenders hope for better times still to come. By contrast, to Spinoza, "the more we strive to live according to the guidance of reason, the more we strive to depend less on hope,"[234] accepting reality as it is, not as we desire it to be.

For Spinoza, as Yovel has it, "history has no special ontological status. It is but the way we humans cut out our experience of natural occurrences from a standpoint which interests us—that of our desires."[235] Spinoza's rejection of teleology resists the human supremacy, progressivism, and inevitability underwriting "Western" conceptions of History. Hegel's repurposing of providence, his glorification of History, and the Christological teleology and totality of his dialectic epitomize what Spinoza critiques. Since there is neither Order nor End in nature, substance is not only not a subject acting *on* nature from beyond or beside it, in realization of some *other*, but nature lacks self-determination, and its unfolding is not the means to the ends of self-realization or the realization of any predetermined aim. For this reason, it is also inappropriate to speak of a "system" or even a "process" in the context of Spinozism, be it in terms of nature as a whole or applied to history. On this register, Althusser,[236] Balibar,[237] Macherey,[238] and Negri[239] falter. To uphold reality as infinite and without a telos is to dispense with confinements and guardrails as much as the pretense of a destination and destiny.

By rejecting teleology and anthropocentrism, alongside the metaphysical and transcendent status with which these endow History, Spinoza extends a strain that pulsates through medieval Jewish philosophy. This contrasts with the Christological approach to temporality, which views it as linearly progressing towards an End. With "the rejection of natural time, or of a time that does not come to an end/judgment," comes, Dobbs-Weinstein notes, "the separation between natural necessity (the domain of mechanical causality, bodies, passions) and human freedom (the domain of history, final causality, reason, free will, and human action)."[240]

The gospel of Progress is guaranteed by transcendent human will, the retreat *from* nature, and claims to human superiority, which are bestowed upon humans by a transcendent God or effectively replace this God. Either option relies on the sovereignties that Spinoza's immanence forecloses. Sovereignties, as we have seen, induce further sovereignties. Unsurprisingly, the Christological doctrine of Progress is at once constructed on a series of hierarchies—culture and nature, mind and body, human and nonhuman, future and present, activity and passivity—and conditions a variety of concomitant hierarchies, including sexgender, race, ability, and class. All of these have combined to license white, European, Christian exploits in domination, expropriation, and genocide. Euphemistically termed "colonialism," these endeavors were executed under the banner of Progress, advancement, and expansion, and just as often, Salvation.

The alliance of History, Progress, and Hope with the sovereign freedoms *to* exploit, *to* dominate, and *to* advance is underwritten by teleology and transcendence. This is why Benjamin and Adorno, in grappling with fascism and genocide, resist "Western," teleological conceptions of history.[241] In an essay from 1940, Benjamin indicts the supremacies of History: "With whom does historicism actually sympathize? The answer is inevitable: with the victor. And all the rulers are the heirs of prior conquerors."[242] As such, "there is no document of culture which is not at the same time a document of barbarism."[243] Only a transcendent disseveration of culture *from* nature allows for the fantasy that "culture" is exempt from exercises in domination and exploitation. So it is that Benjamin, in his interpretation of Paul Klee's *Angelus Novus*, reflects: "Where a chain of events appears before *us*," the angel of history "sees one single catastrophe, which keeps piling wreckage upon wreckage."[244] The angel is driven by a storm and "what we call progress is *this* storm."[245] Contra this "Western" dogma, "the Jews were prohibited from inquiring into the future.... This disenchanted the future, which holds sway over all those who turn to soothsayers for enlightenment."[246] No Jewish thinker has disenchanted the future and decried its soothsayers more than Spinoza.

Teleology is constructed on hierarchies: the effect is subservient to the cause, existence is subsidiary to essence, being subordinate to becoming. It erases singularity, crowning the transcendent telos as Sovereign over all else. When applied to history, this supposes that its purpose is progress, which, as Benjamin shows, is achievable only by exploiting others. Fidelity to such dogmas forces adherents to efface all evidence to the contrary; to discount the violence they visit upon others, which they either deny or construe as mere "bumps" in the march forward. This figures in Adorno's critique of Hegel's philosophy of history and his indictment delivered in 1944: "Millions of Jews have been murdered, and this is to be seen as an interlude and not the catastrophe itself."[247]

Shorting the Longterm

Conventional liberal approaches to history that trumpet Progress as inevitable do not contend that the End is nigh. On the contrary, "reason" manifesting through the spread of liberal ideas, free market economics, and technological improvement guarantees not merely a Future for humans but a better future. Or so the tired teleological tale has it. Yet the rapid acceleration of human-caused global heating disrupts this optimism. Despite the allure of Progress, it is increasingly difficult even for committed liberals to ignore the prospect that human conflicts and pandemics—related to rapid ecological devastation—will continue to wreak significant havoc on human life. The solution, for some, is to be found in "longtermism": "the idea that positively influencing the longterm future is a key moral priority of our time."[248] To William MacAskill, "Longtermism is about taking seriously just how big the future could be."[249] Rather than focusing on humans in the present, longtermism prioritizes future humans: "The future could be wonderful: we could create a flourishing and long-lasting society, where everyone's lives are better than the very best lives today."[250] A future of human flourishing is possible, so long as we commit to it. Despite progress, Toby Ord concedes: "Our present world remains marred by malaria and HIV; depression and dementia; racism and sexism; torture and oppression."[251] But "with enough time, we can end these horrors—building a society that is truly just and humane."[252] It is not at all clear why Ord is convinced that this is possible, let alone probable. This posture is an updated version of Kantian optimism and Hegelian progress. It remains committed to the same teleological hierarchy: the future is privileged over the present. Individual life is subordinated to the "universal" march forward. Such longtermist approaches place all hope in the inevitability of human ingenuity, in the invincibility of human Reason.

By asserting that "future people count," MacAskill is not merely suggesting that they matter but is prioritizing them over people in the present. Not only is there no guarantee that people will exist for as long as his estimates presume—"hundreds of millions of years"[253]—but his perspective actively devalues millions of people alive today. These lives—eight billion of them—or at least most of them, do not really "count." Much as my family murdered in Auschwitz and the Belarussian forests are mere hiccups in the liberal advance forward, many people today are deemed negligible. Our lives have no individual worth, they are but means to the end that is the Future. Singular humans are subordinated to the universal, transcendent construct of Humanity. Such active deprivation of life is advocated by longtermist Nicholas Beckstead: "Saving a life in a rich country is substantially more important than saving a life in a poor country."[254] What supports this conclusion? "Richer countries have substantially more innovation, and their workers are much more economically productive."[255] Striking as this sounds to basic ethical sensibilities, it seems to me that Beckstead is merely stating explicitly what has always been implicit to colonial and capitalist logics: certain lives matter far more than others, and only the lives of those with power and privilege count.

Much of the literature on longtermism focuses on technological development. It is at once concerned with the prospect that advanced technologies like artificial general intelligence might be put towards nefarious ends under the direction of humans or that after surpassing human intelligence, it might overtake humans, exploit them, precipitating their extinction. Yet these catastrophic potential repercussions do not seem to dissuade longtermists from investing their hopes in technology. On the contrary, for MacAskill, technologies *are* the solution to assorted challenges, including declining birthrates, which is a problem because it will lead to economic and by extension, technological "stagnation." To address this, "we might develop artificial general intelligence (AGI) that could replace human workers—including researchers. This would allow us to increase the number of 'people' working on R&D as easily as we currently scale up production of the latest iPhone."[256] For MacAskill, there is "a moral case for space settlement. Though Earth-based civilisation could last for hundreds of millions of years, the stars will still be shining in trillions of years' time, and a civilisation that is spread out across many solar systems could last at least this long."[257] To Toby Ord, colonizing space would "greatly expand our potential lifespan."[258] "If we reach a future of such a scale, we might have a truly staggering number of descendants, with the time, resources, wisdom and experience to create a diversity of wonders unimaginable to us today."[259] It is not clear how he knows of such wonders or why these are desirable. What remains unmistakable, however, are Ord's optimism and hubris.

These longtermists assume not simply that Humanity must have a Future but that securing it is not merely a worthwhile goal, but a top Priority. While they acknowledge factors that might lead to human extinction—nuclear war, artificial intelligence, pandemics—their confidence that humans have the tools to prevent these from happening, if only we cooperate, is unwavering. There is much talk in this literature of "*existential risks*—risks that threaten the destruction of humanity's longterm potential."[260] But considerably less attention is granted to the actual lives of individual people, be they alive today or in some Future. What seems to matter to these philosophers are the abstract, transcendent categories of Humanity and Civilization, rather than specific human lives. Instead of investing in improving the present condition of humans, they prioritize "longterm potential," not what actually is but what they fantasize could be.

To secure the Human Future, Carl Shulman and Nick Bostrom, associated with the Future of Humanity Institute, advocate "embryo selection for cognitive enhancement."[261] Such practices are more commonly known as "eugenics." Their widespread adoption, Shulman and Bostrum claim, would "significantly increase world capital"[262] and "make technological stagnation seem less likely."[263] MacAskill echoes these promises: "If scientists with Einstein-level research abilities were cloned and trained from an early age, or if human beings were genetically engineered to have greater research abilities, this could compensate for having fewer people overall and thereby sustain technological progress."[264]

All of the aforementioned philosophers of longtermism are white men from the United Kingdom, the United States, and Australia, all of whom, uncoincidentally, trained in philosophy departments in the UK and US. As Audra Mitchell and Aadita Chaudhury observe: "Despite their claims to universality . . . these 'end of the world' discourses are more specifically concerned about protecting the future of *whiteness*."[265] Teleology, as we have theorized, is constructed on supremacist rationales, which spawn ever more supremacies. Of concern to these thinkers is the world as *they* know it, from their perch of privilege, and the future to be secured is *their* future, an enhanced version of their present. The fact that millions of people already suffer from the ravages of global heating, food insecurity, and disease is of little interest to these philosophers.

The primary concern of longtermists is the *potential* Future and the prospect of its gloriousness. They concede that many factors might foreclose the technological developments of which they fantasize, especially climate change, pandemics, and nuclear war. Although they recognize that humans and their technologies are mostly responsible for these phenomena, they continue to maintain that technology will save humans. What remains mostly unaddressed is what this means for nonhuman life. To them, not destroying the earth or at least deaccelerating ecological devastation is a goal only insomuch as it will secure the Future of Humanity. The anthropocentrism of longtermism is so brazen, it seems almost too obvious to note. But it is worth underscoring that what animates longtermists is not so much the present and near-term human suffering of climate change and pandemics but that if left unchecked, these could ultimately lead to human extinction. What worth is reality, they maintain, without humans?

To longtermist philosophers, the universe centers on humans, who are correlatively entitled to do with it as they please. Such anthropocentrism also sponsors popular approaches to global heating, which have intensified of late only because the ongoing decimation of ecosystems and nonhuman life is now really threatening humans. Such movements continue to place their hope in human ingenuity and technological development to salvage this state of affairs, seemingly unaware that such advance is what has *caused* the heating of the planet and continues to exacerbate it. The human exceptionalism and purports to human supremacy that sponsor both longtermism and mainstream approaches to global heating remain unwavering, despite considerable evidence that nature is not in our control. Infinite reality does not yield to human desires. Our capacity to reverse the devastating impacts of our actions, to radically alter the course of nature in ways that will only serve us, not to mention rapidly devise ever more fantastical technologies, is limited, despite the bravado of these white "Western" men.

To Spinoza, all beings seek their own advantage.[266] While he denounces human exceptionalism and its pretense to transcendence, he is primarily concerned with human flourishing. Current human suffering, including from global heating, is a concern that Spinozism urges action to address. However, it also stresses that humans are not Special. Reality does not exist *for* us. How it is, is due to the infinite connection of causes, which acts in the absence of guidance and guarantees, without a telos. What seems to us humans, through our anthropocentric lenses as the "End," is merely the End for the life-form that is us (and life-forms most like us). This solicits considering that human extinction, while catastrophic by human standards, might be more than accommodating to other life forms, that the descent of humans need not amount to the apocalyptical End routinely imagined. Since reality was never intended to be and since humans are not "its chief part,"[267] human extinction is a real possibility. By upholding reality as infinite, Spinoza confirms its capacity to constantly *become*, concomitantly affirming that humans are not *privileged* but mere participants in the infinite connection of causes, subject, without exception, to the indirection and insecurity of its immanence.

Order of the Day

The astonishment in response to the emergence of the COVID-19 pandemic is a testament to the continued purchase of anthropocentrism. Despite unceasing warnings from experts the world over, the fact that nature acts in manners dissonant with human needs remains a shock that many individuals, and the systems sustaining them, have not fully absorbed. This partly results from the expectation that reality submits to human desires.

As the appendix delineates, human exceptionalism deludes us into upholding ourselves as superior to nature, perceiving it as inherently ordered, designed to benefit humans, and correlatively, tamable by us. While allowing that reality acts in ways incongruent with human expectations is not groundbreaking, pervasive myths of Progress and the hubris of human Sovereignty *over* nature account for both the disbelief in the exigency of COVID and its continued recalcitrance. Although the pandemic intruded upon such convenient fictions, these remain hard to shirk. Scientific developments—vaccines and antivirals—have blunted the clinical severity of the virus, especially in the acute phase of infection. However, the unbridled optimism in the face of this crisis and the unsubstantiated hope that it was soon to end, reflect fidelity to the belief that nature is fundamentally Ordered or minimally, Orderable, that this is an exceptional circumstance, that human claims to the throne of Exceptionalism remain unthreatened and that humans are still in control.

Fictions of sovereignty *over* nature and fantasies that reality bends to our desires were constitutive of the flawed response to the pandemic. Consider, for example: the initial hesitance to accept that the virus is airborne; the belief that the vaccine would end the pandemic (and that further mitigations, like masking, would be superfluous); the refusal to accept that even vaccinated people contract and spread the virus; the fallacious claim that the virus is not dangerous for children or "healthy" adults; the assertion that "natural" infection confers immunity; and the denial of Long COVID and persistent diminishment of it. Erroneous assertions that new variants would be less severe derive from anthropocentrism. As if the virus is interested in what is convenient for us; as if there is some Law or regulatory mechanism *commanding* it to evolve in ways beneficial to us. As I have told many a friend—much to their consternation—"the virus does not give a damn about you." Nature is indifferent to our preferences. The pandemic is not over just because certain governments, media, and corporations have sovereignly decided that it is, or simply because people are "tired" of caring. The virus does not bow to our dictates. There is no telos, just there, over the horizon.

The response to COVID both initially and still—many years in—was undermined by the hubris that we could easily dominate it. These purports to sovereignty do not exist in a vacuum. As the appendix demonstrates, claims to human exceptionalism rest upon and produce additional sovereignties. The pandemic exposed the interlocking hierarchies structuring our senses of ourselves, systems, and societies. For those with relative health and wealth, the pandemic delivered an unfamiliar feeling of vulnerability. It disrupted a sense of bodily stability and the pleasures of its unimpeded functioning, while showing that all of us are on the precipice of being not "healthy," becoming "disabled." Such risks, as COVID rendered undeniable, are unevenly shared, differing based on sexgender, race, class, and ableness. For Black, indigenous people, other people of color, and migrants, threats to physical safety here in the US have always been present and access to medical care structurally obstructed and prohibitively expensive.

The coronavirus punctured the contrived boundaries regarded as demarcating our Selves. It did so not simply by reminding us that our air is shared, that we rely upon that which is "outside" of us, but more challenging for some to grasp, that we are comprised of, sustained by, and often damaged by that which is "other" to us. The ease with which the virus enters our bodies and wreaks havoc upon it exposes the extent to which our personal confines are permeable, that our human selves, while special to us, are merely vehicles for a virus to thrive. A virus that does not register us as human, a virus that is indifferent to our suffering, a virus that continues to proliferate, despite—at least some—concerted attempts to curtail it.

The ease with which the virus initially spread and continues to mutate and propagate across the world spotlights the meaninglessness of sovereign borders and established geographic hierarchies of center and periphery. Yet the significance of international borders has been reasserted as access to vaccines, antivirals, masks, testing, and medical care still depend upon the country in which one resides. Rather than urging a rethinking of sovereign borders and international relations, the virus has reasserted the significance of these demarcations, rendering visible whose lives matter and whose lives have always been deemed fungible.

Notwithstanding the disparate protections of geography, race, class, sexgender, and ability, the extent to which the government, media, and financial and medical establishments sacrificed all of our health on the altar of "normalcy" and profit exemplifies how teleological rationales remain regnant. The return to "normal"—a normal that was always only livable for some—has been orchestrated under the illusion that the pandemic is over now that it has been formally declared as such, not because it actually *is* over, which is to say not that it has actually ceased being a persistent threat to our health. Hundreds of Americans are still dying each week, tens of thousands are still becoming infected, and the chronic impacts of even mild infections in "healthy" vaccinated people continue to debilitate millions. Here, the conceit of human control over inconvenient natural phenomena shows its face: the pandemic is over because people want it over and not because it actually is over, especially because there is profit to be had. Our health and lives are but means to the end of the further accumulation of capital. Our existences are subservient to the sovereign telos of financial gain. The fact that business is disrupted and profit compromised by the spread of the virus, that workers are routinely infected and too ill to work, and that many are disabled from COVID and unable to work altogether remains beside the point. So long as we pretend it is over, it is over.

The return to "normal" relies on teleology. This is apparent from two related angles. The first is the misrepresentation of COVID as severe only in the acute phase of infection: if hospitalizations are down, the virus must not be that dangerous. While vaccination meaningfully reduces the rate of hospitalization, blunting severe outcomes in the acute stage of infection, this overemphasis on the initial stage of infection, rather than reckoning with its chronic impacts, teleologically presupposes that how things are now (in the acute phase) is how they will be (chronically). It privileges the convenience of the present over likely consequences. This is mirrored by the focus on what is present at hand—a week or two of flu-like symptoms for the "healthy" and vaccinated—rather than concern for the documented neurological, cardiological, immunological, endocrinal, gastrointestinal, and other damage wrought by the virus. This myopia is not due to its novelty: the chronic impacts of other viruses have been proven for decades. Rather, this perspective is driven by the preference not merely for what is convenient now but also by our predilection for Progress. The thinking is that things are always only ever improving; if one is infected with the virus, acutely ill for a relatively short time, even if symptoms may linger, these all, the conventional narrative has it, will resolve linearly, with time, and even more so with antiviral interventions. Harder to digest is the fact that nature does not operate teleologically; it does not progress ever forward. A further instance of the enticements of teleology is perceptible in the unsupported claim that multiple infections are helpful or not really harmful. Exactly the opposite appears to be the case: due to T-cell exhaustion and immunological dysregulation, second infections are worse than first infections, third worse than second infections, and so on.

Hard Truths

Spinoza is committed to discrediting misperceptions of reality. Teleology is at the center of the constellated purports to sovereignty that he disavows. His aim is not only to diagnose these doctrines but to understand *why* people are so drawn to them. Reality appears chaotic. It escapes our attempts to control it. More troubling still, our control over our own selves is truncated. This lack of control precipitates conceits of control. Rather than accepting the disparity of infinity by recognizing that reality exists without a sovereign Overseer, a sovereign Purpose, and a sovereign Guarantor, it is comforting to imagine a sovereign God responsible for all that is and committed to our thriving. Accordingly pacifying are fictions of our sovereignty: over ourselves, over nature, and over other humans. These rely upon contrived hierarchical binaries: god and nature, essence and existence, supernatural and natural, mind and body, culture and nature, universal and individual, abstract and concrete, future and present, cause and effect, self and other, human and nonhuman, male and female, white and nonwhite, center and periphery, whole and part, ends and means, normative and nonnormative, natural and artificial, and on and on. While interpreting reality to confer with our preferences for order may furnish us with a fleeting sense of security, these practices subsidize expanding purports to supremacy. Though superiority may be gratifying and certainly rewarding for those it privileges, Spinoza reminds us of the inconvenient truth: these sovereignties are not only delusive but destructive. The alternative is to accept the discomfort of disparity, the uncertainty of immanence. Recognizing our constitutive lack of control allows us to approximate a semblance of stability amidst a reality that is unruled, unregulated, and unrestrained.

FIVE

Splitting the Difference

Infinity overflows the thought that thinks it.
—EMMANUEL LEVINAS[1]

Can thinking be thought in the absence of sovereignty? Is it possible to conceive reason without crowning it—or even something else, say, God or matter—as sovereign? Might thinking be configured without resort to such fixtures of sovereignty as transcendence and teleology, priority and preeminence, sameness and supremacy? These questions orient this chapter, which essays to rethink Spinoza's approach to reason by exploring the attribute of thought, how thinking happens in humans, and what this means ontologically, epistemologically, and ethically. This is not a simple procedure, not only because of the convolutions that mark such matters of mind, plunging us into puzzles that "Western" philosophy has pondered since Parmenides, but also insomuch as Spinoza's approach to these questions has predominantly been misperceived. Most egregious stand ascriptions of idealism to his program and interpretations that portray thought as ontologically privileged. Such conceptions enthrone Reason as sovereign or the mind as sovereign over body. Moreover, these purports tend to evaporate difference in sameness, which is then elevated as Supreme, as when the difference of the attributes is elided, all thinking assimilated into an Intellect, or the particularities of thinking, context, and embodiment degraded, if not disregarded. Often, these renditions promote the forms of transcendence and teleology that Spinoza's philosophy repudiates. Against these, I educe how Spinoza's commitment to infinity and immanence redounds in an epistemology that refuses to enthrone reason as ontologically Sovereign. Furthermore, by confirming the attributes as different aspects of the same, discounting idealism, and upholding all thinking as modal, particular, and conditioned, Spinoza, I verify, delivers an epistemology divested of the instruments and mechanisms of sovereignty.

Certain prejudices in the scholarship contribute to the misappraisals of Spinoza's conception of reason, mind, and thinking. Most prominent stands the entrenched "Western" reliance on sovereignty to mind reason, as epitomized by Cartesian dualism, Kantian correlationism, and Hegelian dialecticism. Admittedly, the appeal of sovereignties in epistemology is scrutable. There are comforts in embracing dualism, especially its purports to human exceptionalism, transcendence from causal determinism, and unqualified freedom. Accordingly enticing—at least for those professing as much—are pretenses to transcendence from particularity and individuated perspective, by which reason can be heralded as neutral, "objective," and Universal. While these supremacist instruments are examined in the following chapter, here the focus is on a related and more foundational instantiation: the construal of reason as Sovereign and the subordination of all that is to its hegemony. This features in the anthropocentric correlation of being to thinking, wherein all existence is reduced to the human purchase on it. What is, becomes nothing more than *how* it is to humans or more precisely, *certain* humans. Though such takes are understandable—there is no escape from our standpoints—this does not undo their anthropocentrism or decimation of difference. Similarly, purports that reality is guaranteed by the domination of Reason furnish ersatz security by professing to resolve epistemic indeterminacies, contradictions, and uncertainties in an ultimate, absolute Intellect. Such a transcendent Intellect or Mind of God functions much as the illusion of a telos in nature does: it grounds our perceptions and experiences in something Beyond, supplying the delusive order and harmony humans so crave. Similar benefits are discernible in approaches that construe thought and extension as reducibly Same. Without difference, there is no disparity nor the insecurities attendant to it.

A further challenge is that Spinoza is not undertaking to construct a grand epistemological theory or philosophy of mind. His aim is not to defend Reason, to posit its autonomy, or to render everything subject to its critique. On the contrary, part II of the *Ethics*—"On the Nature of the Origin of the Mind"—is bent on delineating "knowledge of the human mind and its blessedness,"[2] which, it becomes clear, is preparatory for making sense of human affects in order to live well. Not only does Spinoza communicate in unfamiliar idioms and revise conventional terminologies, but his outlook is otherwise than what has become expected in "Western" philosophy since at least Descartes and Kant. Unlike Descartes, Spinoza's "epistemology" does not endeavor to design a metaphysical foundation for the New Science. Nor does it seek to secure the Authority of reason, like Kant. Rather, Spinoza's focus is to support readers in approximating better lives. Of course, Descartes and Kant are not uninterested in such concerns; their interventions to reconcile science and reason with religion and morality were intended to benefit society. But approaching Spinoza's *Ethics* with the expectation that it supplies, for example, First Principles systematically validating that we know, how we know, what we know is mistaken. This is not only because Spinoza dispenses with Principles nor because these questions—especially in Cartesian inflection—presuppose skepticisms that Spinoza regards as contrived, but insomuch as this is not his program in the *Ethics*. Such misapprehension contributes to miscues in the scholarship, exemplified by attempts to either smuggle these concerns into his project or evaluate it by the rubrics of prevailing "Western" epistemologies.

Aside from the embrace of the very prejudices that Spinoza disavows—transcendence, anthropocentrism, teleology—which mars the reception of his epistemology, stands a further supremacist prejudice: the ignorance of, and disregard for, the non-"Western" sources informing his approach to reason. This is especially striking with regard to Spinoza's conception of the attributes, which underwrites his construal of humans as minded bodies and bodied minds because in a most decisive passage detailing as much, he references "some of the Hebrews."[3] Without appreciating their doctrine concerning the identity of God, God's thinking, and that which God thinks, it is impossible to absorb Spinoza's approach to reason, perception of what the mind is, and how it operates in humans.

To redress these oversights, this chapter limns critical passages in the *Ethics* and illuminates their contexts as it elucidates Spinoza's epistemology, demonstrating how it divests reason and thinking of sovereignties. Infinite reality, which is of infinite attributes, of which thought is but "one," is not submitted to or secured by its conceptualization. Nor is reality consigned to the human grasp of it. This pressures interpretations that attach idealism as much as parallelism to his program. By disentangling Spinoza's conception of the attributes, I evince how it offers a theoretical model for admitting difference into reality without rendering either it or identity as originary, primary, or sovereign. These commitments to difference reverberate in his construal of thinking, which upholds all thought as modal and so particularized, conditioned, spatial, and temporal. This forecloses the prospect of an Intellect that Knows All or an Idealism that has reality originate in a Mind of God, much as it dispels a View from Nowhere or Absolute Standpoint. This does not mean, however, that Spinoza disregards or deflates reason. On the contrary, he remains sanguine about its promises to enable humans to live well, not because mind can determine body nor body determine mind, but due to an expansive conception of reason, which relies on his construal of mind and body as "one and the same thing." This means that everything a person undergoes is *as* a coordinated being. Mind is nothing but the idea of body, which installs all human thinking in extension. Such immanence and the coordination of mind and body it endues fasten our grip on reality by facilitating knowledge gleaned from our experiences and exposures as well as what Spinoza dubs "common notions" and "intuitive knowledge." Reason positions us to sort through knowledge that we absorb to discern the constraints of its contingencies and universalities, even as we cannot entirely dispense with such baggage. Furthermore, while perceiving things in their distinctions—things as they are in their particularity—is emblematic of intuitive or immanent reasoning, the force of such understanding rests in its affectivity rather than solely in its content.

After introducing and dissecting Spinoza's non-sovereign approach to reason and thinking, the chapter engages with competing takes, specifically Deleuze's interpretation. This is not only because his idealist rendition proffers a particularized instantiation of a current in the literature, which disregards the Jewish sources that condition Spinoza's uncommon approach, but also since it prompts us to explore Deleuze's own project, its appropriation of Spinoza, and the liabilities of its allegiance to epistemological sovereignties. This fidelity manifests in his idealism, which promotes reason as sovereign and defuses difference in Identity. Tarrying with Deleuze punctuates the difference of Spinoza's theory, opening a path for thinking reason and thinking thought otherwise.

Besides Thought

Reality, for Spinoza, is "of an infinity of attributes, of which each one expresses an eternal and infinite essence."[4] Infinite substance must be of infinite attributes because "the more reality or being each thing has, the more attributes belong to it,"[5] meaning "the more powers it has ... to exist."[6] Hence, substance "has an absolutely infinite power of existing,"[7] is "infinite power."[8] With this, as we have traced, Spinoza extrapolates from his medieval Jewish predecessors to conceive substance as the actualization of limitless power, which is its essence, which is its existence, which *is* it. Substance is of unlimited powers—attributes—because excluding anything from it undercuts its infinity. There can be no curbs on how substance can and cannot be, which is why reality is of infinite attributes. But Spinoza makes a further point: each of these attributes is "conceived through itself"[9] and "expresses an essence infinite in its own kind."[10] This is because as an "essence" of substance, an attribute, signifies the infinite ways in which the infinite power that *is* substance is: "each expresses the reality, *or* being of substance."[11] Infinite reality is of an infinity of attributes, infinite in kind.

Despite maintaining that reality is of an infinity of attributes—absolutely infinite power—Spinoza identifies only two attributes: thought and extension. After studying early drafts of the *Ethics*, G. H. Schuller asked Spinoza why "we cannot know more attributes of God than thought and extension?"[12] He responds: "The human Mind, *or* the idea of the human Body, neither involves nor expresses any other attributes of God besides these two. ... So ... the human Mind cannot achieve knowledge of any other attribute of God beyond these."[13] Since humans are of mind and body—thought and extension—their experience is limited to these conditions. Spinoza's reasoning is straightforward enough: how could we know of that which we could not know? Since a "human consists of a Mind and a Body,"[14] these configure but also constrict it. By insisting that reality is of infinite attributes and not *only* thought and extension, Spinoza confirms that what exists is not restricted to or dependent upon that which is human. Within the history of "Western" philosophy, this point is revolutionary in repudiating the anthropocentric reduction of the diversity of all to the sameness of what humans are and the narrowness of their standpoint.

Since each attribute is "conceived through itself" and is infinite in kind, none can be "inferred"[15] from another or "produced by another."[16] Rendering attributes reliant on anything, including each other, would elevate their status and subvert the necessity and infinity of substance. Consequently, no attribute is Primary. Neither thought, nor extension, nor any other attribute is preeminent to or dominant over other attributes. Thus, "modes of each attribute have God for their cause only insofar as God is considered under the attribute of which they are modes."[17] Thought causes ideas and extension causes bodies; ideas do not cause bodies and bodies do not cause ideas. Therefore, infinite reality cannot be subordinated to the supremacy of thought. Reality is not governed by Reason. That would constrain and contain it. This pressures interpretations that anchor Spinoza's philosophy in the Principle of Sufficient Reason[18] or misconstrue his commitment to rationalism—which amounts to the necessity of causal immanence—as subsuming all to the Sovereignty of reason. There is no a priori guarantee that thinking will approximate reality or that being will accommodate its conceptualization. Correspondingly, all that is cannot be regulated by extension, reduced to matter. This eschews a reductionist materialism, a subtlety that certain New Materialist appropriations of Spinoza elide.

The implications of Spinoza's conception of attributes as infinite and substance as of an infinity of attributes, not just those obtaining in humans, remains underrecognized. Prominent readings spanning the interpretative spectrums, across the centuries and still today, have faltered in registering these commitments and their implications. These oversights are exemplified by Hegel's exiguous dismissal of the attributes: "But only *two* are named ... *thought and extension*, and no indication is given of how the infinite multiplicity necessarily reduces to ... this opposition of thought and extension."[19] With this, he commits two missteps. The first is misunderstanding why Spinoza names and focuses exclusively on thought and extension: as human, Spinoza's foothold on reality is restricted to these. Second, Hegel—consistent with his own project—assumes that these constitute an oppositional pairing. Thus, he reduces substance to "the unity of thinking and being."[20] But Spinoza patently indicates otherwise, insisting on "an infinity of attributes," each of which is "conceived through itself" and "expresses an essence infinite in its own kind." This misrepresentation conveniently facilitates Hegel's critique: "Substance is the absolute unity of *thought* and being or extension; it therefore contains thought itself, but only in its *unity* with extension."[21] This is absolutely *not* what substance is. Spinoza even underscores that what he says concerning thought and extension applies to other attributes, for example, "or under any other attribute" and "I understand the same concerning other attributes."[22] Ontologically, thought and extension do not comprise more of a union than either does with another of the infinite attributes or as other attributes do with each other. While thought and extension do come together in modes like humans, Hegel universalizes this particularity, reducing infinite reality to the human experience.

Splitting the Difference 225

Uncorrelated

Construing reality as infinite power actualized in an infinity of ways—attributes—delivers an ontology that decenters humans or at least refuses to restrain what is to how it is for us. This aligns with Spinoza's confutation of anthropocentrism, his identification of this prejudice as deriving from the supposition that "God has made all things for human."[23] Since "humans prefer order to confusion,"[24] they imagine that reality accords with and accommodates their natures and needs, preferences and predilections. This anthropocentrism fosters the anthropomorphic projection of human capacities onto reality, which limits its power. To Spinoza, infinity exceeds the human experience. This stance, as previously demonstrated, is a reformulation of the Maimonidean commitment to God's limitlessness and the human limitations on adequately perceiving, let alone signifying, such limitlessness. The result is an emphatic caution against the anthropocentrism of certain epistemologies, especially the liberties assumed by theories of correlationism.[25]

While Spinoza concedes that we cannot know more or know beyond or know otherwise than our constitutions as the minded bodies or bodied minds that we are, he contests the correlationist supposition that, consequently, what can be known can only be known *for us* or that what is, is *only* as it is to us, as the correlation of thinking and being. Verily, we cannot escape the puzzle: "if there is something outside of thought how can we know it without first having thought it?" But Spinoza's insistence on the infinity of the attributes and resistance to anthropocentrism solicits us to resign from conflating what *is* with what and how *we* know it; what can *be* with what and how it can be known by *us*. The infinite power of existence that *is* substance cannot be conflated with or constrained to that which is human. Although our experiences are structured linguistically, cognitively, phenomenologically, spatially, and temporally, we cannot limit what is to our leases upon it.

Ironically, the seeming humility of correlational thinking—its claim that we can never really know what *is* because of insurmountable epistemic strictures—often functionally entrenches human predominancy by restricting all of reality to the anthropic hold on it. This is typified by assertions foreclosing an in-itself independent of the human Subject. To wit, Hegel's approach renders being and thinking identical and submits all to the particularities of the human standpoint, specifically his Christian standpoint whereby being *becomes* in and as absolute Spirit. By construing reality as infinite power actualized in infinite ways, Spinoza immanentizes the medieval Jewish conception of God as without limits and so uncontainable by human constructs. This delivers an ontology that demotes humans from their perch, refusing the subordination of reality to what and how they are. Correlationism performs a contrasting movement: it replaces the Sovereignty of an anthropomorphically forged God with Reason or with Human Reason, both of which are no less anthropocentric. This promotes human exceptionalism by esteeming the Reason that humans possess as Exceptional and so also humans as Exceptional.

The Right Attribution

What are attributes? The literature is littered in debates about their nature and status.[26] Yet attentive parsing of Spinoza's conception of the attributes, combined with an exploration of the sources that spur it, proves revelatory. Let us start with the initial definition proffered in the *Ethics*: "By attribute I understand what the intellect perceives of a substance, as constituting its essence."[27] Recall that for Spinoza, an essence of substance does not designate a property or thing it possesses but signifies how it exists, how infinite power actualizes. Therefore, each attribute "expresses the reality, *or being* of substance."[28] This is why infinite substance must be of infinite attributes: its power must be limitless. Since each attribute "expresses an essence infinite in its own kind," each is "conceived through itself."[29] Nevertheless, "although two attributes may be conceived to be really distinct (i.e. one may be conceived without the aid of the other), we still cannot infer from that that they constitute two beings *or* two different things."[30] Spinoza's worry is that if the attributes were too distinct, too divisible from substance, this might undercut its status as infinite, imperiling the necessity of its existence. To avoid this, he renders substance of infinite attributes, a "single" reality that actualizes differentially.

Spinoza clarifies that whatever is perceived as "constituting an essence of substance pertains to one substance only, and consequently that the thinking substance and the extended substance are one and the same substance, which is now comprehended under this attribute, now under that."[31] As we have seen, "one" does not denote actual oneness, be it quantitative or qualitative but is an inadequate way of signifying *nothing more than* or *other to* substance. There is "one" reality that is perceivable in a multiplicity of ways. The different essences or attributes of substance are the different manners in which the infinite power that is it actualizes, *how* it is. The precedent for this is found in a doctrine of "some of the Hebrews... that God, God's intellect, and the things understood by God are one and the same."[32] With this principle, as we have explored, certain medieval Jewish philosophers endeavored to reconcile the seemingly multiple attributes or actions credited to God with the imperative to uphold God's unity. To Maimonides, for example, God is the Form of all forms in that God's intellect effectuates all that exists. But this ascription of intellection to God does not mean that God exists independently of God's intellect or God's thoughts. Rather, "He and the thing thought are one thing, which is Himself" or His essence.[33] What cinches such identity is the purport that God's thinking is never potential, only actual. Maimonides follows Aristotle, maintaining that such identity also obtains in humans, for "the intellectually cognizing subject, the intellect, and the intellectually cognized object, are one and the same thing whenever we have an intellect in actu."[34]

At stake for thinkers like Maimonides who maintain that "God, God's intellect, and the things understood by God are one and the same" is the suspicion that attributing distinct faculties or properties to God implies divisibility or multiplicity. This subverts God's singularity, unity, and simplicity, which are deemed theologically fundamental. Maimonides devotes considerable attention to untangling and rebutting the manifold ascriptions of attributes to God that surface in Scripture, theological speculations, and popular opinion. The doctrine that God, God's mind, and God's thoughts "are one and the same thing" is a primary instantiation of these efforts. Against the hypostatization of "essential attributes" of God—living, knowing, possessing power, willing—Maimonides asserts that none of these is *"mussaf 'al 'atsmo"* (added to Himself) or His essence.[35] Rather, these *are* God, *equally* so. Thus, he stresses, concerning the conventional distinction between God's will and intellect: "In our opinion, volition too is consequent upon wisdom; all these being one and the same thing—I mean His essence and His wisdom—for we do not believe in attributes."[36] God's volition is not ontologically distinct from or additive to God. Rather, God's will *is* God's wisdom, which *is* God's essence, which *is* God. All of these are "one and the same."

Maimonides tarries in corroborating that "we do not believe in attributes," devoting considerable space to discrediting intimations to the contrary so as to certify God's simplicity and indivisibility. The primary hurdle confronting his campaign against the ascription of attributes to God is that Scripture is rife with them. It abounds in portrayals of God as doing things and feeling things and seems to characterize God as possessing certain attributes. By the rubrics of Maimonides's theology, all of this is heretical. To neutralize the abundant scriptural evidence against his doctrines, Maimonides contends that all descriptions of God or ascriptions to God of certain attributes reflect the human standpoint and experience rather than how or what God actually is. Across these glosses, Maimonides cites the rabbinic dictum[37] "dibrah Torah kilshon bnei 'adam" (the Torah speaks in the language of humans) to support as much.[38] Whatever qualities or attributes that Scripture attaches to God are "al tsad ha-dimyon be-shleimuteinu ha-muvanot 'etsleinu" (by analogy to perfections in us, as known to us).[39] These serve to convey that God is Perfect by depicting God as possessing that which is perceived as perfect in humans, even as these do not capture how God really is.

Especially problematic for Maimonides is a pericope in Exodus wherein a number of adjectives are ascribed to God, including compassionate, gracious, slow to anger, and abundantly kind. These depictions recur in different combinations in a number of places in Scripture and came to loom large in liturgy and rabbinic lore, which dubbed them as the thirteen *middot* (attributes) of God. To render these attributes consonant with his theology, Maimonides classifies them as attributes of action that do not describe the agent of the action but the actions performed by the agent, as perceived by humans.[40] Cinching his interpretation stands the narrative context preceding the adumbration of these attributes: a dialogue between God and Moses, wherein he asks to be shown *derakhekha* (your ways).[41] Thereupon, God has *kol tuvi* (all of My goodness) pass before Moses, namely, God's "compassion" and "graciousness."[42] Maimonides connects this "goodness" to Genesis, wherein God surveys all that had been created, regarding it as "very good."[43] Thus, Maimonides explains, the "ways"—the good—made known to Moses amounts to knowledge of nature, its interconnections, and God's governance over the universe through compassion, graciousness, and related attributes. The upshot is that what are considered God's attributes do not actually refer to God but to God's actions "in reference to the world."[44] Consequently, "ha-derakhim ve-hamiddot 'ehad" (the ways and the attributes are one and the same).[45] God's ways are God's attributes which are God's actions as apprehended by humans and so, predicated of God. For example, Maimonides expounds, God regulates nature so that embryos can develop and once born, are cared for, protected, and nurtured. Since in humans, the performance of such actions is affective, driven by compassion and concern, Scripture refers to God as compassionate.

So-called "essential attributes" have also only "been thought in reference to the diverse relations that may obtain between God... and the things created by Him."[46] Actions performed by God like willing or exercising power are not reflexive but projective. Consequently, their diversity and multiplicity are not of God but of God's actions in the world. All attributes are "kefi mahshavat bnei 'adam" (per human thought).[47] This is so with notional distinctions made by humans about God, like essential attributes. It equally applies to descriptions of God's productive actions in the world, all of which "are in reference to the multiplicity of His actions and not... a multiplicity subsisting in Him."[48] "We do not say," Maimonides writes, "that God created the heavens by one capacity, the elements by another capacity, the intelligences by another capacity." So too, God does not have a separate capacity by which God has power, wills, and knows. Rather, "God is one and simple, nothing more added."[49] Similarly, the diverse names by which Scripture refers to God "correspond to the actions existing in the world," rather than denoting multiplicity or composition in God. This bears emphasis because most of these are derivative, misleadingly implying that "attributes have real existence" additive to, or distinct from, God.[50]

One and the Same

With the foregoing background on Maimonides, we are now in a position to evaluate Spinoza's invocation of the doctrine embraced by "some of the Hebrews." Importantly, this principle and its premises are referenced several times across his writings. In *Cogitata Metaphysica*, Spinoza affirms: "God's intellect, and God's power and will, by which God has created, understood, and preserves... are not distinguished from one another in any way, except in regard to our thought."[51] Spinoza reprises the point: "In themselves God's will and God's intellect are really one and the same; they are distinguished only in relation to the thoughts we form about God's intellect."[52] He rehearses this in the *Ethics*: "So God's intellect, insofar as it is conceived to constitute God's essence is really the cause both of the essence and the existence of things."[53] Spinoza then remarks how this was "noticed by those who asserted that God's intellect, will and power are one and the same."[54] Those people, of course, are "some of the Hebrews," especially Maimonides. This principle cinches the claim that "the thinking substance and the extended substance are one and the same substance, which is now comprehended under this attribute, now under that."[55] Much as for "some of the Hebrews," God's wisdom, will, and actions are different referents for the same ontological thing, the same actualized power that *is* God. This is precisely what Spinoza is suggesting with regard to the attributes of substance: "Whether we conceive nature under the attribute of extension, or under the attribute of thought, or under any other attribute, we shall find one and the same order, *or* one and the same connection of causes."[56] However we regard it, despite the differences, these are *of* the same reality.

Spinoza's admittance of diversity—infinite attributes—into reality without submitting to multiple realities—multiple substances—exercised his interlocutors and still disquiets readers. After studying early drafts of what became the *Ethics*, Simon de Vries raised the concern that "where there are two different attributes, there are two different substances."[57] In his response, Spinoza includes this definition: "By a substance I understand what is in itself and is conceived through itself. . . . I understand the same by attribute, except that it is called attribute in relation to the intellect."[58] He then remarks: "I say that this definition explains clearly enough what I wish to understand by substance, *or* attribute."[59] Notice how this definition unambiguously construes attributes *as* substances, "or." The only difference is that an attribute is *how* the intellect renders substance definite, how it configures it. This distinction has been regarded as that of "respect"[60] or "aspect"[61] or "perspective."[62] It is not ontological.

The case of "substance" and "attribute" is an instance wherein "one and the same thing can be designated by two names."[63] To explain as much, Spinoza offers two examples. The first: "I say that by Israel I understand the third patriarch; I understand the same by Jacob, the name which was given him because he had seized his brother's heel."[64] This is not simply the banal observation that an individual may have more than one name. Indeed, many of us have multiple names. Rather, Spinoza is accounting for the role that alternate names—at least in Scripture—serve: they express an aspect of a person or an action committed by them and how the power that is that person has been actualized, specifically in relation to or as perceived by others, especially those who name them. With regard to the third patriarch, "Jacob" alludes to his act of cleaving to the heel of his twin at birth,[65] while "Israel" is bestowed in the aftermath of his predawn brawl with the "man" who left him with an injured hip and another name, signifying how he had strived and prevailed.[66] Both of these names of the patriarch reflect experiences that others had of him, how they perceived him. The second example reaffirms this perspectival element: "By flat I mean what reflects rays of light without any change; I understand the same by white, except that it is called white in relation to a human looking at the flat [surface]."[67] Names are relational and perspectival. This is exactly so with substance and attributes: these are different referents for the same thing, which are engendered by different experiences of it, distinct perspectives on it. The upshot is that "substance" and "attribute" are different appellations for that which is "one and the same." Hence, "substances *or* what is the same... their attributes and their affections."[68]

The construal of substance and attribute as different monikers for the same thing accentuates the role they serve in Spinoza's ontology: they furnish language for speaking about different aspects of substance. "Substance" refers to infinite, indeterminate power that is only actual, not potential, whereas "attribute" signifies a particular way in which this indeterminate, infinite power is realized, particularly, as experienced by humans. The human experience involves extended bodies that move and rest. Spinoza deploys "attribute" to refer to the common extended nature of these singular things. All are modal, finite determinations of the infinite, indeterminate power of substance, more specifically the finite determinations of the infinite, indeterminate power of substance *as* extension. Similarly, with thought, the ideas that we have are modal, that is determinate, definite instantiations of infinite, indeterminate power, specifically its power *as* thought. Extension and thought are different names we employ to more precisely nominate the indeterminate, infinite power that is substance. Crucially, this does not mean that without our conception of such that extension and thought would not adhere ontologically, that no bodies or ideas would exist. It simply means that we refer to these aspects of infinite, indeterminate power in these particular ways.

Spinoza refuses to reduce substance to the human standpoint. By maintaining that attributes are how substance is conceived, he means only that these are particular manners in which humans experience and so name the infinite power that is substance. The precedent of "some of the Hebrews" as formulated by Maimonides is salient: God is not *more* than God's self nor is God composed of constitutive parts. Rather, humans speak of God's mind, God's will, God's power, as if they are distinct, although they are same. Similarly, for Maimonides, descriptions of God as compassionate and gracious are but "the ways" in which God's actions are experienced by humans in the world. Yet this does not make them any less real: God's oversight of embryonic development adheres ontologically, irrespective of humans, let alone their ideas about God. What does not adhere ontologically is the distinction between God and God's capacity to enact as much. Those distinctions are only notional. Much as the diverse names by which God is referred to, according to Maimonides, correspond to God's diverse actions in the world and not to God's self because attributes do not exist ontologically distinct from God. Similarly to Spinoza, attributes refer to the ways in which humans experience and describe the powers of substance, and the actuality of these powers is ontologically real irrespective of the human perspective.

The reference to "some of the Hebrews" tenders compounded explanatory force. It offers precedent for conceiving diversity without surrendering identity: God is, God thinks, and God effectuates things into being. These seem like completely different things, a Being, God, who has a mind, and does things. Yet this principle claims otherwise: God is not separate from God's thinking (intellect), which effectuates things (understood by God). These are "one and the same," only distinguished notionally. Likewise, for Spinoza, there is no real distinction between substance and attributes; these are "one and the same thing." Furthermore, Maimonides's theories regarding God's attributes of action furnish Spinoza with a paradigm for admitting diversity into reality without rendering it dependent upon human thought. The "ways and attributes are one and the same," for Maimonides, which means that God acts in a variety of ways that obtain in reality. Such diversity is of God's actions "in reference to the world," not in reference to God. And crucially, the classification of these actions, say as "compassionate" and "gracious," is from the human experience and its perception. Accordingly, for Spinoza, even as substance is same with its attributes, this does not mean that its actualization of these powers is not real. On the contrary, these "ways" are ontologically real, irrespective of the human experience. Moreover, since the power of substance is only actualized, never in reserve, this means that attributes only exist in their actualization, which is only ever modal. This actualization is real. Extension and thought adhere ontologically. Diversity actually exists. The human distinction between substance and its powers, its essence, its attributes is subjective to the human standpoint. Yet diversity inheres ontologically, thought and extension exist objectively. Readers who continue to puzzle over these questions would benefit from actually reading "some of the Hebrews."

Makes a Difference

Through his construal of the attributes, Spinoza furnishes conceptual resources for navigating the dynamics of identity and difference without coronating either as inceptive or sovereign. Consider the familiar approaches. Often, difference is dissolved in absolute identity or rendered dependent upon its dialectical other. Alternatively, difference is defined as determinative. In the former, difference is degraded by its dissolution in identity or in its dependence upon that which is different to it. Identity becomes dominant and is endowed with priority, either as the origin of all or its telos. In the latter, while difference is not subordinated to identity—it retains distinction—its stature is solidified. In such a conception, difference *is* being or difference is the origin or engine of being. Difference is the measure of all. Further, in this instance too, difference retains dependence on its other—identity—that which is different, indeed, transcendent to it. So long as the binary of identity and difference is sustained, it is impossible to avoid both logical deadlock and the pitfalls of sovereignty.

To Spinoza "the thinking substance and the extended substance are one and the same substance, which is now comprehended under this attribute, now under that."[69] Consequently, "a mode of extension and the idea of that mode are one and the same thing, but expressed in two different ways."[70] This universalizes what Spinoza's predecessors applied only to God. For "some of the Hebrews" the identity of God, God's knowledge, and that which God knows are "one," the same non-composite God. Spinoza extends this such that a human mode, despite being of thought and extension, nevertheless constitutes "one" being. Since modes are the finite determinations of infinite, indeterminate power, a mind and body of a given mode are different aspects of the same infinite power. Significantly, despite being "same," mind and body remain irreducible. Spinoza explains: "A circle existing in nature and the idea of the existing circle . . . are one and the same thing, which is explained through different attributes."[71] Yet "God is the cause of the idea of a circle only insofar as God is a thinking thing" and likewise a cause of a circle "only insofar as God is an extended thing."[72] This affirms his claim that ideas cause ideas and extended things cause extended things. There *is* ontological difference. But such difference is of the same reality, although "we can conceive nature under the attribute of thought, or under the attribute of extension . . . we shall find one and the same order, *or* one and the same connection of causes."[73]

By insisting that extension causes extended things and thought causes ideated things, Spinoza rejects both a reductionist idealism and materialism. Neither thought nor extension is sovereign over its other or over any other attribute. When Spinoza explains that extension and thought "are one and the same substance, which is now comprehended under this attribute, now under that,"[74] he is not suggesting that ideated things or extended things do not actually exist ontologically. Nor is he saying as much in conceiving attributes as only "conceptually distinguished."[75] Rather, he is arguing that when it comes to accounting for *how* what exists is as it is, we can differentiate and classify things in two ways: extension or thought. With respect to modes of thought, "we must explain" these as of "the connection of causes, through the attribute of thought alone."[76] Accordingly, modes of extension, "must be explained through the attribute of extension alone."[77] There is difference in reality. Things are explainable only through their actual causes. Yet what causes both "connections of causes"—all that exists—is the infinite, indeterminate power that is substance. Correlatively, this means that everything is equally of substance, equally a determinate actualization of indeterminate power.

Substance—as advocated throughout this book—only exists as modified. The infinite, indeterminate power that is substance, only *is* as finite, determinate modes. Otherwise, the limitlessness of its power and the necessity of its existence would be undercut and it would exist as unactualized. This calibrates a conceptualization of difference that does not devolve into the sovereignty of identity. Because substance is not a being or thing but power in actu, this means that what exists is not grounded in an Identity. There is not first substance and then attributes and then modes, not Identity and only, subsequently, difference. This is not only because substance *is* its attributes but insomuch as attributes are merely the differentiated ways in which humans can "explain" or "conceive of" how or what modes are, but also since modes are how the infinite power that is substance exists. While this contention has been reconfirmed throughout our explorations, it can now be refined: though attributes are the respective manners in which human modes account for what exists, explains them according to different "connections of causes," this conceptualization does not vitiate the veridicality of extended things and ideated things in reality, which exist independent of human perception. What does not exist independent of such perception is the *division* of substance into diverse attributes because substance itself is indivisible. It is indeterminate, indefinite. Hence, absolutely infinite. This means at once that substance can neither be same nor different with itself: it cannot constitute an Identity. Furthermore, this corroborates that there is no identity against which the difference of reality is to be measured. It also confirms that the indeterminate power which is substance cannot be divvied into wholes and parts, categories and subcategories, as this would undermine its singularity, necessity of existence, infinity. With this, Spinoza allows for difference without rendering it sovereign. Singular modes are in a sense all that exist, although these are nothing but finite, determinate actualizations of infinite, indeterminate power. While modes are singular, that of which they are—substance, be it as perceived in thought or extension or both or any other attribute—is not exclusive to any given mode. On the contrary, all that is, is *of* it. Difference adheres ontologically, yet in and of itself cannot properly be considered primary as it is infinite power that is only finitely determined. Similarly, difference cannot exist otherwise than its particularization as singular modes.

Since there are infinite attributes, everything that Spinoza conveys with regard to extension and thought applies to other attributes. This bears punctuation because readers continue to reduce his ontology to the human perspective by adopting doctrines of parallelism.[78] Not only does Spinoza never speak of "parallelism," but several times he reminds readers that what he says about thought and extension are so also with the other attributes. This is exactly the point that concludes a most decisive scholium of the *Ethics*: "I understand the same concerning the other attributes."[79] Irrespective of the attribute in question, "we shall find one and the same order, *or* one and the same connections of causes."[80] The further problem with theories of parallelism is that parallel lines never intersect. Without intersection, how can there really be "one and the same order?" Not only does this pressure the uncompromising claim that everything is *of* substance, but it complicates his unambiguous affirmation that mind and body are "united"[81] and comprise a "union"[82] in humans. This is also why the attributes cannot be ontologically distinct from substance, for then how could they really be "one and the same"?

God Knows Nought

Conceiving Spinoza's reality as indeterminate power that only exists determinately, substance only *as* its modes, forecloses an Infinite Intellect or a Mind of God that adheres ontologically autonomous of modes. Yet honing his explications of how minds think and how thoughts are thought also furnishes evidence to invalidate such readings. Admittedly, Spinoza refers to an "infinite intellect" or "infinite idea" and speaks of God as thinking. But as ever, the meaning of conventional theological and metaphysical terms and concepts undergoes significant revision through his usage of them. While this is not the place to unpack each occurrence of such terms, cognates, and concepts, briefly dissecting a few such instances alongside his overall construal of thought conveys the point and models an interpretive path exploitable in resolving further invocations of this kind.

Spinoza opens part II by demonstrating that "God is a thinking thing"[83] and that "God is an extended thing,"[84] which confirms that thought and extension adhere ontologically. Moreover, "singular thoughts, *or* this or that thought, are modes that express God's nature in a certain and determinate way."[85] The same is the case with extension[86] and modes of other attributes. This means that all singular thoughts and things are determinate expressions of the indeterminate power that is substance, more particularly, determinations of its indeterminate power conceived *as* the attribute of thought or extension. Spinoza corroborates that thought causes thought and extension causes extension: "Modes of each attribute have God for their cause only insofar as God is considered under the attribute of which they are modes."[87] Finite, determinate extended things are the actualization of infinite, indeterminate power *as* extension and not thought, or conversely, and so with other attributes. To be sure that readers grasp this point, he clarifies: "The formal being of things which are not modes of thinking does not follow from the divine nature because [God] has first known the things; rather the objects of ideas follow and are inferred from their attributes in the same way as and by the same necessity as that with which we have shown ideas to follow from the attribute of thought."[88] All singular things are effectuated by that which is like them, for like causes like: extended things cause extended things, ideas cause ideas, and so with other attributes. While Spinoza depicts this point with reference to the attribute of thought, he is not privileging thought. On the contrary, what he says regarding the necessity of like causing like applies *equally* to modes of other attributes. With this, Spinoza explicitly proscribes an idealism whereby God's intellect is responsible for effectuating material things. This diverges from "some of the Hebrews" as much as from Cartesianism.

"In God there is necessarily an idea, both of God's essence and of everything that necessarily follows from God's essence."[89] While this sounds like a familiar claim regarding a transcendent God who Knows and Knows All, this is absolutely not what Spinoza means. Precisely the opposite is at issue, and Spinoza's explicit discounting in this scholium of God as Sovereign is not a coincidence. This proposition simply asserts that since thinking exists in reality, reality can be thought. Subsequent propositions lay out the conditions under which reality can be thought, only modally, only spatially, and so, only partially. But here the moves are more basic. They start with confirming that God "can think infinitely many things in infinitely many modes," which just means that an infinite power of thinking exists, that the infinite power that is reality can be actualized as the power of thought. Since "whatever is in God's power necessarily exists . . . therefore, there is necessarily such an idea and . . . it is only in God."[90] Such an idea of whatever exists is "in God" because "whatever is, is in God, and nothing can be or be conceived without God."[91] By this Spinoza intends that whatever idea there is of God, and that which follows from God's power, exists *in* God and not outside of God because all that exists is *of* it. Differently stated, ideas about reality are *of* reality, modal ideas of reality are *of* reality.

Spinoza proceeds to excoriate those who take "God's power" as "God's free will and right over all things which are."[92] Such people "very often compare God's power with the power of Kings."[93] In this context, the specific problem of such a conception is that it takes God's power as contingent, rather than necessary: as the power to decide, to freely do as it pleases, to act as a human Subject and Sovereign. But "we have shown . . . that God acts with the same necessity by which God understands God's self, i.e. just as it follows from the necessity of the divine nature (as everyone maintains unanimously) that God understands God's self, with the same necessity it follows that God does infinitely many things in infinitely many modes."[94] Since readers are familiar with beliefs that consider God as Knowing All and All Knowing, Spinoza appeals to such doctrines, explaining how just as they consider God's knowledge as necessary, so too, he takes not just God's knowledge but *all* that God does as causally necessary. This means that not only is thinking necessary, not only does thought adhere ontologically but so, too, do all infinite attributes, necessarily, for "God's power is nothing except God's active essence."[95] This is Spinoza's way of confirming that all other attributes or all other things that exist are as equally necessary as thought is. Thinking is not privileged. Moreover, in the subsequent demonstrations it becomes clear that "God's idea"[96] of anything is not more preeminent than God's actions in any other attribute. On the contrary, "the modes of each attribute have God for their cause only insofar as God is considered under the attribute of which they are modes."[97]

But Spinoza's resistance to an idealism in God's mind goes further: "When singular things are said to exist, not only insofar as they are comprehended in God's attributes, but insofar also as they are said to have duration, their ideas also involve existence through which they have duration."[98] If something exists that has duration—is extended—its existence cannot be due to an idea but only to something extended. To depict as much, Spinoza draws a circle with two intersecting lines, D and E. Although infinitely many rectangles can be formed from the segments of lines in this or any circle, since lines have been drawn and labeled D and E, these exist not only because they are "comprehended in the idea of the circle, but also insofar as they involve the existence of those rectangles."[99] This is because they now exist not just in thought but in extension. Here too, Spinoza is not privileging thought, and he is not saying that the idea of these rectangles must exist *in order* for them to exist in extension. Rather, his example serves to distinguish between a singular thing that adheres in thought and does not adhere in extension and, further, to demonstrate that a thing is said to "have duration" *only* if it is extended. The idea of a singular thing cannot effectuate an extended object, period.

Thinking in Place

Despite Spinoza's repeated talk of God causing things or thinking things, it becomes clear that what he intends by such idiomatic phrases is uncustomary. This is further signaled by his positing: "The idea of a singular thing which actually exists has God for a cause not insofar as God is infinite, but insofar as God is considered to be affected by another idea of a singular thing which actually exists . . . and so on, to infinity."[100] Substance is deemed a cause of a singular thing *only* insofar as the indeterminate power that is it, is determined, modified, "affected." To say that substance causes a given thing means that this thing is the effect of a constellation of other singular things that are of the same attribute. Infinite, indeterminate substance causes *only as* its finite, determinate modes, and because substance is not *before* its "decrees," it cannot exist without actualizing its power, cannot be without acting—substance only *is* modally. Hence, "the cause of one singular idea is another idea, *or* God, insofar as God is considered affected by another idea; and of this also insofar as God is affected by another, and so on, to infinity."[101] God causes modally, for God only *does* and *is* modally. But there is more here: "Whatever happens in the singular object of any idea, there is knowledge of it in God, only insofar as God has the idea of the same object."[102] Not only does substance only cause things modally, but substance only knows modally, that is, *as* a mode. This is why substance can only have knowledge of something if such a thing exists materially, if the idea has an object. Differently stated, knowledge of a singular thing only exists if that thing "actually exists" in time and space. The idea of a body is known to substance only *as* the very idea of that body, which must exist. Knowing something is contingent upon spatial and temporal conditions. Glossing this passage, Ursula Renz observes: "Not only does his approach abstain from saying that a single epistemic subject has—or could have—all knowledge; he also implicitly dismisses the claim that there could ever be such an omniscient subject."[103] Indeed, "if there are entities that can only be known from a *view from somewhere* . . . then it must be impossible for anyone to have knowledge of everything by adopting a *view from nowhere*."[104]

While Spinoza upholds the existence of infinite attributes of which humans know but two, the focus on thought and extension as coupled in these propositions reflects not only the limits of his standpoint as human but the imperatives of the exploration: elucidating how thinking happens in humans, which are a "union" of mind and body. Similarly, all of Spinoza's talk of God here serves to explicate how thinking occurs in order to help readers navigate certain hurdles to living well. This is apparent in his unskeptical validation that humans think and exist as they are aware of themselves, a retort to Cartesian dubitability. The veracity of such awareness is clinched by Spinoza's claim that "the first thing that constitutes the actual being of a human mind is nothing but the idea of a singular thing which actually exists."[105] Since a mind, for Spinoza, is not a thing that thinks, but thinking itself, the first thing that constitutes a mind in humans is an idea, and in order for that idea to "actually exist," it needs to be attached to a body. Not only does this reaffirm that all thinking exists spatially and temporally, but "it follows that the human mind is a part of the infinite intellect of God."[106] This is because "when we say that the human mind perceives this or that, we are saying nothing but that God, not insofar as God is infinite, but insofar as God is explained through the nature of the human mind, *or* insofar as God constitutes the essence of the human mind, has this or that idea."[107] When one thinks—has an idea—their doing so is a finite, determinate actualization of the indeterminate, infinite power of thinking. It is infinite power finitely determined as "this or that idea," in this case, the idea is of its body. And since mind is the idea of body, this means that if a mind is thinking, its thinking is attached to a body—it actually exists. This is "the first thing that constitutes the actual being of a human mind," its awareness of itself, its body. Therefore, "if the object of the human mind were not the body, the ideas of the affections of the body would not be in God,"[108] meaning these would not exist ontologically. Significantly, "when we say that God has this or that idea, not only insofar as God constitutes the nature of the human mind, but insofar as God also has the idea of another thing together with the human mind, then we say that that human mind perceives the things only partially *or* inadequately."[109] This makes abundantly clear that Spinoza does not have anything conventional in mind while invoking God's thinking as he is ascribing to God inadequate thinking. Rather, what he means is that when a human mind—a finite, determinate actualization of infinite, indeterminate power as thinking—perceives multiple things simultaneously, this knowledge is incomplete, inadequate. All thinking that happens is "God thinking" insofar as God is nothing but its acts, infinite power that is only actualized finitely.

By insisting that all thinking is modal such that God thinks nought and that minds are ideas of bodies such that all thinking is of a body that exists as extended, Spinoza delivers a resounding blow to the "Western" philosophical valorization of reason as Sovereign. No mind knows All. There is no Supreme intellect or Knower of all. Rather, the infinite, indeterminate power that is reality actualizes in infinite ways, including as thought. Yet this power of thinking is never All Powerful for all thinking is necessarily of a body that exists spatially and temporally. The mind only knows *as* its body. While the ensuing sections unpack the specifics of this arrangement, here it is important to underline how Spinoza installs thinking as particularized and situated. There is no Absolute standpoint, no View from Nowhere, no ideas Transcendent to the conditions under which they are thought. However, divesting thought of such imperiousness does not render it powerless, let alone useless. Nor does it mean that nothing can ever really be known. On the contrary, Spinoza is committed to reason and its role in positioning us to live well, which depends on his contention that we only think *as* bodies, particularized bodies. By divesting reason of sovereignty, refusing to bestow upon it autonomy *from* conditions and domination *over* conditions, while simultaneously confirming it as indispensable to living, Spinoza forges a different course.

Carnal Knowledge

Against the weight of a "Western" philosophical tradition, which since Plato has privileged the faculty of intellection and taken it as *transcending* materiality, Spinoza confirms that all human thinking happens in a body, *as* its body. Yet he equally rejects the elevation of extension: "The body cannot determine the mind to thinking, and the mind cannot determine the body to motion, to rest or to anything else."[110] No attribute is supreme over its other because each "must be conceived through itself, since all attributes have always been in it together, and one could not be produced by another, but each expresses the reality, *or* being of substance."[111] Attributes are "together" because each is the very being, existence, power that *is* substance, all of which are "one and the same substance" only "conceptually distinguished." This dynamic, extrapolated from "some of the Hebrews," positions Spinoza's innovative approach to humans, which upholds the difference of mind and body without resort to hierarchy. Instead of conceiving mind and body through subordination, he upholds their coordination. A singular mode, like substance, is nothing but a certain actualization of power. This power that is a singular mode, at least in humans, expresses itself in extension as well as thought. Yet despite this difference, the mode is still "one and the same thing."[112] Such differentiated sameness accounts for this construal: "The object of the idea constituting the human mind is the body, *or* a certain mode of extension which actually exists."[113] The mind is not a substantially distinct thing attached to a body. It is the idea of the body. It is the existence, the power of a given mode as actualized in thought, much as its body is that very power, that "same thing," actualized in extension.

How are mind and body "one and the same thing"? To grasp what Spinoza is suggesting, it is instructive to reprise his conception of singular things as modes "that express, in a certain and determinate way, God's power, by which God is and acts."[114] Modes are particularized actualizations of power. These fluctuate due to intra-actions that are both external and internal. Spinoza refers to these variations in the "power of acting *or* force of existing" that is a mode as "affections": "By an *affectionem* [affection] of the human essence we understand any constitution of that essence, whether it is innate [or has come from outside], whether it is conceived through the attribute of thought alone, or through the attribute of extension alone, or is referred to both at once."[115] Since mind and body are "one and the same thing," whatever a human mode does, undergoes, and experiences—its affections—are always of mind and body in coordination. If the body acts or is acted upon, so too, does the mind act or is acted upon; if the mind acts or is acted upon, so too does the body act or is acted upon. Such coordination, however, does not mean that every single action or experience is necessarily consciously registered or "referred" to both mind and body. To wit, I do not have conscious ideation of the activities of the mitochondria in the cells of my left pinky. Spinoza is not contending as much but is affirming that whatever a human mode does and endures, it does and endures as the coordination of mind and body.

The affections that a singular mode has are same even as these are "referred" differently to mind and body. In mind these changes in the force of existence that is a mode are actualized as ideas, while in body, as bodily affections. Since "the order and connection of ideas is the same as the order and connection of things," it follows that "the order and connection of ideas happens in the mind according to the order and connection of *affectionum* of the body . . . so vice versa . . . the order and connection of *affectionum* of the body happens as thoughts and ideas of things are ordered and connected in the mind."[116] Whatever a mode does—whether it acts or is acted upon—occurs in coordination and is *of* the same mode, just as attributes are *of* the same reality. The experiences and encounters that a mode endures are impactful and constantly alter its power. "Affectations" are these changes in the "body's power of acting," while affects are "the ideas of these *affectionum*," which transpire "at the same time."[117] This coordinated approach positions Spinoza to account for human behavior and how to more effectively adjust to its variabilities. What is pertinent to impress at present is the consequence of such coordination: it enables the mind to have ideas, for the ideas it has are only as, in, and through its body. This is why "the human mind does not know the human body itself, nor does it know that it exists, except through ideas of *affectionum* by which the body is affected."[118]

Without doubt, complication, or hesitation, Spinoza establishes that we exist as we experience ourselves, as minded bodies or bodied minds. "The first thing that constitutes the actual being of a human mind is nothing but the idea of a singular thing which actually exists,"[119] its body. If this were otherwise then "the ideas of the affections of the body would not be in our mind; but . . . we have ideas of the affections of the body."[120] So, "the object of our mind is the existing body and nothing else."[121] It "follows that a human consists of a mind and body, and that the human body exists, as we are aware of it."[122] Significantly, for Spinoza, mind is knowledge of body: "for the human mind is the idea itself, *or* knowledge of the human body."¹²³ Therefore, "the present existence of our mind depends only on this, that the mind involves the actual existence of the body."¹²⁴ Or, "the essence of the mind" is the very affirmation of "the actual existence of its body."¹²⁵ This relies on Spinoza's basic claim that minds are not things which think ideas but *are* ideas themselves. A mind does not precede or exist independently of the ideas that it thinks. It *is* these ideas. And the first idea of a mind is nothing but its body, which *is* it. Consequently, not only does the mind's knowledge of its body come by way of the ideas it has of the affections of its body, this is also so with regard to knowledge of itself: "The mind does not know itself, except insofar as it perceives the ideas of the affections of the body."¹²⁶ This scheme only works because the affections of the body "agree with the nature of the mind"¹²⁷ as they are "one and the same thing."

Body Check

Spinoza cautions with regard to his conception of mind and body that "no one will be able to understand it adequately, *or* distinctly, unless they first know adequately the nature of the body."¹²⁸ This is why he delineates his theories of bodies, in what has mistakenly been dubbed the "Physical Digression," as if this is tertiary to his focus rather than central to it. Since mind and body are coordinated, a mind that is "more excellent . . . contains more reality" is correlated with the excellence and reality of its object, its body.¹²⁹ A mind is "more capable, the more its body can be disposed in a great many ways."¹³⁰ This is because the mind only knows itself and other things due to the ideas that it has of the affections of its body. Without body, it knows nought. Indeed, it is nought. It has no reality at all. But the more reality a body has—the more affections it has—so the more capable is its mind.¹³¹

By emphasizing the capabilities of the body, Spinoza is not making the banal point that physical health is a prerequisite to thinking and so to living well. Nor is he asserting that physical safety and stable political conditions are critical. While he maintains both of these views, here, Spinoza is articulating a different, less obvious point: since whatever a singular mode experiences, does, or undergoes is always both as mind and body, it follows that the more its body is disposed, the more perceptions its mind has. For example, "an infant or child, has a body capable of very few things, and very heavily dependent on external causes."¹³² Spinoza's aim is to assist readers in becoming more conscious of themselves, of others, and of reality because such a person "is least troubled by evil affects ... by affects contrary to our nature."[133] They live good lives. Reason plays a role in such a life not because mind transcends body or sovereignly commands it, but since with reason, one has "a power of ordering and connecting the affections of their body according to the order of the intellect."[134] The *Ethics* unravels how this is possible. To appreciate as much requires examining Spinoza's understanding of bodies.

Bodies are "composed of a great many individuals of different natures, each of which is highly composite."[135] Pertinently, "the individuals composing the human body, and consequently, the human body itself, are affected by external bodies in very many ways."[136] Consequently, "the human mind perceives the nature of a great many bodies together with the nature of its own body," since bodies are connected with other bodies.[137] Further, "the ideas which we have of external bodies indicate the condition of our own body more than the nature of external bodies."[138] How we experience other modes is primarily determined by the state of our own selves. Yet our hold on ourselves is extremely partial. Not only are we vulnerable to forces both internal and external, conscious and not conscious, which constantly affect us without our consent or control, but knowledge of our bodies, the ideas of its affections, are "not clear and distinct, but confused."[139] What is more, "the idea that constitutes the nature of the human mind is not, considered in itself alone, clear and distinct."[140]

Since the mind knows only its body, which it knows only inadequately, and it gains knowledge of external bodies through the affections of its own body, this means that its knowledge of external bodies is partial and personalized.[141] Such inadequacy is amplified by the fact that its knowledge is gleaned from the affections of its body and correspond to the specificities of its own constitution. We do not autonomously control how our body is affected nor the ideas that our minds form of these affections. This leads to all sorts of mistakes. It is how we imagine things as present even when they are not because, once a body is affected by an external thing, that affectation can only be displaced by another that it excludes. It also explains how ostensibly random thoughts pop into our minds, how associations and memories surface, unconsciously, while asleep—which we call dreams—but constantly too, while awake. All of this happens without our consent. Significantly, because all of these associations, memories, and imaginations are based on actual bodily affections, this anchors all of them, however inadequate, fanciful, and ludicrous, in reality.

Furthermore, because the mind's ideas of the affections of its body are based on affectations from other bodies, which are mostly random, the ideas the mind has of these are inadequate.[142] This is amplified by the fact that our pasts condition how we register present affections by triggering associative memories. For example, when a soldier is affected by imprints in the sand, they immediately think of a horseperson and war, whereas a farmer thinks of a plow and a field. "And so each one, according as they have been accustomed to join and connect the images of things in this or that way, will pass from one thought to another."[143] While these differences reflect the singularity of each mode, shaped by the particularities of its body, experiences, and interconnections, such contingency also confirms the inadequacy of these ideas and our lack of sway over them.

Knowledge of adequate ideas alone does not automatically counter inadequate ideas induced by bodily affectations. Spinoza explains how while looking at the sun, due to how strongly it affects the body, "we imagine it as about 200 feet away from us."[144] Yet even if we know its actual distance, "we nevertheless imagine it as near."[145] Our knowledge of how things are is incapable, in and of itself, of disrupting our imaginings. This is because "inadequate and confused ideas follow with the same necessity as adequate *or* clear and distinct ideas."[146] Like everything, they are causally determined and stay their course. Therefore, "so long as the human mind perceives things from the common order of nature, it does not have an adequate, but only a confused and mutilated knowledge of itself, of its own body and of external bodies."[147]

Stands to Reason

Our susceptibility to forces beyond our command is exemplified by "the affects by which we are daily torn,"[148] which pull us in contrary directions, leaving us conflicted about our desires and uncertain about the future. This, Spinoza argues, makes us miserable. The problem is not simply that we cannot sovereignly control our external encounters. We cannot even direct how these leave us feeling. However, reason can disrupt this disorienting state of affairs with perceptions that are "determined internally," when it "regards a number of things at once, to understand their agreements, differences, and oppositions."[149] Thereby, "it regards things clearly and distinctly."[150] Even though everything the body experiences, the mind does too, precipitating its confused ideas based on the contingencies of its external influences and encounters, since the mind—as much as body—experiences these affections, it can also reorient them. It does this by distinguishing between the "order and connections of the affections of the body" and "the connection of ideas, according to the order of the intellect."[151] While the former reflects the arbitrary, haphazard, and erratic affections one undergoes—the "common order of nature"—the latter "perceives things through their first causes."[152] It grasps what things are and how they have come to be.

In explicating the prospects of reason to stabilize our lives, Spinoza outlines three different forms of knowledge, none of which, despite their constraints, we can do without. The first variety derives from the common order of things and encompasses imagination, universal notions, and opinion. Being entangled in the infinite connection of causes leaves bodied minds or minded bodies vulnerable to external impact and easily flooded by affectations. The problem is that "the human body, being limited, is capable of forming distinctly only a certain number of images at the same time."[153] Consequently, "the mind also will imagine all the bodies confusedly, without distinction, and comprehend them as if under one attribute" such as "Being" or "Thing."[154] This is also the case with "notions they call universal, like Human, Horse, Dog."[155] To cope with such overexposure, humans devise categories and classifications to gain a foothold on reality. Yet, these erase "slight differences" and "determinate number."[156] As such, the mind "imagines distinctly only what they all agree in, insofar as they affect the body"[157] and perceives them in generalized, abstracted ways. Furthermore, "these notions are not formed by all in the same way, but vary from one to another, in accordance with what the body has been more affected by, and what the mind imagines or recollects more easily."[158] Even as we might use the same universal notions, categories, and designations, our singular, mostly random experiences and exposures, coupled with the particularized memories and connections these prompt, condition them to signify different things for different people. These "ways of regarding things"[159] are "the only cause of falsity."[160] They precipitate mutilated knowledge and confusion.

Despite the contingency, partiality, and propensity to falsity of universal notions and opinion, Spinoza does not denigrate them nor suppose that we can dispense with them or imagination. On the contrary, in the *Treatise on the Emendation of the Intellect*, he explains that such knowledge from "random experience" delivers "almost all the things that are useful in life."[161] This encompasses, for example, knowledge that we will die or knowledge that water extinguishes fire, which are known from lived experience and exposures, rather than from perceptions of exactly why these are the case.

Similarly, through reports and the authority of others, we receive knowledge of basic information, like our birthdates and parentage. To Spinoza, knowledge from lived—however random—experience is expansive and essential. Memory is equally critical to functioning, while universal notions, which are responsible for language, time, and numbers, are integral to human flourishing. Therefore, notwithstanding the inadequacies of such knowledge, Spinoza affirms their indispensability. Readings that ascribe to Spinoza a denigration of body and devaluation of imagination miss this complexity.

The second kind of knowledge—"certain ideas *or* notions, common to all humans"[162]—also derives from bodily affections. Yet its form of inferential knowledge is never false but "perceived adequately, *or* clearly and distinctly, by all."[163] This is because "all bodies agree in certain things."[164] Since it concerns bodies and is common to all, "the mind is the more capable of perceiving many things adequately as its body has many things in common with other bodies."[165] The more someone is affected in different ways, especially through agreements with other bodies, the more adequate ideas they have of reality. Such inferential knowledge is exemplified by the recognition of ourselves as a "union of mind and body,"[166] specifically the particularized minded bodies or bodied minds that each of us is. This facilitates knowledge of "the common properties of things" that "we always imagine in the same way."[167] It is adequate because "an idea that excludes the existence of our body cannot be in our mind, but is contrary to it."[168] Spinoza relies on such inference to declare, without hesitation or reservation, that a "human thinks" and "that the human body exists, as we are aware of it."[169]

Such inferential knowledge, common to all bodies of its kind, cinches Spinoza's contention: "There is no affection of the body of which we cannot form a clear and distinct concept."[170] Not only do we have basic, inferential access to, and knowledge of, the affectations of our body, but these are necessarily accurate. This conviction is pivotal to Spinoza's project, indicating that "each of us has—in part, at least if not absolutely—the power to understand themselves and their affects, and consequently, the power to bring it about that they are less acted on by them."[171] What is more, the more capable a body, "the more they have a power of ordering and connecting the affections of the body according to the order of the intellect."[172] To order things according to reason instead of by the random order of nature presupposes expansive, distinct, and particular knowledge of body and its affectations. Not only is it only through the body that one has the ideas of such affectations, but insomuch as the more capable one is of clearly regarding and distinguishing such affectations, the more capable one will be of disrupting the random order of encounters and reordering them according to reason. Such adequate knowledge of self, others, and reality positions one to realize more agreements with others, allowing them to live well.[173]

In addition to universal and common notions, Spinoza discusses the third kind of knowledge, "intuitive knowledge," which "proceeds from an adequate idea of the formal essence of certain attributes of God to the adequate knowledge of the essence of things."[174] To make sense of it, it is instructive to consider the mathematical example that Spinoza offers to depict the different ways of knowing. Based on the ratios between these numbers—1, 2, 3—what is the next number in this proportional series? Spinoza details different ways of approaching this question, which correspond to the three forms of knowledge. A person can rely on knowledge they received from a teacher by following the rule about multiplying the second by the third and then dividing it by the first, leading to 6. Although such a procedure results in the correct number, someone who follows these guidelines without understanding them will not appreciate *why* 6 is the right answer.[175] This is also the case with someone who deduces the answer from trial and error. Both of these are in the realm of universal notions. By contrast, someone might know the next integer "from the common property of proportionals."[176] This knowledge of properties is generalized, not particularized to the specific proportional at hand. Since the person does not grasp the particulars, their understanding remains "outside them,"[177] it relies on "conviction in the intellect," mere "belief."[178] While both of these can be reliable, intuitive knowledge allows someone to know the fourth number is 6 "in one glance" by perceiving "the number to have the second."[179] Such knowledge is immanent, it does not rely on application from rules or deductions from experience or demonstrations. Rather, "through their penetration they immediately see the proportion in all the calculations."[180] Such knowing grasps singular things, in their particularities, their "very essence"[181] and is therefore not prone to error.

There is a further aspect of intuitive knowledge that has been overlooked, yet is crucial for grasping its significance: the immanence emblematic of it. Such perception "is in the person, not outside them."[182] Really perceiving something, knowing it, in its essence, amounts to knowing what it is and how it is, which for Spinoza means what it is in its particularities and how it has come to be as it is in its singularity. Such understanding is not external in the sense of being received from authority or opinion. It is also not external because one actually perceives the thing at hand, as opposed to just knowing it based on experience or prior exposure. This is the Aristotelian form of cognition that "some of the Hebrews" apply to God, whose knowledge of things is not external, but immanent, which dissolves the binary of subject and object. Spinoza follows his predecessors in allowing that humans experience such cognition, at times. By really "getting" the object, knowledge of it is now *of* the thinker, *in* it. The mind is like "a formal cause" of it and in that sense, can be considered "eternal."[183] The immanence of such knowledge induces the most pleasure,[184] which renders it the most powerful form of knowledge.[185] Yet Spinoza confesses, "the things I have so far been able to know by this kind of knowledge have been very few."[186]

Reason not only does not transcend corporeal reality but relies on it. Since humans are minded bodies or bodied minds, binarily distinguishing between these misses Spinoza's conception of humans and its ramifications for living well. Universal notions resulting from the affectations of random experience and received knowledge, despite their liabilities, deliver "almost all the things that are useful in life."[187] Common notions derive from an inherent sense of ourselves, as we are, in our shared reality from perceptions of the affections of our bodies and the attendant ideas we have of them, which to Spinoza, are necessarily accurate. Intuitive knowledge presupposes these other elements, as it refers to perceptions of how things are, in themselves, and their interconnections.

There is another point concerning the power of thinking that bears emphasis. Conceiving adequate ideas helps us navigate the affectations that we undergo through reordering them according to reason, which sorts through and understands things as they are in their particularity. Doing so allows us to grasp "agreements, differences, and oppositions."[188] This contrasts with relying on the affections of random encounters and experiences or the universalized abstractions that we employ to approximate them. Notwithstanding their adequacy, the content of adequate ideas in and of themselves is often insufficient for navigating unstable conditions and the negative affects that accompany them. What proves decisive, as the final chapter addresses, is the affective force of the ideas that we think. The promise of reason, for Spinoza, lies in its affectivity. It is only because the mind, as much as the body, feels, and what it feels, it feels in coordination as a minded body and bodied mind that ideas are powerful enough to meaningfully and consistently impact our lives.

Minding Matter

There are several immediately discernible assets of Spinoza's approach to mind and body. Most blatantly, stands its sidestepping of the puzzles that befall Cartesianism: reckoning with how two substantially distinct things—thought and extension—are united in humans and, further, accounting for what kind of interaction and influence they have over each other. Spinoza lacerates Descartes: "What, I ask, does he understand by the union of mind and body? . . . he had conceived the mind to be so distinct from the body that he could not assign any singular cause. . . . Instead, it was necessary for him to have recourse to the cause of the whole universe, i.e., to God."[189] To account for how two substantially distinct things are united in humans, Descartes resorts to God's sovereign will.[190] These concerns surface in his correspondences with Elisabeth of Bohemia, wherein she pressures his dualism by reflecting on how physical ailments inhibit her philosophizing.[191] If the mind transcends body and governs it, then why does the state of her body impact her mind? Spinoza contests this transcendent, hierarchical arrangement. Since mind and body are irreducibly same, neither can rule its other. By resisting dualism, he reconfigures the scheme. Instead of considering humans as comprised of two substantially distinct things, Spinoza upholds a human mode as "one and the same thing," whose experiences, affections, and encounters—the variations in power that are it—are "referred" or registered differently by mind and body, even as that which it undergoes are the same, of "one and the same connections of causes." Neither mind nor body dominates its other. Rather "one and the same thing" experiences "one and the same order." But this does not mean that reality is constituted by parallel realms. On the contrary, it reflects his basic contention that the same reality can be expressed, experienced, or explained in different ways. At issue is not so much a one-to-one correspondence between everything that happens but a way of accounting for lived experience.

Consider, for example, what happened to me last night: I abruptly experienced a brief, sharp pain on my left ankle. It was followed by a sensation of swelling and then itchiness. My mind registered these affections by deducing that a mosquito pierced my skin with their proboscis and feasted on my blood. In reaction to contact with their saliva, my body released histamine, which triggered inflammation, causing itchiness. Based on common notions—my awareness of myself as bodied and bodied in a specific way—coupled with experience and accumulated knowledge, my mind quickly made sense of these affectations, these alterations in the power that is me. But without these, I could have supposed that my ankle had been severed from my body. Or have imagined that I was attacked by demonic Samael or that a microchip was inserted into my leg. Alternatively, I could have known this was a mosquito but worried that I had been infected with malaria. Yet my reason, thanks to lived experience and collected information, including that malaria is not a biological threat in this geographical zone, foreclosed such concerns. Moreover, since mind and body are not substantially different for Spinoza, the force of my knowledge about these factors affectively determined me to do nothing, rather than recite an incantation, call the FBI, procure chloroquine phosphate, or rush to the emergency room. Equally so, the force of my understanding that scratching the bite would only increase the soreness made me determined not to scratch it, not because my mind overrode my body, commanding my hand not to scratch the bite. Rather, since I am a minded body or bodied mind—"one and the same thing"—the affective power of this understanding determined that I did not do so. Accordingly, that I am "one and the same thing" also explains why as I sit here typing this sentence, endeavoring to think philosophically, my train of thought is disrupted by irritation on my ankle. A dualist like Descartes struggles to reconcile as much.

All for One

Now that Spinoza's non-sovereign conception of reason and non-supremacist construal of the attributes have been examined, we are in a position to consider the divergent take advocated by Deleuze and its duplication in his philosophy. Deleuze's Spinoza is committed to univocity and parallelism, which lead to idealism. Univocity means that "*being is predicated in the same sense* of everything that is, whether infinite or finite."[192] This is because the same attributes formally constitute the essence of substance and formally contain the essence of modes.[193] Similarly, "all forms of being are equal and equally perfect, and there is no inequality of perfection between attributes."[194] While this latter point is correct, Deleuze is mistaken to hypostatize the attributes and construe them as constituting or comprising substance. Such composition supports his logic of univocity, that "there is a unity of the diverse in substance, and an actual diversity of the One in the attributes."[195] More astonishingly, Deleuze actually compromises on the very equality of the attributes that he purports.

Recall that Spinoza renders substance nothing *but* modes. So, equivalence between what is in substance and in modes is meaningless. However, Deleuze's error is not so much his failure to construe substance exactly as I do but his disregard for the sources that inform Spinoza. From Maimonides, as we have seen, Spinoza receives and then revises a model for difference that adheres ontologically, not because the diversity in nature corresponds to diversity in God but since diversity refers to God's actions in the world, not God's self, which remains non-composite. This conditions Spinoza's construal of attributes *as* substance, that is, indivisible such that any distinction between substance and its attributes is notional. Simultaneously, he upholds ontological difference; things extended and things thought do exist in their distinction. Deleuze's univocity delivers the obverse: "Attributes themselves have at once identity of being and distinction of formality. Ontologically one, formally diverse, such is their status."[196]

How does Deleuze come to assemble such a portrait? Rather than heeding Spinoza's remark concerning "some of the Hebrews," he baptizes Spinoza as a Scotist, which is curious because Duns Scotus actually references Maimonides in a related discussion and was aware that his own univocal approach to Divine attributes diverged from Maimonides's. Furthermore, Maimonides is uncompromising on God's simplicity, resisting any compositeness, proscribing "essential attributes," which distinguish between God and features of God.[197] Contributing to Maimonides's polemic against essential attributes is the Christian hypostatization of God's attributes in support of the Trinity. This matters because Scotus's commitment to the Trinity is *precisely* what sponsors his theory of formal distinction. To Scotus, a formal distinction is real—not only in the mind—even as it concerns things that are inseparable. Thus, for Scotus, the formal distinction between each of the Persons of the Trinity and God's essence is real and nevertheless does not subvert unity. Deleuze's assertion that Spinoza's attributes are "ontologically one, formally diverse" is a forced conversion of Spinoza to Christian doctrines. No wonder Deleuze proclaims: "Part One of the *Ethics* may be seen as the unfolding of three triads."[198] There is a trinity of trinities: "attribute-essence-substance,"[199] "perfect-infinite-absolute,"[200] and "attribute-mode-modification."[201] But this Christian supremacist violence is not even the main problem with Deleuze's reading. The real issue concerns its consequences: the dissolution of all difference in the Identity of substance, specifically infinite intellect.

To Deleuze, in Spinoza's philosophy, "God expresses himself in the foundations of the world, which form his essence, before expressing himself in the world. And expression is not simply manifestation, but also constitution of God himself."[202] There are two issues here. The first is the presumption that God constitutes Self before constituting world. Spinoza denies that substance precedes its actions. The second is that God is not constituted by attributes. Rather, attributes are the essence, the power, the ways in which substance actualizes, how it exists. Spinoza never suggests that attributes *constitute* substance, but maintains that they *are* substance. Deleuze acknowledges the evidence—especially the correspondence with de Vries—indicating that attributes are only perceived to be different from substance. Then, he dismisses it: "A philosopher is always led to simplify his thought on some occasion, or to formulate it only in part."[203] If only Deleuze would do us the favor of simplifying his own thought, not to mention his labyrinthine interpretation of Spinoza's thought.

The next misstep that Deleuze commits is his fidelity to parallelism. This derives from his claim that "God acts, or produces, as he understands himself . . . understanding himself necessarily, he acts necessarily."[204] The passage that Deleuze cites (EIIp3schol.) in his footnote to support this assertion does not actually suggest as much. There, Spinoza, as noted above, is burnishing his case that everything substance does, it does necessarily, which he conveys by referencing the conventional belief that God thinks necessarily to show that attributing necessity to God is not heretical. He is not affirmatively positing that God thinks as such. Deleuze then addresses the position of "some of the Hebrews," who he rightly notes were "Jewish Aristotelians" but then wrongly construes as upholding God as "thinking himself."[205] As emphasized in the foregoing, Maimonides denies reflexive activity of God, insisting that God's actions refer to relations with the world. The proviso is that such thinking does not rely on something external to God. But that does not mean that God reflexively thinks God's self, as this entails a form of deficiency in a God that is without limits and so wants for nothing and is perfect. Not only does Deleuze surmise that God thinks God's self, but he presumes how this happens: "In expressing himself formally in attributes he understands himself objectively in an idea,"[206] such that "God necessarily understands himself, just as he explicates or expresses himself."[207] This betrays ignorance of the doctrine of "some of the Hebrews," namely, their commitment to God's unity, which underwrites the principle that "God, God's intellect, and the things understood by God are one and the same."[208] This unity of God's intellect does not privilege God's thinking. The same applies to willing, exercising power, or any other "essential attributes." These are all ontologically same and ontologically same with God because God is nothing but God's existence, which is God's power.[209] This miscue has Deleuze suppose that "attributes are necessarily referred to an understanding that understands them objectively."[210] This devolves into Deleuze's convoluted parallel parallelism.

Despite conceding the imprecision of imputing parallelism to Spinoza, Deleuze embraces and compounds it.[211] Spinoza's alleged parallelism "implies the equality of two things that express the same third thing, and the identity of the third thing as expressed in the other two. The idea of expression in Spinoza at once brings together and grounds three aspects of parallelism."[212] And here we see, once more, Deleuze's fetish for threesomes. The problem is that "one and the same thing" for Spinoza actually means "one and the same thing." It does not mean two things, and it certainly does not mean three things. Neither God nor humans, for Spinoza, constitute Trinities. A human mode is a singular minded body or bodied mind, and it is not comprised of two separate modes that both "express the same third thing." Deleuze proceeds "to confer on the attribute of Thought a singular privilege: the attribute must contain as many irreducible ideas as there are modes of different attributes."[213] Consequently, "the idea of God is thus the cause of all ideas, just as God is himself the cause of all things."[214] Here too, Deleuze mistakenly distinguishes between the power of God to think and the power of God to do, the error against which "some of the Hebrews" militate. In the Maimonidean philosophical tradition that informs Spinoza, unity precludes ontological distinction between God's thinking and God's doing; there are no faculties, attributes, or properties *in* God. Yet to Deleuze, "Spinoza's God is a God who both is, and produces, all, like the One and All of the Platonists; but he is also a God who thinks both himself and everything, like Aristotle's Prime Mover."[215] This spotlights Deleuze's error: the distinction between a God who produces and a God who thinks, exactly what "some of the Hebrews" deny.

The upshot is that "God . . . possesses two equal powers: the power of existing and acting, and the power of thinking and knowing."[216] Deleuze's Trinitarian God has "two sides."[217] What is more, these dual powers are of "the absolute . . . in and through itself, involving them in its radical unity," but this "is not the case with the attributes."[218] Rather "all attributes are equal relative to this power of existing and acting that they condition."[219] Again, this distinction between the powers of substance and its attributes is unfounded. What follows is that "God understands and expresses himself objectively,"²²⁰ such that "God's absolute essence is formal in the attributes that constitute his nature, and objective in the idea that necessarily represents his nature."²²¹ Thereby, thought is elevated above the other attributes: "*Thought thus suffices to condition a power of thinking equal to the power of existing, which is however conditioned by all attributes (including Thought)*."²²² This is because everything relies on God's idea of God's self, which "would remain only potential did not God create in the attribute of Thought the formal being of the idea in which God thinks himself."²²³ This arrangement installs a contrived binary that Spinoza proscribes, that between potential and actual, possibility and necessity. It also distinguishes between God's power of thinking, God's power of thinking Self, and "the formal being of the idea in which he thinks himself," which it then orders hierarchically. The doctrine of "some of the Hebrews" discounts precisely such distinguishing and ranking of God's powers.

Most damning about Deleuze's byzantine construal is how it privileges the attribute of thought. To defend his affirmation that "all attributes are equal" and his concurrent promotion of thought, Deleuze contends: "There does not seem to be any contradiction in this, but rather an *ultimate fact*."²²⁴ Nothing makes for a convincing argument quite like an appeal to "ultimate fact." Not only does the formal being of the idea of God invest God with the capacities that make god God, it secures all else, granting "substantial unity to modes."²²⁵ This is because "ideas that flow from the idea of God itself . . . will have a specific modal unity. The same modification will thus find expression in an infinity of ways in God's infinite understanding."²²⁶ Thereby, "the objects represented by these ideas . . . like their ideas . . . will express one and the same modification."²²⁷ Through the idea of God, "one passes from the unity of substance, constituted by all the attributes that express its essence, to the unity of a modification comprehended in infinite understanding."²²⁸ The reason that Deleuze needs to unite God and thus also modes is because he separates the attributes *from* substance, while also conceiving them as "formally or really distinct."²²⁹ Like Descartes, he then needs to account for their unity, and like Descartes, to do so, he replicates precisely the move for which Spinoza assails Descartes, recourse to God. The only difference is that in Deleuze's version, God's own idea of Self unifies all, rather than God's sovereign Will. But for both, reality is ensured by the alterity, transcendence, originality, preeminence, and superiority of God *or* God's idea. Everything is subordinated to either the Sovereignty of God or the Sovereignty of God's infinite understanding.

Deleuze's reading of Spinoza is disturbing, and not simply due to its convoluted turns, forced points, and contradictory purports. Nor because it misapprehends the Jewish sources that inform Spinoza's theories. Nor even because Deleuze reduces Spinoza's ontology to an idealism of God's mind. Indeed, none of these are novel. Such interpretations were not only advanced by those with manifest Christian agendas, like Hegel. In fact, both Mendelssohn[230] and Maimon[231] read too much Maimonides into Spinoza, construing his immanence as an immanence *in* the infinite intellect. What differentiates Deleuze's rendition is that at every turn he appears to compromise on the very commitments he rightly attributes to Spinoza: instead of ontological equality, we get the priority of thought; in place of true diversity, we get the erasure of difference in the identity of the idea of God; in lieu of immanence we get a transcendence of the infinite intellect. It is one thing for an expositor to attribute certain ideas to a philosopher that are not really theirs. This is understandable, even when not unintended. But to do so while undercutting the very convictions that one claims the philosopher in question actually promotes is a distinct feat, a case of Deleuzian differen*t*iation. Deleuze's prejudices and the priorities of his own project seem to inform his interpretation of Spinoza. Pertinently, both *Expressionism in Philosophy, Spinoza* and *Difference and Repetition* were published in 1968. Through both projects, Deleuze assembles his philosophy. Exploring as much contextualizes his reading of Spinoza.

Before proceeding, it bears emphasis that Deleuze never wavers in Christianizing Spinoza. This surfaces not only in the systematic transubstantiation of Spinoza's theories into Deleuze's philosophy but also manifests in his portrayal of Spinoza's philosophical contributions. Deleuze, together with Félix Guattari, conceptualizes Spinoza's "plane of immanence" as "the nonthought within thought."[232] While the content of this claim will be explicated in the ensuing analysis, what matters here is what they proceed to purport that "the supreme act of philosophy" is "not so much to think THE plane of immanence as to show that it is there, unthought in every place ... that which cannot be thought, which was thought once, as Christ was incarnated once, in order to show that one time, the possibility of the impossible."[233] And so they proclaim: "Spinoza is the Christ of philosophers, and the greatest philosophers are hardly more than apostles who distance themselves from or draw near to this mystery."[234] Deleuze is not satisfied in simply Christianizing Spinoza's ideas, which is par for the course in "Western" philosophy, he must forcibly convert Spinoza himself, much as his converso ancestors were during the Inquisition, under penalty of death. While they were only expected to ritualistically digest the Body of Christ, Spinoza has now been incarnated as Christ *or* the Christ of philosophers to testify to the impossible.

Know Difference

Deleuze's construal of Spinoza's ontology through the distinction between the powers of being and thinking and their reconciliation undermines his interpretation. This same design configures and compromises Deleuze's own program. In both, what salvages the simulated disjunction of thinking and being is an idealism of Identity, notwithstanding Deleuze's professed fidelity to difference. Descrying as much requires digressing through Kant and Maimon because Deleuze leans on Maimon to resolve the problems of Kant's externalism.

Recall that for Kant, humans can never know things in themselves but only their appearances. This is because understanding cannot offer direct access to the sensible realm but only the a priori forms through which we structure that experience. While the passive faculty of sensibility absorbs from the sensible realm through affections of external objects, the faculty of understanding actively constructs this experience based on a priori concepts. Both are needed: "Without sensibility no object would be given to us, and without understanding none would be thought."[235] Yet, "the understanding is not capable of intuiting anything, and the senses are not capable of thinking anything. Only from their unification can cognition arise."[236] Since "the things we intuit are not in themselves as they appear to us," space and time "cannot exist in themselves, but only in us."[237]

Maimon critiques the schism that Kant installs between sensibility and understanding, being and thinking: "How is it conceivable that *a priori* forms should agree with things given *a posteriori*?"[238] Moreover, he questions how a mind that is so "heterogenous" from body is able to conceive matter.[239] These issues would be resolved "if our understanding could produce objects out of itself according to its self-prescribed rules or conditions without needing to be given something from elsewhere."[240] This is exactly what Maimon does: he renders understanding not merely active but constitutive such that "both the matter of intuition (the empirical of intuition) and its form exist only within me."[241] To do so, he relies on the Leibnizian-Wolffian supposition that takes sensibility and understanding to "flow from one and the same cognitive source" and its construal of space and time as "concepts of the understanding of the connections and relations ... of things in general."²⁴² This is possible because "we assume an infinite understanding (at least as idea), for which forms are at the same time objects of thought, or that produces out of itself all possible connections and relations of things (the ideas). Our understanding is just the same, only in a limited way."²⁴³ An infinite understanding or at least the idea of it, which knows All, underwrites all knowing. To Maimon, God ("understanding that actually thinks all these relations"), world ("the intellectual world ... the sum total of all possible objects that can be produced from all possible relations thought by an understanding"), and human soul ("an understanding ... that relates itself to this world so that all possible relations can be thought by it") are "the very same thing."²⁴⁴ The marks of a certain Maimonides and a certain Spinoza are unmistakable.

To further reckon with the given of Kant's sensible experience, Maimon appeals to mathematical differentials, which "produce the relations of different magnitudes themselves from their differentials."²⁴⁵ Similarly, understanding can "determine objects by means of relations" such that "it can legitimately relate different relations to one another *a priori*."²⁴⁶ It "produces unity in the manifold" by thinking an object, "specifying the way it arises or the rule by which it arises."²⁴⁷ Thereby, understanding determines "real objects through thinking a relation that refers to an object in general"²⁴⁸ and its relations with other objects. To Maimon, "differentials of objects are the so-called *noumena;* but the objects themselves arising from them are the *phenomena.*"²⁴⁹ Understanding produces internally, immanent to itself, that which Kant renders external and inaccessible. For Maimon, "space and time are as much concepts as intuitions, and the latter presuppose the former."²⁵⁰ Space and time are conceptual in representing the difference and connections between things and intuitive "in representing the specific relations between particular sensible objects."²⁵¹ These representations are not "outside us" and neither is the "given." They are "purely passive and not active" and arise "in an unknown way."²⁵² Whereas for an infinite intellect all thinking is active and conscious, finite minds only experience this when doing mathematics. This maps onto Maimon's distinction between actuality and possibility: actuality refers to that which is given, its representation in time and space, while possibility signifies "insight into how they arise," its concept.²⁵³ Therefore, "for an infinite understanding, i.e. objectively, everything possible is therefore at the same time actual."²⁵⁴ Yet this leads to a hitch. If differentials genetically produce the given (that which is represented in time and space but not consciously known or even thinkable), how can this be underwritten by an infinite understanding? To resolve this, Maimon claims either the "given intuited by an infinite understanding" is present in it, albeit not thought by it, or it is "a mere idea of the relation of the concept to something outside it."[255]

Difference is afforded prominence in Maimon's program but so is Identity. Aptly, he deems these "relational concepts" such that "one cannot be thought without the other."[256] While relationality induces a possibility of mutuality rather than primacy, it becomes clear that for Maimon, the liaison of identity and difference is hierarchical, with the former invested with supremacy. Differentials are produced *by* understanding through universal rules that are predetermined, which renders difference subsidiary to identity, dissolving particularity in universality. Moreover, these are "universal forms of thought by means of which the understanding brings unity to the manifold."[257] Understanding deploys the differentials that it contrives only to consummate unity. Accordingly, reducing all sensibility, all that is given, all that is outside the mind—be it conscious or not—to understanding flattens difference, dissipating it in the Same. There is not simply no venturing from the Self but all that can be known is within the mind alone.[258] This is duplicated in the infinite intellect, the idea of which secures all finite thinking, which depends upon an understanding that knows All that can be known. Difference is thereby subsumed in Identity. This devaluation of difference aligns with Maimon's remark: "Difference is not actually a special form in its own right, but signifies simply lack of identity, or of objective unity."[259]

Echoing Maimon, Deleuze inducts a system wherein "difference is not phenomenon but the noumenon closest to the phenomenon."[260] To achieve this, he amplifies the internal differences of Leibniz alongside Maimon's advances in "overcoming the Kantian duality."[261] Whereas for Kant, "difference remains external and as such empirical and impure," Deleuze regards "Maimon's genius" as recognizing that "both terms of the difference must equally be thought."[262] Deleuze hails his "internal subjective method of genesis," which upholds an empirical, "outer difference, but also an inner concept of difference."[263] Differentials ground real, genetic, productive thinking in difference, rather than identity. With Maimon, "space-time ceases to be a pure given in order to become the totality or the nexus of differential relations in the subjects, and the object itself ceases to be an empirical given in order to become the product of these relations in conscious perception."[264] Deleuze reframes Maimon's infinite understanding: "which infinite is taken here only as presence of an unconscious in finite understanding . . . of a nonself in the finite self."[265] And here we encounter Deleuze's unthought of thought. For Maimon and Leibniz, "reciprocal determination of differentials does not refer to a divine understanding but to tiny perceptions as representative of the world in the finite self."[266] Thus, "the relation with infinite understanding devolves from it, and not the inverse."[267] While this massages the aforementioned snag in Maimon's scheme, it does not avoid his eclipse of difference. Even if the infinite understanding is not the origin of these differentials, it is their guarantor. Moreover, while such a conceptualization sidesteps the foibles of an Origin that is an Identity, it does not resolve corresponding pressures with regard to how unifying differentials erases difference or renders it subsidiary to Unity.

Responding to critics who deem Maimon's "unthought in thought" contradictory, Deleuze maintains this is only the case if "the faculty of Ideas" only refers to understanding.[268] Instead, for Deleuze, "ideas occur throughout the faculties and concern them all . . . they render possible both the differential object and the transcendent exercise of that faculty."[269] Consequently, "there is thus a point at which thinking, speaking, imagining, feeling, etc., are one and the same thing, but that *thing* affirms only the divergence of the faculties in their transcendent exercise."[270] Thus, "ideas are pure multiplicities which do not presuppose any form of identity in a common sense but, on the contrary animate and describe the disjoint exercise of the faculties from a transcendental point of view."[271] Identity, Deleuze suggests, is overcome if Ideas refer to multiple faculties and if Ideas are uncontained but "swarm in the fracture, constantly emerging on the edges, ceaselessly coming out and going back, being composed in a thousand different manners."[272] Yet to really avoid identity, the self cannot be intact. Deleuze identifies such a move in Kant, who recognizes "a fissure or crack in the pure Self of the 'I think,' an alienation in principle . . . the subject can henceforth represent its own spontaneity only as that of an Other."[273]

The promise of Deleuze's venture to divest from Identity is stymied by his riff on Henri Bergson's virtuality, which suffers the Same problems that Deleuze pinpoints in several predecessors. Although the virtual is said to "possesses full reality by itself," it undergoes a "process" of "actualisation,"[274] which is "a task to be performed or a problem to be solved."[275] Accordingly, its dynamism "incarnates the differential relations, the singularities and the progressivities immanent in the Idea."[276] Deleuze's virtual is nothing but a fresh name for Idealism. Hence, "the virtual . . . is the characteristic state of Ideas: it is on the basis of its reality that existence is produced, in accordance with a time and space immanent in the Idea."[277] which "the Idea is actualized precisely only insofar as its differential relations are incarnated in species or separate qualities, and insofar as the concomitant singularities are incarnated in an extension that corresponds to this quality."[278] Whatever "difference, divergence or differenciation"[279] and "genuine creation"[280] he affords the actualisation of the virtual is undercut by subordinating them to Ideas, which they purposively instantiate. The actual is but the incarnation of incorporeal ideas that precede and determine it. Moreover, notwithstanding Deleuze's embrace of a multiplicity of faculties of understanding, Ideas, which are ontologically privileged, "concern a special faculty to the point that one can say: they come from it."[281] So, "Ideas have a very special relationship to pure thought," constituting the "'differentials' of thought, or the 'Unconscious' of pure thought."[282] Ideas of pure thought are Sovereign. For Deleuze, as Ray Brassier observes, "being is nothing apart from its expression in thought; indeed, it simply *is* this expression."[283]

Ideas for Deleuze are situated at the top of a supposedly "equal being" wherein, really, "things reside unequally."[284] Rather than conceive reality as difference, Deleuze takes it as the differential actualisation of Ideas such that the difference between thinking and being amounts to the difference *of* the incarnation of Ideas in and as being. Like his Idealist reading of Spinoza and like Maimon, notwithstanding his own reservations, Deleuze's philosophy and his commitment to difference is subverted by his enthronement of Ideas. As Knox Peden grasps, this "is counter to the more general Spinozism of Deleuze's effort."[285]

The supremacist eclipsing of difference in the identity of virtuality, which are Ideas, corresponds to Deleuze's surmise that since "it is being which is Difference. . . . it is we and our individuality which remains equivocal in and for a univocal Being."[286] Individuality exists only in relation to the universality of Being. Thus, "a single and same voice for the whole thousand-voiced multiple, a single and same Ocean for all the drops, a single clamour of Being for all beings."[287] Despite the tendentiousness of his reading, Badiou rightly discerns that "Deleuze's fundamental problem is . . . to submit thinking to a renewed concept of the One."[288] Of course, as we have unveiled, Badiou's own philosophy commits this same misstep.

Thinking Otherwise

While Maimon is not unjustified in construing difference and identity relationally, the question is whether it is possible to conceive difference without becoming entrapped in binary logics. Deleuze's negotiation of this complex underscores the difficulties of so doing. Even as they both demonstrate a regard for difference and develop intricate theorizations of it, their commitments are eclipsed by the supremacy of ideas. To suture the disparity in reality, they resort to Ideas as the origin and measure of all. Reason is rendered Sovereign. By contrast, Spinoza refuses to dissever mind from body, conceiving them as irreducible aspects of the same, a same that only exists in and as its actualization. What is more, only ideas cause ideas and only things cause things. Neither is sovereign over its other. Difference adheres ontologically, but it is not the result of, or the means towards, Identity.

This regard for difference is realized in Spinoza's refusal of an infinite intellect independent of its modal actualization. Reality is thinkable, but only modally and, so, partially. All thinking happens in time and space, which renders it subject to the constraints of situatedness and imbrication, confirming all thinking as particular and particularized. Mind and body are "one and the same thing," which means that everything humans undergo is as both mind and body, in coordination. This constrains thinking certain adequate ideas but is also their precondition. While there are salves to supposing a View from Nowhere or Absolute Knowledge, Spinoza's philosophy is distinguished by its refusal of such delusional sovereigns and the sovereignties they secure.

SIX

Off Subject

> Humanity has died in Europe, the United States, and anywhere in the world in which Western Man—that is, White Man/ White Culture—*is* Man and, therefore, Reason.
>
> —LEWIS P. GORDON[1]

Feminist philosophy and decolonial philosophy have uncovered the ways in which prevailing "Western" constructions of the Human validate and perpetuate the supremacy of a specific kind of human over other humans: the white European cis Man. The dualism that sponsors this construal and the superiorities that it ratifies are discernible in certain varieties of Christian theology, especially as inflected by Augustine. Centuries later, these commitments to dualism were fortified by Descartes, for whom the human is essentially a thinking being, endowed with an interior mind that transcends its exterior body and rules over it. This Christian dualistic approach continues to shape "Western" philosophy, science, and culture. However, there is a different approach to humans and reason, which resists the dualism, transcendence, and supremacies of the "Western," Christian, Cartesian program. The decisive voice in this alternative tradition is that of Spinoza whose contributions validate his designation as "the first anti-Cartesian."[2] In arraying his unflinching criticism of Cartesian dualism, transcendence, and freedom, Spinoza draws from the materialist or naturalist Aristotelian currents that pulsate through medieval Islamic and Jewish philosophy. This heritage, which has been marginalized by "Western," Christian philosophy, furnishes Spinoza with the conceptual resources to resist the interconnected "fictions" upon which Cartesianism is founded.

Spinoza's critique of Descartes, as examined in chapter 4, has occasioned the investment of certain feminist philosophers because "the dualistic thinking that subordinated body to mind, passion to reason, and nature to culture, while coding one side of the duality as feminine and passive and the other as masculine and active is alien to Spinoza's monism."[3] Yet what remains unaddressed by feminist readers of Spinoza like Gatens, Lloyd, and Hasana Sharp is the distinctively Jewish background informing his resistance to dualism. Fortunately, a few feminist scholars of Jewish philosophy have tallied as much. Tamar Rudavsky situates Spinoza within a stream of Jewish thought that stretches back to antiquity. Whereas certain Hellenistic Jews and early Christians upheld the soul as the true essence of a human being, the rabbis "invested significance in the body," and "Spinoza's conception of body shares a marked similarity to that of the rabbis."[4] This regard for the body makes him "a philosopher much more congenial to the feminist project than were many of his peers."[5] Similarly, Dobbs-Weinstein has registered the indebtedness of Spinoza's rejection of Cartesianism to the non-dualism of Maimonides and Gersonides. This heritage, she argues, presents a generative rejoinder to "Western" feminisms that merely critique rather than dispense with the Cartesian subject. By turning to these repressed Jewish thinkers, "feminist philosophy can be transformed from an abstract critique of dualism, or anti-dualism, to a concrete mode of a-dualist philosophizing."[6]

Decolonial thinkers continue to highlight the racist and colonialist aspects of the Cartesian legacy. Enrique Dussel has analyzed the colonial resonances of the Cartesian *cogito*, especially its purported transcendence from and superiority over its body. In the Cartesian scheme, Dussel explains, the human body is likened to a pure machine, devoid of quality. Such a "pure machine would not show skin color or race (it is clear that Descartes thinks only from the basis of the white race), and nor obviously its sex (he equally thinks only on the basis of the male sex), and it is that of a European (he doesn't sketch nor does he refer to a colonial body, an Indian, an African slave, or an Asian)."[7] This purport to objectivity or neutrality deprived of quality devolves into the simultaneous erasure of difference in the *cogito* and the domination over those bodies deemed "different." This "quantitative indeterminacy of any quality," Dussel reasons, enables "modern philosophical subjectivity and the constitution of the body as a quantifiable commodity with a price (as is the case in the system of slavery or the capitalist wage)."⁸ When the body is construed mechanistically, lacking particular qualities, it becomes readily exploitable by means of abstraction and so easily commodified.

Sylvia Wynter unpacks the specific complicity of Christianity in the racist calculus of colonialism. She has theorized the ways in which the "Christian Self" is transformed with modernity into the "Rational Self of Man," the construction of which relies upon its others: "the peoples of the militarily expropriated New World territories (i.e., Indians), as well as the enslaved peoples of Black Africa (i.e., Negroes), that were made to reoccupy the matrix slot of Otherness—to be made into the physical referent of the idea of the irrational/subrational Human Other."⁹ To Wynter, the Christian binary of "Spirit/Flesh" morphs into "the new rational/irrational organizing principle and master code."¹⁰ Thereby, the "divinely created difference of substance between rational humans and irrational animals, would also come to be mapped at another 'space of Otherness' . . . that of a projected Chain of Being comprised of differential/hierarchical degrees of rationality."¹¹ This hierarchy "legitimated the large-scale expropriation and mass enslavement of two peoples on the grounds of a naturally determined difference of rational substance between them and their expropriators and slave masters that had, at the same time, made possible the rise and development of the physical sciences as a new order of human cognition."¹² For Wynter, the medieval and late antique ontological hierarchies of Christianity are transmuted, with modernity, into hierarchies of rationality. This comes to underwrite modern philosophy and science—especially bioscience—authorizing colonialism, racism, and the interlaced exploitations of capitalism.

While the solipsism of Descartes's *ego cogito* has been widely critiqued, decolonial thinkers have turned attention to its more pernicious implications: the ways in which it reinforces a colonial posture. Scrutinizing this phenomenon, Nelson Maldonado-Torres dissects the Cartesian formula *cogito, ergo sum*: "From 'I think, therefore I am' we are led to the more complex and both philosophically and historically accurate expression: 'I think (others do not think, or do not think properly), therefore I am (others are-not, lack being, should not exist or are dispensable)."¹³ Here, Maldonado-Torres is oriented by this assessment of Dussel:

The colonizing ego, subjugating the Other, the woman and the conquered male, in an *alienating erotics* and in a mercantile *capitalist economics*, follows the route of the conquering ego toward the modern *ego cogito*. Modernization initiates an ambiguous course by touting a rationality opposed to *primitive*, mythic explanations, even as it concocts a myth to conceal its own sacrificial violence against the Other. This process culminated in Descartes's 1636 presentation of the *ego cogito* as the absolute origin of solipsistic discourse.[14]

For Dussel, the *ego conquiro* aligns with the *ego cogito*. Colonialism relies on the hierarchical opposition between rationality and primitivity, a dualism that is mirrored and reinforced by Descartes's construction of the immaterial *cogito* as the seat of rationality, superior to and dominant over the material body. Glossing a passage from Felipe Guamán Poma de Ayala—the late sixteenth- and early seventeenth-century Quechua thinker who chronicled Spanish colonialism in Peru—Dussel comments: "Guaman discovers the process through which the *ego conquiro*—this expanding, self-centered subjectivity—passes, wildly overcoming all limits in its arrogances, until it culminates in the *ego cogito* based on God himself, as his own mediation to reconstruct the world under his control, at his service, for his exploitation, and among these the populations of the South."[15] The transcendent, independent, sovereign *ego cogito*, modeled after God, coheres with the colonial mindset and the conquest, expropriation, and genocides that it sanctions.

Descartes's configuration of humans as thinking beings and his reduction of them to this capacity have distinctly racist implications. As Emmanuel Chukwudi Eze observes: "Although many of Descartes's views about other things . . . have been defeated by subsequent thinkers, his essential definition of 'man' as a being whose reason for being is 'merely to think' has remained acceptable."[16] This essentialization of reason precipitates the Enlightenment's "race knowledge," whereby "some humans could quite conveniently be philosophically judged as incapable of reason and freedom and unworthy of responsibility."[17] Accordingly, "thanks to modern racial encounters, unreason, whether in the form of emotion or irresponsibility in European anthropology and philosophy, was no longer thought of as located within Europeans."[18] Rather, "its representations would be conveniently located in cultures outside of Europe, against whom anthropology and philosophy must now heteronomously manifest a racialized, white, sovereign reason, order, and humanity."[19] By means of this perverse logic, Eze argues, "the modern idea of humanity is irrevocably linked to a theory of race."[20]

Let me be clear: notwithstanding his resistances to Cartesian dualism, (sadly) neither Spinoza nor his philosophy can be classified as anti-colonial or anti-racist. In fact, his personal biography implicates him, minimally, as proximate to the ravages of colonialism and slavery: his brother Gabriel settled in Barbados and then Jamaica, worked as a "merchant," undoubtedly profiting from slavery and the colonial plunder of the Americas.[21] Spinoza's sister, Rebecca, and her family also settled in the Caribbean; eventually, all of Spinoza's relatives did.[22] This all transpired after Spinoza had departed Amsterdam and ceased working at the family firm; it is not clear what if any contact he maintained with his family members thereafter. Yet, his philosophy, specifically his resistance to Cartesian dualism, proffers resources for resisting certain logics that have subsidized "Western" colonial racism. Although it would be imprecise to blame Descartes's metaphysics directly for the genocide and oppressions of colonialism, as Dussel shows, the Cartesian posture aligns with and bolsters the attitudes that inspired and licensed the crimes of colonialism. Accordingly, as Wynter evinces, the dualisms of Christianity facilitated and morphed into the rational/irrational dualism that shaped "Western" science, colonialism, and capitalism. By disputing the Christian dualisms and sovereignties that conditioned Descartes's *ego cogito*, Spinoza introduces alternatives to the ontotheologies that continue to underwrite much of "Western" culture. Since the mind is as constitutive of the human as is body, classifying humans based on hierarchies of rationality, as will be shown, is plainly illegible to Spinozism. Accordingly inadmissible is the devaluing of body through abstraction to license exploitation and violence.

Spinoza, as we have evinced, is no feminist. But that does not discount the potential that his philosophy carries for conceiving reality and configuring humans without the supremacies that have historically underwritten prevalent "Western" forms of sexism. By conceiving the mind and body as different, irreducible aspects of a mode, Spinoza's philosophy solicits regard for the body, as much as the mind, in all of its particularity. Similarly, while Spinoza's rejection of human exceptionalism and teleology challenge the logics that continue to authorize human domination over animals or the devastation of the environment, it is misguided to portray him—as certain scholars do—as an advocate for animal rights or an environmentalist. While this complex is addressed in the next chapter, here it is sufficient to emphasize that Spinoza's immanence disallows for human exceptionalism. Thinking is not exclusive to humans nor are they reducible to their capacity to think.

The itinerary of this chapter is diverse, even digressive. Its project throughout, however, is to probe Spinoza's rejection of Christian, Cartesian, "Western" dualism. Our foray opens with Augustine, whose dualism, free will, and subjecthood inform Descartes. Highlighting Christian transcendence and the binary hierarchies it produces, including God and World, Spirit and Matter, Man and Woman, Human and Animal, Self and Other, which structure Augustine's and Descartes's systems, positions a contrast with Spinoza's approach, which draws from medieval Jewish Aristotelianism. After tending to Descartes's *cogito*, our study interrogates the promises of, and limits to, its purported universality. First is a further inspection of how the Christian, European, "Western," colonial, and racist projects expose the conceit of the supposed universality and neutrality of reason. Next, pivoting to the legacies of Cartesianism, is an examination of its appeal to seventeenth- and eighteenth-century women thinkers, specifically its claim that all humans are endowed with reason such that if they follow Descartes's method, they can arrive at the truth. Consulting the scholarship positions us to reflect critically on the complexities of sexgender as pertains to the ideas developed by these women and their relationships to Cartesian dualism. Particular attention is tendered to Anne Conway, whose vital monism, I demonstrate, remains tethered to sovereign Christian hierarchies, which limit its potential to position matter as on par with spirit, women as equal to men. These ventures prepare us to study the critique of dualism that Spinoza inducts and his alternative epistemology.

Whereas for Descartes, humans are essentially thinking beings, the mind is distinct from and sovereign over the body, and the will is free, Spinoza exposes the transcendent and teleological fictions underwriting such dualism. By drawing from Maimonides and Gersonides, Spinoza upholds the mind's dependence on body, considers all human thinking as embodied, and construes the mind and body as different, irreducible aspects of a mode. For Spinoza, as corroborated in chapter 5, all human thinking is attached to a body, thought exists in time and space, and is *particular*. This confirms that there can be no neutral standpoint, no absolute viewpoint, no universal Reason. In disrupting the dualism of mind and body, Spinoza, I demonstrate, accordingly dislodges a series of constellated hierarchical binaries, including subject and object, active and passive, internal and external, self and other, and theory and practice. These position an epistemology stripped of familiar seats of sovereignty, including notions of Truth, Method, and the Subject, construed as isolated, autonomous, and transcendent. Critically engaging the literature on this register, including the reflections of Derrida, Deleuze, Althusser, and Macherey, uncovers the difference of Spinoza's epistemology, while highlighting its continuities with medieval Jewish philosophy. Reading Descartes's *Rules* and *Discourse on Method*, in conversation with Spinoza's

The Emendation of the Intellect, exposes the fundamental contrast in their epistemologies and by extension, overall projects. For Descartes, following his prescriptive, formalized, normative Method for capturing Truth serves to condition the individual Self into becoming the Cartesian Subject, to wit, independent Subjects who amass metaphysical truth and scientific knowledge, becoming "lords and masters of nature." Contra these instrumental, entitling, and individualistic goals of the Cartesian undertaking, Spinoza's *Emendation* is focused on the "highest good," which entails recognizing one's place within the immanent connection of causes and interdependence with others. This ethical orientation of Spinoza's epistemology is an inheritance from medieval Jewish and Islamic Aristotelianism. It expresses the basic commitment of Spinoza's philosophy: immanence. Since there is no hierarchy of mind and body, no escape from the connection of causes because humans are equally of mind and body, corporeal existence and material circumstances *matter*. This regard for the concrete—over and against the dualist transcendence of Augustine, Descartes, and Conway—underwrites Spinoza's unrelenting spurning of supremacies. This anti-sovereign impulse has inspired modern Jewish thinkers such as Hess and Marx and, less directly, Adorno. Scanning their ideas at the close of this chapter highlights the emancipatory and egalitarian possibilities unleashed by Spinoza's epistemological refusal of sovereignty, which follows directly from an ontology that is without sovereigns or sovereign pretenses.

A central thesis of this book is that how we perceive reality at once reflects and simultaneously reinforces our commitments. Constructions of reality anchored in purports to sovereignty naturalize it and, in turn, sanction exercises in it. Sovereignties beget further sovereignties. By presenting an ontology stripped of sovereign pretenses, Spinoza denaturalizes sovereignty, rejecting its most pervasive manifestations. This is especially pertinent in the context of reason and rationality, which have conventionally supported human pretenses to superiority and purports to exceptionalism. By rejecting these sovereignties, Spinoza tenders an innovative epistemology, which packs not yet fully tapped potential for thinking reason otherwise.

Kindred Spirits

Descartes conceives reality hierarchically: there is God, the paramount substance, whose existence depends on nothing else, and there are subordinate substances, which "can exist only with the help of God's concurrence."[23]

These substances are thought and extension. Like the Creator/Created binary, the mind and body are hierarchically arranged: the former is privileged and immortal, sovereign over the latter. Like the incorporeal God who is transcendent and sovereign over nature, the incorporeal mind or soul is transcendent to and sovereign over the body. Yovel discerns how these "two asymmetries allow Descartes to preserve and redefine the basic dogmas of Christianity in terms of his New Philosophy," retaining the transcendence of "an all-powerful God separate from the world."[24] While "the second symmetry ... upholds the whole Catholic culture and life-experience that severs the spiritual from the material, soul from body, ascribing all value to the former, deprecating the body as the source of evil, depravity, and damnation, hailing asceticism, and subjecting earthly life to a world of the Beyond which only a bodiless spirit can access."[25] This Christian worldview is rooted in certain Platonic and Neoplatonic principles. For Plato, material bodies are not true substances. What truly is, is relegated to the eternal, immaterial Forms. The immaterial soul endeavors to escape the fetters of the material, to access the realm of the Forms. These debts of Cartesianism to Platonism are often left unacknowledged, although certain readers have recognized as much, such as Christina of Sweden who contended that Descartes offered scant innovations on Plato.[26] In contradistinction to Descartes, Spinoza, as we have charted throughout our study, draws from the naturalist currents of medieval Jewish philosophy, stimulated by medieval Islamic Aristotelianism. Although the extent to which Aristotle considers the intellect to be material or immaterial is debated, what is clear is that he does not subscribe to the substantial dualism of Plato nor to its extreme disseveration of mind from body, divesting body of substance, and its concomitant derogation of body.

Augustine is pivotal to the tradition of Platonic, Neoplatonic, and Christian dualism that Descartes promotes. While the Christology that sponsors the Cartesian project is patent, this feature is seldom mentioned in the literature. Indeed, historically and predominantly still today, "Western" philosophy is *Christian* philosophy. Critically engaging "Western" philosophy, entails naming its profoundly Christian standpoints and suppositions, not to mention its correlative programmatic marginalization of ideas deemed other to it. Although Descartes is celebrated as heralding a "modern" era of new science, even a cursory encounter with his thought showcases its commitments to Christian doctrines. Acknowledging as much is imperative, not only for the basic task of properly grasping his thought but insomuch as it is precisely the principles of this background that account for Spinoza's critiques. Although the ensuing survey focuses on Augustine, other Christian thinkers have also been considered influences on Descartes, including Pedro de Fonseca (1528–1597), Francisco Sánchez (1551–1623),[27] and Gómez Pereira (1500–1567).[28]

Reality, for Augustine, is dualistically structured: there is spirit and there is matter. Spirit is superior to matter. Humans are seen as uniquely endowed with a rational faculty, which is immaterial: "Man was made in the image of God, not according to the form of the body but according to the rational mind."[29] The superior aspect of the soul (*anima*) is the mind (*mens*).[30] To Augustine, humans "are not bodies but intelligible beings, since we are life."[31] Moreover, the entire cosmos, which is willfully created and overseen by God—who is Spirit—is governed by this hierarchical binary of spirit and matter: "First of all he subjects all things to himself, and then the bodily creation to the spiritual, the non-rational to the rational, the earthly to the heavenly, the feminine to the masculine, the weaker to the stronger, the needier to the better endowed."[32] God's sovereignty over reality conduces additional purports to sovereignty that are likewise supported by the subordination of matter to spirit: the mind is supreme over the body, much like rational beings are seen as supreme over non-rational beings. Which means, for example, that humans are supreme over supposedly irrational animals, and men who purportedly possess superior rationality are supreme over women. This essential subordination of women to men, he explains, is signaled by the creation of Eve from Adam.[33]

To Augustine, the human mind is not merely the seat of understanding, knowledge, and memory but also of willing. Much as God presides over reality by exercising free will, God bequeathed this capacity to humans: "He did not give all nature free will, while those he did give it to are higher, more powerful ones so the natures which do not have free will are necessarily subordinate to those which do."[34] The free will divinely apportioned to humans distinguishes them and solidifies their dominion over other beings. Without free will, the human "would lack his pre-eminence in the order of nature."[35]

The final pertinent aspect of Augustine's philosophy is what has come to be known as his *cogito* argument. Against skeptical doubt, he confirms his existence based on his capacity to be mistaken about it: "For if I am mistaken, I exist. He who does not exist clearly cannot be mistaken; and so, if I am mistaken, then by the same token, I exist."[36] Thus, "just as I know that I exist, so also do I know that I know."[37] This procedure and conclusion are reiterated in Augustine's *Trinity*,[38] where he also stresses how knowledge of others beyond the self commences with knowledge of the self, a self that is a mind.[39]

Augustine's mark on Descartes's *Meditations* was already descried by his interlocutors.[40] Although he deflected these suspicions,[41] commentators across the centuries have confirmed as much. To wit, Giuseppa-Eleanor Barbapiccola in the preface to her 1722 translation of his *Principles* writes that Descartes "spread his metaphysics following the beliefs of Saint Augustine."[42] More recently it has been observed: "Augustine is ... responsible for some key elements of what we designate as seventeenth-century 'rationalism' and that we identify especially with Descartes."[43] The most significant of these are dualism and its ramifications: the denigration of the sensible realm, the imperative to withdraw from it to gain knowledge, a knowledge that begins internally and is constituted by the self. This devolves into the reduction of humans to their capacity to think and the subordination of bodies to minds. Whether or not Descartes consciously followed Augustine is beside the point, at least for our purposes. This is because Augustinian doctrines pervaded early modern "Western" philosophy: "In the sixteenth and seventeenth centuries Augustine was the chief human authority and model for many thinkers throughout Latin Christendom who were indifferent or hostile to the thought of Aristotle."[44] The influence of Augustine on Descartes, therefore, is neither unique nor unexpected. Yet it is no less significant for understanding Cartesianism and its sway over "Western" thought. To be sure, their philosophical points of departure are divergent: Augustine is bent on cultivating a relationship with God, while Descartes is focused on inaugurating a metaphysics to secure his mechanistic approach to nature. Despite these differing orientations, Descartes absorbs his basic commitments—transcendence, dualism, free will, the supremacy of reason, and human exceptionalism—from Augustine's Christian program. This inheritance exemplifies a guiding theory of this book: that modern "Western" philosophy tends to recycle, rather than dismantle the hierarchical sovereignties it had previously relegated to God or believed God to have bequeathed to humans. Not only is this phenomenon obscured by the pervasive association of "Western" modernity—especially, its science and philosophy—with so-called secularism, but this refurbishment of sovereignties further obfuscates the ways in which the logics and instruments of sovereignty continue to underwrite "Western" thought.

Taking Exception

While everything is thrown into doubt for Descartes, like Augustine, all that can really be confirmed is the veridicality of his own existence. This affirmation of the *ego cogito*—which cinches both his earlier *Principles* and *Meditations*—is the anchor of his intertwined philosophical and scientific projects. "I am, I exist—that is certain."[45] By which Descartes means: "I am ... in the strict sense only a thing that thinks; that is, I am a mind, or intelligence, or intellect or reason."[46] The actuality of all else, save his own mind, remains uncertain. Even the existence of his own body is but "a probable conjecture."[47] Indeed, "it is certain that I am really distinct from my body, and can exist without it."[48] This reduction of the human to its mind and the detachment of it from body express Descartes's core belief: "The body is always a hindrance to the mind in its thinking."[49] As such, thinking commences with segregating the self from the external realm and turning inwards, which allows Descartes "to achieve, little by little, a more intimate knowledge of myself."[50] All that can truly be known resides inside the self or emerges from it.

After evincing the facticity of his own existence, his "I" that is foremost a "thinking thing," Descartes proceeds—in both *Principles* and *Meditations*—to confirm the existence of God and conclude that said God could not be deceiving him. Therefore, whatever errors Descartes commits are his own, because "we possess two modes of thinking: the perception of the intellect and the operation of the will."[51] Whereas the former is extremely limited, the latter is unlimited and so the cause of error: "The will, on the other hand, can in a certain sense be called infinite."[52] Like Augustine, Descartes considers the will a Divine bequest to humans: "It is above all in virtue of the will that I understand myself to bear in some way the image and likeness of God."[53] The supremacy of willing over that of reasoning is so powerful that in order for Descartes to proceed, he must actively withhold assent to that which he already knows.

Descartes, like Augustine, secures knowledge by validating his own existence and mooring it to an I that thinks and accordingly wills. For both, all knowledge begins in and with the self, a self that is reducible to its capacity to think and is governed by its sovereign free will. This self is *only* its mind, not its body. To think—to be human—is to transcend body, overcome corporeality, and dominate it. The sensual realm is not simply uncertain but delusive. The Christian dualistic elevation of Spirit and denigration of matter sponsors the Cartesian insistence on the disembodied mind and its claim of transcendence from the contingencies of body, space, and time, hence the pretension of a mind that thinks from Nowhere, which continues to suture "Western" conceits of a neutral, "objective," absolute viewpoint.

Not only does Descartes uphold the mind as constitutive of being human, but like Augustine, he maintains that humans monopolize reason: "As regards reason... since it is the only thing that makes us men and distinguishes us from the beasts, I am inclined to believe that it exists whole and complete in each of us."[54] Moreover, not only do "beasts have less reason than men, but that they have no reason at all."[55] Their souls are "completely different in nature from ours,"[56] for the human soul "must be specially created."[57] In fact, no error "leads weak minds further from the straight path of virtue than that of imagining that the souls of the beasts are of the same nature as ours... that after this present life we have nothing to fear or to hope for, any more than flies and ants."[58] From this doctrine of human exceptionalism, it follows, Descartes writes, that we humans are to "make ourselves, as it were, the lords and masters of nature."[59]

Sovereignties engender further sovereignties. The contention that reality is the voluntaristic product of a willful God—Spirit—that transcends corporeal nature and reigns over it validates assertions that humans are fundamentally their minds, which transcend their bodies, over which they preside with free will. This transcendence of mind from body, of will from causal determinism, elevates humans over that which is nonhuman and sanctions human supremacy. Humans, perceiving themselves as singularly forged in the image of God, arrogate a Godlike authority over nature. As Max Horkheimer and Adorno recognize: "The awakening of the subject is bought with the recognition of power as the principle of all relationships. ... In their mastery of nature, the creative God and the ordering mind are alike. Man's likeness to God consists in sovereignty over existence, in the lordly gaze, in the command."[60] Spinoza, as we have seen, critiques the circular logic and narcissistic conceits that underwrite the human pretension to being exclusively forged in the image of God. What is worth emphasizing here is how dualism is necessarily hierarchical and therefore fundamentally supremacist. The construct of a human Subject relies on that which it denigrates as inferior: body, materiality, corporeal nature. Its exclusive possession of Reason and Will facilitate the Subject's domination *over* matter: over body, over materiality, over all of nature. Spirit is the rubric through which humans organize reality. Beings that are seen as only body—nonhuman animals—are taken as inferior and worthy of domination. While humans that are perceived as insufficiently Spirit—historically, anyone who is not a cis white Christian man of European association—are deemed subordinate, primed for subjection.

Soul Crushing

Although Cartesian dualism has been deemed complicit in promoting "Western" sexism, colonialism, and racism, their synergy is not uncomplicated. Descartes's conception of reason does not in and of itself necessarily lead to the sexist and racist construction whereby the white Christian European cis man maintains sole possession of reason or at least has privileged access to it. This complexity has been analyzed by Aimé Césaire. In *Discourse on Colonialism*, he scrutinizes how "Western" intellectual authorities have weaponized reason and supposedly "objective" methods to justify racism and colonialism. Simultaneously, these very scholars undermine the supposed "universality" of Cartesian reason by arrogating it exclusively to themselves and the white race. Condemning "Western" historians, Césaire indicts "their false objectivity, their chauvinism, their sly racism . . . their obsession with monopolizing all glory for their own race."[61] Césaire proceeds to register the racism of social scientists and link it to a contradiction at the core of a "Western" culture that sees itself as heir to Descartes:

their views on "primitivism," their rigged investigations, their self-serving generalizations, their tendentious speculations, their insistence on the marginal, "separate" character of the non-whites and—although each of these gentlemen, in order to impugn on highest authority the weakness of primitive thought, claims that his own is based on the firmest rationalism—their barbaric repudiation, for the sake of cause, of Descartes's statement, the charter of universalism, that "reason. . . . is found whole and entire in each man," and that "where individuals of the same species are concerned, there may be degrees in respect of their accidental qualities, but not in respect of their forms, or natures."[62]

With this, Césaire at once exposes the conceit of supposed objectivity in social science research and concurrently unmasks the contradictory grounds upon which the European colonialist enterprise is constructed. Such research is established on the dualist hierarchies of the "civilized" and "primitive," white and nonwhite, and rational and irrational. In this fraudulent calculus, rationality is claimed as exclusive to "Western," Christian civilization. In supposing as much, these scholars undermine the Cartesian promise that reason is universal, that its transcendence from particularity—body, "nature," place—renders it equally accessible to all. These "Western" scholars accordingly refute Descartes's contention that although individuals of a given species differ by accidental qualities, fundamentally, they are the same, a logic that seems to resist the essentialization of racial difference and the concomitant mapping of it onto manufactured degrees of rationality. Césaire's incisive disclosure of the partial "Western" commitment to Cartesian principles solicits a closer assessment of both the prospects and perils of Cartesianism. On the one hand, it seems to be the case that the transcendence of the *cogito* and the universality of reason promote a more egalitarian conception of reason and rationality. On the other hand, the dualism upon which it rests is subsidized by and in turn underwrites a series of purported sovereignties, including nature and culture, body and mind, rational and irrational, which have historically supported purports to supremacy, including white supremacy, male supremacy, and "Western" supremacy.

The appeal to the universality of reason and its teleological endowment by God to all humans has actually been invoked to resist the ravages of colonialism. In his now celebrated sermon denouncing the enslavement and genocide of indigenous peoples—likely the Taíno—the Dominican friar Antón de Montesinos delivered this rebuke, in 1511, in the colonial city of Santo Domingo during the early decades of the Spanish occupation of Quisqueya, alternately known as Ayiti:

Tell me, by what right or justice do you hold these Indians in such a cruel and horrible servitude? Why do you keep them so oppressed and exhausted, without giving them enough to eat or curing them of the sicknesses they incur from the excessive labor you give them, and they die, or rather, you kill them, in order to extract and acquire gold every day? And what care do you take that they should be instructed in religion, so that they may know their God and creator, may be baptized, may hear Mass, and may keep Sundays and feast days? Are these not men? Do they not have rational souls? . . . Be assured that in your present state you can no more be saved than the Moors or Turks who lack the faith of Jesus Christ and do not desire it.[63]

In this stirring exhortation, de Montesinos—as reported by Bartolome de las Casas—expresses the obvious point: the Taíno people are human beings, as human as their "Western" colonizers. Therefore, enslaving them, killing them, stealing their land, and extracting their resources is unjust. They, like all humans, de Montesinos insists, have "rational souls." Significantly, de

Montesinos seems not only concerned with the injustices of colonialism but also with how these hinder the Christian mission: harsh slave conditions leave no time for missionizing the Taíno people. Indeed, the rigors of slavery prevent them from attending Mass and observing "Sunday and feast days." At risk of stating the obvious, his investment in Christian evangelism limits de Montesinos's universalism.

The rhetorical plea of de Montesinos: "Are these not men? Do they not have rational souls?" presumes that all "men" (humans?) have rational souls and suggests that it is therefore unjust to enslave, kill, and exploit Taíno people. This is patently true, which is why Montesinos's argument—that the Taíno are humans!—threatened the enterprise of his fellow colonists, who demanded that he recant his remarks, which he refused to do, and so was summoned back to Spain to plead his case before Ferdinand II of Aragon. However, the ostensible inclusiveness that underpins de Montesinos's claim to the humanity of the Taíno people is misleading and rests on a series of exclusionary hierarchies. "Men," to the seeming exclusion of other beings, have "rational souls," and these souls, at least implicitly, have been endowed by God to humans, alone. Humans are like God, who is sovereign and therefore are themselves superior to others. To whatever extent de Montesinos rightly maintains that the Taíno people are just as human as he is, such calls for equality are not compellingly delivered from within a system that is constructed on ranks of supremacy, on the naturalization of hierarchy and sovereignty, both in terms of Christianity more generally and as pertains specifically to de Montesinos's own Order and the monarchy under which he operates. Moreover, de Montesinos's missionizing posture undermines the purport to God-granted human equality: it entails the delegitimization of different religions, as evidenced by his remark about the "Moors or Turks" who remain unsaved, not to mention the beliefs, practices, and cultures of the Taíno and other indigenous peoples whom he undertook to missionize.

The limitations that Christian supremacy places on its purported commitment to universality were tallied in our analysis of Hegel's conception of progress, his exclusion of Jews from history, and the "Western" philosophical supersession of the Jewish and "Oriental." Here, it is instructive to highlight one further emblematic instance of how "Western" thought has weaponized reason, monopolizing it. Such rationales are pivotal to Bruno Bauer's campaign against the emancipation of Prussian Jews in the early 1840s. His diatribes—which build on Cartesian reason and Hegelianism—profess that Jews do not possess reason and consequently are unworthy of civil rights: "In the Orient, man does not yet know that he is free and gifted with reason. He does not recognize freedom and reason as his real nature."[64] Jews, as "Oriental," cannot appreciate universal freedom and reason. To Bauer, "the individual as well as the nation which in its thought and deed follows universal laws will progress with history; for universal laws have their base in reason and liberty, they develop with the progress of Reason."[65] However, the basis of the "Jewish national spirit," Bauer alleges, "is lack of ability to develop with history... due to its oriental nature. Such stationary nations exist in the Orient, because there human liberty and the possibility of progress are still limited."[66] The Jewish "national spirit... is dumb and mindless," thus, "no universal truths can emerge from such a shut-in and imprisoned mind."[67] Since reason is the basis of freedom and progress, people—such as Jews—who do not possess reason, are incapable of progress and unworthy of freedom. To Bauer, "human rights... can be possessed only by those who acquire and deserve them."[68] Therefore, Jews, whose lack of reason prevents them from acquiring or deserving rights, should not be granted rights through emancipation.

Cartesian reason and the Christian principles from which it draws, purporting that humans are created in the image of God and endowed with a rational soul, seem to support a certain equality amongst humans and equal access to rationality. Yet forms of colonialism, racism, and antisemitism expose the inconsistent and contradictory ways in which "Western" religious and intellectual figures have applied these doctrines. Similar tensions surface in a cognate debate pertaining to Cartesianism and sexism.

Cartésiennes

Feminist philosophers and thinkers have turned attention to the sexist legacies of Cartesian reason and so-called rationality, tracing how the dualist binary of mind and body has been mapped onto a gender binary. For Susan Bordo this amounts to "the Cartesian 'masculinization' of thought," alongside the attendant denigration of nature and body, which becomes associated with "femininity."[69] This is why, as we have tracked, Spinoza's rejection of dualism has appealed to feminist philosophers. However, while there is a case to be made for a certain kind of sexism deriving from the Cartesian *cogito* or, minimally, a sexism in which it is complicit—incontestably with regard to the Christian principles of transcendence, denigration of body, and the misogyny that informs it—the picture as pertains to Descartes the person and his philosophy is more complex.

While I know of no evidence indicating that Spinoza engaged in philosophical discussions with women or even corresponded with them, Descartes tutored women in philosophy and engaged in philosophical exchanges with them. In fact, his *Passions of the Soul*, which he dedicated to Elisabeth of Bohemia, was penned in response to her interrogations of his dualism. Yet, both Elisabeth of Bohemia and Christina of Sweden were his patrons: he could not but discourse with them. When asked why he did not thoroughly address proofs for the existence of God in his *Discourse on Method*, Descartes responds: "These thoughts did not seem to me suitable for inclusion in a book which I wished to be intelligible in part even to women while providing matter for thought for the finest minds."[70] Beyond this manifest sexism, what is significant is that he wrote with women readers in mind. Why? Instructive context emerges from his correspondences. Regarding Elisabeth of Bohemia, with whom at the time he seems not yet to have been personally acquainted, he writes: "I set far more store in her judgment than by that of those learned doctors whose rule is to accept the truth of Aristotle's views rather than evidence of reason."[71] Similarly, years later, justifying his extended stay in Sweden, Descartes writes: "This country is ... governed by a Queen who possesses in herself more knowledge, intelligence and reason than all the learned churchmen and academics spawned by the fertile lands where I have resided."[72] Notice how Descartes praises both of their intellects by way of contrast with "learned" men. This reflects the philosophical aims of his Method, which sought to inaugurate an entirely new way of thinking, unencumbered by what he perceived to be the errors of Scholasticism.

Women were the ideal recruits to Descartes's philosophy because as systematically excluded from the Schools, they were seen as disburdened of Scholastic biases. Not only would women be most open to it, but all that was required to follow his Method was the ability to read and assimilate what he had written. Cartesianism, "ironic as it may seem, liberated women intellectually and thus psychically, by making it possible for numbers of them to participate in serious mainstream philosophical discourse."[73] Descartes's solicitation of women readers, moreover, "functions to show the specificity of the new philosophy as individual and elitist, even if its vocation is potentially universal."[74] Aside from Elisabeth of Bohemia and Christina of Sweden, other roughly contemporaneous women philosophers also engaged with

Cartesianism, including the English Anne Conway, Mary Cavendish, Mary Astell, and Damaris Masham, while the seventeenth-century French salon became "a major conduit for Cartesian discourse,"[75] incubating a number of *cartésiennes*.[76] In the eighteenth century, the Italian thinkers Maria Gaetana Agnesi and Giuseppa-Eleanor Barbapiccola embraced Cartesian philosophy, while Barbapiccola celebrated what she perceived as Descartes's regard for women thinkers and the specific appeal of his philosophy to women.[77] Clearly, Descartes cultivated a readership of women that spanned centuries.

Notwithstanding contemporary feminist critiques of Cartesianism, the dualistic transcendence of mind from body and professing of the universality of reason proved valuable in advocating for women's rights. Poullain de la Barre's 1673 treatise *On the Equality of the Two Sexes* declares: "Since the mind merely gives its consent, and does so in exactly the same way in everyone, we can conclude that it has no sex."[78] Cartesian ideas and method—alongside that of the Cartesian Antoine Arnauld—were also pivotal to Astell's advocacy for women's education. In *A Serious Proposal to the Ladies*, she explains how because God has endowed all humans with reason, whatever intellectual constraints women are seen to have are socially constructed: "The Incapacity, if there be any is acquired not natural."[79] Indeed, "all may *Think*, may use their own Faculties rightly, and consult the Master who is within them."[80]

The Cartesian universality of reason, its endowment by God to *all* humans, and the accessibility of its Method evidently contains egalitarian potential that was tapped by early modern and modern women thinkers. Scholars point to this data in attempts to counter or at least problematize contemporary feminist critiques of Cartesianism. Yet the tensions cannot be ignored: "Cartesian dualism brought both potential freedom from the prejudice of sex-linked mind and an effacement of value behind objective fact in a discourse whose supposed value-neutrality concealed, among other things, the bias of gender."[81] Accordingly, commentators have underscored how even as women philosophers and the *cartésiennes* were drawn to Cartesianism, they were often quite critical of its dualism.[82] It has been suggested that specifically the identity of these philosophers *as* women informed and conditioned their qualms about, and rebuttals to, Cartesianism. For example, Elisabeth of Bohemia's challenges to dualism have been deemed as emerging from a "woman's point of view,"[83] which supposedly typifies something "distinctive about *women's* thought."[84]

Dually Noted

Before dissecting Spinoza's pointed critiques of the sovereignties that suture Cartesianism, it is illuminating to examine Conway's philosophy. Pertinently, she developed her vitalist monism against the dualisms of Descartes and Henry More and in opposition to the materialisms of Thomas Hobbes and Spinoza. The latter two, she maintains, fail to distinguish between God and other beings.[85] While Conway is influenced by the Cambridge Platonists, especially their reservations about Cartesianism, her ontology is distinguished in its indebtedness to Neoplatonic emanationist principles as refracted through Christianized Lurianic concepts. Notably, she was interlocutors with Francis Mercury van Helmont, who collaborated with Christian Knorr von Rosenroth, the primary translator and editor of *Kabbalah Denudata*, the Christian compendium of select Kabbalistic texts rendered in Latin. Whereas critics of Spinoza castigated his philosophy by associating it with Kabbalah's purported atheism—in denunciations suffused with Christian anti-Jewish tropes—Conway extracts and baptizes Kabbalistic concepts as she constructs her alternative to the supposed heresies of Spinozism, while simultaneously correcting the mistakes of Cartesianism.

Reality, for Conway, is comprised of three hierarchically arranged, distinct, yet interconnected substances or species of being: "God, who is supreme, Christ, the mediator, and creatures who are lowest."[86] All beings—not just humans—are of matter and spirit: "In every visible creature there is body and spirit, or a more active and a more passive principle, which are appropriately called male and female."[87] The body, which is coded as passive and female, is "dark," while spirit, which is active, is "light."[88] Although every being is constituted by spirit and body—really many spirits and bodies[89]—body "is not an essential property of anything."[90] While thus far, her ontology presents as a particularized variety of familiar Christian schemes, Conway infuses these with monist and vitalist elements. Her resistance to Cartesianism is secured with this claim: "The distinction between spirit and body is only modal and incremental, not essential and substantial."[91] The difference is of "degree."[92] As such, "spirit and body are of one original nature and substance."[93] To Conway, "just as God is one . . . just as Christ is one simple Christ . . . likewise all creatures, or the whole of creation, are also a single species . . . many individuals gathered into subordinate species and distinguished from each other modally but not substantially or essentially."[94] Notwithstanding her reproofs of Spinoza, which may partly have been driven by strategic considerations, the influence of a *certain* Spinoza is unmistakable.

Conway's modal conception of body and spirit counters the dualism of Descartes, which she emphasizes, mistakenly divests matter of vitality: "Cartesian philosophy claims that body is merely dead mass ... lacks life and perception of any kind."[95] Like Elisabeth of Bohemia, Arnauld,[96] and Spinoza, Conway turns attention to the puzzles of Cartesianism: how to account for the connection between mind and body, if they are substantially distinct.[97] She likewise underlines how the soul is no less impacted by the experiences of the body.[98] These problems, Conway argues, evaporate "if one admits that the soul is of one nature and substance with the body."[99] Spirits and bodies are connected by "great love and desire,"[100] just as "in every species of animal males and females love each other."[101] Such love, however, is not that of equals, for the soul "surpasses the body by many degrees of life and spirituality."[102]

While Conway accurately identifies several downsides of Cartesianism and makes a case for a certain vitality with which all being is infused, her philosophy remains tethered to the same hierarchical, dualistic principles that underpin both Augustine's and Descartes's philosophies. Her reality is organized hierarchically: there is God, "the highest spirit,"[103] Christ, who is "generated by God rather than made or created,"[104] and finally, creatures, "which are lowest."[105] Moreover, although she considers all "lowest" creatures as "distinguished from each other modally but not substantially or essentially," she considers them as organized into "subordinate species."[106] Accordingly, even as Conway imbues matter with spirit, insisting on its vitality, her system retains the Neoplatonic and Christian dualist denigration of matter. Spirit "is the more excellent of the two,"[107] which is why "the more spiritual a certain creature becomes ... the closer it comes to God."[108] God, is only Spirit and so "has no darkness or corporeality at all, nor any form, image, or figure whatsoever."[109]

The case is similar with Conway's dualist approach to sexgender, her metaphor linking spirit to maleness and body to femaleness, as well as her description of the love—like that between "males and females"—uniting spirit and body. These have been read as reflecting "an equal relationship between male-female couples."[110] And it has been argued that her philosophy "not only blurs the essential distinction between 'male' spirit and 'female' matter, but in fact elevates matter to the status of spirit."[111] However appealing, such interpretations strain credulity as Conway repeatedly describes body negatively and spirit entirely positively. Moreover, she pointedly dispossesses God of matter and underscores the inherent superiority of spirit. Her recurrent association of femaleness with body, much like her sexgendered imagery of love, cannot be dissevered from her rampant denigration of matter and subordination of it to spirit. Conway's monism is unable to transcend its hierarchical moorage: though body and spirit differ only in degree, these degrees are graded and staid. Spirit, light, and "maleness" remain superior, most like God, and thus paramount. This comes as no surprise. Conway's fidelity to Christian supremacies not only impedes her alternative to Cartesianism, it undermines any prospect of equality, be it conceptual or actual. For even if Conway is attempting some form of "feminist" redress—a point I contest— its promise is already undone by the logics of sovereignty and the coalition of naturalized supremacies that steady her system. This phenomenon instantiates a contention that steers this book: ontologizing traits of sovereignty— especially hierarchy, essentialized difference, and preeminence—effectuates the generation of further sovereignties. Is it any wonder that a philosophy constructed on the imbricated sovereignties of God over beings, spirit over matter, mind over body, leads to or reinforces the essentialization of sexgendered difference and its attendant submission of that which is "female" to that which is "male"? Only denaturalizing all purports to supremacy, abrogating the very rationales of sovereignty, can disrupt inequality, let alone occasion its undoing.

The Stupid Cartesians[112]

The difference between the Cartesian and Spinozist epistemological approaches is best captured by Spinoza's remark: "As far as the human mind is concerned, I think it is part of nature too."[113] By this he means that the mind does not transcend nature, is not exempt from causal determinism, and is not exceptional. The mind, like everything that exists, is of the infinite connection of causes. Since there is no escape from nature, this means that ideas are causally determined and the mind is not free to assent or dissent to an idea. The mind, reason, the Subject do not constitute a "dominion within a dominion." In claiming that the mind is *of* nature, Spinoza also means that it cannot transcend its surroundings, dissever itself from the contexts in which it is embedded, or disconnect from the body to which it is attached. As the previous chapter unfurls, all thinking for Spinoza is embodied and particular. This means that what one thinks is conditioned by where they are, who they are, how they are, and with whom they are, both in the present as well as in the past. A further consequence of this is that for Spinoza, thinking is not atomistic: it does not transpire in isolation, neither from other ideas nor from other modes. And, crucially, as chapter 7 explores, thinking is affective.

While for Descartes thinking commences with the purported flight from the sensual realm, the confirmation that the human self is essentially its mind, and the guarantee of a certain disinterested or "neutral" view from nowhere, Spinoza rejects these sovereign pretenses: "The first thing that constitutes the actual being of a human mind is nothing but the idea of a singular thing which actually exists."[114] This affirms both that a mind is not a thing that exists independent of the ideas that it thinks and that a human mind does not exist independent of thinking about something that actually exists. Moreover, this singular thing that actually exists "is the body *or* a certain mode of extension which actually exists."[115] Consequently, "the human body exists, as we are aware of it."[116] Not only is thinking always already entrenched in time and space—*of* an extended body—but this forecloses dubitability or skepticism about body, about self, about world: these exist as we experience them. For Spinoza, there is no distrusting our most basic, direct, phenomenological awareness of ourselves, which is necessarily of ourselves as embodied.

The reason that Spinoza forecloses skepticism about body and extended reality—why the mind (idea) always already knows its body (object)—is because "the human mind is united to the body."[117] Glossing this point, Wolfson explains: "This must be considered the essential point of Spinoza's theory of mind—its inseparability from the body. It runs counter to the entire trend of the history of philosophy down to his time, for everybody before him, for diverse reasons, insisted upon the separability of mind and body."[118] Even as Descartes speaks of the union of mind and body, his union is not only entirely fractious and contingent but completely hierarchical: the self is really only its *cogito*, which transcends its subordinate body, and strives to escape it, while for Spinoza, mind and body are inseparable, "one and the same individual."[119] They are not two distinct substances but irreducible aspects of the same. Neither mind nor body is more constitutive. An upshot of this dynamic is that knowing mind not only entails but requires knowing body.[120] Consequently, the more capable a body is, "so its mind is more capable of perceiving many things at once."[121] Likewise, a body that "has many things in common with other bodies" has a mind that is "more capable."[122] Not only does this discount the Cartesian approach that considers willful escape from corporeality a prerequisite to thinking and knowing, but it reverses the equation that the ideas of the mind *depend* upon body. The body—its conditions, contexts, connections—impacts thinking. Bodies matter, as do connections with others, for adequate thinking is never a solitary affair. In a further reversal of the Christian, Cartesian program, Spinoza does not restrict thought to humans. Although he deems human thinking to exceed that of other modes, this is not because he considers it a unique bequest from God, a proprietary Essence, or even a quality exclusive to being human. Rather, the human mind "surpasses" that of nonhuman animals simply because its body is more capable.[123]

Body Positive

Spinoza's rejection of the dualism that courses through Plato, Augustine, and Descartes is an inheritance from medieval Jewish and Islamic philosophy. As is always the case with Spinoza, he further immanentizes the intuitions and partial commitments that he receives. Consider Maimonides, whose approach in the *Guide of the Perplexed* to these questions combines the naturalist tendencies of Aristotle as transmitted through Ibn Rushd, together with certain Neoplatonic positions. On the one hand, he contends that human thinking is embodied: "The rational faculty is a faculty subsisting in a body and is not separable from it."[124] Mind and body are codependent. The soul, including its rational faculty, is "the form of human."[125] This interdependence of matter and form reflects the influence of Aristotelian hylomorphism, which conceives the soul as the form of body, body as the matter of soul. Throughout his diverse works, not just his medical treatises, Maimonides underscores the extent to which the state of the body impacts and conditions the functioning of its mind. Yet he also embraces certain Neoplatonic principles that downgrade corporeality. Indeed, a tenet of his program is that God is *not* body. Similarly, the "image of God" in which Genesis says that humans are formed, refers specifically to their rational faculty, which distinguishes them from other beings. To Maimonides, reason is what renders humans most *like* God and superior to all else. Furthermore, the rational faculty of the soul, in this approach, is supposed to govern the human body, controlling its desires and behavior. These discrepant approaches precipitated a controversy over Maimonides's thought: his inconsistent position on, and impartial commitment to, doctrines concerning human resurrection after death.

Another precursor to Spinoza's campaign against dualism is the epistemology of Gersonides. Following Aristotle, Gersonides considers thinking as originating in sensation. This is why there is no cognition without embodiment, no human mind (form) exists independent of its body (matter): "That which serves as form is inseparable from that which is related to it as matter."[126] Negotiating the freighted terrain of the soul's immortality—Aristotle's disputed position and the divergent interpretations of Alexander of Aphrodisias and Ibn Rushd—occasions Gersonides to uphold this interdependence of mind and body and to demonstrate their irreducibility. To Gersonides, "it must be that the body is the subject" of the material intellect "via the imaginative faculty."[127] The material intellect—*sekhel ha-heyul'ani*—is actualized through imagination, which is bodied. Sensible experience positions the material intellect to gain knowledge, which is then cognized by the agent intellect, *ha-sekhel ha-po'el*. Such a procedure facilitates true knowledge, including abstractions, mathematical truths, and essences. This happens as the particulars of sensory experience become cognized into universals. For example, the experiences that an individual has of encountering specific pigeons, parakeets, and parrots, would be expressed by *ha-sekhel ha-po'el* as the abstract notion of "birds." What emerges is known as *ha-sekhel ha-niqneh*, the acquired and active intellect (rather than the potential and passive intellect, *sekhel asher ba-koaḥ*). Moreover, the immortal aspect of the soul, Gersonides maintains, is the acquired intellect. Its truths about nature are eternal because nature itself is eternal.[128] This reflects an identity adhering between knowledge of a thing and the thing itself: "the acquired intellect is itself the order obtaining in the sublunar world that is inherent in the agent intellect."[129] Such a dynamic positions the particularized intellects of individual minds to be *of* the agent intellect.[130]

Significantly, for Gersonides, the agent intellect is not a separate or transcendent being, but the particularized immanent activity of thinking itself. In excavating the connections between Gersonides and Spinoza, both Dobbs-Weinstein and Klein underscore as much. They emphasize how for Gersonides, thinking does not transpire through ontologically discrete faculties: the mind distinct from the body, the material intellect distinct from the acquired intellect, but rather how these "are all simultaneously the same and different,"[131] or a "sameness" wherein "the same . . . is always already the different."[132] What Spinoza retains from this tradition and extends further is a commitment to "the inseparability of mind and body and the strictly material origin of *all* knowledge."[133]

Body Politic

Expanding on medieval Jewish Aristotelianism leads Spinoza to uphold mind and body as inseparable, interdependent, irreducible aspects of the same. This implies the imbrication of ideas with embodied conditions and contexts, and correlatively, as the previous chapter details, confirms all thinking as particularized. These resistances to the transcendence of Christian, Cartesian dualism, as we have seen, have appealed to contemporary feminist scholars contesting the "sexless" nature of the Cartesian mind. Since for Spinoza, mind and body are "one and the same," they suggest, there can be no mind that is not already sexgendered. While this is true to the extent that every mind is shaped by its body and its lived experiences *as* a body, including its sexgender, as established in chapter 4, it is problematic to essentialize or reduce any mind to its body, let alone to particular bodily features. What is clear, however, is that Spinoza's immanence renders it impossible to disaggregate the identities, experiences, and contexts of a mode from the ideas that they think. This solicits a more complex approach to the scholarly debate about Cartesianism, sexism, and the reception of it by early modern women thinkers including Elisabeth of Bohemia and Conway, and subsequently, the *cartésiennes*. Their positions on dualism cannot be readily disaggregated from their sexgendered identities, much as it cannot be easily desegregated from their socioeconomic or racial identities. Equally so, however, Spinoza's anti-dualism entails at once the interdependence, yet also the irreducibility of mind and body. While the nuanced theories of dualism that these thinkers advanced cannot be dissociated from their sexgendered identities and their statuses in society, they accordingly cannot be assimilated to these elements alone. Ideas are *of* the mode that thinks them and yet irreducible to any single, sovereign contributing factor.

There is a further ramification emerging from Spinoza's rejection of Cartesian dualism, which is at once more subtle, yet no less fundamental. By positioning not only thought but also extension as distinct attributes of infinite substance, Spinoza contests the traditional denigration of corporeality and the intertwined claim that it cannot be an attribute of God. Both extension and thought are equally of substance. Neither is superior or supreme. There is no demotion of the body, no subjugation of it to the purported domination of the sovereign mind or the will, no grounds on which to devalue it. Whereas Augustine, Descartes, and Conway uphold Christian doctrines that elevate mind or spirit over and above body or matter, Spinoza's ontology undoes such hierarchy. The body matters: not less than the mind, not more than it. But as much as it. Indeed, *as it*, for mind and body are different aspects of the irreducible same.

By valuing the body, insisting upon its significance, stressing how much the state of the body *matters*, Spinoza counters the dominance and dominations of Christian, Cartesian, "Western" transcendence. The pockets of immanence primed by medieval Jewish thinking position his alternative. Upholding the inseparability and irreducibility of mind and body forecloses the abstraction of humans *from* their bodies, a move that decolonial and antiracist thinkers have credited with financing certain racist, colonialist, and capitalist exploitations. Similarly, refusing to reduce humans to their capacity to think and concomitantly affirming body as indispensable as mind, and further, conceiving them as different aspects of the same disqualifies "Western" racist, sexist, and ableist classifications of humans based on manufactured hierarchies of rationality. Such rubrics are illegible from a Spinozist perspective.

Spinoza's approach not only tenders a generative alternative to the supremacies that suture dominant Christian, Cartesian, "Western" stances and the exercises in supremacy they continue to subsidize. It furnishes us with the conceptual resources for appreciating how this happens and why it matters. Demonstrating that all thinking is embodied in time and place, impacted by its situatedness and conditioned by corporeal imbrications, exposes the sundry factors that influence the formation of ideas, while validating that ideas are impactful. They have actual, corporeal, lived effects. Ideas matter, materially. This is why *how* "Western" philosophy conceives of the mind, reason, and truth *matters*. For these have concrete ramifications, including with regard to racism, sexism, colonialism, and capitalism. Contra Descartes, ideas are not isolated, existing in a transcendent realm, with circumscribed boundaries, influential only when consciously assented to and deployed by a sovereign will. Ideas are shaped by and in turn continuously reshape our worlds. This is a critical implication of immanence that spurs the basic critique incubated throughout this book: "Western" philosophy is constructed on the rationales of sovereignty, and this matters because conceptualizations have material implications because ideas are immanent, not transcendent.

But there is more here. Spinoza's rebuttals to Christian, Cartesian dualism turn attention to the series of mutually reinforcing sovereignties that secure it: a sovereign God that stands above material reality willfully presiding over it validates claims that humans are invested with a sovereign free will/reason which is their true essence and which transcends materiality and commands the lowly body subordinated to it. This installs humans as Exceptional, exempting them from causal determinism, while simultaneously glorifying the individual ego that is now upheld as self-founding and self-determining and, on account of its free will, also individually culpable for its actions. This Cartesian transcendence positions thinking as universal, neutral, and most Real, confirming body as particular, contingent, and degraded. Identifying and dissecting these presumptions to sovereignty illuminate and contextualize the oppressions that decolonial, antiracist, and feminist thinkers have linked to dualism. It does this by demonstrating how dualism's complicity in, or sponsorship of, racism, colonialism, sexism, and ableism derives from the sovereign logics that underwrite dualism, especially hierarchy, essentialized difference, and supremacy. The fact that dualism has licensed supremacies, I contend, is not merely not a coincidence nor simply predictable, but inexorable. This is because a system constructed on the rationales of and purports to supremacy cannot but perpetuate further supremacies. The problem, moreover, is not restricted to dualism. Instead, as this book corroborates, dualism is but an instance of the countless ways in which "Western" philosophy relies upon and fosters presumptions to, and exercises in, sovereignties. Redressing the sexism, racism, ableism, and Christian supremacy that are constitutive of "Western" philosophy entails reversing these logics and inculcating alternatives divested of sovereign pretenses.

Since a human mode is equally of mind and body, the only legitimate conception of a human is one that recognizes them as embodied and, specifically, as embodied in their particularity. This upholds the indispensability of concrete, material, lived circumstances to who and how a mode is and so what they think. Ideas cannot be readily abstracted from the particularities, interests, and desires of the individuals who think them. By rejecting all transcendence, Spinoza disregards the Cartesian pretense to impartiality, disinterestedness, and "objectivity." This means that all of our conceptions are conditioned (some more than others, but all are nonetheless conditioned). How "Western" philosophy conceives of, say, the mind is conditioned by the countless unconscious and conscious inclinations, experiences, and priorities of the individual philosophers admitted into its ranks. Exposing the conceits of the *cogito* to think freely and neutrally undoes the interested fiction at the heart of "Western" philosophy: its purport to thinking disinterestedly, absolutely, and so, universally. Its claim to thinking the Universal and monopolizing such Universality—as Césaire pinpoints—is conditional and conditioned. Descartes promotes specifically this fantasy in order to secure his performative dissolution of all fantasies, to functionally screen it from precisely such critique. "Western" philosophy's delusions of neutrality and universality, coupled with its systematic marginalization of alternatives that contest as much, shield it from, or at least forestall, just redress.

Truth Be Told

The sovereignties that secure Descartes's conception of humans—transcendence, hierarchy, supremacy, exceptionalism, free will—certify the ego as *cogito*. This induction of human *as* their capacity to think installs the conditions of thinking as primary, effectively positioning epistemology and its concerns as philosophically foremost. Aptly, the epistemology that Descartes contrives is devised on the precise rationales and instruments of sovereignty that facilitated his designation of human as exceptionally rational, invested with individual free will, unencumbered by causal determinism, and superior to other beings. This dependence on sovereignty acutely manifests in Descartes's method and conception of truth, which he manufactures to remedy his simulated doubt about everything. Starting with his earliest publication—*Descartes's Principles of Philosophy*—Spinoza begins to expose the fictions clasping Descartes's scheme. Across his oeuvre, Spinoza disassembles Cartesianism, exposing the symbiotic pretenses to sovereignty that stay it. This prompts his alternative epistemology, which divests method and truth of sovereign traits, while also refusing to moor them to an individual, sovereign, free Subject. Thereby, Spinoza not only models how to think without sovereignty but how to think thinking non-sovereignly.

To Descartes, suspicion is a prerequisite to truth. Knowing commences with doubting "everything as far as possible."[134] What keeps this enterprise in check is "free will," which "enables us always to refrain from believing things which are not completely certain and thoroughly examined."[135] By means of this escapade, Descartes confirms that which cannot be doubted—"I am thinking, therefore I exist"—the self who is doing the doubting, "is the very first thing we come to know when we philosophize in an orderly way."[136] The rehearsal of this scheme in *Meditations* reprises these elements: through methodical doubt, the self is born as Thinking, validating its truths by dint of its free will. Elaborating on "the freedom of will," Descartes claims, "the scope of the will is wider than that of the intellect" and is "the source of . . . error and sin."[137] With this maneuver, Ravven observes, "Descartes performed a radical reversal of the classical worldview, thoroughly Christianizing even thinking itself. Knowledge was now to be viewed as resulting from a free act of the resolve of the will, while cognitive error was recast as a willful failure or rebellious refusal to use reason."[138] By contrast, as Ludwig Meyer underscores in his preface to Spinoza's first publication, "the will is not distinct from the intellect, much less endowed with that liberty which Descartes ascribes to it; that that faculty of affirming and denying is a mere fiction."[139]

While Descartes overcomes his performative doubt through exercising free will, which assents to the truth, Spinoza carefully uncovers the interlocking conceits that cinch this procedure. Against Descartes, he reasons that truth does not require a transcendent external sign and certainly not a transcendent will to validate it. Rather, "there is something real in ideas, through which the true are distinguished from the false."[140] This is why, one "who has a true idea at the same time knows that they have a true idea, and cannot doubt the truth of the thing."[141] An idea, for Spinoza, is "something real in itself."[142] Whereas Descartes renders ideas passive, relegating their veridicality to the sovereignty of a transcendent verifying ego and transcendent rubrics of validation, to Spinoza, ideas are not something "mute, like a picture on a tablet,"[143] but active. They have force in and of themselves. To know, therefore, is already to be certain: "What can there be which is clearer and more certain than a true idea, to serve as a standard of truth? As the light makes both itself and the darkness plain, "sic veritas norma sui et falsi est" (so truth is the standard both of itself and of the false).[144] Or as he puts it to Albert Burgh in response to his pressing Spinoza about how he knows that his own philosophy is better than others: "est enim verum index sui, et falsi" (the true is the indicator both of itself and of the false).[145]

Recall that for Spinoza, Truth, in the metaphysical sense, is a construct. Like all universal, abstract terms, it is a human contrivance that misrepresents how things really are: "Those who seek certainty in the things themselves are deceived in the same way as when they seek truth in them."[146] Neither certainty nor truth is in things. Rather, trueness inheres in ideas. In this stance, Derrida descries "a critique . . . of a transcendentalized and abstract truth that pretends to be defined outside the sign to which it gives the true idea through itself."[147] To Spinoza, contra Descartes, there is no Truth independent of ideas. There are only true ideas. This liberation of truth from subjection to that which transcends it correlates with its emancipation from the authority of a transcendent Subject who verifies it. As grasped by Althusser, Spinoza dispenses with the "*criterion of truth*," which "only represents a form of Jurisdiction, a Judge to authenticate and guarantee the validity of what is True."[148]

Readers including Althusser, Derrida, and Macherey correctly discern in Spinoza's notion of truth as *norma sui* a critical rejoinder to the fancies of Cartesian transcendence. What they miss, however, is that Spinoza is not the first to conceive of truth in this manner. Consider, for example, a passing remark by Crescas that surfaces in the context of his speculations on infinity (ideas that Spinoza references):[149] "ve-ha-'emet 'ed le-'atsmo hu u-maskim me-kol tsad" (truth is its own testimony and agrees with itself in all regards).[150] Crescas is here enunciating a Hebrew version of Aristotle's axiom, "For everything that is true must in every respect agree with itself."[151] This formulation appears in a variety of medieval Hebrew texts, including biblical commentaries and philosophical works. I surmise that Spinoza's notion of truth as its own sign is indebted to this Hebrew idiomatic riff on Aristotle. Deploying this adage of Aristotle, which Spinoza likely encountered indexed in Hebrew, appears to be another overlooked instance wherein he draws from the font of medieval Jewish ideas to counter the transcendences that command "Western" philosophy.

Thinking Straight

While Descartes maintains that "we need a method if we are to investigate the truth of things,"[152] for Spinoza, "method is nothing but a reflexive knowledge, or an idea of an idea."[153] It does not precede thinking but *is* thinking: "Because there is no idea of an idea, unless there is first an idea, there will be no method unless there is first an idea."[154] Consequently, "the true method is the way of truth itself."[155] It expresses, says Macherey, "the real movement of thought."[156] With this, Spinoza revises the notion of method, depriving it of a priori, independent, external status. Consequently, "true method" is not an instrumental, teleological program through which to arrive at a transcendent, predetermined Truth but is that very truth itself, in and as its production.

Since ideas are active, real, and productive, to understand something entails understanding *how* it has come to be, to understand the necessary causal involvements and intra-actions that effectuate it.[157] Thus, adequate knowledge encompasses perception of a thing "through its essence alone, or through knowledge of its proximate cause."¹⁵⁸ Thereby, ideas are deduced from "one real being to another real being, in such a way that we do not pass over to abstractions and universals,"¹⁵⁹ whereas "confused ideas"—inadequate ideas—"are like conclusions without premises."¹⁶⁰

To depict what Spinoza is describing, it is instructive to consider artificial intelligence. Currently, AI is an effective aggregator of information based on what has been inputted into the databases available to it for processing. Since the results it delivers come from inputted data, rather than constructive thoughts, they are like Spinoza's "conclusions without premises." AI, at the moment, lacks the capacity to produce truths because it does not *understand* the information that it collects and stores; it does not conceive ideas. While the machine can deliver the what—assuming that the data from which it draws are accurate—it lacks the insight to account for the how and the why. As Spinoza underscores: "A true idea shows how and why something is, or has been done."¹⁶¹ From this perspective, AI is a plagiarist or parrot, bereft of actual understanding. It is a memorizer and aggregator but not a thinker; it cannot think ideas in and as their production. The "knowledge" that a machine "possesses" is superficial precisely because it does not conceive the truths that it collects. To Spinoza, a true thought "is distinguished from a false one not only by an extrinsic, but chiefly by an intrinsic denomination."¹⁶² This is why "if someone says, for example, that Peter exists, and nevertheless does not know that Peter exists, that thought, in respect to him is false, or, if you prefer, is not true, even though Peter really exists."¹⁶³ Accordingly, "this statement, Peter exists" is only true to one "who knows certainly that Peter exists."¹⁶⁴

Spinoza's regard for adequate understanding as conceiving something through its causes aligns with what is known as synthesis and stands in contrast with two alternatives. The first—addressed in previous chapters—is the reliance on abstract universals and transcendentals, which erase particularities, inhibiting perception of a given thing. The second type of method that Spinoza resists is that of analysis, which Descartes favored in metaphysics. Analysis proceeds from effects to causes rather than from causes to effects.¹⁶⁵ "Spinoza's Anticartesianism is fully manifest," Deleuze explains, in his preference for synthesis over analysis.¹⁶⁶ A further upshot to Spinoza's preference, as Macherey appreciates, is that "synthetically determined, the process of knowledge no longer views things such as they are for me: it grasps them such as they are in themselves."¹⁶⁷ This allows thinking to be "liberated from the finalist illusion, which proceeds by a projection from me."¹⁶⁸

Taking knowledge as the conception of things in and as their actual intra-active effectuation avoids the self-centered conceits of teleologically oriented thinking.

Rule Over

To discover the truth, Descartes renounces his education and conceptions, undertaking "to reform my own thoughts and construct them upon a foundation which is all my own."[169] This abdication of all prior and probable knowledge, which is suspiciously cast under the pale of absolute doubt, allows him to start thinking rightly, *his way*. Such thinking is only possible by means of a standardized method that he develops and proceeds to prescribe to his readers. This course is comprised of "reliable rules which are easy to apply," such that "if one follows them exactly, one will never take what is false to be true . . . but will gradually and constantly increase one's knowledge till one arrives at a true understanding of everything with one's capacity."[170] Through strict adherence to Descartes's predetermined, universalized method, readers are trained to think by progressively ascending from simple ideas to more complex ones, until reaching their limit.

Spinoza rejects Descartes's performed ignorance, not only because a true idea cannot be doubted but insomuch as thinking does not commence. This is exemplified by his axiomatic declaration: "human thinks."[171] We are in thought, already thinking.[172] However inadequate or rudimentary these ideas may be, "other ideas will be deduced from them, and these again will interact with other ideas."[173] Mocking Cartesian doubt and its rules, Spinoza professes that "to prove the truth and good reasoning, we require no tools except the truth itself and good reasoning."[174] This expresses his declination of Descartes's hierarchical, overdetermined, and instrumentalized approach to thinking.

In *Discourse on Method*, Descartes writes: "As regards reason or sense . . . it exists whole and complete in each of us."[175] This ostensibly egalitarian belief, as we have seen, appealed to certain seventeenth- and eighteenth-century women thinkers. However, the emancipatory potential contained in this principle is vitiated by the hegemony of Descartes's method, which prescribes in advance the precise course to be undertaken, correcting for the fact that "we direct our thoughts along different paths and do not attend to the same things."[176] Through his method, thinking becomes *the same for all people*. All people can be instructed in how to think *just like Descartes thinks*.

All minds can be subordinated to Descartes's domineering Mind. Since for Descartes the I, the Subject, the Self thinks and *is* its very capacity to think, his project undertakes to subject other minds to his own, urging their submission to his teleological path to truth. To be clear, Spinoza's *Emendation* is also invested in elucidating how to think adequate ideas. However, because for Spinoza method is reflexive and truth is not an object perceived by a subject but "the way of truth itself," thinking is not subordinated to a prescribed itinerary or Subject. Moreover, his focus is not on instituting uniform rules to be followed. Rather, Spinoza turns attention to the teleological fictions that stake Cartesian epistemology, its controlled progression, contrived tautness, and constrained flexibility. Thinking for Spinoza does not advance in a predetermined Order, in deference to a hierarchical, formalized path. Rather, as everything, it acts causally and immanently, which may seem unsystematic and untidy compared with the Cartesian blueprint, yet reflects the necessary causal interactions that *are* reality, which defy the anthropic predilection for order.

Following rules, for Descartes, ensures not only certitude about the truth but also its comprehensiveness: "If a child who has been taught arithmetic does a sum following the rules, he can be sure of having found everything the human mind can discover regarding the sum he was considering."[177] By contrast, Spinoza does not think that adequate ideas are grasped by rote adherence to rules. To depict as much, he also turns to an arithmetic example, his series of proportionals, discussed in the previous chapter. Certain people know the next integer in the series "because they have not forgotten that procedure which they simply heard from their teachers, without any demonstrations,"[178] while "others will construct a universal axiom from an experience with simple numbers."[179] Although such people deduce the correct answer, they do not understand *why* that number is the next integer in the series, as they are merely adhering to a rule. By contrast, immanent or "intuitive knowledge" entails grasping ratios and the interconnection between the numbers, *why* the number is next in the series and not simply *that* it is next.

While there is dispute in the scholarship about the consistency and even possibility of Descartes's method, what is evident is that method occupies a central place in his project. The proper method leads to attaining "knowledge of all things," an "all-embracing knowledge."[180] Method is the means to the telos of systematic, comprehensive, scientific, and metaphysical truth. Crucially, method generates the Subject of truth by directing it towards the teleological fulfillment of its potential.[181]

Subject Lessons

Divesting from all previous knowledge is critical to becoming a Cartesian Subject of science and philosophy. Descartes positions himself as the model of such a Method. Abjuring his formal Scholastic education amidst doubt and the corresponding retreat into solitude form the backdrop of both his *Discourse* and *Meditations*. This performed ignorance, suspicion, and escape leave him "free to converse with myself about my own thoughts."[182] Unsurprisingly, such isolation facilitates reflections on the self. In his *Discourse*, Descartes quickly recognizes that various enterprises, including architecture, urban planning, legal systems, true religion, and the sciences are best when instituted by an individual rather than through collaboration.[183] Truths are discovered by an individual, "a single man is much more likely to hit upon them than a group of people."[184] Through even more enforced seclusion, he comes to grasp the illusoriness of all that he knows. All *but* himself. And so, "*I am thinking, therefore I exist*" becomes "the first principle of the philosophy I was seeking."[185] Certitude about the self is now the First Principle of philosophy and by extension the sciences, which Descartes's metaphysics secures. The self—Descartes's self—is the foundation upon which all truth rests. Following his course trains readers to pursue truth, amass knowledge, and become "the lords and masters of nature."[186]

Examining Spinoza's project in the *Emendation* accentuates his divergences from Cartesianism. It opens with a disclosure, likely based on his difficulties working for and subsequently leaving his debt-straddled family business: "After experience had taught me that all the things which regularly occur in ordinary life are empty and futile . . . I resolved at last to try to find out whether there was anything which would be the true good."[187] While Spinoza, like Descartes, opens with a personal reflection, unlike him, Spinoza does not abjure his education or knowledge, question all that he knows and all that is, nor does he seek to retreat from the world. Most significantly, unlike Descartes, Spinoza is not "seeking the truth in the sciences"[188] but "the true good." Experience has taught him that people mistakenly regard "wealth, honor, and sensual pleasure"[189] as the highest good, although these often prove destructive.[190] While he intends to ascertain the good, he underscores that "good and bad are said of things only in a certain respect."[191] These are relative, anthropic constructs. What Spinoza desires is "knowledge of the union that the mind has with the whole of nature"[192] and seeks "to acquire such a nature, and to strive that many acquire it with me."[193] His is a collaborative undertaking: "The highest good is to arrive—together with other individuals if possible—at the enjoyment of such a nature."[194] Experiencing as much entails knowledge of "our nature," alongside knowledge of "as much of the nature of things as is necessary," in order to infer "the differences, agreements and opposition of things," to grasp "rightly what they can undergo and what they cannot," and finally, "to compare [the nature of things] with the nature and power of human."[195] Instructing the mind on how to think more adequate ideas by recognizing the implications of our embeddedness in the infinite connection of causes, how our ideas are causally determined, how everything immanently intra-acts, is critical to "the good life." This commitment takes more robust shape in the *Ethics*, where Spinoza explores the prejudices that inhibit adequate ideas and ethical living.

Whereas thinking for Descartes entails transcendence of nature, escape from the corporeal realm, and solitary introspection, for Spinoza, the opposite is the case: the highest good *is* knowledge of one's place within the infinite and immanent connection of causes. Such understanding encompasses recognizing both that humans are embodied, *of* nature, and social: "It is necessary, *first* to understand as much of nature as suffices for acquiring such a nature; *next* to form a society of the kind that is desirable, so that as many as possible may attain it as easily and surely as possible."[196] Spinoza proceeds to adumbrate the other elements necessary for the highest good: "moral philosophy," children's education, medicine, and "mechanics."[197] This orientation aligns with the Aristotelianism he inherits from medieval Jewish philosophy. Rather than "mastering" and "lording" nature, he is committed to the comparatively humbler and far less predictable quest to enjoy goodness with others.

No Doubt

While Descartes strives to free himself from doubt by exercising his free will to affirm his existence, Spinoza exposes how such fictions of freedom are what precipitate this doubt and doom the entire scheme. Descartes's exemption of human thinking from nature leads him to uphold the mind as Exceptional, and so its conceptions as subject to affirmation or denegation by the free will that supersedes it. By ridiculing this program and presenting his alternative, Spinoza turns attention to the coalition of purports to sovereignty that buttress it.

The reason that Cartesians doubt everything, fearing that they are being duped—by a demon or a dream—is because they misapprehend reality, supposing, Spinoza explains, that "the soul can, by its own force alone, create sensations or ideas, which are not of things . . . they consider it, to some extent, as like God."[198] Dissevering the mind from nature by upholding its autonomy leads them to doubt everything, which reinforces the corresponding assertion "that we, or our soul, has such a freedom that it compels us, or itself"[199] and can affirm or deny ideas. Once Cartesians accept such fictions of sovereign freedom, they circularly reinforce them, devolving into "madness."[200] Spinoza has little patience for such exploits because he refuses to accept that we can perceive something and simultaneously deny it. Contra the duped Cartesians, to Spinoza "we ought not to fear in any way that we are feigning something, if only we perceive the thing clearly and distinctly."[201] This is for two interconnected reasons: the first is that to know is already to be certain, and the second is because thinking is *of* nature and not apart from it. This correlates with Spinoza's contentions that we simply know that we are minded bodies and bodied minds and that such knowledge is in the realm of common notions, known adequately by all.

Much like we do not freely determine to affirm or deny our dreams while dreaming them, wakeful thinking is no different.[202] "Doubt is nothing but the suspension of the mind concerning some affirmation or negation."[203] There is no faculty of willing that stands independent of, let alone superior to, the intellect: "There is no absolute, *or* free, will, but the mind is determined to will this or that by a cause which is also determined by another, and this again by another, and so to infinity."[204] The mind is causally determined not only to think but to affirm or deny ideas; it does not *choose* to do so. Thus, "inadequate and confused ideas follow with the same necessity as adequate, *or* clear and distinct ideas."[205] Doubt and denial of an idea is not the result of a superior, external faculty disaffirming it but is due to the inadequacy of that idea or the presence of another idea that limits it. These are causally determined not sovereignly dictated.[206] Against Christian dualism Spinoza maintains: "The will and intellect are one and the same."[207] Therefore, "an idea, insofar as it is an idea, involves an affirmation or negation."[208]

The claim that the mind is sovereign, that it can fabricate all sorts of things, presumes that humans exist *independent* of extension, that a sovereign boundary demarcates their personal internal worlds from a shared external realm. Against such transcendence and freedom, Spinoza's causal immanence maintains: "The order and connection of ideas is the same as the order and connection of things."[209] Ideas do not exist *other* to reality but are *of* it: "Whether we conceive nature under the attribute of extension, or under the attribute of thought... we shall find one and the same order, *or* one and the same connection of causes."[210] Thought and extension are not separate realities but different ways in which the same reality is expressed.

Drop the Subject

What salvages Descartes, amidst his unnerving doubt about everything, is his recognition of his own self as a *thinking* being who freely wills. Burnishing the Augustinian "I" enables Descartes to "found" what is seen to be modernity. It is hard to overestimate the impact of the Cartesian Subject on "Western" philosophy and culture. Contemporary feminist, antiracist, and decolonial thinkers are not its only modern critics. Aspects of their critiques align with concerns that were leveled by philosophers in the late nineteenth century and throughout the twentieth century.

Nietzsche stresses the circularity of the Cartesian *cogito*: "Man's three 'inner facts,' the things he believed in most firmly—the will, the mind, the I—were projected out of himself: he derived the concept of Being from the concept of the I, and posited the existence of 'things' after his own image, after his concept of the I as cause."[211] The Spinozist thrust of this remark is startling, but not surprising: Nietzsche deemed Spinoza to be his *Vorgänge* (precursor) and kindred spirit who rescued him from "lonesomeness."[212] They both grasp the ways in which our subjectivity colors our experience and perceptions. By grounding reality and all knowledge in the *ego* and its knowledge of itself, Descartes and philosophies indebted to him cannot escape the dead end that is the self.

Even as phenomenology turned attention to consciousness and direct experience, Husserl's indebtedness to Cartesianism sustains, if not reinforces, the hegemony of the Subject. By contrast, Heidegger critiques the *cogito* to build his case about philosophy's forgetting of *Dasein*. To Heidegger, Descartes privileges the *cogitare*, neglecting the *sum*.[213] While this is true, Heidegger's corrective—the centering of *Dasein*—reduplicates the human exceptionalism that sponsors Cartesianism. Later, Heidegger sharpened his critique, observing that Descartes's task was "to create the metaphysical ground for the freeing of man to freedom considered as self-determination that is certain of itself."[214] This willful freedom, derived from the Self, is constitutive of modern science and technology: "Man has become the *subiectum*. He can, therefore, determine and realize the essence of subjectivity—always according to how he conceives and wills himself."[215] Then, he proceeds with this recognition, which is striking considering the year is 1938: "Man as the rational being of the Enlightenment is no less subject than man who grasps himself as nation, wills himself as people [*Volk*], nurtures himself as race and, finally, empowers himself as lord of the earth."[216] Clearly, Heidegger—not unlike decolonial and antiracist thinkers!—appreciated the gross ramifications of the Cartesian Subject, its freedom, and its self-constitution by grasping the ways in which it colludes with and inspires supremacist ideologies and sovereign domination. Such lucid recognition by Heidegger seems only to fortify the case against him for his Nazism.[217]

Spinoza, as we have seen, rejects the autonomy, dualism, and atomism that underwrite the Cartesian Subject. His critique inspired Hess's resistance to individualism, much as it did Marx's criticism of the constraints of idealism and liberalism. In the twentieth century, diverse French thinkers such as Cavaillès, Gueroult, and Deleuze found resources in Spinoza's philosophy for countering the perceived irrationalism of phenomenology and for negotiating certain puzzles of psychoanalytic consciousness,[218] while Spinoza also positioned Althusser to navigate the excesses of Cartesian subjectivity. Allied Marxists, including Balibar, Negri, and Macherey also turned to Spinoza to debilitate the Subject. More recently, theorists of New Materialism have invoked Spinoza as guiding their erasure of the Subject. Not unsurprisingly, Spinoza's treatment of the Subject, or what is meant by it, is more nuanced than such accounts suggest.

In his seminar on psychoanalysis, Althusser links the subject of psychology to the subject of philosophy. Expectedly, Descartes is presented as responsible for uplifting the subject and Spinoza as inaugurating its critique. Althusser expounds: "Why is there this emergence of a subject of truth as the constitution of truth itself? It's an extremely important phenomenon because it's the origin of the whole of 'Western' philosophy, and the refutation that Spinoza gives of it is a refutation that has disappeared into history."[219] By "opposing" truth and error, by rendering "error as the exterior of a truth," Descartes installs "a philosophy of the subject that decides between truth and error,"[220] which emerges from "the moral and religious categories of the subject of imputation."[221] By contrast, Spinoza "critiques the constitution of the subject (psychological subject, ethical subject, and philosophical subject) as being imposed by the structure of the imaginary . . . by a social structure that necessarily produces this subject."[222] Althusser revisits these concerns in reflecting on his "detour *via* Spinoza," which was necessary for understanding Marx's "detour *via* Hegel."[223] To Althusser, Spinoza's philosophy, "by its radical criticism of the central category of imaginary illusion, *the Subject* . . . reached into the very heart of bourgeois philosophy, which since the fourteenth century had been built on the foundation of the legal ideology of the Subject."[224] This "resolute anti-Cartesianism" contrasts with Hegelianism, which despite criticizing subjectivity, accommodates the Subject.[225] Althusser subsequently allies Spinoza and Hegel on these very questions claiming that for both "there is no theory of knowledge," which is to say, "no theory of an a priori guarantee of truth of its scientific, social, moral, and political effects."[226]

While Althusser rightly identifies Spinoza as dispensing with the Cartesian *cogito* and the "Western" juridical approach to truth, his conception of the imagination and three kinds of knowledge is suspect.[227] It upholds a rigid distinction between imagination and knowledge, which teeters on the edges of idealism, notwithstanding Althusser's claims to materialism. This aligns with Deleuze's projection of idealism onto Spinozism. Not coincidentally, they both attribute parallelism to Spinoza. Yet for Spinoza, the mind is not a being that thinks ideas but the very ideas themselves and its constitutive idea is its body, which *is* it, immanently embedded in the infinite connection of causes.

Raising an Object(ion)

Commentators are justified in discerning in Spinoza a forceful rejection of the delusive transcendence and teleology that underwrite the Cartesian *cogito*, its purported sovereignty, and by extension, the "Western" Subject. However, Spinoza's epistemology is more nuanced. It is true that Spinoza liberates Truth from a Guarantor or Guarantee, from an external Authority. Yet such interpretations overemphasize the strains in Spinoza's philosophy that relegate truth solely to its coherence, ascribing to him a causal or coherence theory of truth. The *Emendation*, as we have seen, emphasizes the non-subjective claim that "truth is its own sign." This is reiterated in the *Ethics*: "By adequate idea I understand an idea which, insofar as it is considered in itself, without relation to an object, has all the properties, *or* intrinsic denominations of a true idea."[228] Here, adequacy is seen as inhering within ideas; trueness is not external to an idea nor an element *added* to it. However, Spinoza also offers this seemingly conflicting axiom: "A true idea must agree with its object."[229] It appears that Spinoza not only did not consider these positions conflictual—coherentism and correlationism—but conceived them as complementary.

Spinoza was asked to explain "the difference between a true idea and an adequate idea."[230] He responds: "I don't recognize any difference between a true idea and an adequate one,"[231] but then proceeds to note how truth "concerns the agreement of the idea with its object," while adequacy "concerns the nature of the idea itself."[232] Truth is *extrinsic* to an idea, while adequacy is intrinsic, immanent to thought. Spinoza's reservations about this distinction concern its reliance on the quarantining of subject and object, inside and outside, which contravenes the rudiments of his ontology, rendering either the object as mere representation or the mind as enclosed.[233] Precisely *because* mind is the idea of body—all human thinking is embodied—ideas do not exist in an ontologically distinct realm.

While Descartes anxiously worries about the validity of his access to the external world and subsequent centuries of "Western" philosophy fixate on negotiating this apparent disjunction, Spinoza discounts such divides. Not only do we already know that we are thinking, but thinking is always embodied because the mind *is* the idea of the body. Furthermore, the mind *acts*. Spinoza deems an idea "a concept of the mind"[234] and offers this gloss: "I say concept rather than perception, because the word perception seems to indicate that the mind is acted on by the object. But concepts seem to express an action of the mind."[235] Because the mind acts, "insofar as it has adequate ideas, it necessarily does certain things, and insofar as it has inadequate ideas, it necessarily undergoes other things,"[236] hence this equivalence: "insofar as we understand, *or* insofar as we act."[237] Since the mind is active, the *Ethics* is concerned with exploring how to think more adequate ideas, how such active thinking enables living well.

Fundamentally, what Spinoza resists in the Cartesian worldview is transcendence: not only the transcendence of the *cogito* and that of free will, which dissevers mind from body, but accordingly, the transcendent ontological boundaries that isolate the human Subject or Self from the world perceived as beyond it. This sovereign border precipitates the unease that Descartes is dreaming, it is why he needs to expend so much effort to confirm his own existence, which becomes the grounds upon which all else is established. For Spinoza, for whom there are no a priori confines delimiting existences, for whom causes and effects intra-act, there is no ready separation between subject and object.[238] Mind *is* the idea of body, which is its object.

Rejecting transcendence levels not only the hierarchical, sovereign binaries segregating mind from body, human from nature, will from intellect, but consequently that of subject from object.

Sharp Practice

To Spinoza, mind and body are "one and the same individual."[239] The commitments of "some of the Hebrews," as we have seen, position Spinoza to repel the Christian promotion of Spirit over matter and contest the Augustinian/Cartesian dualism that follows therefrom. Without transcendence, there can be no privileging of mind over body, no reduction of a human to its mind, no construction of thinking as exceptional. The "Western" severing of mind from body anchors the notion of a will that freely captains the actions of the body over which it dominates. Within the logics of dualism, the body, which acts, can only be spurred to do so by means of an intentionality that precedes it and presides over it. Such a setup construes action as directed by an independent agent that exercises its autonomous and unbounded will. Spinoza exposes the anthropocentric and teleological fantasies that anchor this scheme. There is no escape from body, no sovereign will, and the mind is not superior to the body, which *is* it. This Jewish immanence of Spinoza proved a critical resource for subsequent materialists.

Beginning in the 1830s, revolutionary and socialist German-Jewish thinkers, including Heinrich Heine, Hess, and the young Marx, uncovered emancipatory and egalitarian resources in Spinoza's ontological and epistemological resistance to hierarchy.[240] This positioned their distinct critiques of idealism, capitalism, liberalism, and individualism, much like Spinoza inspired Johann Jacoby's advocacy for social democracy and Jakob Stern's Marxist socialism. Significantly, the political commitments of all of these thinkers and their resort to Spinoza in formulating them cannot be disaggregated from their own identities as German-Jews agitating for civil rights nor, correlatively, from their perception of Spinoza's Jewishness. Yet the twentieth-century Marxist investment in Spinoza typified by Althusser, Macherey, Balibar, and Negri are oblivious to this constellation of Jewish radical Spinozists, save Marx himself, whose own Jewishness like that of Spinoza proves immaterial to them.

Marx observed: "The philosophers have only *interpreted* the world, in various ways; the point, however, is to *change* it."[241] Spinoza's philosophy testifies to how these activities are not only not in opposition but coincident. This explains Spinoza's appeal to socialist thinkers, revolutionaries, and to Marx himself.

In "The Philosophy of the Act," published in 1843—two years before Marx's "Theses on Feuerbach"—Hess undertakes to bridge the gap between thought and being. What captures his concerns are the constraints of the German philosophical revolution and the French political revolution both of which, in his estimation, have left freedom unrealized. At the crux of these failures lie dualisms and the alienations they beget. Hess opens with Descartes, asserting that his scheme fails because it cannot move beyond the *cogito*, introducing "only a proof of thinking, of the act of the spirit."[242] What is needed is for "the philosophy of spirit to become the philosophy of the act."[243] This entails recognizing the "identity" between "the thinking and thought about, between the subject and the object."[244] Hess endeavors to overcome the "dead end"[245] in which spirit finds itself when it is dissociated from the thought-about, left suspended in reflection. Whereas Fichte starts with the self-conscious "I" that determines itself as fact and act—in a move of both knowing and doing—Hess leads with the act. Without a schism between the thinking and the thought-about, the "I," the self, "is in constant motion, just as life."[246] It is neither stable nor isolated as Descartes has it. Consequently, when the "I" perceives "itself as its own activity, it is perceiving all activity, all life, with the same certainty."[247] This entails—here a certain Hegelianism manifests—"the act of the self becoming another."[248]

While Ludwig Feuerbach descried the limits of the *cogito* and its privileging of thought over being, Hess refuses to follow his course and resolves this by simply reversing the hierarchy. The problem *is* the binary. It must be razed so that "all oppositions fade away."[249] Thusly, "the philosophy of the spirit" *becomes* "the philosophy of the act."[250] Spinoza's rejection of Cartesian dualism and insistence that extension and thought are equally *of* substance, that a human is equally of body and mind, provoke Hess's critique and theorization of activity. To Hess, "the basis of the free act is the *Ethics* of Spinoza."[251]

Throughout the essay, Hess excavates, with not an immodest amount of fervidness, the ways in which the supremacist logics of dualism sponsor additional forms of domination and alienation. In a move that echoes Spinoza's critique of how abstractions misrepresent reality and universals efface difference, Hess asserts that dualism falsely abstracts the individual, absorbing it into the universal. This erasure of the individual occurs in the epistemic sundering of self from reality. Religion and politics, likewise, situate "the abstract universal on one side, and the material individual in opposition to it" through "the *absolutism* of the heavenly and earthly *tyrants over slaves*."[252] In both, universality is the "negation of all individuality" such that "all separate existences vanish before God and the monarch."[253] This leaves individuals "cut off from one another, rather than bound together" and so "opposed to one another."[254] These oppressive vestiges of dualism, Hess contends, are responsible for the failures of both German philosophy and French liberalism to deliver freedom.

The Young Hegelians, says Hess, have merely replaced Hegel's Absolute Spirit with the State, positioning "the universal" against the "individual."[255] Similarly, the revolutionary French institution of rights has not delivered on its promises because they remain abstract and centered on the I: "the majesty and sovereignty of the one has transformed itself into the majesty and sovereignty of everyone."[256] While "previously the abstract universal ruled in the form of the one over the particular, and oppressed the individual, now the abstract individual rules in the form of the many over the universal."[257] Hess then reproofs the reliance on individual freedoms: "To what end? For the benefit of private interests and private opinions, which intend to strangle overlordship to death through the 'free competition' of truth and justice! What is this democracy but the domination of the individual will under the name of 'subjective' or 'personal' freedom? How does it really differ from the domination of one person?"[258] The abstract rights that liberalism grants to individuals does not promote freedom but pits individuals against each other through competition, engendering further alienation and domination. Indeed, "what did the revolution achieve after all? Its freedom and equality... turned out to be just another form of slavery.... the abstract individual achieved domination."[259] To Hess, "as long as dualism has not been overcome everywhere, in the spirit as in social life, freedom has not yet been victorious."[260] Nodes of these arguments were reprised and popularized by Marx's early writings: "Theses on Feuerbach" pivots on a critique of dualism, while the limits of liberalism to secure emancipation and the ways in which it reproduces the alienation of religion are central to "On the Jewish Question."[261]

The Spinozist-Hessian-Marxist subversion of the dualisms of mind and body, subject and object, being and doing reverberates into the twentieth century through a stream of Jewish materialism that courses through Freud, Benjamin, and Adorno. Particularly salient is Adorno's dissection of how modern "Western" philosophy fails to overcome the binary of thinking and being, subject and object, while perpetuating the dominations constitutive of dualism, which reinforces the exploitations of capitalism. To Adorno, with the idealist dissevering of subject and object: "Mind then arrogates to itself the status of being absolutely independent—which it is not: mind's claim to independence announces its claim to domination. Once radically separated from the object, subject reduces the object to itself."[262] Hegel and Fichte merely tinker with the formula, retaining its hierarchies by situating the subject as the condition for consciousness. In a remark strikingly reminiscent of Hess, Adorno observes: "The doctrine of the transcendental subject faithfully discloses the precedence of the abstract, rational relations that are abstracted from individuals and their conditions."[263] Husserl's phenomenological response, which takes the conditioned as unconditioned and renders "the derivative as primary," proves no less oppressive.[264] This reversal serves capitalism, allowing the individual to be "consoled and exalted with the attributes of creative power, absolute rule, and spirit."[265] Not dissimilarly, Adorno elsewhere decries Henri Bergson's alternative as devolving into "an undifferentiated tide of life" that inducts "a cult of irrational immediacy, of sovereign freedom in the midst of unfreedom."[266] Replacing the transcendental subject with intuition—as does Bergson—is no less dualistic than Cartesianism and Kantianism and is equally doomed: "The causal-mechanical mode was no more affected by the intuitive one than the bourgeois establishment was by the relaxed unself-consciousness of those who owe their privilege to that establishment."[267] Against these dominations constitutive of dualism, Adorno proposes "differentiation without domination, with the differentiated participating in each other."[268]

In "Marginalia on Theory and Praxis," Adorno further tussles with dualism: "A consciousness of theory and praxis must be produced that neither divides the two such that theory becomes powerless and praxis becomes arbitrary, nor refracts theory through the archbourgeois primacy of practical reason proclaimed by Kant and Fichte."[269] Rather, "thinking is a doing, theory a form of praxis."[270] Accordingly, "praxis does not proceed independently of theory, nor theory independently of praxis."[271] This does not amount to an identity whereby one is subordinated to the other, as certain Marxists construe the relation, for such a "false identity" sustains "the principle of domination."[272] Through probing the linkages between Spinoza, Hess, Marx, and Adorno on this complex, Goetschel posits: "Jewish modernity is critical to the rethinking of the theory-praxis problem."[273]

While the legacies of Descartes's Christian dualism have been deemed complicit in facilitating or at least perpetuating certain forms of sexism, racism, and ableism, alongside the annihilations and exploitations of colonialism and capitalism, Spinoza's Jewish anti-dualism has inspired movements agitating for equality and mobilizing against oppression. Hess's socialism is a case in point—alongside its uptake by Marx and Marxists—actualizing the promise that Spinoza's immanence carries for countering forms of supremacy and domination.

Identity Politics

Spinoza's critique of Cartesianism uncovers the sovereignties that anchor it. His alternative, which conceives mind *as* body is without the rationales of domination or the hierarchies of binarization. This is apparent in his rejection of a domineering Method, renunciation of Truth as transcendent, instrumental, and teleological, and in his repudiation of the *cogito* as isolated, autonomous, and free. While these strides have received attention in the scholarship, what has largely been unrecognized—save for the important work of the few aforementioned scholars—is the Jewish background that informs Spinoza's unprecedented renunciation of Cartesian dualism. Exploring Augustine's philosophy at the start of this chapter contextualizes Descartes's program and spotlights the Christian roots of his dualism. Such Christian dualism, which is seeded by Platonic and Neoplatonic tendencies, contrasts with the more naturalist or materialist commitments of medieval Aristotelianism as refracted through philosophers like Ibn Rushd and Maimonides. This tradition was suppressed by Christian, Latin, "Western" culture through bans, censorship, and marginalization. Considering the supremacies that certain feminist, decolonial, and antiracist thinkers perceive as derivative of Christian, Cartesian, "Western" dualism, and in light of the imbricated sovereignties this chapter implicates dualism in promoting, it seems apposite to pressure the presumed inevitability of this course. By pondering, for example, the conduits of thinking, conceptions of humans, and construals of rationality that may have gained traction in "Western" philosophy, if not for the supremacy of a very specific brand of Christian thought. Had Christian Europe not censured the Islamic and Jewish strands of Aristotelian naturalism and its glimmers of immanence, might its ideas and actions—which this tradition insists are inseparable—have taken a different, less oppressive course?

If Spinoza's philosophy and its Jewish influences had not been so thoroughly denounced and dismissed, might modern "Western" philosophy have developed a more robust alternative to Descartes, a less sovereign conception of reason, humans, and reality? Or, is it the case, as certain strands of decolonial philosophy and feminist philosophy might argue, that these ideas *became* regnant precisely *because* of the forms of domination that they license. What we think and why we think it, the ideas that become most influential, as Marx reminds us—in a move unmistakably influenced by Spinoza's appendix to part I—are so precisely because they are the ideas of those in power, and the ideas of those in power are such because they serve their interests.[274] It bears emphasizing how this line of inquiry is incoherent by the precepts of Augustinian, Cartesian, "Western" dualism. Such ruminations are foreclosed by a posture that presumes the mind to transcend its body, to exist in a realm *beyond* the corporeal. The specks of Jewish immanence that Spinoza absorbs from Maimonides and Gersonides rebuff such dissevering of mind from body, confirming all thinking in humans as tethered to a body that exists in time and space. This coincides with the ethical investment that fuels this tradition, its focus on life lived in society, its decidedly political orientation. Spinoza inherits all of this, amplifying its potency and punctuating its ramifications. From the affirmation that a human mind depends upon its body, it follows that the conditions of the body matter for the ideas being thought. Whereas Descartes constructs his project on the conceit of retreat from the corporeal realm, Spinoza insists not only that such escape is delusional but that, on the contrary, *where* an idea is thought, *when* it is thought, by *whom* it is thought are all constitutive of it. Material circumstances are not simply nontrivial, they are decisive: context matters. There is no indifferent thinking, no neutral standpoint, no ideas from Nowhere. For Spinoza, the dependence of mind on body means that it is not possible to disaggregate an idea from the minded body or bodied mind that perceives it. All ideas are conditioned by the particularities of the person thinking it, their identities, their experiences, their memories, their predilections, and their desires, both conscious and unconscious.

Adequately deliberating, let alone resolving our counterfactual puzzle is, needless to say, impossible. However, what deserves to be ventilated is that for Spinoza—in consonance with the clusters of Jewish immanence that precede him—because all thinking is *of* a body that exists spatially and temporally, all ideas are conditioned, which confirms that ideas are always already political and ethical. They are political in the sense that ideas can never be unconditioned, indifferent, or dissociated from the confluence of circumstances under which they are thought. Ideas are never born from a neutral, "objective," disinterested standpoint. All ideas—philosophies—are political in that they have real, lived, actual impacts precisely because there is no retreat from the corporeal because thinking is embodied, active, productive. Furthermore, ideas are political in that all ideas derive from and so ipso facto concern actual bodied minds or minded bodies that live and feel and desire. These minded bodies are imbricated with other minded bodies in the infinite connection of causes, which collapses the sovereign boundaries dissevering self from other. Untangling the consequences of being a human mode entangled with others, a human mode that is equally of mind and body, and so a human mode who is constitutively non-sovereign is the undertaking of the ensuing chapter.

SEVEN

Human Interest

> Acted on, I act still, but it is hardly this "I" that acts alone, and even though, or precisely because, it never quite gets done with being undone.
> —JUDITH BUTLER[1]

How are humans to be? This is the primary concern animating Spinoza's *Ethics*. Its wager is that living well is causally necessary and immanent to reality. This means that ethics is possible without relying on transcendent sovereignties like God or the Good. These render norms a priori through Divine command or Natural Law and Morality, professing that humans are inherently bound to certain standards, presupposing that good and evil or right and wrong exist in reality independent of anthropic construction. Similarly, for Spinoza, ethics cannot in principle be anchored in a Duty that renders a mode subservient to a standard, rubric, or end that transcends it such as Ideals, the Law, or the Other. Nor can ethics be secured by coercion through notions of Willpower, Self-control, and Goal-setting. Furthermore, ethics cannot be guaranteed by submission to Reason or Rationality. All of these rely on the logics and technologies of sovereignty, which undercut the commitments of Spinoza's ontology. To Spinoza, such doctrines are erroneous and ineffective; they misrepresent reality and take humans not as they are but as we want them to be. By contrast, he imparts a way of living that emerges from how reality is and so what the actual nature of humans is.

Tendering such an ethics requires overturning the constellated purports to sovereignty that sponsor competing accounts. The most commanding prejudice is the belief that humans are sovereign over themselves, invested with free will. This fantasy derives from and reinforces anthropocentrism, which promotes human exceptionalism and supremacy. Such a perspective rests on a constellation of imbricated sovereign binaries and hierarchies anchored in Platonic and Christian dualisms that place Spirit above matter, God above nature, and so also the human soul or mind above the causal necessity associated with corporeal nature. This is how freedom comes to be perceived as *opposed* to causal determinism. Spinoza certifies how the prospect of unfettering ourselves from nature, from the infinite connection of causes, from our bodies, our pasts, our desires is delusional. Ethics is not in tension with our natures. If it exists, as everything, it must be necessary, immanent, *of* the nature of reality. So, he elucidates how living ethically is in our natures and how living well is possible without purport to sovereignty and its dominations.

Spinoza's most immediate disputant is Descartes who upholds humans as endowed with reason and free will. This chapter opens by exploring such Christian dualism, which places humans above nature, rendering them entirely responsible for their deeds and superior to nonhuman animals. Human failure to act virtuously results from a weak soul that submits to passions and succumbs to irrationality. The legacies of this approach are palpable in currents of liberalism and neoliberalism that idolize self-sufficiency and castigate individuals, rather than structural conditions for, say, poverty, addiction, and chronic illness. Its echoes are discernible in varieties of cognitive behavioral therapy that assail irrationality as the cause of disordered feelings or forms of toxic positivity that blame our bad feelings on insufficiently rosy outlooks. The Cartesian stance also persists in attitudes that consider humans exceptional, uniquely rational, fundamentally different from other beings. Against these currents, the so-called "nonhuman turn"[2] decenters humans. New Materialists including Jane Bennett and Rosi Braidotti have seen in Spinoza an inspiration for their projects. Yet I adduce how their attempts to unseat humans from their sovereign perch reproduce the most oppressive "Western," Christian sovereignties. The alternative Spinoza introduces derives from the immanence of his medieval Jewish philosophical forebears.

Spinoza's conception of living well is based on his ontology, specifically his understanding of the imbrication of all humans within the infinite connection of causes. As we have seen, this allows him to dismantle the contrived binaries of nature and culture, self and other, natural and unnatural. In this chapter, these insights are expanded by taking a closer look at his redefinition of conatus, desire, and affect. Not only are these not unique to humans, but I elucidate how Spinoza's theorization of each of these is divested of sovereign pretenses, and in demonstrating as much, I also rebut certain tropes in the scholarship. Since a mode is nothing but its conatus, its force of existing, this means that what a thing is, is nothing but *how* it is, which discounts the binaries of mind and body, essence and existence, being and doing. The conatus that is a mode is shaped and reshaped by its conditions, interactions, feelings, and thoughts both past and present, which exemplify the singularity of each mode. Against human exceptionalisms that consider our actions the results of a transcendent will or executive decision-making, Spinoza demonstrates how they are causally determined, driven by conscious and unconscious desires. To change how we act, we need to change our desires, *who* we are. Relying on cost-benefit analyses and the conceits of self-control to make us act well fail because they depend on the delusions of dualism: that our minds are other to our bodies, that we are other to our conditions, that we are other to our impulses, pasts, and contexts.

Instead, Spinoza introduces a capacious rendition of affects or emotions or feelings, which construes them neither as representational nor merely reactive but as ontological adjustments in the force, power, acting that *is* a mode. This is why feelings cause real effects in reality, why they are so hard to contain, and why they are constitutive of who we are. Since we are minded bodies or bodied minds, these ontological fluctuations are neither merely cognitive nor corporeal. Feelings are of both mind and body, which are "one and the same individual." With this, Spinoza topples the hierarchical binary of feelings and thoughts, emotions and cognitions. The mind feels as much as the body. This is critical to his approach to moderating affects: because thinking feels, what we think changes who we are, what we desire, and so also *how* we are. Whatever role there is for reason to impact how we live depends not on the truth of our ideas alone but on their affective force.

Spinoza recognizes how conceptions of humans as above nature, in command of themselves and so superior to other beings, would be a hindrance to apprehending his ideas. This is why he elucidates his ontology and epistemology before turning to directly address the affects and how best to live. Despite his efforts, scholars continue to misinterpret his theories, attaching to them the very prejudices he repudiates. Throughout this chapter, a farrago of the "Western," Christian sovereignties often attributed to Spinoza's ethics are scrutinized and debunked. These include constructions of his ethics that incorporate teleology; construe rationality as commanding; interpret the conatus as an Essence; uphold passions and affects as really distinct; consider good and bad as real; and conceive virtue as other to our natures. Particular attention is granted to misapprehensions about his conception of an individual mode. Rather than dissolving the self, Spinoza's construal of desire upholds singularity. Taking a look at his approach to self-esteem and suicidality exposes the extent to which who we are is entangled with how others perceive us, how the boundaries between self and other are porous, and how infrequently we are the adequate causes of our actions, feelings, ideas, and desires. This exemplifies how interdependence with others can be advantageous yet also destructive, while spotlighting the constitutive role of social structures in shaping us.

The contention that living well is natural, immanent, and necessary is fastened by Spinoza's claim that we incline towards what makes us feel good, and what makes us feel good is good for us and so is good for those like us. We enact such good through realizing "agreements" with others, which is how it is that ethics is *of* our natures. Although we often enact "disagreements," this does not discount how in principle we conatively impel towards what feels good, which is good for us and necessarily for those like us. In unpacking as much, I verify how classifications of Spinoza as promoting "self-interest" and "egoism" result from the coercion of "Western" sovereignties onto his program. Furthermore, his conception of agreements upholds the particularity of different kinds of modes, stressing the constraints of connecting meaningfully with nonhuman animals, which pressures certain ecologies and animacies.

The chapter ends by elucidating the conclusion of the *Ethics*, which the scholarship mostly sidelines or smothers with Christian, "Western," liberal dogmas. I evince how it strategically invokes morality and religion—transcendent, teleological constructs—in order to affect readers ethically. This move, I show, traces back to the dénouement of Maimonides's *Guide of the Perplexed*. Crucially, a careful reading and contextualization of these final propositions indicates that the experience described entails no transcendence from materiality. Rather, Spinoza is sketching the experience of wellness or "freedom," which accompanies realizing agreements with others.

Breaking Free

Dogmas of human exceptionalism stretch into the "Western" past; they are perceptible in ancient Near Eastern origin stories, including accounts in Genesis. They also hold sway in Greek philosophy, especially Platonic dualism, which presumes human privilege, maintaining that freedom is possible through dominating and overcoming corporeality in pursuit of the Good. Such commitments, fused with early Christian doctrines, position the free will that Augustine celebrates and Descartes consolidates. The legacies of these approaches permeate "Western" liberalism, especially the freedom, individualism, and rationality it venerates.

Augustine calibrates his conception of humans on the purport that they were created in God's image, endowed with an incorporeal mind that encompasses knowledge, memory, and free will. "But he did not give all nature free will, while those he did give it to are higher . . . so the natures which do not have free will are necessarily subordinate to those which do."[3] Free will cinches human "pre-eminence in the order of nature."[4] Although humans are partly of matter, they are chiefly of Spirit. Just as God freely supersedes passive nature, so too, the human mind can freely overcome nature[5] by exercising its free will, which dominates the rest of its mind and body.[6] Through "free voluntary decision" humans can even control reflexes.[7] This capacity renders humans culpable for sin: "The cause of evil is the free decision of our will, in consequence of which we act wrongly and suffer your righteous judgment."[8] This dualism, the freedom attendant to it, and the transcendence on which it rests form the bedrock of the Cartesian freedom that Spinoza assails.

To be human, for Descartes, is to be possessive of intellect and free will. Thus, "it is a supreme perfection in man that he acts voluntarily, that is, freely; this makes him in a special way the author of his actions and deserving of praise for what he does."[9] Our foibles derive from "a defect in the way we act or in the use we make of our freedom."[10] Free will is a Divine bequest to humans who "bear in some way the image and likeness of God."[11] God's sovereign will, which Descartes likens to that of a monarch,[12] is the model for human will, which is infinite[13] and indivisible.[14] Much like a transcendent God is superior to nature and rules over it, humans are superior to other beings, invested with a soul which transcends nature. This doctrine positions humans to be "the lords and masters of nature."[15]

The hallmarks of this Christian approach manifest in the liberal fetish of freedom. This is constructed on the hierarchical binaries that Augustine and Descartes celebrate: the transcendence of God's will over nature sponsors the transcendence of human will over nature; the dominance of mind over body; the promotion of human culture and rationality over irrationality; the privileging of individual choice over concrete, collective conditions. In this tradition, freedom is the supremacist exercise of individual will by a human Subject who is liberated from corporeal nature, and so dominant over it, over body, over animals. The freedom *from* nature redounds into the freedom *to* subjugate. This conception spurs liberal notions of individualism, which in the United States devolve into conceptions of individual rights that sanction harming others, as with rights to bear arms or rights to defy mask mandates. My individual freedom operates by superseding yours, taking precedence over the common good. Since hierarchical binaries and exclusions are mutually reinforcing and reproducing, this approach routinely invests only *certain* individuals with robust freedom: differently abled people, pregnant people, and trans youth are deemed unworthy of full individual freedom. Their physical bodies circumscribe their metaphysical rights.

The Augustinian and Cartesian investiture of free will onto humans serves to render individuals responsible for their actions. Without free will, the apparatuses of Divine punishment, human guilt, and confessionary submission become meaningless. God's willful sovereignty relies upon the sovereignty bestowed upon *individual* humans who are deemed *individually* culpable for their deeds. Since individuals are freely capable of transcending their bodies, their desires, their circumstances and teleologically *choosing* their actions, they alone are to blame for their deeds. Such articles of faith suffuse neoliberal culture and policies. The mythology of "pulling oneself up by their bootstraps" and "rugged individualism" and "just changing your attitude" are its most familiar slogans. These shibboleths exonerate those with actual power—governments, institutions, and corporations—from taking responsibility for the ramifications of the systemic inequities and injustices that they produce, perpetuate, and from which they profit. People, they say, are sovereignly in control of themselves and their actions, so epidemics of poverty, violence, and chronic illness are due to the cumulative bad choices made by individuals or, when being generous, the choices also made by individual members of their "nuclear" families. Their suffering has nothing to do with racism, capitalism, colonialism, ongoing policies of disinvestment, and dehumanization. Even more contextual approaches tend to diagnose and treat these conditions as individual rather than societal disorders. To be sure, treating a single person for, say, type 2 diabetes or clinical depression requires personalized care. But this necessarily individualized approach ought not to contribute to the absolution of the system from culpability, allowing the epidemic to persist, while manufacturing ever more opportunities for profiteering from the endless proliferation of chronic illnesses and disability. Moreover, faulting individual patients for their conditions serves to place the burden on them to care for themselves. This focus on individual choice not only excuses society from responsibility for actively producing the circumstances that effectuated this suffering but it also routinely dismisses the nonbiological factors that contribute to diseases and the ways in which personal and generational stress and trauma dispose people to a coalition of ailments, chronic and acute.

Human Touch

To Spinoza, everything is an effect of causes and in turn the cause of effects, entangled in the infinite connection of causes. This deprives all modes, including humans, of exceptional status, exclusion from causal determinism, and escape from immanence. Since all that exists is *of* the infinite connection of causes, there are no given borders and transcendent boundaries in reality. With this claim, Spinoza, as we have registered, disrupts the binary of nature and culture and the anthropocentric sovereignties underwriting it. All modes are of the same reality: "nature." For example, a coho salmon migrating to saltwater, a thought of this coho salmon, a caricature of this coho salmon, a dream of this coho salmon, an NFT of this coho salmon, a symphony about this coho salmon, this coho salmon poached and plated, are equally *of* the infinite connection of causes. Just like you and me. We are all finite, determinate modes of infinite, indeterminate substance. We are all also constituted by countless modes: the sensation of pain that the coho salmon and I experience is a mode, as is the blood coursing through our veins, the herring in our bellies, and the microbiota in our guts. So too, the pixels that comprise the NFT of this coho salmon, the vibrations of the cello in the first movement of the symphony about it, and the memory I have of having eaten it.

Does this mean that there is no difference between this coho salmon and my thought of it? How about this coho salmon and the economic system through which I came by it? Absolutely not. Appreciating as much distinguishes Spinoza's approach from competing materialisms. There are countless differences between these modes, to name a few: some were alive and are now dead, others were never alive; some are modes of thought, others are modes of extension; some are more localized, others are more dispersed; some are fish and modes of fish, others are human modes and modes of humans. Furthermore, the coho salmon exists in a way different from, say, the abstract legal rights granted to members of the Quinault nation to capture, kill, consume, and transact the coho salmon. These rights are modes of thought, which means that they are different from, say, the 6PPD-quinone toxicant leached from automobile tires contaminating the waterways in which the coho salmon was spawned. Even as both are real, for Spinoza, the latter adheres ontologically, whereas the former is a "being of reason." More importantly, he emphasizes the complex imbrication and intra-action of both kinds of modes.

Since thought and extension are "one and the same," Spinoza refuses to binarily side with either Nature or Culture. Humans are not exceptional, period. Yet he devotes considerable attention to deconstructing the particularly human prejudices that inhibit recognizing as much. This concern with both "nature" and "culture" explains Spinoza's appeal to materialists of the naturalist, ecological, animist strand as well as those of the Marxist, feminist, social constructivist variety. What is often missed, however, is that for Spinoza, these go hand in hand, precisely *because* humans—like all modes—are particularized determinations of infinite reality. We cannot transcend nature, free ourselves from it, let alone dominate it. This actuality leads us to devise conceptual and concrete sovereignties that allow us to feel otherwise, to feel superior, to feel exceptional. Such interplay makes living well so difficult, as the challenges of being human are not just "natural" nor are they merely "social" or "cultural."

The *Ethics* contends that living well is possible without transcendence, without fleeing our bodies or freeing ourselves from nature. But this does not reduce everything that is human to nature in the biological, ecological sense. To Spinoza, what is conventionally labeled "culture" is "natural," in the sense that as everything, it emerges and exists immanently, is causally determined. The upshot is that it can also be causally redetermined, disrupted, and remade. This is a prospect of ethics. Thus, he critiques human institutions and their oppressions, recognizing that because they emerged naturally, that is, immanently, they can be dismantled, naturally, immanently.

By dissecting prejudices, Spinoza exposes how they rely on "modes of reason" like abstractions, universals, and transcendentals. These interrogations betray the contingency of such constructs, underscoring the extent to which they are determined by our conditioned desires and particularized contexts. While these critiques orient Spinoza's project and prompt the alternatives that he advances, it is misguided to distill this demystifying posture into a privileging of the ontological over and above the epistemological, the cultural, or the anthropic. Spinoza is not out to valorize what is *real*, that is, exclusively what exists concretely in "nature." This is not only because his philosophy rejects precisely such a contrived binary, nor because it is impossible to transcend the human standpoint, but more pressingly, because to dispense with modes of thinking is to dispense with humans altogether: there is no point to an ethics that sees matters not as they are but as we want them to be.

Reducing all the artifacts of being human to being just like everything else makes ethics useless and impossible. This is why I am skeptical of New Materialists like Rosi Braidotti who link themselves to Spinoza while advocating for a "becoming animal" and a "post-humanism."[16] Accordingly concerning is the ascription to Spinoza of "anti-humanism."[17] Though he does not think humans are special, privileged, or exceptional, his entire oeuvre attends to the particularities of being human and how complicating these are. Consequently, asserting that for Spinoza "we could even construct a moral theory for hippopotamuses and rocks" misses the point.[18] It also implies that morality exists independent of its human invention, which he repeatedly underscores is not the case. Sharp's project of "renaturalization" is closer to the mark, although I hesitate about its implicit promotion of nature and the natural, notwithstanding her disavowals.[19] Spinoza *de*naturalizes human conceits—especially sovereignty—imploring us to accept that we are not supra-nature. But his resistance to fantasies of being *above* nature does not amount to a "renaturalization." Furthermore, "renaturalization" suggests a teleological Return to a former state that never was. It also risks transforming nature or the natural into a new sovereign. The continued weaponization of Nature to promote cishetsexism, racism, and ableism is a case in point.

Material Differences

While theoretical enterprises that put humans in their place are not without merit, as observed throughout this book, attempts to dismantle a given sovereign often tend merely to replace it with another sovereign or, minimally, perpetuate certain features of sovereignty. Calls to make humans *more* animal hazard transforming Human into Animal. Redressing anthropocentrism by making humans just like nonhuman animals or just like things deteriorates into a counterproductive anthropomorphizing that sovereignly heaves anthropic constructs *onto* nature, creating all others in the Human image. This deprives other existents of their particularity, solipsistically universalizing the human experience. In the most grievous instances, such moves dehumanize certain humans by denying the particularly human elements of their suffering. Bennett's vital materialism exemplifies such tendencies.

In *Vibrant Matter: A Political Ecology of Things*, Bennett undertakes to "theorize a vitality intrinsic to materiality... to detach materiality from the figures of passive, mechanistic or divinely infused substance."[20] The problem is that "vitality" is a human construct, much like her "vibrancy" and "liveliness"[21] and, more worryingly, her "agency" of things and "culture of things."[22] I do not mean to suggest that modes that are not human do not possess aspects of what it is that we signify by these terms, but to highlight the limits to projects founded on anthropomorphization. Bennett is not unaware of her anthropomorphizing and even justifies it: "We need to cultivate a bit of anthropomorphism... to counter the narcissism of humans in charge of the world."[23] It is not clear to me how narcissism is disrupted by rendering all other things in our image. Besides, must the worth of something rest in its sameness to us?

Rather than interrogating the "Western" supremacies that underwrite its prized conceits of activity, vitality, agency, liveliness, and Culture—not to mention their historic weaponization through sexism, racism, colonialism, and ableism—Bennett seeks to endow all beings with these traits. Instead of creating God in our image, the contemporary approach is to create *everything* in our image. In lieu of questioning the theological and scientific privileging of activity, Bennett reinforces it: "The vital materialist affirms a figure of matter as an active principle... materialities that are active and creative without needing to be experienced or conceived as partaking in divinity or purposiveness."[24] Yet her "vitality" aligns with traditional depictions of God and is "intrinsically resistant to representation."[25] Like the "absolute" it is "not an object of knowledge... no-thing at all."[26] But this vitality, this "thing-power," is in everything, so "everything is, in a sense, alive."[27] Thereby, Activity, Creativity, Vitality, and Liveliness become the new sovereigns: the essence of all, the source of everything, which transcends human intelligibility. By critiquing universal, abstract constructs—including "human" and "thing" and "being"—Spinoza dissects the deficits of totalizing classifications like those Bennett promotes. At issue here is not merely the anthropic categories she thrusts onto bottle caps, electrical circuits, and dead rats, but also her situatedness: all the kinds of factors that social, cultural, historical, and economic materialisms have taught us to interrogate. Precisely the prejudices Spinoza helps to deconstruct.

Bennett is not oblivious to the tension between reacting to the perils of anthropocentrism with a solution that is decidedly of the human perspective. Parroting a narrow version of this critique (through a reductive parody of poststructuralism), she asks: " 'Is it not, after all, a self-conscious, language-wielding human who is articulating this philosophy of vibrant matter?"[28] She responds: "It is not so easy to resist, deflect, or redirect this criticism."[29] Yet Bennett then proceeds to remind us of the bacteria on the human elbow, the aid offered by parasitic helminth worms to the human immune system, and "other instances of cyborgization" which demonstrate that "human agency is always an assemblage of microbes, animals, plants, metals, chemicals, word-sounds, and the like."[30] This is not under debate. Even the theologians and mechanists she decries—as we saw with Augustine and Descartes—considered the human body part of nature. The difference is that they conceived something else as unique to humans, a mind or soul, which enables agency. Against this, she grants all things seemingly equal agency: "insofar as anything 'acts' at all, it has already entered an agentic assemblage: for example Hurricanes-FEMA-GlobalWarming; or StemCells-NIH-Souls; or Worms-Topsoil-Garbage; or Electricity-Deregulation-Fire-Greed; or E.Coli-Abattoirs-Agribusiness."[31] Familiarity with her analysis of these groupings is unnecessary to recognize that they all include something conventionally deemed "natural" and something conventionally seen to be "artificial" or "cultural." Bennett continues her defense: "The voice of reason or habit is, however, unlikely to be mollified by such tactics and will again grasp for that special something that makes *human* participation in assemblages radically *different*."[32] She is right that there is nothing essentially special or inherently unique about human participation in assemblages. But that does not mean that humans are exactly like everything else and everything else is exactly like humans. Moreover, obviating differences, that is, discrepancies in capacities and imbalances in power between humans and nonhumans, comes at a steep ethical price: it erases the particular, overwhelmingly *human* ingredient in, say, global warming, deregulation, and agribusiness.

By inverting the classic hierarchy, rendering nature sovereign, and merely universalizing traditionally human features like activity, culture, and vitality, Bennett's project amounts to little more than a reappropriation of antique Christian sovereignties. This reliance on Christology is not merely theoretical nor even subtle. Throughout the book, she leans on Catholic doctrines to evangelize for New Materialism. This is strikingly manifest when Bennett concludes the book by incanting a "kind of Nicene Creed" for "would-be vital materialists": "I believe in one matter-energy, the maker of things seen and unseen. I believe that this pluriverse is traversed by heterogeneities that are continually *doing things*."[33] Here, the one God becomes matter-energy, maker of all things. Reality is One, unified, reducible to a single thing, while "doing things" morphs into a sovereign measure and feature of all. The "pluriverse" and "heterogeneities" she invokes are effectively erased through totalization. Particularity is dissolved in Christian universality. Bennett continues: "I believe it is wrong to deny vitality to nonhuman bodies, forces, and forms, and that a careful course of anthropomorphization can help reveal that vitality, even though it resists full translation and exceeds my comprehensive grasp."[34] Instead of Jesus Christ rising, with unique vitality, to save certain humans, Bennett enters as the savior to reveal to us the saving grace of vitality, however much it transcends our lowly comprehension. Bennett's credo then concludes: "I believe that encounters with lively matter can chasten my fantasies of human mastery, highlight the common materiality of all that is, expose a wider distribution of agency, and reshape the self and its interests."[35] Much like an encounter with the Son of God chastens believers into a life of humility and submission, the vital materialist is to be redeemed from their haughtiness by confessing to the agency in all things. Rather than granting this creed and its trafficking in theological sovereignties further exegetical attention, I will instead expose the violence that her invocation commits and how it encapsulates the ethical constraints of her program.

By revamping the Nicene Creed and recommending it to her disciples, Bennett displays willful indifference to the brutal history associated with this distinctly human artifact. The actual words of this creed and the doctrines it expresses have been weaponized by Christians for over 1,600 years. The Church ordained colonial conquest of lands and peoples deemed to be without "culture" was sponsored by this creed, which was simultaneously forced upon indigenous peoples through missionizing and dispossession. My own Ashkenazi Jewish ancestors were marginalized and murdered because they refused to confess certain principles pronounced by this creed. Jews have penned countless liturgical texts in memory of actual communities and concrete individuals whose lives were taken because they did not accept the "Lord Jesus Christ" as their "salvation." Certain of these works are still recited—weekly—by Jews across the world, centuries after these atrocities. I share as much and turn to the personal to highlight the ethical bankruptcy of vital materialisms that glorify the agency and vitality of bottle caps but fail to take human power and history seriously.

It seems ironic that in proselytizing for vital materialism, Bennett discounts the actuality that here on earth, only we humans have the kinds of cultures that produce such creeds, valorize them, and cajole or coerce others to embrace them, precisely as she does. Only such human culture, such history, renders meaningful the significance of her mission to "bear witness to the vital materialisms that flow through and around us"[36] and track the "vital things that will rise up."[37] These turns of phrase have resonance only because of their cultural histories (however oppressive). Despite her disdain for the poststructuralist investment in language, Bennett undertakes "developing a vocabulary and syntax for, and thus a better discernment of, the active powers issuing from nonsubjects."[38] Rather than offering fresh concepts, she renovates weathered artifacts by wresting them from their particular, historical contexts. In the process, she fails to "bear witness" to their violent pasts that "rise up." My family was deemed too lacking in Christian vitality, activity, Spirit, to be worthy of life. But for Bennett, we need not resurrect such historic matters, these are immaterial, precisely the kind of thing a Jew, entrapped in particularism, would say. What matters is the imperative to universalize vitality by transubstantiating all matter into actants, incarnating them with life. Conveniently for her, unlike the victims of historic Christian missionizing, forced conversions, and crusades, her nonhuman victims—stem cells, berries, dead rats—notwithstanding the inflated agency she affords them, cannot remonstrate against her crusade.

In disagreeing with Bennett, it seems that I am in good company, for despite her liberal (in both senses) appropriation of Spinoza, she concedes: "It would be too much to say that Spinoza was a vital materialist."[39] This she gets right, albeit for the wrong reason: à la Deleuze, she converts Spinoza into an idealist. To Bennett, he is not materialist enough. Throughout her scattered remarks on Spinoza, his ontology is freighted with the dualism, oneness, and essentiality that have been staples of Christianized misinterpretations for centuries.

The ethical hurdles of Bennett's gospel are twofold. Grounding ethics in the likeness of things to us humans does not eschew human narcissism, it refurbishes it. Furthermore, it diverts attention from the effects of distinctly human phenomena. By this I mean not only the ways in which exactly the notions that she glorifies and universalizes, like vitality, agency, and culture, have been wielded to erect hierarchies between humans in order to justify the supremacy of, for example, white Christian Europe, but also that only by tending to the particularly destructive power that humans exercise might there be a prospect of curtailing it. This is especially the case with ecological matters, with which she is especially concerned. How can the effects of global warming be mitigated if humans are seen as mere actants amongst many others? Instead of attending to the inequity in power, the imbalance between human destructive impacts on the environment and those of the nonhumans with whom we are entangled and of which we are comprised, Bennett attempts to colonize everything with liberal democracy by introducing a "political ecology of things."

For Bennett, humans are not the only beings who engage in political acts. To burnish this point, she turns to worms. First, she references Darwin's observations of how certain worms plug their burrows at night, which, he concludes, reflects intelligence. To Darwin, such actions are not unlike that of humans, which Bennett glosses to mean that worms "make apparently free, or at least unpredictable, decisions based on the available materials."[40] Next, Bennett takes us—by citation of Bruno Latour—to the Amazon, specifically to an area where there are trees more typical of the savanna than the rainforest. She does not qualify this assessment by reminding us that this geological classification is anthropic, that this curiosity seems only to puzzle humans, namely, those researching this specific part of the vast, diverse Amazon (we are never told where in the vast "Amazon" this transpired). In any case, researchers wonder: "How was the border between savanna and forest breached?"[41] This question presupposes a fixed border between the savanna and forest, rather than a dynamic "assemblage." No matter. It seems that "for reasons unknown to humans" worms gathered "at the border," which produced aluminum, transforming the soil into terra more suitable to the growth of forest trees. To Bennett, this demonstrates how "worms play a more important part in the history of (that part of) the world than most persons would suppose."[42] Let us bracket the imprecision of this sweeping conclusion and its premise of contrived ignorance because more concerning is her conclusion: "The task at hand for humans is to find a more horizontal representation of the relation between human and nonhuman actants in order to be more faithful to the style of action pursued by each."[43] Subtending Bennett's presentation of this extremely limited study is the presumption of the very dichotomy she claims to want to dismantle: humans as *other* to nature. She makes no mention of the millions of humans who lived in the Amazon and who impacted its terrain through very human things like agricultural cultivation and elaborate civilization over thousands of years. I mention as much not to discount the particular role of worms in this particular ecosystem with regard to this particular phenomenon but to tag this erasure of human settlement and seeming implication of some "pristine" ecosystem as untouched by humans. Updated research—her study is from the mid '90s—documents the human role in the foresting of the Amazon, including transitions from savanna to jungle.[44]

But this is a digression, however vital. The main point of Bennett's interest in Latour's Amazonian worms is that such "agency" and "free" decisions render the acts of worms "political." Much as it is considered "a political act, for example, when people distribute themselves into racially and economically segregated neighborhoods, even if, doing so, they are following a cultural trend and do not explicitly intend, endorse, or even consider the impact of their movements on, say, municipal finances, crime rates, or transportation policy."[45] There are, Bennett asserts, "many affinities between the act of persons dragging their belongings to their new homes in the suburbs and the acts of worms dragging leaves to their burrows or migrating to a savanna-forest border."[46] This analogy broadcasts the ethical impoverishment of her project: yes, worms and humans both drag things into their dwellings. But when a worm does so, their decision is not the product of systemic racism nor does it perpetuate it. In her attempt to elevate worms to the status of humans, Bennett actively devalues certain humans, cheapening the lives of those harmed by racism, while exonerating those who sustain it. These are the kinds of oversights that surface when attending to anthropic constructs like ideology and power becomes passe. Taking nonhuman things seriously must not come at the cost of also taking human things seriously, especially the oppressive things that humans *actively* do to other humans.

This indifference to the particularities of human suffering is not an isolated oversight; it appears to be a programmatic feature of Bennett's materialism. Consider her advocacy for a "vital materialist theory of democracy" that dispenses with our "prejudice" against nonhumans.[47] There is a precedent for such a move: "Surely the scope of democratization can be broadened to acknowledge more nonhumans in more ways, in something like the ways in which we have come to hear the political voices of other humans formerly on the outs."[48] The following sentence makes clear that those "formerly on the outs" are enslaved people and women. Just as Black people and women were denied equal rights but now (at least in principle) have them, so too, it is time to overcome our "prejudice" against nonhumans. In delivering this equivalence, Bennett never addresses how the sovereign features of vitality, agency, and creativity with which she wants to imbue all things—spools of thread, fire, dead rats—have for most of "Western" history been apportioned unequally based on hierarchies of sexgender, race, and ability. Instead, she uncritically implores their universalization.

In both content and form, Bennett's program to decenter humans reproduces the logics and mechanisms of sovereignty. Whereas for Spinoza—whose name she invokes no less than twenty-nine times throughout the book—how we perceive reality both reflects our ethical commitments and in turns configures them, tellingly, Bennett seems to disaffirm such a linkage: "I do not think there is any *direct* relationship between, on the one hand, a set of ontological assumptions about life or matter and, on the other hand, a politics."[49] Evidently, she does not appreciate the politics that subsidizes her materialism nor its political implications. This is what results from a disregard for the particularities of being human, the particularities of human oppression.

Overcoming the false binaries of human and nonhuman, nature and culture, material and immaterial entails the recognition of their imbrication. At the outset of the study, Bennett declares: "I pursue a materialism in the tradition of Democritus-Epicurus-Spinoza-Diderot-Deleuze more than Hegel-Marx-Adorno. It is important to follow the trail of human power to expose social hegemonies (as historical materialists do). But my contention is that there is also public value in following the scent of nonhuman, thingly power, the material agency of natural bodies and technological artifacts."[50] Had she read Spinoza more attentively she may have realized that his philosophy dismantles the binary she erects between the nonhuman natural and the human cultural and social (hence, Spinoza's inspiration not only to Deleuze, but to Hegel and Marx). It unmasks her either/or as not merely illusory but injurious. For Spinoza, the two are imbricated: precisely *because* we humans are *of* nature—inconsistent, non-sovereign, conditioned—we produce cultural objects, ideas, prejudices that are ethically compromising. Social hegemonies reflect our humanness, which *is* natural, rather than super-natural. Moreover, if culture, as Bennett tells us, is "infused . . . with biological, geological, and climatic forces,"[51] this means that particularly human aspects of culture are also equally impacting and impacted by these elements. It is why, say, global warming is effectuated by colonialism, racism, capitalism, neoliberalism, and in turn reinforces the supremacies upon which they are constructed and which they perpetuate. Despite her talk of dispensing or decentering human constructs, her program is anchored in classic "Western" sovereignties, including Christian supremacy; anthropomorphism; the fetishization of agency, vitality, and creativity; and the indifference to the particularities of social inequities and the humans who suffer under their torments.

Staying Power

To Spinoza, everything that exists—singular things—are particularized ways in which infinite power exists, *how* it is. A singular thing is "the power, *or* striving, by which it strives to persevere in its being," which "is nothing but the given, *or* actual, essence of the thing itself."[52] The striving, the conatus of a thing, is its essence. Yet essence, for Spinoza, is not foundational or fixed. It does not transcend the thing—it *is* it. What modes are is *how* they are. Similarly, essence is not a telos. Rather, essence simply is the persistence, the enactment of the power that is a mode, which is only actual, never potential. Spinoza explicitly criticizes those who "distinguish between the thing itself and the striving that is in each thing to preserve its being."[53] Such people err because "though the thing and its striving to preserve in its being are distinguished by reason, or rather verbally . . . they are not in any way really distinct."[54] The conatus is not a feature possessed by modes, it *is* them, for "acting, living, and preserving in our being (these signify the same thing)."[55] Acting *is* existing *or* living, which *is* persisting.[56]

If the essence of a mode is its acting, this means that essence is not separable from existence. Although Spinoza asserts that the essence of substance is its existence, whereas that of modes depends on substance, this does not affirm a distinction obtaining between the essence of modes and their being. Rather, this underscores how the infinite and indeterminate power that is substance only exists as its finite, determinate modes. Everything *is* its conatus, not just humans but all things, including salamanders, salmonella, and sulfuric acid. All modes—like substance itself—are nothing but their acts, the power that is their persistence. Moreover, actions for Spinoza are expansive: they are not limited to, say, the action of typing this sentence. Actions are all the different alterations in the power that is a mode, encompassing feelings, sensations, inclinations, associations, recollections, and thoughts. We are as much the affections of our body, the coalition of exposures we have absorbed, the accumulation of our memories, as we are the ideas that we cogitate, for mind and body are "one and the same individual."[57]

Spinoza's take abjures several transcendent and teleological sovereignties often attached to identity, while toppling the binaries commonly hitched to it: self and other, essence and existence, being and doing, nature and nurture, nature and culture. There is no essence that is external, other, above, or beneath a mode that defines or determines it; no True self awaiting potentiation; no given Presence. This is also because power is never in reserve but only actualized, so the force, the acting that is each of us, can only be *as* it is. Furthermore, if the essence of a singular thing is nothing but its doings, this means that what or who it is, is never stable. Since modes are susceptible to external and internal forces that constantly alter their power, this affirms that identity fluctuates and modes are not isolated. Who we are is effectuated as much by our interconnections, exposures, and contexts as it is by anything internal, of the Self, which also means that no singular aspect determines identity. We are not reducible to ourselves nor to our relations but are of their coincidence, which is singular. No determinate actualization of power, no singular thing is same with another because identity exists *as* the particularities of constitution, context, and conditioning. While there is nothing special or unique about such facets, any particular coalescence of biological, cultural, linguistic, social, geographic, or temporal factors coupled with the countless exposures, encounters, and experiences a mode undergoes, render them distinct. Contra misconceptions touted by Hegel and Conway and others that Spinoza disallows for modal individuality, his conatus actually upholds the irreducible singularity that *is* each mode. Conceiving the essence of a mode as nothing but *how* it is affirms difference without rendering it sovereign, a priori, or fixed. Similarly, the difference between a human, a hedgehog, and a herpes virion is not essential or given but concerns their actions, their capacities, *how* they are, and the same also with respect to the difference *between* humans, *between* hedgehogs, *between* herpes virions.

This conception of the conatus allows Spinoza to refer all that happens to immanent, causal determinism. Singular things are as they are based on the force of their causes. Once something is caused to be, it will persist, retaining its force, until it is interrupted by something more powerful, which might enhance or deplete the arrangement of power that is it. This applies to everything. It pertains to specific modes like the cell membrane of a single cell in my index finger or to an ensemble of modes like the cellular system of my entire body, or to my idea of a cell, however imprecise. Such persistence of things explains how in drafting the previous sentence, my thought about cells caused memories of my tenth-grade biology teacher to surface, together with the scent of green tea that she sipped and so also the boredom I experienced during her lectures. And now also, pangs of guilt about how less than solicitous I was during them. All of these thoughts, recollections, and feelings are as they are based on their causation—however unconscious or unintended—and will persist unless disrupted by more impactful forces: a different thought, a different affect, a different memory. With this construal of the conatus, Spinoza applies Descartes's principle of motion—"each and everything, in so far as it can, always continues in the same state"[58]—to everything that is, not just extended bodies.

A Royal Pain

The only thinker and text that Spinoza explicitly cites in his *Ethics* are Descartes and his *Passions of the Soul*, penned in response to Elisabeth of Bohemia's challenges to his dualism. Three salient concerns surface in their exchanges. The first is that Elisabeth of Bohemia pressures the purported independence of the mind over the body, observing how the conditions of the body impact the mind. Yet Descartes mostly upholds his contention that a "free mind" can control its thinking, "no matter what indisposition the body has."[59] Second, to Descartes, the body shackles the mind, "takes away its freedom."[60] Finally, he argues: "The force of the passions consists only in overwhelming and subjecting reason to them."[61] By contrast, she maintains "there are passions that do carry us to reasonable actions."[62]

Despite the capacity of the soul to dominate the body, Descartes concedes in his *Passions* that sometimes conflicts arise, for which the body is responsible.[63] But the "strongest souls ... can most easily conquer the passions and stop the bodily movements which accompany them."[64] The soul is to conduct "battle," furnished with "proper weapons" to subjugate the body to its sovereign will.[65] "There is no soul so weak that it cannot, if well-directed, acquire an absolute power over its passions."[66] Therefore, "the weakest souls could acquire absolute mastery over all their passions if we employed sufficient ingenuity in training and guiding them."[67] Since everyone is capable of dominating their passions through exercising free will, people are worthy of esteem or blame for their actions. This "renders us in a certain way like

God by making us masters of ourselves."[68] The *Passions* concludes by asserting that "the chief use of wisdom lies in its teaching us to be masters of our passions,"[69] which correlates with the conclusion of his *Discourse*, calling upon humans to be "the lords and masters of nature."[70] Both instances of "mastery" rest on the hierarchical logics of dualism: God over nature, mind over body, human over nature, all of which are possible by means of free will, which transcends nature and is thus able to rule over it.

The sovereign logics that underwrite Descartes's insistence on the capacity of the transcendent, free, active will to overcome the passive body, of rationality to teleologically direct action, and of the individual culpability and failure that follow when this does not transpire remain pillars of "Western" culture. These figure in self-help literature, campaigns for "self-care," and cognitive behavioral therapy, which all rely on fantasies that we can autonomously overcome debilitating circumstances and freely control our thoughts to think positively and "succeed." When this does not happen, the individual is to be faulted for their bad feelings, bad conditions, and bad attitude. The problem is not reality itself nor oppressive material conditions. Rather, the atomized self is to blame for its failure to regulate, optimize, and realize its "potential." So it is that anxiety, depression, and suicidality are privatized conditions, the results of bad personal choices, insufficient rationality, and negative dispositions. Varieties of cognitive behavioral therapy, for example, pinpoint irrationality as the cause of disordered feelings, which result from distorted perceptions of ourselves, others, and reality. Correcting our thoughts is key to "happiness," since we are reducible to our minds.

Will Away

The Christian, Cartesian system rests upon its construction of a sovereign God, which is the model for the sovereign Human Subject. Surely, Spinoza has in mind Descartes—amongst others—when he explains that people mistakenly attribute free will to God as "they very often compare God's power with the power of Kings."[71] The infinity of substance deprives it and the modes that are it of autonomy, free will, transcendence, and teleology. Substance is by necessity, and "humans, like other things, act from the necessity of nature."[72]

Why are people so committed to free will? Both Augustine and Descartes reason that in the absence of free will it makes no sense for God to reward and punish humans for their behavior. This concern surfaces in Spinoza's correspondences with Lambertus van Velthuysen, who accuses Spinoza of "atheism" because, as Spinoza writes, "he thinks I take away God's freedom and subject him to fate."[73] The upshot of this for Velthuysen is that "no room is left for any divine governance or providence; the whole distribution of punishments and rewards is destroyed."[74] Spinoza's response anticipates reproach that rejecting free will renders "all wickedness . . . excusable" and underscores that "evil humans are no less to be feared nor are they any less harmful, when they are necessarily evil."[75] The fact that actions are causally determined—immanently necessitated—rather than transcendently directed or willfully elected does not detract from the evilness of certain deeds. It merely undermines the construct of a purportedly independent, free agent as solely culpable for their actions.

Not only does the notion of a free, sovereign God subsidize the conceit of a free, sovereign Human but as is the case with sovereignties, they instate evermore hierarchies. So, advocates of free will, Spinoza bemoans, "attribute the cause of human impotence, not to the common power of nature, but to some vice in human nature, which they therefore bewail, or laugh at, or disdain."[76] The fiction of free will promotes a culture of success or failure that warrants ostracizing those who succumb to "vices." Thus, "he who knows how to censure more eloquently and cunningly the weakness of the human mind is held to be Godly."[77] Spinoza is alluding to Descartes but also religious figures who employ free will to condemn humans as weak and sinful. Today, such castigations are delivered by politicians and psychologists, eager to censure individuals for their "failings." This neoliberal ethos of personal achievement absolves society of responsibility for human "vices" like poverty, addiction, and mental illness, promoting a culture that marginalizes and dehumanizes people in such circumstances, furthering the very conditions that engendered these "vices." Just like past religious leaders who had a vested interest in sustaining their hierarchical system, contemporary neoliberals advocate as much to perpetuate their interests.

Spinoza remarks: "That famous human freedom everyone brags of . . . consists only in this: that humans are conscious of their appetite and ignorant of the causes by which they are determined."[78] Thus, "the madman, the chatterbox, and a great many people of this kind believe that they act from a free decision of the mind, and not that they are set in motion by an impulse."[79] Since "this prejudice is innate in all humans, they are not so easily freed of it."[80] The delusion of freedom, the desire to be free, is almost ingenerate. Addressing our question—why humans are so attached to free will—it seems that at least part of the reason is simply *how* we are: "Though experience teaches quite abundantly that there is nothing less in human's power than to restrain appetites, and that often, when humans are torn by contrary affects, they see the better and follow the worse, they still believe themselves to be free."[81] But, Spinoza reinforces: "I deny that we are free in anything," if by free what is meant is contravention of causal determinations.[82]

In the preface to part III of the *Ethics*, Spinoza expounds on the human preference to see itself as constituting a "dominion within a dominion," exempted from immanent, causal determinism. People want to perceive themselves as invested with "absolute power," the sole determinants of their actions. Descartes, Spinoza writes, "believed that the mind has absolute power over its own actions," and strained to show how "the mind can have absolute dominion over its affects," but "in my opinion, he showed nothing but the cleverness of his understanding."[83] Throughout these passages, Spinoza depicts the Christian, Cartesian position as reliant upon "dominion," "free decision," and "decrees." Such "juridical-political"[84] terminology signals how purports to sovereignty are mutually reinforcing. The hierarchical, sovereign approach to mind and body is subsidized by parallel claims to absolute power, the freedom to dominate, and the license to subjugate that suffuse politics and religion.

Against these conceits to exceptionalism and the domination it commissions, Spinoza insists that the mind cannot determine the body to act. What is more, like everything that exists, "the mind is determined to will this or that by a cause which is also determined by another, and this again by another, and so on to infinity."[85] Since there is no transcendence from causal intra-action, the mind "cannot be a free cause of its actions."[86]

Consumed by Desire

Without sovereign free will and executive decision-making, what drives human action? Spinoza's alternative rests on his nondualism. Mind and body are "one and the same thing" only "conceptually distinguished." The same being undergoes and does the same things, which can be registered bodily or mindedly. Accordingly, "the decision of the mind ... and the determination of the body by nature exist together—or rather are one and the same thing."[87] Decisions of the mind are not only not loftier than the determinations of the body, they are same with it because whatever a minded body or bodied mind does or undergoes is coordinated as "one and the same individual."

Moreover, the decisions of the mind, like the determinations of the body, are not sovereignly decided but driven by desire *or* appetite. Although "desire" signifies an appetite accompanied by conscious awareness, "between appetite and desire there is no difference"[88] because "whether a human is conscious of their appetite or not, the appetite still remains one and the same."[89] There is also no difference between so-called will and desire or impulse and desire. All of these are different names for the same "strivings of human nature."[90] Thus, "desire is human's very essence, insofar as it is conceived to be determined, from any given affection to it, to do something."[91] Or "appetite is the very essence of human, insofar as it is determined to do what promotes their preservation."[92] Appetite *or* desire is the essence of humans because the conatus that is a mode is its actions, its strivings, which are determined by its affections, the alterations in the force that is it.

While other thinkers elevate the mind and its "decisions" or "wills" over the body and its brute appetites, Spinoza considers all of these same and uses "desire" to denote as much: "By the word desire I understand any of human's strivings, impulses, appetites, and volitions."[93] All we do is driven by desire. This has two significant implications. The first is that without desire there can be no action. We cannot will ourselves to do anything whether in deference to commands, be they internal or external, or in submission to some ideal or principle. Rather, in order to act—to even be, to persist in existing—there must be desire, conscious or unconscious. The second point is that desires "vary as the human's constitution varies,"[94] which means that desire is particular and personalized. What we do is determined by the singular medley of experiences, exposures, and encounters that we undergo, which in turn condition our desires, forming and reforming them.

Turning Beet Red

What determines our desires? Like everything, these are causally effectuated through internal and external intra-action. Desires can be "conceived through the attribute of thought alone, or through the attribute of extension alone, or referred to both at once."[95] We can speak of, say, my desire to sip chilled borscht on this sweltering afternoon, which can be conceived as a desire of extension, since I am peckish. Yet this desire is also conceivable in thought, as the recognition that said borscht will cool me, nourish me, and satisfy me, or we can simply say that I—the minded body or bodied mind that is me—desire it. This desire comes from learned experience, positive associations, and possibly also fond memories, not to mention my predilection for colorful fare and complex flavors, paired with my knowledge of the many nutrients it contains. Convenience is also critical: the borscht is prepared, sitting in the refrigerator. These are the most obvious ingredients coalescing into my supremely low stakes act of savoring this soup. Importantly, although these factors may be disaggregated in our after-the-fact analysis, from Spinoza's perspective, the grumblings in my stomach, my mind's registering of this affectation, and my subsequent move to quell it are coordinated.

On the one hand, electing to depict Spinoza's theory of desire with an edible delight is possibly not the most illuminating. No one can deny that culinary preferences are determined by our desires (and the conditions and resources available to satisfying them). Moreover, the food in question is nutritious, so I cannot pretend that there was a tension between my hankering for it and some rational desire not to consume foods that might harm me. If this were the case, then we could have considered the process of my determination to enjoy or not enjoy it, unpacking the conceit of so-called willpower, much as we could have weighed the ethics of my consumption if the borscht did not belong to me, but it does. This was an easily quenchable desire with no major countervailing impulses or commitments. But the simplicity of this example and its mundanity is precisely the point. It captures the scandal of Spinoza's undertaking: to analyze human affairs without Exceptionalism, insisting that all of our actions emerge through processes just like those that facilitated my consumption of the borscht. Everything we do is driven by desires. Even the weighty, consequential actions that we take are causally determined and conditioned by our conscious desires and unconscious appetites. The fact that human action is prompted by conative desires makes us no different from nonhuman animals in this respect.

There is nothing sovereign about my determination to relish the borscht. I was hangry, so I paused my writing to ingest it, without really thinking about it. While such experiences are routine, Spinoza's controversial point is that much of what we do comes to pass in this manner. As he allows, "the causes of buildings, of paintings, and of things of this kind" can emerge from "nature alone, insofar as it is considered to be only corporeal,"[96] by which Spinoza does not mean that no thinking is ever involved in architectural and artistic production. Nor does he mean that buildings and art make themselves but that skilled architects and artists might fabricate even remarkable works in the absence of conscious planning or deliberative reflection, the kind of experience that we might describe as "being in the flow." Since people are so wedded to models of sovereign decision-making and purports that mind is sovereign over body, they do not understand "what the body can do" without being "guided by the mind."[97]

I did not choose my desire for chilled borscht, I did not elect to like it, nor can I properly be said to have autonomously decided to consume it. Sure, I was not coerced into eating it, but since my act of so doing is profoundly conditioned, it is not a Free act. In Spinoza's parlance we could say that I was a more active rather than passive cause. Furthermore, my previous experiences with borscht were indispensable to my determination to enjoy it. Such past experiences, which often evade our sovereign awareness, explain why it is that you might be thinking about borscht right now. Why you might be tickled to taste my borscht or why you might be repelled by such fantasies, considering your distaste for beetroot or the caraway accenting it. Or because it was over a bowl of chilled borscht that your lover ended your liaison, nine years ago, and you still cannot shake that painful association. Maybe your tolerance for this illustrative example has peaked, and your patience with me and my borscht are waning. All of these factors will determine your reception of what I am conveying, and yet none of it can properly be said to have been sovereignly *chosen* by you. For Spinoza, this is the case in all matters.

There is a further significant way in which Spinoza disrupts the sovereignties of decisionism. If I asserted that this chilled borscht is "good," you would have shaky grounds on which to contest the claim. This is because, conventionally, we regard judgments of taste as determined by personal desires. Accordingly, if I meant "good" in the sense of nourishing or fortifying and therefore good for me to consume, this, too, would be hard to disprove. And if my valence of "good" signifies that it is good because it sated me, was pleasurable, and refreshing, you would have limited grounds on which to protest. For Spinoza, the same considerations are operative with all value judgments: "We neither strive for, nor will, neither want, nor desire anything because we judge it to be good; on the contrary, we judge something to be good because we strive for it, will it, and desire it."[98] Good and evil are immanent expressions of our lived and learned affective experiences. When we say that something is "good, or evil," this signifies "what is useful to, or harmful to, preserving our being . . . increases or diminishes, aids or restrains, our power of acting."[99] It represents "nothing but an idea of joy or sadness."[100] Good and evil are modes of thinking—ideas—that our minds attach to certain affects. Consuming the borscht was delightful, which in Spinoza's idiom means that I was affected with joy. This feeling of joy is expressed in the mind as the idea of good: "Knowledge of good and evil is nothing but the affect itself, insofar as we are conscious of it."[101] Crucially, "this idea is not really distinguished from the affect itself, *or* from the idea of the body's affectation; it is only conceptually distinguished from it."[102]

Acting Out

"Minds, however, are conquered not by arms, but by love and nobility."[103] This applies to ourselves as much as to relations with others. Spinoza's ethics is anchored by the recognition that in order to live rightly, we cannot be coerced to do so but must *desire* to do so. Since we are determined by desires rather than sovereign decisions, in order to alter our actions, we need to adjust our desires, *who we are*. This dispenses with the teleology of traditional ethics: we cannot will ourselves to be otherwise, we cannot force ourselves to be a certain way, we must actually *be* otherwise, which means that our *desires* must be otherwise. Clarifying as much and adumbrating its implications is the focus of the final three parts of the *Ethics*.

The crux of this program concerns the affects, which Spinoza reconstrues by wresting them from association with a passive, irrational, detached body. Affects are alterations in the power of existing that *is* a mode and "the ideas" of those changes.[104] The force that is a mode fluctuates constantly, and while these variations can be registered differently in the mind or the body, they express the same changes.[105] Sometimes we are the "adequate cause" of these changes, while most of the time, we are only a "partial, *or* inadequate" cause.[106] Significantly, enhancements in the power of existing that is us affect us with joy, while decreases in power affect us with sadness. At issue here is neither Power or Joy as such but Spinoza's way of expressing how generally, when we persist in our beings, when we are not hindered or harmed by ourselves or others, we feel good, we are affected with "joy," whereas when we are hindered or harmed by ourselves or others, we feel bad, we are affected with sadness. The upshot is that since affects are actual changes in who we are, understanding them, how they function, and what sway we may have over them is critical to adjusting who we are and so how we live.

With his approach to affect, Spinoza capaciously redefines what might conventionally be termed "feelings" or "emotions" (in our analysis, these are used interchangeably). Affects are neither mere representations of changes that we undergo nor are they byproducts of these changes. Rather, affects *are these very changes*. They adhere ontologically. Feelings alter the power of acting, of existing, that is a mode because affects are active and effectuate actual changes in reality. For example, the feeling of sadness alters a given mode, adjusting its power, which is its acting. When someone is sad, they disengage and withdraw, their sadness decreases their power such that performing certain activities is now more effortful and strenuous. This is what Spinoza means in construing affects as alterations in the power of a mode, its existence. Moreover, this sadness not only influences the power of that given mode and its capacity to act, but it impacts the modes with which it is connected. When I see a sad person, I, too, am impacted. By altering both of us, this sadness transforms ontological conditions; it adjusts both of our states and changes our relations, which has further consequences for us and others. Affects are not contained or easily containable because they are actual modifications in reality that have repercussions.

Spinoza's nondualism entails a further expansion of feelings: because mind and body are the same thing only "conceptually distinguished," it is not only the body that feels. Rather, "the mind feels those things that it conceives in understanding."[107] Thinking is affective. Whatever prospects there are for reason to help us live center on the affectivity of thinking, on how ideas transform us and so also our desires. Ideas are powerful because they are not mute pictures on a tablet but actual changes in the arrangement of power that is us, which effectuates additional changes. For Spinoza, when the mind thinks "inadequate *or* confused ideas," it becomes sad for "the mind's power of acting is diminished or restrained."[108] Accordingly, when the mind conceives adequate ideas, "it also rejoices . . . insofar as it acts."[109] This is because its power is enhanced, which means that it alters the state of the mode that is doing the thinking, changing its force, producing real effects "related to joy or desire."[110] Clear and distinct ideas increase the power of a mode, adjust its constitution, and augment its capacities. These ideas now have a "greater force of existing," experiencing more "reality than before."[111] This change has ramifications for the mode, causally influencing and conditioning their desires, which is why "desire is also related to us insofar as we understand."[112] Thinking feels, what we think alters who we are, which *is* our desires and so also *how* we are.

For Descartes, passions are *caused* by the body.[113] Therefore, dominating the body combats the passions either through willpower or habituated discipline. Spinoza overturns this: the passions are not *caused* by the body nor can the mind captain the body, for mind and body "are one and the same thing." As such, passions cannot be quashed or chastened into submission. Furthermore, he dispenses with the binary opposition whereby reason is *opposed* to passions: passions and affects are the same thing, what distinguishes them is whether or not an individual is an adequate or inadequate cause of them. Passions may be of the mind as much as they are of the body. Additionally, thinking can morph a given passion into an action.[114] Accordingly, there is no inherent difference between a desire of which we are an inadequate, partial cause and of which we are an adequate cause.[115] Activity and passivity are not binarily opposed so much as spectrally in flux.

Hard Feelings

Spinoza is committed to explicating the seemingly inconsistent, disadvantageous, and irrational things that we do. Rather than "laugh" or "condemn" human affairs, he investigates the causes effectuating our idiotic and destructive actions. This approach rebuts the allied stances of "theologians" and "stupid Cartesians" who fault poor discipline, feeble willpower, and irrationality for such behaviors. Today, such views finance neoliberal gospels of self-help and positive psychology that blame people for their "unproductive" emotional states. Such doctrines absolve unjust—racist, capitalist, sexist—structures for our suffering, insisting that rational thinking, positive attitude, and effort are enough to overcome our bad feelings and optimize our "best selves." By contrast, Spinoza pinpoints the constitutive factors that curtail our control and condition our feelings, ideas, and behaviors.

To Spinoza, we humans are never the sovereign cause of our affects, ideas, or actions. Our power is "infinitely surpassed by the powers of external causes,"[116] and we "do not have an absolute power to adapt things outside us to our use."[117] This deficit of freedom is due to the fact that we are not isolated, atomistic beings but entangled in the infinite connection of causes upon which we depend and from which there can be no extrication. Such imbrication explains why often, without our awareness, let alone consent, it happens that an affect "stubbornly clings" to us.[118] What is more, we are not in control of how our bodies and minds register these external forces, how our past experiences and particular inclinations respond to stimuli.

Since our minds are the ideas of our bodies and we have ideas of the affectations of our bodies and our bodies are comprised of diverse and variable modes, which are suspended amidst the diverse and variable conditions that are the "common order of nature," most of what we feel and think is determined by fortuitous encounters and experiences that linger in our memories.

This is how it happens that "one and the same object can be the cause of many and contrary affects."[119] Similarly, we may like or dislike something for no clear reason due to unconscious associations of multiple, simultaneous affects. Anything, therefore, "can be the accidental cause of joy, sadness, or desire"[120] or "hope or fear."[121] Instead of pathologizing our proneness to desires and feelings that do not serve us, Spinoza uncovers their causes, stressing how these are unavoidable aspects of being human, rather than indications of individual failure.

We often believe things that defy reason because "we easily believe the things we hope for, but believe with difficulty only those we fear."[122] This is how "superstitions" proliferate. It explains how we remain attached to beliefs, dreams, and goals that seem either irrational or unattainable. There is a *reason* that people are drawn to conspiracy theories. Likewise, there is a *reason* that we hold on to unachievable, debilitating fantasies: they make us feel better in the present, rendering our miserable lives a bit more livable. In contemporary affect theory such coping mechanisms have been dubbed "cruel optimism."[123] As Spinoza explains, we are prone to affirm things that bring us joy,[124] especially in the present, and disaffirm that which brings us sadness, particularly future sadness. This inclination also explains certain loves and hates that conflict with reason, experience, and what we know to be in our best interests.[125]

As the disparate arrangement of countless modes, we are exceedingly prone to unstable, disempowering feelings and desires. This is how we come to harbor inclinations and drives that may unintentionally hurt us and others. We are "daily torn" by affects.[126] Such "contrary affects" are why people regularly "do not know what they want."[127] Often a single, forceful desire persists "without regard to our health as a whole"[128] or best interests.[129] Another complication is the fact that affects toward present things are more powerful than past or future things.[130] Hence, "we value most the pleasures of the moment."[131] Rather than castigating us to "think of the consequences" and "put mind over matter," Spinoza examines *why* doing so is so difficult.

Since we are constituted by our particular desires and conditioned by our encounters and experiences, "the desire of each individual differs from the desire of another as much as the nature, or essence, of the one differs from the essence of the other."[132] There is a singularity to our desires, which *are* us. We have different experiences, we feel things differently, we have different constitutions. Conflicts and disagreements arise not because we *want* them nor because we do not know that they harm us and others but because we are mostly driven by inconsistent, incoherent, inconstant desires, and often enough these do not coincide with the inconsistent, incoherent, inconstant desires of others.[133]

Delusions of freedom are a major cause of sadness and conflict. Although we are prone to promote what brings us joy and prevent what brings us sadness, these conceptions are often based on mistaken judgments and inflated perceptions of our powers.[134] This is how we come to erroneously think of ourselves as the sole *cause* of our joy or sadness. Exaggerated notions of our freedom precipitate the sadness of "repentance,"[135] while the "joy accompanied by the idea of some deed which we believe we have done from a free decision of the mind" is known as "self-esteem."[136] To Spinoza, "because humans believe themselves free, these affects are very violent."[137] Such purports to sovereignty lead us to blame ourselves for doing what is deemed "wrong" and praise ourselves for doing what is considered "right."[138] These ideas of right and wrong, and the good or bad feelings that come from our alignment or misalignment with these values, Spinoza emphasizes, are socially constructed, especially through parenting and education.[139] Since "humans consider themselves to be free," they fault or hate others, esteem or adore them, based on the perceived freedom of their actions.[140]

Our entanglement with other humans is a primary cause of our feelings, which condition our desires, which are who we are and so how we act. Spinoza refers to this phenomenon as the "imitation of the affects" and "emulation" of desire. These account for, among other things, how we come to: like things that we think others like us like and dislike things that others like us dislike;[141] like someone or something when it affects those we like or others like us with joy and so also dislike things that affect us and others with sadness;[142] want what we like to like us in return;[143] dislike those who dislike us;[144] like those who like us;[145] dislike those who dislike that which we like;[146] and are saddened when those we like are saddened.[147] Our susceptibility and interconnectedness with others is part of being human, and while this induces bad feelings and desires, it correspondingly engenders good feelings and desires.

Missed Connections

We are not merely dependent upon others but constituted by them. This dynamic can enhance the conatus that is a mode or vitiate it. However, commentators routinely miss the interconnection that configures and sustains modes, as in readings that mistakenly attach to Spinoza an "egoism" and "individualism" based on a misapprehension of what he means by "self-interest."[148] Or, they emphasize modal entanglement—like Balibar's transindividuality—yet slight the disabling aspects of such intertwinement.[149] For Spinoza, we become mimetically, especially in our early years but throughout life. Yet imitation can also undercut individual and societal flourishing as when we imitate bad feelings that cultivate insalubrious desires, corrosive to ourselves and others. Taking a closer look at Spinoza's reflections on self-esteem and suicidality exemplifies these complexities.

Self-approval or self-esteem is defined by Spinoza as "a joy born of the fact that a human considers themselves and their own power of acting."[150] Such "*acquiescentia in se ipso summum quod sperare possumus*, is the highest thing for which we can hope."[151] Feeling good about our own power, which *is* who we are, is the best of feelings because these are not teleological: "No one strives to preserve their being for the sake of any end."[152] Further, "because self-esteem is more and more encouraged and strengthened by praise . . . and on the other hand, more and more upset by blame . . . . we are guided most by love of esteem and can hardly bear a life in disgrace."[153] Our self-esteem is linked to how others perceive us. While verily attested by lived experience, Spinoza's emphasis on this has been overlooked.

Even as Spinoza recognizes the assets of affirmation from others, he registers its deficits. Since our *acquiescentia in se ipso* (self-esteem) is so dependent upon others, "everyone is anxious to tell their own deeds, and show off their powers . . . and that humans, for this reason, are troublesome to one another."[154] What is more, because approbation feels good, "it can easily happen that one . . . imagines themself to be pleasing to all, when they are burdensome to all."[155] Furthermore, the desire for affirmation can lead us to seek it from the wrong people, such as "the multitude," which is "fickle and inconstant."[156] The trouble with courting public opinion is not only that it generates anxiety, requires constant exertion, and "gives rise to a monstrous lust of each to crush the other," but when it "ceases, the self-esteem ceases."[157]

There is a further complexity to self-esteem and our interlacements with others. We feel good the more we "distinctly" imagine our actions, "distinguish them from others, and consider them as singular things."[158] This is why people are most glad "when they consider something in themself which they deny concerning others."[159] Hence, "humans are naturally inclined to hate and envy."[160] Since people like feeling singular, "if they relate what they affirm of themself to the universal idea of human or animal, they will not be so greatly gladdened."[161] Similarly, they feel bad upon realizing their "actions are weaker, compared to others' actions."[162] These bad feelings spur one to "wrongly interpreting their equals' actions" or to "magnifying their own as much as they can."[163] However, comparing ourselves to others can be salutary, as when someone "conceives their lack of power because they understand something more powerful than themself."[164] In such an instance, this person "understands themselves distinctly, *or* . . . their power of acting is aided."[165] Appreciating how we stand in comparison to others is necessary to preserving ourselves, not merely in cases of, say, impending physical injury but as concerns our ideas, feelings, and desires, which are equally crucial.

We are embedded in society and rely upon others for our basic needs. To Spinoza, these needs are not merely things like food and shelter but also our feelings, especially self-esteem, which is critical to our persistence, not to mention flourishing. This underpins Spinoza's remarks on death by suicide.[166] Suicide results from someone being "completely conquered by external causes contrary to their nature"[167] because "that a human should, from the necessity of their own nature, strive not to exist, or to be changed into another form, is as impossible as that something should come from nothing."[168] The external forces that can impel suicide are not merely physical as when, for example, someone is physically coerced to stab their own heart with a sword.[169] Rather, Spinoza recognizes that circumstances may compel someone to kill themself and cites the example of Seneca. No one forced him to kill himself, but the situation was such that doing so was preferable to the alternative of being killed by others. Likewise, someone may kill themself "because hidden external causes so dispose their imagination, and so affect their body, that it takes another nature, contrary to the former."[170]

By underscoring how external and contrary forces cause suicide, Spinoza at once reaffirms his resistance to sovereign free will and individualism, while spotlighting the centrality of societal norms and structures to well-being. Instead of "blaming the victim" or merely condemning suicide, Spinoza appreciates how suicide, as Steven Barbone and Lee Rice descry, "is always a symptom of the failure of life-giving and reinforcing contingencies within the environment itself."[171] Surges in deaths by suicide "can be seen, from a Spinozistic perspective, as an indictment not of the suicidal person, but our collective failure to produce environments which support inbuilt tendencies for self-preservation."[172] People kill themselves because our systems do not maintain life. Or more precisely, they are designed for the promotion of some life, at the cost of other life. Present capitalist, racist, sexist, ableist, transphobic, and xenophobic conditions actively devalue certain lives, rendering them unlivable. Suicide, from this perspective, while ostensibly an individual act, is really collective. Our structures concretely slay people. Since feelings are real changes in the capacities of a mode, the kinds of bad feelings—estrangement, desperation, abjection, loneliness, hopelessness—that precipitate suicide are not pathologies nor misperceptions of reality but real modifications in people caused by circumstances that overpower their capacity to live.

To Spinoza, "we can never bring it about that we require nothing outside ourselves to preserve our being, nor that we live without having dealings with things outside us."[173] Despite the destructive impacts of sociality, we cannot live without it, which is why not living at all is sometimes the only option. In their glosses on Spinoza's approach to suicide, Butler observes: "The desire to live implicates desire in a matrix of life that may well, at least partially, deconstitute the 'I' who endeavors to live," as "the 'I' is already responsive to alterity in ways that it cannot always control."[174] To be, for Spinoza, is to be composed of and entangled with others, embedded in a connection of causes that makes, remakes, and unmakes who and so how we are.

Vested Interests

Human existence, like that of all modes, is *conative*, propelled by a tendency to persist in being. When the force that is a given mode perdures or is enhanced, they feel good and this good feeling inclines them to continue persisting.[175] This compulsion to doing what feels good abides unless disrupted by countervailing forces, internal or external. To Spinoza, whatever seems to facilitate these good feelings is deemed "good" and whatever disturbs them is "evil." Therefore, doing good—living well—amounts to doing the things that feel good, perpetuate, or enhance our existence. This is why living ethically is living itself: "No one can desire . . . to act and live well, unless at the same time they desire to be, to act, and to live . . . to actually exist."[176] Or, the desire "to live blessedly, *or* well, to act . . . is the very essence of human."[177] Living well is immanent to human existence. It *is* the conatus. Hence, "the striving to preserve oneself is the first and only foundation of virtue."[178] Here and throughout, Spinoza capitalizes on the dual resonances of "virtue": it means both doing good and power.[179] This synonymy assists his redefinition of living as living virtuously: persisting in power, existing, living at all is coincident with living ethically. Significantly, "no one strives to preserve their being for the sake of any end"[180] or "for the sake of anything else."[181] Since living, acting, persisting *is* the very existence of a mode, doing so cannot be transcendent to it, external to it, other than it. Doing good is never teleological.

The actions that perpetuate our existence are those that make us feel good, affect us with joy.[182] Things which make us feel good "agree" with our nature,[183] whereas those that affect us with sadness "disagree" with our nature, are "contrary to us."[184] And "the more a thing agrees with our nature, the more useful, *or* better it is for us . . . the more a thing is useful to us, the more it agrees with our nature."[185] What most agrees with our natures are things with which we have the most in common. "Nothing can agree more with the nature of any thing than other individuals of the same species."[186] As such, those who "live among such individuals as agree with their nature, their power of acting will thereby be aided and encouraged."[187] Importantly, because other humans are most like us, the agreements that are good for us are necessarily also good for them. Therefore, one who actualizes such agreements wants "nothing for themselves that they do not desire for other humans," so "they are just, honest, and honorable."[188]

By confirming that living ethically is nothing but living itself, Spinoza delivers an ethics divested of teleology and transcendence. We are *conatively* inclined to persisting in our beings, which feels good, and whatever feels good *is* good, and what most allows us to perdure and so feels most good is maintaining agreements with those most like us, other humans, and because we share a nature, what is most good for us is also most good for them.

Despite this feat but also because of it, Spinoza was acutely cognizant of the resistance it would encounter by those committed to an ethics constructed on the sovereignties of transcendence and teleology. He allows that his approach might unsettle readers "who believe that this principle—that everyone is bound to seek their own advantage—is the foundation, not of virtue and morality, but of immorality."[189] This concern is not misplaced; scholars over the centuries and still today continue to either critique or champion the conatus as promoting varieties of "self-interest," "egoism," and "individualism." These reservations miss what Spinoza is after: an ethics that is *not* constructed on the supremacies that moor the hegemonic alternatives. Notions of coercing, submitting, dominating ourselves into acting well are deluded and so ineffective. Only an ethics based on how things really are, on how humans *really* are, has any promise.

Classifications of "egoism" and "individualism" miss the scope of Spinoza's point that what is good for an individual human mode is enacting agreements with other human modes. This is only the case because humans are of the infinite connection of causes, interconnected with other modes, primarily those most like it. From the outset, they exist as the effect of external causes, but they also cause effects, impacting those around them and in turn being impacted by them. Such mutuality is constitutive. Furthermore, readings of the conatus and Spinoza's ethics as "selfish" are premised on the very pragmatic functionalism that he decries: they presume that modes executively decide or consciously elect to enact agreements with other humans *because* it serves them. Spinoza's claim is that enacting agreements with others *is* the very nature of a mode, which they do without purpose, end, or objective, solely because they incline towards what feels good and what feels good *is* such persistence. Yet this is not because they want to persist or intend to persist or elect to persist, rather since they *are* this very persistence, this very desire, this very doing. It makes no sense to construe the conatus as "self-interest" or "self-advantage," as if there is a self that exists *before* its existence or *other* to it, a desire that exceeds it. To be is to be "interested" or "advantaged" in persisting, and this aligns with the persistence of others like it who are equally "interested" or "advantaged," which is why my interest coincides with your interest. So-called self-interest or self-advantage is always already collective.

A Whole Different Beast

"So let the satirists laugh as much as they like at human affairs, let the theologians curse them, let melancholics praise as much as they can a life that is uncultivated and wild, let them disdain humans and admire lower animals."[190] But humans, Spinoza proceeds to explain, can provide for their needs most fully by "helping one another" and "only by joining forces can they avoid the dangers that threaten on all sides."[191] By now, it is quite obvious how Spinoza's approach counters that of satirists who scorn human idiocy as well as theologians who condemn succumbing to desire. What commands attention is his aside about melancholics keen on "nature" and animals. To Spinoza, "it is much preferable . . . to consider the deeds of humans, rather than those of the lower animals."[192] Since we are most like other humans, investigating their behavior is more valuable than interrogating that of animals. This spotlights a particular aspect of Spinoza's resistance to anthropocentrism: though humans are not exceptions to nature and not inherently superior to other modes, this does not mean they are same with them. This point remains salient, considering our foregoing assessment of Bennett's political ecology of things. The problem with her politics is that humans are quite different from amoebas, antelopes, and apes, not to mention acacia trees, amanita basii, and actinomycetota. Even if we might interact with some of them, consume some of them, and depend on some of them, our differences from these other modes limit intra-actions with them. Other humans agree most with our natures, which is why living rightly depends upon enacting agreements *specifically* with them.

Although "we cannot in any way doubt that the lower animals feel things," the affects of nonhuman animals "differ from humans' affects as much as their nature differs from human nature."[193] For example, "both the horse and the human are driven by lust to procreate; but the one is driven by equine lust, the other by a human lust. So also the lusts and appetites of insects, fish, and birds must vary."[194] There is a *particularity* to desire. While such distinction can be generalized to a certain species, there is differentiation within a group as the desires of any singular mode are shaped by their constitution, relationships, experiences, and circumstances. So, "there is no small difference between the gladness by which a drunk is led and the gladness a philosopher possesses."[195] The challenges of such differences is "why many . . . have preferred to live among the lower animals rather than among humans."[196] Despite human discord, Spinoza insists that "more advantages than disadvantages follow from their forming a common society."[197]

In the Augustinian and Cartesian worldview, humans stand above animals in the hierarchy of nature. This is because animals are without "understanding or thought."[198] Animals "imitate or surpass us only in those of our actions which are not guided by our thought."[199] They "act naturally and mechanically, like a clock which tells the time better than our judgment does."[200] The actions of nonhuman animals are automatic, not free. Spinoza, of course, dispels the anthropocentrism and human exceptionalism underpinning this approach. Humans are not fundamentally different from nonhuman animals nor do they possess transcendent, supernatural capacities. Thought is not exclusive to humans, and "many things are observed in the lower animals that far surpass human ingenuity."[201] Yet, this does not lead Spinoza to care much for their welfare: "The law against killing animals is based more on empty superstition and womanish compassion than sound reason."[202] With this sexist turn of phrase, he means that prioritizing animal needs over human needs is misguided: "I do deny that we are therefore not permitted to consider our own advantage, use them at our pleasure, and treat them as is most convenient for us. For they do not agree in nature with us, and their affects are different in nature from our human affects."[203]

To certain sensibilities, Spinoza's callousness to the suffering of nonhuman animals is unsettling. However, it makes sense within the context of his philosophy, which is at once unequivocally non-anthropocentric but equally resistant to replacing the supremacy of humans with another sovereignty. Much as he decries the anthropomorphic crowning of a sovereign God, he is equally suspicious of glorifying the nonhuman, be it through romanticizing "wild" nature or communing with nonhuman animals. This is not because nonhuman animals are bad or inferior but since he is focused on human thriving. By decrying individuals who decamp from human society, Spinoza is criticizing the hubris of such renunciation and spotlighting the egoism that drives it. As Sharp explains: "The zoophile marks Spinoza's concern with a deification of nature as the inversion of human arrogance."[204] This is also why he is suspicious of those who turn animals into models for human emulation.[205]

Spinoza's conception of all modes as equally of substance and constrained by immanent causal determinism explains why German Romantics like Heine, modern deep ecologists like Arne Naess, and contemporary New Materialists have been inspired by him. Yet his ontology upholds difference between different natures within "species" and across them: "However fond one may be of a dog or a horse, one cannot share with them the affective mutuality that characterizes human relationships."[206] Spinoza takes difference seriously. Our difference from nonhuman animals in our affects and so also our actions pressures the prospects for developing community, let alone conducting politics with nonhuman animals, not to mention objects, as Bennett imagines, much as it accentuates the totalizing sameness underwriting visions of human-animal, human-tree, human-aluminum democratic association.

The primacy that Spinoza places on enacting agreements with other modes aligns with Maimonides who repeatedly stresses that "living beings" are driven by "the pursuit of what agrees with them and for the avoidance of what disagrees."[207] This speaks to his stance on the particularity of animal desires, which is quite similar to Spinoza's comment about the singularity of human, equine, and other animal lusts.[208] To Maimonides, the animating force—soul—of each species differs from others and so, too, their sensations.[209] Yet unlike Spinoza, Maimonides considers humans uniquely possessive of a God-given rational faculty. This promotes human flourishing, including the development of tools and arts, which require cooperation, necessitating life in society.[210] Even as Maimonides regards humans as exceptional, he maintains, "we should not inflict pain gratuitously without any utility... we should intend to be kind and merciful even with a chance animal, except in a case of need... for we must not kill out of cruelty or for sport."[211] To Maimonides, animals feel love as much as pain, "there being no difference regarding this pain between man and other animals."[212]

Know That Feeling

Clasping Spinoza's ethics is the claim that living well is natural and flows immanently from the nature of humans. Modes are nothing but causally determined, particularized forces that incline to persist. They *are* this power. Such persistence feels good and whatever feels good *is* good. Since what agrees with a mode feels good and is good and modes agree most with those with whom they share a nature, they incline towards such agreements, which are good for themselves and others. This means that a human mode is naturally, immanently, necessarily inclined to enacting agreements with other humans. These agreements *are* ethical actions. Living well is therefore not simply possible but natural and necessary, and it follows directly from Spinoza's ontology. With this in mind, we can examine his advice for living well, which derives from his approach to reason and conception of ideas as active and affective.

Reason supports our inclination towards that which feels good, most basically through knowledge about ourselves as embodied and connected with others. Thus, "the mind is more capable of perceiving many things adequately as its body has many things in common with other bodies."[213] The more someone is affected in different ways, the more they develop adequate ideas about reality and so the more exposures they have to that which feels good. Similarly, perceiving things clearly and distinctly, "to understand their agreements, differences, and oppositions,"[214] delivers knowledge concerning agreements conducive to continued good feelings.

"Only insofar as humans live according to the guidance of reason, must they always agree in nature."[215] This is *not* because reason ordains someone to help others nor because it disciplines them into acting "rationally." Such constructions rely on the transcendence of mind over body and the concomitant teleological submission to a transcendent ethical principle. Rather, Spinoza means that perceiving adequate ideas causally determines us to act in ways that cultivate agreements with others. This is because ideas are affective and affects change us, modifying our desires, altering who we are. In this case, adequately perceiving what is good for us by understanding more about what agrees with our natures, especially other humans, makes us feel good, inclining us to sustain these good feelings and agreements, which also feel good for them, so they, too, incline towards these agreements. Therefore, "insofar as humans live according to the guidance of reason, they must do only those things that are good for human nature, and hence for each human."[216]

"The greatest virtue of the mind is to know god . . . *or* to understand things by the third kind of knowledge."[217] Such knowledge entails understanding singular things as they are in themselves—their "very essence"[218]— and their interconnections with other things. This is why one "who has a body capable of a great many things, has a mind which considered only in itself is very much conscious of itself, and of God, and of things,"[219] whereas an infant, who has comparatively limited capacities and experiences, is "conscious of almost nothing of itself, or of god, or of things."[220] Spinoza values the third way of knowing because it is the most affectively powerful. In his example of the mathematical proportional, knowledge of the third kind is "clear knowledge which comes not from being convinced by reason, but from being aware of and enjoying the thing itself."[221] Such understanding is intuitive *or* immanent and so more pleasurable. Similarly, its affective force—its good feeling—leaves one desirous of more: "The more the mind is capable of understanding things by the third kind of knowledge, the more it desires to understand them by this kind of knowledge."[222]

To Spinoza, one "who knows things by this third kind of knowledge passes to the greatest human perfection . . . is affected with the greatest joy, accompanied . . . by the idea of themselves and their virtue."[223] Since perfection correlates with power, the more power one has, the more perfect they are. Crucially, the power of such knowledge lies in its affectivity, which follows from its immanence: "We have more power if we understand the proportion itself than if we understand the rule of proportion."[224] Indeed, "the power of an effect is defined by the power of its cause,"[225] in this instance, one's intuitive grasp of the proportion. The immanence or intuitiveness of such knowledge conduces its affectivity: because this understanding derives from the self, rather than from reliance on external authority or received knowledge, it causes *really* good feelings. This is the purport of Spinoza's affirmation that one "led by reason. . . . complies with no one's wishes but their own, and does only those things which they know to be the most important in life, and therefore desires greatly."[226] Rather than promoting self-interestedness or individualism, he is emphasizing how really grasping something, understanding it immanently, feels fabulous and is therefore affectively forceful. The more intuitively *or* immanently someone understands singular things, in themselves, and their interconnections, the more they will desire salubrious agreements with others and so the more they will realize them.

Reason figures prominently for Spinoza because thinking is active and affective. This is what the final moves of the *Ethics* convey. Describing the pleasure that accompanies clear, distinct, adequate ideas about singular things—self and others—in their interconnections demonstrates how reason impacts our lives. It allows us to know more things about ourselves, others, and reality, the experience of which affects us with good feelings. These good feelings alter who we are by modifying our desires, stimulating us to *conatively* enact more agreements with others, eliciting more good feelings. This is how ethics is immanent, of human nature, causally necessary.

Pushing over the Goal

Construing human action as affective, as oriented by desires, rather than objectives, allows Spinoza to approach human behavior without resort to a telos. Not only does he reject notions of the mind or will commanding the body to act towards a specific end, but he denies that adequate ideas are teleological. This is why the pleasure, enjoyment, and joy—good feelings—of thinking clear and distinct ideas are important; they are what conduce further adequate ideas. Moreover, due to their affective force, these ideas alter the person, adjusting their desires, inclining them towards actions that promote agreements with others. These adjusted desires are the byproducts of these ideas. They are not their intended ends. Reason does not transcendentally or teleologically command, direct, or guide action. Rather, its affectivity immanently alters who we are and how we act, indirectly and non-sovereignly.

The final proposition of the *Ethics* underscores this non-teleology: "Blessedness is not the reward of virtue, but virtue itself . . . because we enjoy it, we are able to restrain our lusts."[227] Adequate ideas engender good feelings—enjoyment and joy—which affectively modify us, altering our desires, inclining us towards agreements with others, which elicit further joy, bolstering these desires, compelling ever more actions of their kind. This is the blessedness to which Spinoza refers: the good that comes from living in agreement with other humans. A wise, free person acts in this way not because they intend to constrain their affects or to experience salutary agreements but because they "enjoy it." And so, they want more of it.

The non-teleological aspects of Spinoza's approach rebut the goal-oriented creeds of neoliberalism. This is apparent from two interrelated facets of his theory. The first is the insight that commanding the self to do something is not merely impossible but relies on a debilitating conception of how we operate. In order to alter our actions, we must alter who we are—our desires, inclinations, propensities—which is only possible affectively. The force of adequate ideas rests on the good feelings they induce, which spur further ideas promoting those feelings, fortifying those desires. Merely setting a transcendent goal, independent of the felt, embodied, genuine desire to achieve it, will never work, Spinoza tells us. Which is why teleologically oriented self-improvement often leaves people feeling dejected and disempowered. The disappointment from our inabilities to "accomplish" our goals affects us with bad feelings like sadness and failure, making it that much harder to "accomplish" whatever that initial goal had been. Moreover, we are complex beings, rife with unconscious desires and feelings, which make us profoundly resistant to change. We will continue as we are, unless more forceful, enduring affects tousle us, disrupting who we are and therefore how we act.

Much as we are not in control of how we feel—as we are continuously flooded with affects that compete with and undermine any particular goals towards which we might aim—we are even less in command of the multifarious external factors that affect us. This configures the second asset of Spinoza's non-teleological approach. The dogmas of achievement, optimization, and progress, which underwrite neoliberal doctrines of self-help, place the onus on the individual to overcome their circumstances, transform themselves through willpower and grit. By renouncing teleology, Spinoza unmasks the inability of an individual to transcend their surroundings, while turning attention to the unfortunate fact that change—"achieving a goal"—transpires not due to outside coercion or deference to an external imperative but through actual modifications in who we are and what we desire. Such alterations can happen when our conditions become otherwise but not by pretending that we can transcend these conditions. There can be no goal above or beyond who we are. Whatever transformation is possible is only ever immanent. Who we are is modified affectively, inclining us towards different activities, which are the marks of a different reality.

Moderating the Affects

Against Cartesian free will and faculties of mind, for Spinoza, the only capacity a mind has is thinking, the ideas that *are* it. Further, since mind and body are "one and the same individual," reason cannot sway us through hegemony. Rather, the force of the mind rests in the ideas that are it and not so much in their truth content but their affectivity: "No affect can be restrained by the true knowledge of good and evil insofar as it is true, but only insofar as it is considered as an affect."[228] This anchors the practices that Spinoza advances for moderating affects. Crucially, this advice, I suggest, is critical to his undertaking in part V, which not only analyzes the affects but affectively impacts readers by deploying the strategies he outlines.

At the crux of Spinoza's advice is this assertion: "To every action to which we are determined from an affect which is a passion, we can be determined by reason, without that affect."[229] This is because "an affect which is a passion ceases to be a passion as soon as we form a clear and distinct idea of it."[230] The act of clearly and distinctly perceiving a passion transforms it from a passive affect into an active one. What had been externally caused is now internally reconfigured. Thereby, one becomes an adequate cause of the affect. The asset of being an adequate cause, as we have seen, is that its effects are more forceful and have more staying power. By probing the affects, Spinoza helps readers foster clear and distinct ideas about them, supporting their negotiation of them.

A further strategy for coping with affects concerns reordering them by connecting them to clear and distinct ideas.[231] What had been externally, passively caused is altered through active rearrangement. This is possible because "the appetite by which a human is said to act, and that by which they are said to be acted on, are one and the same."[232] Rather than quashing desires, reason adjusts them in ways that attenuate their force. Likewise, since we are conditioned by exposures and our memories of them, Spinoza proposes a practice of reassociation: connecting the idea of an affect with other ideas, so that when the affect is experienced, the idea of it will now be attached to several other ideas, blunting its power. Assemblages of clear and distinct ideas of affects have staying power, so when a person undergoes affects contrary to them, these "will have to accommodate themselves to it more and more, until they are no longer contrary to it."[233] Spinoza's exploration of the affects does exactly this: it promotes connections and associations that will persist in the memories of readers and resurface when they experience these affects.

Another technique that Spinoza advocates is "to conceive a correct principle of living, *or* sure maxims of life, to commit them to memory, and to apply them constantly to the particular cases frequently encountered in life."[234] This is not saying that subjecting ourselves to these norms will restrain affects nor that mere knowledge of these principles will translate into action. Rather, "in this way our imagination will be extensively affected by them, and we shall always have them ready."[235] Maxims are useful in handling powerful affects because the more that we think about something, the more firmly it stays in our memories, and the more readily it can be recalled, not because we choose to recall it but since the associations and connections that we have formed with it will be causally triggered by the experience of the affect now associated with it. The influence of such teachings is not in their truth content or our understanding of their validity but in our familiarity with them, our repeated awareness of and involvement with them.

For the Love of God

To Spinoza, as we have tallied, living well is of our natures. It is a causally necessary, immanent aspect of reality. No teleology or transcendence, coercion or submission is required, in principle, for living ethically. However, due to our lack of sovereignty over ourselves, others, and reality, doing so, and doing so consistently, and in concert with others, is difficult. This challenge does not render his program utopian in the sense of being imaginary or unrealizable. It is no more utopian than positing, for example, that it is possible, considering the ways of immanent causation, for all the fig trees in the world to bear an abundance of succulent fruit in their times. For any given fig tree, if not unfavorably impacted by external forces more powerful than it or internally disrupted by disagreements between the countless modes that comprise it, could yield a cornucopia of figs, in season. Spinoza's position on ethics is no different. Allowing that often humans do not act ethically— because reality is unstable and they are prone to external and internal forces that disrupt their power, and so their capacity to persist in enacting what is good for them, which is necessarily also good for other humans—does not contradict or undercut his theory. It merely corroborates the obvious: living well is tricky.

Spinoza is no naïf. He details, as we have seen, why doing good routinely eludes us. Due to the instability of reality, our imbrication with others, our lack of self-awareness, inconsistency, and unreliability, humans devise certain institutions like morality, the state, and religion to support living well. As the *Ethics* and the *Theological-Political Treatise* detail, frequently, such transcendent, teleological constructs do more harm than good. Still, he maintains, these are useful to a point, as when they promote the common good. To do this, the state exercises sovereignty, depriving humans of "their natural right."[236] But if "humans lived according to reason," consistently enacting agreements, which are good for themselves and so for others, there would be no need for a sovereign state, its moral norms, and coercive force.[237]

By leaning on religion and morality, Spinoza commits a further concession to transcendences and teleology: "Whatever we desire and do of which we are the cause insofar as we have the idea of God . . . I relate to religion. The desire to do good generated in us by our living according to the guidance of reason, I call morality."[238] Spinoza tenders both courses to his readers, addressing clear and distinct ideas, which nourish the "desire to do good," while intoning on the register of religion by deploying God as a means of promoting this "desire to do good." These are not mutually exclusive. They both aim to conduce in readers the desire to live well. There is a rhetorical sleight of hand in his equation of "morality" with reason. Considering how consistently he decries normative morals, stressing that they are transcendent, teleological, anthropic constructs, which defy reason and are often ethically debilitating, suspicion is due. Spinoza, I maintain, strategically deploys the idioms and ideas of religion and morality in ways that do not entirely undermine his ontology, while also delivering enough rhetorical force to affectively impact his religiously and morally committed readers and simultaneously insulate himself from criticism.

In his example of the proportional, someone who follows the external rule that their teacher taught them about proportions, without fully understanding it, arrives at the same answer as the person who intuitively perceives the proportional. Spinoza leans on religion, morality, and laws of state in a similar way: he tolerates the teleological submission to their transcendent norms in order to affect people to live well. This aligns with positions in the *Theological-Political Treatise* and *Political Treatise* about how following certain religious, moral, and state laws, whether one understands them or not, cultivates harmonious living. As he makes plain: "Especially necessary to bring people together in love, are the things which concern religion and morality."[239] Moreover, people "find it difficult to bear ... what is *thought* dishonorable, *or* that someone rejects the accepted practices of the state."[240] Hence, Spinoza condones state authority and morality.

Since the forces of adequate ideas are constantly imperiled by contrary affects, Spinoza advises practices of reconnection, association, and maxims to counter bad feelings. These very techniques, I propose, are harnessed through invocations of God, love, and religion at the end of the *Ethics*. Unfortunately, much of the literature continues to read Spinoza a bit too uncritically, a bit too literally, which has led to the dismissal of part V and the misattribution of teleological and transcendent commitments to him.

If we follow what is written about love, joy, and reciprocity in parts III and IV, it becomes patent that by deploying "God" in part V, Spinoza is trafficking in a familiar idiom, only to redefine its valence. Even as this utilization of God subverts the purports of Spinoza's ontology, I maintain that his maneuvers are intentionally nonbinary: whether a reader is persuaded by Spinoza's immanent account of ethics or inspired by his strategic resort to transcendence, both affect the reader, altering who they are and so what they desire and how they act. The final moves of the *Ethics* can be read as "religious" insofar as Spinoza invokes God in discussing the third kind of knowledge. At the same time, it can be read—and considering the balance of evidence *ought* to be read—as pointing towards Spinoza's redefinition of God *or* substance *or* nature. The more someone clearly and distinctly understands themselves (a finite, determinate mode of infinite, indeterminate substance), reality (infinite, indeterminate substance), and other things (other finite, determinate modes of substance), the more they are affectively impacted, which modifies their desires, and so their actions, inclining them towards agreements with others.

Actualizing such agreements *is* blessedness, the concrete, corporeal experience of living in harmony with others and tolerating the causal necessity of that which, despite one's best efforts, exceeds their control. Such living is possible because they experience a certain *acquiescentia*, which affects them, so they desirously incline to continue living in such a way, enabling a *vera animi acquiescentia* (true peace of mind). Spinoza even flags his technique: "One who desires to aid others by advice or by action, so that they may enjoy the highest good together" ought to speak "generously of human's virtue *or* power, and how it can be perfected, so that humans, moved not by fear or aversion, but only by an affect of joy, may strive to live as far as they can according to the rule of reason."[241] This is what Spinoza endeavors in part V: to affect readers, making them feel good, which modifies their desires and so how they are. To do so, he relies on the kinds of maxims and cultural associations that he advises for modifying affects.

Spinoza's Guide

In promoting an ethics divested of transcendence and individualism, Spinoza is oriented by Maimonides in three salient ways. The first concerns religion, which for Maimonides serves two functions: "the welfare of the soul and the welfare of the body."[242] A prerequisite to the welfare of the soul is that of the body, since one cannot think if one is "in pain or is very hungry or is thirsty or is hot or is very cold."[243] Even as Maimonides maintains that reason distinguishes humans, unlike Descartes he centers bodily wellness. This instantiates the practical role that religion and philosophy serve in this heritage.

The second connection is that for Maimonides, the welfare of body and soul rely on a functioning society, which is achieved through limiting the power of individuals, so they "do that which is useful to the whole" and acquire "moral qualities."[244] Religious commandments facilitate social and political life, securing individual and communal well-being. These are interdependent. Satisfying the basic human needs of food and shelter requires "political association, it being already known that man is political in nature."[245] This resounds in Spinoza's remark: "They can hardly, however, live a solitary life; hence, that definition which makes the human a social animal has been quite pleasing to most. And surely we do derive, from the society of our fellow humans, many more advantages than disadvantages."[246]

The third facet concerns Maimonides's claim that Scriptural commandments are concerned with three things: "opinions, moral qualities, and political civic actions."[247] Certain laws teach true opinions or correct misguided opinions—prejudices—that people maintain. Due to social conditioning these are especially intransigent, and Maimonides devotes considerable attention to dislodging them but soberingly assesses: "Man has love for, and the wish to defend, opinions to which he is habituated and in which he has been brought up and has a feeling of repulsion for opinions other than those."[248] Scripture, Maimonides argues, makes concessions to such opinions, legislating practices that conflict with rational truths because the ancient Israelites could not be expected to fully dissociate from their experiences and milieus. Since norms are culturally and socially specific, Scripture traffics in erroneous anthropomorphisms. Spinoza's devotion to dismantling prejudices aligns with Maimonides's practice. Moreover, his deployment of God and religion in the *Ethics*—despite undermining his ontology—actualizes Maimonides's theory of religion as an accommodation to the fickleness of being human. Contextualizing as much elucidates both of their projects.

Space disallows for delineating all the ways in which Spinoza's invocations of God are subverted by his ontology and the overwhelming balance of evidence against teleological and transcendent readings[249] of part V.[250] Yet tending to the valence of his "love of God" sufficiently obviates the thrust of such misinterpretations. Despite its ostensible conventionality, Spinoza recasts the valence of such love. This strategy is affective: it placates certain readers even as it affects them ethically. By relying on the cultural associations that readers have, Spinoza enacts his theories regarding how desires are conditioned by pasts and contexts, while also leaning on his advice regarding the role of maxims and associations in moderating affects.

Spinoza defines love in general as "nothing but *joy with the accompanying idea of an external cause*."[251] Yet there is another type of love: "*joy accompanied by the idea of an internal cause* [*acquiescentiam in se ipso*,]"[252] an acquiescence, a complacency with one's own self. Recall his definition of self-esteem: "*Acquiescentia in se ipso* is a joy born of the fact that a human considers themself and their power of acting."[253] This is Spinoza's "love of God," which affects one with *vera animi acquiescentia*. These are the good feelings that accompany knowledge of the third kind whereby one is "conscious of themself and of God,"[254] themselves *as* the determinate, finite act of the indeterminate, infinite power that is reality. In describing this *mentis acquiescentia*, Spinoza cites his definition of self-esteem and then glosses: "This joy is accompanied by the idea of oneself . . . it is also accompanied by the idea of God as its cause."[255] The third kind of knowledge is an immanent, intuitive knowing wherein one actively conceives rather than passively perceives. This matters because "the more perfection each thing has, the more it acts and the less it is acted on."[256] Such immanence is why "the mind's intellectual love of God is the very love of God by which God loves themself."[257] Thereby, Spinoza appeases readers attached to conventional notions of God and simultaneously gestures towards his main point: the more someone perceives singular things in their particularity, the more powerfully they appreciate what is and is not in their control—after having done their duty[258]—so the more they are affected with a certain acquiescence, contentment, or satisfaction.

Then, Spinoza asserts: "From this it follows that insofar as God loves themself, they love humans, and consequently that God's love of humans and the mind's intellectual love of God are one and the same."[259] This can be read as saying that modal love of God is coincident with God's love of modes *or* it can mean that God's love is nothing but modal love. Blessedness consists "in a constant and eternal love of God, *or* in God's love for humans."[260] Since nothing exists in potential but is only actual and God is infinite substance, which is nothing but finite modes, this love of God is love for other humans, which amounts to salubrious agreements with them, living well. This affects one with good feelings, *acquiescentia*. Spinoza continues, "this love, *or* blessedness, is called glory in the sacred Scriptures—not without reason. For whether this love is related to God or to the mind, it can rightly be called *acquiescentia*, which is really not distinguished from glory."[261] Scholars are divided on which precise mention of "glory"—in Hebrew, *kavod*—Spinoza has in mind.[262] This is fair, considering that *kavod* in its various conjugations appears nearly two hundred times in Hebrew Scripture. However, I suggest that Spinoza intends a verse that Maimonides interprets at a critical passage in the *Guide of the Perplexed*, which he reiterates at its conclusion.

To revise what is meant by God's attributes, Maimonides glosses an episode in Exodus. Deputized with leading the Israelites, Moses beseeches God for guidance: "If, I have found favor in your eyes, pray, let me know Your ways, that I may know You."[263] He asks: "Show me, pray, your glory" (*kevodkha*).[264] Then, God's "goodness," meaning that God is "gracious" and "compassionate," is to pass before Moses.[265] Maimonides interprets this "goodness" as referring to the created world in its interconnections and God's governance over it through God's "ways."[266] God's attributes are "actions proceeding from God . . . in reference to the world."[267] The sway of this is unmistakable in Spinoza's claim: "Perfecting the intellect is nothing but understanding God, God's attributes, and God's actions. . . . the ultimate end of the human who is led by reason . . . is . . . to conceive adequately both themself and all things that fall under their understanding."[268] Knowing God is knowing reality, specifically knowing about oneself and others in order to enact agreements with them.

God's attributes of action, for Maimonides, are "moral qualities": compassion, graciousness, and so on. Thusly, he paraphrases Moses's request to know God's ways: "I need to perform actions that I must seek to make similar to Thy actions in governing them."²⁶⁹ To know God's attributes is to imitate them: "For the utmost virtue of man is to become like unto Him ... as far as he is able;²⁷⁰ which means that we should make our actions like unto His."²⁷¹ Spinoza takes this further: knowing God's attributes is synonymous with understanding singular things, in order, as we have seen, to realize agreements with them. God is infinite, indeterminate power, which only exists as its finite, determinate modes, and clearly and distinctly perceiving singular modes facilitates good living. Kavod *is* experiencing such goodness.

I propose that Spinoza is not merely following Maimonides or appropriating his teachings or even doing both simultaneously, depending on the interpretive register. His moves may be read as delivering a commentary on the conclusion of the *Guide*, which ends by interpreting these verses: "Let the wise person not boast in their wisdom, nor the mighty glory in their might, let the rich not boast in their riches; but in this may one who boasts boast: understanding and knowing Me, for I am the Lord doing kindness, justice and righteousness in the land, for in these I delight, said the Lord."²⁷² Glory, Maimonides explains—referencing his previous analysis—is not merely apprehending God's actions but enacting them. This means "it is My purpose that there should come from you *loving-kindness, righteousness, and judgment in the earth*."²⁷³ Glory is knowing God's ways by embodying God's attributes by living ethically. The *Theological-Political Treatise* echoes this: "God ... asks no other knowledge from humans than the knowledge of divine justice and loving-kindness, i.e., such attributes of God as humans can imitate."²⁷⁴ It then cites the same verses from Jeremiah, refers to the aforementioned verse from Exodus,²⁷⁵ and explains, "when Moses wants to see and to come to know ... God reveals only those attributes which display justice and loving-kindness."²⁷⁶

Right before the *Guide* ends, it discusses a hierarchy of human perfection: possessions, bodily constitution, moral habits, and rational virtues. The problem with perfection of moral habits is that it amounts to the "disposition to be useful to people; consequently it is an instrument for someone else."²⁷⁷ It is "not an end in itself."²⁷⁸ Moral habits are teleological. By contrast, only perfection of rational virtues is not contingent upon an end. Maimonides's point is rendered visible by the final sentence of the *Guide*, which reiterates that knowing God—possessing rational virtues—entails imitating God: "The way of such an individual, after he has achieved this apprehension, will always have in view *loving-kindness, righteousness, and judgment*, through assimilation to His actions."[279] A natural consequence of understanding God *is* acting ethically; an effect of understanding God's ways—God's kind, gracious oversight of nature—is embodying these traits. Spinoza's *Ethics*, I propose, actualizes what Maimonides essays: an ethics divested of teleology. Thus, for Spinoza, the immanent effect of adequately understanding oneself, others, and reality is that one enacts agreements with others, experiencing goodness. Spinoza fills in what Maimonides leaves unsaid: the reason that someone who apprehends God *or* nature is necessarily one who acts morally is due to the *affective* force of such understanding.

Let us return to love. For Maimonides, love of God is commensurate with knowledge of God, which amounts to understanding the kind ways in which God oversees nature. The "intellect which overflowed from Him ... toward us is the bond between us and Him."[280] This linkage can be fortified through love of God. The more passionate this love, the firmer the connection. Moses, Aaron, and Miriam experienced as much and "died in the pleasure of this apprehension due to the intensity of passionate love."[281] Spinoza's reading of Maimonides would be that because thinking is affective, the more someone understands God, to wit, God's kindness, so the more they come to love God. Such love alters the desires and so the actions of this person, so that they *live* these virtues. In the *Ethics*, Maimonides's God becomes nature, the infinite connection of causes in which a mode is entangled, so this love is not a union with an Other. It is finitely determined love. Moreover, this love is not Love but the *acquiescentia*—the *kavod*—that a person experiences in perceiving by the third kind of knowledge. Such understanding immanently affects them, adjusts their desires, inclining them to actualizing agreements with others and so experiencing blessedness, goodness.

Feeling Free

The *Ethics* concludes by returning to a concern with which it opens: freedom. It proffers this initial definition: "That thing is called free which exists from the necessity of its nature alone, and is determined to act by itself alone."[282] The "freedom" of substance is its necessity. This repudiation of "God's power" as "the power of kings," especially as manifest in avowals of "God's free will and right over all things," is the initial stride in Spinoza's denaturalization of sovereignty and the freedom constitutive of it.[283] Thus, "no one will be able to perceive rightly the things I maintain unless they take great care not to confuse God's power with the human power or right of kings."[284] This prejudice derives from the anthropomorphic projection of purported human traits onto God *or* nature, as humans decided "there was a ruler, or number of rulers of nature, endowed with human freedom."[285] Because humans sees themselves as free, constituting "a dominion within a dominion," they suppose that "human disturbs, rather than follows, the order of nature, has absolute power over their actions, and is determined only by themself."[286] The *Ethics* devotes considerable space to dislodging the human prejudice to being free and its mutually reinforcing delusions of transcendence: that mind controls body, that reason is supreme, that humans are exceptional, that humans are consistent, that humans are in control. Spinoza discredits this coalition of sovereignties and discloses how they not only misrepresent reality but make living well unrealizable. Instead, he elucidates his alternative, which upholds humans as nonexceptional, dependent, conditioned, disparate, and unfree.

Part V is entitled: "On the Power of the Intellect *or* on Human Freedom." Here, Spinoza transmits his final redefinition of freedom, equally anchored in the necessity of causal determinations. Freedom is not about sovereign decisionism, sovereign autonomy, sovereign domination. It concerns how reason might position us to live well and, likewise, the constraints to doing so. Reason is not supreme, and mind cannot discipline the body into submission for "humans, like other things, act from the necessity of nature." The different form of freedom that Spinoza envisions starts with absorbing that "freedom does not take away the necessity of acting. It assumes it."[287] This repudiates freedoms constructed on exceptionalist liberation *from* causal determinations and its attendant license *to* subjugate body, others, nature. It accordingly refuses the autonomous individualism that accompanies such Christian, Cartesian, "Western," liberal, neoliberal constructions because "imagining a thing as free can be nothing but simply imagining it while we are ignorant of the causes by which it has been determined to act."[288] Nothing that we do is unconditioned, undetermined, or unpredicated. We cannot direct our minds to think, let alone command our bodies; we cannot discipline our bad feelings nor commission our bad memories away; we cannot reign over the unconscious or conscious prejudices, associations, and preferences that we have nor can we direct ourselves to like or dislike, desire or disdain anyone or anything at all. So much of what makes us who we are and how we are comes to pass without our consent or even awareness. If we cannot sovereignly oversee our own selves, we certainly cannot superintend others, our contexts, our interconnections because "human power is very limited and infinitely surpassed by the power of external causes."[289] We are constitutionally disempowered.

Rather than coping with the disparities of reality and incongruities of being human by manufacturing fictions of control, Spinoza maintains that reason not only corroborates otherwise but positions a different approach. It forces us to accept our limitations while affirming our imbrication with others. Certain "Western" attitudes suppose one is "free to the extent that they are permitted to yield to their lust,"[290] that freedom concerns exemption *from* constraint and excess *to* indulge. Or, alternatively, one must submit to the "bondage" of morality and religion from which they will ultimately be disburdened and for which they will "receive a reward."[291] Spinoza excavates and overturns the logics staying these dogmas. Not only is there no rebate that awaits but there is no remit from immanence. Living well does not entail transcendent norms or teleological fancies. Often, such fictions inhibit as much by advocating practices and doctrines that misrepresent the nature of reality and so also, human nature. Instead, Spinoza ventures that ethics is not only possible but necessary, it is in our natures and so *of* reality. Experiencing as much *is* freedom. "Acting from reason is nothing but doing those things which follow from the necessity of our nature."[292] Thus, "a free human ... desires the good directly ... acts, lives, and preserves their being,"[293] as they incline towards what is good for them, which is necessarily good for others like them, realizing agreements with others. This *is* Spinoza's "salvation, or blessedness, *or* freedom."[294] Freedom is the experience of salutary agreements with others, which are staked upon the particularities of our desires, interconnections, and contexts. Such immanent freedom is nothing but the enjoyment of concrete, collective goodness, however provisional.

To experience Spinoza's "freedom" requires assimilating that Freedom is a conceit. It entails recognizing that we are constitutively unsovereign: not sovereign over ourselves, not sovereign over others, not sovereign over reality. This involves liberating ourselves from the fiction of independence from imbrication, emancipating ourselves from the fantasy of domination, and releasing ourselves from the fetish of sovereignty. It demands submission to the disparity of reality.

Abbreviations and Citational Practices

Works of Spinoza
CM — *Cogitata Metaphysica* (appendix to DPP)
DPP — *Descartes' Principles of Philosophy*
E — *Ethics (Ethica)*
HG — *Hebrew Grammar*
KV — *Short Treatise on God, Human and Well-Being (Korte Verhandeling)*
Letter — *The Letters (Epistola)*
TIE — *Treatise on the Emendation of the Intellect (Tractatus de Intellectus Emendatione)*
TP — *Political Treatise (Tractatus Politicus)*
TTP — *Theological-Political Treatise (Tractatus Theologico-Politicus)*

References to Spinoza's *Ethics* use this abbreviation and citation system:
Roman numeral = part
ax = axiom
app = appendix
cor = corollary
dem = demonstration
DA = definition of the affects
def = definition
ex = explanation
GDA = general definition of the affects
lem = lemma
p = proposition
post = postulate
pref = preface
schol = scholium

Works of Descartes

All citations are from *The Philosophical Writings of Descartes*. 3 volumes. Edited and translated by John Cottingham, Robert Stoothoff, and Dugald Murdoch (third volume also by Anthony Kenny). Cambridge University Press, 1984–1991.

Citations to the first two volumes are denoted by CSM followed by the volume and page number and for the third volume by CSMK followed by the page number.

Notes

Preface
1. This book, amongst other things, undertakes to disrupt the very construct of the so-called "Western," exposing the forms of domination, especially the Christian supremacy, Eurocentrism, anti-Judaism, and racism that underwrite it. To signal as much and to avoid reifying, let alone validating, it here and throughout, the word appears in quotation marks.
2. Hegel, *Lectures on the History of Philosophy: Medieval and Modern*, 258.
3. Hegel, *Encyclopedia of the Philosophical Sciences in Basic Outline*, §151, 224.

Introduction
1. Wittgenstein, "Whence the Feeling That Our Grammatical . . ." §88, 305e.
2. Cited in Goetschel, "Theory-Praxis: Spinoza, Hess, Marx, and Adorno," 19.
3. Baracchi, *Aristotle's Ethics as First Philosophy*, 8.
4. Throughout this book, quotations from Spinoza that use sexgendered pronouns as the default have been altered to nonbinary pronouns, when appropriate. This is not intended to portray Spinoza's writing with anachronistic inclusivity but reflects how in the *Ethics* he often uses the Latin *homo*, which denotes the nongendered "human," even as translations have mostly rendered it as "man." Citations from most of Spinoza's writings, with occasional modifications (based on consultation with Spinoza's *Opera*) are taken from Curley's *The Collected Works of Spinoza*. Translations from *Hebrew Grammar* are from Shirley's *Spinoza: Complete Works*, also with occasional adjustments.
5. EIIp3schol.
6. Ibid.
7. EIapp.
8. Letter 58.
9. Ibid.
10. EIIIpref; TP II.6.

365

11. See Löwith, *Meaning in History*; Blumenberg, *The Legitimacy of the Modern Age*; Funkenstein, *Theology and the Scientific Imagination*; Wynter, "Unsettling the Coloniality of Being/Power/Truth/Freedom"; Gillespie, *The Theological Origins of Modernity*.

12. See Kelsen, *Der soziologische und der juristische staatsbegriff*; Kelsen, "God and State," 61–82; Schmitt, *Political Theology*; Schmitt, *Political Theology II*; Agamben, *Homo Sacer*.

13. See Kelsen, *Der soziologische* and "God and State"; Schmitt, *Political Theology* and *Political Theology II*; Kantorowicz, *The King's Two Bodies*; Elshtain, *Sovereignty*.

14. EVp6dem.

15. Althusser, "The Underground Current of the Materialism of the Encounter," 168.

16. Bloch, *Avicenna and the Aristotelian Left*.

17. H. A. Wolfson, *The Philosophy of Spinoza*, vol. 1, vii.

18. Ibid.

19. Strauss, *Spinoza's Critique of Religion*.

20. Roth, *Spinoza, Descartes and Maimonides*, 145.

21. Harvey, "*Ishq, ḥesheq*, and *amor Dei intellectualis*"; Harvey, "A Portrait of Spinoza as a Maimonidean"; Harvey, "Spinoza and Maimonides on Teleology and Anthropocentrism"; Harvey, "Spinoza on Biblical Miracles"; Harvey, "Spinoza and Maimonides on True Religion."

22. Dobbs-Weinstein, "The Ambiguity of Imagination and the Ambivalence of Language in Maimonides and Spinoza"; Dobbs-Weinstein, "Maimonidean Aspects in Spinoza's Thought"; Dobbs-Weinstein, *Spinoza's Critique of Religion and Its Heirs*, 28–29, 34, 48, 86, 88.

23. Ravven, *The Self-Beyond Itself*, 183–239.

24. See also Pines, "The Philosophical Sources of the *Guide of the Perplexed*," xcvi, xcviii, c; Pines, "Spinoza's *Tractatus Theologico-Politicus*, Maimonides and Kant"; Pines, "Spinoza's *Tractatus Theologico-Politicus* and the Jewish Philosophical Tradition"; Pines, "On Spinoza's Conception of Human Freedom and of Good and Evil"; Hyman, "Spinoza's Dogmas of Universal Faith in the Light of their Medieval Jewish Background"; Fraenkel, "Maimonides' God and Spinoza's *Deus sive Natura*"; Whitman, *An Examination of the Singular in Maimonides and Spinoza*.

25. Dobbs-Weinstein, "Gersonides's Radically Modern Understanding of the Agent Intellect"; Dobbs-Weinstein, "Thinking Desire in Gersonides and Spinoza"; Harvey, "Gersonides and Spinoza on Conatus"; Klein, "Spinoza's Debt to Gersonides"; Klein, "'Something of It Remains.'"

26. For Islamic philosophy's influence on Spinoza via Jewish philosophy, see Hyman, "Spinoza on Possibility and Contingency"; Fraenkel, "Spinoza and Philosophy and Religion"; Fraenkel, "Reconsidering the Case of Elijah Delmedigo's Averroism and Its Impact on Spinoza"; Ogden, "Avicenna and Spinoza on Essence and Existence"; Manekin "Spinoza and the Determinist Tradition."

27. "Decolonial" originates in the effort to recover lands and properties stolen by

colonial forces. Here I use this term metaphorically, while recognizing its contested, unsettled valence, hoping (perhaps not too naively) that in so doing, I am not committing another form of violence.

28. See Dussel, "Anti-Cartesian Meditations"; Eze, *Achieving Our Humanity*; Maldonado-Torres, "On the Coloniality of Being, Contributions to the Development of a Concept"; Wynter, "Unsettling the Coloniality of Being/Power/Truth/Freedom."

29. Deleuze notes Spinoza's familiarity with Jewish Aristotelianism: Deleuze, *Expressionism in Philosophy*, 101; makes a passing claim about "Arab and Jewish philosophy" 54; and mentions Spinoza's Jewish intellectual background (323). These are unaccompanied by elaboration, let alone substantive treatment.

30. Israel makes a case for Spinoza's influence on "revolutionary" Jewish thinkers in *Revolutionary Jews*. He has also argued for Spinoza's influence on liberalism in Israel, *Democratic Enlightenment*.

31. Matysik, *When Spinoza Met Marx*.

32. See Rose, *Jewish Philosophical Politics in Germany*, 200–270.

33. See Avineri, *Karl Marx*, 4–8.

34. Goetschel, *Spinoza's Modernity*.

35. Goetschel, "Theory-Praxis: Spinoza, Hess, Marx, and Adorno."

36. Dobbs-Weinstein, *Spinoza's Critique of Religion and Its Heirs*, 12.

37. See Bernard, "Psychotherapeutic Principles in Spinoza's *Ethics*"; Yovel, *Spinoza and Other Heretics*, 136–66; Balibar, *Spinoza, the Transindividual*, 137–91; Goetschel, *Spinoza's Modernity*, 286fn1; Whitebook, "Spinoza and Freud."

38. Nadler, *Spinoza*, 71–75; Israel, *Spinoza*, 49–54, 154–57, 171.

39. Israel, *Spinoza*, 50.

40. van Sluis and Musschenga, *De boeken van Spinoza*.

41. Leibniz, *Die philosophischen Schriften*, vol. 3, 545.

42. Bayle, "Spinoza," vol. 4.

43. Nirenberg, *Anti-Judaism*, 340.

44. Goldenbaum, "The *Pantheismusstreit*," 345.

45. Conway, *The Principles of the Most Ancient and Modern Philosophy*, 64.

46. Hegel, *Lectures on the History of Philosophy: Medieval and Modern Philosophy*, 252.

47. Hegel, *Encyclopedia*, §151, 224.

48. Hegel, *Lectures on the History of Philosophy: Medieval and Modern Philosophy*, 283.

49. Ibid., 257.

50. See Dobbs-Weinstein, *Spinoza's Critique of Religion*, 45–51; Rose, *Jewish Philosophical Politics*, 93–105; Nirenberg, *Anti-Judaism* 397–407; and Yovel, *Spinoza and Other Heretics*, 44–49.

51. Macherey, *Hegel or Spinoza*, 19–24.

52. Althusser, *Essays in Self Criticism*, 134, 136.

53. Lærke, "Aspects of Spinoza's Theory of Essence," 11.

54. Norris, "Spinoza and the Conflict of Interpretations."
55. Badiou, "What Is a Proof in Spinoza's *Ethics*?" 39.
56. Norris "Spinoza and the Conflict of Interpretations."
57. Vardoulakis and Voss, "Introduction."
58. Montag, "Preface," x–xi.
59. Vardoulakis and Voss, "Introduction," 2.
60. Derrida, "Shibboleth," 54.
61. Hegel, *Lectures on the History of Philosophy: Medieval and Modern Philosophy*, 286.
62. Ibid., 287.
63. See Mendelssohn, "To the Friends of Lessing" in *Last Works* 147–76; "Letter to Elise Reimarus" in Altmann, *Moses Mendelssohn*, 609.
64. See Maimon, *The Autobiography*, 58, 63–64, 197.
65. Cohen, *Spinoza on State and Religion, Judaism and Christianity*.
66. See Levinas, *Totality and Infinity*, 87, 105, 218–19.
67. See Buber, *The Origin and Meaning of Hasidism*, 90–112; Buber, *Eclipse of God*, 10–14.
68. See Schwartz, *The First Modern Jew*; Schwartz, *Spinoza's Challenge to Jewish Thought*.
69. See E. R. Wolfson, *Heidegger and Kabbalah*.
70. More, "Henry More to Robert Boyle: 14 December 1671."
71. Bauer, *The Jewish Problem*, 11.
72. Ibid.
73. Žižek, *Organs Without Bodies*, 29.
74. See Dobbs-Weinstein, "The Ambiguity of the Imagination and the Ambivalence of Language in Spinoza and Maimonides," 105–6.
75. EIp11.
76. EIVpref.
77. Lorde, "The Master's Tools Will Never Dismantle the Master's House," 112.
78. Letter 55.
79. Letter 56.
80. Althusser, "On Spinoza," in *Essays in Self-Criticism*, 132.
81. EIIp49schol.IV§d.
82. EIIp3schol.

Chapter 1

1. Karen Barad, "Transmaterialities," 413.
2. EIIp3schol.
3. EIp11.
4. EIVpref.
5. EIIp7schol.
6. Augustine, *On Genesis*, 55.
7. Descartes, CSMK.23.

8. Aristotle, *Metaphysics*, in *The Complete Works of Aristotle*, 1072b1.
9. Avicenna, *The Metaphysics of* The Healing, 8.4, 273.
10. Ibid., 1.6, 30.
11. Maimonides, *Guide of the Perplexed*, II.1, 238; see also II.1, 248.
12. EIp11dem.
13. EIp8schol.2.II
14. EIdef1.
15. EIaxiom2.
16. EIdef3.
17. EIdef2; EIdef6.
18. EIp7.
19. Letter 60.
20. Descartes, *Meditations*, CSM II.28.
21. Ibid., CSM II.34.
22. Descartes, *Objections and Replies*, CSM II.116.
23. Ibid., CSM II.165–70.
24. Ibid., CSM II.168–69.
25. See Marion, *On the Ego and on God*, 139–160.
26. Heidegger, "The Onto-Theo-Logical Constitution of Metaphysics," in *Identity and Difference*, 72.
27. Ibid., 71.
28. Derrida, *The Beast and the Sovereign, II*, 207.
29. Macherey, *Hegel or Spinoza*, 16.
30. Here and throughout this book, I adjust translations of Spinoza that deploy gendered pronouns when referring to God. In this case, I have done so by inserting "God" instead of "he" and "itself" instead of "himself." While I would prefer to replace all gendered pronouns with the nonbinary they/them in the case of pronouns attached to God, I worry that readers might impute an unintended plurality or multiplicity. In sentences wherein Spinoza uses gendered pronouns to describe substance *or* nature, I tend to replace them with the nongendered "it." This variance is not to suggest any distinction between what Spinoza denotes by the terms, substance, nature, and God, but to maintain linguistic specificity, as many of his employments of "God" appear in the context of rebuttals and revisions to competing theories attached to traditional notions of God. Often, Spinoza's own use of the moniker strategically enhances the persuasive force of his arguments by cloaking them in traditional jargon.
31. EIp25schol.
32. EIp15.
33. EIp15schol.
34. EIp25cor.
35. EIp4dem.
36. EI6cor.
37. EIp8.

38. EIp4.
39. EIp7.
40. EIp18dem.
41. EIp18.
42. KV, II.16.
43. Ibid.
44. EIIp7schol.
45. Ibid.
46. Ibid.
47. Abraham ibn Ezra on Exodus 34:6, *Perush ibn Ezra 'al ha-Torah*.
48. See the ensuing analysis in this chapter.
49. Gersonides, *The Wars*, III.XII.
50. Aristotle, *Metaphysics*, in *The Complete Works of Aristotle*, 1072b1.
51. Ibid.
52. Aristotle, *On the Soul*, in *The Complete Works of Aristotle*, 430b1.
53. Aristotle, *Metaphysics*, in *The Complete Works of Aristotle*, 1075a1.
54. Ibid., 1074b1.
55. Aristotle, *On the Soul*, 430a1.
56. Excerpts from the *Guide of the Perplexed* are mostly from Pines's English translation. Sometimes, I cite from Ibn Tibbon's Hebrew translation, specifically, the 1551 edition with commentaries that Spinoza had.
57. See also, Maimonides, *Mishneh Torah*, Hilkhot Yesodei ha-Torah 2.10.
58. Maimonides, *Guide of the Perplexed*, I.68, 163.
59. Ibid., 164.
60. Maimonides, *Moreh Nevukhim*, I.69, 51b.
61. Maimonides, *Guide of the Perplexed*, I.68, 165.
62. Ibid.,163.
63. Ibid., III.20, 483.
64. Ibid., 482.
65. Ibid., 485.
66. Maimonides, *Moreh Nevukhim*, III.21, 148b.
67. Ibid.
68. Maimonides, *Mishneh Torah*, Hilkhot Yesodei ha-Torah 2.10.
69. Maimonides, *Guide of the Perplexed*, I.72, 184.
70. Samuel I, 25:26; see also Genesis 42:15.
71. Maimonides, *Guide of the Perplexed*, I.68, 163.
72. See also ibid., I.53, 122–23; *Mishneh Torah*, Hilkhot Yesodei ha-Torah 2.10.
73. Maimonides, *Guide of the Perplexed*, I.53, 122.
74. Ibid., I.69, 169.
75. Ibid.
76. Maimonides, *Moreh Nevukhim*, I. 68, 50a.
77. Ibid, *Guide of the Perplexed*, II.12, 279.
78. Ibid., III.21, 485.

79. Maimonides, *Moreh Nevukhim*, III.32 160a.
80. CM II, vii.
81. Ibid.
82. Ibid.
83. Ibid.
84. Ibid., II.iii.
85. Ibid., II.vi.
86. Ibid., II.vii.
87. Ibid., II.iii.
88. Ibid., II.vii.
89. Ibid.
90. See Mendelssohn, *Philosophical Writings*, 105–11; "To the Friends of Lessing," *Last Works*, 160–65.
91. Fraenkel, "Maimonides' God"; Harvey, "A Portrait of Spinoza as a Maimonidean," 162; Pines, "The Philosophic Sources," xcvi; H. A. Wolfson, *The Philosophy of Spinoza*, ii, 24–28.
92. Maimonides, *Guide of the Perplexed*, II. Introduction, 239.
93. Maimonides, *Mishneh Torah*, Hilkhot Yesodei ha-Torah 1.7.
94. Maimonides, *Guide of the Perplexed*, II. Introduction, 239.
95. Ibid., II.1, 248.
96. Ibid., I.26, 56.
97. EIIp7schol.
98. Maimonides, *Guide of the Perplexed*, III.9, 437.
99. Ibid., I.35, 81.
100. Ibid., III.9, 437.
101. Ibid.
102. Ibid.
103. Ibid.
104. EIp8.
105. EId6.
106. EIp14.
107. EIp15schol.
108. EIp14cor.1.
109. EIp15schol.
110. Maimonides, *Guide of the Perplexed*, III.19, 477.
111. Ibid., III.20, 483.
112. EIp9.
113. EIp11schol.
114. Ibid.
115. Ibid.
116. Letter 36.
117. Ibid.
118. Ibid.

119. EIp3.
120. Aristotle, *Metaphysics*, in *The Complete Works of Aristotle*, 1074b1.
121. CM II, vi.
122. EIp17schol.
123. Ibid.
124. EIp33schol.2.
125. Ibid.
126. EIIp3schol.
127. Ibid.
128. EIapp.
129. EIp17.
130. EIp17cor.2.
131. Ibid.
132. EIp32.
133. EIp32dem.
134. Letter 42.
135. Letter 43.
136. Ibid.
137. Descartes, *Principles*, CSM I.206.
138. Augustine, "The Literal Meaning of Genesis," in *On Genesis*, VI.26, 316.
139. Descartes, CSMK.23.
140. Ibid.
141. Ibid.
142. Ibid., CSMK.25.
143. Ibid.
144. Ibid., CSMK.235.
145. Ibid., CSMK.358–59.
146. Maimonides, *Guide of the Perplexed*, II.19, 302–303; II.20, 312–314; III.13, 452; III.13, 454.
147. Ibid., I.69, 170.
148. Ibid., II.19, 302.
149. Ibid., III.14, 456.
150. Ibid., I.69, 170.
151. Harvey, "A Third Approach to Maimonides' Cosmogony-Prophetology Puzzle," 297.
152. CM, II.vii.
153. Ibid. Also, TTP, IV.23.
154. EIp17schol.
155. Ibid.
156. Israel, *Spinoza*, 50.
157. Herrera, *Gate of Heaven*, 158.
158. Ibid., 159.

159. The term "intra-action" is borrowed from Barad, *Meeting the Universe Halfway*, 33.
160. EIa4.
161. EIa5.
162. EIIp45.
163. EIIp45dem.
164. EIIp49dem.
165. EIp28schol.
166. Ibid.
167. Spinoza's definition of *noun* is expansive, such that verbs are to him, a kind of noun. Most Hebrew words "have the force and properties of nouns" (*Hebrew Grammar*, in *Spinoza: Complete Works*, V). Yet "all Hebrew nouns . . . are derived from forms of verbs" (*Hebrew Grammar*, VIII).
168. *Hebrew Grammar*, XII.
169. Ibid.
170. Ibid.
171. The root—ד.ק.פ. *p. q. d.* meaning to visit, call upon, install, or reckon is that rarest of roots to appear in all seven different structures in Hebrew Scripture. This is surely why Spinoza uses it here. See Numbers 1:47 and Ibn Ezra's commentary there.
172. EIp17dem.
173. KV, I.2.
174. Ibid.
175. EIp8.
176. EIp8dem.
177. EIdef2.
178. Letter 36.
179. Ibid.
180. See Dea, "The Infinite and Indeterminate in Spinoza"; Hallett, *Benedict de Spinoza*, 20; Macherey, *Hegel or Spinoza* 150–62; For divergent takes: H. A. Wolfson, *The Philosophy of Spinoza* I.138; DeLire, "Spinoza's Metaphysics of Infinity," 69–108; Deleuze, *Expressionism in Philosophy*, 74.
181. Letter 36.
182. CM, II.iii.
183. EIdef6.
184. EIp11schol.
185. Ibid.
186. EIapp.
187. EIp34.
188. EIp11schol.
189. EIIp3schol.
190. Ibid.

191. For substance as activity/action, see Hallett, *Benedict de Spinoza*, 13; Dea, "The Infinite and Indeterminate in Spinoza"; Macherey, *Hegel or Spinoza*, 142–62; di Poppa, "Spinoza and Process Ontology."
192. EIp34dem.
193. EIp36dem.
194. EIp25cor.
195. *Hebrew Grammar*, in *Spinoza: Complete Works*, V.
196. EIp11cor.
197. For allied claims, see Hübner, "Spinoza's Thinking Substance"; Moder, *Hegel and Spinoza*, 140; Morfino, *Plural Temporality*, 29–31; Hallett, *Benedict de Spinoza*, 13; Macherey, *Hegel or Spinoza*, 200.
198. EIIp3schol.
199. EIp33schol.2.
200. While EIp1 describes substance as "prior in nature to its affections" this does not mean chronologically prior but that substance is self-caused. Similarly, EIp16cor.3 renders substance as "first cause," meaning that modes depend on it.
201. EIp15dem.
202. EIp6cor.
203. EIdef5.
204. EIp4dem.
205. CM II.v.
206. EIp8schol.2.
207. EIpdef3.
208. EIp29schol.
209. EIdef7.
210. See Letter 12.
211. EIp8schol.2.
212. EIp29schol.
213. EIp25.
214. EIp34dem.
215. Engels, "Dialectics of Nature," *Marx and Engels: Collected Works*, 25:510.
216. Klein, "Nature's Metabolism," 193.
217. Negri, *The Savage Anomaly*, 65.
218. Macherey, *Hegel or Spinoza*, 145.
219. Ibid., 200.
220. Hegel, *The Science of Logic*, 474.
221. Deleuze, *Difference and Repetition*, 40.
222. EIIIp7.
223. EIIp10dem.
224. EIp36dem.
225. EIp36.
226. EIp28.
227. EVp6dem.

228. Balibar, *Spinoza, the Transindividual*, 48.
229. EIIIpref.
230. Letter 6.
231. EIIp13post.I
232. Letter 32.
233. EIIp13lem3A2def.
234. EIIp13post.III.
235. Letter 32.

Chapter 2
1. E. R. Wolfson, *Heidegger and Kabbalah*, 174.
2. Heidegger, *Identity and Difference*, 61.
3. Badiou, *Theoretical Writings*, 41.
4. Badiou, *Being and Event*, 42.
5. Hegel, *Lectures on the History of Philosophy: Medieval and Modern Philosophy*, 252.
6. Ibid.
7. Ibid.
8. Ibid., 253.
9. Ibid., 254.
10. Ibid., 257.
11. Ibid., 256.
12. Ibid., 260
13. Ibid., 281.
14. Ibid., 286.
15. Ibid., 288.
16. Ibid.
17. Ibid.
18. Ibid., 286.
19. Ibid., 289.
20. Ibid., 280.
21. Ibid., 258.
22. Hegel, *Encyclopedia*, §151, 224.
23. Ibid., 289.
24. Ibid., 287.
25. Ibid.
26. Ibid., 288.
27. Ibid.
28. Ibid.
29. Hegel, *Encyclopedia*, §151, 224.
30. Ibid.
31. Hegel, *Science of Logic*, 212.
32. Ibid., 474.

33. Hegel, *Lectures on the History of Philosophy: Medieval and Modern Philosophy*, 262.
34. Hegel, *Lectures on the Philosophy of History*, 179.
35. Ibid.
36. Ibid.
37. Hegel, *Lectures on Philosophy of Religion*, 360.
38. Ibid.
39. Ibid., 371.
40. Ibid., 365.
41. Ibid., 361.
42. Hegel, *Encyclopedia*, §151, 224.
43. For Hegel's anti-Judaism, see Nirenberg, *Anti-Judaism*, 397–407; Librett, *Orientalism and the Figure of the Jew*, 129–75; Mack, *German Idealism and the Jew*, 42–62; O'Regan, "Hegel and Anti-Judaism"; Yovel, *Dark Riddle*.
44. Hegel, *Lectures on the Philosophy of History*, 91.
45. Ibid., 177.
46. Librett, *Orientalism and the Figure of the Jew*, 13.
47. Bayle, *Dictionaire historique et critique*, "Spinoza."
48. Ibid., "Zenon."
49. Letter 70.
50. Letter 72.
51. Leibniz, *Philosophical Papers and Letters*, 555.
52. Ibid., 502.
53. Ibid., 507.
54. Ibid.
55. See also, ibid:196–204, 502, 507, 533, 554–55, 559, 583, 594, 663.
56. Leibniz, *Theodicy*, 69.
57. Ibid., 397.
58. Ibid., 81.
59. Ibid.
60. See Franks, "Inner Anti-Semitism or Kabbalistic Legacy?"; Franks, "Nothing Comes from Nothing"; Popkin, "Spinoza, Neoplatonic Kabbalist?"; O'Regan, "Hegel and Anti-Judaism."
61. Basnage, *The History of the Jews*, 294.
62. Beiser, *The Fate of Reason*, 61.
63. Jacobi, *The Main Philosophical Writings*, 187–88.
64. Ibid.
65. Ibid., 233–34.
66. Ibid., 346.
67. Ibid., 342.
68. Ibid., 231.
69. Ibid., 209–10.
70. Ibid., 210.

71. Ibid., 233.
72. Jacobi and Mendelssohn, *Die Hauptschriften zum Pantheismusstreit*, 140.
73. Librett, "Humanist Antiformalism as a Theopolitics of Race," 240.
74. Jacobi, *The Main Philosophical Writings*, 503.
75. von Sömmering, *Ueber die körperliche Verschiedenheit des Negers vom Europäer*, 77–78.
76. Jacobi and Mendelssohn, *Die Hauptschriften zum Pantheismusstreit*, 360–61.
77. See Rosenstock, *Philosophy and the Jewish Question*, 79–122.
78. Mendelssohn, *Last Works*, 157.
79. Ibid., 158.
80. Ibid.
81. See Altmann, *Moses Mendelssohn*, 731; Rosenstock, *Philosophy and the Jewish Question*, 113–16.
82. Mendelssohn, *Last Works*, 149–50.
83. Ibid., 150.
84. Goldenbaum, "The *Pantheismusstreit*," 340.
85. Beiser, *The Fate of Reason*, 45.
86. Goldenbaum, "The *Pantheismusstreit*," 340–41.
87. Goetschel, *Spinoza's Modernity*, 178.
88. Ibid., 179.
89. Franks, "Inner Anti-Semitism or Kabbalistic Legacy?," 276.
90. Mack, *German Idealism and the Jew*.
91. See Mendelssohn's letter in Altmann, *Moses Mendelssohn*, 609; Nicolai, *Über meine gelehrte Bildung*, 44.
92. Maimon, *The Autobiography*, 58.
93. Ibid.
94. Ibid.
95. Ibid.
96. Ibid.
97. Maimon, *Maaseh Livnat ha-Sapir*, 459.
98. Mendelssohn, *Last Works*: 98–100, 103, 107–9.
99. E. R. Wolfson, *Heidegger and Kabbalah*, 336.
100. E. R. Wolfson, "Heeding the Law Beyond the Law," 228.
101. TTP, IX.
102. Exceptions include: Klein, "Nature's Metabolism"; Lærke, "Spinoza's Monism? What Monism?"; Macherey, *Hegel or Spinoza*, 104; Melamed, "Why Spinoza Is Not an Eleatic Monist (or Why Diversity Exists)."
103. CM, I.5.
104. Ibid.
105. Ibid.
106. Descartes, *Principles*, CSM I.212.
107. CM, I.4.

108. Ibid.
109. Letter 50.
110. Ibid.
111. Ibid.
112. See Letter 12.
113. Letter 50.
114. See EIp5; EIp6; EIp8; EIp14; EIp15.
115. See Euclid, *Elements* 7:2.
116. Letter 50.
117. Ibid.
118. Maimonides, *Guide of the Perplexed*, I.57, 132.
119. See Aristotle, *Metaphysics*, in *The Complete Works of Aristotle*, X.2.
120. Maimonides, *Guide of the Perplexed*, I.57, 132.
121. Ibid., I.56, 130.
122. Ibid., 130–31.
123. Crescas, *Light of the Lord*, 106.
124. Ibid., 102.
125. See Letter 81.
126. Ibid.
127. Ibid.
128. Ibid.
129. Ibid.
130. Ibid.
131. Ibid.
132. EIapp.
133. See Kletenik, "To Infinity, Not Beyond: Spinoza's Ontology of the Not One."
134. EIdef6.
135. Letter 12.
136. Ibid.
137. Ibid.
138. EIp8schol.2.
139. Ibid.
140. EIIp40schol.1.
141. Ibid.
142. Ibid.
143. Ibid.
144. Ibid.
145. EVp29schol.
146. Letter 12.
147. Ibid.
148. Ibid.

149. EIdef2; EIp8dem.
150. EIdef6.
151. Letter 36.
152. Ibid.
153. Letter 50.
154. EIp13.
155. EIp12.
156. EIp12dem.
157. EIp13schol.
158. EIp15schol.2.
159. Ibid.
160. Ibid.
161. Ibid.
162. Ibid.
163. Ibid.
164. Ibid.
165. Ibid.
166. Ibid.
167. Ibid.
168. Ibid.
169. Ibid.
170. Ibid.
171. KV, I.2.
172. Ibid.
173. Ibid.
174. Ibid.
175. EIIp13lem.7schol.
176. Maimonides, *Guide of the Perplexed*, I.72, 184.
177. Ibid., 186.
178. Ibid., 190.
179. Ibid., 187.
180. Letter 32.
181. EIIp13lem.7schol.
182. Ibid.
183. Letter 32.
184. Ibid.
185. EIIp13def.
186. Ibid.
187. Letter 32.
188. EIIp13post1.
189. Klein, "Nature's Metabolism," 207.
190. Roth, *Spinoza*, 82.

Notes to Chapter 2

191. Macherey, *Hegel or Spinoza*, 12.
192. Hegel, *Lectures on the History of Philosophy: Medieval and Modern Philosophy*, 283.
193. Jacobi, *The Main Philosophical Writings*, 187.
194. Hegel, *Lectures on the History of Philosophy: Medieval and Modern Philosophy*, 283.
195. Hegel, *Science of Logic*, 512.
196. Ibid.
197. Ibid.
198. Yovel, *Spinoza and Other Heretics*, 45.
199. Ibid.
200. Yovel, *Dark Riddle*, 99.
201. Rose, *Jewish Philosophical Politics in Germany*, 95.
202. Dobbs-Weinstein, *Spinoza's Critique of Religion and Its Heirs*, 48.
203. Ibid., 47.
204. Ibid., 48.
205. Hegel, *Lectures on the History of Philosophy: Medieval and Modern*, 22.
206. Ibid, *Lectures on the History of Philosophy: Greek Philosophy*, 99.
207. Hegel, *Lectures on the History of Philosophy: Medieval and Modern*, 1.
208. Ibid., 552.
209. Ibid., 547.
210. Ibid.
211. Ibid., 552.
212. Macherey, *Hegel or Spinoza*, 11.
213. Ibid., 12.
214. Ibid., 19–24.
215. Althusser, "On Spinoza," in *Essays in Self Criticism*, 134, 136.
216. See Ravven, "Hegel's Epistemic Turn—or Spinoza's?," 195.
217. Žižek, *Organs Without Bodies*, 30.
218. Ibid., 29.
219. Žižek, *The Parallax View*, 8–9.
220. Ibid., 42.
221. Žižek, *Less Than Nothing*, 381.
222. Moder, *Hegel and Spinoza*, 6.
223. Ibid.
224. Ibid.
225. Ibid., 7.
226. Ibid.
227. Hegel, *The Phenomenology of Spirit*, 11.
228. Althusser, "On Spinoza," in *Essays in Self-Criticism*, 138.
229. Hegel, *Encyclopedia*, 225.
230. Hegel, *Lectures on the History of Philosophy: Medieval and Modern*, 552–53.
231. Ibid., 547.

232. Macherey, *Hegel or Spinoza*, 120.
233. Letter 54; see Crescas, *Or Adonai*, in H. A. Wolfson, *Crescas' Critique of Aristotle*, 106.
234. Deleuze, *Expressionism in Philosophy*, 182.
235. Braidotti, *The Posthuman*, 56.
236. Althusser, "On Spinoza," in *Essays in Self-Criticism*, 141.
237. Della Rocca, *Spinoza*, 33; see also Della Rocca, "The Elusiveness of the One and the Many in Spinoza: Substance, Attribute, and Mode."
238. Bennett, *A Study of Spinoza's Ethics*, 76.

Chapter 3
1. Adorno, *Negative Dialectics*, 379.
2. Hegel, *Science of Logic*, 60.
3. Ibid.
4. See O'Regan, *The Heterodox Hegel*, 147.
5. Hegel, *Science of Logic*, 61.
6. Ibid.
7. Ibid., 212.
8. Ibid.
9. Ibid., 474.
10. Ibid.
11. Ibid., 212.
12. Hegel, *Encyclopedia*, 225.
13. Badiou, *Theory of the Subject*.
14. Derrida, "My Chances / *Mes Chances*."
15. Diderot contrasts Spinoza with Epicureanism: "Spinosa," *Encyclopédie*.
16. Letter 55.
17. Letter 56.
18. See Morfino, *Plural Temporality*, 72–88.
19. Lucretius, *On the Nature of Things*, 1.150–59, 7.
20. Ibid., 4.379, 110.
21. Ibid., 1.951–1051, 29–31.
22. Ibid., 2.1048–89, 61–62.
23. Strauss, *Spinoza's Critique of Religion*, 45.
24. See Nail, *Lucretius I*, 11.
25. Lucretius, *On the Nature of Things*, 2.219–20.
26. Ibid., 2.221–26.
27. Ibid., 2.253–56.
28. See Hegel, *Encyclopedia of the Philosophical Sciences*, 155.
29. See Hegel, *Science of Logic*, 134.
30. Ibid., 134–35.
31. Marx, *Marx and Engels: Collected Works*, 1:37.
32. Ibid., 50.

33. Ibid.
34. Ibid.
35. Deleuze, *Expressionism in Philosophy*, 60.
36. Deleuze, *Spinoza*, 26.
37. Deleuze, "Gueroult's General Method for Spinoza," in *Desert Islands*, 50.
38. Deleuze, *The Logic of Sense*, 268.
39. Ibid., 270.
40. Ibid., 269.
41. Ibid., 279.
42. See Montag, *Althusser and His Contemporaries*, 187.
43. Althusser, *Philosophy of the Encounter*, 169.
44. Ibid., 190.
45. Ibid., 176.
46. Ibid.
47. Ibid., 174.
48. See Letter 36; Letter 50.
49. To some, dark matter complicates this.
50. See Descartes, *Principles*, CSM I.225–30.
51. DPP, IIp3.
52. Ibid., IIp3d.
53. Letter 13.
54. EIp15schol.
55. Descartes, *Principles*, CSM I.230
56. Ibid.
57. Ibid., CSM I.231.
58. Ibid., CSM I.231–32.
59. Ibid.
60. Ibid., CSM I.201.
61. Ibid., CSM I.232.
62. Ibid.
63. Ibid., CSM I.240.
64. Ibid. Angle brackets in original.
65. Ibid.
66. Letter 81.
67. EIp13dem.
68. KV, I.2.
69. Ibid.
70. Ibid.
71. Ibid.
72. EIp33schol.2.
73. Hegel, *The Science of Logic*, 59.
74. EIp1.
75. Aristotle, *Physics*, in *The Complete Works of Aristotle*, 211b13.

76. Ibid., 212a30.
77. Ibid., 213b32–34.
78. Ibid., 216b7–11.
79. Ibid., 203b28–29.
80. Crescas, "Or Adonai," Book I, Part 2, 195, in H. A. Wolfson, *Crescas' Critique of Aristotle*.
81. Ibid., 199.
82. Ibid., 201.
83. Crescas, "Or Adonai," I, 2 Ch. 1,199.
84. See H. A. Wolfson, *The Philosophy of Spinoza*, 281; Harvey, *Physics and Metaphysics in Ḥasdai Crescas*, 29–30; Fraenkel, "Ḥasdai Crescas on God as Place of the World and Spinoza's Notion of God as '*Res Extensa*'"; Rudavsky, "Time, Space, and Infinity."
85. de Herrera, *Gate of Heaven*, 64. Parentheses in original.
86. Grant, *Much Ado About Nothing*, 263.
87. EIax1.
88. EIp15.
89. Morton, *Realist Magic*, 47.
90. Ibid.
91. Ibid.
92. Ibid.
93. Harman, *Tool-Being*.
94. Ibid., 52.
95. Ibid., 113.
96. Ibid.
97. Ibid., 183.
98. Ibid., 62.
99. Ibid., 63.
100. See Harman, *Object-Oriented Ontology*.
101. Ibid., 17.
102. Ibid.
103. Ibid., 17–18.
104. Ibid., 73.
105. Ibid., 64.
106. Ibid., 53.
107. Ibid., 102.
108. Ibid., 199.
109. Ibid.
110. Ibid., 200.
111. Ibid., 75.
112. Ibid.
113. Ibid.
114. Ibid.

115. Ibid.
116. Ibid.
117. Ibid.
118. Ibid.
119. Ibid., 76.
120. Ibid., 56.
121. Ibid., 76.
122. Ibid.
123. Ibid.
124. Ibid.
125. Proverbs, 25:11.
126. Maimonides, Introduction, in *Guide of the Perplexed*, I, 12.
127. Ibid.
128. Sheldon also registers Morton's apophaticism: "Dark Correlationism," 139.
129. Harman, *Weird Realism*.
130. Morton, *Realist Magic*, 164–65.
131. For a similar observation, see Sheldon, "Dark Correlationism," 141.
132. Morton, *Realist Magic*, 72.
133. Ibid., 137.
134. Ibid.
135. For Badiou's Spinoza, see Gillespie, "Placing the Void: Badiou on Spinoza"; Hallward, *Badiou: A Subject to Truth*, 168–71.
136. Badiou, *Being and Event*, 113.
137. Ibid., 116.
138. Ibid., 119.
139. Ibid., 113.
140. Ibid., 114.
141. Ibid., 120.
142. Ibid., 86.
143. Ibid., 23.
144. Ibid., 24.
145. Ibid., 52.
146. Ibid.
147. Ibid., 55.
148. Ibid., 59.
149. Ibid.
150. Ibid., 54.
151. Ibid., 58.
152. Ibid., 97.
153. Ibid., 184.
154. Ibid., 184–85.
155. Ibid., 185.
156. Ibid., 188.

157. Badiou, "Spinoza's Closed Ontology," in *Theoretical Writings*, 87.
158. Ibid.
159. Ibid., 88.
160. Ibid.
161. Ibid.
162. Ibid., 92.
163. Ibid., 89.
164. Ibid.
165. Ibid.
166. Ibid.
167. Ibid., 93.
168. Ibid.
169. Ibid.
170. Badiou, "The Question of Being Today," in *Theoretical Writings*, 37.
171. Badiou, *Being and Event*, 176.
172. Ibid., 178.
173. Ibid., 55.
174. Ibid., 189.
175. Ibid., 174.
176. Ibid., 216.
177. See Bensaïd, "Alain Badiou and the Miracle of the Event"; Badiou, "L'émancipation, c'est celle de l'humanité tout entire."
178. See Badiou, "The Event as Trans-being," in *Theoretical Writings*, 104.
179. For Žižek's Spinoza, see Ravven, "Hegel's Epistemic Turn—or Spinoza's?"; Williams, "Thinking the Space of the Subject *Between* Hegel and Spinoza"; Stolze, "Hegel or Spinoza."
180. Žižek, *Organs Without Bodies*, 31.
181. Ibid.
182. Žižek, *Less Than Nothing*, 368.
183. Ibid., 368–69.
184. Ibid., 369.
185. Ibid., 376.
186. Ibid.
187. Ibid., 377.
188. Ibid., 376.
189. Ibid., 377.
190. Žižek, *Absolute Recoil*, 385.
191. Ibid., 393–94.
192. Ibid., 394.
193. Ibid., 396.
194. Ibid., 397.
195. Žižek, *Less Than Nothing*, 958.
196. Ibid., 959.

197. Žižek, *Absolute Recoil*, 412.
198. Ibid., 413.
199. Žižek, *Less than Nothing*, 947.
200. Ibid., 949.
201. Ibid.
202. Ibid., 925.
203. Žižek, *Absolute Recoil*, 389.
204. Ibid.
205. Ibid., 393.
206. Ibid.
207. Žižek, *Less Than Nothing*, 912.
208. Žižek, *Absolute Recoil*, 387.
209. See also Žižek, *Disparities*, 31; *Incontinence of the Void*, 277.
210. Macherey, *Hegel or Spinoza*, 11.
211. Moder, *Hegel and Spinoza*, 131.
212. Ibid.

Chapter 4

1. Luxemburg, "The Beginning," 344.
2. EIVpref.
3. Althusser, "The Only Materialist Tradition," 7.
4. EIapp.
5. Ibid.
6. Ibid.
7. Ibid.
8. Ibid.
9. Ibid.
10. Ibid.
11. Ibid.
12. Ibid.
13. Ibid.
14. Ibid.
15. Ibid.
16. Ibid.
17. Ibid.
18. Ibid.
19. Ibid.
20. Ibid.
21. Ibid.
22. Marx, "The German Ideology," 172.
23. EIapp.
24. Ibid.
25. Ibid.

26. EIVpref.
27. Ibid.
28. Ibid.
29. Ibid.
30. Ibid.
31. Ibid.
32. Ibid.
33. Ibid.
34. Ibid.
35. Ibid.
36. EIp33schol.2.
37. del Lucchese, "The Mother of All Prejudices," 145.
38. EIVpref.
39. Ibid.
40. Ibid.
41. Ibid.
42. Ibid.
43. EVp6schol.
44. EIVpref.
45. Ibid.
46. Letter 51.
47. Ibid.
48. Ibid.
49. Letter 53.
50. Ibid.
51. Letter 54.
52. Ibid.
53. Ibid.
54. Ibid.
55. Letter 55.
56. Ibid.
57. See Xenophanes, *The Texts of Early Greek Philosophy*, 109.
58. Letter 56.
59. EIapp.
60. Ibid.
61. Ibid.
62. Ibid.
63. Harvey, "Spinoza and Maimonides on Teleology," 43.
64. Maimonides, *Guide of the Perplexed*, III.13, 452.
65. Ibid., 454.
66. Ibid., III.12, 442.
67. Ibid., III.453.
68. Ibid., 24–25.

69. Ibid.
70. Ibid.
71. Philo, *On the Creation*, in *The Works of Philo*, I.28.
72. Ibid., I.22.
73. Ibid., I.27.
74. Ibid., I.28.
75. EIapp.
76. Ibid.
77. Ibid.
78. Ibid.
79. Maimonides, *Guide of the Perplexed*, III.19, 479.
80. Ibid.
81. Ibid.
82. EIapp.
83. Ibid.
84. EIp33schol.2.
85. Funkenstein, *Theology and the Scientific Imagination*, 192.
86. Descartes, *The World*, CSM I.93.
87. Descartes, *Principles*, CSM I.240.
88. Descartes, CSMK.23.
89. EIIIpref.
90. Ibid.
91. EIVp57schol.
92. EIVapp.
93. EIVp50schol.
94. EIIIp2schol.
95. TTP, IV.
96. Ibid.
97. Ibid.
98. Ibid.
99. Ibid.
100. Letter 31.
101. Letter 30.
102. Letter 32.
103. Ibid.
104. See Mason, "How Things Happen," 17–36; Campos, *Spinoza's Revolution*, 77–80.
105. EIp17.
106. EIp17dem.
107. EIIp40schol.1.
108. EIIp40schol.2.
109. Letter 33.

110. Garber, "God, Laws, and the Order of Nature"; Garret, *Meaning in Spinoza's Method*, 29–31, 35–54; Rutherford, "Spinoza's Conception of Law."
111. Totaro, "Law and Dissolution of Law in Spinoza," 385.
112. Ibid., 386.
113. Ibid., 388.
114. Ibid., 389.
115. EIVpref.
116. Ibid.
117. Ibid.
118. Ibid.
119. EIIp40schol.1.
120. Ibid.
121. See Goetschel, "Spinoza's Dream"; Rosenthal, "'The Black, Scabby Brazilian.'"
122. See Lord, "Outside of Human Nature."
123. EIapp.
124. Ibid.
125. Ibid.
126. TTP, XVII.
127. KV, VI.
128. EIapp.
129. Fanon, *Black Skin, White Masks*, 73.
130. Mbembe, *Out of the Dark*, 227.
131. Appiah, "Race, Culture, Identity," 37.
132. Mills, *Blackness Visible*, 48.
133. Letter 56.
134. See Bottici, *Anarchafeminism*, 130–16; Gatens, ed. *Feminist Interpretations of Spinoza*; James, "The Power of Spinoza"; Sharp, "Spinoza and Feminism"; Sharp, "Feminism and Heterodoxy."
135. Gatens, *Imaginary Bodies*, 131.
136. KV, I.6.
137. Ibid.
138. Ibid.
139. Ibid.
140. Ibid.
141. Ibid.
142. Ibid.
143. EVp24.
144. EIIp40schol.1.
145. Ibid.
146. Ibid.
147. Ibid.

148. Ibid.
149. Ibid.
150. Ibid.
151. Ibid.
152. EIapp.
153. Fausto-Sterling, *Sexing the Body*, 87.
154. EIapp.
155. Butler, *Gender Trouble*, 11.
156. EIIp40schol.1.
157. KV, I.6.
158. Lloyd, *Part of Nature*, 161.
159. Ibid.
160. Ibid.
161. Ibid., 164.
162. Ibid., 162.
163. Ibid., 164.
164. Ibid., 166.
165. Ibid., 165.
166. Ibid., 167.
167. Ibid.
168. EIIp7schol.
169. Ibid., 162.
170. Gatens, *Imaginary Bodies*, 133.
171. Ibid., 139.
172. Ibid., 131.
173. Ibid., 132.
174. Ibid.
175. Ibid.
176. Ibid.
177. Ibid.
178. Ibid., 149–50.
179. KV, I.10.
180. Gatens, *Imaginary Bodies*, 52.
181. Ibid., 57.
182. Ibid., x.
183. Ibid., 2.
184. Ibid., 4.
185. Ibid., 8.
186. Ibid., 9.
187. Ibid.
188. Ibid.
189. Ibid., 14.
190. Ibid., 13.

191. Ibid.
192. Ibid., 16.
193. Ibid.
194. Ibid.
195. Ibid., 13.
196. Ibid., 15.
197. Ibid., 11.
198. Ibid., 14.
199. Walsh, "Twenty Years Since 'A Critique of the Sex/Gender Distinction,'" 213.
200. Gill-Peterson, *A Short History of Trans Misogyny*, 144.
201. EIIIpref.
202. Maimonides, *Guide of the Perplexed*, II.48, 410.
203. Pines, "Studies in Abul-Barakāt al-Baghdādī's"; Altmann, "Free Will and Predestination."
204. See Ravven, *The Self Beyond Itself*, 183–239.
205. See Klein, "Spinoza's Debt to Gersonides"; Klein, "'Something of It Remains.'"
206. See Manekin, "Spinoza and the Determinist Tradition."
207. Descartes, *Meditations*, CSM II.40.
208. Ibid., CSM II.54.
209. Descartes, *Principles*, I.32, CSM I.204.
210. Descartes, *Meditations*, CSM II.18.
211. Ibid., CSM II.40.
212. Descartes, *Discourse*, CSM I.142–43.
213. Augustine, "The Literal Meaning of Genesis," in *On Genesis*, VIII, 372.
214. EIVp5cor.
215. EIIp13schol.L7.
216. EIIIp2schol.
217. Tallbear and Willey, "Introduction: Critical Relationality," 5.
218. TP, VII.
219. Ibid., XI.
220. Ibid.
221. Ibid.
222. EIapp.
223. Riskin, *The Restless Clock*, 18.
224. Ibid., 19.
225. Ibid., 18–19.
226. Ibid., 19.
227. Kant, "Idea for a Universal History with a Cosmopolitan Purpose," in *Political Writings*, 41.
228. Ibid.
229. Ibid., 42.

230. Ibid.
231. Ibid., 52.
232. Ibid.
233. Ibid., 53.
234. EIVp47schol.
235. Yovel, *Spinoza and Other Heretics*, 23.
236. Althusser, "The Underground Current of the Materialism of the Encounter," 190.
237. Balibar, *Spinoza and Politics*, 122.
238. Macherey, *Hegel or Spinoza*, 59, 77, 203–4.
239. Negri, *The Savage Anomaly*, 160–62, 194; Negri, *Subversive Spinoza*, 17–18, 45–49.
240. Dobbs-Weinstein, *Spinoza's Critique of Religion and Its Heirs*, 37–38.
241. For more on Spinoza, Benjamin, and Adorno, see Dobbs-Weinstein, *Spinoza's Critique of Religion and Its Heirs*.
242. Benjamin, "On the Concept of History," 391.
243. Ibid., 392.
244. Ibid.
245. Ibid.
246. Ibid., 397.
247. Adorno, *Minima Moralia*, 55.
248. MacAskill, *What We Owe the Future*, 4.
249. Ibid., 4–5.
250. Ibid., 6.
251. Ord, *The Precipice*, 22.
252. Ibid.
253. Ibid., 189.
254. Beckstead, "On the Overwhelming Importance of Shaping the Far Future," 11.
255. Ibid.
256. MacAskill, *What We Owe the Future*, 156.
257. Ibid., 189.
258. Ord, *The Precipice*, 20.
259. Ibid.
260. Ibid.
261. Shulman and Bostrom, "Embryo Selection for Cognitive Enhancement."
262. Ibid., 89.
263. Ibid., 90.
264. MacAskill, *What We Owe the Future*, 156.
265. Mitchell and Chaudhury, "Worlding Beyond 'the' 'End' of 'the World,'" 310.
266. EIVp37schol.1.
267. TTP, VI.

Chapter 5

1. Levinas, *Totality and Infinity*, 25.
2. EIIpref.
3. EIIp7schol.
4. EIdef6.
5. EIp9.
6. EIp11schol.
7. Ibid.
8. EIapp.
9. EIp10.
10. EIp16dem.
11. EIp10schol.
12. Letter 63.
13. Letter 64.
14. EIIp13cor.
15. Letter 64.
16. EIp10schol.
17. EIIp6.
18. For example: Della Rocca, *Spinoza*; Lin, "The Principle of Sufficient Reason in Spinoza."
19. Hegel, *The Science of Logic*, 473.
20. Hegel, *Lectures on the History of Philosophy: Medieval and Modern*, 153.
21. Hegel, *The Science of Logic*, 472.
22. EIIp7schol.
23. EIapp.
24. Ibid.
25. This term is from Meillassoux, *After Finitude*, 5.
26. See Bennett, *A Study of Spinoza's Ethics*; Curley, *Behind the Geometrical Method*; Della Rocca, *Representation and the Mind Body Problem in Spinoza*; Guéroult, *Spinoza I*; Hallett, *Benedict de Spinoza*, 16–18; H. A. Wolfson, *The Philosophy of Spinoza*, I, 146–57.
27. EIdef4.
28. EIp10schol.
29. EIp10.
30. EIp10schol.
31. EIIp7schol.
32. Ibid.
33. Maimonides, *Moreh Nevukhim*, I.69, 51b.
34. Maimonides, *Guide of the Perplexed*, I.69, 165–66.
35. Maimonides, *Moreh Nevukhim*, I.47, 29a.
36. Maimonides, *Guide of the Perplexed*, II.19, 302.
37. See for example, Sifra Kedoshim 10; Sifre Numbers (Shelah); b. Berakhot 31b; b. Yevamot 71a; b. Bava Metsia 31b; b. Avodah Zarah 27a.

38. See TTP, VI.
39. Maimonides, *Moreh Nevukhim*, I.53, 35a.
40. Maimonides, *Guide of the Perplexed*, I.52, 119.
41. Exodus 33:13.
42. Exodus 33:19.
43. Genesis 1:31.
44. Maimonides, *Guide of the Perplexed*, I.54, 125.
45. Maimonides, *Moreh Nevukhim*, I.54, 36a.
46. Maimonides, *Guide of the Perplexed*, I.53, 122.
47. Maimonides, *Moreh Nevukhim*, I.53, 35a.
48. Maimonides, *Guide of the Perplexed*, I.52, 119.
49. Maimonides, *Moreh Nevukhim*, I.53, 35a.
50. Ibid., I.61, 43b.
51. CM II.viii.
52. TTP, IV.
53. EIp17schol.
54. Ibid.
55. EIIp7schol.
56. Ibid.
57. Letter 8.
58. Letter 9.
59. Ibid.
60. Hallett, *Benedict de Spinoza*, 17.
61. Dobbs-Weinstein, "Gersonides's Radically Modern Understanding of the Agent Intellect."
62. Klein, "Aristotle and Descartes in Spinoza's Approach to Matter and Body"; Klein, "Spinoza's Debt to Gersonides."
63. Letter 9.
64. Ibid.
65. Genesis 25:26.
66. Ibid., 32:29.
67. Letter 9.
68. EIp4dem.
69. EIIp7schol.
70. Ibid.
71. Ibid.
72. Ibid.
73. Ibid.
74. EIIp7schol.
75. EIVp8dem.
76. EIIp7schol.
77. Ibid.

78. Some duplicate parallelism, see Deleuze, *Expressionism in Philosophy*; Guéroult, *Spinoza II*; Melamed, *Spinoza's Metaphysics*.
79. EIIp7schol.
80. Ibid.
81. EIIp13schol.
82. EVpref.
83. EIIp1.
84. Ibid.
85. EIIp1dem.
86. EIIp2dem.
87. EIIp6.
88. EIIp8cor.
89. EIIp3.
90. EIIp3dem.
91. EIp15.
92. EIIp3schol.
93. Ibid.
94. Ibid.
95. Ibid.
96. EIIp4.
97. EIIp6.
98. EIIp8cor.
99. EIIp8schol.
100. EIIp9.
101. EIIp9dem.
102. EIIp9cor.
103. Renz, *The Explainability of Experience*, 141.
104. Ibid.
105. EIIp11.
106. EIIp11cor.
107. Ibid.
108. EIIp13dem.
109. EIIp11cor.
110. EIIp2.
111. EIp10schol.
112. EIIp7schol.
113. EIIp13.
114. EIIIp6dem.
115. EIIIDA1ex.
116. EVp1.
117. EIIIdef3.
118. EIIp19.

119. EIIp11.
120. EIIp31dem.
121. EIIp13dem.
122. EIIp13cor.
123. EIIp19dem.
124. EIIp11schol.
125. EIIIGDAex.
126. EIIp23.
127. EIIp23dem.
128. EIIp13schol.
129. Ibid.
130. EIIp14.
131. EIIIGDA.
132. EVp39schol.
133. EVp39dem.
134. Ibid.
135. EIIp13post.I.
136. EIIp13post.III.
137. EIIp16cor.1.
138. EIIp16cor.2.
139. EIIp28.
140. EIIp28schol.
141. EIIp25.
142. EIIp17schol.
143. EIIp18schol.
144. EIIp35schol.
145. Ibid.
146. EIIp36.
147. EIIp29schol.
148. EIVp44schol.
149. EIIp29schol.
150. Ibid.
151. EIIp18schol.
152. Ibid.
153. EIIp40schol.1.
154. Ibid.
155. Ibid.
156. Ibid.
157. Ibid.
158. Ibid.
159. EIIp40schol.2.
160. EIIp41.
161. TIE, 18.

162. EIIp38cor.
163. Ibid.
164. Ibid.
165. EIIp39cor.
166. EIIp13schol.
167. EVp7dem.
168. EIIIp10.
169. EIIp13cor.
170. EVp4.
171. EV4schol.
172. EVp39dem.
173. EVp39schol.
174. EIIpschol.2.
175. KV, II.1.
176. EIIpschol.2.
177. KV, II.1.
178. Ibid.
179. Ibid.
180. Ibid.
181. EVp36schol.
182. KV, II.1.
183. EVp31.
184. EVp27dem.
185. KV, II.1; EIVp66schol.
186. TIE, 22.
187. TIE, 18.
188. EIIp29schol.
189. EVpref.
190. Descartes, *Principles*, CSM.213.
191. Elisabeth of Bohemia and Descartes, *The Correspondence*, 88–90, 93–94, 99–101.
192. Deleuze, *Expressionism in Philosophy*, 63.
193. Ibid., 102–3.
194. Ibid., 81.
195. Ibid.
196. Ibid., 66.
197. Maimonides, *Guide of the Perplexed*, I.50, I.53.
198. Deleuze, *Expressionism in Philosophy*, 95.
199. Ibid., 82.
200. Ibid.
201. Ibid., 111.
202. Ibid., 80–81.
203. Ibid., 61.

204. Ibid., 100.
205. Ibid., 101.
206. Ibid.
207. Ibid., 102.
208. EIIp7schol.
209. Noncapitalization of *same* in this sentence is intentional.
210. Ibid., 101.
211. Ibid., 109.
212. Ibid., 110.
213. Ibid., 114.
214. Ibid., 116.
215. Ibid., 117.
216. Ibid., 118.
217. Ibid.
218. Ibid.
219. Ibid., 120.
220. Ibid.
221. Ibid.
222. Ibid., 122.
223. Ibid., 124.
224. Ibid.
225. Ibid., 127.
226. Ibid.
227. Ibid.
228. Ibid., 128.
229. Ibid., 127.
230. Mendelssohn, "Morning Hours," in *Last Works*, 98–100, 103, 107–9.
231. Maimon, *The Autobiography*, 62–64.
232. Deleuze and Guattari, *What Is Philosophy?*, 59.
233. Ibid., 59–60.
234. Ibid., 60.
235. Kant, *Critique of Pure Reason*, B74.
236. Ibid., B75.
237. Ibid., B59.
238. Maimon, *Essay on Transcendental Philosophy*, 63, 37.
239. Ibid.
240. Ibid.
241. Ibid., 205, 109.
242. Ibid., 64–65, 38.
243. Ibid., 63–65, 38.
244. Ibid., 207, 110.
245. Ibid., 355, 183.
246. Ibid., 356, 184.

247. Ibid., 33, 22.
248. Ibid., 206, 109.
249. Ibid., 32, 22.
250. Ibid., 18, 14.
251. Ibid.
252. Ibid., 203, 108.
253. Ibid., 249, 131.
254. Ibid.
255. Ibid., 251, 132.
256. Ibid., 110, 63.
257. Ibid., 111, 64.
258. Ibid., 205, 109.
259. Ibid., 11, 64.
260. Deleuze, *Difference and Repetition*, 222.
261. Ibid., 173.
262. Ibid.
263. Deleuze, *The Fold*, 89.
264. Ibid.
265. Ibid.
266. Ibid.
267. Ibid.
268. Ibid, *Difference and Repetition*, 193.
269. Ibid.
270. Ibid., 194.
271. Ibid.
272. Ibid., 164.
273. Ibid., 58.
274. Ibid., 211.
275. Ibid., 218.
276. Ibid.
277. Ibid., 211.
278. Deleuze, *Desert Islands*, 100.
279. Deleuze, *Difference and Repetition*, 212.
280. Ibid.
281. Ibid., 164.
282. Ibid.
283. Brassier, *Nihil Unbound*, 203.
284. Deleuze, *Difference and Repetition*, 37.
285. Peden, *Spinoza Contra Phenomenology*, 241.
286. Deleuze, *Difference and Repetition*, 39.
287. Ibid., 304.
288. Badiou, *Deleuze*, 10.

Chapter 6

1. Gordon, *Fanon and the Crisis of European Man*, 8–9.
2. Yovel, "Spinoza, the First Anti-Cartesian."
3. Sharp, "Spinoza and Feminism," 427.
4. Rudavsky, "Feminism and Modern Jewish Philosophy," 331.
5. Ibid., 331–32.
6. Dobbs-Weinstein, "Thinking Desire in Gersonides and Spinoza," 56.
7. Dussel, "Anti-Cartesian Meditations," 21.
8. Ibid.
9. Wynter, "Unsettling the Coloniality of Being/Power/Truth/Freedom," 266.
10. Ibid., 300.
11. Ibid.
12. Ibid., 305.
13. Maldonado-Torres, "On the Coloniality of Being," 252.
14. Dussel, *The Invention of the Americas*, 48.
15. Dussel, "Anti-Cartesian Meditations," 44.
16. Eze, *Achieving Our Humanity*, 5.
17. Ibid., 42.
18. Ibid.
19. Ibid.
20. Ibid.
21. Dias and van der Tak, "Spinoza, Merchant and Autodidact," 185–87.
22. Israel, *Spinoza*, 185.
23. Descartes, *Principles*, CSM I.210.
24. Yovel, "Spinoza, the First Anti-Cartesian" 124.
25. Ibid.
26. Åkerman, *Queen Christina of Sweden and Her Circle*, 49.
27. Sánchez's family were Jewish conversos.
28. See Dussel, "Anti-Cartesian Meditations."
29. Augustine, *On the Trinity*, 12.12, 91.
30. Ibid., 15.7, 178.
31. Ibid., 61.
32. Augustine, "The Literal Meaning of Genesis," in *On Genesis*, VIII, 372.
33. Ibid., 380.
34. Ibid., 371.
35. Ibid., 342.
36. Augustine, *The City of God Against the Pagans*, 484.
37. Ibid.
38. Augustine, *On the Trinity*, 15.12, 21.
39. Ibid., 8.6, 14.
40. See Arnauld, CSM II.138–53.
41. Descartes, CSMK.159, CSMK.232.
42. Barbapiccola, "Preface to René Descartes's Principles of Philosophy," 65.

43. Wilson, "Descartes and Augustine," 47.
44. Menn, *Descartes and Augustine*, 4.
45. Descartes, *Meditations*, CSM II.17.
46. Ibid, CSM II.18.
47. Ibid, CSM II.51.
48. Ibid, CSM II.54.
49. Ibid, CSMK.336.
50. Descartes, *Meditations*, CSM II.24.
51. Descartes, *Principles*, CSM I.204.
52. Ibid., CSM I.204.
53. Descartes, *Meditations*, CSM II.40.
54. Descartes, *Discourse*, CSM I.112.
55. Ibid., CSM I.141.
56. Ibid.
57. Ibid.
58. Ibid.
59. Ibid., CSM I.142.
60. Horkheimer and Adorno, *Dialectic of Enlightenment*, 6.
61. Césaire, *Discourse on Colonialism*, 49.
62. Ibid.
63. de las Casas, *Witness*, 67.
64. Bauer, *The Jewish Problem*, 13.
65. Ibid.
66. Ibid., 12.
67. Ibid., 39.
68. Ibid., 22.
69. Bordo, *The Flight to Objectivity*, 9.
70. Descartes, CSMK.86.
71. Ibid., CSMK.214.
72. Ibid., CSMK.375.
73. Perry, "Radical Doubt and the Liberation of Women," 172.
74. Pellegrin, "Cartesianism and Feminism," 567.
75. Harth, "Cartesian Women," 214.
76. O'Neill, "Women Cartesians, 'Feminine Philosophy,' and Historical Exclusion," 233.
77. Barbapiccola, "Preface to René Descartes's Principles of Philosophy," 55–56.
78. Poullain de la Barre, "On the Equality of the Two Sexes," 82.
79. Astell, *A Serious Proposal to the Ladies*, 59.
80. Ibid., 168.
81. Harth, "Cartesian Women," 12.
82. O'Neill, "Women Cartesians."
83. Broad, *Women Philosophers of the Seventeenth Century*, 15.
84. Ibid.

85. Conway, *The Principles of the Most Ancient and Modern Philosophy*, 64.
86. Ibid., 28.
87. Ibid., 38.
88. Ibid.
89. Ibid., 39.
90. Ibid., 38.
91. Ibid., 40.
92. Ibid., 56.
93. Ibid., 61.
94. Ibid., 31.
95. Ibid., 63.
96. Arnauld, CSM II.139–44.
97. Conway, *Principles of the Most Ancient and Modern Philosophy*, 56.
98. Ibid., 58.
99. Ibid.
100. Ibid., 46.
101. Ibid., 47.
102. Ibid., 58.
103. Ibid., 42.
104. Ibid., 25
105. Ibid., 28.
106. Ibid., 31.
107. Ibid., 42.
108. Ibid.
109. Ibid., 9.
110. Broad, *Women Philosophers of the Seventeenth Century*, 79.
111. Borcherding, "Loving the Body, Loving the Soul," 34.
112. Letter 68.
113. Letter 32.
114. EIIp11.
115. EIIp13.
116. EIIp13cor.
117. EIIp13schol.
118. H. A. Wolfson, *The Philosophy of Spinoza*, II, 53.
119. EIIp21schol.
120. EIIp13schol.
121. Ibid.
122. EIIp39cor.
123. EIIp13schol.
124. Maimonides, *Guide of the Perplexed*, I.72, 192.
125. Ibid., I.49, 91.
126. Gersonides, *War of the Lords*, I.V, 145.
127. Ibid.

128. Ibid., I.XI, 213.
129. Ibid.
130. See Klein, "Spinoza's Debt to Gersonides," 20.
131. Klein, "'Something of It Remains.'"
132. Dobbs-Weinstein, "Gersonides's Radically Modern Understanding of the Agent Intellect," 198.
133. Ibid., 209.
134. Descartes, *Principles*, CSM I.193.
135. Ibid., CSM I.194.
136. Ibid., CSM I.194.
137. Descartes, *Meditations*, CSM II.40–41.
138. Ravven, *The Self Beyond Itself*, 179.
139. DPP, Preface.
140. TIE, §70.
141. EIIp43.
142. TIE, §34.
143. EIIp43schol.
144. Ibid.
145. Letter 76.
146. CM I.6.
147. Derrida, "Language and Discourse on Method," 65.
148. Althusser, "Elements of Self-Criticism," in *Essays in Self-Criticism*, 137.
149. See Letter 12.
150. Crescas, "Or Adonai," I, 2 Ch. 1 in H. A. Wolfson, *Crescas' Critique of Aristotle*, 195.
151. Aristotle, *Prior Analytic*, in *The Complete Works of Aristotle*, I.32.
152. Descartes, *Rules*, CSM I.9.
153. TIE, §38.
154. Ibid.
155. TIE, §36.
156. Macherey, *Hegel or Spinoza*, 43.
157. TIE, §85; EIax4.
158. TIE, §19.
159. TIE, §99.
160. EIIp28dem.
161. TIE, §85.
162. TIE, §69.
163. Ibid.
164. Ibid.
165. Descartes, CSM II.110.
166. Deleuze, *Expressionism in Philosophy*, 160.
167. Macherey, *Hegel or Spinoza*, 55.
168. Ibid.

169. Descartes, *Discourse*, CSM I.118.
170. Descartes, *Rules*, CSM I.16.
171. EIIax2.
172. Macherey, *Hegel or Spinoza*, 50.
173. TIE, §41.
174. TIE, §44.
175. Descartes, *Discourse*, CSM I.112.
176. Ibid., 111.
177. Ibid., CSM I.121.
178. TIE, §23.
179. Ibid.
180. Descartes, *Rules*, CSM I.16.
181. Dika, *Descartes's Method*, 347.
182. Descartes, *Discourse*, CSM I.116.
183. He concedes that science requires others: ibid., CSM I.149.
184. Ibid., CSM I.119.
185. Ibid., CSM I.127.
186. Ibid., CSM I.142.
187. TIE, §1.
188. Descartes, *Discourse*, CSM I.111.
189. TIE, §3.
190. TIE, §7.
191. TIE, §12.
192. TIE, §13.
193. TIE, §14.
194. TIE, §13.
195. TIE, §25.
196. TIE, §14.
197. TIE, §15.
198. TIE, §60.
199. Ibid.
200. TIE, §61.
201. TIE, §60.
202. EIIpschol.3b.
203. TIE, §80.
204. EIIp48.
205. EIIp36.
206. EIIpschol.3b; EIIp17schol.
207. EIIp49cor.
208. EIIp49cor.2.
209. EIIp7.
210. EIIp7schol.
211. Nietzsche, *Twilight of the Idols*, 28.

212. Nietzsche, *Sämtliche Briefe*, 6:101.
213. Heidegger, *Being and Time*, 46.
214. Heidegger, "The Age of the World Picture," 81.
215. Ibid., 84.
216. Ibid.
217. For Heidegger's Nazism, see E. R. Wolfson, *The Duplicity of Philosophy's Shadow*.
218. See Peden, *Spinoza Contra Phenomenology*.
219. Althusser, *Psychoanalysis and the Human Sciences*, 81.
220. Ibid., 83.
221. Ibid.
222. Ibid., 85.
223. Althusser, "Elements of Self-Criticism," in *Essays in Self-Criticism*, 134.
224. Ibid., 136.
225. Ibid., 136–37.
226. Althusser, "The Only Materialist Tradition," 5.
227. Ibid.
228. EIIdef4.
229. EIax6. See also EIIp32.; EIIp32dem.
230. Letter 59.
231. Letter 60.
232. Ibid.
233. See Klein, "Dreaming with Open Eyes," 159n13.
234. EIIdef3.]
235. EIIdef3ex.
236. EIIIp1.
237. EIIIp58.
238. See Dobbs-Weinstein, "Thinking Desire in Gersonides and Spinoza," 62–63.
239. EIIp21schol.
240. See Matysik, *When Spinoza Met Marx*; Rose, *Jewish Philosophical Politics in Germany*, 200–271.
241. Marx, "Theses on Feuerbach," 145.
242. Hess, "The Philosophy of the Act," 249.
243. Ibid., 264.
244. Ibid., 249.
245. Ibid., 250.
246. Ibid., 251.
247. Ibid.
248. Ibid.
249. Ibid., 264.
250. Ibid.
251. Ibid., 267.

252. Ibid., 260.
253. Ibid.
254. Ibid., 255.
255. Ibid., 264–65.
256. Ibid., 261.
257. Ibid.
258. Ibid., 262.
259. Ibid., 261.
260. Ibid., 259.
261. Marx names Hess as an influence: Marx, "Economic and Philosophic Manuscripts," in *The Marx-Engels Reader*, 68.
262. Adorno, "On Subject and Object," in *Critical Models*, 246.
263. Ibid., 248.
264. Ibid.
265. Ibid.
266. Adorno, *Negative Dialectics*, 8.
267. Ibid.
268. Adorno, "On Subject and Object," 247.
269. Adorno, "Marginalia on Theory and Praxis," in *Critical Models*, 261.
270. Ibid.
271. Ibid., 276.
272. Ibid., 265.
273. Goetschel, "Theory-Praxis," 16.
274. Marx, "The German Ideology," 172.

Chapter 7

1. Butler, *Senses of the Subject*, 16.
2. Grusin, *The Nonhuman Turn*.
3. Augustine, "The Literal Meaning of Genesis," in *On Genesis*, VI.26, 371.
4. Ibid., 342.
5. Ibid., 357–58.
6. Ibid., 370.
7. Ibid., 390.
8. Augustine, *Confessions*, 161.
9. Descartes, *Principles*, CSM I.205.
10. Ibid.
11. Descartes, *Meditations*, CSM II.40.
12. Ibid., CSMK.23.
13. Descartes, *Principles*, CSM I.204.
14. Descartes, *Meditations*, CSM II.40.
15. Descartes, *Discourse*, CSM I.142.
16. Braidotti, *The Posthuman*.
17. Melamed, "Spinoza's Anti-Humanism."

18. Ibid., 161n56.
19. Sharp, *Spinoza and the Politics of Renaturalization*.
20. Bennett, *Vibrant Matter*, xiii.
21. Ibid., xvi.
22. Ibid., 5.
23. Ibid., xvi.
24. Ibid., 93.
25. Ibid., xvi.
26. Ibid., 3.
27. Ibid., 117.
28. Ibid., 120.
29. Ibid.
30. Ibid.
31. Ibid., 121.
32. Ibid.
33. Ibid., 122.
34. Ibid.
35. Ibid.
36. Ibid., x.
37. Ibid., 3.
38. Ibid, ix.
39. Ibid., 118.
40. Ibid., 97.
41. Ibid., 98.
42. Ibid., 97.
43. Ibid., 98.
44. See Levis, et al. "Persistent Effects of Pre-Columbian Plant Domestication on Amazonian Forest Composition"; Lombardo et al. "Early Holocene Crop Cultivation and Landscape Modification in Amazonia."
45. Bennett, *Vibrant Matter*, 98.
46. Ibid.
47. Ibid., 108.
48. Ibid., 109.
49. Ibid., 84.
50. Ibid., xiii.
51. Ibid., 115.
52. EIIIp7dem.
53. CM I.6.
54. Ibid.
55. EIVp24.
56. EIIIGDAexp.
57. EIIp7schol.
58. Descartes, *Principles*, CSM I.240.

59. Elisabeth of Bohemia and Descartes, *The Correspondence*, 107.
60. Ibid., 107.
61. Ibid., 110.
62. Ibid., 110–11.
63. Descartes, *Passions*, CSM I.346.
64. Ibid., CSM I.347.
65. Ibid.
66. Ibid., CSM I.348.
67. Ibid.
68. Ibid., CSM I.384.
69. Ibid., CSM I.404.
70. Ibid., *Discourse*, CSM I.142–43.
71. EIIp3schol.
72. EVp10schol.
73. Letter 43.
74. Letter 42.
75. Letter 58.
76. EIIIpref.
77. Ibid.
78. Letter 58.
79. Ibid.
80. Ibid.
81. Ibid.
82. Ibid.
83. EIIIpref.
84. Montag, "Commanding the Body," 147.
85. EIIp48.
86. EIIp48dem.
87. EIIIp2schol.
88. EIIp9schol.
89. EIIIpDA1.
90. Ibid.
91. Ibid.
92. EIIIpDA1ex.
93. Ibid.
94. Ibid.
95. Ibid.
96. EIIIp2schol.
97. Ibid.
98. EIIIp9schol.
99. EIVp8dem.
100. Ibid.
101. Ibid.

102. Ibid.
103. EIVappI.
104. EIIIdef3.
105. EIIIp11.
106. EIIIdef2.
107. EVp23schol.
108. EIIIp59dem.
109. EIIIp58dem.
110. EIIIp59.
111. EIIIGDA.
112. EIIIp58dem.
113. Descartes, *Passions*, CSM I.328; 338–39.
114. Evp3.
115. Evp4schol.
116. EIVp2.
117. EIVapp.XXXIII.
118. EIVp6.
119. EIIIp17dem.
120. EIIIp15.
121. EIIIp50.
122. EIIIP50schol.
123. Berlant, *Cruel Optimism*.
124. EIIIp28.
125. EIIIp26.
126. EIVp44schol.
127. EIIIp2schol.
128. EIVp60schol.
129. EIIIp44schol.
130. EIVp9; EIVp60schol.
131. EIVapp.XXX.
132. EIIIp57dem.
133. EIVp35schol.
134. EIIIp51schol.
135. EIIIDA.XXVII.
136. EIIIDAXXVIex.
137. EIIIp51schol.
138. EIIIDAXXVIIex.
139. Ibid.
140. EIIIp49schol.
141. EIIIp26.
142. EIIIp27cor1.
143. EIIIp34.
144. EIIIp40.

145. EIIIp41.
146. EIIIp45.
147. Ibid.
148. See Nadler, "Spinoza's Moral Philosophy"; Marshall, "Moral Realism in Spinoza's *Ethics*."
149. Balibar, *Spinoza, the Transindividual*.
150. EIIIDAXXV.
151. EIVp52schol.
152. EIVp25.
153. EIVp52schol.
154. EIIIp55schol.
155. EIIIp30schol.
156. EIVp58schol.
157. Ibid.
158. EIIIp55schol.
159. Ibid.
160. Ibid.
161. Ibid.
162. Ibid.
163. Ibid.
164. EIVp53dem.
165. Ibid.
166. EIIp49schol.; EIVp18schol.; EpIV20schol.; Letter 23.
167. EIVp18schol.
168. EIVp20schol.
169. Ibid.
170. Ibid.
171. Barbone and Rice, "Spinoza and the Problem of Suicide," 241.
172. Ibid.
173. EIVp18schol.
174. Butler, "Spinoza's *Ethics* Under Pressure," 76–77.
175. EIIIp11.
176. EIVp21.
177. EIVp21dem.
178. EIVp22cor.
179. EIVdef8.
180. EIVp52schol.
181. EIVp25.
182. EIVp31.
183. EIVp29.
184. EIVp30.
185. EIVp31cor.
186. EIVappIX.

187. EIVappVII.
188. EIVp18schol.
189. Ibid.
190. EIVp35schol.
191. Ibid.
192. Ibid.
193. EIIIp57schol.
194. Ibid.
195. Ibid.
196. EIVapp.XIII.
197. Ibid.
198. Descartes, CSMK.302.
199. Ibid.
200. Ibid.
201. EIIIp2schol.
202. EIVp37schol1.
203. Ibid.
204. Sharp, *Spinoza and the Politics of Renaturalization*, 193.
205. EIVp35.
206. James, "Spinoza on the Constitution of Animal Species," 370.
207. Maimonides, *Guide of the Perplexed*, I.46. Also I.26, I.49, II.Introduction, II.1, II.4, II.10, III.17.
208. See Bernstein, "Love and Friendship in Spinoza's Thinking," 8n10.
209. Maimonides, *Shemoneh Peraqim*, 1.3.
210. Maimonides, *Guide of the Perplexed*, I.72, 191.
211. Ibid., III.17, 473–74.
212. Ibid., III.48, 599.
213. EIIp39cor.
214. EIIp29schol.
215. EIVp35.
216. EIVp35dem.
217. EVp27dem.
218. EVp36schol.
219. EVp39schol.
220. Ibid.
221. KV, II.2.
222. EVp26.
223. EVp27dem.
224. KV, II.21.
225. EVax.2.
226. EIVp66schol.
227. EVp42.
228. EIIIp14.

229. EIVp59.
230. EVp3.
231. EVp4schol.
232. Ibid.
233. EVp7dem.
234. EVp10schol.
235. Ibid.
236. EIVp37schol.2.
237. Ibid.
238. EIVp37schol.1.
239. EIVapp.XV.
240. Ibid.
241. EIVapp.XXV.
242. Maimonides, *Guide of the Perplexed*, III.27, 510.
243. Ibid., 511.
244. Ibid., 510.
245. Ibid., 511.
246. EIVp35schol.
247. Maimonides, *Guide of the Perplexed*, III.31, 524.
248. Ibid., I.31, 67.

249. For readings that refuse transcendence, see Klein, "Materializing Spinoza's Account of Human Freedom"; Klein, "'Something of It Remains'"; Bernstein, "Love and Friendship in Spinoza's Thinking."

250. See EVp39dem.; EVp41schol.
251. EIIIDAVI.
252. EIIIp30schol.
253. EIIIDAXXV.
254. EVp31schol.
255. EVp32dem.
256. EVp40.
257. EVp36.
258. EIVapp.XXXII.
259. EVp36cor.
260. EVp36.
261. Ibid.

262. See H. A. Wolfson, *The Philosophy of Spinoza*, 311–16; Harvey, "'Ishq, hesheq, *and* amor Dei intellectualis"; Harvey "The Biblical Term 'Glory' in Spinoza's *Ethics*."

263. Exodus 33:13.
264. Exodus 33:18.
265. Exodus 33:19.
266. Maimonides, *Guide of the Perplexed*, I.54, 124.
267. Ibid., 125.

268. EIVapp.IV.
269. Maimonides, *Guide of the Perplexed*, I.54, 125.
270. See Sifre Devarim 11:49; b.Talmud Sotah 14a. See also Maimonides, Mishnah Torah Hilkhot De'ot, 1.6; Maimonides, Sefer Ha-Mitsvot, *'Aseh* 8.
271. Maimonides, *Guide of the Perplexed*, I.54, 125.
272. Jeremiah 9:22–23.
273. Maimonides, *Guide of the Perplexed*, III.54, 637.
274. TTP, XIII.20.
275. Exodus 34:6–7.
276. TTP, XIII.20
277. Maimonides, *Guide of the Perplexed*, III.54, 635.
278. Ibid.
279. Ibid., 638.
280. Ibid., 621.
281. Ibid., 627.
282. EId7.
283. EIIp3schol.
284. Ibid.
285. EIapp.
286. EIIIpref.
287. TP, II.11.
288. EVp5dem.
289. EIVAXXXII.
290. EVp41schol.
291. Ibid.
292. Ep59dem.
293. EIVp67dem.
294. EVp36schol.

Bibliography

Spinoza's Works
Spinoza, Benedict de. *The Collected Works of Spinoza*. Edited and translated by Edwin Curley. 2 vols. Princeton University Press, 2016.
———. *Complete Works*. Edited by Michael Morgan and translated by Samuel Shirley. Hackett, 2002.
———. *Œuvres, vol. IV: Ethica/Éthique*. Edited by Fokke Akkerman and Piet Steenbakkers and translated by Pierre-François Moreau. Presses Universitaires de France, 2020.
———. *Opera Posthuma*. Amsterdam: 1677.
———. *Spinoza: Opera*. Edited by Carl Gebhardt. Winter, 1925.
———. *The Vatican Manuscript of Spinoza's "Ethica."* Edited by Leen Spruit and Pina Totaro. Brill, 2011.

Other Works
Åkerman, Susanna. *Queen Christina of Sweden and Her Circle: The Transformation of a Seventeenth-Century Philosophical Libertine*. Brill, 1991.
Adorno, Theodor. *Critical Models: Interventions and Catchwords*. Translated by Henry W. Pickford. Columbia University Press, 1998.
———. *Minima Moralia: Reflections from Damaged Life*. Verso, 2005.
———. *Negative Dialectics*. Translated by E. B. Ashton. Continuum, 1973.
Agamben, Giorgio. *Homo Sacer: Sovereign Power and Bare Life*. Translated by Daniel Heller-Roazen. Stanford University Press, 2017.
Althusser, Louis. *Essays in Self-Criticism*. Translated by Grahame Lock. NLB, 1976.
———. "The Only Materialist Tradition." In *The New Spinoza*, edited by Warren Montag and Ted Stolze. University of Minnesota Press, 1997.

———. *Psychoanalysis and the Human Sciences*. Translated by Steven Rendall. Columbia University Press, 2016.

———. "The Underground Current of the Materialism of the Encounter." In *Philosophy of the Encounter, Later Writings, 1978–87*, translated by G. M. Goshgarian. Verso, 2006.

Altmann, Alexander. "Free Will and Predestination in Saadia, Bahya, and Maimonides." In *Essays in Jewish Intellectual History*. University Press of New England, 1981.

———. *Moses Mendelssohn: A Biographical Study*. Oxford: The Littman Library of Jewish Civilization, 1973.

Appiah, K. Anthony. "Race, Culture, Identity: Misunderstood Connections." In *Color Consciousness: The Political Morality of Race*. Princeton University Press, 1996.

Aristotle. *The Complete Works of Aristotle*, 2 vols. Edited by Jonathan Barnes. Princeton University Press, 1984.

Astell, Mary. *A Serious Proposal to the Ladies*. Edited by Patricia Springborg. Broadview Literary Texts, 2002.

Augustine. *The City of God Against the Pagans*. Translated by R. W. Dyson. Cambridge University Press, 2013.

———. *The Confessions*. Translated by Maria Boulding. New City Press, 1997.

———. *On Genesis*. Translated by Edmund Hill. New City Press, 2002.

———. *On the Trinity, Books 8–15*. Translated by Stephen McKenna. Cambridge University Press, 2002.

Avicenna. *The Metaphysics of* The Healing. Translated by Michael E. Marmura. Brigham Young University Press, 2005.

Avineri, Shlomo. *Karl Marx: Philosophy and Revolution*. Yale University Press, 2019.

Badiou, Alain. *Being and Event*. Translated by Oliver Feltham. Continuum, 2005.

———. *Deleuze: The Clamor of Being*. Translated by Louise Burchill. University of Minnesota Press, 2000.

———. "L'émancipation, c'est celle de l'humanité tout entière," *Revue Ballast*, April 27, 2015. https://www.revue-ballast.fr/alain-badiou-lemancipation-cest-celle-de-lhumanite-tout-entiere/.

———. *Theoretical Writings*. Translated by Ray Brassier and Alberto Toscano. Bloomsbury, 2015.

———. *Theory of the Subject*. Translated by Bruno Bosteels. Continuum, 2009.

———. "What Is a Proof in Spinoza's *Ethics*?" In *Spinoza Now*, edited by Dimitris Vardoulakis. University of Minnesota Press, 2011.

Balibar, Étienne. *Spinoza and Politics*. Translated by Peter Snowdon. Verso, 2008.

———. *Spinoza, the Transindividual*. Translated by Mark G. E. Kelly. Edinburgh University Press, 2020.

Baracchi, Claudia. *Aristotle's Ethics as First Philosophy*. Cambridge University Press, 2007.

Barad, Karen. *Meeting the Universe Halfway: Quantum Physics and the Entanglement of Matter and Meaning.* Duke University Press, 2007.
——. "Transmaterialities: Trans*/Matter/Realities and Queer Political Imaginings." *GLQ* 21, no. 2/3 (2015): 387–422.
Barbapiccola, Giuseppa-Eleanora. "Preface to René Descartes's Principles of Philosophy." In *The Contest for Knowledge: Debates over Women's Learning in Eighteenth-Century Italy.* Translated by Rebecca Messbarger and Paula Findlen. University of Chicago Press, 2005.
Barbone, Steven, and Lee Rice. "Spinoza and the Problem of Suicide." *International Philosophical Quarterly* 34, no. 2 (1994): 229–41.
Basnage, Jacques. *The History of the Jews, from Jesus Christ to the Present Time.* Translated by Thomas Taylor. T. Bever, and B. Lintot, 1708.
Bauer, Bruno. *The Jewish Problem.* Translated by Helen Lederer. Hebrew Union College-Jewish Institute of Religion, 1958.
Bayle, Pierre, et al. "Spinoza." In *Dictionaire historique et critique: Cinquieme edition, revue, corrigée, et augmentée.* Leyden, 1740.
Beckstead, Nicholas. "On the Overwhelming Importance of Shaping the Far Future." PhD diss., Rutgers University, 2013. Proquest (3597734).
Beiser, Frederick C. *The Fate of Reason: German Philosophy from Kant to Fichte.* Harvard University Press, 1987.
Benjamin, Walter. "On the Concept of History." In *Walter Benjamin, Selected Writings*, vol. 4, 1938–1940. Translated by Edmund Jephcott et al. Belknap Press, 2003.
Bennett, Jane. *Vibrant Matter: A Political Ecology of Things.* Duke University Press, 2009.
Bennett, Jonathan. *A Study of Spinoza's Ethics.* Hackett, 1984.
Bensaïd, Daniel. "Alain Badiou and the Miracle of the Event." In *Think Again: Alain Badiou and the Future of Philosophy.* Edited by Peter Hallward. Continuum, 2004.
Berlant, Lauren. *Cruel Optimism.* Duke University Press, 2011.
Bernard, Walter. "Psychotherapeutic Principles in Spinoza's *Ethics*." In *Speculum Spinozanum 1677–1977*, edited by Siegfried Hessing. Routledge & Kegan Paul, 1977.
Bernstein, Jeffery. "Love and Friendship in Spinoza's Thinking." *NASS Monograph* 9 (2000):1–15.
Bloch, Ernst. *Avicenna and the Aristotelian Left.* Translated by Loren Goldman and Peter Thompson. Columbia University Press, 2019.
Blumenberg, Hans. *The Legitimacy of the Modern Age.* Translated by Robert M. Wallace. MIT Press, 1966.
Borcherding, Julia. "Loving the Body, Loving the Soul: Conway's Vitalist Critique of Cartesian and Morean Dualism." In *Oxford Studies in Early Modern Philosophy*, edited by Donald Rutherford. Oxford University Press, 2019.
Bordo, Susan. *The Flight to Objectivity: Essays on Cartesianism and Culture.* State University of New York Press, 1987.

Bottici, Chiara. *Anarchafeminism*. Bloomsbury Publishing, 2021.
Braidotti, Rosi. *The Posthuman*. Polity Press, 2013.
Brassier, Ray. *Nihil Unbound: Enlightenment and Extinction*. Palgrave Macmillan, 2007.
Broad, Jacqueline. *Women Philosophers of the Seventeenth Century*. Cambridge University Press, 2003.
Buber, Martin. *Eclipse of God: Studies in the Relation Between Religion and Philosophy*. Princeton University Press, 2016.
———. *The Origin and Meaning of Hasidism*. Translated by Maurice Friedman. Horizon Press, 1960.
Butler, Judith. *Gender Trouble*. Routledge, 1990.
———. "Spinoza's *Ethics* Under Pressure." In *Senses of the Subject*. Fordham University Press, 2015.
Campos, Andre. *Spinoza's Revolution in Natural Law*. Palgrave Macmillan, 2012.
Casas, Bartolome de las. *Witness: Writings of Bartolome de las Casas*. Translated by George Sanderlin. Orbis Books, 1971.
Césaire, Aimé. *Discourse on Colonialism*. Translated by Joan Pinkham. Monthly Review Press, 2000.
Cohen, Hermann. *Spinoza on State and Religion, Judaism and Christianity*. Translated by Robert S. Schine. Shalem Press, 2014.
Conway, Anne. *The Principles of the Most Ancient and Modern Philosophy*. Cambridge University Press, 1996.
Crescas, Hasdai. *Light of the Lord* (Or Hashem). Translated by Roslyn Weiss. Oxford University Press, 2018.
Curley, Edwin. *Behind the Geometrical Method: A Reading of Spinoza's* Ethics. Princeton University Press, 1988.
Dea, Shannon. "The Infinite and Indeterminate in Spinoza." *Dialogue* 50 (2011): 603–21.
Deleuze, Gilles. *Desert Islands and Other Texts, 1953–1974*. Translated by Michael Taormina. Semiotext(e): 2004.
———. *Difference and Repetition*. Translated by Paul Patton. Columbia University Press, 1994.
———. *Expressionism in Philosophy: Spinoza*. Translated by Martin Joughin. Zone Books, 1992.
———. *The Fold: Leibniz and the Baroque*. Translated by Tom Conley. The Athlone Press, 1993.
———. *The Logic of Sense*. Translated by Mark Lester with Charles Stivale. Columbia University Press, 1990.
———. *Spinoza: Practical Philosophy*. Translated by Robert Hurley. City Light Books, 1988.
Deleuze, Gilles, and Félix Guattari. *What Is Philosophy?* Translated by Hugh Tomlinson and Graham Burchell. Columbia University Press, 1994.

DeLire, Luce. "Spinoza's Metaphysics of Infinity." PhD diss., Johns Hopkins University, 2023.
Della Rocca, Michael. *Spinoza*. Routledge, 2008.
———. "The Elusiveness of the One and the Many in Spinoza: Substance, Attribute, and Mode." In *Spinoza in Twenty-First Century American and French Philosophy: Metaphysics, Philosophy of Mind, Moral and Political Philosophy*, edited by Jack Stetter and Charles Ramond. Bloomsbury Academic, 2019.
———. *Representation and the Mind Body Problem in Spinoza*. Oxford University Press, 1996.
Derrida, Jacques. *The Beast & the Sovereign, II*. Translated by Geoffrey Bennington. University of Chicago Press, 2011.
———. "Language and Discourse on Method." Translated by Willi Goetschel and Warren Montag. *Bamidbar: Journal of Jewish Thought and Philosophy* 1, no. 2 (2011): 60–96.
———. "My Chances / *Mes Chances*: A Rendezvous with Some Epicurean Stereophonies." In *Psyche: Inventions of the Other*. Stanford University Press, 2007.
———. "Shibboleth: For Paul Celan." In *Word Traces: Readings of Paul Celan*, edited by Aris Fioretos. Johns Hopkins University, 1994.
Descartes, René. *The Philosophical Writings of Descartes*. 3 volumes. Translated by John Cottingham et al. Cambridge University Press, 1984–1991.
Dias, A. M. Vaz, and W. G. van der Tak. "Spinoza, Merchant and Autodidact." *Studia Rosenthaliana* 16 (1982):105–95.
Diderot, Denis, and Jean d'Alembert, eds. *L'Encyclopédie, ou, Dictionnaire raisonné des sciences, des arts, et des métiers, par une societé des gens de lettres*. Paris, 1751–72.
Dika, Tarek. *Descartes's Method: The Formation of the Subject of Science*. Oxford University Press, 2023.
di Poppa, Francesca. "Spinoza and Process Ontology." *Southern Journal of Philosophy* 48, no. 3 (September 2010): 272–94.
Dobbs-Weinstein, Idit. "The Ambiguity of Imagination and the Ambivalence of Language in Maimonides and Spinoza." In *Maimonides and his Heritage*, edited by Idit Dobbs-Weinstein et al. State University of New York Press, 2009.
———. "Gersonides's Radically Modern Understanding of the Agent Intellect." *Meeting of the Minds: The Relations Between Medieval and Classical Modern European Philosophy, Recontres de Philosophie Médiévale* 7, (1998): 191–213.
———. "Maimonidean Aspects in Spinoza's Thought," *Graduate Faculty Philosophy Journal* 17, no. 1/2 (1994):153–74.
———. *Spinoza's Critique of Religion and Its Heirs: Marx, Benjamin, Adorno*. Cambridge University Press, 2015.
———. "Thinking Desire in Gersonides and Spinoza." In *Women and Gender in Jewish Philosophy*, edited by Hava Tirosh-Samuelson. Indiana University Press, 2004.

Dussel, Enrique. "Anti-Cartesian Meditations: On the Origin of the Philosophical Anti-Discourse of Modernity." Translated by George Ciccariello-Maher. *Journal for Cultural and Religious Theory* 13, no. 1 (2014): 11–53.

———. *The Invention of the Americas: Eclipse of "the Other" and the Myth of Modernity.* Translated by Michael D. Barber. Continuum, 1995.

Elisabeth of Bohemia and René Descartes, *The Correspondence Between Elisabeth of Bohemia and René Descartes.* Translated by Lisa Shapiro. University of Chicago Press, 2007.

Elshtain, Jean Bethke. *Sovereignty: God, State, and Self.* Basic Books, 2008.

Engels, Friedrich. *Marx and Engels: Collected Works*, 50 vols. International Publishers, 1975–2006.

Euclid. *The Thirteen Books of Euclid's Elements.* Translated by Thomas L. Heath. Dover Publications, 1956.

Eze, Emmanuel Chukwudi. *Achieving Our Humanity: The Idea of the Postracial Future.* Routledge, 2001.

Ezra, Abraham ibn. *Perush ibn Ezra 'al ha-Torah.* 3 vol. Edited by Asher Veizer. Mossad Harav Kook, 1996.

Fanon, Frantz. *Black Skin, White Masks.* Translated by Richard Philcox. Grove Press, 2008.

Fausto-Sterling, Anne. *Sexing the Body: Gender Politics and the Construction of Sexuality.* Basic Books, 2020.

Fraenkel, Carlos. "Ḥasdai Crescas on God as Place of the World and Spinoza's Notion of God as 'Res Extensa.'" *Aleph* 9, no. 1 (2009): 77–111.

———. "Maimonides' God and Spinoza's *Deus sive Natura.*" *Journal of the History of Philosophy* 44, no. 2 (2006): 169–215.

———. "Reconsidering the Case of Elijah Delmedigo's Averroism and Its Impact on Spinoza." In *Renaissance Averroism and Its Aftermath: Arabic Philosophy in Early Modern Europe*, edited by Anna Akasoy and Guido Giglioni. Springer, 2013.

———. "Spinoza and Philosophy and Religion: The Averroistic Sources." In *The Rationalists: Between Tradition and Innovation*, edited by Carlos Fraenkel et al. Springer, 2010.

Franks, Paul. "Inner Anti-Semitism or Kabbalistic Legacy? German Idealism's Relationship to Judaism." In *Glaube und Vernunft / Faith and Reason*, edited by Jurgen Stolzenberg and Fred Rush. De Gruyter, 2010.

———. "'Nothing Comes from Nothing': Judaism, the Orient, and Kabbalah in Hegel's Reception of Spinoza." In *The Oxford Handbook of Spinoza*, edited by Michael Della Rocca. Oxford University Press, 2017.

Funkenstein, Amos. *Theology and the Scientific Imagination, from the Middle Ages to the Seventeenth Century.* Princeton University Press, 1986.

Garber, Daniel. "God, Laws, and the Order of Nature: Descartes and Leibniz, Hobbes and Spinoza." In *The Divine Order, the Human Order, and the Order of Nature: Historical Perspectives*, edited by Eric Watkins. Oxford University Press, 2013.

Garret, Aaron. *Meaning in Spinoza's Method.* Cambridge University Press, 2003.

Gatens, Moira, ed. *Feminist Interpretations of Benedict Spinoza*. Pennsylvania State University Press, 2009.
———. *Imaginary Bodies: Ethics, Power and Corporeality*. Routledge, 1996.
Gersonides, Levi. *The Wars of the Lord*. 3 vols. Translated by Seymour Feldman. The Jewish Publication Society, 1984–1999.
Gill-Peterson, Jules. *A Short History of Trans Misogyny*. Verso, 2024.
Gillespie, Michael. *The Theological Origins of Modernity*. University of Chicago Press, 2008.
Gillespie, Sam. "Placing the Void: Badiou on Spinoza." *Angelaki: Journal of Theoretical Humanities* 6, no. 3 (2001): 63–77.
Goetschel, Willi. "Spinoza's Dream." *Cambridge Journal of Postcolonial Literary Theory* 3 no. 1 (2016): 39–54.
———. *Spinoza's Modernity: Mendelssohn, Lessing, and Heine*. University of Wisconsin Press, 2004.
———. "Theory-Praxis: Spinoza, Hess, Marx, and Adorno." *Bamidbar: Journal of Jewish Thought and Philosophy* 2 (2013): 16–28.
Goldenbaum, Ursula. "The *Pantheismusstreit*." In *Spinoza's Ethics, A Collective Commentary*, edited by Michael Hampe et al. Brill, 2011.
Gordon, Lewis P. *Fanon and the Crisis of European Man: An Essay on Philosophy and the Human Sciences*. Routledge, 1995.
Grant, Edward. *Much Ado About Nothing*. Cambridge University Press, 1981.
Grusin, Richard, ed. *The Nonhuman Turn*. University of Minnesota Press, 2015.
Guéroult, Martial. *Spinoza I: Dieu*. Aubier-Montaigne, 1968.
———. *Spinoza II: L'Âme*. Aubier-Montaigne, 1974.
Hallett, H. F. *Benedict de Spinoza: The Elements of his Philosophy*. The Athlone Press, 1957.
Hallward, Peter. *Badiou: A Subject to Truth*. University of Minnesota Press, 2003.
Harman, Graham. *Object-Oriented Ontology: A New Theory of Everything*. Pelican Books, 2017.
———. *Tool-Being: Heidegger and the Metaphysics of Objects*. Open Court, 2002.
———. *Weird Realism: Lovecraft and Philosophy*. Zero Books, 2012.
Harth, Erica. "Cartesian Women." In *Feminist Interpretations of René Descartes*, edited by Susan Bordo. The Pennsylvania State University Press, 1999.
———. *Cartesian Women: Versions and Subversions of Rational Discourse in the Old Regime*. Cornell University Press, 1992.
Harvey, Warren Zev. "The Biblical Term 'Glory' in Spinoza's *Ethics*." *Iyyun* 48 (1999): 447–49.
———. "Gersonides and Spinoza on Conatus." *Aleph* 12, no. 2 (2012): 273–97.
———. "'Ishq, hesheq, *and* amor Dei intellectualis." In *Spinoza and Medieval Jewish Philosophy*, edited by Steven Nadler. Cambridge University Press, 2014.
———. *Physics and Metaphysics in Ḥasdai Crescas*. J. C. Gieben, 1998.
———. "A Portrait of Spinoza as a Maimonidean." *Journal of the History of Philosophy* 19, no. 2 (1981): 151–72.

———. "Spinoza on Biblical Miracles." *Journal of the History of Ideas* 74, no. 4 (2013): 659–75.

———. "Spinoza and Maimonides on Teleology and Anthropocentrism." In *Spinoza's Ethics*, edited by Yitzhak Melamed. Cambridge University Press, 2017.

———. "Spinoza and Maimonides on True Religion." In *A Companion to Spinoza*, edited by Yitzhak Melamed. Wiley Blackwell, 2021.

———. "A Third Approach to Maimonides' Cosmogony-Prophetology Puzzle." *Harvard Theological Reviews* 74, no. 3 (1981): 287–301.

Hegel, G. W. F. *Encyclopedia of the Philosophical Sciences in Basic Outline*. Cambridge University Press, 2010.

———. *Lectures on the History of Philosophy: Greek Philosophy to Plato*. Translated by E. S. Haldane. University of Nebraska Press, 1995.

———. *Lectures on the History of Philosophy: Medieval and Modern Philosophy*. Translated by E. S. Haldane and Frances H. Simson. University of Nebraska Press, 1995.

———. *Lectures on the Philosophy of History*. Translated by Ruben Alvarado. Wordbridge Publishing, 2011.

———. *Lectures on the Philosophy of Religion*. Edited by Peter C. Hogden. Oxford University Press, 2006.

———. *The Phenomenology of Spirit*. Translated by Terry Pinkard. Cambridge University Press, 2018.

———. *The Science of Logic*. Translated by George di Giovanni. Cambridge University Press, 2010.

Heidegger, Martin. "The Age of the World Picture." In *Off the Beaten Track*, translated by Julian Young and Kenneth Haynes. Cambridge University Press, 2002.

———. *Being and Time*. Translated by Joan Stambaugh. State University of New York Press, 2010.

———. *Identity and Difference*. Translated by Joan Stambaugh. University of Chicago Press, 2002.

Herrera, Abraham Cohen de. *Gate of Heaven*. Translated by Kenneth Krabbenhoft. Brill, 2002.

Hess, Moses. "The Philosophy of the Act." In *Socialist Thought: A Documentary History*. Edited by Albert Fried and Ronald Sanders. Aldine Publishing Company, 1964.

Horkheimer, Max, and Theodor Adorno. *Dialectic of Enlightenment: Philosophical Fragments*. Translated by Edmund Jephcott. Stanford University Press, 2002.

Hübner, Karolina. "Spinoza's Thinking Substance and the Necessity of Modes." *Philosophy and Phenomenological Research* 92, no. 1 (2014) 1–40.

Hyman, Arthur. "Spinoza's Dogmas of Universal Faith in the Light of Their Medieval Jewish Background." In *Biblical and Other Studies*, edited by Alexander Altmann. Harvard University Press, 1963.

———. "Spinoza on Possibility and Contingency." In *Meeting of the Minds: The Relations Between Medieval and Classical Modern European Philosophy (Acts of the International Colloquium, Boston College, June 14–16, 1998)*. Brepols, 1998.

Israel, Jonathan. *Democratic Enlightenment: Philosophy, Revolution, and Human Rights 1750–1790*. Oxford University Press, 2013.

———. *Revolutionary Jews: From Spinoza to Marx: The Fight for a Secular World of Universal and Equal Rights*. University of Washington Press, 2021.

———. *Spinoza: Life and Legacy*. Oxford University Press, 2023.

Jacobi, Friedrich Heinrich. *The Main Philosophical Writings and the Novel Allwill*. Translated by George di Giovanni. McGill-Queen's University Press, 1994.

Jacobi, Friedrich Heinrich, and Moses Mendelssohn. *Die Hauptschriften zum Pantheismusstreit zwischen Jacobi und Mendelssohn. Herausgegeben und mit einer historischkritischen Einleitung versehen*. Edited by Heinrich Scholz. Reuther & Reichard, 1916.

James, Susan. "The Power of Spinoza: Feminist Conjunctions: Susan James Interviews Genevieve Lloyd and Moira Gatens." *Hypatia* 15, no. 2 (2000): 40–58.

James, Susan. "Spinoza on the Constitution of Animal Species." In *A Companion to Spinoza*, edited by Yitzhak Melamed. Wiley Blackwell, 2021.

Kant, Immanuel. *Critique of Pure Reason*. Translated by Paul Guyer and Allen W. Wood. Cambridge University Press, 1998.

———. "Idea for a Universal History with a Cosmopolitan Purpose." In *Kant: Political Writings*, edited H. S. Reis. Cambridge University Press, 2011.

Kantorowicz, Ernst H. *The King's Two Bodies: A Study in Medieval Political Theology*. Princeton University Press, 1957.

Kelsen, Hans. *Der soziologische und der juristische staatsbegriff: kritische untersuchung des verhältnisses von staat und recht*. Verlag von J. C. B. Mohr, 1922.

———. "God and State." In *Essays in Legal and Moral Philosophy*. Translated by Peter Heath. D. Reidel Publishing Company, 1973.

Klein, Julie R. "Aristotle and Descartes in Spinoza's Approach to Matter and Body." *Graduate Faculty Philosophy Journal* 26, no. 2 (2005): 157–76.

———. "Dreaming with Open Eyes: Cartesian Dreams, Spinozan Analyses." *Idealistic Studies* 33, no. 2/3 (2003): 141–59.

———. "Materializing Spinoza's Account of Human Freedom." In *Freedom, Action, and Motivation in Spinoza's Ethics*, edited by Noa Naaman-Zauderer. Routledge, 2019.

———. "Nature's Metabolism: On Eating in Derrida, Agamben, and Spinoza." *Research in Phenomenology* 33 (2003): 186–217.

———. "'Something of It Remains': Spinoza and Gersonides in Intellectual Eternity." In *Spinoza and Medieval Jewish Philosophy*, edited by Steven Nadler. Cambridge University Press, 2014.

———. "Spinoza's Debt to Gersonides." *Graduate Faculty Philosophy Journal* 24, no. 1 (2003): 19–43.

Kletenik, Gilah. "To Infinity, Not Beyond: Spinoza's Ontology of the Not One." In *New Paths: Essays in Honor of Professor Elliot Wolfson*, edited by Glenn Dynner et al. Purdue University Press, 2024.

Lærke, Mogens. "Aspects of Spinoza's Theory of Essence: Formal Essence, Non-

Existence, and Two Types of Actuality." In *The Actual and the Possible: Modality and Metaphysics in Modern Philosophy*, edited by Mark Sinclair. Oxford University Press, 2017.

———. "Spinoza's Monism? What Monism?" In *Spinoza on Monism*, edited by Philip Goff. Palgrave Macmillan, 2012.

Leibniz, Gottfried Wilhelm. *Die philosophischen Schriften*. 7 vols. Edited by C. I. Gerhardt. Georg Olms, 1965.

———. *Philosophical Papers and Letters*. Translated by Leroy E. Loemker. Kluwer Academic Publishers, 1989.

———. *Theodicy: Essays on the Goodness of God, the Freedom on Man and the Origin of Evil*. Translated by E. M. Huggard. Open Court, 1985.

Levinas, Emmanuel. *Totality and Infinity: An Essay on Exteriority*. Translated by Alphonso Lingis. Duquesne University Press, 1969.

Levis, C., et al. "Persistent Effects of Pre-Columbian Plant Domestication on Amazonian Forest Composition." *Science* 355, no. 6328 (2017): 925–31.

Librett, Jeffery. "Humanist Antiformalism as a Theopolitics of Race: F. H. Jacobi on Friend and Enemy." *Eighteenth-Century Studies* 32, no. 2 (1998–99): 233–45.

———. *Orientalism and the Figure of the Jew*. Fordham University Press, 2014.

Lin, Martin. "The Principle of Sufficient Reason in Spinoza." In *The Oxford Handbook of Spinoza*, edited by Michael Della Rocca. Oxford University Press, 2018.

Lloyd, Genevieve. *The Man of Reason: "Male" and "Female" in Western Philosophy*. Routledge, 1984.

———. *Part of Nature: Self-Knowledge in Spinoza's Ethics*. Cornell University Press, 1994.

Lombardo, Umberto, et al. "Early Holocene Crop Cultivation and Landscape Modification in Amazonia." *Nature* 581 (2020): 190–93.

Lord, Beth. "Outside of Human Nature: Spinoza on Affective Difference." *In Circolo: Rivista di filosofia* 10 (2020): 421–32.

Lorde, Audre. "The Master's Tools Will Never Dismantle the Master's House." In *Sister Outsider: Essays and Speeches*. Crossing Press, 2007.

Löwith, Karl. *Meaning in History*. University of Chicago Press, 1957.

Lucchese, Filippo del. "The Mother of All Prejudices: Teleology and Normativity in Spinoza." *Parrhesia* 32, no. 1/2 (2020): 145–70.

Lucretius. *On the Nature of Things*. Translated by Martin Ferguson Smith. Hackett Publishing, 1969.

Luxemburg, Rosa. "The Beginning." In *The Rosa Luxemburg Reader*, translated by William D. Graf. Monthly Review Press, 2004.

MacAskill, William. *What We Owe the Future*. Basic Books, 2022.

Macherey, Pierre. *Hegel or Spinoza*. Translated by Susan M. Ruddick. University of Minnesota Press, 2011.

Mack, Michael. *German Idealism and the Jew: The Inner Anti-Semitism of Philosophy and German Jewish Responses*. University of Chicago Press, 2003.

Maimon, Solomon. *The Autobiography of Solomon Maimon: The Complete Translation*. Translated by Paul Reitter. Princeton University Press, 2018.

———. *Essay on Transcendental Philosophy*. Translated by Nick Midgley et al. Continuum, 2010.

———. *Maaseh Livnat ha-Sapir*. Edited by Gideon Freudenthal. *Tarbiz* 86 (2019): 440–78.

Maimonides, Moses. *The Guide of the Perplexed*, 2 vols. Translated by Shlomo Pines. University of Chicago Press, 1963.

———. *Mishneh Torah*. 14 vols. Mahadurat Shabtai Frenkel, 2001.

———. *Moreh Nevukhim: 'im perush Shem Tov ve-'im perush ha-'Efodi*. Alvise Bragadin, 1551.

Maldonado-Torres, Nelson. "On the Coloniality of Being, Contributions to the Development of a Concept." *Cultural Studies* 21, no. 2/3 (2007): 240–70.

Manekin, Charles. "Spinoza and the Determinist Tradition." In *Spinoza and Medieval Jewish Philosophy*, edited by Steven Nadler. Cambridge University Press, 2014.

Marion, Jean-Luc. *On the Ego and God*. Translated by Christina M. Gschwandtner. Fordham University Press, 2008.

Marshall, Colin. "Moral Realism in Spinoza's *Ethics*." In *Spinoza's Ethics: A Critical Guide*, edited by Yitzhak Melamed. Cambridge University Press, 2017.

Marx, Karl. "The German Ideology." In *The Marx-Engels Reader*, edited by Robert C. Tucker. W. W. Norton & Company, 1978.

Marx, Karl. *The Marx-Engels Reader*, edited by Robert C. Tucker. W. W. Norton & Company, 1978.

Marx, Karl, and Frederick Engels. *Marx and Engels: Collected Works*. 50 vols. International Publishers, 1975–2006.

Mason, Richard. "How Things Happen: Divine-Natural Law in Spinoza." *Studia Leibnitiana* 28 no. 1 (1996): 17–36.

Matysik, Tracie. *When Spinoza Met Marx: Experiments in Nonhumanist Activity*. University of Chicago Press, 2022.

Mbembe, Achille. *Out of the Dark: Essays on Decolonization*. Columbia University Press, 2021.

Meillassoux, Quentin. *After Finitude: An Essay on the Necessity of Contingency*. Bloomsbury, 2010.

Melamed, Yitzhak. "Spinoza's Anti-Humanism: An Outline." In *The Rationalists: Between Tradition and Innovation*, edited by Carlos Fraenkel et al. Springer, 2010.

———. *Spinoza's Metaphysics: Substance and Thought*. Oxford University Press, 2013.

———. "Why Spinoza Is Not an Eleatic Monist (or Why Diversity Exists)." In *Spinoza on Monism*, edited by Philip Goff. Palgrave Macmillan, 2012.

Mendelssohn, Moses. *Last Works*. Translated by Bruce Rosenstock. University of Illinois Press, 2012.

———. *Philosophical Writings*. Translated by Daniel O. Dahlstrom. Cambridge University Press, 1997.

Menn, Stephen. *Descartes and Augustine*. Cambridge University Press, 1998.

Mills, Charles. *Blackness Visible: Essays on Philosophy and Race.* Cornell University Press, 1998.

Mitchell, Audra, and Aadita Chaudhury. "Worlding Beyond 'the' 'End' of 'the World': White Apocalyptic Visions and BIPOC Futurisms." *International Relations* 34, no. 3 (2020): 309–32.

Moder, Gregor. *Hegel and Spinoza: Substance and Negativity.* Northwestern University Press, 2017.

Montag, Warren. *Althusser and His Contemporaries: Philosophy's Perpetual War.* Duke University Press, 2013.

———. "Commanding the Body: The Language of Subjection in *Ethics* III, P2S." In *Spinoza's Authority Volume I: Resistance and Power in* Ethics, edited by Kiarina Kordela and Dimitris Vardoulakis. Bloomsbury Academic, 2018.

———. "Preface." In *The New Spinoza*, edited by Warren Montag and Ted Stolze. University of Minnesota Press, 1997.

More, Henry. "Henry More to Robert Boyle: Monday, 14 December 1671." In *Electronic Enlightenment Scholarly Edition of Correspondence*, edited by Robert McNamee et al. Version 3.0. University of Oxford, 2022.

Morfino, Vittorio. *Plural Temporality: Transindividuality and the Aleatory Between Spinoza and Althusser.* Haymarket Books, 2014.

Morton, Timothy. *Realist Magic: Objects, Ontology, Causality.* Open Humanities Press, 2013.

Nadler, Steven. *Spinoza: A Life.* Cambridge University Press, 1999.

———. "Spinoza's Moral Philosophy." In *A Companion to Spinoza*, edited by Yitzhak Melamed. Wiley Blackwell, 2021.

Nail, Thomas. *Lucretius I: An Ontology of Motion.* Edinburgh University Press, 2018.

Negri, Antonio. *The Savage Anomaly: The Power of Spinoza's Metaphysics and Politics.* Translated by Michael Hardt. University of Minnesota Press, 1991.

———. *Subversive Spinoza: Uncontemporary Variations.* Translated by Timothy S. Murphy et al. Manchester University Press, 2004.

Nicolai, Friedrich. *Über meine gelehrte Bildung, über meine Kenntniß der kritischen Philosophie und meine Schriften.* Berlin, 1799.

Nietzsche, Friedrich. *Sämtliche Briefe: Kritische Studienausgabe in 8 Bänden.* Edited by Giorgio Colli and Mazzino Montinari. Deutscher Taschenbuch Verlag, 2003.

———. *Twilight of the Idols.* Translated by Duncan Large. Oxford University Press, 1998.

Nirenberg, David. *Anti-Judaism: The Western Tradition.* W. W. Norton & Company.

Norris, Christopher. "Spinoza and the Conflict of Interpretations." In *Spinoza Now*, edited by Dimitris Vardoulakis. University of Minnesota Press, 2011.

Ogden, Stephen R. "Avicenna and Spinoza on Essence and Existence." In *A Companion to Spinoza*, edited by Yitzhak Melamed. Wiley Blackwell, 2021.

O'Neill, Eileen. "Women Cartesians, 'Feminine Philosophy,' and Historical Exclusion." In *Feminist Interpretations of René Descartes*, edited by Susan Bordo. The Pennsylvania State University Press, 1999.

Ord, Toby. *The Precipice: Existential Risk and Humanity*. Hachette Books, 2020.

O'Regan, Cyril. "Hegel and Anti-Judaism: Narrative and the Inner Circulation of the Kabbalah." *Owl of Minerva* 28 (1997):141–82.

———. *The Heterodox Hegel*. State University of New York Press, 1994.

Peden, Knox. *Spinoza Contra Phenomenology: French Rationalism from Cavaillès to Deleuze*. Stanford University Press, 2014.

Pellegrin, Marie-Fréderque. "Cartesianism and Feminism." In *The Oxford Handbook of Descartes and Cartesianism*, edited by Steven Nadler et al. Oxford University Press, 2019.

Perry, Ruth. "Radical Doubt and the Liberation of Women." In *Feminist Interpretations of René Descartes*, edited by Susan Bordo. The Pennsylvania State University Press, 1999.

Philo. *The Works of Philo, Completed and Unabridged: New Updated Edition*. Translated by C. D. Yonge. Hendrickson Publishers, 1993.

Pines, Shlomo. "On Spinoza's Conception of Human Freedom and of Good and Evil." In *Studies in the History of Jewish Thought*, edited by Warren Zev Harvey et al. Jerusalem: The Magnes Press, 1997.

———. "The Philosophical Sources of the *Guide of the Perplexed*." In Moses Maimonides, *The Guide of the Perplexed*, translated by Shlomo Pines. University of Chicago Press, 1963.

———. "Spinoza's *Tractatus Theologico-Politicus*, Maimonides and Kant." In *Studies in the History of Jewish Thought*, edited by Warren Zev Harvey et al. The Magnes Press, 1997.

———. "Studies in Abul-Barakāt al-Baghdādī's Poetics and Metaphysics." *Studies in Philosophy, Scripta Hierosolymitana* 6 (1960): 195–98.

Popkin, Richard. "Spinoza, Neoplatonic Kabbalist?" In *Neoplatonism and Jewish Thought*, edited by Lenn Goodman. State University of New York Press, 1992.

Poullain de la Barre, François. "On the Equality of the Two Sexes." In *Three Cartesian Feminist Treatises*, translated by Vivien Bosley. University of Chicago Press, 2002.

Ravven, Heidi M. "Hegel's Epistemic Turn—or Spinoza's?" *Idealistic Studies* 33, no. 1/2 (2003): 195–202.

———. *The Self-Beyond Itself: An Alternative History of Ethics, the New Brain Sciences and the Myth of Free Will*. The New Press, 2013.

Renz, Ursula. *The Explainability of Experience: Realism and Subjectivity in Spinoza's Theory of the Human Mind*. Oxford University Press, 2018.

Riskin, Jessica. *The Restless Clock: A History of the Centuries-Long Argument over What Makes Living Things Tick*. University of Chicago Press, 2016.

Rose, Sven-Erik. *Jewish Philosophical Politics in Germany, 1789–1848*. Brandeis University Press, 2014.

Rosenstock, Bruce. *Philosophy and the Jewish Question: Mendelssohn, Rosenzweig, and Beyond*. Fordham University Press, 2010.

Rosenthal, Michael. "'The Black, Scabby Brazilian': Some Thoughts on Race and Early Modern Philosophy." *Philosophy and Social Criticism* 31, no. 2 (2005): 211–21.

Roth, Leon. *Spinoza, Descartes and Maimonides*. Clarendon Press, 1924.

Rudavsky, Tamar. "Feminism and Modern Jewish Philosophy." In *The Cambridge Companion to Modern Jewish Philosophy*, edited by Michael L. Morgan and Peter E. Gordon. Cambridge University Press, 2007.

———. "Time, Space, and Infinity." In *The Cambridge History of Jewish Philosophy: From Antiquity Through the Seventeenth Century*, edited by Steven Nadler and Tamar Rudavsky. Cambridge University Press, 2009.

Rutherford, Donald. "Spinoza's Conception of Law: Metaphysics and Ethics." In *Spinoza's "Theological-Political Treatise": A Critical Guide*, edited by Yitzhak Melamed and Michael Rosenthal. Cambridge University Press, 2010.

Schmitt, Carl. *Political Theology: Four Chapters on the Concept of Sovereignty*. Translated by George Schwab. University of Chicago Press, 1985.

———. *Political Theology II: The Myth of the Closure of Any Political Theology*. Translated by Michael Hoelzl and Graham Ward. Polity Press, 2008.

Schwartz, Daniel B. *The First Modern Jew: Spinoza and the History of an Image*. Princeton University Press, 2012.

———. *Spinoza's Challenge to Jewish Thought: Writings on his Life, Philosophy, and Legacy*. Edited by Daniel B. Schwartz. Brandeis University Press, 2019.

Sharp, Hasana. "Feminism and Heterodoxy: Moira Gatens's Spinoza." *Philosophy Today* 63, no. 3 (2019): 795–803.

———. "Spinoza and Feminism." In *A Companion to Spinoza*, edited by Yitzhak Melamed. Wiley Blackwell, 2021.

———. *Spinoza and the Politics of Renaturalization*. University of Chicago Press, 2011.

Sheldon, Rebekah. "Dark Correlationism: Mysticism, Magic, and the New Realisms." *symplokē* 24, no.1/2 (2016): 137–53.

Shulman, Carl, and Bostrom, Nick. "Embryo Selection for Cognitive Enhancement: Curiosity or Game-Changer?" *Global Policy* 5, no. 1 (2014): 85–92.

Sluis, Jacob van, and Tonnis Enno Musschenga. *De boeken van Spinoza*. Rijksuniversiteit Groningen Universiteitsbibliotheek, 2009.

Sömmering, Samuel Thomas von. *Ueber die körperliche Verschiedenheit des Negers vom Europäer*. Varrentrapp und Wenner, 1785.

Stolze, Ted. "Hegel or Spinoza: Substance, Subject and Critical Marxism." *Crisis and Critique* 1, no. 3 (2014): 355–69.

Strauss, Leo. *Spinoza's Critique of Religion*. Translated by E. M. Sinclair. University of Chicago Press, 1997.

Tallbear, Kim, and Angela Willey. "Introduction: Critical Relationality: Queer, Indigenous, and Multispecies Belonging Beyond Settler Sex and Nature." *Imaginations* 10, no. 1 (2019): 5–15.

Totaro, Pina. "Law and Dissolution of Law in Spinoza." In *A Companion to Spinoza*, edited by Yitzhak Melamed. Wiley Blackwell, 2021.

Vardoulakis, Dimitris, and Voss, Daniela. "Introduction: Spinoza's Provocation." *Parrhesia* 32 (2020): 1–2.

Wachter, Johann Georg. *Der Spinozismus im Jüdenthumb, oder, die von dem heutigen Jüdenthumb und dessen Geheimen Kabbala Vergötterte Welt*. Wolters, 1699.

Walsh, Mary. "Twenty Years Since 'A Critique of the Sex/Gender Distinction': A Conversation with Moira Gatens." *Australian Feminist Studies* 19, no. 44 (2004): 213–24.

Whitebook, Joel. "Spinoza and Freud: Psychoanalytic Reflections on Immanence, Finitude and Emancipation." *Graduate Faculty Philosophy Journal* 42, no. 2 (2021): 335–52.

Whitman, Norman L. *An Examination of the Singular in Maimonides and Spinoza: Prophecy, Intellect, and Politics*. Palgrave Macmillan, 2020.

Williams, Caroline. "Thinking the Space of the Subject *Between* Hegel and Spinoza." In *Between Hegel and Spinoza: A Volume of Critical Essays*, edited by Hasana Sharp and Jason E. Smith. Bloomsbury, 2012.

Wilson, Catherine. "Descartes and Augustine." In *A Companion to Descartes*, edited by Janet Broughton and John Carriero. Blackwell Publishing, 2008.

Wittgenstein, Ludwig. "Whence the Feeling That Our Grammatical . . ." In *The Big Typescript: TS 213, German-English Scholars' Edition*, translated by Charles Grant Luckhardt and Maximilian A. E. Aue. Wiley Blackwell, 2005.

Wolfson, Elliot R. *The Duplicity of Philosophy's Shadow: Heidegger, Nazism, and the Jewish Question*. Columbia University Press, 2018.

———. "Heeding the Law Beyond the Law: Transgendering Alterity and the Hypernomian Perimeter of the Ethical." *European Journal of Jewish Studies* 14 (2020): 215–63.

———. *Heidegger and Kabbalah: Hidden Gnosis and the Path of Poiēsis*. Indiana University Press, 2019.

Wolfson, Harry Austryn. *Crescas' Critique of Aristotle: Problems of Aristotle's Physics in Jewish and Arabic Philosophy*. Harvard University Press, 1957.

———. *The Philosophy of Spinoza: Unfolding the Latent Processes of His Reasoning*. 2 vols. Harvard University Press, 1934.

Wynter, Sylvia. "Unsettling the Coloniality of Being/Power/Truth/Freedom: Towards the Human, After Man, Its Overrepresentation—An Argument." *CR: The New Centennial Review* 3, no. 3 (2003): 257–337.

Xenophanes. *The Texts of Early Greek Philosophy: The Complete Fragments and Selected Testimonies of the Major Presocratics*, Part I. Translated and edited by Daniel W. Graham. Cambridge University Press, 2010.

Yovel, Yirmiyahu. *Dark Riddle: Hegel, Nietzsche, and the Jews*. The Pennsylvania State University Press, 1998.

———. "Spinoza, the First Anti-Cartesian." *Idealistic Studies: An Interdisciplinary Journal of Philosophy* 33, no. 2/3 (2003): 121–40.

———. *Spinoza and Other Heretics: Adventures in Immanence.* Princeton University Press, 1989.
Žižek, Slavoj. *Absolute Recoil: Towards A New Foundation of Dialectical Materialism.* Verso, 2014.
———. *Disparities.* Bloomsbury Academic, 2016.
———. *Incontinence of the Void: Economic-Philosophical Spandrels.* MIT Press, 2017.
———. *Less Than Nothing: Hegel and the Shadow of Dialectical Materialism.* Verso, 2012.
———. *Organs Without Bodies: On Deleuze and Consequences.* Routledge Classics, 2004.
———. *The Parallax View.* MIT Press, 2009.

Index

Note: All titles are by Baruch Spinoza unless otherwise indicated.

ableism, 187–88, 288, 289, 306–7, 314–15, 319, 341–42
absolute, the: becoming self and, 118; God and, 66, 172, 255; infinity and, 102, 118; spirit and, 225–26, 306; substance and, 83; teleology and, 20, 35, 116, 161; wholeness and, 115–16
Adorno, Theodor, 24, 124, 210, 274, 305–6
affect: adequate ideas and, 354; as adhering ontologically, 335–36; animal, 345–46, 347; causation and, 337–39, 348, 352, 356; as change in who we are, 312, 335–36, 348, 349–51; cruel optimism and, 338; culture modifying, 355; external causes and, 337–38; force of morality and, 359; free will and, 350; gender as, 198; good and, 254–55, 313, 342–44, 347–50, 351, 359; ideas and, 242, 249, 348, 349, 351; immanence and, 348–49; intuitive knowledge and, 348, 354, 359; maxims and, 352; moderation of, 312, 351–52, 356; modes and, 312, 335–36, 338, 350–51, 354–55, 356; ontology and, 312, 335–36; power to exist and, 335–36; reason and, 39, 249, 312, 336–37, 349, 351–52; redefinition of, 335; thought and, 30, 336, 349, 359; value judgments and, 334–35, 339. *See also* desire
affect, power and: alteration of power and, 244, 247, 250–51, 335–36, 338, 351–52; comparative power and, 340–41, 354–55, 356; intuitive knowledge and, 348, 356; as modes, 312; power to exist and, 335–36
affections: of being, 96; of the body, 240, 241–46, 247–48, 249, 327; desire and, 332; essence and, 241–42; God's attributes and, 47–48, 54, 66; ideas and, 242–43, 244–46, 247, 249; Kant and, 257; mind as one and the same with the body and, 241–42, 244–46, 251, 312, 327; modes and, 49, 72, 241–42, 250, 326–27; reality and, 243; of substance, 48, 49, 68, 100, 231, 374n200

431

agency: Christianity and, 83, 110; God and, 44, 57–58; humans and, 110, 320 (*see also* free will, human claims to); as its actualization, 71; mind/soul enabling, 320; modern science and, 207; monarchs and, 57–58 (*see also* sovereignty); naturalism and, 207; substance as not having, 40, 56, 57–58, 61, 74, 207; as synergistic, 63; of things, 203, 207, 319, 320–21, 322–25 (*see also* vital materialism). *See also* free will

agreements. *See* living well

Althusser, Louis: appendix to Part I (*Ethics*) and, 168; the Cartesian subject and, 300–301; causal immanence and, 119; the clinamen and, 155–56, 163; Hegelian dialectics and, 116; a Lucretius-Spinoza connection and, 125, 128–29, 132, 133, 161–62; materialism and, 133, 161; Spinoza as erased and, 12, 300; Spinoza as structuralist and, 119, 133; Spinoza's anti-teleology and, 21, 113; truth and, 291–92; the void and, 132, 133–34; Žižek and, 155

animals: affect and, 345–46, 347; desire and, 333, 346; human sovereignty over, 271, 274–75; human use of, 345–46; as lacking free will, 345; as lacking rationality, 271, 274–75, 345–47; making humans like, 318–19, 344–45, 346; souls and, 274, 346

anthropocentrism: being and, 220; causal necessity and, 99; COVID and, 214–15; desire and, 207, 208–9, 214–15; epistemology and, 99, 225–26; ethics and, 322–23; evolutionary biology and, 206–7; free will and, 310–11, 345 (*see also* God, anthropomorphizing of: as model of human will); ghosts/divine creatures and, 176–78, 369n30; Hebrew Scripture and, 179–80, 227–28, 355–56; infinity and, 99, 224; longtermism and, 213–14; nature as serving humans and, 170, 171–76, 188–89, 195, 207, 215, 225, 274; the negative and, 144, 163; normativity and, 186; oneness and, 105–6; order and, 181, 182, 185, 187, 225, 323; particularity and, 319, 344–45; reason and, 225–26; sameness and, 223; surprise and, 155–56; teleology and, 36, 170, 173, 177, 179, 207, 208; value judgments and, 187, 296, 310; vital materialism and, 319–20, 321, 322–23; worldviews and, 41, 120, 148, 170. *See also* God, anthropomorphizing of

anthropomorphism: ghosts/divine creatures and, 177–78, 369n30; Hebrew Scripture and, 356; of nature, 319; ontology and, 148, 171; as prejudice, 168; purposeful action and, 207; teleology and, 168–70, 173, 179, 203, 207; vital materialism and, 319–20, 321, 326

anti-dualism, 48, 202, 263–64, 266–67, 287, 288–89, 303, 304, 307. *See also* binaries; dualism; mind, as one and the same with the body

anti-Judaism: acknowledged in scholarship, 110–11; Christianity's supersession of Judaism and, 20–21, 85, 109–10, 111, 114, 277; Christian supremacy and, 21, 31, 92–93, 95, 110–13, 281, 321–22; Hegel and, 77–78, 82–85, 88, 98, 110–11, 115 (*see also* Hegel, G. W. F. (Spinozism as Oriental and)); ignored/normalized in scholarship, 21–22, 77–78, 86, 112–13, 114; Judaism as Oriental and, 18, 20, 82–85, 113–14, 277 (*see also* Hegel, G. W. F. (Spinozism as Oriental and); Orientalism); Kabbalah and, 87, 89, 281; misreading Spinoza

and, 18–22, 77–78, 82–86, 89–90, 94, 98, 110–11, 115. *See also* antisemitism; Jacobi, Friedrich Heinrich; Judaism; *Spinozastreit*, the
antisemitism, 19, 92–93, 278. *See also* anti-Judaism
Appiah, Kwame Anthony, 190
Aristotle: the Aristotelian Left and, 12–13; being and, 106; causation and, 181–82; critique of Democritus, 130; the eternity of the world and, 142, 143; as heretical to Christianity, 143; the infinite and, 98, 140; materialism and, 12, 263–64, 307; naturalism and, 11–12, 14–15, 34, 136; the nature of matter and, 52, 54–55, 64, 71; oneness and, 80; ontology and, 136; thought as sovereign and, 49, 54–55; transcendent categories and, 191; the Unmoved Mover and, 44, 45, 80, 142, 254; the void and, 125, 140–41, 142; *Metaphysics*, 4, 55
Aristotle, influence on Jewish and Islamic philosophy of: Crescas and, 136, 140–41, 143; dualism and, 38, 285; ethics and, 269, 297; exceptionalism and, 203; the first mover as God and, 45; Gersonides and, 203, 286; God's knowledge/thought and, 50, 56, 66, 227, 248–49, 253; God's will and, 56; human exceptionalism and, 203; ignored in scholarship, 11–12, 37; immanence and, 307; Maimonides and, 4, 11–12, 34, 45, 50, 52, 66, 136; mind/body as interdependent and, 287; modern Jewish philosophy and, 16; naturalism/materialism and, 4, 43, 120, 263–64, 270, 285, 307; Spinoza's education and, 367n29; thought originating in sensation and, 286; transcendence and, 292; truth and, 292; the void and, 36, 125, 143

artificial intelligence (AI), 212, 293
Astell, Mary, 280
atheism, Spinoza accused of: Christian supremacy and, 18, 21–22, 83–85; destabilizing sovereignty and, 123; Jacobi and, 77, 88, 89, 94; Jewishness and, 24, 25, 86, 87–88, 90, 120; Kabbalah and, 18, 21, 24, 89, 281; Mendelssohn and, 51–52; Orientalism and, 85; van Velthuysen and, 58–59, 329–30
atomism: being and, 130, 165; Epicurus and, 128, 130, 131, 132; God and, 135; Hegel and, 130–31; identity and, 81, 130; indivisibility and, 80, 128, 135–36, 144, 161, 165; Lucretius and, 125, 128, 152, 165 (*see also* clinamen, the); Object-Oriented Ontology and, 148–49; Scholasticism and, 126; Spinoza's proposed alignment with, 35, 36, 125, 132–33, 161–62; Žižek and, 157
attributes: as actualizing power, 236; beyond thought and extension, 223, 235; as conceived through themselves, 223–24; definition of, 226–29, 230; Deleuze and, 251–55; desire and, 332; elided difference of, 219; emanation and, 70; essence and, 223, 226–27, 232, 248, 251, 253, 254–55; God as cause of, 223–24, 236; grammar and, 67; Hegel's dismissal of, 224; human perception and, 223–24, 227–29, 232, 234, 239, 246, 253; individuality and, 306; indivisibility and, 103, 234–35, 252; like causing like and, 236, 238–39; matter as, 55; modal actualization and, 232; modes as finite and, 231, 233; modes of, 223–24, 236; parallelism of, 197–98, 199–200, 235; Spinoza's sources and, 221; substance as, 68, 83, 103–4, 224, 226, 230–35, 241,

attributes (cont.)
251–55; univocity and, 252. See also extension; God, attributes of; thought

attributes, hierarchy and: absence of hierarchy and, 99, 223, 234, 237–38, 241; attributed to Spinoza, 43, 78; perfection and, 251; thought as superior and, 237–38, 254–55 (see also mind, supremacy over body of)

attributes, infinite: adhering ontologically, 237; diversity and, 63, 221–22, 230; of God, 54; infinite power and, 222–24, 226; infinite substance and, 103–4, 224, 226; Lucretius and, 129; thought/extension and, 54–55, 73, 99, 103–4, 137, 221–24, 235, 239

attributes, infinite substance and: absence of hierarchy and, 99; decentering humans and, 225; extension and, 105, 137, 144; infinite attributes and, 103–4, 224, 226; kinds of modes and, 73, 235; perfection/limitlessness and, 54–55, 226; the power of existing and, 65–66, 222–23; understanding substance and, 63; without multiple substances, 230

attributes, power and: differing from substance, 231, 254–55; as essence, 253; as God, 229–30; indeterminate power and, 236, 238; perception of reality and, 232; power conceived as attributes and, 236, 238; the power of existing and, 54, 65–66, 222–23, 254; as the power that is substance/reality, 225–27, 241. See also extension; thought

Augustine: conception of God, 45, 59; dualism and, 10, 27–28, 38, 263, 272, 315; free will and, 33, 59, 203–4, 271, 314–15, 329–30; human mastery of nature and, 345; influence on Descartes, 45, 59, 203–4, 270–74, 299,
307, 314–15; knowledge of the self and, 271–73; rationalism and, 272, 274; spirit and matter and, 204, 267–68, 270–72; teleology and, 208

Badiou, Alain: being and, 150; the exceptional event and, 151, 152, 153–55, 165; infinity and, 99; Lucretius and, 36, 128, 132; the multiple and, 118; oneness and, 82, 94, 153, 154, 261; the real and, 146; sovereignty and, 149, 153–55; the void and, 149–54, 165

Balibar, Étienne, 72, 209, 300, 303, 340

Barad, Karen, 40

Barbapiccola, Giuseppa-Eleanor, 272, 280

Barbone, Steven, 341

Bauer, Bruno, 25, 277–78

Bayle, Pierre, 18, 25, 86

Beckstead, Nicholas, 211–12

being: absolute/pure, 139, 159; affections of, 96; anthropocentrism and, 220; Aristotle and, 106; atomism and, 130, 165; Badiou and, 150; becoming and, 152–53, 210, 225–26; the being/nothingness binary and, 126, 128, 139, 161, 163, 165–66 (see also nothingness); as composed of entanglement, 194, 202, 342; Dasein and, 299; Descartes' cogito and, 273, 290; difference and, 233, 261; Eleaticism and, 161, 165; equality of, 251; hierarchy of, 62; immanence and, 152; indivisibility of, 80, 161, 165; infinite, 72; infinite substance and, 99, 165; Maimonides and, 106–7; mathematics of, 152; of the mind, 242, 284; misreading Spinoza and, 253–54, 256, 257, 261; mutually exclusive with the real, 158; the negative corrupting, 165; Parmenides and, 80, 128, 130, 161, 165; as primordial, 164, 165; reality as individual being and, 106–7; the soul and, 107; sover-

eignty and, 165; universality of, 261; the void and, 150, 161
being, thought and: being as thinking, 261, 265–66, 273, 290, 295, 296, 299, 303; misreading Spinoza and, 253–54, 256, 257, 261
Benjamin, Walter, 16, 210
Bennett, Jane, 39, 319–26, 345, 346
Bennett, Jonathan, 119
Bergson, Henri, 260, 306
binaries: activity/passivity, 49–50, 62, 63–64, 209, 264, 281, 319, 337 (*see also* cause and effect); being/non-being (positive/negative), 124–25, 126, 128, 139, 158–59, 161–63, 165–66 (*see also* nothingness); constraining infinity, 79; culture/nature, 168, 205, 208, 209, 264, 276, 316; East/West, 20–21, 82, 85 (*see also* Orientalism); freedom/necessity, 34, 40, 42, 75, 209; hierarchy in general and, 38, 78, 117, 118–19, 218; identity/difference and, 233; immanence and, 48–49, 156–57, 168; indeterminacy and, 117, 138; infinite/finite, 118, 122, 154 (*see also* modes, as finite); infinite substance and, 117–19; logics of supremacy and, 79–80, 118, 126, 200, 218, 262, 274; natural/unnatural, 168, 202, 205, 311; nature/culture, 168; one/multiple, 118, 151; potential/actual, 49, 52, 255, 258; rational/irrational, 265–66, 267, 271, 275–76, 311; sexgender and, 192–93, 195–97, 198–200, 206, 271, 278; spirit/action, 304; subject/object, 63–64, 249, 304; thought/extension as, 224, 304; thoughts/feelings as, 312; Trinitarian thinking amplifying, 157. *See also* dualism; hierarchy; mind, supremacy over body of; positive and negative; spirit and matter

Black people, 90, 216, 265, 325. *See also* racism
Bloch, Ernst, 12–13
bodies: affections of, 240, 241–46, 247–48, 249, 327; capability of, 243–44, 247–48, 284–85, 348; colonial, 264–65; as comprised of modes, 108, 337–38; Descartes and, 264–65, 273, 278–79, 336–37 (*see also* mind, supremacy over body of (Descartes and)); as extension, 223–24, 231, 240, 284; finitude of, 52, 140 (*see also* modes, as finite); God's corporeality and, 52, 56, 111, 287 (*see also* Trinity, the); human experience and, 223; imagination and, 244; immanence and, 288; individual freedoms and, 315; inferential knowledge and, 247; intra-action and, 108, 193; Judaism as, 90; lack of unity and, 53; as metaphor, 106–7; normativity and, 192–94, 195–96; passivity and, 329; as purposive, 181; the soul and, 282–83, 285; Spinoza's sources and, 264, 268, 285–87, 308; Spinoza's theorization of, 243–45; the void and, 130, 134, 140–41, 143; welfare of, 355. *See also* embodiment; mind, as one and the same with the body; sexgender
Bordo, Susan, 278
Bostrom, Nick, 213
Boxel, Hugo, 30, 129, 176–78
Boyle, Robert, 134, 184
Bradwardine, Thomas, 143, 164
Braidotti, Rosi, 119, 311, 318
Brassier, Ray, 261
Butler, Judith, 194, 310, 342

capitalism, 211–12, 264–66, 267, 288, 303, 305–6
Catholicism, 90, 270, 321. *See also* Christianity

causal determinism: the actions of substance and, 58, 61, 176; adequate ideas and, 347–48; atheism and, 58–59; the conatus and, 327–28; Crescas and, 203; epistemology and, 283; free will and, 203, 204, 274, 298, 311, 333, 360; God as beyond, 182; humans as exempt from, 41, 220, 288–89, 316, 331, 360 (*see also* transcendence); humans as subject to, 183, 298, 330–31; of ideas, 283, 308–9; immanence and, 184, 317, 327–28, 330, 346; Jacobi's rejection of, 89; knowledge of effect and, 63; the natural and, 205; no exemptions from, 33, 41, 73, 283, 331, 360; politics and, 308–9; suicide and, 341; thought and, 283–84, 297, 298, 308–9

causal determinism, desire and: affects and, 337–39, 348, 356; changing desire and, 312, 348, 359; decision-making and, 332–35; ethical action and, 335, 361; intra-action and, 202, 332–33; lack of autonomy and, 204, 333–34; particularity and, 345

causal immanence: absence of hierarchy and, 48–49, 63, 64; Althusser and, 119; existence without guides and, 181; God and, 48; Hegel's appropriation of, 110; the infinite connection of causes and, 42, 47–48, 63, 72, 76, 214, 269, 297, 301; Maimonides and, 52; modal intra-action and, 185; necessity of, 224; negating the cause/effect binary, 156–57; reflexive activity and, 64; rejecting transcendence, 48–49, 205; self-causation and, 47–48, 131, 136–37; substance as, 47–48, 63, 68, 72, 98, 136, 298–99. *See also* causes, infinite connection of; substance

causal necessity: absence of hierarchy and, 237; anthropocentrism and, 99; disavowing individualism, 360; epistemology and, 99; free will and, 61, 203, 360; lack of telos and, 174; living well and, 310, 354, 360; mind as superior to, 311; natural laws as, 181–82, 185; particularity and, 191; as threat to Christian doctrine, 95, 311

causation: adequate causes and, 313, 335, 337, 351; affective association and, 352; Aristotle and, 181–82; commonality and, 55–56, 103; the conatus and, 328; difference and, 132; divine creation and, 181; efficient, 46, 175, 185, 187; God as causing but not caused and, 44–46, 50–51, 55–56, 62, 135, 142; God's interruption of, 58; intra-action and, 184–85, 202, 332–33; logics of, 46; modes and, 72, 185, 238, 312; natural, 59, 203; no escape from, 73 (*see also* transcendence); Object-Oriented Ontology and, 146; oneness and, 81, 132; order and, 152; perception of, 246; power and, 74–75, 156–57, 234, 238, 327, 337, 348, 352–53; sexgender and, 198; structural, 155; substance as matrix of, 106, 238. *See also* first causes; self-causation

cause and effect (active/passive): analysis and, 293–94; dismantling of, 40, 42–43, 63–64, 70, 131; effect confused for cause, 181–82, 188, 206–7; hierarchy and, 46, 62, 70, 210; immanence and, 72, 119; intra-action and, 302–3; power and, 348

causes, infinite connection of: adequate ideas and, 297; as God as substance as nature, 41–42, 359; human contrivance of transcendence and, 182; imagination and, 73, 341; immanence and, 42, 47–48, 63, 72, 76, 214, 269, 297, 301; interdependence with others and, 38, 269, 311–12;

intra-action and, 69, 73, 297, 344; modes of thought and, 234; as necessity, 185; as reality, 72–73, 74, 76, 106, 107, 214, 316; sexgender and, 194; shaping desires, 202, 359; substance as indeterminate and infinite and, 234, 316; as without exception, 42, 73, 100, 168, 182, 214, 283, 311, 316; as without purpose, 175, 182, 185–88, 194, 207–8, 214. *See also* reality, infinity and

causes, infinite connection of (entanglement and): absence of hierarchy and, 74; being as composed of, 194, 202, 342; causing affects, 337; disallowing exceptionalism, 74, 316; infinity and, 72; involvement and, 63; knowledge formation and, 246; living well and, 297, 343–44; mind and body as one and the same and, 202, 246, 301; modes and, 175, 194, 359; nature and, 359; transcendence refused by, 316

Césaire, Aimé, 275, 276, 289–90

Chaudhury, Aadita, 213

Christianity: agency and, 83, 110; Aristotle and, 12, 143; Catholicism, 90, 270, 321; causal necessity as threat to, 95, 311; Christianizing of Kabbalah and, 19, 35, 87–88, 281; Christianizing of Spinozism and, 19, 23, 88, 92, 93, 113, 252, 256–57; colonialism and, 265, 276–77, 321–22; epistemology and, 10, 225–26, 268; faith as essential to, 88–89; the Fall and, 159; freedom and, 83, 85, 89, 314–15; free will and, 59, 89, 203, 267–68, 271, 273, 288–89 (*see also* Descartes, René: free will and); German Idealism and, 92–93, 94, 119–20, 122; God as transcendent and, 49, 59, 270 (*see also* God, as transcendent); Hegel and, 20–21, 23, 35, 78, 109–14, 116, 120, 277; heresy and, 12, 24–25, 143; Jewish atheism and, 18, 25, 85; *Kabbala Denudata* and, 19, 87–88; naturalism and, 95; New Materialism and, 320, 326; persecution of Jews and, 17, 95, 321–22; the self and, 265; sovereignty and, 43, 44–45, 59, 109, 311, 312–13, 319, 321, 329; Spinozism as threat to, 18–19, 83, 88–89, 95; spirit's supremacy over matter and, 49, 282–83, 287, 303, 311, 331; supersession of Judaism and, 20–21, 85, 109–10, 111, 114, 277; transmuted as rationality, 265. *See also* philosophy, "Western" (as Christian); Scholasticism, Christian; Spirit; supremacy, Christian; Trinity, the

Christina of Sweden, 270, 279–80

Christology: evaluating Spinozism and, 22, 77; Hegel and, 77, 84, 85, 111, 113, 116–17, 209; underpinning "Western" philosophy, 9, 77–78, 120, 270, 321

cisness, 28, 195–96 263, 275. *See also* sexgender

clinamen, the: Althusser and, 155–56, 163; the conatus and, 132–33, 161; the event and, 151; indeterminacy and, 130, 132; Lucretius and, 35–36, 125, 130, 131, 151, 161, 165; materialism and, 133; positive/negative and, 133, 165; substance and, 132, 161; universality and, 165; the void and, 128, 130–31, 132

Cogitata Metaphysica, 51, 60, 229

cognitive behavioral therapy, 311, 329

Cohen, Hermann, 24

colonialism: binary difference and, 20, 189–90, 264–66; the body and, 264–65; Christianity and, 265, 276–77, 321–22; Descartes and, 264–67, 275, 289, 306–7; discourses of

colonialism (*cont.*)
  reason and, 266, 275–77; expropriation and, 110, 265; progress and, 209–10; racism and, 38, 275–76; Spinoza's ties to, 30, 266–67; "Western" philosophical foundations of, 14–15, 265. *See also* decolonization
conatus, the: causation and, 328; the clinamen as, 132–33, 161; desire and, 333; as essence, 312–13, 326, 332; living well and, 312, 342, 343, 349; the mode as, 312, 326, 327, 332, 339; self-interest and, 343–44
Conway, Anne, 19, 38, 281–83, 287, 327
corporeality, 52, 56, 111, 287. *See also* bodies; God, as incorporeal
correlationism, 145–46, 220, 225–26, 301–2
COVID, 214–17
Crescas, Hasdai, 97–98, 125–26, 136, 140–43, 164, 203, 292
culture: absence of hierarchy and, 317; defining reason/humanity and, 263, 266, 275, 277, 315, 321–22; history and, 210, 322; human hegemonies and, 321–22, 325–26; human political action and, 324; individual culpability and, 329–30; modifying affect and, 355; as of nature, 205, 317, 325; neoliberal, 315, 330; normativity and, 356; rationality and, 315; sex-gender and, 197, 199, 264; superiority over nature, 168, 205, 208, 209, 264, 276, 316; of things, 319–21, 322, 323; "Western", 77, 143, 199, 267, 275, 307, 329 (*see also* Christianity; philosophy, "Western"; West, the)

decolonization: anti-Judaism and, 94; the Cartesian legacy and, 263, 264–66, 288, 289, 307–8; of infinity, 119–20; metaphorical, 366n27; recuperating sources and, 14–15

Deleuze, Gilles: attributes and, 251–55; as Christianizing Spinoza, 252, 256–57; defending Spinoza from Hegel, 35–36, 128–29, 132, 161; difference and, 251–57, 259–60; God and, 253–54; idealism and, 37, 119, 222, 257, 260–61; identity and, 37, 259, 260; Jewish Aristotelianism and, 367n29; a Lucretius–Spinoza connection and, 35, 125, 128–29, 132–33, 161–62; Maimon and, 259–60; misreading Spinoza and, 251–56; parallelism and, 253–54; prejudices and, 256; Spinoza's immanence and, 256; Spinoza's sources and, 252, 253–54, 255, 256; Spinoza's synthesis and, 293–94; the substance–mode relationship and, 70; thought and, 254–55, 256; the Trinity and, 254; univocity and, 21, 118, 119, 155, 251–52, 261; the void and, 165; Žižek's rejection of, 161
Della Rocca, Michael, 119
democracy, 206, 303, 305, 323, 324–25, 346
Democritus, 80, 128, 129, 130, 131, 157, 161, 325
Derrida, Jacques, 23, 47, 128, 291, 292
Descartes, René: Augustine's influence on, 45, 59, 203–4, 270–74, 299, 307, 314–15; Christianity and, 9, 59, 263, 270–71, 272, 279, 296, 329 (*see also* dualism, Cartesian: solidifying Christian dualism); Conway's "correction" of, 281–82; critique of Scholasticism, 279; in the *Ethics*, 44, 328; extension and, 48–49, 103–4, 134–35, 197, 250, 269–70, 304; free will and, 59, 61, 183, 203–4, 288, 290–91, 297–98, 314–15, 329–30; God and, 45, 46–47, 59–60, 61, 104, 203–4, 273 (*see also* God, as incorporeal: Descartes and; sovereignty, God and: Descartes' conception of);

human mastery of nature and, 203–4, 269, 274, 296, 314–15, 328–29, 345; human reason and, 274–76, 278, 297–98; the infinite and, 98; influence on "Western" philosophy, 3, 14–15, 265–66, 299–302, 307–8 (*see also* dualism, Cartesian); intellectual engagement with women, 279–80; laws of nature and, 183, 184; method of, 268–69, 279, 280, 290, 293–96; the neutral view and, 264–65, 284; the New Science and, 59, 221, 270; principle of motion of, 328; racism/colonialism and, 264–67, 275, 289, 306–7; the subject and, 38, 264, 269, 290, 296, 299–301, 304, 315, 329; substance and, 49, 103, 162; teleology and, 295, 301; truth and, 269, 290–92, 300–301; the void and, 36, 125, 134, 135–36; *Discourse on Method*, 268–69, 279, 294; *Meditations*, 272, 273, 290, 296; *Passions of the Soul*, 279, 328–29; *Principles*, 272, 273, 290. See also dualism, Cartesian

Descartes, René (mind over body and): the body as causing passions and, 336–37; colonial legacy of, 264–67, 275–76, 289, 306–7; as constituting humans, 274, 290; distinctness and, 250, 268, 273, 281–82, 284, 287; doubting and, 239, 271, 290–91, 294, 296, 297–98, 302; human exceptionalism and, 290, 297–98; matter and, 64; mind as transcendent and, 183, 194, 196, 264, 266, 284, 288–89, 328, 331; thought beginning with sensual rejection and, 194, 284, 285, 288, 295, 297, 308

Descartes, René (mind over body and, *cogito* and): Althusser and, 300–301; Augustine and, 271–72, 273; being and, 273, 290; circularity of, 299; colonial legacy of, 264–67, 275–76, 289, 306–7; *Dasein* and, 299; Hess's critique of, 304; neutrality and, 289–90; sexism and, 278–79; transcendence and, 264, 276, 284, 301, 302, 307

Descartes, René (transcendence and): free will and, 288–89; human exceptionalism and, 302, 314, 315; mind over body and, 183, 194, 196, 264, 266, 284, 288–89, 328, 331; nature and, 203, 297; truth and, 291. See also dualism, Cartesian (transcendence and)

desire: action and, 332–33, 335, 349; affection and, 332; animals and, 346; anthropocentrism and, 207–9, 214–15; attributes and, 332; change and, 335–36, 348–51, 354, 359; conditioning sovereignty, 75; corporeality and, 201–2; as doing, 62; entanglement with others and, 339–41, 343, 349–50, 353; essence and, 332, 335, 336, 338, 342, 344; free will and, 58, 89, 285, 330–31, 334, 339, 344, 360; ideas and, 289, 308–9, 336, 348–50, 354; infinite reality and, 214; injurious, 340; for knowledge, 348; linking spirit and body, 282; normativity and, 186, 200, 202, 205; for order, 181; particularity and, 332, 345; past experience and, 334; reason and, 348–49, 351; for right living, 335, 340, 342–43, 348–49, 353–55, 359, 361; for security, 105–6; self-expression and, 119; shaping belief, 176, 318; singularity and, 313, 338; Spinoza's definition of, 332; teleology and, 335, 349–50; transcendence of, 315; value judgments and, 173, 188–89, 334, 339, 344; as who we are, 338, 339; as will, 332. *See also* affect; prejudices desire, causal determinism and: affects and, 337–39, 348, 356; changing desire and, 312, 348, 359; decision-making and, 332–35; ethical action and, 335, 361; intra-action and, 202, 332–33; lack of autonomy and, 204, 333–34; particularity and, 345

difference: absence of sovereignty and, 221–22, 230, 233–35, 241, 256; being and, 233, 261; causation and, 132; colonial bodies and, 264; the conatus and, 327; denied to God, 42; domination and, 58, 264–65, 306; erasure of, 116, 219, 232, 246, 252, 256, 260, 264–65, 320–21 (*see also* sameness); human/animal, 274, 277, 344–46; identity and, 233, 257, 259; Jewish, 91–93 (*see also* otherness, Jewish); limiting intra-action, 345; Lucretius and, 152; Maimon and, 259, 260; modes and, 234–35; as non-originary, 221–22; oneness and, 81–83, 112; the same and, 286; subordinate to ideas, 261; superiority and, 20, 41, 208; the Trinity and, 252; as uncomfortable, 220. *See also* binaries; dualism; exceptionalism; otherness

difference, attributes and: absent of hierarchy, 221–22, 230, 233–35, 241, 256; God and, 68; ontological difference and, 252; perception of reality and, 246; sexgender and, 197–98, 219–20

difference, essentialized: binaries and, 28, 36, 289; generation of sovereignties and, 283; hierarchy and, 44–45, 48, 55, 118; immanence reversing, 48–49; otherness and, 78; race and, 276; rejection of, 41–43, 45, 48, 55–56, 63, 69–70, 72; sexgender and, 193, 198–99, 206; sexism and, 206; as teleological, 191; "Western" reliance on, 44; wholeness and, 188–89. *See also* essence

Discourse on Method (Descartes), 268–69, 279, 294

disinterestedness, 6, 10–11, 284, 289–90, 309. *See also* view from nowhere, the

Dobbs-Weinstein, Idit, 16, 111, 209, 264, 286

domination: difference and, 264–65, 306; dualism and, 305–6; freedom and, 33, 209–10, 315, 331; free will and, 61, 314, 328–29, 343, 360, 361; God as sovereign and, 58, 171, 204; Hegel and, 109–10; ideas and, 308; individual freedom and, 305; of mind over body, 273–74, 287–88, 303, 305–6, 328, 331, 336–37 (*see also* mind, supremacy over body of); nature and, 195, 204, 215–16, 267, 274–75, 317; normativity and, 186, 264–65; progress and, 209–10; of reason, 220, 240, 300; spirit and, 118 (*see also* spirit, supremacy of); the universal and, 304–5; validation of, 28, 33, 58, 308. *See also* hierarchy; sovereignty; supremacy

dualism: abstracting the individual and, 304–5; Christian, 49, 168, 263, 267, 270, 303, 306–7, 311; as hierarchical, 14–15, 38, 48–49, 59, 274, 289, 304, 306; Kantian, 257–58, 259; logics of, 304–5, 329; logics of supremacy and, 38, 274, 289, 304, 307, 329; thought and extension and, 224, 304; transcendence and, 184, 220, 303. *See also* binaries

dualism, Cartesian: Augustine and, 203–4, 272, 303, 308, 314–15; the *cartésiennes* and, 280, 287; colonial legacy of, 264–67, 275–76, 289, 306–7; delusion of free will and, 202–3, 314 (*see also* freedom: Descartes and; free will: Descartes and); Elisabeth of Bohemia's challenges to, 279, 328; God as incorporeal and, 45, 104, 135–36, 270, 282, 287, 314–15; God's will and, 250, 255; Lloyd and, 197; sexgender and, 202, 278–80; as solidifying Christian dualism, 49, 168, 263, 267, 270, 303, 306–7. *See also* Descartes, René; mind, supremacy over body of: Descartes and

dualism, Cartesian (transcendence and): the *cogito* and, 273–74, 284–85, 291, 297, 301, 302; extension as its own substance and, 103; free will/reason and, 250, 263, 288–89, 329; immanence and, 48–49, 167–68; influential ideas and, 308; laws of nature and, 183; minds lacking particularity and, 196, 276; sexism and, 278–80; transcendence as fundamental and, 303, 314–15. *See also* God, as transcendent; mind, as one and the same with the body

Dussel, Enrique, 264–66, 267

Ein Sof, 77, 81, 89, 93–95, 102, 120, 142, 180. *See also* Kabbalah

Eleaticism: attributed to Spinoza, 18, 35, 83, 86, 125, 127, 128, 161–62; nonbeing and, 161, 165; oneness and, 80, 127, 128, 130, 137, 162, 165

Elisabeth of Bohemia, 250, 279–80, 328

emanation: infinite power and, 70; Kabbalah and, 89, 95, 117, 180; Neoplatonism and, 281; as Oriental, 84, 127; overflow and, 55–56; transcendence and, 62

emancipation, Jewish, 19, 25, 85, 88, 91, 92, 277–78, 305

embodiment: elided difference and, 219; modal existence and, 194, 289; as of nature, 297; sexgender and, 194, 196, 197, 200–201, 202; thought and, 197, 268, 283–86, 287–88, 302. *See also* bodies; mind, as one and the same with the body

end. *See* teleology

Engels, Friedrich, 70

Enlightenment, the, 18–19, 88–92, 208, 266, 300

entanglement: of human and nonhuman, 323; modal, 175, 194, 339, 340, 359; of the One and infinity, 80–81; of order and final causes, 181; with other humans, 339–42, 343, 349–50, 353; of self and perception, 313. *See also* causes, infinite connection of (entanglement and)

Epicurus, 87, 128–30, 131, 132, 133, 161, 325

epistemology: anthropocentrism and, 99, 225–26; causation and, 99, 283; Christian theology and, 10, 225–26, 268; dualism and, 10, 268, 286, 304; Gersonides and, 203, 286; as intertwined with ontology and ethics, 30–31, 74, 113, 219, 269, 312, 318; knowledge and, 238, 239; living well and, 221, 312; misreading Spinoza and, 221; mistakes of, 129, 187, 190, 295 (*see also* prejudices; teleology); nothingness and, 148; ordering reality and, 100; primacy of, 2–4, 290; reason and, 10, 219–21, 269, 290, 295, 301; sovereignty and, 220, 221–22, 225–26, 268–69, 290, 303 (*see also* method; subject, the; truth); transcendence and, 203

essence: affections of humans and, 241–42; appearance and, 146; attributes and, 223, 226–27, 232, 241, 248, 251, 253, 254–55; biology and, 178, 188–89, 193–94, 199–202; the conatus as, 312–13, 326, 332; desire and, 332, 335, 336, 338, 342, 344; difference and,

essence (cont.)
70, 79, 198, 338–39 (see also difference, essentialized); as existence, 326; free will and, 288–89; of God, 66, 252–53; God's knowledge/thought and, 50, 51, 60–61, 227, 236–37; God's oneness and, 97, 104, 252; infinity of substance and, 65–66, 103; knowledge of, 226–27, 248, 348; the mind and, 67, 203, 243, 287; modes and, 72, 99–100, 251, 326, 327; numbers as inadequate to, 100; purpose and, 178; reason and, 288–89; the self and, 327; sexgender and, 193, 198, 281, 287; the soul as, 264; sovereignty of, 194; of substance, 69; teleology and, 191, 326; as unfindable, 147, 148; as unfixed, 326, 327; uniqueness and, 96–97; vital materialism and, 319; as without transcendence, 327. See also difference, essentialized

essence, power and: actualization of as substance, 223, 226, 232; attributes and, 253; God's power as God's essence and, 66; infinity and, 69, 223; modes and, 72, 326; as never potential/reserve, 327; as substance's essence, 68–69

ethics: agreement with others and, 313, 343, 347, 359; anthropocentrism and, 322–23; causal redetermination and, 317; desire for living well and, 335, 342–43, 352, 361; difficulty of, 352–53; God's attributes and, 357–59; the highest good and, 269, 296–97; human particularity and, 318; immanence and, 310, 311, 361; life lived in society and, 308, 361; Maimonides and, 355–56, 357–59; prejudices compromising, 325; teleology of, 335, 343, 359. See also living well; morality

Ethics: citation of sources in, 43–44, 328 (see also Spinoza, Baruch (sources and influences)); early drafts of, 86, 223, 239. See also epistemology; God; immanence; infinity; living well; ontology; substance

Ethics, appendix to Part I: human exceptionalism and, 202, 216–17; Marx and, 308; prejudices and, 5–7, 57–58, 181–83, 190, 202–3, 205; teleology and, 168–69, 173–74, 207–8

event, the, 151–52, 153–54, 155. See also Badiou, Alain

evil: affect and, 351; body as source of, 270; vs. falsehood, 180; free will and, 314, 330, 339; judgments of the imagination and, 179–80; living well and, 243–44, 334, 342; as mode of thinking, 173, 334–35; nature and, 188; normativity and, 310; teleology and, 173, 175, 179. See also good

exceptionalism: the event and, 151, 152, 153–55, 165; God as having, 44–45, 46–47, 48, 52, 104, 125, 171, 172 (see also God, as sovereign/monarch; God, as transcendent); God as lacking, 40–41, 85–86; hierarchy and, 171, 208, 331; mind as absent of, 283

exceptionalism, human: absence of mind/body hierarchy and, 317; appendix to Part I (*Ethics*) and, 202, 216–17; Aristotle and, 203; dualism and, 107, 168, 171, 172–73, 180, 184, 203–4, 207, 220; entanglement disallowing, 74, 316; fictions of sovereignty and, 8, 107, 180, 215–16, 217; Hebrew Scripture and, 285, 314; humans as modes and, 168; humans as of nature and, 184, 214; humans as other to nature and, 172–73, 180, 184, 203, 324; human souls and, 274, 277; independence from extension and, 298–99; the infinite connection of causes and, 73, 182, 316; long-termism and, 213–14; mind/reason and, 225–26, 271, 274–77, 280, 288–90, 297, 346–47; nature as having human ends and, 170–74, 207, 215, 274; relation to affects and, 312; teleology and, 170, 208, 276; transcendence and, 48–49, 89, 172–73, 302, 303, 314, 315; vital materialism and, 320

exceptionalism, human (free will and): causal determinism and, 220, 333, 360; mind over body and, 290, 297–98; as prejudice, 310–11, 360; the self and, 273, 299–300; a sovereign God and, 203–4, 271, 274–75, 288–89, 297–98, 360; superiority to nature and, 345, 360

extension: as attribute of substance, 105, 137, 141, 197–98, 199–200, 287, 304; attributes beyond, 223, 235; as binary with thought, 224, 304; bodies as, 223–24, 231, 240, 284; causal immanence and, 298–99; Descartes and, 48–49, 103–4, 134–35, 197, 250, 269–70, 304; desire and, 332; divisibility and, 104, 105, 135, 137; duration and, 238; extended substance same as thinking substance and, 229–30, 233; extension causing extension and, 233–34, 236, 262; as finite and determinate, 236; God and, 54–55, 105, 135, 137, 236, 269–70; Hegel and, 224, 225–26; human experience and, 223, 284; human independence from, 298–99; idealism proscribed by, 238; ideas and, 261; inclusion in good things, 54; indeterminacy and, 231; as infinite, 54–55, 73, 99, 103–4, 137, 221–24, 235, 239; infinite substance and, 104, 105, 137, 141, 144, 231; limits of mind and, 223, 226; modes of, 49, 197; as modification of substance, 49, 53–56, 64, 134–35; ontology and, 53–54, 224, 231, 234, 235, 236, 237, 240, 253–54; reality and, 284; sexgender and, 197–98, 199–200; thought and, 48–49, 220, 222, 241, 252, 317. *See also* bodies

Eze, Emmanuel Chukwudi, 266

Fanon, Frantz, 189
Farabi, al-, 4, 50, 203
feminisms: anti-dualism and, 264; Cartesian sexism and, 278–80; construction of the human and, 263; logics of sovereignty and, 27, 283; misogyny of, 201–2; sexgender and, 36–37, 196–202; TERFism and, 28; "Western", 264. *See also* Gatens, Moira; Lloyd, Genevieve
Feuerbach, Ludwig, 304, 305
Fichte, Johann Gottlieb, 304, 306
first causes, 34, 40, 61, 74, 142, 155, 163, 246
freedom: authority and, 33; binary with necessity, 34, 40, 42, 75, 209; Christianity and, 83, 85, 89, 314–15 (*see also* free will, human claims to: Christianity and); deficit of, 337; delusion of, 167, 306, 330–31, 339; Descartes and, 59–60, 202, 203–4, 220, 263, 298, 299–300, 314, 328 (*see also* free will, human claims to: Descartes and); to dominate, 33, 209–10, 315, 331; dualism and, 220; as exercise of individual will, 315, 361; from extension, 298–99; as fiction, 33, 297–98; God's lack of, 26, 73, 74, 330 (*see also* free will, God and); God's presumed possession of, 5–6, 7, 57–58, 59–60, 170, 203–4 (*see also* free will, God and); human belief in, 5–6, 33, 58, 59, 170, 172, 203, 360; individualism and, 14–15, 305, 306;

freedom (cont.)
Jewish form of, 16; Jews as not recognizing, 84, 110, 120, 277–78; liberalism and, 305, 314–15; the mind and, 283; modes' lack of, 33, 73; naturalization of, 6; ontology and, 6; as opposed to causal determinism, 311; Plato and, 314; from prejudice, 280; reason as basis of, 278; Spinoza's redefinition of, 39, 40, 71, 313, 359–60, 361; spiritual, 83, 85; substance and, 58, 61, 62, 83, 329, 359; unrealized, 304, 305; the West and, 33, 112, 314; worthiness of, 266, 278, 315. *See also* sovereignty

free will: ableism and, 314–15; affect and, 350; animals as lacking, 345; causation and, 203–4, 274, 298, 333, 360; as creating doubt, 297; essence and, 288–89; the first cause and, 61; Maimonides and, 203; memory and, 360; modes' lack of, 73; as prejudice, 330–31; Spinoza's redefinition of, 359–61 (*see also* freedom: Spinoza's redefinition of); truth and, 290–91. *See also* agency

free will, God and: anthropomorphizing God and, 57, 168–69, 170, 172, 207–8, 271, 288–89, 314 (*see also* God, as sovereign/monarch); creation and, 45, 56, 59–60, 250, 255, 274; God as lacking, 40–41, 56–59, 60, 61, 73, 98, 237; God as lacking exceptionalism and, 40–41, 85–86; God's power and, 57, 59–61, 66, 237; necessity and, 58–59, 61. *See also* God, as sovereign/monarch; God, as transcendent

free will, human claims to: affirming existence and, 297–98; anthropocentrism and, 310–11, 345; anthropomorphizing God and, 57, `68–169, 170, 172, 207–8, 271, 288–89, 314; Augustine and, 59, 203–4, 314–15, 329–30; Christianity and, 59, 89, 203, 267–68, 271, 273, 288–89; culpability for actions and, 314, 315, 328–30, 339, 361; as delusion, 330–31, 339; Descartes and, 59, 61, 203, 273, 288, 290–91, 297–98, 314–15, 329–30; desire and, 58, 89, 285, 330–31, 334, 339, 344, 360; domination and, 61, 314, 328–29, 343, 360, 361; ethics and, 310–11, 335; evil and, 314, 330, 339; as gift from God, 59, 271, 314; good and, 87, 314, 339; human belief in, 6, 59, 172; humans as lacking, 86, 89, 203, 291, 298, 330, 334, 339; individualism and, 305; liberalism and, 314–15; as license to indulge, 361; the logics of dualism and, 303; the logics of sovereignty and, 329; Lucretius and, 130; mind overcoming nature/body and, 274, 288–89, 314–15, 329, 360 (*see also* nature: human mastery of); neoliberalism and, 33, 39, 315–16, 330, 337, 350, 360; the soul and, 59, 311; teleology and, 170, 209, 315, 335, 350; transcendence and, 209, 273; voluntarism and, 28–29, 183, 203–4; "Western" culture and, 329; willpower and, 333, 336, 337, 350. *See also* exceptionalism, human (free will and)

Freud, Sigmund, 16, 305

Gatens, Moira, 191, 197–202
Gersonides: Aristotle and, 203, 286; epistemology and, 203, 286; as heretical, 24–25; immanence and, 14, 39, 49, 308; influence on Spinoza and, 13, 17, 37; Jewish reception of, 17; Maimonides on Aristotle and, 12, 136; mind as interdependent with body and, 268, 286, 308; nondualism and, 264; ontology and, 286; "Western" neglect of, 22

Gill-Peterson, Jules, 201–2

God: the absolute and, 66, 172, 255; as active, 66; agency and, 44, 57–58 (*see also* free will, God and); alterity and, 74, 117, 141, 158, 255; Aristotle and, 45, 50, 56, 66, 227, 248–49, 253; atomism and, 135; Augustine's conception of, 45, 59; causal determinism and, 182; causal immanence and, 48; causation interrupted by, 58; as cause of attributes, 223–24, 236; as causing but not caused, 44, 45–46, 50–51, 55–56, 62, 135, 142; as corporeal, 56, 111, 287 (*see also* Trinity, the); Descartes and, 45, 46–47, 59–60, 61, 72, 104, 203, 273 (*see also* God, as incorporeal); difference and, 42, 68; essence of, 50, 51, 60–61, 66, 227, 236–37, 252–53; as essence of the human mind, 67; as exceptional, 44–45, 46–47, 48, 52, 104, 125, 171–72 (*see also* God, as sovereign/monarch; God, as transcendent); exceptionalism denied to, 40–41, 85–86; as existing modally, 238–39, 357; extension and, 54–55, 105, 135, 137, 236, 269–70; first causes and, 34, 74, 163; as Form, 50–51, 55; good and, 54, 57, 60, 228, 357–58; Hebrew Scripture and, 44, 52–53, 56, 80, 227–29, 231–32, 357–59; human knowledge of, 53, 56, 179–80, 203, 225, 228–29, 231–32, 357–59 (*see also* Maimonides); identified with reason, 48; as immanent materiality, 53; immutability and, 50, 52, 80–81, 135, 183; as indeterminate, 55, 102, 142, 358; infinity and, 50, 52, 54–55, 57, 60, 172, 186, 237, 358 (*see also* substance, as infinite); intellect of, 60–61, 66; Jewish and Islamic medieval philosophy and, 46, 102, 103, 225–26, 236 (*see also* Ibn Rushd; Ibn Sina; Maimonides); knowledge and, 239, 248–49, 253; lack of sovereignty and, 5–6, 8, 11, 24, 26, 41, 57, 74; living well and, 353; love of, 356–57, 359; as necessary existent, 34, 45–46, 52, 54, 59, 69; nothingness and, 36, 125–26, 133, 137, 141–43, 154, 155, 159, 164–66; Object-Oriented Ontology and, 145–46; otherness and, 170–71; as paramount substance, 269–70; particularity and, 191; potentiality of, 57; as preexistent, 142–43, 252–53; recycled concepts of, 272; redefinition of, 41, 42, 45–46, 354; revelation of, 112, 116; as self-caused, 46–47, 69; self-knowledge of, 50, 51, 59, 237; as spirit, 84, 204, 282; supremacy over reality and, 7, 41, 48–49, 59–60 (*see also* God, as sovereign/monarch); teleology and, 169; as thinking itself, 49–50, 253, 255; thought and, 49–52, 55, 56–57, 59, 227, 235–37; vitality and, 319, 321; the void as, 125–26, 141–42, 143, 154, 155, 164, 165–66; as world and human soul, 258. *See also* free will, God and; substance

God, anthropomorphizing of: free will and, 57, 169, 170, 172, 207–8, 271, 288–89, 314 (*see also* God, as sovereign/monarch); glorifying humans, 178, 207–8, 319, 330; God as model for the subject, 329; God's perfection and, 228; God's power as king's power and, 40, 41, 51, 57–58, 61–62, 171–72, 237, 329, 359–60; human ends and, 170–74, 179, 225; human responsibility and, 315; human superiority and, 170, 171–73, 274, 277, 288–89; making sense of God and, 52–53, 56–58, 97–98, 228; mastery of the self and, 203–4, 328–29; order and, 181, 182, 225; rejection of,

God, anthropomorphizing of (*cont.*) 61–62, 203, 346; replacing with reason and, 226; sexgender and, 369n30; transcendence and, 203, 209

God, attributes of: affections of, 47–48, 54, 66; anthropomorphism and, 97–98; corporeality and, 287; differences in, 68; ethics and, 357–59; extension and, 55, 236; as of God/God's unity and, 54, 60, 68–69, 227–29, 232, 252, 253–54; Hebrew Scripture and, 56, 227–28, 231–32, 357–59; imitation of, 357–58; intuitive knowledge and, 248; Maimonides and, 227–29, 231–32, 252, 254, 357–59; oneness/unity and, 54, 60, 68–69, 227–29, 232, 252, 253–54; power as, 227, 229–30, 231, 253–54; transcendence and, 55; the void and, 155, 165–66

God, as incorporeal: causing the corporeal and, 55; Descartes and, 45, 104, 135–36, 137, 270, 282, 287, 314–15; ghosts and, 176, 177; God as spirit and, 282–83; God's exceptionalism and, 40–41; God's indivisibility and, 104; Jewish philosophical tradition and, 52–53, 103, 110, 137, 285; sovereignty and, 204, 270, 274; transcendence and, 48, 52, 55, 270, 274; the void and, 135–36, 141–42

God, oneness/unity of: Aristotle and, 54; God's attributes and, 54, 60, 68–69, 227–29, 232, 252, 253–54; God's incorporeality and, 53; God's knowledge and, 50; God's power and, 84, 237, 254; God thinking itself and, 253, 255; Hebrew Scripture and, 50, 80–81; human exceptionalism and, 107; ideas of God as of God and, 237; Kabbalah and, 80–81, 93 (*see also* Ein Sof); Maimonides and, 50, 51–52, 60, 93–94; as mode of thinking, 96–97; oneness of creation/substance and, 137, 281; power and, 84, 237, 254; as relative mode of speaking, 96, 97–98; Spinoza's Jewishness and, 77, 82–83, 84, 98, 110, 113–14, 115; the Trinity and, 82, 83, 252. *see also* Trinity, the

God, perfection of: acting for an end and, 170, 172; anthropocentrism and, 228; extension and, 105, 135, 137; imperfection and, 54–55, 57, 102, 135; Maimonides and, 52–53, 54, 55, 56, 228, 253

God, power of: actualization and, 56–57, 66, 229–30; as attribute, 227, 229–30, 231, 253–54; as contingent, 57, 61, 237; expressed in modes, 241; as God's essence, 66, 237; God's free will and, 57, 59–61, 66, 237; God's infinitude and, 52, 55, 57, 60, 172, 237, 358; God's intellect and, 60–61, 66; God's oneness and, 84, 237, 254; God's power as king's power and, 40, 41, 51, 57–58, 61–62, 171–72, 237, 329, 359–60 (*see also* God, as sovereign/monarch); God's self-generation and, 46–47; as limited, 55, 56–57, 61, 143; power to exist and, 254, 255; as ranked, 253–54, 255; as unlimited, 59–60, 66, 135, 172, 183, 270

God, as sovereign/monarch: absolute power and, 61–62; begetting other sovereignties, 41, 271; comfort of, 182, 218, 220; contingent power and, 237; Descartes' conception of, 59–60, 136, 203–4, 255, 266, 329; domination and, 58, 171, 204; the *ego cogito* and, 266; erasure of particularity and, 305; free will and, 40, 41, 45, 58, 169; God divested of, 26, 27, 34, 40–41, 57–59, 60–61, 171, 207–8 (*see also* free will: God's lack of); laws of nature and, 183; nothingness/the void and, 125–26, 141–43, 154, 155, 164–66; oneness and, 51, 107; order and, 171, 182; prejudices rooted in, 168–73; reward/punishment and, 58–59, 172, 189, 315, 329–30, 361; teleology and, 174, 180, 191

God, as sovereign/monarch (anthropocentrism and): as approximations of God, 228; exceptionalism of human will and, 203–4, 271, 274–75, 288–89, 297–98, 360; God's power as king's power and, 40, 41, 51, 57–58, 61–62, 171–72, 237, 329, 359–60; human responsibility and, 315; human superiority and, 170, 171–73, 274, 277, 288–89; as model of human will, 169, 170, 172, 207–8, 314

God, as transcendent: anthropocentrism and, 203, 209; attributes and, 55; Christian dogma and, 49, 59, 270; ensuring reality and, 117–18, 135–36, 255; free will and, 59; human superiority and, 209; immanence disallowing, 170; incorporeality and, 48, 52, 55, 270, 274; to nature, 49, 110; the negative and, 148, 159, 163; otherness and, 170–71; substance as modes disallowing, 235–36; transcendence denied and, 40–41, 42 (*see also* free will, God and)

God *as* substance *as* nature, 41–42, 74

God *or* nature, 40–41, 42, 174, 191

God *or* substance, 40–41, 42

God *or* substance *or* nature, 27, 65, 354

Goetschel, Willi, 16, 92, 306

good: affect and, 254–55, 313, 342–44, 347–50, 351, 359; common, 315, 353, 361; free will and, 87, 314, 339; God and, 54, 57, 60, 228, 357–58; judgments of the imagination and, 179–80; living well and, 243–44, 269, 296–97, 313, 335, 342–44, 347–50, 352–55, 361; as mode of thinking, 173, 334–35; nature and, 188; normativity and, 186, 187, 310; ontological, 191; Plato and, 80, 314; teleology and, 57, 173, 174, 175, 179, 342–43, 353; vs. truth, 180. *See also* evil

Gordon, Lewis P., 263

Guide of the Perplexed (Maimonides), 4, 17, 50, 52, 60, 147–48, 285, 313, 357

Harman, Graham, 145, 146

Hebrew Grammar, 43, 64, 373n167

Hebrew Scripture: alternate names as aspects and, 230; anthropocentrism and, 179–80, 227–28, 355–56; correction of prejudices and, 355–56; God as causing but not caused and, 44, 52–53; God as having free will and, 56; God's attributes and, 56, 227–28, 231–32, 357–59; God's unity and, 80, 227–28, 229; harmonizing with philosophy, 148; human exceptionalism and, 285, 314; internal and external meaning and, 147; morality and, 355, 357–58; no God without creation and, 70; root words in, 357, 373n171; Spinoza's education and, 16–17; teleological ranking and, 180; the *Tractatus Theologico-Politicus* and, 24. *See also* Maimonides; Talmud, the

Hegel, G. W. F.: appropriation by Levinas, 24; appropriation of Spinoza, 20–21, 78, 109–10, 111–12, 113, 114, 116; atomism and, 130–31; attributes and, 224; becoming and, 126–27, 152–53, 225–26, 304; binaries and, 117–18, 224; Christianity and, 20–21, 35, 78, 109–13, 116, 120, 277; Christology and, 77, 84, 85, 111, 113, 116–17, 209; the connection of causes and, 156; domination and,

Hegel, G. W. F. (*cont.*)
109–10; extension and, 224, 225–26; history of philosophy of, 20–21, 78, 82, 109, 110–13, 114–15, 116; Jacobi and, 77, 78, 88; Jewish otherness and, 78, 111–12, 116; Jewish particularity and, 25; the logics of supremacy/sovereignty and, 27, 78, 109, 114–18, 122; misreading Maimonides and, 111; modes and, 110, 160; philosophy of history of, 20–21, 78, 85, 114, 209, 210, 211, 277; pure being and, 139; self-determination and, 131; Spinoza's indispensability to, 109, 161; spirit and, 10, 20, 21, 82–83, 84, 111, 112–13, 225–26, 305; the subject and, 84, 301, 306; substance and, 77, 83, 84, 110, 115, 152, 160, 224; supersession of Spinoza and, 21, 77, 78, 84, 85, 109–10, 111–14; teleology and, 115–16, 209, 211, 277; totality and, 35, 114–15, 118, 209, 305; the Trinity and, 20, 21, 77, 83, 85, 110–11, 113; unity of thought and extension and, 224–26; wholeness and, 115–16, 150; Žižek and, 113, 126, 139, 156, 157, 160–61; *Lectures on the History of Philosophy*, 82–83, 113; *The Science of Logic*, 83–84, 139

Hegel, G. W. F. (dialectic system of): Althusser and, 116; binaries and, 117–18; as Christological, 209; difference and, 233; the logics of supremacy/sovereignty and, 78, 114–18, 122; Lucretius and, 132; the negative and, 84, 110, 115, 117, 139, 156, 157, 160; ontology and, 114–15; reason and, 220; sameness and, 132, 151; substance and, 114–18, 127–28; teleology and, 35, 115–16, 209; the Trinity and, 111; Žižek and, 155–56, 159

Hegel, G. W. F. (misreading Spinoza and): anti-Judaism and, 77–78, 82–85, 88, 98, 110–11, 115; appropriation of concepts and, 110; Christian supremacy and, 78, 110–13, 120; decontextualization and, 114; destabilizing Hegelianism and, 112; Eleatic identity and, 125, 137, 161; emanation and, 70, 127; the geometrical method and, 87, 116; infinity and, 102, 110, 111, 115, 117, 127, 152, 224; Jacobi and, 88; the logics of sovereignty and, 114–15; modal individuality and, 327; the negative and, 82–85, 110, 125, 126, 127–28, 149–50, 152, 162; oneness and, 77, 82–83, 84, 98, 110, 113–14, 115; ontology and, 114–15; scholarly ignoring/replication of, 77–78, 110–11, 112–14; substance and, 70, 77, 79, 110, 115, 224; unity and, 127; unity of thought and extension and, 224

Hegel, G. W. F. (Spinozism as Oriental and): history of philosophy and, 111; infinity and, 119–20, 127; Jews as lacking reason and, 277–78; Moder and, 114; oneness and, 82–85, 98, 113–14; otherness and, 115–16; substance and, 77; supersession and, 109–11, 113–14

Hegel, G. W. F. (the negative and): generative negativity and, 83–84, 110, 126–28, 132, 163; misreading Spinoza and, 82–85, 110, 125, 126, 127–28, 149–50, 152, 162; nothingness as God and, 164–65; teleology and, 117; the void and, 131–32, 145, 164; Žižek and, 156, 157

Heidegger, Martin, 47, 82, 145, 154, 299–300

Heine, Heinrich, 15, 303, 346

Herrera, Abraham Cohen de, 61, 95, 142

Hess, Moses, 3–4, 15, 300, 303, 304, 305, 307

hierarchy: of activity over passivity, 49–50, 62, 64, 255; attempts to place in Spinozism, 43; attributes and, 43, 78, 237–38, 251, 254, 255; begetting hierarchy, 205, 330 (*see also* sovereignty, begetting sovereignties); of being, 62; capitalism and, 265; cause and effect and, 46, 62, 64, 70, 156; control and, 218; difference and, 44, 45, 48, 55, 79, 118, 178, 233, 259; dualism and, 48–49, 59, 274, 289, 304, 306, 329 (*see also* binaries); emanation and, 180; eugenics and, 213 (*see also* ableism; racism); exceptionalism and, 41, 45, 171, 208, 310–11, 331; geographic, 216; between humans, 189, 215–16, 315, 323, 325, 330 (*see also* ableism; colonialism; racism; sexism); of infinity over finitude, 118; mathematical, 151, 154; matter and, 42, 48–49, 204, 271, 285; naturalization of, 48, 171, 189, 277; in nature, 122, 345; Neoplatonism and, 62, 285; not adhering ontologically, 74; oneness and, 79, 81, 121–22; order and, 180, 295; otherness and, 78, 81, 154; of perfection, 358; politics and, 331; of positive over negative, 115, 117, 158–59; rationality and, 204, 265–66, 267, 275–77, 288; reality and, 44, 55, 72, 106, 121, 180, 269–70, 281–83; of reason over substance, 48 (*see also* mind, supremacy over body of; reason, sovereignty/supremacy of); in scholarship on Spinoza, 31, 70; sexgender and, 200, 201, 206, 281, 282–83 (*see also* sexism); of subject over object, 64, 306; teleology and, 116, 165, 172, 174, 180, 182, 188, 209–10, 211; within thought, 255, 295; transcendence and, 7, 52, 81, 116, 118–19, 122, 267–68, 302–3, 314–15; "Western" over Oriental, 20–21, 78, 85, 109–10, 112–14, 116, 277; "Western" reliance on, 43, 44, 122, 272; wholeness and, 116, 193. *See also* binaries; domination; mind, supremacy over body of; sovereignty; supremacy

hierarchy, absence of: attributes and, 63, 99, 223, 234, 237–38, 241; causal necessity and, 237; culture and, 317; difference and, 221–22, 230, 233–35, 241, 256; entanglement and, 74; immanence and, 48–49, 63, 64, 70, 156–57, 168; infinite being and, 72; intra-action and, 72–73; mind as one and the same with the body and, 241, 250, 262, 287–88, 303, 317, 331–32; nature and, 42, 73, 74, 318, 320–21; ontology and, 42–43; reason and, 37, 241, 250, 351; shaping revolutionary/socialist thought, 303–7

hierarchy, substance and: causation and, 47, 63, 70; classical primacy and, 41; Conway and, 281, 282–83; Descartes and, 269–70; misreading Spinoza and, 78; substance as its modes and, 69, 119; volition and, 56

Horkheimer, Max, 274

humans: agency and, 110, 320; animals and, 271, 274–75, 318–19, 344–46; belief in free will and, 6, 58, 59, 172 (*see also* free will, human claims to); dehumanizing of, 315–16, 319, 324–25, 330, 341–42; hierarchy between, 189, 215–16, 315, 323, 325, 330 (*see also* ableism; colonialism; racism; sexism); lack of free will and, 86, 89, 203, 291, 298, 330, 334, 339 (*see also* free will, human claims to); as like animals, 318–19, 344–45, 346; as like things, 319–20, 323–24; materiality of, 129, 274; memory as critical to, 247; as of nature, 184, 202–3,

humans (*cont.*)
204, 214, 324, 360; nature as serving, 170, 171–76, 179, 188–89, 195, 207, 215, 225, 274; nature mastered by, 203–4, 214–16, 269, 274, 296, 314–15, 328–29, 345; perfection of, 167, 187, 203, 228, 314, 348, 354–55, 357, 358; as separate from nature, 208, 311, 324 (*see also* exceptionalism, human); as subject to causal determinism, 183, 298, 330–31; as telos of creation, 180. *See also* anthropocentrism; anthropomorphism; bodies; culture; exceptionalism, human; living well; longtermism; mind; prejudices; soul, the; transcendence, human

humans, as modes: affect and, 338; affection and, 241–42, 250; agreements with others and, 343–44, 347; attributes and, 224, 231; difference and, 208, 316–17; experience of others and, 244; mind and body in coordination and, 241–42, 250, 254, 289 (*see also* affect; mind, as one and the same with the body); substance and, 137, 231

humans, perception and attributes and: difference and, 253; ideas and, 239–40; infinite reality/attributes and, 223–25; perception by others and, 230–31; perception of God and, 232; thinking in extension and, 222

Husserl, Edmund, 299, 306

Ibn Ezra, Abraham, 14, 24, 49
Ibn Gabirol, Solomon, 12, 13, 62
Ibn Rushd, 11–12, 136, 142, 143, 203, 285
Ibn Sina, 11–13, 45, 50, 56, 60, 136, 203
idealism: Adorno and, 306; Christian supremacy and, 92; Deleuze and, 37, 119, 222, 257, 260–61; hierarchy of attributes and, 234; of identity, 257;

like causing like as proscribing, 234, 236, 237–38, 257; particularity as foreclosing, 222; reason and, 262; Spinoza's sources and, 236; "Western" supremacy and, 92

idealism, attributed to Spinoza: Althusser and, 301; attributes and, 221; Bennett and, 321; Deleuze and, 119, 251, 256, 257, 261, 301; German Idealism and, 78; Maimon and, 93–94; Mendelssohn and, 51–52

Idealism, German: antisemitism and, 92–93; Christianizing Spinoza, 88, 113; Christian supremacy and, 92–93, 94, 119–20, 122; connecting Spinoza to Parmenides, 128; influence of Jacobi and, 88; misreading Spinoza and, 21–22, 78, 109, 119–20, 124, 139 (*see also* Hegel, G. W. F. (misreading Spinoza and)); monopolization of reason and, 38; Spinoza's Jewishness and, 88, 92–93, 94, 113, 119–20; "Western" supremacy and, 119–20. *See also* Hegel, G. W. F.; Kant, Immanuel; Schelling, Friedrich Wilhelm Joseph

ideas: of affections, 242–43, 244–46, 247, 249; affect of, 242, 249, 348, 349, 351; in the bodied mind, 242–43, 249, 284, 308 (*see also* mind, as one and the same with the body); as causally determined, 283, 308–9; deduction of, 292–93; desire and, 289, 308–9, 336, 348, 349–50, 354; difference subordinate to, 261; domination and, 308; doubt and, 298; extension and, 261 (*see also* mind, as one and the same with the body); first causes and, 246; of God as of God, 237; ideas of power and, 308; immanence and, 261; memory conditioning, 308, 351–52; as mind, 284, 301; mind as, 243, 351; modes as, 242; as multiplicities,

260; as not transcendent, 240; ontology of, 302, 317; as privileged, 261, 262; as real in themselves, 291; Spinoza's definition of, 302; Spinoza's true ideas and, 301–2; thought causing, 223–24 (*see also* mind, as one and the same with the body); as through the body, 242–43, 284, 308 (*see also* embodiment: thought and; mind, as one and the same with the body); truth and, 291–92, 293, 301–2. *See also* thought

ideas, adequate: action and, 302, 336, 347–48; affect and, 249, 354; causal determinism and, 347–48; commonality with others and, 247, 347; danger to, 354; happening in time and space, 262; inadequate ideas and, 245; inferential knowledge and, 247; the infinite connection of causes and, 297; intuitive knowledge and, 248; living well and, 302; particularity and, 249; pleasure of, 336, 347–50; prejudices inhibiting, 297; rules and, 295; Spinoza's definition of, 301–2

identity: absolute, 82, 83; abstract, 127; atomism and, 81, 130; Deleuze and, 37, 259, 260; diversity/difference and, 232, 233, 256, 257, 259, 327; dominance of, 233; Eleaticism and, 137, 161; false, 306; immutability and, 79, 206; indeterminacy and, 40; indivisibility and, 101, 105; lack of stability and, 108–9, 327; otherness and, 81–82; reality as system of, 165; the self and, 260, 327; substance as constituting, 115, 152–53, 252; substance as not constituting, 115, 120–21, 125, 138, 139, 156, 160, 234–35. *See also* sexgender

imagination: aids of, 98, 100, 104, 121, 352; as bodied, 244, 286, 341; as of

the infinite connection of causes, 73, 341; knowledge and, 246–47, 301; order and, 181, 185, 190–91, 192; sexgender and, 177, 190–91, 192, 196; value judgments and, 179–80, 184

immanence: absence of hierarchy and, 48–49, 63, 64, 70, 156–57, 168; affect and, 348–49; alterity and, 62, 63; as anti-supremacist, 307–8; Aristotle and, 307; Badiou and, 152; being and, 152; binaries and, 48–49, 156–57, 168; bodies and, 288; Cartesian dualism and, 15, 37, 48–49, 167–68, 303; causal determinism and, 184, 317, 327–28, 330, 346; cause and effect and, 72, 119; the clinamen and, 156; Deleuze and, 256; Ein Sof and, 142; embodied thought and, 308; essentialized difference and, 48–49; ethics and, 310, 311, 361; generation and, 161; Gersonides and, 14, 39, 49, 308; God as immanent materiality and, 53; Hegel and, 20, 114, 156, 160; ideas and, 261; individualism disallowed by, 15; infinity and, 35, 37, 99, 103, 107, 123; Jewish medieval philosophy and, 25, 29, 34–35, 39, 49, 51–52, 168, 288, 311; of knowledge, 248–49, 258, 295, 348, 356, 359; living well and, 310, 311, 312, 342; Lucretius and, 131; Maimon and, 256, 308; Maimonides and, 14, 39, 49, 51–52, 168; materialism and, 53; Mendelssohn and, 256; naturalism and, 14, 15–16; nature and, 205; of the negative, 144; no escape from, 316, 361; nothingness and, 144; opposed to emanation, 89; placing all modes within nature, 168; power and, 40, 68, 70, 156–57, 225–26, 238; of reality, 99, 103, 123, 187, 205, 226; return to self and, 115; sovereignty denaturalized by, 43–44; sovereignty disallowed by, 10, 169,

immanence (cont.)
    209; Spinoza's sources of, 14, 49, 168, 225–26, 269, 288, 303, 308–9 (see also Gersonides; Ibn Ezra, Abraham; Maimonides); as stable, 160; supremacy and, 63; teleology disallowed by, 169–70; of thought, 38, 53, 286, 287, 288, 295; transcendence and, 169–70, 187; value judgments and, 334; "Western" philosophy marginalizing, 14, 29. See also causal immanence
impartiality, 23–24, 93, 285, 289. See also view from nowhere, the
indeterminacy: binaries and, 117, 138; the clinamen and, 130, 132; difference and, 264–65; epistemic, 220; as essence, 69; God and, 55, 102, 142, 358; identity and, 40; the infinite connection of causes and, 234, 316; modes and, 107, 185; negating oneness and, 115. See also power, indeterminate; substance, as indeterminate
indigenous people, 91, 216, 265, 276–77, 321, 324
individualism: attributed to Spinoza, 340; bodies and, 315; causal necessity disavowing, 360; the conatus and, 343–44; denied, 83; domination and, 305–6; as fantasy, 33; free will and, 305, 306; individuals as composed of individuals and, 108; liberalism and, 15, 33, 305, 315; neoliberalism and, 315–16; the self and, 304–5, 313; as "Western" principle, 20, 21, 28–29, 77, 83, 252. See also exceptionalism; transcendence
infinity: the absolute and, 102, 118; as act, 79 (see also modes); alterity of, 117–18; anthropocentrism and, 99, 224; Aristotle and, 98, 140; Badiou and, 99; of being, 72; binaries constraining, 79; as composed of the finite, 35, 41, 63, 120–21, 152 (see also modes); decolonization of, 119–20; Descartes and, 98; desire and, 214; Ein Sof and, 94; entanglement of the One with, 80–81; essentialized difference and, 72; of extension, 54–55, 73, 99, 103–4, 137, 221–24, 235, 239; first causes and, 61; God and, 50, 52, 54–55, 57, 60, 172, 186, 237, 358 (see also substance, as infinite); Hegel and, 20, 102, 110, 111, 115, 117, 119–20, 127, 152; hierarchy over finitude, 118; immanence and, 35, 37, 99, 103, 107, 123; of intellect, 152, 235–36, 239, 252, 256, 258, 259, 262; Jewish medieval philosophy and, 34–35, 102; laws of nature disallowed by, 186; Lucretius and, 129; nature and, 119, 121, 137, 169; the negative encompassed by, 131; the negative precluded by, 83–84, 101–2, 115, 125, 127, 139, 152–53; as nonbinary, 35–36, 79–80, 117, 122, 156–57; oneness and, 82, 84, 98–100; the positive as, 117; preexisting the finite and, 102, 115, 117–18, 120, 125; sovereignty disrupted by, 34–35, 115, 122, 169, 186; Spinoza's conception of as deficient, 83–84, 102, 115, 117, 127, 152–53; supremacy of, 117–18; teleology and, 117–18, 119, 136, 167, 173–74, 187; thought and, 54, 223–24, 237, 259; transcendence and, 34, 84, 102, 117, 119, 187; of understanding, 255, 258–60; as unquantifiable, 98–100, 104, 120–21; "Western" philosophy and, 34–35, 165, 167; wholeness and, 76, 101, 115–16, 119, 120–21, 162–63; of will, 273. See also attributes, infinite; causes, infinite connection of; power, infinite; reality, infinity and; substance, as infinite

infinity, modes and: measuring infinity and, 98; modes as existence of infinite, indeterminate power, 66, 69–70, 162–64, 233–35, 326, 358; modes comprising infinity and, 120–21, 162, 234, 316, 326. *See also* modes, as actualized/enacted power

intra-action: absence of hierarchy and, 72–73; as agreement, 74, 108; bodies and, 108, 193; causation and, 69, 73, 184–85, 202, 297, 302–3, 332–33, 344; coherence and, 74, 184–85, 301; desire and, 202, 332–33; difference limiting, 345; dissolving boundaries, 74; lack of control of, 202; modes and, 108, 184, 185, 241, 317, 345; as nonhierarchical, 72–73; reality and, 34, 73

Jacobi, Friedrich Heinrich, 18–19, 77–79, 88–92, 93, 94

Judaism: as atheist, 18, 24, 25, 86, 87–88, 90, 120; bodies and, 90; Christianity's supersession of, 20–21, 85, 109–10, 111, 114, 277; conversion to, 87–88; as discrediting Spinozism, 18–22, 24, 83–84 (*see also* Hegel, G. W. F. (Spinoza as Oriental and)); exclusion from history and, 25, 85, 111, 112, 210, 277, 278; ignored in Spinoza's philosophy, 15–16, 19 (*see also* Spinoza, Baruch (sources and influences)); Lessing and, 19, 88–89, 90, 91, 92, 109; natural religion and, 91; oneness and, 82–85; particularity and, 20, 25, 113–14, 322; as pivot between East and West, 85; reason and, 88–92; reduced to Kabbalah, 18, 87–88; as rendering Spinozism malleable, 23; Spinoza's early education and, 16–17; as static, 20, 87. *See also* anti-Judaism; emancipation, Jewish; Kabbalah; Mendelssohn, Moses; Orientalism; otherness, Jewish; philosophy, Jewish medieval

Judaism, Hegel's conception of: God and, 84, 110; oneness and, 84, 85–86, 98, 113–14; as Oriental, 77, 82–85, 98, 109–10, 114, 116, 277–78; as other, 93, 111–12, 116; particularity and, 20, 25, 113–14; supersession and, 110–11

Judaism, Spinoza's identity and: Basange and, 88; Bayle and, 18, 25, 86; German Idealism and, 88, 92–93, 94, 113, 119–20; Hegel and, 85–86, 98, 116 (*see also* Hegel, G. W. F. (Spinozism as Oriental and)); Jacobi and, 89–90 (see also *Spinozastreit*, the); Kabbalah and, 17, 87–88, 94–95, 119–20; Mendelssohn and, 91–92, 95; minimizing sources and, 15, 120; modern Jewish philosophers and, 24, 303; More and, 25; "purified" Spinozism and, 91–92; as scandalous, 18–22, 91–93; Spinoza's self-conception and, 17–18; Žižek and, 113–14

Kabbalah: atheism and, 18, 21, 24, 86, 87–88, 89, 281; Christianization of, 19, 35, 87, 88, 281; Ein Sof and, 77, 80–81, 89, 93–95, 102, 120, 142, 180; emanation and, 89, 95, 117, 180; Jewish medieval philosophy and, 95; Judaism reduced to, 18, 87–88; *Kabbala Denudata* and, 19, 87–88; Maimon's commentary on, 93–94; Neoplatonism and, 62, 95; oneness and, 35, 80–81, 86, 88, 94, 102; ontology and, 95; origin of the world and, 142; Spinoza's education and, 17, 95; Spinoza's Jewish identity and, 17, 87–88, 94–95, 119–20; transcendence undermined by, 24; wholeness and, 94

Kant, Immanuel: antisemitism and, 92; the authority of reason and, 221; Christianity and, 9; dualism and, 257–58, 259; knowledge and, 257; nothingness and, 145; progress and, 208, 211; the self and, 260

Klein, Julie R., 70, 108, 286

Knorr von Rosenroth, Christian, 87–88, 281

knowledge: adequate, 292–93; artificial intelligence and, 293; of the body, 242, 244, 247–48, 298 (*see also* mind, as one and the same with the body); common notions and, 152, 222, 249, 250–51, 298; desire for, 348; of effect, 63; entanglement and, 246; epistemology and, 238, 239; experience of others and, 247; forms of, 246–49; of God, 53, 56, 179–80, 203, 225, 228–29, 231–32, 357–59 (*see also* Maimonides); God's knowledge and, 239, 248–49, 253; God's self-knowledge and, 50, 51, 59, 237; imagination and, 246–47, 301; immanent, 248–49, 258, 295, 348, 356, 359; inferential, 247; infinite understanding and, 255, 257–60; intuitive, 248–49, 295, 348, 353–54, 356, 359; Kant and, 257; lived experience and, 246–47, 250–51, 334; Maimon and, 257–60; memory as form of, 247; originating in the body, 30; of other bodies, 244–45, 247, 309, 347; power and, 348, 356; of the self, 248, 271–73, 356–57, 359 (*see also* Descartes, René (mind over body and, *cogito* and)); synthesis vs. analysis and, 292, 294; universal notions and, 192, 246–47, 248, 249. See also thought; truth

Lacan, Jacques, 150, 155, 157–58, 160–61, 163

Lectures on the History of Philosophy (Hegel), 82–83, 113

Leibniz, Gottfried Wilhelm, 18, 19, 86–87, 88, 257–58, 259, 260

Lessing, Gotthold Ephraim, 19, 88–89, 90, 91, 92, 109

Levinas, Emmanuel, 24, 219

liberalism: free will and, 33, 314–15; individualism and, 15, 33, 305, 315; progress and, 32, 210–11 (*see also* longtermism); self-sufficiency and, 311; sexgender and, 202; socialist critiques of, 15; vital materialism and, 323

Librett, Jeffery, 90

living well: adequate ideas and, 302; affecting methods and, 353–54; agreements with others and, 343, 345–49, 354–55, 357, 359, 361; causal necessity and, 310, 354, 360; challenges to, 317, 360, 361; the conatus and, 312, 342, 343, 349; entanglement and, 297, 343–44; epistemology and, 221, 312; ethics and the desire for, 335, 342–43, 352, 361; evil and, 243–44, 334, 342; feeling good and, 254–55, 313, 342, 343–44, 347–50; good and, 243–44, 269, 296–97, 313, 335, 342–44, 347–50, 352–55, 361; immanence and, 310, 311, 312, 342; Maimonides and, 355–59; as natural, 347, 352; ontology of, 311, 336, 347; reason and, 222, 240, 245–49, 347–49, 353–55, 360–61

Lloyd, Genevieve, 196–97

longtermism, 211–14

Lorde, Audre, 29

Lucretius: atomism and, 125, 128, 152, 165; the clinamen and, 35–36, 125, 130, 131, 151, 161, 165; connected to Spinoza, 35, 125, 128–29, 132–33, 161–62; difference and, 152; Marx and, 128, 131–32, 144; mention by

Spinoza, 129; the multiple and, 154; nothingness and, 129; wholeness and, 153; Žižek and, 36
Luria, Isaac, 87, 117, 142, 180, 281
Luxemburg, Rosa, 167

MacAskill, William, 211, 212, 213
Macherey, Pierre, 21, 70, 109, 112, 161, 292
Maimon, Salomon: Deleuze and, 259–60; difference and, 259, 260; immanence and, 256, 308; influence of Spinoza and Maimonides on, 257–58; Kabbalist commentary and, 93–94; knowledge and, 257–60; a Spinoza-Kabbalah connection and, 93–94; Spinoza's Jewishness and, 24; totality and, 259–60
Maimonides: free will and, 203; God as accessed through nature and, 203; God as incorporeal and, 52–53, 64, 285; God as limitless and, 102, 225; God as perfect and, 52–53, 54–55, 56, 228, 253; God as thinking and, 50–51, 54–55, 56, 227, 253; God's attributes and, 227–29, 231–32, 252, 254, 357–59; God's unity/oneness and, 60, 97–98, 227–29, 231–32, 233, 252, 254; God's will and, 60–61, 227; Hegel's misreading of, 111; as heretical, 24–25; the human body as purposive and, 181; immanence and, 14, 39, 49, 51–52, 168; interpretation of Aristotle, 11–12, 34, 45, 50, 52, 66, 136; mind as dependent on body and, 268; nature as not serving humans and, 179; Neoplatonism and, 51, 62; non-dualism and, 264; Object-Oriented Ontology and, 146, 147; prejudices and, 27, 355–56; reality as individual being and, 106–7; religion's function and, 355; Spinoza's education and, 17; Spinoza's reconception of, 60–61, 66, 225, 229–30, 231–32, 233; thinking as embodied and, 285, 308; *Guide of the Perplexed*, 4, 17, 50, 52, 60, 147–48, 285, 313, 357; *Mishneh Torah*, 50
Maldonado-Torres, Nelson, 265–66
Marx, Karl, 36, 128, 131–32, 144, 171, 300, 305, 308
materialism: Althusser and, 133, 161; Aristotle and, 12, 263–64, 307; the clinamen and, 133; disrupting the ego's sovereignty, 16; hierarchy of attributes and, 234; immanence and, 53; medieval Jewish and Islamic philosophy and, 12, 29–30, 307; modern Jewish, 305–6; New Materialism, 15, 27, 39, 224, 300, 321, 346 (*see also* Bennett, Jane; Braidotti, Rosi); particularity and, 316–17; socialist critique and, 15; sovereignty of reason and, 224; vital materialism, 319–26, 345, 346; "Western" philosophy censoring/marginalizing, 10, 11–12, 143, 307; Žižek's definition of, 159–61
matter: as divisible, 52, 53, 55, 135; as finite, 52; free will and, 59; God and, 48, 49, 52–54, 55, 59, 135, 204, 283; human thought and, 49; Lucretius and, 129–30, 131 (*see also* atomism; clinamen, the); mind's conception of, 257; modal difference and, 104, 125; oneness and, 119; as passive, 49–50, 55, 64, 281; potentiality of, 52, 55; reduction to, 224; as of substance, 48–49; substance as not, 71, 101, 138, 162–63; vitality of, 282 (*see also* materialism: vital materialism). *See also* bodies; extension; substance
matter, as inferior: Christianity and, 204, 271, 273–74, 282–83, 303, 311; free will and, 314, 338; removing hierarchy and, 42, 48–49; the subject's domination and, 274–75;

matter, as inferior (*cont.*)
"Western" philosophy and, 56. *See also* mind, supremacy over body of
Matysik, Tracie, 15
Mbeme, Achille, 189–90
Meditations (Descartes), 272, 273, 290, 296
memory: affections of the body and, 244–45; artificial intelligence and, 293; association and, 74, 184, 245, 246, 328, 332–33, 337–38; Augustine's theory of mind and, 314; conditioning ideas, 308, 351–52; as critical to human functioning, 247; cultural, 321–22; as a form of knowledge, 247; free will and, 360; moderating affect and, 351–52; modes and, 74, 316, 327; perception of reality and, 246; Spinoza's theory of, 184
Mendelssohn, Moses: defense of Spinozism, 19, 51–52, 88–89, 91–92, 93–95; immanence and, 256; Jewish emancipation and, 88, 91; a Spinoza-Kabbalah connection and, 93, 94
method: Cartesian truth and, 268–69, 279, 290, 293–96; colonialism and, 275; geometrical, 87, 116, 152; Maimon and, 259; sovereignty and, 290; Spinozist truth and, 292–94, 295, 301, 307
Meyer, Ludwig, 291
Mills, Charles, 190
mind: as active, 302; all knowing as within, 259; dependence on the body, 11, 242–43, 250, 268, 285, 286, 308; as finite, 258; God as essence of, 67; as ideas, 243, 351; as incorporeal, 270, 314; Kant and, 257; knowing as its body, 240, 242–43; limited to thought and extension, 223, 226; the material intellect and, 286; modes as ideas and, 242; as self, 273, 284; Spinoza's theorization of, 220–21, 239–43, 283, 284; as thinking itself, 239, 284; union with nature, 296–97; as without transcendence, 283. *See also* rationality; reason; thought

mind, as one and the same with the body: absence of hierarchy and, 241, 250, 262, 287–88, 303, 317, 331–32; affections and, 241–42, 244–46, 251, 312, 327; as aspects of a mode, 268; coordination of mind and body and, 241–42, 243, 249, 262, 331–32; desire and, 202, 332–33, 336–37; embodied thought and, 197, 268, 283–84, 285–86, 287, 288, 302; feelings and, 249, 336; ideas as through the body and, 242–43, 249, 284, 308; irreducibility and, 284, 287–88; knowledge of other bodies and, 244–45, 247, 309, 347; mind as of nature and, 283, 298; mind as the idea of body and, 222, 240, 241, 302–3, 337; mind's knowledge of the body and, 242, 244, 298; modes and, 241, 243, 254, 309; perception of reality and, 222, 225, 246, 247, 249, 298; precluding parallelism, 235; reason and, 222, 351; sexgender and, 194, 197–98, 201, 287; Spinoza's influences and sources and, 221, 268, 286, 308

mind, supremacy over body of: Augustine and, 203–4, 271–72, 303, 308, 314–15; begetting further supremacies, 205; being human and, 273–74; body as hindrance and, 273, 328; domination and, 306; free will and, 263, 314, 315, 328–29; human creativity and, 333–34; mind as transcendent and, 274, 315; the rational/irrational binary and, 265 (*see also* rationality; reason); the self as mind and, 273, 284, 290, 295, 296, 299; as superior aspect of the soul, 271 mind, supremacy over body of (Descartes and): colonial legacy of, 264–67, 275–76, 289, 306–7; Conway and, 282; Elisabeth of Bohemia and, 250; free will and, 263 (*see also* free will: Descartes and); human mastery of nature and, 203–4; misreading Spinoza and, 220; the nature of God and, 203, 270, 315 (*see also* God, as incorporeal: Descartes and); the passions and, 328, 336–37; the senses as delusive and, 273–74, 284; sexism and, 278–79, 287; Spinoza's laws of nature and, 183

Mitchell, Audra, 213

Moder, Gregor, 114, 163

modes: affections and, 49, 72, 241–42, 250, 326–27; of attributes, 223–24, 236; bodies as comprised of, 337–38; as both mind and body, 243; causation and, 72, 185, 238, 312; as their conatus, 312, 326, 327, 332, 339, 343; coordination and, 242; desire and, 345; as determinate, 72, 101, 236; difference and, 235, 345; differentiated sameness and, 241; distinction of spirit and body and, 281–82; divested of oneness, 76; divisibility and, 104–5, 137–38, 139; embodiment and, 194; entanglement of, 175, 194, 339–40, 359; essence and, 72, 99–100, 251, 326, 327; ethics and, 310; extension and, 49, 197, 233; freedom and, 33, 73; God existing modally and, 238–39, 357; Hegel and, 110, 160; as interconnected, 73–74, 100, 107–9, 317, 339–40; irreducibility and, 145, 191, 327; as lacking purpose, 173, 175, 178, 182, 194; measuring infinity and, 98; as negation, 127; normativity and, 186, 188, 194; as not preexisting substance, 164; oneness and, 35, 83–84, 156, 255; order as, 185; particularity and, 39, 66, 191–92, 195, 289, 312, 316–17, 345; power of, 72, 176, 242; as production of substance, 66–67, 149; as reality, 74–75, 102, 205, 316–17; singularness and, 254; substance and coincidence with, 125, 139, 162–63, 164, 326; substance as of its modes, 41, 67–71, 234, 238, 251–52, 316, 346 (*see also* modes, as actualized/enacted power); thinking of, 67, 287

modes, as actualized/enacted power: alteration of power and, 326–27, 335–36; essence and, 326; as existence of infinite, indeterminate power, 66, 69–70, 162–63, 164, 233–35, 326, 358; the mind of God and, 235–36; as of modes but not same with them, 125, 138–39, 164; modification of substance and, 67; nonbinariness and, 139; particularity and, 241, 326–27, 358; substance as irreducible to modes and, 162; substance not preexisting modes and, 67–68, 69, 102, 120, 138, 160; substance only existing as, 71–72, 101–2, 115, 120–21, 156–57, 160, 162–63

modes, as finite: actions and, 67, 69, 72, 101, 102; attributes and, 231, 233; boundaries and, 108; comprising infinity, 120–21, 162, 234, 316, 326; growth and decay and, 137; involvement and, 63; mind/body as aspects of the same and, 233; nonbinary reality and, 117; substance as its modes and, 68; the void and, 149

modes, humans as: agreements with others and, 343–44, 347; attributes and, 224, 231; difference and, 208, 316–17; experience of others and, 244; mind and body in coordination and, 241–42, 250, 254, 289 (*see also* affect; mind, as one and the same with the body); substance and, 137, 231

458 *Index*

monism: attributed to Spinoza, 21–22, 31, 35, 78, 119, 162, 264; Conway and, 38, 268, 281–83. *See* oneness
Montag, Warren, 23
Montesinos, Antón de, 276–77
morality: affective force of, 359; Cartesian truth and, 300–301; as dependent on its human invention, 318; God's attributes and, 357–59; Hebrew Scripture and, 355, 357–58; laws of, 353–54; Liebniz and, 87; limiting individual power and, 355; longtermism and, 211, 212; need for moral philosophy and, 297; New Materialism and, 318; normativity and, 310, 353; reason and, 353; religion and, 89, 353–54, 355, 361; self-interest and, 343; supporting living well, 353–54, 359; teleology and, 358. *See also* ethics
More, Henry, 25
Morton, Timothy. *See* Object-Oriented Ontology

naturalism: agency and, 207; Aristotle and, 11–12, 14–15, 34, 136; immanence and, 14, 15–16; Lucretius and, 132; medieval Jewish and Islamic philosophy and, 12, 13, 29–30, 95 (*see also* Aristotle, influence on Jewish and Islamic philosophy of); as against the negative, 133; suppression of, 12. *See also* causal determinism; causal necessity
nature: absence of hierarchy and, 42, 73, 74, 318, 320–21; absence of normativity and, 36; anthropomorphizing of, 319; as both thought and extension, 233; as eternal, 286; global heating and, 211, 213–14; global warming and, 320, 323, 326; God as creating laws of, 59, 204; God as not separate from, 41, 73, 133; God as transcending, 58; God *or* nature, 40–41, 42, 174, 191; God *or* substance *or* nature, 27, 65, 354; human mastery of, 203–4, 214–16, 269, 274, 296, 314–15, 329, 345; humans as separate from, 208, 311, 324; human sovereignty over animals and, 271, 274–75, 314; human use of animals and, 345–46; immanence and, 205; as infinite, 119, 121, 137, 169 (*see also* substance, as infinite); lack of sovereignty and, 26; laws/order of, 180–86, 188, 193–94, 203, 204, 208, 215; as limited, 110; mind as of, 283, 298; mind's union with, 296–97; as perfect, 167, 176, 187, 191; as reality, 73, 316; redefinition of, 27; as requiring governance, 106–7; as serving humans, 170, 171–76, 179, 188–89, 195, 207, 215, 225, 274; sexgender and, 190–91, 192–94, 200; the soul transcending, 59, 314; as sovereign, 320–21; substance as, 68; as without purpose, 193, 204, 207–9, 215–16. *See also* reality; substance
negative, the: the clinamen as against, 133; as corrupting being, 165; Eleaticism and, 125; as finite, 117; infinity precluding, 83–84, 101–2, 115, 125, 127, 139, 152–53; Spinoza as rejecting, 133–34, 138–39, 150, 152; as of substance, 144, 163; the void and, 130–32, 165. *See also* nothingness; sovereignty, nothingness/the void and; void, the
negativity, generative: configuring the Hegelian dialectic, 110, 115; as excluding a generative positive, 156; Object-Oriented Ontology and, 163; Spinozism as lacking, 84, 139, 151 (*see also* Hegel, G. W. F. (the negative and): misreading Spinoza and); the void and, 130–31, 132, 154. *See also* nothingness

Negri, Antonio, 70, 209, 300, 303
neoliberalism: free will and, 33, 39, 315–16, 330, 337, 350, 360; progress and, 208; self-sufficiency and, 311
Neoplatonism, 12, 62, 95, 281, 282, 285, 301
New Materialism, 15, 27, 39, 224, 300, 321, 346. See also Bennett, Jane; Braidotti, Rosi
New Science, 59, 221, 270
Nietzsche, Friedrich, 154, 299
nonbinariness: infinity and, 35–36, 79–80, 117, 122, 156–57; modes as actualized power and, 139; of reality, 36, 80, 117, 165, 194
normativity: absence of, 26, 36, 167; anthropocentrism and, 186; bodies and, 192–94, 195–96; culture and, 356; desire and, 186, 200, 202, 205; domination and, 186, 264–65; modes and, 186, 188, 194; morality and, 186, 187, 310, 353; nature and, 186–90, 194; ontology and, 186–87; prejudices of, 187, 356; reality and, 167, 185, 201–2; sexgender and, 192–94, 195; sovereignty and, 186–89; specificity of, 356; as supremacist, 186, 189; teleology and, 186–87; as transcendent, 186, 187, 193–94, 201, 310, 353, 361; transness and, 195; "Western" ethics and, 3. See also ableism; racism; sexism
nothingness: Adorno and, 124; as anthropic, 144; Badiou and, 149–53, 154; the being/nothingness binary and, 139, 163; in contemporary thought, 134; Ein Sof as creating, 142–43; epistemology and, 148; God and, 36, 125–26, 133, 137, 141–43, 154, 155, 159, 164–66; Kant and, 145; less than nothing and, 157, 158, 160; Lucretius and, 129; ontology and, 144–49, 151–52, 158, 160–61; ontotheology and, 36, 126, 140, 143, 144–46, 155, 157, 159, 164–65; Parmenides and, 125, 126–27, 128, 161, 165; as pervasive, 145; power and, 127, 133, 139; preceding creation, 180; as primary/originary, 36, 142, 155; as productive, 144, 145 (see also negativity, generative); universality of, 145; Žižek and, 157, 158–59. See also negative, the; sovereignty, nothingness/the void and; void, the
numbers, 96–100, 247, 248, 295. See also infinity

objectivity: Cartesian claims to, 29–30, 38, 220, 264, 273–74, 275, 280, 289, 308–9; as fiction, 10–11, 173; God and, 253–55; the infinite connection of causes and, 11; infinite intellect and, 258; inherent antagonism and, 160; miracles and, 154; obscured theology and, 169; of thought and extension, 232; unity and, 259. See also view from nowhere, the
Object-Oriented Ontology, 36, 126, 144–46, 148–49, 154, 156, 163, 164–65
Oldenburg, Henry, 106, 107, 134, 184–85, 204
oneness: Badiou and, 82, 94, 153, 154, 261; the diffracted void and, 158; Eleaticism and, 80, 128, 130, 137; erasure of difference and, 112; hierarchy and, 121–22; as immobile, 83; incompletion and, 160, 163; Kabbalah and, 35, 80–81, 86, 88, 94, 102; the Lacanian real and, 158; misreading Spinoza and, 82, 83, 119; in multiplicities, 150; the one as displaced and, 158; as Oriental, 20, 35, 77, 80, 82–85, 98; sovereignty and, 78–79, 81–82, 116, 117–18; Spinoza's repudiation of, 80, 96, 98, 100–101, 102,

oneness (*cont.*)
105–7, 153. *See also* identity; indivisibility; unity

ontology: actualized power and, 225, 227, 229–30, 231–32; affect and, 312, 335–36; anthropomorphism and, 171; difference and, 232–33, 235, 252, 262, 346; freedom and, 6; German-Jewish thinkers and, 303; of ideas, 302, 317; laws of nature and, 182, 186; of living well, 311, 336, 347; mathematical, 87, 99, 116, 150, 151–52, 154, 157; modes and, 189, 208, 235–36, 312; New Materialism and, 15, 27, 39, 224, 300, 321, 346 (*see also* Bennett, Jane; Braidotti, Rosi); normativity and, 186–87; privilege in, 74, 198, 207–9, 219–20, 261; redefinition and, 72; religious/moral idioms and, 353–54, 356; resisting oneness and, 26, 35, 76–77, 82; sex-gender and, 167, 190–91, 194, 195, 196–97, 198; social and political philosophy and, 5, 169, 190, 325; of sovereign traits begetting sovereignties, 283; thought and extension and, 224, 231, 234, 235–36, 237, 240, 253–54; vital materialism and, 319–26, 345, 346; "Western" (*see* binaries; dualism; free will; hierarchy; oneness; sovereignty; teleology; transcendence). *See also* atomism; causal immanence; immanence; naturalism; Object-Oriented Ontology; substance; *individual philosophers*

ontology, misreading Spinoza and: absence of hierarchy and, 42–43; being and thinking and, 253–54, 256, 257, 261; difference and, 252, 256; the Hegelian dialectic and, 114–15; laws of nature and, 186; nothingness and, 151–52, 158, 160–61; oneness and, 76–77, 119; parallelism and, 235, 253–54; teleology and, 174; vital materialism and, 322, 325

ontology, Spinoza's sources and: Aristotle and, 136; extension and, 53–54; Gersonides and, 286; immanence and, 49; infinite substance and, 65; Kabbalah and, 95; lack of mention in the *Ethics*, 43–44; Maimonides and, 51–52, 254, 256, 356

ontotheology: Maimonides and, 148; nothingness and, 36, 126, 140, 143, 144–46, 155, 157, 159, 164–65; oneness and, 94, 98, 153–54, 158. *See also* teleology; transcendence

Ord, Toby, 211, 212

order: anthropocentrism and, 181, 182, 185, 187, 225, 323; causation and, 152, 181, 295; desire for, 181; epistemology and, 100; God and, 171, 181–82, 225; hierarchy and, 55, 180, 295; imagination and, 181, 185, 190–91, 192; as merely apparent, 152; as modes, 185; nature and, 180–86, 193–94, 203, 204, 208, 215; prejudices of, 181–82; reality and, 100, 184, 185, 218; reason and, 247–48, 249; sovereignty and, 171, 180, 182, 188

Orientalism: anti-Judaism and, 18, 20, 84, 86, 113–14, 277; atheism and, 85, 86, 87, 120; Bayle and, 18; emanation and, 84, 127; hierarchy of "Western" over Oriental and, 20–21, 78, 85, 109–10, 112, 113–14, 116, 277; Jews lacking reason and, 277–78; Judaism as Oriental and, 77, 82–85, 98, 109–10, 114, 116, 277–78 (*see also* Hegel, G. W. F. (Spinozism as Oriental and)); oneness and, 20, 35, 77, 80, 82–85, 98

otherness: binaries and, 78; Christianity and construction of, 85; defining the rational self and, 265; essentialized difference and, 78; God as other and, 170–71; hierarchy and, 78, 81; of humans to nature, 324; identity and, 81–82; lacking substance and, 23; subjugation and, 265–66 (*see also* colonialism)

otherness, Jewish: Hegel and, 93, 111–12, 116 (*see also* Hegel, G. W. F. (Spinozism as Oriental and)); Jews as Oriental and, 93, 115, 116, 119–20, 277–78; Jews as outside history and, 25, 85, 111, 112, 210, 277–78; misreading Spinoza and, 119–20, 161; "Western" philosophy and, 78, 93. See also *Spinozastreit*, the

paganism, 85, 89, 113

pantheism, 18, 19, 85, 88, 95, 127

parallelism: attributed to Spinoza, 198, 221–22, 235, 251, 253–54, 301; of attributes, 197–98, 199–200, 235

Parmenides: being and, 80, 128, 130, 161, 165; nothingness and, 125, 126–27, 128, 161, 165

particularity: adequate ideas and, 249; anthropocentrism and, 319, 344–45; causation and, 191, 345; desire and, 332, 345; dissolved, 115, 259; erasure of, 116, 191, 293, 304–5, 319–21; ethics and, 318; as foreclosing idealism, 222; God and, 191; of humans, 318; infinite power and, 326; intuitive knowledge and, 248–49; Judaism and, 20, 25, 113–14, 322; materialism and, 316–17; of nature, 187; oneness and, 112, 115, 127; perception and, 293; reality and, 191; reason and, 17, 276; self-esteem and, 340–41; sexgender and, 192; of suffering, 324; of thought, 240, 262, 268, 287

particularity, modes and: actualized/enacted power and, 66, 241, 326–27, 358; causation and, 189; desire and, 345; kinds of modes and, 316–17;

lived experience and, 244–45, 289, 312; sexgender and, 191–92, 195

Passions of the Soul (Descartes), 279, 328–29

Peden, Knox, 261

philosophy, Islamic medieval: God as necessary and, 46; historicism and, 25; Ibn Rushd and, 11–12, 136, 142, 143, 203, 285; Ibn Sina and, 11–13, 45, 50, 56, 60, 136, 203; immanence and, 14, 15–16, 25, 49; Plato's influence on, 4; politics and, 3, 4, 5, 10; rationalism and, 25; "Western" marginalization of, 10, 11–12, 110. See also Aristotle, influence on Jewish and Islamic philosophy of

philosophy, Jewish medieval: anthropic metaphors of reality and, 106–7; causal determinism and, 203; Crescas and, 97–98, 125–26, 136, 140–43, 164, 203, 292; emanation and, 89, 95; epistemology and, 268–69; extension and, 55; God as incorporeal and, 55, 103; God as limitless and, 53–54, 102, 225–26; God as necessary and, 46; God's intellect creating material things and, 236; historicism and, 25; Ibn Ezra and, 14, 24, 49; Ibn Gabirol and, 12, 13, 62; immanence and, 25, 29, 34–35, 39, 49, 51–52, 168, 288, 311; infinity and, 34–35, 102; Kabbalah and, 95; naturalism and, 12, 13, 29–30, 95; Neoplatonism and, 62, 95; ontology and, 53–54; Plato's influence on, 4; politics and, 3, 4, 10; rationalism and, 14, 24, 25, 90; resistance to dualism and, 264; substance and, 223; temporality and, 209, 210; unity and, 254; "Western" marginalization of, 10, 11–12, 13–14, 35, 116, 120, 122 (*see also* philosophy, "Western" (censorship/marginalization of thought philosophy, Jewish medieval (cont. and)). See also Aristotle, influence on Jewish and Islamic philosophy of; God, attributes of; Kabbalah; Maimonides

philosophy, modern: atomism and, 35–36; Christian supremacy and, 9, 77–78; ignoring Spinoza, 24; Spinoza as testing-point of, 21, 109; Spinoza's Jewishness and, 17, 24; subjectivity and, 264–65; teleology and, 85; the theory–praxis problem and, 306; the void and, 164. See also Object-Oriented Ontology; vital materialism; *individual philosophers*

philosophy, "Western": anti-Judaism of, 77, 112–14; Augustine's influence on, 271–72, 307; Cartesian influence on, 3, 14–15, 265–66, 299–302, 307–8 (*see also* dualism, Cartesian); censorship of Aristotle and, 12, 143, 307; claims to universality and, 289–90, 319–20; colonialism and, 14–15, 265; converting Eastern concepts, 20–21, 78, 85 (*see also* supersessionism); critiques of Spinozim, 14, 18, 20 (*see also* Hegel, G. W. F.; Jacobi, Friedrich Heinrich); fictions of, 10–11, 289–90 (*see also* disinterestedness; neutrality; objectivity); importance of Jewish ideas to, 16, 109, 161; infinity and, 34–35, 165, 167; the Jewish other and, 78, 93 (*see also* Orientalism); longtermism and, 211–14; misreading Spinoza and, 15, 20–21, 22, 27, 35, 111–14, 120, 122 (*see also* Hegel, G. W. F. (misreading Spinoza and)); New Materialism and, 15, 27, 39, 224, 300, 321, 346; politics as separate and, 3, 4, 5, 10–11; reason as sovereign and, 37, 240, 265, 271–72, 277, 288 (*see also* reason, sovereignty/supremacy of); sovereignty as framing, 8–9, 26, 28–30, 34, 109, 114, 122–23, 165, 288–89 (*see also* domination; sovereignty); sovereignty of mind over matter and, 56, 241, 284, 288 (*see also* mind, supremacy over body of); Spinozism as threat to, 18–19, 78; telos of history and, 112, 113–14, 208; treatment of term, 365n1; vital materialism and, 319–26, 345, 346. See also anthropocentrism; domination; dualism; exceptionalism, human; feminisms; free will; hierarchy; individualism; nothingness; supremacy; teleology; transcendence; *individual philosophers*

philosophy, "Western" (as Christian): Christianizing Spinoza and, 19, 256–57; Christian supremacy and, 9–10, 77–78, 84–85, 112, 113–14, 263, 272, 289, 307–8 (*see also* Hegel, G. W. F.); Christology and, 77, 78; dualism and, 263, 270 (*see also* dualism, Cartesian; dualism: Christian; mind, supremacy over body of); Hegelian history and, 112; minimizing/occluding sources and, 11–12, 14; misreading Spinoza and, 21–22, 23, 24; politics as separate and, 3, 4; sovereignty as frame and, 9–10, 29, 109, 122; Spinozism as threat and, 18–19. See also Descartes, René; exceptionalism, human; Hegel, G. W. F.; hierarchy; individualism; Kant, Immanuel

philosophy, "Western" (censorship/marginalization of thought and): Aristotle and, 4, 12, 263; Christian supremacy and, 13–14, 15, 16, 270, 307–8; claims to universality and, 289–90; ignorance of diversity and, 113; immanence and, 14, 29; infinity and, 35, 122; materialism and, 10, 11–

12, 143, 307; misreading Spinoza and, 22, 31, 120, 122; naturalism and, 10, 11–12; otherness and, 270; Spinozist anti-Cartesian dualism and, 263–64; Spinozist infinity and, 122

Plato: dualism and, 48, 270, 307, 314; free will and, 314; the good and, 80, 314; influence on medieval Jewish and Islamic philosophy, 4; influence on "Western" philosophy, 13, 38; interpretations of Spinoza and, 22; oneness and, 80, 254; reality as individual being and, 106; spirit/thought's supremacy over matter and, 241, 311; transcendence and, 44, 241; universality and, 191

Plotinus, 44–45, 62, 80

Political Treatise, 2, 206, 353–54

politics: causal determinism and, 308–9; common good and, 355; culture and, 324; hierarchy and, 331; inseparability from philosophy, 3, 4, 5, 10, 308; nonhuman things and, 323, 324, 325, 345, 346; ontology and, 5, 169, 190, 325; *Political Treatise* and, 2, 206, 353–54; separation from philosophy, 3, 4, 5, 10–11, 169; sovereignty and, 1–2, 8–9, 25; *Theological-Political Treatise* (*Tractatus Theologico-Politicus*) and, 2, 24, 184, 353–54, 358. *See also* democracy

positive and negative (something/nothing): Badiou and, 149–55; the clinamen and, 133, 165; evasion of, 158; the positive as superior and, 115, 117, 125; rejection of primordial forms of, 162, 163; rejection of the binary and, 124–25, 126, 138, 139, 155; Žižek and, 157, 165. *See also* negative, the; nothingness; substance; void, the

Poullain de la Barre, François, 280

power: of acting, 176, 241, 242, 334, 336, 340, 341, 343, 356; alteration of, 242, 326–27, 335–36, 338; of atoms, 133; causation and, 234, 337, 348, 352–53; as constitutive of substance, 66, 67, 70, 71, 99–100, 101–2, 115, 234 (*see also* modes, as actualized/enacted power); as contingent, 57, 61, 237; creative, 306; desire/willpower and, 310, 331, 333, 334, 336, 337, 339, 350–52 (*see also* free will, human claims to; self-esteem); exoneration of, 315; expressed in modes, 241 (*see also* modes, as actualized/enacted power); finite, 52; human, 203, 360–61 (*see also* free will, human claims to); ideas of, 308; imbalances of, 320, 323, 326; immanent, 40, 225–26; infinite substance and, 66, 67, 68, 69, 70, 71, 72, 80, 101; knowledge and, 348, 356; lack of, 54, 175, 341; limitation of, 55–57, 61, 66, 143, 225, 234, 355, 360–61; modes and, 250, 336, 347 (*see also* modes, as actualized/enacted power); morality and, 355; naturalization of, 122–23, 171, 205–6, 308; nature and, 271, 300, 320, 322, 323, 330; negativity/nothingness and, 127, 133, 139; ontology and, 225, 227, 229–30, 231–32; operations of, 197; perfection and, 348; as principle of all relationships, 274; racism as serving, 189, 190; responsibility and, 315; self-generation and, 46–47; sex⁄gender and, 196–98, 206; of things, 319, 320, 322, 324, 325; thought and, 249, 254–55, 257, 297, 336; as unlimited, 59–60, 66, 135, 172, 183, 270; virtue and, 242–43, 342; vital materialism and, 321–25. *See also* affect, power and; attributes, power and; colonialism; essence, power and; free will; God, power of; substance, power constituting power, actualization of: attributes and, 230, 231, 241; God and, 56–57, 66, 229–30; the infinite connection of causes and, 74–75, 327; infinite substance and, 66, 67, 68, 70, 71, 72, 101; nonbinary infinity and, 80, 117, 156–57. *See also* modes, as actualized/enacted power

power, actualization of (substance as): absence of identity and, 234; attributes and, 231; causation and, 156–57, 238; divisibility/indivisibility and, 138; essence and, 223, 226, 232; immanence and, 70, 238; incomplete reality and, 120–21; as of modes but not same with them, 125, 138–39; ontological realness of, 232; substance as insubstantial and, 71, 99–100; substance as not preexistent and, 67–68, 70, 101–2, 115, 117; unity and, 120. *See also* modes, as actualized/enacted power

power, indeterminate: attributes and, 231, 236, 238, 239–40; causation and, 234, 238; divisibility/indivisibility and, 105; as extension, 231; infinity and, 66, 138–39; mind and body as same and, 233; only existing determinately, 71, 74–75, 105, 138 (*see also* modes, as actualized/enacted power); self-knowledge and, 356; singularity of, 235

power, infinite: attributes and, 223, 225, 231, 236; the connection of causes and, 234; as essence of substance, 69, 223; of existing, 54, 65–66, 222–23, 225, 326; existing as modes, 41, 70, 120, 138–39, 234–36, 326, 358 (*see also* modes, as actualized/enacted power); indeterminacy and, 66, 138–39; as necessary of existence, 68, 162, 185; reality and, 225–26, 240; a telos as subverting, 170; thought and, 237, 239–40

power, as never potential/reserve: essence and, 327; God as active and, 56–57, 66, 229–30; immanence and, 68, 156–57; incomplete reality and, 121; lack of teloi and, 208; modes and, 125, 138, 232; necessity of nature and, 187; perfection and, 176; Spinoza's redefinition of substance and, 41

power, to exist: affect and, 335–36; the conatus and, 326; God and, 254, 255; infinity of, 54, 65–66, 222–23, 225, 326; living well and, 342–43; reality and, 54, 222–23; as substance, 241. *See also* being

prejudices: appendix to Part I (*Ethics*) and, 5–7, 57–58, 181–83, 190, 202–3, 205; compromising ethics, 325; Deleuze and, 256; free will as, 310–11, 330–31, 360; furthering misperceptions, 202; inhibiting adequate ideas, 297; inhibiting understanding, 5, 6, 31, 40, 43, 168–69, 170–71, 317; language as repository of, 27; Maimonides and, 27, 355–56; modes of reason and, 317–18; nature as purposive and, 170–74, 176, 179; of normativity, 187, 356; of order and confusion, 181–82; Scriptural correction of, 355–56; sovereignty and, 168–73, 310–11, 330–31; supremacy and, 32–33, 220, 221; teleology and, 168–69, 174, 205. *See also* anthropocentrism; anthropomorphism; exceptionalism: human; free will; teleology; transcendence

Principle of Sufficient Reason, the, 37, 224

Principles (Descartes), 272, 273, 290

progress, 32, 208–11, 215, 217, 278

psychoanalysis: consciousness and, 300; the other and, 115

psychology: human failure and, 330,

337; pop, 33; sexgender and, 199; the subject and, 300–301
purpose. *See* teleology

racism: Cartesian influence on, 265–67, 275–76, 289; colonialism and, 38, 275–76; *ego cogito* and, 266; race as interpreted nature and, 189–90; reason and, 266, 275–76; scientific, 90, 266, 275–76; as serving power, 189–90; Spinoza's, 30, 187–88, 266–67; systemic, 324; teleology and, 188

rank. *See* hierarchy

rationalism: Aristotelian, 4; Augustine and, 272, 373; Cartesian, 38, 275; medieval Jewish, 14, 24, 25, 90; nature as lacking, 208; phenomenology and, 300; scientific racism and, 275–76; Spinoza's sources of, 25, 224 (*see also* Gersonides; Ibn Ezra, Abraham; Maimonides). *See also* reason

rationality: animals as lacking, 271, 274–75, 345, 346–47; Christianity transmuted to, 265; culture and, 315; hierarchy and, 204, 265–66, 267, 275–76, 288; humanity in God's image and, 271; insufficient, 329; as not guaranteeing ethics, 310; the rational self and, 265; the soul and, 276–77, 285; teleology of, 329; women as inferior and, 271. *See also* mind; reason

Ravven, Heidi, 291

reality: affections and, 243; anthropic metaphors for, 106–7; atomism and, 161; attributes and, 225, 226–27, 241; causal immanence and, 295; as difference, 261; as disparate, 32, 108; diversity and, 230, 232, 234, 252; divested of sovereignty, 74; epistemology ordering, 100; extension and, 284; as finite, 118, 121–22, 127; God's interruption of causation and, 58; God's supremacy over, 7, 41, 48–49, 59–60 (*see also* God, as sovereign/monarch); God's transcendence ensuring, 117–18, 135–36, 255; as hierarchical, 269–70, 281, 282; as immanent, 187; as incomplete, 120–21; as individual being, 106–7; intra-action and, 34, 73; as lacking purpose/meaning, 173, 186–87, 204, 207, 218; modes and, 69, 71–72, 74–75, 102, 205, 262, 316–17; as nonbinary, 36, 80, 117, 165, 194; normativity and, 167, 201–2; oneness and, 80–82, 100–101, 105–7, 118, 120–21, 321; order and, 184–85, 218; particularity and, 191; as perfect, 176, 187; power to exist and, 54, 222–23, 226; proto-reality and, 159–60; the Rift and, 146; as self-caused, 42; as stable, 165; as system of identity, 165; as thinkable, 237, 262; transcendence and, 81, 185, 255; as ungoverned by reason, 224; unity and, 51–52, 83, 121–22; as variable, 108; "Western" conception of origin of, 44–45, 48, 63. *See also* causes, infinite connection of; hierarchy, reality and; nature; substance

reality, infinity and: constant becoming and, 214; desire and, 214; disallowing supremacy of thought, 223–24; immanence and, 99, 103, 123, 187, 205, 226; infinite attributes and, 129, 221, 222–24, 226, 230; the infinite connection of causes and, 41–42, 61–63, 69, 72–76, 106–7, 156, 194, 214, 316; infinite power and, 225–26, 240 (*see also* modes, as actualized/enacted power); Lucretius and, 131; teleology and, 167, 207. *See also* causal determinism; modes; substance, as infinite reality, perception of: attributes and, 232, 246; body as one and the same with the mind and, 222, 224–25, 246, 247, 249, 298; effect on perception in general, 11, 41, 121–22, 169, 171–72, 269, 288; ethics and, 325; human limitation and, 234; as illusion, 146–47; Marx and, 171; memory and, 246; multiple ways of, 226–27; as not neutral, 30; universalizing and, 246

reason: affect and, 39, 312, 349; anthropocentrism and, 225–26; beings of, 68, 100, 105, 137, 198, 266, 317; as disembodied, 196 (*see also* mind, supremacy over body of); as distinguishing humans, 272, 274, 355; as distinguishing substance and modes, 68; as essence, 288–89; essentialization of, 266; exception from, 46; God as self-caused and, 47; God identified with, 48, 285; Jacobi's attacks on, 18–19, 88–90; as Jewish, 88–89, 90, 91–92; Jews as lacking, 277–78; laws of nature and, 183–84; living well and, 222, 240, 245–49, 347–49, 353–55, 360–61; longtermism and, 211; mind–body interdependence and, 37, 251; as neutral, 38, 220, 264–65, 268, 289–90, 308–9; as not guaranteeing ethics, 310; order and, 247–48, 249; particularity and, 17, 276; the passions and, 328, 336–37; precluding a need for hope, 208; the Principle of Sufficient Reason and, 37, 224; progress and, 278; racism and, 266, 275–76; reality as ungoverned by, 224; as reliant on the body, 249; transcendence and, 38, 276; universalization of, 12, 19, 38, 220, 275–76, 278, 280, 294; white "Western" culture and, 263, 266, 275–76; wholeness and, 137. *See also* Enlightenment, the; mind

reason, sovereignty/supremacy of: absence of mind/body hierarchy and, 37, 241, 250, 351; affective ideas and, 349; all thought as modal precluding, 240; causal immanence and, 224; Christianity and, 10, 267; the *ego cogito* and, 266, 267, 290, 297–301; free will and, 360; God subsumed in, 47; idealism and, 262; infinite reality precluding, 223–24; Kant and, 221; pure thought and, 261; "Western" philosophy and, 37, 240, 265, 271–72, 277, 288. *See also* mind, supremacy over body of

redefinition: of affect, 335; anti-dualism and, 39; Descartes and, 270; disrupting sovereignty and, 27, 39, 40–41, 42, 71; of freedom, 39, 40, 71, 313, 359–60, 361; of God, 41–42, 45–46, 354; of living, 342–43; misapprehension of, 42–43; of natural law, 184–85; of nature, 27; ontology and, 72; of substance, 27, 34, 41–42, 71; as subversive, 27, 42, 129

Renz, Ursula, 239
Rice, Lee, 341
Riskin, Jessica, 207
Rojtburd, Oleksandr, xv, xvi
Romantics, German, 19, 20, 85, 88, 92
Rose, Erik-Sven, 111
Roth, Leon, 13, 108
Rudavsky, Tamar, 264

sameness: anthropocentrism and, 223, 319; dialectic of, 132, 151; difference and, 219, 223, 286; differentiated, 241; reduction of sensibility to understanding and, 259; of thought and extension, 220, 224, 225–26, 298–99; as trait of sovereignty, 78–79, 219; vital materialism and, 346. *See also* oneness; unity; wholeness

Schelling, Friedrich Wilhelm Joseph, 19, 88, 159

Scholasticism, Christian: atomism and, 126; Descartes' critique of, 279, 296; God as causing but not caused and, 46; God's will and, 59; Rightist Aristotelianism and, 12–13; univocity and, 252; value judgment and, 179; the void and, 126, 143, 164

Science of Logic, The (Hegel), 83–84, 139

Schuller, G. H., 223

Scripture. *See* Hebrew Scripture

self, the: becoming and, 18, 115, 118; boundaries with others and, 204, 309, 313; the Cartesian subject and, 269, 296, 299, 304; Christian, 265; constant motion of, 304; entanglement with perception, 313; essence and, 327; as experience, 284; as finite, 259–60; free will and, 273, 299–300; identity and, 260, 327; individuality and, 304–5, 313; as its existence, 344; Maimon and, 259; mastery of, 110, 203–4, 321, 328–29, 337, 350 (*see also* free will, human claims to); mind as, 273, 284, 290, 295, 296, 299; the negative and, 115, 127, 130–31; oneness and, 81, 84; the rational self and, 265; return to, 115, 117; transcendence and, 302; vital materialism and, 321. *See also* Descartes, René (mind over body and, *cogito* and); individualism

self-causation: causal immanence and, 47–48, 131, 136–37; Descartes and, 46–47; God and, 46–47, 69; reality and, 42; substance and, 46–47, 48, 136, 138, 374n200; the void and, 154

self-consciousness, 111, 112, 304, 320, 353

self-determination, 131, 289, 299–300, 310, 312. *See also* free will, human claims to

self-esteem, 313, 339, 340–41, 350, 356

self-knowledge, 248, 259, 271–73, 296, 299, 304, 356–57, 359

sexgender: absent from the mind, 280, 287; anthropocentrism and, 176–78, 369n30; binaries and, 192, 195–97, 198–200, 206, 282–83; body as one and the same with the mind and, 194, 197, 198, 201, 287; Cartesian dualism and, 202, 278–80; causation and, 194, 198; Conway and, 282–83; culture and, 197, 199, 264; denaturalization of sex and, 194–96, 200, 201; difference and, 193, 197–99, 206, 219–20; embodiment and, 194, 196, 197, 200–201, 202; essence and, 193, 198, 281, 287; extension and, 197–98, 199–200; feminisms and, 36–37, 196–202; hierarchy and, 200, 201, 206; imagination and, 177, 190–91, 192, 196; liberalism and, 202; modes of thought and, 190–91, 198, 199–200, 287; naturalizing stereotypes of, 197, 199, 206, 282–83; nature and, 190–91, 192–94, 200; normativity and, 192–95; ontology and, 167, 190–91, 194, 195, 196–97, 198; particularity and, 191–92, 195; power and, 196–98, 206; teleology and, 36–37, 178, 192–93; transcendence and, 194–95. *See also* cisness

sexism, 177–78, 187–88, 190, 197, 199, 206, 279, 345–46

Sharp, Hasana, 318, 346

Short Treatise on God, Human and Well-Being, 48, 64, 105, 137

Shulman, Carl, 214

soul, the: animal-human difference and, 274, 277, 346; the Aristotelian Left and, 12; being and, 107; bodily experience influencing, 282, 355; causal necessity and, 311; control of the passions and, 328; denied independence of, 83; enabling agency,

soul, the (*cont.*)
320; as essence, 264; free will and, 59, 298, 311, 328; human exceptionalism and, 274, 277, 278, 314, 320, 346–47; as immaterial, 270; immortality of, 286; Kabbalah and, 87, 93–94; mind and, 271; as one with the body, 282; rationality and, 276–77, 278, 285, 346–47; substance and, 87, 258; supremacy over the body of, 270, 282–83, 285, 328 (*see also* mind, supremacy over body of); as transcending nature, 59, 314; transience of, 86; welfare of, 355. *See also* spirit

sovereignty: Aristotle and, 49–50, 54–55; atheism destabilizing, 123; Badiou and, 149, 153–55; being and, 165; causation and, 62–63, 117–18; Christian sources of, 43, 44–45, 59, 109, 311, 312–13, 319, 321, 329; Conway and, 281–83; definition of, 7, 9; desire conditioning, 75; difference and, 79, 235, 283; of the East/West binary, 20; of the end/purpose, 7–8 (*see also* teleology); entitlement to, 8–9; epistemology and, 9, 220–22, 225–26, 268–69, 290, 303 (*see also* method; subject, the; truth); of essence, 194; essentialized difference and, 283; ethics and, 38–39, 310–11, 317, 339, 343; as framing "Western" philosophy, 109, 122–23, 165, 272, 288–89, 313, 326 (*see also* domination); human exceptionalism and, 39, 73, 107, 180, 215–16, 217, 317 (*see also* free will, human claims to; God, anthropomorphizing of); human mastery of nature and, 203–4, 214–16, 269, 274, 296, 314–15, 329, 345; of humans over animals, 271, 274–75; identity and, 234, 327; immanence disallowing, 10, 169, 209; infinite substance as removing, 117, 129, 165, 169; infinity removed from ontotheology and, 76; intuition and, 306; laws of nature and, 183, 185–86; living well and, 352–53; modes divested of, 35, 73, 76, 108–9, 190, 202, 327; national borders and, 216; naturalization of, 75, 121, 122–23, 169, 171, 178, 208, 269, 277 (*see also* God, anthropomorphizing of; God, as sovereign/monarch); of nature, 320–21 (*see also* vital materialism); nature as having human ends and, 170–74, 207, 215, 274; normativity and, 186–89; notions of history and, 37, 208–9; oneness and, 78–79, 81–82, 116, 117–18; order and, 171, 180, 182, 188; persistent appeal of, 122–23; of philosophy, 29–30; political/legal theory and, 1–2, 8–9, 25, 169; prejudices and, 168–69; reality and, 5, 34, 40, 41–42, 71–72, 74–76, 123, 165; reception of Spinoza and, 122; sexgender and, 178, 190–96, 201, 202; of the soul, 328 (*see also* mind, supremacy over body); of the state, 305, 353–54; substance *as* God *as* nature and, 41; substance as immanent cause and, 98; substance as insubstantial and, 65, 69, 71; substance as without volition and, 56, 57–58; substance dispossessing, 7, 43, 136–37; transcendence dislodging, 175; universality as, 192–93. *See also* domination; God, as sovereign/monarch; individualism; mind, supremacy over body of; power; reason, sovereignty/supremacy of; supremacy

sovereignty, begetting sovereignties: beyond assumed categories, 8–9; COVID and, 215–16; denaturalizing sovereignty and, 45; dismantling sovereignties and, 318–21, 325, 326; the East/West binary and, 20; exceptionalist human reason and, 271, 274; extension and, 48; God as sovereign/monarch and, 41, 171, 177–78, 204, 271, 274, 277, 288–89, 315, 330; naturalizing sovereignty and, 75, 171, 177–78, 269; ontologizing sovereign traits and, 283; prejudices and, 169, 310–11, 330–31; progress and, 209

sovereignty, denaturalization of: anthropocentrism and, 11, 75; disrupting sovereignty and, 75; divesting God of sovereignty and, 34, 41–42, 359–60; humans as of nature and, 204, 318, 325; immanence and, 43–44; the infinite connection of causes and, 63; perception of reality and, 5–9, 269; as resource, 30; sovereignty begetting sovereignties and, 6–7, 45, 75; substance as without volition and, 56, 57–58

sovereignty, disrupting: attributes and, 233–34, 287–88, 297–99; binaries and, 42, 79, 117, 126, 155, 162, 165, 205, 268; causal determinism and, 39, 316–17, 331–35, 337, 341–42; causal immanence and, 47, 136–37, 269 (*see also* immanence: absence of hierarchy and); contesting supremacy and, 118; denaturalizing sovereignty and, 75; God divested of sovereignty and, 26, 171, 207–8; humans divested of sovereignty and, 29; infinity and, 34–35, 115, 122, 165, 169; like causing like and, 262; reality divested of sovereignty and, 26, 29, 41–43, 297–98; reason divested of sovereignty and, 29, 238–40, 244; redefinition and, 27, 39, 40–41, 42, 71; refusing new alternatives and, 7, 26, 165–66; Spinoza's Jewish sources and, 80; substance as insubstantial and, 139; the void and, 35, 36. *See also* mind, as one and the same with the body

sovereignty, God and: Descartes' conception of, 59–60, 136, 203–4, 255, 266, 329; God as exemplar and, 7, 33, 44, 45, 46, 49 (*see also* free will: God as having; God, anthropomorphizing of; God, as sovereign/monarch); God divested of, 26, 27, 34, 40–41, 57–59, 60–61, 171, 207–8 (*see also* free will: God's lack of); nothingness/the void and, 125–26, 141–43, 154, 155, 164–66; prejudices rooted in, 168–73. *See also* God, as sovereign/monarch

sovereignty, logics of: Badiou and, 149, 153–55; binaries and, 79–80, 118, 126, 200, 218, 262, 274; Cartesianism and, 27, 43; Christianity and, 9, 29, 36, 39, 43, 44–45; configuring "Western" philosophy, 9, 10, 29–30; denaturalizing sovereignty and, 75; ethics and, 310–11; feminisms and, 27, 283; free will and, 7, 329; Hegel and, 27, 78, 109, 114–15, 116–18, 122; New Materialism and, 27; Object-Oriented Ontology and, 27, 36; reproduced in critique, 21; vital materialism and, 39. *See also* domination; exceptionalism, human; hierarchy; idealism; parallelism; progress; supersessionism; supremacy; teleology; transcendence

sovereignty, nothingness/the void and: Badiou and, 153–55, 156; Crescas and, 125–26, 140–43; God and, 125–26, 141–43, 154, 155, 164–66; Hegel and, 84, 110, 117, 139, 156, 157, 160; Object-Oriented Ontology and, 36, 126, 144–49; Žižek and, 157–59

sovereignty, of mind: Cartesian dualism and, 11, 183, 250, 268, 269–70, 284, 287, 290–92; ontological privileging and, 219. *See also* mind, supremacy over body of

Spinoza, Baruch: as baptized/Christianized, 88, 92, 93, 113, 252, 256–57; conflict of interpretation and, 22–25; Kabbalah as discrediting, 18, 21, 24, 88, 89, 93, 94, 281 (see also *Spinozastreit*, the). See also atheism, Spinoza accused of; *Ethics*; Hegel, G. W. F. (misreading Spinoza and); Judaism, Spinoza's identity and; living well

Spinoza, Baruch (biography): education, 16–17, 95, 367n29; expulsion from Amsterdam's Jewish community, 17, 24, 25, 171, 267; family move to Caribbean, 267; overview, 15, xv–xvi

Spinoza, Baruch (sources and influences): acknowledged in scholarship, 16, 86, 264; anti-Cartesianism and, 263–64, 267–69, 270, 285, 306–8, 311; attributes and, 60–61, 68, 221, 226–27, 229, 231–33, 241; bodies and, 264, 268, 285, 286, 287, 308; causal determinism and, 203; citation in the *Ethics* and, 31, 43–44, 328; Deleuze and, 252, 253–55, 256; epistemology and, 268–69; God's corporeality and, 55; God's necessity and, 54, 55; idealism and, 236; ignored in scholarship, 43, 113, 222, 264; immanence and, 49, 53, 168, 225–26, 249, 269, 288, 303, 308–9 (see also Gersonides; Ibn Ezra, Abraham; Maimonides); infinity and, 102; as lens for reading Spinoza, 31; living well and, 297; materialism/naturalism and, 11–12, 13; mind and body as one and the same and, 303; minimizing of, 11–12, 13–14, 15–16, 120 (see also philosophy, Islamic medieval; philosophy, Jewish medieval); misunderstanding of, 16; modes and, 65, 68; Neoplatonism and, 95; oneness and, 80–81, 98, 102; pushed to different conclusions, 24–25, 43–44, 95; rationalism and, 25, 224 (see also Gersonides; Ibn Ezra, Abraham; Maimonides); Spinoza's education and, 16–17; substance as the actualization of limitless power and, 222–23, 225–27; teleology and, 14–15, 209; transcendence and, 14–15, 24, 292; unity and, 24; Wolfson and, 13. See also Aristotle, influence on Jewish and Islamic philosophy of; Maimonides; ontology, Spinoza's sources and; philosophy, Islamic medieval; philosophy, Jewish medieval

Spinoza, Baruch (works): *Cogitata Metaphysica*, 51, 60, 229; *Hebrew Grammar*, 43, 64, 373n167; *Political Treatise*, 2, 206, 353–54; *Short Treatise on God, Human and Well-Being*, 48, 64, 105, 137; *Theological-Political Treatise (Tractatus Theologico-Politicus)*, 2, 24, 184, 353–54, 358; *Treatise on the Emendation of the Intellect*, 246, 269, 295, 296, 301

Spinozastreit, the, 20, 77–79, 88–92, 93, 94. See also Jacobi, Friedrich Heinrich

spirit: action and, 304; becoming of, 20, 118, 225–26; in God, 82; God as, 204, 271, 274, 282; God separated from, 83; Hegel's history of philosophy and, 112; infusing matter, 282; as mode, 83; teleology of, 85, 116, 117; as universal, 20. See also soul, the

spirit, supremacy of: Augustine and, 204, 271; the body as source of evil and, 270; Christianity and, 10–11, 49, 282–83, 287, 303, 311, 331; Conway and, 282–83, 287–88; Descartes and, 49, 59, 268, 270, 273–74,

282, 287–88; ghosts and, 176–77; God as spirit and, 204, 271, 274, 282; human free will and, 310–11; legacy of, 9–11; nonhuman animals and, 274–75; Plato and, 241, 311

spirit and matter: as active/passive, 281; Augustine and, 204, 267–68, 271, 314; Conway and, 281–83; as parts of the irreducible same, 287–88; as rational/irrational, 265

Strauss, Leo, 13, 129

subject, the: the absolute as, 35; body as, 286; as capacity to think, 295; Cartesian, 38, 264, 269, 290, 296, 299–301, 304, 315, 329; domination of the object and, 306; exercising will and, 315; God and, 237, 329; Hegel and, 84, 301, 306; human supremacy and, 225–26, 274; as transcendent, 291–92; as without omniscience, 239

substance: affections of, 48, 49, 68, 100, 231, 374n200; as attributes, 230–31, 232; as a cause, 63, 156; the clinamen and, 132, 156, 161; coincidence with its modes and, 125, 139, 162–64, 326; dispossession of sovereignty by, 7, 43, 136–37; as divisible, 135–36, 137, 139; encompassing subject, 115; freedom and, 58, 61, 62, 83, 329, 359; as given, 152–53; God as, 54, 83; having knowledge only modally, 239; Hegel and, 77, 83, 84; human perception of, 231 (*see also* reality, perception of); as immobile, 110, 138; as indivisible, 103–5, 134, 137–39, 162, 164; as irreducible to its modes, 107, 108, 139; as of its modes, 63–64, 65, 67–72, 137–38, 234; as lacking purpose, 173–76; as lacking volition/will, 56, 57–58, 61, 360; matter as of, 48–49; movement and, 135–36; as not matter, 71, 101, 138, 162–63; as not preexisting its modes, 125, 133, 138, 139, 156–57, 164, 183, 238; the other as lacking, 23; as preexisting its modes, 149, 253; redefinition of, 27, 34, 41, 42, 71; as self-caused, 46–48, 136, 138, 374n200; as stable, 160; as subject, 20, 110, 156, 209; as substantial, 149; transcendence and, 55, 136. *See also* attributes; God; immanence, of substance; matter; nature; reality

substance, as indeterminate: causation and, 238; coincidence with modes and, 125, 162–64; identity and, 234–35; indivisibility and, 235; insubstantiality and, 101 (*see also* modes, as actualized/enacted power); modal change and, 137; perfection and, 65, 102; power as attributes and, 236; resisting limitation and, 65

substance, as indeterminate (infinity and): change in substance and, 105; the connection of causes and, 234, 316; existing as finite and determinate acts, 71–72, 74–75, 117 (*see also* modes); infinite/limitless power and, 101, 102, 138–39; irreducibility and, 162–63, 164; power of existing and, 65–66; substance as not whole and, 115

substance, as infinite: attributes as realizing power and, 231; Badiou and, 149, 151–52; being and, 99, 165; causation and, 49, 238; coincidence with modes and, 125, 162–63, 326; definition of modes and, 68; disruption of binaries and, 117–19; existing beyond human experience, 225; extension and, 104, 105, 137, 141, 144, 231; foreclosing the negative, 83–84, 101, 102, 115, 125, 127, 139, 152–53; identity and, 234–35; immanence and, 41, 48, 49, 103, 124, 163, 169, 185; incompletion and, 120–21, 160, substance, as infinite (*cont.*) 163–64; indivisibility and, 104–5; infinite activity and, 79, 105, 125, 127–28, 138–39, 162; infinite attributes and, 222–23, 224, 226–27; infinite power of existing and, 223, 226, 231; involvement and, 63; irreducibility to modes and, 162; as key to Spinoza's ontology, 54, 76, 99, 104, 106, 119, 169–70, 225; laws as descriptive and, 182–83; the necessary of existence and, 48, 54, 65, 144, 162, 174, 329; as nongenerative, 115; not comprising a totality, 101, 105–7, 120–21, 153, 156, 163; perfection and, 127–28, 167, 170, 172; power and, 66, 67, 68, 69, 70, 71, 72, 80, 101 (*see also* modes, as actualized/enacted power); self-causation and, 46; singularity and, 103; sovereignty removed by, 165, 169; substance as insubstantial and, 94, 162, 163–64; teleology proscribed by, 136; a telos as undermining, 173–74; transcendence proscribed by, 136; unfinishedness and, 120–21. *See also* attributes, infinite; immanence, of substance (infinity and); substance, as indeterminate (infinity and)

substance, as insubstantial, 163–64; indeterminacy and, 101; sovereignty and, 65, 69, 71, 139; substance as actualized power and, 34, 71, 99–100, 138 (*see also* modes, as actualized/enacted power); substance as infinite and, 94, 162, 163–64

substance, as the necessary of existence: causal necessity and, 58; God thinking necessarily and, 253; infinity and, 48, 54, 65, 144, 162, 174, 329; lack of freedom and, 329; the laws of nature and, 185; as substance's essence, 69

substance, oneness and: actualized infinite power negating, 138; features of oneness and, 101; indeterminacy negating, 76–77, 94, 115; infinity and, 76–77, 96–97, 138, 156, 158, 160; Kabbalah and, 35, 88; Liebniz's critique of Spinoza and, 86–87; as Oriental, 20, 35, 77, 80, 82–85, 98; qualities of, 96, 101 (*see also* identity; immutability; indivisibility); unfinishedness negating, 120–21; unity of, 83–84; Žižek and, 156

substance, power constituting: absence of identity and, 234; attributes and, 66, 231; causation and, 156–57, 238; divisibility/indivisibility and, 138; essence and, 69, 223, 226, 232; everything as equally of, 234; immanence and, 70, 238; incomplete reality and, 120–21; as of modes but not same with them, 125, 138–39 (*see also* modes, as actualized/enacted power); nonbinary reality and, 80; ontological realness of, 232; substance as insubstantial and, 71, 99–100; substance as not preexistent and, 67–68, 70, 101–2, 115, 117; unity and, 120

substance as insubstantial: power constituting substance and, 71, 99–100

suicidality, 329, 340, 341–42

supersessionism: of Christianity over Judaism, 20–21, 85, 109–10, 111, 114, 277; Hegel and, 77, 78, 84, 85, 109–10, 111–13, 114

supremacy: the Cartesian subject and, 290, 300; the conatus and, 343; embodied thought and, 288; fetishization of, 9; of the future, 211, 212–13; of God over reality, 6, 7, 41, 48–49, 58–60 (*see also* God, as sovereign/monarch); of history, 210; of ideas, 262; of identity, 259, 261; immanence and, 63; of the infinite, 117–18; infinite reality and, 72; normativity and, 186, 189–90; prejudices and, 32–33, 220, 221; of the soul, 270, 282–83, 285, 328; substance and, 34, 70; teleology and, 32, 37, 116, 167, 174, 188, 209, 213 (*see also* progress); transcendence and, 170–71; of unity, 81, 121–22, 260; of universality, 26; wholeness and, 116, 118. *See also* attributes, hierarchy and; hierarchy; mind, supremacy over body of; reason, sovereignty/supremacy of; sovereignty; spirit, supremacy of

supremacy, Christian: anti-Judaism and, 21, 31, 92–93, 95, 110–11, 281, 321–22; baptizing Spinoza and, 252; blocking natural connection with God, 91; Conway and, 282–83; Descartes and, 263, 272; dismissing Spinoza's influences and, 13–14, 16, 22, 307; German Idealism and, 92–93, 94, 119–20, 122; Hegel and, 20, 21, 23, 35, 78, 110–13, 114, 120, 277; idealism and, 92; misreading Spinoza and, 21–24, 31, 35, 80, 95, 252; modern philosophy and, 9, 77–78; as philosophical lens, 95; scholarly complicity with, 78, 112–14; Spinoza accused of atheism and, 18, 21–22, 83–85; Spinozism as Oriental/atheist and, 18, 20–22, 35, 83–85, 109–10, 114, 120, 123 (*see also* Orientalism); supersession of Judaism and, 110, 277; threatening natural truth, 91; universality and, 277; vital materialism and, 39, 323, 325–26; "Western" philosophy and, 9–10, 14, 15, 16, 23, 77–78, 84–85, 112–14, 270, 289, 307–8 (*see also* dualism, Cartesian; Hegel, G. W. F.). *See also* Christianity; *Spinozastreit*, the

supremacy, human: formation in God's image and, 271, 273, 274, 278, 285, 314; free will and, 6, 7, 8, 310–11, 314–15; human experiential knowledge and, 225–26; longtermism and, 214; mastery of nature and, 203–4, 269, 274, 296, 314–15, 328–29, 345, 360; over nonhuman life, 171, 213–14; rejection of teleology removing, 167–68, 171, 207–9; the subject and, 225–26, 274. *See also* anthropocentrism

supremacy, logics of: binaries and, 79–80, 118, 126, 200, 218, 262, 274; dualism and, 38, 274, 289, 304, 307, 329; Hegel and, 78, 109, 116, 117. *See also* hierarchy

supremacy, "Western": assimilation of Eastern concepts and, 78, 85; classical languages and, 43; Descartes and, 263; difference and, 20; dismissing Spinoza's influences and, 13–14, 15–16, 22, 221; dualism of reason and, 276; German Idealism and, 119–20; Hegel and, 35, 112–14, 120; idealism and, 92; misreading Spinoza and, 21–22, 35; scholarly complicity with, 114; social injustices and, 29; Spinozism as Oriental and, 18, 20, 35, 78, 114, 120; vital materialism and, 319, 325–26. *See also* Orientalism; philosophy, "Western"

supremacy, white, 20–21, 263, 276. *See also* colonialism; Orientalism; otherness

Tallbear, Kim, 205
Talmud, the, 17, 93. *See also* Hebrew Scripture
teleology: the absolute and, 20, 35, 116, 118; Althusser and, 21, 113; anthropocentrism and, 36, 170, 173, 177, 179, 207, 208; anthropomorphism

teleology (*cont.*)
and, 168–70, 173, 179, 203, 207; appendix to Part I (*Ethics*) and, 168–69, 173–74, 207–8; Augustine and, 208; the being/nothingness binary and, 139, 163; causal necessity and, 174; Christian Trinitarianism and, 85; Christological, 209; Descartes and, 295, 301; desire and, 335, 349, 350; essence and, 191, 326; essentialized difference and, 191; of ethics, 335, 343, 359; of evolutionary biology, 206–7; free will and, 170, 209, 315, 335, 350; God and, 169, 174, 180, 191; Hegel and, 115–16, 117, 209, 211, 277; hierarchy and, 116, 165, 172, 174, 180, 182, 188, 209–10, 211; of history, 112, 113–14, 208; human exceptionalism and, 170, 208, 276; human supremacy and, 167–68, 171, 207–8, 209; immanence disallowing, 169–70; infinity and, 117–18, 136, 167, 173–74, 187; laws of nature and, 183, 186; the less than nothing and, 157; modern philosophy and, 85; morality and, 57, 173, 174, 175, 179, 342–43, 353, 358; nature as nonpurposive and, 169–70, 172–74, 177–79, 188, 204, 208–9; normativity and, 186–87; nothingness/the void and, 138, 139, 157, 160, 163–65; ontology and, 174; prejudices and, 168–69, 174, 205; of progress, 32, 208–11, 217; racism and, 188; of rationality, 329; sexgender and, 36–37, 178, 190–91, 192–94; Spinoza's sources and, 14–15, 209; spirit and, 10, 21, 85, 112, 116, 117; substance and, 71, 124, 173–74; as subverting infinite power, 170; supremacy and, 32, 37, 116, 167, 174, 188, 209, 213 (*see also* progress); supremacy of the future and, 211, 212–13; telos as sovereign and, 7–8, 174;

transcendence and, 172, 191, 350; truth and, 295, 307; of the whole over the part, 193

Theological-Political Treatise (*Tractatus Theologico-Politicus*), 2, 24, 184, 353–54, 358

thought: absence of autonomous control and, 244; the absence of sovereignty and, 219–20, 237; as action, 306; as actualizing power, 237, 239–40; as affective, 336, 359; as attribute of substance, 255, 287, 298–99, 304, 332; beginning with sensual rejection, 194, 284, 285, 288, 295, 297, 308; as being, 265–66, 273, 290, 295, 296, 299, 303; as of the body, 239, 240–41, 284–85; causal determinism and, 283–84, 297, 298, 308–9; as causing ideas, 223–24; difference and, 257–60; as embodied, 30, 37, 268, 285, 286–88, 309; in extension, 222, 241, 252, 317; as finite, 259; as finite and determinate, 236, 239–40; as given, 152; God and, 49–52, 54, 55, 56–57, 227, 235–37, 269–70; hierarchy within, 255, 295; human experience and, 223, 284; as immanent activity, 38, 53, 286, 287, 288, 295; the infinite intellect and, 259; infinite reality disallowing supremacy of, 223–24; method as, 292; mind as ideas themselves and, 243, 351; as modal, 222, 223–24, 231, 236–37, 240; as not exclusive to humans, 285, 345; as not in isolation, 284; ontology and, 224, 231, 234, 235–37, 240, 253–54; particularity of, 240, 262, 268, 287; preeminence of, 55, 56, 254–56 (*see also* mind, supremacy over body of; reason, sovereignty/supremacy of); split as intellect and will, 273; the subject/object binary and, 304; synthesis vs. analysis and,

293–94; thinking substance same as extended substance and, 229–30, 233, 287; thought causing thought and, 233–34, 236, 262, 294; transcendence and, 96, 288; truth and, 291–92, 293, 301–2. *See also* Descartes, René (mind over body and, *cogito* and); ideas

thought, modes of: analogies as, 107; the connection of causes and, 234; Descartes and, 273; dispensing with, 318; numbers as, 96, 98–99; ontological adherence of, 317; sexgender and, 190–91, 198, 199–200, 287; universals as, 96; value judgments as, 173, 175, 179, 184, 334–35

Totaro, Pina, 186

transcendence: anthropocentrism and, 105–6; Aristotle and, 14–15, 191, 292; Augustine and, 45; Badiou and, 154; the being/nothingness binary and, 139; beyond God, 57; denied to God, 40–42; of desire, 315; of difference, 118–19; dualism and, 184, 220, 303 (*see also* dualism, Cartesian (transcendence and)); the *ego cogito* and, 266; emanation and, 62; entanglement and, 316; epistemology and, 203; essence and, 327; free will and, 209; God as having, 49, 58, 62, 159; hierarchy and, 52, 81, 116, 118–19, 122, 267–68, 302–3, 314–15; human contrivance of, 182; human exceptionalism and, 48–49, 89, 172–73, 302, 303, 314, 315; ideas and, 240; immanence and, 48–49, 169–70, 187, 205; impossibility of, 73; infinity and, 34, 102, 117, 119, 187; Kabbalah and, 24; the laws of nature and, 185; Maimonides and, 106–7, 203; mind and, 274, 283, 315; modes as of substance and, 317; normativity and, 186, 187, 193–94, 201, 310,

353, 361; *object a* and, 158, 160, 165; objectivity and, 10–11, 289; Object-Oriented Ontology and, 145–46, 149; oneness and, 81; Plato and, 44, 241; purposive nature and, 181; of the real, 158; reason and, 38, 276; the self and, 302; sexgender and, 194, 195; the soul and, 59, 314; sovereignty and, 175; Spinoza's sources and, 14–15, 24, 292; substance and, 55, 124, 136, 174; supremacy and, 170–71; teleology and, 172, 191, 350; thought and, 96, 288; universality and, 191; vital materialism and, 319–20, 321; the void and, 141, 160; the whole and, 116. *See also* Descartes, René (transcendence and); dualism, Cartesian (transcendence and); God, as transcendent

transcendence, human: human exceptionalism and, 48–49, 89, 107, 172–73, 203, 302–3, 314–15; humans as lacking, 108–9, 182, 183–84; as universal construct, 211, 212

transcendence, universality and: categories and, 100, 185, 187, 189, 191–92, 195, 201; longtermism and, 211, 212; reason and, 276, 289; teleology and, 191

transness, 28, 193–94, 195, 200–201, 202

Treatise on the Emendation of the Intellect, 246, 269, 295, 296, 301

Trinity, the: Deleuze and, 254; dynamicity of, 20, 77, 83; evolution toward, 85, 110; Hegel's critique of Spinoza and, 20, 21, 77, 83, 85, 110–11, 113; medieval Jewish thought and, 95; "Western" individuality and, 20, 21, 77, 252; Žižek and, 157

truth: as construct, 291; Crescas and, 292; Descartes and, 269, 290–92, 300–301; free will and, 290–91; the

truth (cont.)
    individual and, 296; method and, 292–93, 295–96, 307; teleology and, 295, 307; as tool for proving truth, 293, 294, 295, 301–2; true ideas and, 301–2; understanding and, 292–93

unity: bodies' lack of, 53; as dynamic, 83, 127; as immobile, 83–84; knowledge/understanding and, 259; modes and, 255; Plotinus and, 44–45, 62; reality and, 51–52, 121–22; substance irreducible to, 105–7, 115; supremacy of, 8, 121–22, 260. See also God, oneness/unity of; oneness; wholeness

universality: of being, 261; categorical consensus and, 192; Christian supremacy and, 277; cishet white Christian male claims to, 10, 213; the clinamen and, 165; as contingent, 195; Descartes' method of truth and, 294; domination and, 304–5; erasing particularity, 191, 293, 304–5, 319–20, 321; of human experience, 319; inferential knowledge and, 247, 286; laws of nature and, 185, 187, 189, 191; modes of thought and, 96, 173; of nothingness, 145; number and, 100; perception of reality and, 246; Plato and, 191; of progress, 211; of reason, 12, 19, 38, 220, 275–76, 278, 280, 294; as sovereignty, 192–93; of spirit, 20; the state and, 305; supremacy of, 26; transcendence and, 191; unity and, 259; universal notions and, 192, 246–48, 249; vital materialism and, 319–21, 322, 323, 324–25; "Western" philosophy and, 289–90, 319–20. See also transcendence, universality and

unnaturalness, 168, 202, 205, 311

Velthuysen, Lambertus van, 58–59, 329–30

view from nowhere, the, 222, 239, 240, 262, 268, 274, 284, 308

vital materialism, 319–26, 345, 346

void, the: Althusser's association with Spinoza, 132–34; Aristotle's rejection of, 125, 140–41, 142; Badiou and, 149–53; being and, 150, 161; Crescas and, 36, 125–26, 140–43, 164; Descartes' rejection of, 135–36, 162; dialectical mediation and, 127–28; Ein Sof and, 142; as God in disguise, 125–26; matter and, 129–30; motion within (clinamen), 128, 130–31, 132; as self-caused, 154; Spinoza's definition of, 134, 144; Spinoza's rejection of, 125, 133–34, 138–39, 149, 161–62; tension and, 160; transcendence and, 141, 160. See also negative, the; nothingness

volition, 56, 58, 59, 60–61, 203, 227, 332. See also free will

Vries, Simon de, 230, 253

Wachter, Johann Georg, 18, 19, 87–88, 89–90, 94

West, the: binary with the East, 20–21, 82, 85 (see also Orientalism); culture of, 77, 143, 199, 267, 275, 307, 329 (see also philosophy, "Western"); feminisms of, 264; freedom and, 33, 112, 314; hierarchy of West over East and, 20–21, 78, 85, 109–10, 112–14, 116, 277; individualism as principle of, 20, 21, 28–29, 77, 83, 252; reliance on essentialized difference, 44; reliance on hierarchy, 43, 44, 122, 272; treatment of term, 365n1; the Trinity and individuality in, 20, 21, 77, 252 (see also supremacy, Christian); white culture's emphasis on reason and, 263, 266, 275–76. See also philosophy, "Western"; supremacy, "Western"

wholeness: as being of reason, 137; essentialized difference and, 188–89; Hegel's embrace of, 115–16, 150; hierarchy and, 116, 193; the human body and, 188; individuality and, 50; infinity and, 76, 101, 105–9, 115–16, 119, 120–21, 162–63; Kabbalah and, 94; Lucretius and, 153; Parmenides and, 128. *See also* indivisibility; oneness; unity

Willey, Angela, 205

willpower and, 310, 333, 336, 337, 350

Wittgenstein, Ludwig, 1

Wolfson, Elliot R., 76, 94, 284

Wolfson, Harry Austryn, 13

Wynter, Sylvia, 265, 267

Yovel, Yirmiyahu, 111, 209, 270

Žižek, Slavoj: Hegel–Spinoza opposition and, 156, 160–61; Lacan and, 156, 157–58, 159–60, 165; Lucretius and critique of Spinoza, 36; the nothing/something binary and, 157, 158–59; Spinoza's Jewishness and, 25, 113–14; Spinoza's rejection of negativity and, 155; the void and, 155–61, 165

Cultural Memory in the *Present*

Eyal Peretz, *American Medium: A New Film Philosophy*

Jensen Suther, *True Materialism: Hegelian Marxism and the Modernist Struggle for Freedom*

Jean-Luc Marion, *Cartesian Questions III: Descartes Beneath the Mask of Cartesianism*

Walter Benjamin, *On Goethe*

Elliot R. Wolfson, *Nocturnal Seeing: Hopelessness of Hope and Philosophical Gnosis in Susan Taubes, Gillian Rose, and Edith Wyschogrod*

Severo Sarduy, *Barroco and Other Writings*

David D. Kim, *Arendt's Solidarity: Anti-Semitism and Racism in the Atlantic World*

Hans Joas, *Why the Church?: Self-Optimization or Community of Faith*

Jean-Luc Marion, *Revelation Comes from Elsewhere*

Peter Sloterdijk, *Out of the World*

Christopher J. Wild, *Descartes' Meditative Turn: Cartesian Thought as Spiritual Practice*

Eli Friedlander, *Walter Benjamin and the Idea of Natural History*

Helmut Puff, *The Antechamber: Toward a History of Waiting*

Raúl E. Zegarra, *A Revolutionary Faith: Liberation Theology Between Public Religion and Public Reason*

David Simpson, *Engaging Violence: Civility and the Reach of Literature*

Michael Steinberg, *The Afterlife of Moses: Exile, Democracy, Renewal*

Alain Badiou, *Badiou by Badiou*, translated by Bruno Bosteels

Eric Song, *Love against Substitution: Seventeenth-Century English Literature and the Meaning of Marriage*

Niklaus Largier, *Figures of Possibility: Aesthetic Experience, Mysticism, and the Play of the Senses*

Mihaela Mihai, *Political Memory and the Aesthetics of Care: The Art of Complicity and Resistance*

Ethan Kleinberg, *Emmanuel Levinas's Talmudic Turn: Philosophy and Jewish Thought*

Willemien Otten, *Thinking Nature and the Nature of Thinking: From Eriugena to Emerson*

Michael Rothberg, *The Implicated Subject: Beyond Victims and Perpetrators*

Hans Ruin, *Being with the Dead: Burial, Ancestral Politics, and the Roots of Historical Consciousness*

Eric Oberle, *Theodor Adorno and the Century of Negative Identity*

David Marriott, *Whither Fanon? Studies in the Blackness of Being*

Reinhart Koselleck, *Sediments of Time: On Possible Histories*, translated and edited by Sean Franzel and Stefan-Ludwig Hoffmann

Devin Singh, *Divine Currency: The Theological Power of Money in the West*
Stefanos Geroulanos, *Transparency in Postwar France: A Critical History of the Present*
Sari Nusseibeh, *The Story of Reason in Islam*
Olivia C. Harrison, *Transcolonial Maghreb: Imagining Palestine in the Era of Decolonialization*
Barbara Vinken, *Flaubert Postsecular: Modernity Crossed Out*
Aishwary Kumar, *Radical Equality: Ambedkar, Gandhi, and the Problem of Democracy*
Simona Forti, *New Demons: Rethinking Power and Evil Today*
Joseph Vogl, *The Specter of Capital*
Hans Joas, *Faith as an Option*
Michael Gubser, *The Far Reaches: Ethics, Phenomenology, and the Call for Social Renewal in Twentieth-Century Central Europe*
Françoise Davoine, *Mother Folly: A Tale*
Knox Peden, *Spinoza Contra Phenomenology: French Rationalism from Cavaillès to Deleuze*
Elizabeth A. Pritchard, *Locke's Political Theology: Public Religion and Sacred Rights*
Ankhi Mukherjee, *What Is a Classic? Postcolonial Rewriting and Invention of the Canon*
Jean-Pierre Dupuy, *The Mark of the Sacred*
Henri Atlan, *Fraud: The World of Ona'ah*
Niklas Luhmann, *Theory of Society, Volume 2*
Ilit Ferber, *Philosophy and Melancholy: Benjamin's Early Reflections on Theater and Language*
Alexandre Lefebvre, *Human Rights as a Way of Life: On Bergson's Political Philosophy*
Theodore W. Jennings, Jr., *Outlaw Justice: The Messianic Politics of Paul*
Alexander Etkind, *Warped Mourning: Stories of the Undead in the Land of the Unburied*
Denis Guénoun, *About Europe: Philosophical Hypotheses*
Maria Boletsi, *Barbarism and Its Discontents*
Sigrid Weigel, *Walter Benjamin: Images, the Creaturely, and the Holy*
Roberto Esposito, *Living Thought: The Origins and Actuality of Italian Philosophy*
Henri Atlan, *The Sparks of Randomness, Volume 2: The Atheism of Scripture*
Rüdiger Campe, *The Game of Probability: Literature and Calculation from Pascal to Kleist*
Niklas Luhmann, *A Systems Theory of Religion*
Jean-Luc Marion, *In the Self's Place: The Approach of Saint Augustine*
Rodolphe Gasché, *Georges Bataille: Phenomenology and Phantasmatology*
Niklas Luhmann, *Theory of Society, Volume 1*
Alessia Ricciardi, *After La Dolce Vita: A Cultural Prehistory of Berlusconi's Italy*
Daniel Innerarity, *The Future and Its Enemies: In Defense of Political Hope*
Patricia Pisters, *The Neuro-Image: A Deleuzian Film-Philosophy of Digital Screen Culture*

For a complete listing of titles in this series, visit the Stanford University Press website, www.sup.org.